McNae's Essential Law for Journalists

McNae's
essential law for journalists

Twentieth Edition

David Banks   Mark Hanna

Honorary Consultants: Tom Welsh and Walter Greenwood

OXFORD
UNIVERSITY PRESS

OXFORD
UNIVERSITY PRESS

Great Clarendon Street, Oxford OX2 6DP

Oxford University Press is a department of the University of Oxford.
It furthers the University's objective of excellence in research, scholarship,
and education by publishing worldwide in

Oxford New York

Auckland Cape Town Dar es Salaam Hong Kong Karachi
Kuala Lumpur Madrid Melbourne Mexico City Nairobi
New Delhi Shanghai Taipei Toronto

With offices in

Argentina Austria Brazil Chile Czech Republic France Greece
Guatemala Hungary Italy Japan Poland Portugal Singapore
South Korea Switzerland Thailand Turkey Ukraine Vietnam

Oxford is a registered trade mark of Oxford University Press
in the UK and in certain other countries

Published in the United States
by Oxford University Press Inc., New York

British Library Cataloguing in Publication Data
Data available

Library of Congress Cataloging in Publication Data
Data available

Typeset by Newgen Imaging Systems (P) Ltd., Chennai, India
Printed in Great Britain
on acid-free paper by
Ashford Colour Press Ltd., Gosport, Hampshire

ISBN 978-0-19-955645-8

10 9 8 7 6 5 4 3 2

To my wife, Sarah, and my sons, Joseph and William – for constant support and welcome diversion

D.B.

To my wife Linda, my son Rory, my mother Mary, and my father Michael

M.H.

Preface

The world of journalism is changing fast. It remains an exciting career, and a protection for democracy. But its challenges grow more demanding. For example, the development of websites to publish both newsroom-crafted journalism and 'user generated material' – e.g. comments, reports, photographs and video footage submitted by readers, listeners, and viewers – means that some decisions on what can be published legally and ethically must be made more quickly than ever in fierce competition for 'exclusives' and to retain audiences.

This edition of *McNae's Essential Law for Journalists* – the twentieth edition – introduces major changes to the book, to respond further to this new environment, to the relentless increase in recent years of statute affecting journalism, and to the rapid development of jurisprudence since the European Convention on Human Rights was incorporated in 2000 into the United Kingdom's law.

Structure of the book

Regular users of *McNae* will notice that this edition, as well as referring to changes in the law which have occurred since the nineteenth edition was published in 2007, alters the chapter structure of previous editions and the organisation of content within chapters. For example, the continuing integration of media 'platforms' – print, broadcast, and internet – prompted us to dispense with separate chapters on online and broadcast journalism. Material pertinent to online publication and broadcasting occurs throughout this edition (the term 'publish' should usually be read as including broadcasting).

Because of this technological convergence, we have, in some contexts where previous editions referred to newspapers and magazines, used the term 'media organisations'. This term is not wholly satisfactory, in particular where the point being made also applies to freelance journalists or to an individual running a website or 'blogging'. But we felt it to be the most practical option.

In another change, we have introduced a separate chapter – ch. 8 – to provide more explanation of the reporting restrictions in sexual offences law, after several prosecutions in recent years of newspapers which breached the anonymity of victims of such crimes. The Sexual Offences Act 2003 increased the number of crimes covered by this anonymity provision. We felt that this increase, and what may be growing pressure on some newsrooms, including on editing and subbing operations – pressure caused by manpower reductions and by the demands of publishing online as well as in print – justified a deeper focus on reporting restrictions generally. We have also expanded explanations of restrictions arising from juveniles' involvement in court cases, including ASBO proceedings (ch. 7). Sadly, in 2008 and 2009 hundreds of journalists in the UK, many with decades of experience, have been made redundant because of economic recession. It may be that young reporters will need, more than ever, to stand on their own feet as regards understanding and complying with restrictions in crime and court coverage, and in avoiding libel and other legal pitfalls.

We have also reorganised and expanded content to create new, separate chapters on the family courts (ch. 11), on the *Reynolds* defence in libel law (ch. 20), and on the law on terrorism and counter-terrorism (ch. 33), as responses to developments in these legal fields. There is also a new, separate chapter on 'Children and privacy' (ch. 26).

There are changes too to the book's page design, including greater use of cross-referencing and of bullet points. We hope this will help highlight to students and trainees what needs to be learnt for the exams of the National Council for the Training of Journalists (NCTJ) and that experienced journalists will also welcome these new features.

→ glossary   One change concerns the book's glossary, on pages 573 to 578. A legal term which within a chapter is in blue text, flagged by a margin reference to the glossary, as shown here, is defined in the glossary for easy reference.

McNae remains a book for the entire journalism community – in part a primer for trainees and students, but also a reference volume and law refresher for seasoned reporters, writers, newsdesks, and editors.

As authors, we would be grateful if readers tell us what they think of changes made in this edition, and about its content generally. Our email addresses are below.

Significant legal developments since the last edition

This book deals with media law as it applies in England, Wales, and Northern Ireland (and retains a separate chapter for law applicable only in Northern Ireland). Since 2007 significant legal developments include:

- the Government's decision to 'open up' family law proceedings in county courts and the High Court by giving reporters a better right of admission to such cases – see Late News, p. xxix, and ch. 11;

- a modernisation of the system of tribunals which dispense 'administrative justice', with new rules on what can be disclosed from their proceedings – see ch. 15;

- the abolition of the common law offences of blasphemy and blasphemous libel – see ch. 21;

- the creation in the Counter-Terrorism Act 2008 of a new (and vague) offence to outlaw the eliciting and publication of information about a police officer or a member of Her Majesty's forces or of the UK intelligence services, if the information 'is of a kind likely to be useful' to a terrorist – see ch. 33;

- the creation of a new offence to outlaw the stirring up of hatred on the grounds of sexual orientation – see ch. 34 and Late News, p. xxix.

The Coroners and Justice Bill 2009, which as this edition went to press was progressing, in most respects, fairly smoothly in Parliamentary debates, will if it becomes law:

- enable a magistrate to make an 'investigation anonymity order' to keep secret the identity of a person assisting the police during investigations of homicide by gun or knife when the suspect is likely to be involved in a gang of teenagers or young adults – see ch. 2;

- define the circumstances in which the identity of a prosecution witness can be kept secret from the defence (and thereby from the public);

- reform the coroner system generally – see ch. 14;

- seek to prevent criminals from profiting from the sale of memoirs of their crimes.

However, in May the Government announced it would, by dropping two clauses from the Bill, abandon its controversial plans for 'non-jury' inquests. It had intended that such inquests would be held in certain circumstances, e.g. if evidence involved 'national security' matters, and be presided over by a High Court Judge, not by a coroner.

See the McNae Online Resource Centre for updates on the Bill and for more detail on its implications for journalists if and when it becomes law. See also Late News.

A welcome development in October 2007 was the Government's abandonment of proposals to change how public authorities calculate the cost of meeting requests made under the Freedom of Information Act 2000. Had the proposals become law they would have severely restricted use of the Act by journalists and others. Less welcome was the first usage of a Ministerial veto to block a request made under the Act. This occurred in early 2009 – see ch. 28.

Among significant rulings by courts since 2007 are:

- the decision by a Crown court judge to throw out the prosecution case against *Milton Keynes Citizen* reporter Sally Murrer, who had been charged with aiding and abetting misconduct in a public office after it was alleged that police information was leaked to her. In what newsrooms hope will be an influential example of judicial protection of journalism, the judge thus upheld Sally's rights under Article 10 of the European Convention – see ch. 32;

- the extension of the *Reynolds* libel defence to cover books – see ch. 20;

- the High Court award of £60,000 privacy damages to Max Mosley for the *News of the World*'s revelations about his sex life – see ch. 24;

- the decision of Belfast High Court to ban the media from publishing photographs of, or the whereabouts of, a convicted murderer being assessed in the community for permanent release at the end of his sentence – see ch. 9. This is the latest in a line of similar judgments, suggesting that the granting of such anonymity may become established judicial practice as regards people convicted in notorious cases who are due to be considered for release from prison – see ch. 9. See also Late News for a similar case.

Acknowledgements

Tom Welsh and Walter Greenwood, former authors of *McNae*, acted as honorary consultants to this edition. For more than 30 years as authors of previous editions (having edited thirteen editions of *McNae*, starting with the seventh edition) they ensured the success of *McNae* and its reputation as the 'bible' of newsrooms. We, as a new author team, owe them a great debt for their encouragement and guidance as this edition was written.

Our thanks are also due to: Heather Brooke, author of *Your Right to Know*; Amanda Ball, senior lecturer at Nottingham Trent University; Bob Whitehouse, former justices' chief executive for County Durham; and Mike Dodd, legal editor of the Press Association. They provided comment on draft passages in the book and/or suggested material for inclusion. Mike Dodd is also editor of the Press Association's *Media Lawyer* journal, an invaluable source of news in this field. See www.medialawyer.press.net/.

Our colleagues on the NCTJ media law examinations board have given continued support. We are also grateful to Jo Butcher, the NCTJ's chief executive, and to staff at Oxford University Press – in particular Philippa Groom, Angela Griffin, Rekha Summan, and Susan Faircloth – for all their advice and patience.

We also thank the Judicial Studies Board and Her Majesty's Courts Service for permitting use of diagram material, the Press Standards Board of Finance (Pressbof) for permitting reproduction of the Editors' Code used by the Press Complaints Commission, and Ofcom for allowing us to cite extracts from its Broadcasting Code.

The main body of the text of this edition was completed in February 2009, but it was possible to add some late news until May 2009.

David Banks, d.banks3@btinternet.com
Mark Hanna, m.hanna@sheffield.ac.uk

This book bears the name of its first author, the late Leonard McNae, who was Editor of the Press Associations Special Reporting Service. Its first edition was published in 1954.

Summary Contents

Detailed Contents

| Part 5 | Photography, filming, and videoing | 541 |

Late News

The Coroners and Justice Bill 2009

In May 2009 the Government announced that, because it lacked cross-party support in the House of Lords, it would remove from the Bill the proposal that in certain circumstances – e.g. to stop 'national security' matters becoming public – a Home Secretary could decide that an inquest be held without a jury. The Bill had proposed that such a 'non-jury inquest' would be presided over by a High Court judge, not by a coroner, with wide discretion to exclude public and reporters. See ch. 14. Critics welcomed this 'secret inquests' plan being dropped. But the Government insisted it still needed 'to protect sensitive material' from being made public in inquests. Justice Secretary Jack Straw said that if, exceptionally, the Government felt it 'not possible to proceed with an inquest under the current arrangements', the circumstances of a death could instead be ascertained by an inquiry held under the Inquiries Act 2005. Critics point out this Act permits Ministers to decide that an inquiry's proceedings be held in private – see ch. 15.

Another clause in the Bill seeks to abolish section 29JA of the Public Order Act 1986. This section was a 'free speech' proviso inserted by the House of Lords when the Criminal Justice and Immigration Act 2008 amended the 1986 Act to create the offence of stirring up hatred on the grounds of sexual orientation. The section states that discussion or criticism of sexual conduct or practices or urging persons to refrain from or to modify such conduct is not, in itself, to be taken to be threatening or intended to stir up such hatred. The Government's explanatory notes to the 2009 Bill state that the removal of the section will not affect 'the threshold' required for the offence to be prosecuted. See ch. 34.

The 'opening up' of family cases in the High Court and county courts

After controversy about the family courts system lacking transparency, the Justice Secretary, Jack Straw, in April 2009 laid statutory instruments before Parliament to amend procedural rules governing family cases in the High Court, county courts, and magistrates Courts. The Government had said that it wanted reporters to routinely gain admission to family cases in these courts, though judges and magistrates will retain some power to exclude them. However, the media expressed concern about the extent to which the new procedural rules will allow reporters to cover such cases. See the Online Resource Centre for this book for more details of this measure. Reporters wishing to attend such cases will need an identity card accredited in the UK Press Card scheme. See www.ukpresscardauthority.co.uk/. There was no news by April 2009 of when the Government intended to reform the complex layers of reporting restrictions which apply in respect of family cases. However, Justice Secretary, Jack Straw announced that month that he had decided, after 'further reflection', <u>not</u> to introduce legislation to reverse the precedent set in *Clayton v Clayton*. That judgment determined that automatic anonymity for a child involved in proceedings under the Children Act 1989 ceases to apply when the case is concluded. That judgment will continue, then, to have scope to improve the transparency of such concluded proceedings. See also ch. 11.

Anonymity for murderer

In February 2009 in the High Court Mr Justice Silber ordered that a man convicted of three notorious murders some decades ago should not be identified in media reports. The Parole Board was due to consider whether he should be released from prison, where he has been since those convictions. His lawyers applied for him to have anonymity, arguing that media exposure might compromise arrangements being made for his future. The judge was being asked to decide whether the Justice Secretary, Jack Straw, should be ordered to place the man in an open prison prior to possible release. The judge said he would review the anonymity provision when he handed down judgment on the open prison issue. Please check the Online Resource Centre, where an update on this case will be posted. See also Preface, and see ch. 9 for other examples of such anonymity being granted by the High Court.

Section 46 order prevented

At Blackpool magistrates court journalist David Graham, head of Lancashire-based freelance agency Watsons, successfully opposed an application made under section 46 of the Youth Justice and Criminal Evidence Act 1999 that a barrister who was a witness should have anonymity in reports of an assault case. Mr Graham argued that no other complainant at court that day would be given such privilege of anonymity The case concerned the barrister being assaulted by a client. The application for the section 46 order was made by the Crown Prosecution Service on the basis that it would improve the quality of the barrister's evidence (*Media Lawyer*, 7 April 2009). See also chs 9 and 13 on section 46 orders.

Breach of the Magistrates' Court Act 1980

At the time *McNae* went to press a legal restriction continued to prevent publication of details of Jewish Chronicle Newspaper Ltd's conviction in 2008 for breach of the 1980 Act. This conviction is referred to briefly in ch. 4. Please check the Online Resource Centre, where an update on this case will be posted when possible.

Breach of section 8 of the Contempt of Court Act 1981

In May 2009 *The Times* newspaper was fined £15,000 after the High Court ruled it had breached section 8 of the Contempt of Court Act 1981, which protects the confidentiality of jury deliberations. The Attorney General alleged contempt arose when the paper reported in 2007 that a man who was jury foreman in a manslaughter case was questioning the majority, 'guilty' verdict, which he had opposed. He had approached the paper. It quoted him on how jurors took an early vote, and on the role played by complicated, medical evidence. He and the paper denied contempt. *The Times* said the European Convention on Human Rights protected freedon of expression. It had identified no other juror. But Lord Justice Poll said the disclosures 'offended against the secrecy of the jury room.' The Attorney General was awarded £27,426 costs, against the paper. It said it would seek leave to appeal. The foreman was fined £500 for contempt (*The Times*, 13 and 23 May 2009). For section 8 law, see ch. 9.

Home Office guidance to aid photography in public places

In April 2009 the Home Office Minister, Shahid Malik, said that guidance would be issued to police to help ensure that people are not unnecessarily stopped from taking photographs in public places. His statement followed protests by media photographers and others about officious and unjustified use of counter-terrorism law by police. See ch. 35 for the background to these concerns.

Another celebrity gets court protection from paparazzi

In March 2009 the pop star Lily Allen became the latest celebrity to secure a High Court injunction to prevent harassment by photographers. Her lawyer said she had been constantly harassed for months by paparazzi. The court order forbade photographers from following her or going within 100 metres of her home. See *Media Lawyer*, 16 March. For detail of similar cases, see also chs 23, 24, and 35.

PCC warning on pictures reproduced from social networking sites

In March 2009 the Press Complaints Commission warned in its annual report that media reproduction of pictures found on social networking sites – such as Facebook – could breach the Editors' Code of Practice, used by the PCC to adjudicate on ethics. After sudden deaths, some bereaved relatives had complained about media use of such pictures (portraying events in the life of those who had died). The PCC said that insensitive use of such pictures could breach the code's clause 5 concerning intrusion into grief. Its report said there could also be a copyright issue, though this was not a matter for the PCC. See also ch. 1 on the PCC's role, chs 24, 26, and 35 on privacy issues concerning photographs, and ch. 27 on copyright.

Max Mosley libel action

After his successful action against the *News of the World* for breach of privacy, the Formula 1 chief, Max Mosley, began a libel action against the paper in March 2009. See also ch. 24 for detail of his privacy action.

Editors' Codebook updated

A second edition of the Editors' Codebook was published in March 2009. The Codebook – written by Ian Beales, secretary of the Editors' Code Committee, see p. 17 – provides updated guidance and case studies on interpretation of the Editors' Code of Practice. See www.editorscode.org.uk/.

Control of costs in defamation cases

In February 2009 the Government published a consultation paper on reform of costs in defamation cases. The Justice Minister, Bridget Prentice, said the effect of excessive costs could sometimes force defendants to settle unwarranted claims.

Measures under consideration were:

- mandatory cost capping;
- limiting hourly rates; and
- requiring the courts to look at proportionality of costs.

The consultation followed a campaign by lawyers representing publishers and broadcasters who had criticised the 'chilling effect' that conditional fee agreements were having on freedom of speech. See also ch. 17.

Justice Ministry looks at libel and the internet

In March 2009 the Justice Ministry said it was investigating the issue of libel and the internet, in particular the rule which means each download of an article is fresh publication. Claimants have one year to take action for material in print media, but the rule in the Duke of Brunswick case (1849), that each publication can give rise to a separate action, means that online archives containing defamatory articles leave publishers open to a libel action for much longer if that material is downloaded. The Justice Ministry investigation was due to lead to a consultation paper. For an explanation of the current law in this context, see ch. 18.

Guide to the Online Resource Centre

McNae's Essential Law for Journalists is accompanied by an Online Resource Centre that features a range of helpful resources for students, journalists and lecturers. These resources are free of charge and are designed to complement the book. This Online Resource Centre can be found at: www.oxfordtextbooks.co.uk/orc/mcnaes20e/

For students and journalists

Regular updates

The Online Resource Centre provides updates on changes in media law which have occurred since this book was published, and includes updates on ethical matters, e.g. any new guidance issued to journalists by the Press Complaints Commission. This indispensable online resource enables you to be informed of developments in these fast-moving fields.

Extra materials/information

For some areas of law, the Online Resource Centre provides additional information. Where such further information can be found on the Online Resource Centre, this is flagged in the margin or text of the book at the relevant point. For example, the book's ch. 31, on the Official Secrets Acts of 1911 and 1989 explains these statutes, and further detail of this complex law is made available in an expanded version of this chapter on the Online Resource Centre.

Web links

The Online Resource Centre provides web links to all 'Useful Websites' listed in the book. These relate to areas of law and ethics covered in it and are organised by chapter for easy reference.

For students

Glossary

For easy reference, the Online Resource Centre contains the glossary of legal terms used regularly in the book.

Podcasts

Podcasts offering recordings in audio and video of lectures covering the NCTJ syllabus are available on the Online Resource Centre, and are suitable for download to PC, Mac or iPod/MP3 player.

For lecturers

Lecturers can access the 'Lecturer Resources' on the Online Resource Centre; this part of the site is password-protected. Each registration is individually checked to ensure the security of this part of the site.

Registering is easy: click on the 'Lecturer Resources' on the Online Resource Centre, complete a simple registration form which allows you to choose your own username and password, and access will be granted within 48 hours (subject to verification).

Test bank

The test bank, part of the 'Lecturer Resources', is a fully customisable resource containing ready-made questions and assessments with which to test your students. It offers versatile testing tailored to the contents of the book and there are questions in several different formatting including multiple choice, true/false and essay style questions.

The test bank is downloadable into Questionmark Perception, Blackboard, WebCT, and most other virtual learning environments capable of importing QTI XML. It is also available in print format.

1

Introduction

Chapter summary

This chapter gives an overview of law particularly affecting journalism. It sets out the origins and sources of UK laws, and explains the hierarchy of the court system in England and Wales. It outlines the vital benefits of freedom of expression, and the role and responsibility of journalists to use this freedom, and to be vigilant to protect it. This chapter explains how the UK's full adoption of the European Convention on Human Rights has led to rapid developments in law directly affecting the media. These developments are explored in later chapters. Bodies which regulate and self-regulate media ethics in the UK are introduced in this chapter.

The United Kingdom has a tradition of a 'free press'. When compared with the authoritarian censorship which stifles liberty in some other nations, the UK's laws allow journalists much freedom. But some other democracies bestow greater freedom on the media than the UK does. As this book will show, the description of the UK media as a 'free press' must be qualified, because there are many prohibitions on what can be published.

Journalists have no rights in UK law distinct from those of other UK citizens – except in a few circumstances explained in later chapters. Yet journalists' capacity and responsibility to enhance democratic debate are special. The importance of this role was emphasised in 2000 by the House of Lords, the highest court in the land, when it ruled that a press conference was a 'public meeting' as regards defamation law, a ruling which gave the media greater protection against libel actions.

The purpose of the press conference which gave rise to that particular case was to raise support for a convicted prisoner. The senior law lord, Lord

see ch. 19, p. 343

Bingham said the press representatives at it could either be regarded as members of the public themselves, or as 'the eyes and ears of the public, to whom they report'. Lord Bingham said in the same judgment:

❝ In a modern, developed society it is only a small minority of citizens who can participate directly in the discussions and decisions which shape the public life of that society. The majority can participate only indirectly, by exercising their rights as citizens to vote, express their opinions, make representations to the authorities, form pressure groups and so on. But the majority cannot participate in the public life of their society in these ways if they are not alerted to and informed about matters which call or may call for consideration and action. It is very largely through the media, including of course the press, that they will be so alerted and informed. The proper functioning of a modern participatory democracy requires that the media be free, active, professional and enquiring. ❞

The extent to which journalists are 'free, active, professional and enquiring' is, of course, regularly an element of discussions and debate.

→
see ch. 12 Other judgments have recognised that court reporters exercise an essential, watchdog role on the justice system.

The constitutional position of journalism is analysed by Fenwick and Phillipson in their book, *Media Freedom under the Human Rights Act* (Oxford University Press, 2006).

▌ Freedom of expression

Freedom of expression, the important right which in a democracy journalists share with other citizens, includes the right to communicate information and ideas. Without this freedom, democratic life would be impossible.

Unlike some other countries, the UK has no written constitution, so the rights of its people are said to be 'residual'. This means that the constitutional position is that its citizens are free to do whatever law does not prohibit. Until recently they had no legal code to help define and guarantee the extent of their freedoms. Then in 2000 the European Convention on Human Rights was adopted directly into UK law (see below, p. 9), and this provided its first codification of human rights, including that of freedom of expression.

Like other freedoms, however, freedom of expression may be restricted by the law. Most citizens, including journalists, believe it is reasonable for there to be some restrictions on this freedom. For example, the law must strike a balance between the media being free to expose wrongdoing and an individual being able to defend his/her reputation from baseless attacks. The law of defamation – libel and slander – tries to strike that balance. There are also, for example, laws which make certain, potentially harmful statements illegal, e.g. incitement of racial hatred.

see chs 17–21, and ch. 34

This book is largely concerned with restrictions. But it also seeks to show how journalists can, through vigilance and knowledge of the law, uphold freedom of expression when it is improperly infringed. For example, ch. 13 of this book, 'Challenging the courts', should help journalists achieve this.

Freedom of expression has been so highly valued in the United Kingdom, and the tradition of this freedom has been so strong, that for many years statutory restrictions on it were kept to a minimum. But in the 55 years since the first edition of this book was published, Parliament has made many inroads into that freedom, passing a number of Acts which restrict the journalist's ability to report, particularly in coverage of court cases. For example, before the Contempt of Court Act 1981 it was rare for a judge to order journalists to postpone the reporting of a criminal trial. But once that power had been codified in the Act, its use became frequent. The principle of open justice, discussed in chs 12 and 13, was thus eroded.

see ch. 16, p. 289

Many people believe such legislation restricts freedom of expression too severely. It was assumed that the Human Rights Act 1998 would provide better protection for this freedom, because section 19 of the Act created a requirement that a Minister introducing a Bill into Parliament must declare that its provisions are compatible with the European Convention, including thereby a commitment to freedom of expression. But journalists have been disappointed to find that the declaration has been attached to a number of Bills which bore little evidence of having been examined to safeguard such freedom. Recent examples include the Coroners and Justice Bill 2009, which sought to increase the potential for secrecy in the inquest system, and the Counter-Terrorism Act 2008, which created a new and vague offence of 'eliciting information' as regards questions asked about police and military personnel.

see chs 14 and 33

In the absence of a written constitution, freedom of expression in Britain has depended traditionally on two constitutional bulwarks in law – jury trial and the rule against prior restraint.

◗ Jury trial

The history of the development of freedom of expression in the UK has several instances of journalists and others being brought before the courts, charged with offences arising from publications which riled the Government of the day. But some such defendants were then found not guilty by independently minded juries, sometimes in flagrant disregard of the strict legal position. An example of such a jury decision was the acquittal in 1985 of Clive Ponting, a civil servant whose conscience led him to leak government information, and who was then prosecuted for breaching official secrets law. Since that acquittal no journalists had, by the time this book went to press, been prosecuted to trial for breach of that law. A main factor in officialdom's reluctance to use such law to prosecute journalists seems to be that successive UK Attorney Generals have been unsure whether juries would convict.

→
see ch. 31

The legal scholar Albert Dicey wrote: 'Freedom of discussion is, then, in England little else than the right to write or say anything which a jury, consisting of 12 shopkeepers, think it expedient should be said or written.' However, though jury decisions can be unpredictable, the lesson of history is that juries – being drawn from the general population – are more likely to acquit defendants, including journalists, for actions in dissent from government policy than judges would be. See ch. 6 for more detail on the jury system.

◗ The rule against prior restraint

A system of government censorship died out in England in 1695, and in the next century the jurist Sir William Blackstone said: 'The liberty of the press…consists in laying no previous restraints on publication, and not in freedom from censure for criminal matter when published.'

The 'rule against prior restraint', as it is known, developed in UK law to safeguard freedom of expression against forms of censorship. For example, in libel law – a branch of civil law – this principle means that judges will, other than in very exceptional cases, refuse to grant an application that a media organisation should be prevented by court order from publishing material. Any remedy for a person who claims to be defamed will therefore have to be through an action, after publication, for damages.

→
see chs
17–20

Injunctions stopping publication are more likely to be granted by judges when a media organisation plans to air matter which an individual argues will breach his/her privacy or which a party claims will breach a duty of confidence owed to it. Such an injunction will usually be imposed initially as an interim measure, before any full hearing at court of whether such publication would be lawful. The media organisation gagged by such an injunction will then have to decide if the story is worth the heavy legal costs it could incur should it argue at a full hearing for publication to be allowed, but lose the case.

→ see chs 23 and 24

UK governments have controversially used the injunction procedure to prevent publication of information which, Ministers have claimed, would damage the State's interests if aired. For example, in the series of cases in the 1980s relating to the book *Spycatcher* the then Government used the law of breach of confidence to prevent – by means of injunctions against the media – publication of stories it claimed breached official secrets law. The injunctions were enforced by the use of the law of contempt of court, which is dispensed by judges sitting without juries.

→ see chs 23 and 31

When drafting the Human Rights Act 1998, the Government responded to media concern that the historic rule against prior restraint had been undermined by some court judgments. The Act's section 12 requires that before issuing an injunction which will affect the right to freedom of expression, a court must be 'satisfied that the applicant is likely to establish that publication should not be allowed', and that the party planning to publish the material must usually be given notice of the attempt to impose such an injunction, to allow him/her to argue against it – see p. 388.

The public interest

There is no single, comprehensive definition in law of the concept of 'the public interest'. But in the context of journalism, if 'the public interest' is argued in a legal case to justify information being published, this usually means that the information's value to society is argued to be particularly high, or potentially so. It is, for example, in the public interest to warn people of a particular criminal or that a politician is misleading them. Similarly, a public interest criterion is used to justify the waiving of normal ethical restraints when reporters gather information – e.g. the waiving of the usual ethical prohibition on use of subterfuge. But, as judges have regularly reminded journalists, such a criterion of the public interest does not necessarily apply to material, e.g. a 'kiss and tell' story, which greatly interests the public.

→ see below, p. 17 and ch. 23, p. 394

However, there is also a general 'public interest' in the law allowing a very broad range of material to be published. Even if the social benefits of a particular story, or of a particular opinion being aired, are not immediately obvious, there may well be some, and freedom of expression includes personal rights – e.g. the right of individuals to describe their own experiences, or to comment on events involving others, whether or not this is likely to be deemed by a judge to be of social benefit.

There is also a different kind of 'public interest', yielding other personal and social benefits, in individuals subject to media attention being able to enforce legal rights to privacy and to protect their reputation – rights fully explained later in this book. The courts sometimes have to decide, for example in privacy or libel actions, which type of public interest should prevail.

▌ Sources of law

In the UK, whether an action – including, for example, publication – is recognised as being legal or illegal is determined by consideration of various sources of law, sometimes referred to as 'authorities'. The main sources of the law have traditionally been custom, precedent, and statute. Now the European Convention on Human Rights and the judgments of the European Court of Human Rights, forming new precedents, are becoming an increasingly important source – see below.

Custom

When the English legal system began to take shape in the Middle Ages, royal judges were appointed to administer the 'law and custom of the realm'. This part of the law was called 'common' – that is, common to the whole kingdom – in contrast to that which was particular or special, such as ecclesiastical law or local law.

Precedent

→ glossary   As judges applied the common law to the cases before them, their decisions were recorded by lawyers. This process continues. Records of leading cases give the facts considered by the court, and the reasons given by it for its decision. The UK has a hierarchy of courts, as do most other countries. A decision made by a lower court can be challenged by appeal to a higher court. The decisions on law made by the higher courts are thereafter binding on all lower courts, and so shape their future rulings. The decisions are known as 'precedents', and the system as 'case law', and precedents evolve the common law.

Figure 1 is a diagram of the hierarchy of the courts in England and Wales. The nature and role of these courts is explained further in later chapters. A judgment of the House of Lords (which will be known from October 2009 as the **Supreme Court**) is binding on all other UK courts apart from Scottish →glossary criminal courts. The House of Lords/Supreme Court judges can refuse to follow their earlier decisions, if they decide this is justified. If their interpretation of a point of law is contrary to the intentions, policies, or wishes of the Government, the effect of such a ruling can be reversed only by new legislation.

Below the House of Lords/Supreme Court, decisions of the Court of Appeal bind the High Court and the lower courts. Decisions of High Court judges, though binding on all lesser courts, can be disregarded by other High Court judges – although they do so reluctantly because the tradition of unanimity is strong.

Equity

The common law is supplemented by the rules of equity. In non-legal usage, equity means fairness and impartiality. In the law, the term encompasses these meanings but also refers to a system of doctrines and procedures which have developed through the centuries alongside common law. These rules of equity give judges the flexibility to make rulings which they believe are just in a case's particular circumstances. The 'maxims of equity' express such principles. They include: 'He who comes into equity must do so with clean hands.' This refers to the principle that someone who has improperly violated the rights of others has thereby reduced his/her chance of getting a court to enforce obligations those people owe to him/her.

Statutes and statutory instruments

Common law, supplemented by equity, remains the basic law of the land, but increasingly it is being modified or changed by statute – that is, by Acts of Parliament, law drafted at the instigation of, and approved by, politicians in the House of Commons and the House of Lords. These Acts are referred

Chapter 1

Figure 1 Hierarchy of the courts.

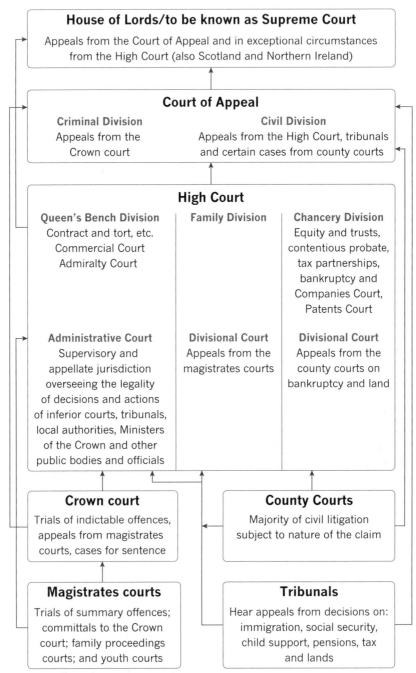

House of Lords/to be known as Supreme Court
Appeals from the Court of Appeal and in exceptional circumstances from the High Court (also Scotland and Northern Ireland)

Court of Appeal

Criminal Division
Appeals from the Crown court

Civil Division
Appeals from the High Court, tribunals and certain cases from county courts

High Court

Queen's Bench Division
Contract and tort, etc.
Commercial Court
Admiralty Court

Family Division

Chancery Division
Equity and trusts, contentious probate, tax partnerships, bankruptcy and Companies Court, Patents Court

Administrative Court
Supervisory and appellate jurisdiction overseeing the legality of decisions and actions of inferior courts, tribunals, local authorities, Ministers of the Crown and other public bodies and officials

Divisional Court
Appeals from the magistrates courts

Divisional Court
Appeals from the county courts on bankruptcy and land

Crown court
Trials of indictable offences, appeals from magistrates courts, cases for sentence

County Courts
Majority of civil litigation subject to nature of the claim

Magistrates courts
Trials of summary offences; committals to the Crown court; family proceedings courts; and youth courts

Tribunals
Hear appeals from decisions on: immigration, social security, child support, pensions, tax and lands

Figure reproduced by permission of Her Majesty's Courts Service.

to as primary legislation. Their interpretation by the courts gives rise to a great number of new precedents. UK governments have made increasing use of secondary legislation known as **statutory instruments**. Parliament frequently uses Acts to enshrine broad principles in legislation, but delegates the detailed framing of the new law – and therefore of its intended effect – to the departmental Minister concerned, who will cause this law to be set out in regulations or rules. These are called statutory instruments. They become law under powers given in the primary legislation. Statutory instruments are also used to phase legislation into force gradually, for administrative convenience.

→ glossary

European regulations and directives

Under the European Communities Act 1972, the UK is part of the European Union, and EU treaties and other EU law are thus part of UK law. The EU's Council and its Parliament agree regulations and directives which are legally binding on member states, e.g. on copyright matters, as part of a raison d'etre of the EU to encourage trade between member states, and therefore their wealth creation, by harmonising relevant law throughout its area. EU regulations apply in the form in which they are drawn up. But states decide how directives should be implemented, through their own legislation.

see ch. 27, p. 452

The European Court of Justice, based in Luxembourg, clarifies – for the national courts of EU member states – how EU legislation should be interpreted. This court can rule, for example, on allegations that EU law has been infringed by a member state, e.g. to gain advantage in trade. The court can penalise a state for such infringement. This court is not to be confused with the European Court of Human Rights, see below.

▌ The European Convention on Human Rights

As a response to the repression and genocide of totalitarian regimes – e.g. Germany under the Nazis, Communism under Stalin – Western European nations signed a treaty after World War Two to create the Council of Europe, a body to promote individual freedom, political liberty, and the rule of law. The Council of Europe preceded and is independent of the European Union, and has a different role. The work of the Council led to a further treaty – the

European Convention for the Protection of Human Rights and Fundamental Freedoms. This is usually referred to by its shortened title, the European Convention on Human Rights. The Convention came into force in 1953, setting out the freedoms which must be protected by its signatory nations, which include the UK. These freedoms include the right to life itself, freedom from torture, and freedom of expression, see below. Forty-seven nations are signatories to it, i.e. they have adopted it. The Convention created the European Court of Human Rights (ECtHR), based in Strasbourg. Individuals can take a case to this court to argue that a signatory nation has failed to protect them from, or to sufficiently compensate them for, a breach of a Convention right by a public authority. This definition of public authority includes national governments, local government bodies and other state agencies, but also judicial institutions. Therefore the Convention has very wide application, because if a private body or a person violates an individual's human rights, the Convention is breached if that nation's court system is asked, in either criminal or civil law (see below), to stop or to adequately remedy that violation but fails to do so. The ECtHR requires an individual to have exhausted all possibility of appeals within his/her nation's court system before asking it for justice. At the Strasbourg court, cases are argued between the individual, or more usually by his/her lawyers, and lawyers representing the nation thus accused of failing to uphold the Convention. The names of the cases decided there reflect this, e.g. Peck versus the United Kingdom, or von Hannover versus Germany.

The ECtHR can, if it rules for the individual, order the nation to pay compensation and to take general measures to avoid any future similar breach of the Convention. The Council of Europe's Committee of Ministers (which is comprised of the chief Foreign Ministers of the signatory nations) will check if the relevant nation has obeyed the judgment. The ECtHR's judgments, though not binding on the courts of signatory nations, nevertheless have influenced how judges in them approach the law, and how national legislation is drafted.

The Human Rights Act 1998

The Human Rights Act 1998, which came into force on 2 October 2000, has greatly increased the influence of the Convention and the ECtHR on UK courts, because the Act integrated the Convention into UK law. Now an individual can require any UK court to consider, in the context of any case, his/her rights under the Convention – he/she does not have to wait to take a case

see
Useful
Websites,
below

see ch.
24, pp.
401 and
402

to Strasbourg for those rights to be specifically considered, though he/she can still try that as a last resort if he/she feels the UK courts were unjust.

The Act says that:

(1) a UK court determining a question in connection with a Convention right must take account of decisions of the ECtHR;

(2) new UK legislation must be compatible with the Convention rights, and old and new legislation must be construed so far as possible to conform with Convention rights;

(3) UK courts have no power to strike down legislation that is incompatible with Convention rights, but may declare it to be incompatible, leaving it to the discretion of the relevant government Minister, if he/she considers that there are compelling reasons, to introduce amending legislation;

(4) it is unlawful for UK public authorities to act in any way that is incompatible with Convention rights.

Prior to 2000 UK law did recognise fundamental human rights, having evolved over centuries to do so. However, a general right of privacy – as specified in the Convention's Article 8, see below – did not previously exist in UK law. And some experts argue that freedom of expression was also insufficiently protected. The adoption of the Convention directly into UK law has required judges to systematically consider the extent to which Convention rights need upholding in any particular case, and to develop a transparent methodology to decide and explain why in some situations one Convention right can override another. Since 2000 these requirements have triggered rapid development of case law.   → glossary

For journalists, the most important part of the Convention is Article 10, which says in part: 'Everyone has the right to freedom of expression. This right shall include freedom to hold opinions and to receive and impart information and ideas without interference by public authority.'

Article 10 makes clear that restrictions on this right have to be justified. They must be 'necessary in a democratic society, in the interests of national security, territorial integrity or public safety, for the prevention of disorder or crime, for the protection of health or morals, for the protection of the reputation or rights of others'.

The Article states also that the restrictions must be 'prescribed by law' – this means they should not be imposed without legal basis or more widely than law permits.

As this book explains, journalists wanting to exercise their rights under Article 10 may find Article 8, which protects privacy, is argued against them. Article 8 would be a basis for a lawsuit by an individual to prevent publication of a story about his/her personal life, or of a picture or film which is argued to breach his/her privacy, or for a lawsuit to seek damages if such material has already been published. A reporter arguing against an order made by a court to give a witness or defendant anonymity in media reports can refer to Article 10 and may find Article 8 is cited in counter-argument.

→
see ch. 24

→
see ch. 13

> See Appendix 1, p. 565, for the text of both these Articles, and of others.

Weighing competing rights

Various precedent judgments have set out methodology which a court should use to decide in any particular case whether one Convention right should prevail over another, e.g. Article 10 over Article 8.

A leading case is *Re S (A Child) (Identification: Restrictions on Publication)* [2004] UKHL 47. In that House of Lords judgment, Lord Steyn said:

❝ First, neither article has *as such* precedence over the other. Secondly, where the values under the two articles are in conflict, an intense focus on the comparative importance of the specific rights being claimed in the individual case is necessary. Thirdly, the justifications for interfering with or restricting each right must be taken into account. Finally, the proportionality test must be applied to each. For convenience I will call this the ultimate balancing test. ❞

As the rest of this judgment makes clear, Lord Steyn was emphasising that the particular circumstances of each case must be intensely considered to decide which Convention right – and therefore which party to the argument – prevails in each matter to be decided. That focus must weigh the respective importance to each party, in the case's circumstances, of the right it claims. But the assessment may also need to address what outcome is most important for society, i.e. for the public interest (see above, p. 5). *Re S* concerned whether a particular defendant in a pending criminal trial should have anonymity in media reports of it, to help shield her young son from the effects of the publicity of the trial, because of his privacy rights under Article 8. Lord Steyn and his fellow law lords agreed with the argument made by media organisations, claiming rights under Article 10, that the public interest in unrestricted coverage of the trial would be too greatly harmed if such anonymity was granted.

 See ch. 11, p. 185, for more detail of this judgment. For more detail of the public interest in unrestricted media coverage of court cases, see ch. 12.

The legal principle of 'proportionality', referred to by Lord Steyn, will continue to be important. Judges in such cases will consider whether the media's intrusion into someone's privacy is disproportionate to the public interest value in the story. If a judge decides there is no such value, or it is low, he/she is much less likely to regard such intrusion as legal. The principle of proportionality also means that an order a court makes to prevent matter being published must not have a disproportionate effect on the media. For example, if a court considers that one item of information should not be published, it should not impose an order which stops the rest of the story being aired.

Other Articles in the Convention – for example, Article 6 (the right to a fair trial) and, exceptionally, Article 2 (the right to life) and Article 3 (freedom from torture) – have been cited in legal argument and judgments about the potential consequences of media reports.

 see Appendix 1, p. 565, ch. 9, p. 137–8

▌ Divisions of the law

There are two main divisions of the law – criminal law and civil law.

Criminal law deals with offences that are deemed to harm the whole community and thus to be an offence against the sovereign. A Crown court case is therefore listed, if a John Smith is accused of an offence, as *R v Smith*. 'R' stands for Regina (the Queen) or Rex (the King), depending on who is reigning at the time, and 'v' stands for 'versus'.

 see chs 2–8 for more detail on criminal law

When speaking about this case, however, a lawyer would generally refer to it as 'The Queen (or the King) *against* Smith'.

Civil law concerns disputes between individuals and organisations in financial matters, or about other entitlements, and includes the redress of wrongs suffered, e.g. through medical negligence. Civil law also includes the resolution of disputes between couples, e.g. in divorce actions.

 See chs 10 and 11 for more information on civil law.

A case in which John Smith is sued by Mary Brown will be known in writing as *Brown v Smith*. Lawyers will speak of the case as 'Brown *and* Smith' (our italics).

In practice, the two divisions in law overlap to some degree. Many acts or omissions are not only 'wrongs' for which the injured party may recover compensation, but also 'offences' for which the offender may be prosecuted and punished. A road accident may lead to a claim for damages and also to a prosecution for dangerous driving. Similarly, breaches of copyright, usually dealt with in the civil courts, may in certain circumstances be regarded as criminal offences, and be dealt with in the criminal courts.

→
see ch. 27

Young reporters must be careful to remember the basic differences between civil and criminal law. It would be wrong, for example, to say that a defendant in a county court – a civil court – is being 'prosecuted'. That is the language of the criminal courts, where the *defendant* is the person accused of a criminal offence. In civil courts the party taking legal action, known formerly as the plaintiff and after 1999 as the **claimant**, is said to sue the other party. The party sued is known as the *defendant* – but if he/she loses that civil case it is wrong to say that he/she has been 'found guilty': he/she is 'held liable'.

→ glossary

A reporter should not describe the civil court's order as a sentence. The term sentence is used only in criminal courts.

▌ The legal profession

Lawyers are either solicitors or barristers.

By tradition and practice, solicitors are the lawyers who deal directly with the client – e.g. a defendant in a criminal case or a party needing advice or to be represented in a civil law matter. Solicitors advise the client. They prepare the client's case, taking advice, when necessary, from a barrister specialising in a particular branch of the law – although solicitors themselves increasingly specialise. Solicitors may represent their clients in court, but in the past have generally been allowed to do so only in the lower courts – that is, the magistrates courts and the county courts. From 1993, solicitors with a record of experience as advocates and who have gained a higher courts qualification have been allowed to appear in the higher courts, where they compete with barristers in representing clients. Solicitors can represent an accused person in the Crown court in an appeal from a magistrates court or in a committal for sentence when they have represented the person in the lower court. They can also appear in the High Court in formal or unopposed proceedings, and in proceedings when judgment is delivered in open court following a hearing in chambers (in the judge's private room) at which they conducted the case for their client. In court, a solicitor wears a gown but no wig.

→ glossary

In other cases, the solicitor 'briefs' (instructs) a barrister to conduct the case. The title 'solicitor' derives from this procedure: on behalf of their clients, solicitors 'solicit' the services of a barrister.

Solicitors for misconduct may be 'struck off the roll' – the roll is the national list of solicitors – or suspended for a period. In that case, they are unable to practise.

Barristers are so called because they practise at the 'bar' of the court. Originally, the bar was a partition or barrier separating the judges from laypeople attending court. Nowadays, there is no physical barrier in most courts.

Barristers are known, singly or collectively, as 'counsel'. In court reporting, it is a common error to apply the word to solicitors, but this is incorrect.

Except for certain conveyancing matters, counsel have until recently not been allowed to accept instructions directly from lay clients. They had to be instructed by solicitors. Now, however, there is direct access to barristers for other professions such as surveyors, accountants, and town planners seeking legal advice in their fields.

Barristers wear a wig and gown in the higher courts, the Crown courts, and in the county courts, but not in the magistrates courts.

Successful barristers who have been practising for at least 10 years may apply to the Lord Chancellor for appointment as a **Queen's Counsel**. If this → glossary application is successful, they are said to 'take silk' because henceforth they will wear a gown of silk instead of cotton. They use the letters QC after their names.

The terms Queen's Counsel and King's Counsel are interchangeable: which is used depends on whether the reigning monarch is a queen or king.

For unprofessional conduct, barristers may be censured, suspended, or disbarred – that is, deprived of their standing as a barrister and therefore unable to practise.

▌ Legal posts in government

There are three senior government posts that have traditionally been held by lawyers – the Lord Chancellor, the Attorney General, and the Solicitor General. Until the passage of the Constitutional Reform Act 2005, the Lord Chancellor was head of the judiciary, but that legislation ended this role, which is now held by the Lord Chief Justice (see ch. 6, p. 81). This change was made to give further effect to the principle that the judiciary is, and is seen to be, independent and separate from any government. The Lord

Chancellor remains responsible for the general workings of the justice system, as political head of the government department which is now known as the Ministry of Justice. The Lord Chancellor as this edition of *McNae* went to press in 2009 is Jack Straw, Secretary of state for Justice.

The Act also created a Judicial Appointments Commission to take on the work of identifying candidates to be appointed as judges.

The main duty of the Attorney General and the Solicitor General, the holders of which posts are known as the two 'law officers', is to advise the government of the day on legal matters. Some holders of the post of Attorney General have been Ministers of Cabinet rank. The Attorney General or, in his/her absence, the Solicitor General, conducts the prosecution in certain important types of cases. The Lord Chancellor and the law officers change with a change of government.

Regulation and self-regulation of the media

→ see Useful Websites, below

→ see Useful Websites, below

Commercial TV and radio stations in the UK are subject to statutory regulation on who owns them, how programmes are transmitted, and on programme content, including journalism. The regulating body is the Office of Communications (Ofcom), which has power to fine a broadcasting organisation which breaches regulations. It can close down a commercial broadcaster, or a 'pirate one', which operates illegally in the UK. The BBC is subject to regulation by Ofcom in some respects, but is also self-regulated by the BBC Trust. Ofcom's Broadcasting Code sets out ethical rules for broadcast journalists, and their employers will face Ofcom admonishment or sanctions if a rule is adjudged to have been broken. The ethical code for BBC journalists is the BBC Editorial Guidelines, which incorporate elements of the Ofcom code. Broadcasting is thus subject to statutory regulation because politicians have historically regarded it as a medium which, were it to fall into the wrong hands, has particular power to offend the public or to be harmful, e.g. by transmission of pornography to children, by inflammation of communal tensions, by incitement to violence, or by distortion of news to manipulate people's political views. Regulation has also been necessary to govern access to the airwaves – e.g. to protect the radio channels of the emergency services from interference. But digitilisation and the growth of the internet have weakened this particular rationale. The system of statutory regulation and the BBC's constitution require that broadcast journalists must in their output be politically impartial.

The UK's newspapers and magazines, apart from some anti-monopoly legislation, are not subject to any statutory control on who owns them, or to any statutory regulation of their journalism's ethics. They are therefore free to be politically partisan. But this industry has created and funds a self-regulatory body, the Press Complaints Commission – which has elements of independence from the industry – to adjudicate on complaints about newspapers' and magazines' editorial output, including that on their websites, or about the information-gathering activities of their journalists. The code of practice used by the PCC to determine adjudications and to guide journalists on ethics is drawn up by a committee of editors, not by the PCC itself and is therefore formally known as the Editors' Code, though it is commonly referred to as the PCC code. The PCC's only direct sanction is to shame an editor by ensuring that any adjudication against his/her newspaper or magazine is published in it. But the PCC argues that this sanction has proved effective. A journalist or editor who grossly or persistently breaches the code risks being fired by his/her employer. The Editors' Code is reproduced in full in Appendix 2, p. 568.

→ see Useful Websites, below

The law exams of the National Council for the Training of Journalists (NCTJ) include questions on parts of the Editors' Code. Later chapters of this book emphasise its ethical guidance in the context of various legal topics. But it can be noted here that the Code's clause 4 states that:

> i) Journalists must not engage in intimidation, harassment or persistent pursuit.
>
> ii) They must not persist in questioning, telephoning, pursuing or photographing individuals once asked to desist; nor remain on their property when asked to leave and must not follow them. 〞

Its clause 10 states that:

> i) The press must not seek to obtain or publish material acquired by using hidden cameras or clandestine listening devices; or by intercepting private or mobile telephone calls, messages or emails; or by the unauthorised removal of documents or photographs; or by accessing digitally-held private information without consent.
>
> ii) Engaging in misrepresentation or subterfuge, including by agents or intermediaries, can generally be justified only in the public interest and then only when the material cannot be obtained by other means. 〞

→ See above, p. 5 and Appendix 2, p. 572

Both these clauses are among those subject to the code's 'public interest' exceptions.

▦ Recap of major points

- The media are the eyes and ears of the general public.

- A free media are an essential element in maintaining parliamentary democracy.

- In general journalists in the UK have no legal rights to gain information, or to publish it, beyond those enjoyed by other citizens.

- The European Convention on Human Rights has codified fundamental freedoms, including that of freedom of expression.

- Journalists must be alert to challenge unreasonable or unlawful restrictions on this freedom.

- Two constitutional bulwarks protect freedom of expression in the UK – jury trial and the rule against prior restraint.

- Sources of UK law include custom, precedent, equity, statutes and statutory instruments, and European Union regulations.

- The two main divisions of the law are criminal law and civil law, and journalists need to use correctly the legal terms appropriate for the type of court they are reporting.

- Codes of ethics guide journalists in their work.

🌐 Useful Websites

www.echr.coe.int/echr/ The 'Basic Texts' link leads to the full text of the Convention
   European Court of Human Rights

www.ofcom.org.uk/
   Ofcom

www.bbc.co.uk/guidelines/editorialguidelines/
   BBC Editorial Guidelines

www.ofcom.org.uk/tv/ifi/codes/bcode/
   Ofcom Broadcasting Code

www.pcc.org.uk/
   The Press Complaints Commission

Part 1

Crime, courts, and tribunals

Crime: media coverage prior to any court case

Chapter summary

All journalists need general knowledge of criminal law, for accurate reporting and to avoid committing contempt of court. This chapter explains the standard of proof needed to convict someone of a crime. It also provides a grounding in police powers of arrest and to detain. Crime reporters are well-versed in detention time limits, which can dictate – for example – how a murder investigation develops. This chapter explains how criminal prosecutions begin, and indicates the range of prosecuting agencies. Some contempt and libel pitfalls are noted here, but are explained further in other chapters. This chapter also outlines law which aims to keep secret the identities of police informants.

▶ Standard of proof in criminal law

For anyone to be convicted of a criminal offence, guilt must be admitted or – as a general principle – must be proven in court 'beyond reasonable doubt'. This is the standard of proof in criminal law which police or other investigative agencies therefore aim to achieve when gathering evidence. This principle is sometimes referred to as 'the presumption of innocence', i.e. people accused of crime are not required to prove they are innocent, because it is for the prosecution to prove they are guilty.

▌ Arrest without warrant

Under the Serious Organised Crime and Police Act 2005, police can arrest a person who has committed, or is committing, an offence (however minor), or is about to commit one, or anyone for whom there are reasonable grounds to suspect of such conduct. But the police officer also has to have reasonable grounds for believing the arrest is necessary to achieve one of the purposes specified in the Act. For example, the officer must think an arrest necessary to allow 'prompt and effective investigation' of the offence or to prevent prosecution of the offence being hindered by that person disappearing; or to get his/her true name and address; or to save him/her or others from injury; or to prevent him/her damaging property or obstructing the highway. In some circumstances police and prosecutors may seek an arrest warrant, i.e. authorisation by a magistrate, see below. To make an arrest, police can legally use 'reasonable force' to overcome resistance.

Members of the public can make what is sometimes termed 'a citizen's arrest'. But statute and legal precedent tightly prescribe, more than for a police arrest, when a 'citizen's arrest' is lawful. For example, the person arrested must be, or be reasonably suspected of, committing an **indictable offence** (i.e. not a minor offence).

→ glossary
→
see ch. 3
on offences

▌ Police questioning of suspects

A person under arrest is usually taken to a police station. A suspect who attends a police station voluntarily has no obligation to stay there, unless arrested. Police may decide, e.g. because of responses to questioning, to arrest a person who attended voluntarily. Statements that someone is 'helping with inquiries' or 'detained for questioning' are sometimes issued by police.

→ glossary
→
see
ch. 16,
covers
contempt
law

- Journalists should check whether the suspect is truly detained, i.e. under arrest, rather than helping police voluntarily, because an arrest **automatically** makes the case 'active' under the Contempt of Court Act 1981, affecting what can be published about it. As this book will explain, this Act protects the justice process. Media organisations which breach the Act's provisions face heavy penalties.

▶ Limits to detention by police, prior to any charge

Suspects are often detained under arrest by police for hours without any charge so they can be questioned. By law, to protect civil liberties, no person can normally be detained for more than 24 hours. If they have not been charged within that period they must be released. This period runs from the time of arrest or from when the suspect was brought into the police station, depending on circumstances. Under the Police and Criminal Evidence Act 1984, a police officer of superintendent rank or above can authorise that someone suspected of an indictable offence be detained for a further 12 hours, i.e. up to a total of 36 hours. If police apply to a magistrates court for a further extension, it can authorise the person's detention for up to a further 36 hours. If a further application is made, the court cannot extend this detention beyond a maximum total of 96 hours, i.e. 96 hours since detention began. The Act stipulates that the magistrates must **not** sit in open court when hearing applications for extended detention, so the public and reporters cannot attend these hearings. The Terrorism Act 2006 permits a person suspected of a terrorism offence to be detained without charge for a longer period – to a maximum of 28 days.

→ for the definition of a charge, see below, p. 24

If any person arrested is later released without being charged, and decides to sue the police for damages, alleging 'false arrest' or 'wrongful imprisonment' or both the success of any such lawsuit will depend on whether he/she was indeed deprived of liberty and, if so, whether the police grounds to detain him/her were unreasonable in the particular circumstances.

→ see p. 158 and p. 552 on such lawsuits →glossary

A suspect's friends or solicitor can, if they consider his/her detention to be unlawful, apply to the High Court for a writ of **habeas corpus** to attempt to secure his/her release, a procedure centuries old, now rarely used. In medieval Latin 'habeas corpus' means 'You should have the body [person]', referring to the writ's requirement for the police or other authorities to bring the person to the court to justify why he/she has been detained.

▶ The Crown Prosecution Service

Most prosecutions are the responsibility of the Crown Prosecution Service (CPS), a government department. It has local bases serving each of the 43

see Useful Websites, below on CPS

police areas in England and Wales. The head of the CPS is the Director of Public Prosecutions. It is independent of police. But it has the duty to advise and direct them in all investigations, except for those into the most minor crimes. The CPS decides, in all major cases involving police investigation, whether a suspect should be prosecuted, and if so, what the charge(s) should be.

- A charge is a formal accusation, giving the alleged offender basic details of the crime he/she is accused of. It is one of the ways in which a prosecution begins, and therefore means the case is due to go to court.

When a person detained at a police station is charged, he/she should be given the charge in written form. But he/she may have been charged orally, before that document is ready.

If a suspect is not charged, but the police want more time to complete investigations, he/she can be given **police bail** to return to a police station at a later date. He/she may be questioned further then, and be charged, or be told he/she will not be prosecuted.

Ch. 16 explains this law

As stated above, under the Contempt of Court Act 1981 when an arrest is made that case becomes 'active', so beginning the time in which the media must, to obey the Act, exercise care in what is published about that case.

- If there is no arrest, the case first becomes 'active' if and when the suspect is charged orally or – if there is no oral charge when a charge is served in writing; or when a summons or arrest warrant is issued for him/her, see below if he/she has not by then been charged.

If the suspect is released from arrest without charge, but is on police bail, the case remains 'active' during the time span of that bail, but ceases to be 'active' if and when the period of police bail ends without arrest or charge.

▌ Decisions on whether to prosecute

When considering whether suspects should be prosecuted, Crown Prosecution Service lawyers assess each case's evidence and circumstances to decide if there is 'a realistic prospect of conviction'. If the case passes that test, they then consider if it is in the public interest to prosecute. In almost all serious cases, consideration of the public interest leads to a decision to prosecute.

See the Code for Crown Prosecutors, under Useful Websites, below.

▮ Limits to detention by police, after any charge

Once a person has been charged police questioning of him/her must stop, except in some limited, prescribed circumstances. The person, if he/she remains under arrest, must by law be brought before a magistrates court on the day he/she was charged or the following day, excepting Sundays, Christmas Day, or Good Friday. Alternatively, after being charged the person may be released from arrest and given police bail to attend the court.

Lawyers employed by the CPS, using police-gathered evidence, conduct such prosecutions in court, except those for some minor offences for which the police handle the prosecuting process.

→
see chs 4 and 5 on what happens in Court

▮ Other prosecution agencies in the public sector

Other governmental agencies investigate and prosecute offences falling within their particular fields of responsibility. For example: local authorities can prosecute property landlords for breach of tenants' rights, and prosecute local traders under consumer protection laws; the Serious Fraud Office, a government department, investigates and prosecutes serious and/or complex fraud; the Department for Business, Enterprise and Regulatory Reform (formerly the Department of Trade and Industry) can, under company law, investigate businesses and refer evidence to other investigators or prosecutors (e.g. the police or the Serious Fraud Office); the Revenue and Customs Prosecutions Office prosecutes people accused of tax fraud, and some of those accused of drug smuggling and money laundering.

▮ Laying/presenting of information; summonses; requisitions; fixed penalties

The decision whether to prosecute may be taken quickly, e.g. soon after an arrest, or after weeks or months if such time is needed to gather evidence.

If the case is to be pursued, the prosecution can then begin either with a charge, e.g. after a final questioning of the suspect, or by the 'laying of information' before a magistrate. In the latter procedure, an allegation that a crime has been committed by the alleged perpetrator is supplied, either orally or in writing, to a magistrate. The magistrate will, without at that stage any full consideration of the evidence, issue a summons.

- A summons is a formal document, issued by a magistrates court, setting out one or more crime allegations in similar detail to a charge. It can be served on someone by being handed to them, being left at their address or by post. It requires them to attend the court on a specified date to respond to the allegation(s).

A summons is therefore another means of starting a prosecution. At court, the allegation(s) in the summons becomes the charge(s), there put verbally to the person, who – whether he/she arrives in answer to police bail, or under arrest, or in response to a summons or to a requisition (see below) – is there termed 'the defendant'. The Criminal Justice Act 2003 replaces, for specified 'public prosecutors' including those acting for the CPS, the 'laying of information' for a summons with a new, streamlined procedure known as 'written charge and requisition', whereby:

- a written charge is issued by the prosecuting agency, and is sent to or otherwise served on the accused person, and this documentation includes a requisition, i.e. a formal notification giving a date and time for him/her to turn up at the magistrates court.

This new procedure was already operative in some districts in 2009. Also, the term 'laying of information' has been changed for relevant cases involving public prosecutors to the 'presenting of information' to modernise terminology.

Summonses and requisitions are mainly used routinely for minor offences. In some such cases, documentation enclosed allows the accused person to admit the offence with no need to attend the magistrates court. They thereby accept a 'fixed penalty' fine. It can be paid by post. Fixed penalty notices, imposing a fine, are also handed out directly by police officers to people who, in what seem to be straightforward cases, have been witnessed committing an offence permitted in law to be dealt with by such procedure, e.g. speeding. Other enforcement agencies also use fixed penalty notices, e.g. council litter wardens hand them to people seen dropping litter. Anyone who wishes to challenge such a notice has the right to do this in a magistrates court, which will decide, after considering evidence, if the alleged offence is proved. If so, a fine must be paid. Failure to respond to such a fixed penalty notice, either by paying the fine or by challenging it within a specified time-scale, will lead to a summons to attend the court.

▶ Arrest warrants

Magistrates can issue an arrest warrant, if sworn, written information is laid before them that a person has committed an indictable offence, or any summary offence punishable by imprisonment, or as regards any offence if that the person's address is not sufficiently established for a requisition or summons to be served.

→ glossary

→
see
ch. 3 on
offences

- An arrest warrant is a formal document in which a magistrate empowers any police officer to arrest the suspect wherever he/she is located in the UK, and for him/her to be brought to the magistrates court.

This is another way, therefore, to initiate a prosecution. It can be used for a suspect 'on the run'. Such a warrant is generally sought when it has not been possible to serve a summons or requisition, or there has been no response to one. Sometimes when an arrest warrant is issued, it is 'backed for bail', thus allowing the person, after being arrested and having completed certain formalities at the police station, to be released on bail to attend the magistrates court at a future date. An arrest warrant is also sought by police to instigate extradition proceedings.

The issue of an arrest warrant is another of the triggers which make the case 'active' under the Contempt of Court Act 1981. It may already be active if a summons has been issued or a written charge has been served.

→
see ch.
16 on
Contempt
law

▶ 'Private prosecutions'

An individual citizen can, by the laying of information before a magistrate, initiate a prosecution to seek to prove that someone is guilty of a crime, even if police, the CPS, or any other public prosecuting agency has already concluded there is no or insufficient evidence. This capacity for any citizen to launch such a 'private prosecution' is seen as a fundamental right to counter-balance any inertia or partiality by police or other such agencies when crime is alleged. However, a magistrate has discretion to refuse to issue a summons if, for example, he/she has information that the allegation is frivolous or vexatious. After being launched, a private prosecution may quickly become unsustainable because, for example, an individual citizen lacks the investigatory powers given in law to police, and/or may not understand relevant law. To protect the civil liberties of those accused, no one can be tried for certain serious offences, e.g. murder, without the Director of Public Prosecutions being informed of the case. The law allows the CPS to take over the conduct of a 'private prosecution', and therefore also to withdraw the case. Also, the Attorney General can stop private prosecutions.

→
see p. 15 about Attorney General

Some private organisations prosecute, e.g. the Royal Society for the Prevention of Cruelty to Animals, which is a charity, regularly and successfully conducts 'private prosecutions' as part of its work, even though it has no special powers to assist it in collecting evidence. In 2007 such RSPCA prosecutions for cruelty to or neglect of animals led to 1,104 defendants being convicted.

▶ The risk of libel in media identification of crime suspects

A media organisation may discover that someone is being investigated by the police or any other agency, e.g. if the person is under arrest. If at that stage it publishes the suspect's name or other detail identifying him/her in this context, the suspect could successfully sue the media organisation for libel if the investigation does not lead to a criminal prosecution. Publishing a statement that someone is under such investigation, even when this is factually correct, is defamatory because it creates an inference that the person may be guilty. If the inference is unfounded, the media organisation may be unable to defend it in any subsequent libel case. If a spokesperson for a governmental agency, e.g. the police or CPS or a local council, officially releases to the media, for publication, the name of the individual under investigation/arrest, then the media can safely publish it, relying on the libel defence of qualified privilege if all the defence's requirements are met.

→
see ch. 17, p. 306 on inferences

→
see ch. 19 on this privilege

In reality, when reporting high-profile investigations, especially if a celebrity or public figure is a suspect, media organisations may choose, within the fierce competition to break news, to publish the suspect's name before any charge/summons/requisition, even when a libel risk exists. A media organisation may take this risk after deciding that the person is unlikely to launch a libel action because, for example, a celebrity or politician may not wish to alienate the media by suing. Or the media may take the risk because police leaks or other information suggest that a charge is sure to follow. If the person is charged, a libel action over pre-prosecution publicity becomes less likely, because any damage this publicity causes to the person's reputation will usually be dwarfed by, or indistinguishable from, damage caused by reports of subsequent court proceedings which the media can safely publish with 'privilege' protection.

However, the general danger in publishing allegations or inference of guilt is well illustrated by the £550,000 libel settlement paid in 2008 by Express Newspapers for suggestions in articles – which the newspaper group conceded were entirely untrue – about Kate and Gerry McCann, including the false allegation that they caused the death of their three-year-old daughter Madeleine, who disappeared during a family holiday in Portugal in 2007 and is feared abducted. The settlement was paid to the Find Madeleine campaign. Another example of such libel danger is the 2009 case in which a man accepted £50,000 damages from the BBC after it wrongly reported he had been charged with fraud.

ACPO guidelines on police naming of suspects

Guidelines issued to police forces by the Association of Chief Police Officers (ACPO) state that generally people under investigation should not be named to the media prior to any charge but that some details, e.g. that the person is 'a 27 year old Brighton man', may be released, provided they do not identify the suspect. Under these guidelines, an adult can and will, with certain exceptions, be identified by police to the media – by name, age, and occupation – once he/she has been charged, with details also to be provided about the charge and forthcoming court appearance. ACPO's guidelines accept that 'in exceptional circumstances' it may be in the public interest for police to release a suspect's name prior to any charge. When the media already have the name, and seek confirmation of it, the name may be confirmed by police, the guidelines add.

 see Useful Websites, below, for ACPO guidelines

However, the Queen's Bench Divisional Court ruled in 1991 that the press has no automatic right to be told by the police the name of a person being investigated or who has been charged with a criminal offence (*R v Secretary of State for the Home Department, ex p Westminster Press Ltd* [1991] *The Times* 18 December).

▶ Media identification of those assisting the police

→

see chs 7
and 9 on
such
orders

Once court proceedings have begun, a court may, under various statutes, make an order forbidding the identification of a witness in any media report of the case. In a youth court case, for example such anonymity protection is automatically bestowed on a juvenile witness.

In some circumstances, the law applies anonymity protection, in respect of a victim, potential witness, or police informant, *before* any court proceedings begin in a case being investigated by police.

Under the Serious Organised Crime and Police Act 2005, sections 86–89, it is an offence, punishable by up to two years in jail, to disclose, at any time, the new identities (e.g. the changed names and new addresses) of informants given such new lives as part of police protection under the Act, or to disclose other arrangements in such protection. Obviously, this prohibition reflects the potential risk to informants of violence or intimidation. The new identity can be given before or after any relevant court proceedings begin. The Act, which is not aimed specifically at the media, sets out limited defences for anyone accused of disclosing information about the new identity, e.g. there is no liability if the disclosure was made with the agreement of the protected person and was not likely to endanger anyone's safety.

→

see
useful
Websites
below, on
SOCA

In the Coroners and Justice Bill 2009, it is proposed that a magistrate – if requested by the police or by specified public prosecutors, including the Director of Public Prosecutions – can make without holding a court hearing an 'investigation anonymity order' in respect of someone assisting or willing to assist the police or the Serious Organised Crime Agency during investigations into suspected murder or manslaughter. But the Bill specifies that such an order should only be made if the death was caused by a gun or knife and if the person likely to have committed the offence was, when it was committed, aged at least 11 but under 30 and was likely to have then been a member of a similarly aged 'group' which was apparently engaged in crime.

This proposal is part of the Government's plans to counter the intimidating effect of street gang culture among young people, which makes it hard to secure information about such killings. The proposal is not aimed directly at the media, but to keep secret generally and indefinitely the identity of those specified by such orders as being actual or potential informants in such investigations. The Bill's explanatory notes make clear that, under this proposed law, once such an order is made it will be a criminal offence for anyone to disclose (other than officially within internal communications inside an investigating or a prosecuting agency) any information that would or might identify this person to others as someone who is such an informant or is willing to be one. The proposed penalty for such disclosure is a fine or a jail term of up to five years or both. It would be seem possible, for example, for a crime reporter, even if nothing is published, to be guilty of such disclosure if he/she verbally tells someone else that such a person is assisting the police. However, the Bill proposes that anyone accused of breach of the order will have a defence if he/she did not know and had no reason to suspect either that the order had been made or that the information disclosed would breach it; or if the disclosure was made to someone already aware that the person subject to the order was or was willing to be such an informant. The Bill proposes that a magistrate, if requested by a relevant investigating or prosecuting agency or by the person protected by the 'investigation anonymity order', can discharge it, i.e. cancel it, if there has been a material change of circumstances since it was imposed.

Though section 44 of the Youth Justice and Criminal Evidence Act 1999 contains provision to prohibit media reports from identifying, after police begin to investigate an alleged crime, anyone under 18 who allegedly is either the crime's victim, or a witness to it or its perpetrator, this part of the Act concerning such juveniles has not become law, and in 2009 the Government apparently had no plans to put this section into effect.

⠿ Point for consideration

It is, in most circumstances, illegal (and unethical) for the media to identify in reports of sexual offences people who are or who are alleged to be victims of such crimes, e.g. rape. See ch. 8.

 See Online Resource Centre for general ethical considerations in covering crime; the illegality of listening to the radio traffic of the emergency services and airports; and the illegality of advertisements for the return of stolen goods, if there is a 'no questions asked' pledge.

⠿ Recap of major points

- A criminal prosecution is initiated:
    - by a person being charged e.g. at a police station, or

- by a magistrate issuing a summons or arrest warrant, or
- by the written charge and requisition procedure.

■ The initial court appearance for someone thus formally accused of a crime will always be at a magistrates court, though the most serious cases can only be dealt with subsequently by a Crown court. See chs 3, 4, 5 and 6.

■ When covering crime stories, there are contempt of court dangers, because an arrest, a charge, a summons, or an arrest warrant makes a case 'active' under the Contempt of Court Act 1981.

■ When covering crime stories, there are defamation dangers, because of the libel risk in identifying, prior to any charge/summons/requisition, anyone as being suspected of, or under investigation for, a crime.

■ But if the police or another governmental agency, in an official statement, identifies a person as a suspect, it is safe in libel law to report the statement.

■ When covering crime stories, there are ethical considerations, see Online Resource Centre.

🌐 Useful Websites

www.cps.gov.uk/
Crown Prosecution Service

www.cps.gov.uk/about/principles.html
Code for Crown Prosecutors

www.acpo.police.uk/asp/policies/Data/magguidelines.pdf
Association of Chief Police Officers (ACPO) Media Advisory Group – Guidance Notes

www.pcc.org.uk/news/index.html?article=OTA=/
Press Complaints Commission guidance note 'on the reporting of people accused of crime'

www.soca.gov.uk
Serious Organised Crime Agency

Crimes: categories and definitions

Chapter summary

To avoid breaching reporting restrictions which are designed to help ensure trials are fair, journalists covering magistrates courts must know the difference between indictable-only, either-way, and summary crimes. This chapter explains what these categories and 'strict liability' mean. In crime and court stories, some offences/charges can be misrepresented if their definitions are misunderstood by journalists. This could lead to libel problems. This chapter provides definitions of offences including robbery and fraud, which often feature in reports. Reporting restrictions and libel dangers are fully explained in other chapters, as indicated by cross-references.

▎ Categories of criminal offences

Criminal charges, and therefore the offences they allege, are grouped into three main categories: indictable-only, either-way, and summary, as explained below. Journalists need to be able to distinguish between these three categories. **Automatic** reporting restrictions make it illegal to include certain details in media reports of some hearings at magistrates courts. Whether such restrictions apply depends on the category of the charge/ offence as well as on procedures followed by these courts.

 See chs 4 and 5 for full explanation of these restrictions and procedures

→ glossary

1) **Indictable-only offences** These are the most serious crimes, punishable by the longest prison terms, e.g. murder, rape, robbery. Therefore such a charge, though processed in its early court stage by a magistrates court, can only be dealt with by a Crown court. If the charge is denied, there will be a jury trial there. A defendant who pleads guilty to or is found guilty of such a charge will be sentenced there by a judge. Crown court judges have greater sentencing powers than magistrates. The term 'indictable-only' derives from the term 'indictment', the name for the document used to record the charge(s) against a defendant at a Crown court. An indictable-only charge can also be referred to as 'triable only by indictment'.

→
see ch. 6
on Crown
courts

→ glossary

2) **Either-way offences** Such charges can be dealt with either at a Crown court or at a magistrates court, hence the term 'either-way'. In this category, a magistrates court may decide a particular case is so serious that only a Crown court can deal with it, or if the magistrates court decides it can deal with the case, the defendant may exercise his/her right to opt for a Crown court trial, i.e. by jury. In general, either-way offences are regarded as being of a lesser magnitude of criminality than indictable-only crimes. Nevertheless, the either-way category includes very distressing and harmful offences, e.g. theft, burglary, sexual assault, and assault causing grievous bodily harm.

→
see also
ch. 4 and
ch. 6

   • Indictable-only and either-way charges are referred to collectively as 'indictable' charges, because both categories share the possibility of jury trial at Crown court, though, as indicated above, it can be determined that an either-way case will be dealt with by magistrates in **summary proceedings**, i.e. as it if were a summary offence, see below. Among legal agencies, there is not always consistency in whether the terms indictable-only and either-way are hyphenated.

→ glossary

→ glossary

3) **Summary offences** These are, compared to the other two categories, minor offences, e.g. common assault, drunkenness, and are likely to be relatively straightforward to deal with, e.g. speeding, **drink driving**. So, summary charges are in almost all cases dealt with in magistrates courts. People charged with summary offences have no right of jury trial, but generally benefit from being dealt with more quickly, by the magistrates, whether in trials or sentencing than defendants who end up at Crown court. So, 'summary proceedings' means 'proceedings in a magistrates court'. Chapter 4, p. 47 and 50, mentions circumstances in which a Crown court may deal with a summary charge. A prosecution for a summary offence has to begin within six months of the

→ glossary

date on which it was allegedly perpetrated – otherwise it cannot be prosecuted. This is in recognition that most such crimes are relatively minor. There is no such time limitation for prosecution of either-way or indictable-only offences.

▌ Defining criminality

There are two elements in most crimes:

- an act which is potentially criminal – which lawyers refer to as the actus reus (which they pronounce, in lawyers' Latin, 'actus reeus'); and
- a guilty mind – referred to as the mens rea ('menz reeah'), which, broadly speaking, means that such an act was carried out, or planned or attempted, with guilty intent, i.e. the perpetrator knew he/she was acting, or intending to act, in a way which is morally wrong.

It is a general, legal principle that a prosecutor has to prove both elements. So, in the crime of murder (see below, p. 36) the actus reus is that of killing someone, and the mens rea is that the act was done with 'malice aforethought'. If there is no such **malice**, a killing may be a lesser crime, e.g. manslaughter → glossary (see below), or – depending on the circumstances – not a crime at all, i.e. a tragic accident.

Strict liability

However, the law also recognises that, for a safe and just society to exist, there must be some crimes for which it is not necessary for prosecutors to prove guilty intent. Such offences are said to be of 'strict liability', and are also called 'absolute offences'. For example, a motorist who exceeds the speed limit commits an offence, even if he/she did not intend to or realise how fast he/she was driving. A motorist who drives with too much alcohol in his/her blood commits an offence, even if he/she did not intend to breach the alcohol limit. Failure to purchase a TV licence when owning a television set is also a strict liability offence.

    Strict liability, when it applies, removes or strictly limits any legal → glossary defences to a prosecution. It can be seen a practical solution to deter harmful or anti-social conduct which would otherwise, in many cases, be difficult or impossible to prove in respect of the extent to which mens rea – a guilty mind – existed. It is particularly important for journalists to understand this concept, in that some of the criminal offences which arise if certain matter is published are of strict liability, e.g. if matter is published which breaches the Contempt of Court Act 1981.

see ch.
16, pp.
274–275

▶ Definitions of crimes

Failure to understand the definitions of some crimes sometimes causes problems for journalists. For example, a crime which is theft is sometimes referred to in stories and headlines as a **robbery**. This not only makes the media organisation appear foolish to anyone who spots the mistake, but also puts it at risk of a libel action, particularly if such error occurs in a court report, because robbery is a more serious offence, involving violence or threatened violence. The definitions of crimes given below are simplified, and so in some instances would not satisfy a lawyer. For fuller definitions, see the CPS website's Legal Guidance section, listed below under Useful Websites.

→ glossary

see
ch. 19 on
accuracy
in court
reports

Crimes against people

Murder The unlawful killing of another human being 'with malice aforethought' – that is, with the intention to kill or cause grievous bodily harm. An adult convicted of murder must be sentenced to life imprisonment. Indictable-only.

Manslaughter The unlawful killing of another person, but in the absence of malice aforethought. Manslaughter can be a charge in its own right. But a jury in a murder trial can, if it finds the defendant not guilty of murder, in some circumstances convict him/her of manslaughter as an alternative verdict. Indictable-only.

Corporate manslaughter An offence for which an organisation, including companies, government departments, and police forces, can be convicted if it causes a person's death in the circumstance of a gross breach of a duty of care owed to that person, if the way in which its activities were managed or organised by its senior management was a substantial element in that breach. Indictable-only.

Causing or allowing the death of a child or vulnerable adult An offence introduced in the Domestic Violence, Crime and Victims Act 2004. It closes a former, legal loophole through which, for example, a couple whose child dies because of physical abuse inflicted in their household could escape justice by blaming each other, making it impossible to prove which of them was the killer. This offence enables both such partners to be prosecuted. It can also be used against relatives in the same household who failed to protect such a child or a vulnerable adult from such lethal abuse. Indictable-only.

Infanticide The killing of an infant under 12 months old by its mother, when the mother's mind is disturbed as a result of the birth. Indictable-only.

Aiding suicide Helping another person to commit suicide or to attempt suicide. Indictable-only.

Assault, common assault, battery, assault by beating The law's evolution in such cases has created overlapping definitions, in that the legal term 'assault' can mean an attack or a hostile act, e.g. a threatening gesture, which causes another person to fear an attack. Either type of act must be proven as intentional or reckless. The charge of common assault can allege such a threat and/or the element of 'battery', i.e. an attack by unlawful application of force/violence. Journalists should not assume, therefore, that a common assault charge necessarily implies a physical attack. Alleged battery can also lead to a charge of 'assault by beating'. These charges tend to be used if no, or only transient or trifling, bodily injury is allegedly caused (e.g. a push can be a common assault) and are summary, unless there are allegedly racial or religious motives in the assault, in which event they are either-way.

Assault occasioning actual bodily harm A charge, often abbreviated as ABH, alleging an assault (i.e. a threat and/or attack, see above) which caused harm. The harm need not be permanent but must be more than transient and trifling. The harm caused could be a psychiatric illness. Lawyers sometimes refer to ABH as 'a section 47 offence', a reference to this section of the Offences Against the Person Act 1861. Either-way.

Wounding or inflicting grievous body harm (GBH) These charges derive from the 1861 Act's section 20, and overlap in their definitions. It must be proved that the perpetrator intended or foresaw causing some harm, and – depending on which charge the prosecutor chooses – that the harm caused was a wound or grievous (i.e. serious) harm which was not or not only a wound. Either such charge, in full form, includes the term 'malicious', e.g. 'malicious wounding'. A 'wound' is the slicing-through or breakage of skin, and can be a mere cut. But a wounding charge tends to be used only if there is a serious wound. A GBH charge tends to be used, for example, if the harm includes broken bone, or led to substantial loss of blood, and/or extended medical treatment and/or permanent disfigurement and/or permanent disability. These charges are either-way.

Wounding 'with intent'/inflicting grievous body harm 'with intent' Under section 18 of the 1861 Act, the wounding or GBH is deemed to have been 'with intent' if there is intent to cause GBH or to resist 'lawful apprehension'. Such a charge is indictable-only. It carries a maximum penalty of life imprisonment.

Rape Indictable-only. For its definition, the definitions of other sexual offences, and for detail of the anonymity protection in law for victims/alleged victims of sexual offences, see ch. 8.

Crimes against property

Theft The dishonest appropriation of property belonging to another with the intention of permanently depriving the other of it (Theft Act 1968). Either-way. The act of theft is stealing. Do not refer to the offence as robbery.

Robbery Theft by force (i.e. violence), or by threat of force. Indictable-only.

Handling Dishonestly receiving goods, knowing or believing them to be stolen; or dishonestly helping in the retention, removal, disposal, or sale of such goods. Either-way.

Burglary Entering a building as a trespasser, and then

- stealing or attempting to steal from it;
- or inflicting or attempting to inflict grievous bodily harm to anyone in it;
- or making such trespassing entry to a building with:
  - intent to steal,
  - or intent to inflict GBH,
  - or intent to do unlawful damage.

Generally, burglary is an either-way charge, though in some circumstances it is indictable-only.

Aggravated burglary The act of burglary while armed with a firearm, imitation firearm, or any other weapon. Indictable-only.

Fraud Under the Fraud Act 2006, there are now general offences of fraud, defined as conduct 'with a view to gain or with intent to cause loss' involving either:

- a dishonest making of a false representation (e.g. using a credit card dishonestly, or using a false identity to open a bank account); or

- a dishonest failure to disclose information when under a legal duty to disclose (e.g. failure, when applying for health insurance, to disclose a heart condition);

- dishonest abuse of a position (e.g. an employee swindling money from his/her employer).

The Act also includes a fraud offence of obtaining services dishonestly. Older fraud charges, such as obtaining property or services by deception, created by earlier legislation (e.g. Theft Act 1968), survive transitionally, their use dependent on when the alleged offences occurred. Conspiracy to defraud remains a **common law** offence. Fraud offences are either-way, but if the allegation is deemed by a relevant public prosecutor as of sufficient 'seriousness or complexity', it is treated as indictable-only. Such fraud offences can encompass multimillion pound scams involving companies used to commit the crime or as its victims.

→ glossary

→ see transfer procedure, ch. 4, p. 59

Blackmail Making an unwarranted demand with menaces with a view to gain. This offence could be a threat to reveal to other people an embarrassing secret, or embarrassing photos, unless money is paid. But it could be another type of extortion, e.g. a threat to a supermarket company that goods on its shelves will be contaminated unless money is paid. Indictable-only.

Taking a vehicle without authority This offence does not imply an intention to deprive the owner permanently and so should not be confused, either in text or headline, with theft. It can be reported, for example, that such a defendant took a car, but not that he/she stole it, though he/she may have abandoned it miles from where the owner parked it. The offence is sometimes referred to on court lists as TWOC (taking without owner's consent), and can cover conduct known colloquially as 'twocking' or 'joy-riding'. Summary.

Aggravated vehicle taking When a vehicle has been taken (as above) and, before it is recovered, someone is injured, or the vehicle or other property is damaged, because of how it was driven. Either-way.

Motoring crimes

Dangerous driving A person drives a motor vehicle dangerously if the way he/she drives falls far below what would be expected of a competent and careful driver, or if it is obvious the vehicle is in a dangerous state (e.g. because of what is attached to or carried in it). Either-way.

Causing death by dangerous driving This replaced the former offence of causing death by reckless driving. Indictable-only.

Careless or inconsiderate driving Driving a motor vehicle without due care and attention or without reasonable consideration for others. The level of bad driving that must be proved for either such offence is considerably less than that required to be proved in cases of dangerous driving. Summary.

Causing death by careless or inconsiderate driving Either-way.

Driving under the influence of drink or drugs Driving a motor vehicle despite the ability to do so being thus impaired. Summary.

Driving with excess alcohol Driving a motor vehicle at a time when the proportion of alcohol in the driver's body exceeds the prescribed limit; that is, 80 milligrammes of alcohol in 100 millilitres of blood, 35 microgrammes of alcohol in 100 millilitres of breath, or 107 milligrammes of alcohol in 100 millilitres of urine. Summary.

Causing death by careless driving when under the influence of drink or drugs The driver must be unfit to drive through drink or drugs; or must have consumed excess alcohol (as above); or must have failed to provide a specimen. Indictable-only.

NB: When reporting drink-driving cases at court, a journalist should realise that it may not be fair or accurate (and therefore could be a libel problem – see ch. 19, pp. 338–339) to describe a driver who has consumed more than the prescribed limit of alcohol as 'drunk'. He/she may only be marginally over the limit. It is safe to use the term 'drunk' if and as it is used in open court, or – in the event of a conviction – if the evidence clearly merits it.

Some other noteworthy crimes

Perjury Knowingly giving false evidence after taking an oath as a witness to
 tell the truth in court, or in an affidavit, or to a tribunal. Indictable-only.

Perverting the course of justice This offence could involve interference with or threatening a witness or juror, or concealing evidence, or giving false information to the police, or making a false allegation. Indictable-only.

Wasting police time A lesser offence than the two above, though it too may involve making a false allegation. It could also occur if somebody falsely claims to police that he/she has information material to an investigation. Summary.

Kerb-crawling The colloquial term for the offence, usually committed by men in streets frequented by prostitutes, of 'soliciting' (which, in this context, means offering to pay for sex) from a motor vehicle in such a manner to cause annoyance to the person approached (who may be a local resident, not a prostitute) or to others in the neighbourhood. Summary.

Other prostitution-related offences Though it is not an offence to be a prostitute, it is an offence for a prostitute to loiter in a public place, or to 'solicit' there (which means, in this context, to approach another person to offer sex in return for money). It is also an offence, for one's own gain, either to incite someone to be a prostitute or to 'control' a prostitute in his/her prostitution; or to run a brothel (which, hence, are usually advertised as 'saunas' or 'massage parlours', though, obviously, such descriptors can be accurate for a legitimate business). A person alleged to be the victim of incitement to be, or of control of, a prostitute, or of 'trafficking' for prostitution, is legally entitled to anonymity in media reports of the case, under sexual offence law.

see ch. 8

⠿ Recap of major points

- There are three main categories of criminal offences/charges:
  - Indictable-only, which can only be dealt with by a Crown court;
  - Either-way, which can be dealt with by a Crown court or a magistrates court, depending on what the magistrates court decides or on the defendant's choice – see ch. 4;
  - Summary – almost all such cases are dealt with by magistrates. There is no right of Crown court trial, i.e. by jury, for such offences – see ch. 5.
- Both indictable-only and either-way charges may be referred to as 'indictable'.
- If an offence is of 'strict liability', the defendant can be convicted even if he/she had no clear 'intent' to do wrong.
- If a media organisation fails to report an offence or charge accurately, it may be successfully sued for libel by the defendant in that case – see also ch.19.

🌐 Useful Websites

www.cps.gov.uk/legal/index.html
  Crown Prosecution Service Legal Guidance

4

Magistrates courts: the most serious criminal cases

Chapter summary

Magistrates, in terms of caseload, are the primary dispensers of justice. Anyone formally accused of a criminal offence is required to appear before them, except those who accept fixed penalties – see ch. 2. Magistrates courts govern the outcome of around 95 per cent of all criminal court cases, i.e. the vast majority of summary charges, and most either-way charges (see ch. 3 for categorisation of offences). But some defendants appear in a magistrates court only en route to a Crown court appearance. This chapter explains who magistrates are, the limits on their sentencing powers, and what bail is. It also explains how magistrates process, in preliminary hearings, those cases – the minority – bound for the Crown court. These are usually the most newsworthy. This chapter also explains how → glossary **automatic** reporting restrictions limit what can be published immediately from these preliminary hearings. Other reporting restrictions are covered in chs 7, 8, and 9. Ch. 5 gives detail of how some criminal cases are entirely dealt with by magistrates. Ch. 6 explains the Crown Courts. The law of contempt of court is primarily dealt with in ch. 16 and libel considerations in court reporting in ch. 19. Other aspects of court reporting are explained in ch. 12.

▶ Who are magistrates?

The role of magistrates originates in the twelfth century. They retain their ancient title of 'justices of the peace', abbreviated to 'JPs'. Almost all are volunteer, part-time magistrates, known as lay magistrates. They embody the British constitutional tradition that those who decide verdicts are, in most instances, not professional judges but are drawn directly from local communities (an ethos also embodied in the Crown court jury system, see ch. 6). Recruitment strategy seeks to ensure that people from a range of social backgrounds are chosen as magistrates. There are around 30,000 lay magistrates. They get expenses and an allowance for any loss of income incurred because of time spent on court duties. They are trained in court procedures.

There are more than 300 magistrates courthouses in England and Wales.

When lay magistrates try a case, there must be at least two. A trial by magistrates is known as a **summary trial**. One magistrate is sufficient for →glossary some court duties. Magistrates also sit in youth courts and deal with some fields of civil law, as later chapters explain. When more than one magistrate sits in a court hearing, one acts as chair and announces decisions. In court, magistrates are advised on law and procedure by a justices' clerk or one of his/her staff – both of whom are legally trained. An appeal can be made to the High Court for **judicial review** to challenge a magistrates court's inter-

→
see also
ch. 6,
p. 92 on
judicial
review

pretation of the law.

 See also Online Resource Centre ch. 4: More about magistrates.

District judges

In addition to lay magistrates, there are, particularly in city districts of high caseload, professional magistrates (i.e. they get a wage) known as **district** →glossary **judges**, appointed after at least seven years' experience as a solicitor or barrister. They are usually asked to deal with lengthy or complex cases. Until August 2000 a district judge was officially termed a **stipendiary magistrate** →glossary (from the Latin term stipend, meaning a wage) and is still sometimes called, in court slang, 'the stipe'. A district judge has power to try cases with no other magistrate. However, for convenience, this chapter and others will generally refer to 'magistrates' (i.e. plural) sitting in court, because two or three lay magistrates sit in many hearings.

In the simplest, summary cases, magistrates may be able to deal with the defendant on his/her first appearance. But many cases need adjourn-

→
see
ch. 5 on
summary
proceed-
ings
→glossary

ment to allow time for preparations for a summary trial or for magistrates to sentence, or, if heading for Crown court, to await a hearing there. Therefore magistrates frequently need to decide whether to grant a defendant **bail** or **remand** him/her to prison custody until the case's next date.

▌ Bail

Bail is the system by which a defendant is given his/her liberty until the case's next court date, if he/she undertakes to return to court then and in the meantime to obey any conditions of bail imposed by the court.

Conditions usually include that he/she continues to live at his/her home address, and may require a defendant to report regularly to a police station, as a check that he/she has not fled the district.

Under the Bail Act 1976, as a general rule a defendant must be granted bail unless one or more of the following circumstances apply:

- the court is satisfied there are substantial grounds for believing that if bail is granted
  - he/she will abscond, or
  - commit another offence, or
  - obstruct the course of justice (e.g. by disposing of evidence or interfering with witnesses);

- the court decides he/she should be sent to prison in custody for his/her own protection, e.g. if the crime alleged has so angered the local community that there is risk of mob violence to him/her;

→

see ch. 3, pp. 33–34 on offence categories

- he/she is alleged to have committed an **indictable-only offence** or an **either-way offence** at a time when he/she was on bail granted in an earlier case;

- he/she is already in prison, serving a jail sentence;

- there is not yet sufficient information available for the court to make a decision on bail.

To inform decisions on bail, the court will be told of any relevant previous convictions a defendant has, and will be given, by the prosecuting lawyer, some detail of evidence, beyond what is stated in the charge(s), of the crime alleged. A defence lawyer arguing for bail may give the defendant's view of events which led to the charge(s). A court must give reasons for any refusal of bail.

Unless there are exceptional circumstances, bail cannot be granted to a defendant charged with murder, manslaughter, or rape if he/she has previously been convicted of such an offence. In 2009, the Government proposed in the Coroners and Justice Bill that magistrates should no longer be empowered to hear a bail application by a defendant charged with murder, and that instead he/she should make the application to a Crown court.

→

see preface, p. ix

Bail need not be granted to a drug user who refuses to undergo drugs assessment or follow-up treatment.

- In some cases, a court will, as an extra safeguard, insist that the defendant has a **surety** before bail is granted.

→ glossary

A surety is someone – e.g. a relative or friend of the defendant – who guarantees the defendant will 'surrender' to bail, i.e. turn up at court on the required date. The surety agrees to forfeit a sum of money, fixed by the court, if the defendant absconds.

A surety can be jailed if subsequently, in the event of the defendant absconding, he/she cannot pay the agreed sum.

To fail to surrender to bail is a criminal offence in itself. In slang, a defendant who absconds is said to 'jump' bail. A court will issue an arrest warrant for him/her, see p. 27.

If bail is refused by magistrates the defendant may apply to a judge at Crown court for bail. The prosecution, if the alleged offence is one punishable by jail, can – by appealing to a Crown court judge – challenge a magistrates court's decision to grant bail, and until that appeal is resolved the defendant will be kept in custody.

→
see also ch. 12, p. 198 on bail hearings

▮ Magistrates' sentencing powers

If a defendant is convicted in a summary trial, magistrates can punish him/her by:

- sentencing him/her for a jail term of up to six months for a single offence, if law sanctions jail for that particular crime, and in total for up to 12 months for more than one such offence if the court decides these sentences should run consecutively, see below;

- imposing a fine, with the actual amount depending on statute for that offence and any discretion the court has. Broadly speaking, magistrates cannot impose a fine of more than £5,000. There are exceptions, e.g. an employer can be fined up to £20,000 for breach of health and safety law. Failure to pay a fine could lead to a jail sentence being imposed instead.

Summary proceedings, and magistrates' other powers of punishment for defendants convicted in these proceedings, are primarily explained in

→ glossary

ch. 5. But the limits of magistrates' punishment powers are also relevant to this chapter, see below.

- Consecutive sentences – that is, two or more jail sentences running one after the other – may be imposed when the defendant is convicted of more than one offence. For example, if a sentence of six months is imposed as consecutive to a sentence of three months, the defendant is thereby sentenced overall to nine months in prison.

- Sentences may, however, be imposed to run concurrently. **Concurrent sentences** are those where the defendant is sentenced overall only for the length of the longest sentence imposed. In the above example, this would be six months.

→ glossary

> See also Online Resource Centre, ch, 4: Changes enshrined in the Criminal Justice Act 2003, concerning law due to increase magistrates' sentencing powers.

▶ Preliminary hearings for cases with potential of jury trial

→
see ch. 3, p. 34 on indicta-ble-only offences

A defendant charged with an indictable-only offence e.g. murder, **robbery**, or rape, cannot be tried or sentenced by magistrates because they do not have the power to impose a sufficiently heavy sentence on anyone convicted of such a serious crime.

Indictable-only charges – 'Sending for trial'

When a defendant on an indictable-only charge appears before a magistrates court, this is classed as a **preliminary hearing**, because the case is merely en route to Crown court, where judges have greater power to sentence if there is a conviction. But such preliminary hearings are often of great news interest, particularly the first appearance in court of someone accused of a notorious crime. In preliminary hearings, the magistrates' role is limited to deciding on bail, to formally sending the case to Crown court 'for trial' and to procedural preparations for the Crown court stage. This **sending for trial** may well occur on the defendant's first appearance before magistrates. The phrase indicates the potential for jury trial, even if in any particular case there may ultimately be no such trial, e.g. if at Crown court the defendant

→ glossary

→ glossary

pleads guilty. In indictable-only cases, no formal plea (i.e. of guilty or not guilty) is taken from the defendant at the magistrates court, because this is done later, at a Crown court **arraignment**, see ch. 6, p. 78.

→ glossary

Automatic reporting restrictions severely limit what can be published immediately from these preliminary hearings of indictable-only cases at magistrates courts. See below, p. 51.

:::: Point for consideration

When a defendant on an indictable-only charge is sent for trial, magistrates have discretion to also send to Crown court any either-way or summary charge, if punishable by jail or disqualification from driving, related to the indictable-only charge, e.g. if these offences allegedly occurred in the same incident.

Either-way charges – mode of trial procedure

There are also preliminary hearings in magistrates courts for *either-way cases*. These hearings are for decisions on bail and, in each case, for procedure which determines at which venue it will be dealt with, i.e. whether it will be heard by the magistrates, and so be treated as a *summary* case, or by a Crown court.

→ see ch. 3, p. 34 on offence categories

In such a preliminary hearing, the defendant is asked, usually on his/her first appearance in the case, to indicate to the magistrates how he/she <u>intends</u> to plead, i.e. guilty or not guilty, to any either-way charge faced. Eliciting this 'indication' is known as the plea-before-venue procedure.

- If the defendant indicates he/she intends to plead 'guilty', then this is automatically treated as a formal plea of guilty, and so he/she is thus convicted of that offence, and will at that hearing or a later one be sentenced by magistrates <u>unless</u>, after hearing more detail of the offence, and of any relevant previous conviction(s) he/she has, they decide their punishment powers are insufficient, and that the defendant should therefore be **committed for sentence** to the Crown court, for a judge there to sentence him/her.

→ see above, p. 64 on committed for sentence

- If the defendant indicates he/she will plead 'not guilty', a **mode of trial hearing** follows, usually immediately, in which the magistrates, after hearing from prosecution and defence about the alleged crime, decide if the case can be dealt with in a summary trial, i.e. by magistrates.
  - If they decide the alleged either-way crime is too serious for this (i.e. in the event of a conviction, magistrates' punishment powers would be insufficient), the case will be adjourned for a **committal**

→ glossary

hearing before another set of magistrates who will decide if there is sufficient evidence for the case to go to Crown court. See below for explanation of committal hearings.

- If magistrates agree to offer a summary trial – a decision which is known as the magistrates 'accepting jurisdiction' – the defendant is then asked if he/she wants summary trial or jury trial. If jury trial is chosen the case will be adjourned for a committal hearing. If summary trial is chosen, the defendant is asked to enter a formal plea of not guilty, and the trial will subsequently take place in the magistrates court, after adjournment to permit preparations.

When deciding in the mode of trial procedure whether to offer a summary trial, magistrates accept at face value the prosecutions account of evidence. But if the defendant wants summary trial, they listen to defence arguments about why the case is suitable for this. A defendant who chooses jury trial is said to 'elect' this.

See also Figure 2, which shows how an either-way case is processed in a magistrates court, and either is dealt with there or may be committed for Crown court trial, as this chapter explains. See ch. 5 generally for detail on automatic reporting restrictions on pre-trial hearings in summary proceedings, and for procedure in summary trials.

See also Online Resource Centre, ch. 4: Changes enshrined in the Criminal Justice Act 2003.

Either-way offences – committal hearings

 → glossary   If, in the **mode of trial hearing**, a magistrates court refuses to offer a summary trial for a denied either-way case, or the defendant exercises his/her right to trial by jury, then the case proceeds to a further type of preliminary hearing – a committal hearing – at the magistrates court, almost certainly at a later date.

In a committal hearing, one or more magistrates will examine the evidence to decide if it is sufficient for the defendant to be '*committed for trial*' on any charge to the Crown court.

In this function, magistrates are known as 'examining justices'. The prosecution will secure such committal if it proves at that hearing that there is → glossary   'a case to answer', sometimes referred to as a **prima facie** case, on at least one charge. This is a low burden of proof. It by no means suggests that the defendant will be convicted on that charge at Crown court. In most instances, the defence does not argue against committal, so magistrates commit such

Figure 2 Processing of either-way cases in Magistrates courts.

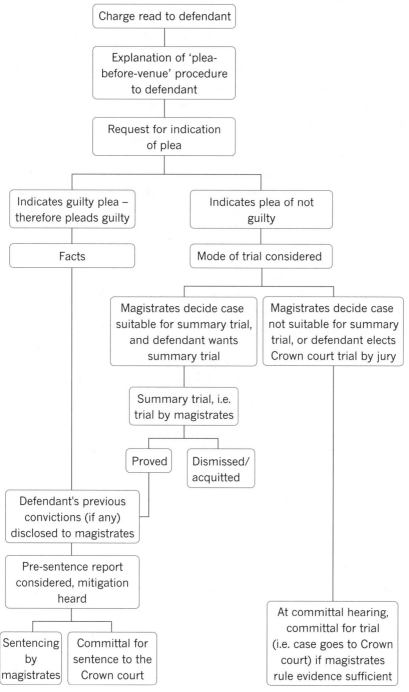

Design of figure used by permission of Judicial Studies Board.

defendants without considering any evidence. But if the defence argues there is no case to answer, the examining justices make their decision after considering the prosecution's written evidence, e.g. witness statements as documents. No witnesses are called in person. No defence evidence is submitted.

If magistrates, when considering any charge, consider there is insufficient prosecution evidence, they will **discharge** the defendant as regards that charge. He/she may be committed for trial on some charges but be discharged on others.

If the defendant is thus discharged, this should not be described as an acquittal on that charge – because there has been no trial. A discharged defendant will not normally be prosecuted again for that particular alleged crime. But it is possible, though rare, for him/her to be charged with it again, if further evidence comes to light, so initiating another prosecution. It is also possible – though again, rare – for the prosecution, after a discharge, to seek to resurrect the charge on the existing evidence by seeking a voluntary **bill of indictment**, see below, p. 60.

There is no provision for the written evidence in a committal hearing to be made available to the media. Reporting restrictions under section 8 of the Magistrates' Courts Act, while in force, forbid publication of evidence anyway (see below, p. 51). But if magistrates decide to discharge a defendant, the Act states that as much of these written statements as has been accepted as evidence shall be read aloud unless the court otherwise directs; and that when such a direction is given (against reading the evidence aloud), an 'account' must still be given orally in court of such evidence.

When an either-way charge is committed for trial, magistrates have discretion to commit with it any related **summary offence**, e.g. if it allegedly occurred in the same incident.

> See also Online Resource Centre, ch. 4: Changes enshrined in the Criminal Justice Act 2003, concerning law due to abolish committal hearings.

⸬ Point for consideration

Indictable-only charges used to be subject to committal hearings, so news reports from previous decades, for example of murder cases, may refer to these. But now indictable-only charges are *sent for trial*, see p. 46.

▶ Automatic reporting restrictions on preliminary hearings in indictable-only and either-way cases

Restrictions, in section 8 of the Magistrates' Courts Act 1980, as amended by other Acts, automatically apply to media reports of preliminary hearings at magistrates courts of indictable-only and either-way cases. So these restrictions thus apply to hearings held to decide on bail in such a case, and to send or transfer it to the Crown court for trial, and to committal hearings. The effect is that these restrictions govern media coverage of any proceedings at a magistrates court in which a case retains the potential of being determined later by jury trial at Crown court. The purpose of the restrictions is to prevent prejudice to such jury trials, as explained below. The restrictions are designed to prevent publication of:

➔ Transfer is explained on p. 54

- any reference to evidence in the case, apart from what is encapsulated in the wording of charge(s), and
- any previous convictions the defendant has, and
- any other material with potential to create such prejudice.

Evidence As indicated above, pp. 44 and 48, some evidence is outlined for magistrates to make decisions on bail, and – in either-way cases – during the mode of trial procedure, and is considered in any contested committal hearing. But it may be that some evidence thus presented in a magistrates court will not figure later in any jury trial of the case. For example, in pre-trial stages at Crown court the defence may persuade a judge there that a prosecution witness's testimony is so unreliable that it should be ruled inadmissible, i.e. the jury should not be told of it. Or evidence that a defendant confessed to the crime, to police or to someone else, could be ruled inadmissible if the judge accepts that the confession was made under improper duress or that evidence of it was fabricated. Yet if the media, when covering a preliminary hearing before magistrates, immediately report such evidence, there is a possibility that anyone reading, viewing, or listening to such a report will later be selected to be a juror in the Crown court trial of that case. Such a person may, during that trial, recall from those earlier media reports detail of evidence, e.g. a discredited confession, that he/she was not supposed to know. This would contaminate the jury's consideration of the case, and could result in a defendant being unfairly convicted.

➔ see ch. 6, p. 76 on juries

Previous convictions Generally, in accordance with the principle of the 'presumption of innocence', see ch, 2, p. 21, a Crown court jury will not be told of any previous conviction(s) a defendant has. Jurors are usually expected to reach a verdict solely on the facts of the particular case in that trial, not on what the defendant has done further back in the past. But if the media were to report, when covering a preliminary hearing at a magistrates court, any such previous conviction mentioned in it, e.g. when magistrates were deciding whether to grant bail. This could alert the public, and therefore potential jurors, to a defendant's criminal past. For a jury to have such knowledge could be extremely prejudicial, e.g. make it more likely to form a poor view of the defendant.

Other material with potential to create such prejudice could occur in various forms. For example, some defendants appear before magistrates before investigation into their alleged criminality is complete. In a rape case the police may be checking other unsolved rapes, to see if the defendant is responsible for them too. Magistrates may be told about these checks by a prosecutor opposing bail. But it may be that no additional charges follow, through lack of evidence. Yet, if the media report, from such a preliminary hearing, police suspicion that the defendant may have committed further (uncharged) crime, someone on a jury trying, for example, a (single) rape charge may recall the earlier suggestion that the defendant could be a serial rapist. This recollection could prove prejudicial to that trial.

The scope of the section 8 restrictions

The restrictions in the 1980 Act function by specifying what <u>can</u> be published from such preliminary hearings. This is restricted to the following categories of information (expressed here in a form which simplifies them, with some explanation added):

- the name of the court (e.g. Sunderland magistrates court) and the magistrates' names;
- the names, addresses, and occupations of the parties, including the defendant(s), and of witnesses, and the ages of the defendant(s) and witnesses;
- the charge(s), or a summary of it/them;
- the names of any legal representatives engaged in the proceedings, e.g. solicitors or barristers acting for the defence or prosecution;
- if proceedings are adjourned, the date and place to which they are adjourned;

- 'arrangements as to bail', i.e. whether bail was granted or refused, and, if it was granted, any bail conditions and surety arrangement (see pp. 44–45, above);
  - as regards cases in which bail is refused, the usual interpretation of the restrictions is that the media should <u>not</u> report why the prosecution opposed bail or any reasons the magistrates gave for refusing it – because such matter could be prejudicial;
- whether **legal aid** was granted;   →glossary
- in any case, it is also safe to publish the bare fact that reporting restrictions are in force, since to do so cannot in itself be prejudicial.

As regards a committal hearing, under the section 8 restrictions the media can, in addition to the categories above, report:

- any decision of the magistrates to commit any defendant to Crown court for trial; if a defendant is committed for trial, the charge(s), or a summary of it/them, on which he/she is committed, and the name of the Crown court to which he/she is committed.

- when there is more than one defendant, and one is committed for trial, any decision on the 'disposal of the case of any defendant not committed for trial, e.g. that there was a discharge because of insufficient evidence.

If, in a case where there is more than one defendant, one of them unsuccessfully asks for the section 8 reporting restrictions to be lifted, see below, p. 56, the bare fact that the court declined to lift them can be reported.

⠿ Points for consideration

In the 1980 Act, the term 'parties' would encompass any individual who had initiated the case in a private prosecution. The scope given within the Act's restrictions to report some detail of witnesses is now largely vestigial. Witnesses used to give evidence in person at committal hearings. But now evidence is presented there in written statements (see above, p. 48).   → see ch. 2, p. 27 on private prosecutions

As regards scope given to report whether there has been for each charge a **committal for trial** or not, this, on any logical interpretation, permits reporting that a case has been 'sent for trial' or 'transferred' (see below, pp. 46 and 56).   →glossary

 See Online Resource Centre, ch. 4: More on the section 8 reporting restrictions.

Liability and penalty for breach of the section 8 restrictions

Under the Act, 'any proprietor, editor or publisher' of a newspaper or periodical can be prosecuted for such a breach. In the case of a TV or radio programme, 'the body corporate which provides the service' and any person whose 'functions in relation to the programme correspond to those of an editor of a newspaper' can be prosecuted. The maximum fine is currently £5,000. The Attorney General has to consent to such prosecutions.

see ch. 16, p. 284

- A breach of reporting restrictions may also, if it occurs at a time when it causes a trial to be aborted, leave a media organisation liable, under the Courts Act 2003, to paying the costs of the aborted trial.

Examples of breaches of section 8

There have been several prosecutions for media reports which breached the section 8 restrictions, or similar restrictions imposed by a forerunner statute.

see late News p. xxx

In 2008 Jewish Chronicle Newspaper Ltd, publisher of the *Jewish Chronicle*, was fined £1,000 after the paper published such a report. In 1996 Graham Glen, the former editor of *The Citizen*, Gloucester, and the paper's owners, were each fined £4,500 by Gloucester magistrates for the contents of a report of the first appearance in the magistrates court of Fred West, accused of several murders. This report accurately reflected this preliminary hearing but breached section 8 by including a statement made there that West had confessed, to police, to killing one of his daughters, i.e. a reference to evidence.

Reporting denials of guilt and choice of jury trial

The media, when reporting preliminary hearings covered by the reporting restrictions in section 8, routinely publish:

see p. 47, on trial procedure

- basic protestations of innocence, i.e. that a defendant intends to deny the charge, either as voiced (if it is an either-way charge) in the plea-before-venue procedure or as otherwise asserted in comment from the dock, or through a solicitor (procedurally, the defendant who ends up at Crown court for trial cannot make a formal plea to that charge until he/she appears there);
- that a defendant, in an either-way case, has chosen trial by jury.

Although publication of such information is beyond what strict application of section 8 would permit, the media feel safe in reporting these facts, because:

- it seems only fair to the defendant to quote denial of guilt – if made in relation to the only charge faced, or to all charges – and that jury trial was chosen;

- publishing such matter cannot logically be deemed prejudicial to an eventual jury trial.

However, the media should be wary, when the restrictions apply, of reporting:

- anything which suggests that a defendant will later enter a mixture of pleas, e.g. quotes suggesting he/she will admit a charge while denying another/others. To publish matter, prior to a trial of a denied charge, stating or implying he/she has made or will make an admission to any charge could be prejudicial to that trial, if the jury is not told of such an admission;
- any defamatory detail in a denial of guilt. For example, if a defendant in a preliminary hearing shouts 'I've been framed by police', a media organisation which reports this, while restrictions still apply, could conceivably be successfully sued by police officers in the case as regards the defamatory effect created. Publication of such a claim after restrictions cease to apply will be safely protected by absolute or qualified privilege, if the requirements of either of these libel defences are met.

see ch. 19 on privilege

Describing the courtroom scene, and background information

The media also routinely report, even when restrictions apply, scene-setting information from such preliminary proceedings, e.g. that the hearing lasted 10 minutes, what the defendant wore in the dock, and that he/she 'spoke only to confirm their name and address'. Such material can hardly be deemed likely to affect potential jurors who read such a report.

Almost daily, media organisations publishing such reports of preliminary proceedings add to them background material about the defendant and/or the alleged crime, even though reporting restrictions apply. It can be argued that such background material, from sources other than the court hearing, is not itself a report of the court proceedings and so does not contravene section 8 of the 1980 Act. But the Contempt of Court Act 1981 would cover matter from other sources added to a court report. To avoid breach of that Act such extraneous matter should not create a substantial risk of serious prejudice, see ch. 17. Mingling, without sufficient care, such background material into a court report could create such a risk, e.g. potential jurors who see/hear the report could draw strong, wrong inferences about what the case evidence is. To avoid this, an option for the media, when they want to report on an alleged crime incident and to report that the alleged perpetrator has already appeared in a preliminary hearing, is to run items segregated by page design or by separate narrative. For example, each item could have its own headline – a story on the alleged incident, conforming to contempt law and not citing matter from the court hearing, and then a separate report solely of the preliminary hearing, conforming to the 1980 Act's restrictions.

When do the section 8 restrictions cease to apply?

These restrictions cease to apply in four circumstances.

1) *Restrictions are lifted if a defendant requests this* Under the 1980 Act magistrates are required to make an order lifting restrictions if the sole defendant wants this. If a case has more than one defendant each must be allowed to make representations before a decision on lifting the restrictions is taken. If any of the defendants object, restrictions may only be lifted if the magistrates decide it is in the interests of justice to do so. A defendant may want restrictions lifted so that the media can report detail of why the defence contests prosecution evidence. For example, a defendant's solicitor may wish to publicise, by means of a full media report of the preliminary hearing before magistrates, a request for witnesses to come forward, to help corroborate at the eventual jury trial the defendant's evidence, including

→ glossary any alibi.

- Even if the restrictions are lifted at a defendant's request, the media should not, for as long as the case retains the potential of being decided by jury trial, publish the previous convictions of any defendant in the case, even if such have been revealed in the preliminary proceedings.

If the restrictions are lifted the 1980 Act itself does not prevent the media reporting such information, but wider contempt law still applies. Pre-trial publication of previous convictions is so foreseeably potentially prejudicial that, it could be argued, the section 4 defence in the Contempt of Court Act 1981, which normally protects fair and accurate reports of court hearings,

→
see also
ch, 16,
on this
defence

may not be held to apply.

The 1980 Act specifies that if there is disagreement between defendants on whether section 8 restrictions should be lifted, their representations to magistrates on this issue, even if a lifting order is then made, should not be reported, i.e. while the case retains potential for being decided by jury.

However, the fact that such a lifting order was made can be reported immediately within the report.

In 1972 the High Court ruled that once lifted, the restrictions cannot be reimposed (*R v Blackpool Justices, ex p Beaverbrook Newspapers Ltd* [1972] 1 All ER 388; [1972] 1 WLR 95). In another case, the High Court ruled that if reporting restrictions were to be lifted they had to be lifted in respect of all defendants in the hearing (*Leeds Justices, ex p Sykes* [1983] 1 WLR 132).

As indicated above, in a case involving more than one defendant magistrates can lift the section 8 restrictions at the request of one defendant even if another defendant objects to this. The magistrates, to pay some heed to any such objection, could choose to use other law – section 4(2) of the Contempt of Court Act 1981 – to temporarily prohibit the media from reporting part of the preliminary hearing, e.g. a reference to particular evidence. Magistrates could thus use the 1981 Act if they felt such prohibition would prevent a substantial risk of prejudice to the eventual jury trial of a defendant who wanted the 1980 Act's section 8 restrictions to remain in force. However, guidelines issued by the Judicial Studies Board suggest that magistrates should not normally use this 1981 Act power after they have decided to lift the section 8 restrictions.

see ch. 16, p. 289

2) *The restrictions automatically cease to apply if and when, for an either-way charge, it becomes clear that the defendant is to be dealt with summarily, i.e. by magistrates, not by the Crown court* See p. 47, above, for explanation of the mode of trial procedure. A defendant, in that procedure, may indicate an intention to plead guilty to an either-way charge (and thereby formally pleads guilty to it). Alternatively he/she may accept a proffered option of summary trial (i.e. by magistrates) as regards a denied either-way charge. In either eventuality the section 8 restrictions no longer apply in respect of that part of the preliminary proceedings relating to any such charge, because this procedure has thus determined that there will be no jury trial of it. It may be that there are co-defendants in the same hearing and that they opt for jury trial – or, indeed, have already been committed for jury trial – on the same or a linked charge. Even if this is the case, section 8 will not apply in respect of what is related in court about the defendant who is to be dealt with summarily, in respect of that charge. This is true whether he/she admits the charge or not.

see Useful Websites, below

However, as regards a denied either-way charge, which the mode of trial procedure has determined is to be tried summarily, the position changes again, after the section 8 restrictions lapse. As soon as the defendant enters a formal plea of not guilty, other (virtually identical) reporting restrictions automatically begin to apply to pre-trial proceedings, in respect of that charge, occurring after that plea is entered. These restrictions have been introduced by newer law under section 8C of the Act, and are explained in ch. 5, see p. 64.

In respect of any other charge faced by the same defendant due, after the mode of trial procedure, to be considered in a committal hearing, the section 8 restrictions continue to apply, unless they cease under conditions 1) above, or 3) below.

3) *Restrictions automatically cease to apply if magistrates decide there is insufficient evidence to commit a defendant in an either-way case for Crown court trial, or they decline to send a defendant for trial on an indictable-only offence* As outlined above, p. 50, magistrates can discharge a defendant at a committal hearing if they consider there is insufficient evidence for an either-way charge he/she faces. In a case involving only one defendant, the section 8 reporting restrictions automatically cease to apply if he/she is discharged on all charges faced. A full report of all preliminary proceedings in the case could then be published. But the section 8 restrictions will continue to apply if, in a case involving more than one defendant, any of them is committed for trial.

In an indictable-only case, magistrates can refuse to send such a charge for trial if they decide there has been abuse of legal process in the prosecution (though such a decision is rare). If there is only one defendant in the case, and this decision means that he/she will definitely not face a jury trial on any charge in it, then the section 8 restrictions cease to apply. But if a hearing involves other charges, on which the defendant is sent for jury trial, or the hearing involves any other defendant in the case being sent for trial, or involves any defendant awaiting a committal hearing, the section 8 restrictions should be regarded as applying to it.

4) *The restrictions automatically expire when the proceedings against all defendants in the case have been concluded – i.e. no jury trial remains pending* The section 8 restrictions cease to apply to a case at the conclusion of all proceedings in it. This can safely be construed to be when all defendants, in all the proceedings involved (e.g. if there are several trials in the same case) have been either convicted or acquitted at Crown court, or the case against all of them has been withdrawn by the prosecution, or dismissed by the Crown court judge.

After such conclusion, evidence aired or submissions made at any preliminary hearing at a magistrates court – including any committal hearing – weeks or months earlier can be fully reported, if still thought newsworthy. For example, the media may wish to highlight evidence which, for legal reasons, the jury did not hear, perhaps to give a fuller picture of the defendant or to scrutinise how the crime was investigated.

 See Online Resource Centre, ch. 4, for an illustrative example of a newspaper reporting evidence aired at a preliminary hearing months after it occurred.

Libel considerations

Provided a report of preliminary proceedings is published as soon as practicable after the section 8 restrictions are lifted or expire, it will be regarded as a contemporaneous report and so enjoy the protection of absolute privilege in libel law, provided other requirements of the defence are met.

 see ch. 19

▌ Transfer of cases to Crown court

Committal hearings were abolished more than a decade ago for two types of either-way charges: those alleging serious and complex fraud, and those alleging sexual and/or violent crimes in which a child (e.g. the alleged victim) is due to be a witness. The Criminal Justice Act 1987, as regards such fraud cases, and the Criminal Justice Act 1991, as regards such cases involving children, introduced a procedure whereby such charges are swiftly 'transferred' by magistrates, without consideration of the strength of evidence, to Crown court. Parliament passed this law to minimise delay in the pre-trial processing of such cases because:

- complex fraud cases will already have undergone many months, perhaps several years, of investigation and preparation, and need to be tried while witnesses' memories of events remain as fresh as possible;

- a child's welfare, and ability to give accurate evidence, can suffer if he/she has a court appearance hanging over them for months.

This transfer procedure is similar to the 'sending for trial' process now used for indictable-only offences. Reporting restrictions under section 8 of the Magistrates' Courts Act 1980, described above, apply to hearings before magistrates where notice requiring such transfer is served by the prosecution.

 See also Online Resource Centre, ch. 4: Changes enshrined in the Criminal Justice Act 2003, concerning law due to abolish transfer procedure for such charges, replacing it with 'sending for trial'.

▌ Voluntary bill of indictment

→ glossary

If magistrates decide not to send an indictable-only case or commit an either-way case for jury trial, a prosecutor can apply to a High Court judge for it to be sent to Crown court directly. If the judge agrees, a draft **indictment**, setting out the charge(s) against the defendant, called a voluntary bill of indictment, is sent to the Crown court to become the actual indictment there. Because magistrates' decisions are usually respected by prosecution agencies, this procedure is rarely used. Exceptionally, it may be used in other circumstances, e.g. if a defendant disrupts a committal hearing.

▦ Recap of major points

- There are two types of magistrate – lay magistrates and district judges.
- Magistrates deal with the majority of criminal court cases.
- But the most serious cases, including all indictable-only charges, are dealt with by Crown courts because magistrates have limited powers to sentence in the event of a conviction.
- An indictable-only case will, at a preliminary hearing in a magistrates court, be 'sent for trial' to the Crown court.
- Whether a denied either-way case will be dealt with by magistrates or by a Crown court is determined in the 'mode of trial' procedure. Magistrates may refuse to try it. A defendant can choose trial by jury.
- If magistrates refuse to try an either-way charge, or the defendant makes the choice of jury trial, that charge will subsequently be considered by magistrates in a committal hearing – another type of preliminary hearing – and in it the defendant will be committed to the Crown court for trial if magistrates decide there is sufficient evidence.
- Reporting restrictions under section 8 of the Magistrates' Courts Act 1980 automatically apply to media reports of a case's preliminary hearing(s) in the magistrates court if the case has potential for jury trial.
- If a defendant admits an either-way offence, magistrates may sentence him/her, but may decide to commit him/her to Crown court for sentence.
- In magistrates (and Crown) courts, a defendant may be granted bail until his/her case's next hearing, but otherwise is remanded to prison custody.

🌐 Useful Websites

www.jsboard.co.uk/publications/rrmc/index.htm
Judicial Studies Board guidance on reporting restrictions at magistrates courts

This site also gives access to the Judicial Studies Board's Adult Bench Book, which guides magistrates on decisions on whether an either-way case is suitable for summary trial.

5

Magistrates courts: summary cases

Chapter summary

Court hearings in which defendants are sentenced or tried by magistrates are known as summary proceedings. Many such cases allege minor crimes. But some are serious enough for a convicted defendant to be jailed. This chapter explains the procedures for trial and sentencing by magistrates. It sets out the **automatic** reporting restrictions which apply to media reports of some pre-trial hearings in magistrates courts. Other relevant reporting restrictions are explained in chs 7, 8, and 9. General information about magistrates courts is in ch. 4. The law of contempt of court is primarily dealt with in ch. 16, and libel considerations in court reporting in ch. 19. The court reporter's role in ensuring open justice is explained in ch. 12.

→glossary

▌ The taking of pleas

→
see ch. 2
for detail
on cat-
egories of
charges

In magistrates courts, defendants who face a summary charge or summary charges are, during their first or a subsequent appearance, asked by the court clerk how they plead. If they plead guilty to a charge, they are thereby convicted of it. The case will usually need to be adjourned to a later date for magistrates to pass sentence, e.g. if a 'pre-sentence report' is needed – see below.

If a defendant pleads not guilty to a summary charge, a very minor offence may be tried there and then. But in most instances a contested case will be adjourned until a date when magistrates can try it. When a case is first adjourned, the magistrates must decide, unless it is a minor one, if **bail** is to be granted.

→glossary

Defendants who plead guilty in a magistrates court to an **either-way** charge or who are convicted of such a charge after choosing in the mode of trial procedure to be tried by magistrates, can also be sentenced by them. In these instances an either-way charge is being treated as if it were a **summary** charge.

→ see ch. 4, p. 47

▶ Sentencing by magistrates when guilt is admitted

In sentencing hearings for a charge admitted, the prosecution first outlines the crime. If there is a dispute about the facts of the admitted offence, magistrates must accept the defence version unless the prosecution wants to prove its version in what is known as a **Newton hearing**. The court will also consider a written statement made by any victim of the crime about how it has affected them, if such a statement has been made. Before sentence is passed, the defence is given the opportunity to make a speech of mitigation. This is a request, citing any extenuating circumstances, for the court to be as lenient as possible. The speech is usually delivered by the defence lawyer, if the defendant has one. A defendant may also ask for other offences to be 'taken into consideration'.

→ glossary

→ see also ch, 9, 141 on derogatory mitigation

Offences to be taken into consideration' – often referred to by the acronym TIC, and which should not be confused with previous convictions – are crimes admitted by the defendant although he/she has not been charged with them.

The defendant brings these crimes to the court's attention so that he/she can be sentenced for these at the same time as for the charged offence(s).

The advantage to the defendant in admitting such uncharged crimes is that (a) it removes the possibility of future prosecution for them, and so the defendant can (it is hoped) concentrate, after any punishment, on starting a fresh life; and (b), through such frank admission he/she gains credit with the court, especially if police knew little about these uncharged crimes, and so he/she hopes to be punished more leniently than if his/her guilt for them were to be uncovered subsequently.

Magistrates also consider any 'pre-sentence report' felt to be needed about the defendant's background. These are prepared by probation officers. See Useful Websites, below, for detail of their work.

Magistrates can, depending on what the law specifies for the relevant offence, jail a defendant for up to six months for a single offence, and for

→

see also
ch. 4,
p. 45–46
on sen-
tencing

up to 12 months for more than one offence if the jail sentence for each is imposed to be consecutive, or can impose a fine. A court's options for sentences other than immediate jail or a fine are listed below, p. 71–73. Courts are encouraged by procedural rules to explain sentencing decisions when they are announced, see p. 87.

❙ Committal for sentence

A defendant convicted of an either-way charge in a magistrates court can be committed by it for sentence to the Crown court if magistrates – because of what they have heard in the case's detail and/or about any previous conviction(s) the defendant has – believe their powers are insufficient to adequately punish him/her. A Crown court judge can impose longer jail terms.

→glossary

A committal for sentence is very different from a **committal for trial** the procedure explained on p. 48. Both are possibilities in an either-way case. But in the latter circumstance, the potential for jury trial still exists, because whether the defendant is guilty remains undetermined. Therefore if a case is committed for trial automatic reporting restrictions will normally continue to apply to media reports of all the case's hearings in the magistrates court,

→

see ch 4,
pp. 51–59
on these
restric-
tions

under section 8 of the Magistrates' Courts Act 1980, until the Crown court conclusion of the case. But if a case is **committed for sentence**, then these restrictions have already ceased to apply, having ceased when, in the mode of trial procedure, the defendant pleaded guilty or chose to be tried by magistrates on that charge. Such admission or that choice, as regards that charge, normally ends its potential for jury trial, and so the section 8 restrictions lapse in respect of it.

> → See also ch. 4, p. 47 on mode of trial procedure and Figure 2, p. 49, which illustrates the various ways in which either-way charges can be dealt with by magistrates, including committal for sentence and committal for trial.

❙ Section 8C reporting restrictions on pre-trial hearings in summary proceedings

→glossary

When a denied charge is heading for a **summary trial** (i.e. trial by magistrates), magistrates may hold a pre-trial hearing to rule on applications made by the prosecution or defence concerning any dispute on the admissibility of evidence or on points of law. In such a hearing, the magistrates may also make other decisions relating to procedure or bail. Under section 8C of the Magistrates' Courts Act 1980, as inserted into it by the Courts Act 2003, automatic reporting restrictions severely limit what can be immediately published from these pre-trial hearings in **summary proceedings**. These section 8C restrictions are a fairly recent addition to media law. They came into effect in 2005. Their scope, set out in detail below, is best understood by reference to their purpose. This, according to what can be read in or construed from the official 'Explanatory Notes' to the 2003 Act, and from what was stated in Parliamentary debate, is to prevent prejudice should a case undergo an unexpected change in its trial venue. An example is a case that was initially heading for summary trial, with no obvious potential for jury trial, but nevertheless ends up being tried by a jury in a Crown court. The section 8C restrictions are also designed to prevent prejudice to any case 'linked' to the contested summary case but due to be tried by jury. →glossary

An unexpected change in a case's trial venue could occur, for example, in the following circumstances:

a) In an either-way case, decisions made by magistrates and the defendant in the mode of trial procedure, see ch. 4, p. 47, might initially determine that it will be tried by magistrates. However magistrates, after hearing more of the case evidence in a pre-trial hearing or after the summary trial begins, might decide after all that the case is too serious for them to deal with, and so commit it for trial to the Crown court.

b) As regards a summary charge, or an either-way charge initially determined to be tried summarily, magistrates might learn in a pre-trial hearing or after the summary trial has begun, that the case is strongly 'related', i.e. linked, to an **indictable-only** or either-way case already sent or committed for jury trial. In such circumstances they could then decide that both cases should be dealt with in one combined case at the Crown court, and so halt the summary proceedings by using statutory powers to send or commit the 'related' summary case to that Crown court. →glossary

In the circumstances outlined above, matters raised in a magistrates court could, if published contemporaneously in a media report, be read by people who could later end up on the case's jury at Crown court. Such matter might include any previous conviction a defendant has, e.g. mentioned during decisions on bail, or argument on admissibility of evidence. Yet – to ensure a fair trial at Crown court – a jury is not normally told of such matters during the trial. Therefore the purpose of the section 8C restrictions, as regards relevant

→

see ch. 4,
on sec-
tion 8

pre-trial hearings in summary proceedings, is the same as that of older restrictions in section 8 of the 1980 Act. The latter apply – to prevent prejudice to any eventual jury trial – to media reports of **preliminary hearings** in magistrates courts for indictable-only or either-way cases which have (more consistently and obviously) retained, en route to Crown court, such potential for jury trial.

However, the section 8C restrictions can be seen as legislative 'over-kill', because they apply automatically to *all* pre-trial hearings in summary proceedings after a 'not guilty' plea is made. Yet the majority of such cases <u>will</u>, as expected at the time that plea is made, be resolved in a summary trial, having at no stage much prospect of ending up in a Crown court.

The scope of the section 8C reporting restrictions

These automatic restrictions prevent the media reporting from cases at magistrates courts in which the defendant has formally pleaded not guilty;

- any rulings made subsequently by magistrates in pre-trial hearings on admissibility of evidence and points of law, and any order made in them to discharge or vary such a ruling;

- the proceedings, in those hearings, concerning applications for such rulings and for such orders, including legal argument and discussion about such matters (i.e. whether or not such a ruling or order is made).

The Act defines a pre-trial hearing as any hearing occurring after the defendant has pleaded not guilty but prior to magistrates starting to hear prosecution evidence at the trial. Section 8C, therefore, does not prevent this plea being contemporaneously reported.

While these restrictions are in force, the media can only report seven categories of information from such application proceedings in pre-trial hearings. These categories are (expressed here in simplified form):

- the name of the court and the magistrates' names;

- the names, ages, home addresses, and occupations of the defendant(s) and witnesses;

- the charge(s), or a summary of it/them;

- the names of solicitors and barristers in the proceedings;

- if the case is adjourned, the date and place to which it is adjourned;

- any arrangements as to bail;

 glossary
- whether **legal aid** was granted.

⬚⬚⬚⬚ **Points for consideration**

The restrictions prevent publication of any reference to evidence beyond what is encapsulated in the wording of the charge. It is safe to publish the bare fact that reporting restrictions are in force, since to do so cannot in itself be prejudicial.

As regards the phrase 'any arrangements as to bail', the safest course for journalists is to follow the usual interpretation of the similar, older restriction – applying to a different type of hearing – in section 8 of the 1980 Act.

see ch. 4, p. 53

The home addresses which may be published are stated in legislation to be those current 'at the time of their inclusion' in what is published, <u>and</u> those 'at any relevant time', a phrase which encompasses former addresses which were current on the date of, or during the time span of, the alleged offence(s). If a report refers to a defendant's former address or includes a picture or footage of it, it should make clear he/she no longer lives there, otherwise there may be a libel problem with the current occupant(s), because people may think them linked to the court case.

Section 8C's explicit restriction on publication of pre-trial argument about and rulings on evidence and points of law is apparently a 'belt and braces' approach, since its limitation of reports to the seven categories cited above has the same effect. If a journalist wanted to report such a pre-trial hearing, it would be safe, just as it is for hearings covered by the Act's section 8, to include in the report neutral (i.e. non-prejudicial) description of the court scene and neutral background information.

see ch. 4, p. 55

When do the section 8C restrictions cease to apply?

The magistrates can choose to lift the section 8C reporting restrictions, wholly or in part, to allow the media to publish contemporaneously fuller reports of such pre-trial applications, and of any ruling or order made in such hearings.

If any defendant objects to such lifting of the restrictions, the court may lift them only if satisfied that this is in the interests of justice.

If there are such objections, they and any representations made to the court about them (i.e. argument in court about whether the restrictions should be lifted) cannot be reported until the 'disposal', see below, of the case, even if restrictions are lifted earlier in other respects.

If not thus lifted by the magistrates, the section 8C restrictions automatically cease anyway when the case is 'disposed of'. Under the section this means when, in respect of all charges faced, all defendants in the case are either acquitted or convicted, or if the case is dismissed by the court (e.g. because of insufficient evidence, see below) or the prosecutor decides not to proceed with it.

So, for example, at the end of the trial, a media organisation could then publish a report of evidence ruled inadmissible some weeks or months previously in a pre-trial hearing, or of any ruling made in it, should such information still be deemed newsworthy.

Liability for breach of the section 8C restrictions

A proprietor, editor, or publisher can be prosecuted for a report which breaches these restrictions. The maximum fine is currently £5,000. The Attorney General has to consent to any prosecution for an alleged breach.

▌ Procedure in summary trials

A trial at a magistrates court can often be reported fully and contemporaneously by the media. No restrictions under the 1980 Act apply to reports of the trial itself, but reporting restrictions could apply under other law.

→

see chs 7, 8, and 9 on other restrictions

→ glossary

In trials, the defence knows beforehand what evidence the prosecution intends to call because this is set out in documents which the prosecution must disclose pre-trial to the defence. Similarly, the defence is required to disclose, pre-trial, some information to the prosecution, e.g. any **alibi** the defendant relies on.

In a trial before magistrates, the procedure (as it is normally implemented) is:

- The prosecutor can make an opening speech, to outline to the magistrates the alleged facts of the case.

- Witnesses are then each called to give evidence. Each is required to swear an oath that he/she will give truthful evidence.

- The prosecution witnesses are called first, and each is asked questions by the prosecutor to elicit their evidence-in-chief (i.e. evidence given in questioning by the side which called them). Leading questions are not normally permitted in it, see below, p. 70. The defence has opportunity to cross-examine each prosecution witness, and the prosecution may then re-examine them.

- At the end of the prosecution evidence, the defence may submit, for any or all charges faced, that there is no case to answer because, the defence argues, it is already clear that the prosecution cannot meet the standard of proof required. If the magistrates agree with any such defence submission, they will dismiss the charge. Otherwise, or if any charge is not subject to such a submission, the trial continues.

see ch. 2, p. 21 on standard of proof

- Any defence witnesses are then called. These may include the defendant, whether represented by a solicitor or conducting his/her own case. The defendant cannot be compelled to testify. But a prosecutor is allowed to comment adversely on the fact of a defendant over 14 choosing without good cause not to give evidence.

- Defence witnesses, including a defendant who testifies, are questioned in their evidence-in-chief by the defence (though again, leading questions are usually prohibited). They can be cross-examined by the prosecutor, and then re-examined by the defence.

- When the court has heard all the witnesses, the defence may address the court in a closing speech, arguing how the facts and the law should be interpreted. Either side may, with permission, address the court twice in total, either in opening or closing speeches, but the defence must be given opportunity to make the last speech.

- If the magistrates feel a charge is not proved, they will acquit the defendant in respect of it.

- If they find him/her guilty on any charge, he/she is thereby convicted of it.

The magistrates will proceed, either then or at an adjourned hearing, to sentence the defendant, following procedure similar to that in cases in which the defendant admits the offence, see above, p. 63. They will hear mitigation, be told of any relevant previous convictions he/she has, and hear more about the defendant's background in a pre-sentence report.

 See ch. 6, p. 87–88, for the national protocol agreed by the Crown Prosecution Service and police, after discussions with media representatives, on what prosecution material, e.g. police photographs of exhibits and defendants, can be released to the media for publication in background features after a trial ends.

After a conviction, a magistrates court can reopen a case, for it to be heard anew by a different set of magistrates, in circumstances in which this would be in the interests of justice, e.g. if a person has been tried in his/her absence.

Reluctant witnesses

A witness (other than a defendant) can be compelled to give evidence if a court issues a witness summons or an arrest warrant for him/her. Magistrates have power to commit to custody for up to a month or to fine any such person who refuses to be sworn or to give evidence. But a person cannot be compelled to give evidence against his or her spouse or co-habitee, except where the spouse or co-habitee is charged with an offence against him or her or their children, and in a few other circumstances.

- If a witness appears to be refusing to testify or to go back on the statement he/she made to the investigators, the court can deem him/her to be a hostile witness – that is, someone who can be asked leading questions by the side which called him/her.

- A leading question is one which suggests what answer is expected. 'Did anything happen after that?' is not a leading question. 'Did you then see a man with a knife?' is a leading question.

Reference during a trial to a defendant's 'bad character'

see ch. 2, p. 21 on this principle

As a general rule, prosecutors in trials – either in a magistrates or Crown court – cannot refer to any previous conviction(s) a defendant has, because – to comply with the principle of the presumption of innocence – the focus is on evidence for the charge(s) being tried, not on any conviction(s) in his/her past. But evidence of previous misconduct (which includes crime and other reprehensible behaviour) can be introduced at trial if relevant to an important issue between the defence and prosecution. This includes evidence to correct a false impression given by the defendant, or about whether the defendant has a propensity to commit offences of the kind with which he/she is charged, or if the defendant has made an attack on another person's character.

▌ Appeal routes from magistrates courts

To contest a ruling by magistrates (including one made when they sit in a youth court, see ch. 7) on a point of law, the defence and prosecution both have a right of appeal to the High Court, by means of the 'case stated' procedure, and the defence can in other types of challenge ask the High Court for a **judicial review**.

A defendant can appeal to a Crown court against a conviction by magistrates, or the severity of the sentence they impose.

→ See ch. 6, pp. 92 and 93, for more detail on these High Court and Crown court roles.

Punishment other than by immediate jail or a fine

See above, ch. 4, pp. 45–46 as regards magistrates' powers to impose jail terms with immediate effect, and fines.

Magistrates (and Crown court judges) have a range of other sentence options, including a suspended sentence if they feel the defendant deserves such leniency.

- If a defendant is given a suspended sentence, he/she does not have go to jail unless he/she commits a further offence, for which a jail sentence could be imposed, during the period the sentence is suspended.

So, for example, a jail term of six months can be suspended for two years. If the defendant commits no other offence punishable by jail in those two years, the suspended sentence lapses. If a jail sentence is suspended, this should always be made clear in a media report of the case. It is incorrect to suggest that such a defendant has been immediately jailed. This could create a libel problem because the impression is given that the defendant was punished more severely than he/she actually was. Therefore an inference is created that the crime was worse than it was, and consequentially there is some risk that a defendant could successfully sue for defamation. The sentence options outlined below are also available to both magistrates and Crown courts, though the latter, in that they deal with the most serious crimes, are less likely than magistrates to use them.

see also ch. 17, p. 306 on inferences

- A community order – this means a defendant is ordered by the court to carry out one or more of a number of requirements, which could include:
  - unpaid work in the community under the direction of a probation officer;
  - adherence to a curfew, e.g. to stay at home during evenings and nights, a requirement which normally includes the defendant wearing an electronic 'tag' to help check he/she is adhering to the curfew;

- having treatment to reduce dependency on drugs or alcohol;
- going to an attendance centre for a specified number of hours to have 'structured' group sessions to reflect on his/her misbehaviour, the sessions being a restriction on his/her leisure time.

- An absolute discharge – this means that the court feels that no punishment, other than the fact of the conviction, is necessary.

- A conditional discharge – this means that the court has not immediately imposed or specified any punishment, but states that if the defendant commits any other offence within a period laid down by the court, e.g. a year, he/she is liable to be punished for the first offence as well as for the subsequent conviction.

Neither of the above discharge outcomes, both being the result of a conviction by guilty plea or by verdict of guilty, should be confused with a **discharge** in a committal hearing, a term which means that evidence was considered insufficient for a charge to be tried.

→

see ch. 4, p. 48 on com- mittal hearings

A court has powers to order a defendant to make restitution to a crime victim, e.g. to pay compensation for personal injury, or for loss or damage to goods.

A court can in suitable cases defer a decision on sentence to a specified date within six months of the conviction, to assess the defendant's conduct in that period – for example, to see if he/she actually fulfils a requirement of reparation to the crime victim.

It can also order confiscation of a motor vehicle used in the furtherance of

→ glossary

theft, including shoplifting.

A magistrates court can vary or rescind a sentence within 28 days of its original decision.

▌ Binding over and restraining orders

In law which originates in the fourteenth century, courts have power to 'bind over' a person 'to keep the peace'. The power can be used to resolve

→ glossary

without trial minor allegations of **assault**, threatening behaviour, or public disorder, in that sometimes the prosecution will drop a charge if the defendant agrees to be thus 'bound over'. But the power can also be used after an acquittal or conviction on such a charge if it is felt the defendant could be involved in a future breach of the peace. A witness can also be bound over, for the same reason. When binding over, the court specifies a sum of money which the person is required to pay to the court if he/she breaches the peace, e.g. by such violent or threatening conduct, within a period specified by the court. NB: Because a binding over order can be made against a person without him/her being convicted of a crime, journalists in reports of such cases should be careful not to imply that a conviction occurred if it did not. A binding over order is regarded as a preventative measure in civil law, not as a punishment.

Under other law – the Domestic Violence, Crime and Victims Act 2004 – a court may impose a restraining order on a defendant, even one acquitted at trial, to protect another person from harassment.

▌ Section 70 committal

If the prosecution apply for it, magistrates may make an order under section 70 of the Proceeds of Crime Act 2002 committing the case of a convicted defendant to Crown court for a hearing there to decide whether there should be a confiscation order to seize property obtained as a result of criminal conduct. No automatic reporting restrictions apply to such committal hearings, because the defendant has already been convicted.

▦ Recap of major points

- Magistrates try summary charges and, if they choose to and the defendant agrees, either-way cases.
- Trials and sentencing at magistrates courts are known as summary proceedings.
- Automatic reporting restrictions, under section 8C of the Magistrates' Courts Act, inserted there by the Courts Act 2003, limit what the media can report from some pre-trial hearings in summary proceedings.
- But the actual trial at a magistrates court can often be reported fully and contemporaneously.
- A magistrates court has a range of sentencing options if a defendant is convicted there because of a guilty plea or in a trial.

- In either-way cases the magistrates, if they think their power to punish a convicted defendant is insufficient, can commit him/her to the Crown court for sentence.

🌐 Useful Websites

www.probation.homeoffice.gov.uk/
   National Probation Service

www.cjsonline.gov.uk/
   The Government's 'Criminal Justice System Online'

6

Criminal cases in the Crown courts and appeal courts

Chapter summary

This chapter explains how Crown courts deal with the most serious criminal cases, and the role of the jury. It outlines the work of the High Court, the Court of Appeal, and the House of Lords/**Supreme Court** in criminal law. It also explains → glossary
how **automatic** reporting restrictions limit what the media can publish from pre- → glossary
trial and preparatory hearings at Crown courts. Other reporting restrictions are covered in chs 7, 8, and 9. The law of contempt of court is primarily dealt with in ch. 16 and libel considerations in court reporting in ch. 19. The court reporter's role in ensuring open justice is explained in ch. 12.

▌ Roles at Crown courts

The Crown courts deal with the most serious criminal cases. The most famous Crown court is the Central Criminal Court in London – known as the Old Bailey. There are Crown courts at 77 locations in England and Wales, organised in seven administrative regions, still referred to as 'circuits'. This term, from the era of horse-drawn transport, reflects the fact that judges travelled round regional courthouses in a regular sequence to deal with caseload. Some judges still commute to more than one courthouse.

Whereas magistrates in **summary proceedings** rule on matters of → law, decide whether guilt is proven, and can after convictions decide on

see ch. 5

punishment, in Crown courts there is division of such roles, in that:

- judges rule on law and decide what sentence is imposed on convicted defendants; and

- in trials juries decide whether each charge is proved, see below.

A Crown court trial can proceed without a jury in certain, rare circumstances, leaving the judge to decide the verdict(s).

▌ Who are jurors?

A jury in a Crown court trial in England or Wales consists of 12 people – the jurors – aged between 18 and 70, selected at random from the electoral rolls for the districts served by that Crown court. Those selected are sent a summons, requiring them to turn up for jury service. Some groups of people are disqualified from jury service, e.g. those due to face a criminal trial themselves, and anyone jailed in the previous 10 years. See Useful Websites, below.

▌ Types of Crown court judges

Three types of judges sit in Crown courts:

- High Court judges, i.e. those who can sit in the High Court (see below, p. 91) *and* Crown courts. These are referred to formally as Mr Justice Smith, or Mrs Justice Smith. They wear distinctive red robes for criminal cases. Only they can try the most serious offences, such as murder, because they are regarded as the most experienced judges.

- **Circuit judges**, who are referred to as Judge John Smith or Judge Mary Smith. They must be barristers of at least 10 years' standing or be solicitors who have been recorders.

- **Recorders**, who are part-time judges. They are barristers or solicitors who have held 'right of audience' (i.e. the right to represent clients) at Crown court. Recorders are usually referred to as the Recorder, Mr John Smith or Mrs Mary Smith.

⠿ Points for consideration

Exceptions to the above status of recorder are the Recorder of London, the historic title for one of the senior full-time judges who sit at the Central Criminal Court. Additionally, some cities have bestowed the honorary title of 'Recorder of –' on the senior circuit judge who carries out ceremonial duties.

Up to four magistrates may sit with judges at Crown court trials. But this is not obligatory and such magistrates' real contribution is in discussing sentence with the judge.

The recruitment and selection of judges is primarily the responsibility of the independent Judicial Appointments Commission.

→ see Useful Websites, below

▌ Lawyers at Crown court

Prosecutions at Crown court are conducted by barristers, and barristers usually appear for the defence. Solicitors have 'right of audience' in the court in some circumstances. A court clerk, who is legally trained, sits in each Crown court in front of the judge, to assist in administration and procedures.

→ see ch.1, p. 14 on legal profession

▌ Routes to Crown court

A defendant's case (apart from any that are there following an appeal, see below, p. 91) reaches a Crown court because it has been:

- **sent for trial** by magistrates, if it is an **indictable-only** charge, all of which can only be dealt with by a Crown court, or
- **committed for trial** by magistrates, if it is an **either-way** charge, or
- **transferred** by magistrates, if it is an either-way fraud case deemed serious or complex, or is an either-way case involving an alleged sexual or violent crime <u>and</u> a child witness, or
- sent for trial by a High Court judge by means of a *voluntary* **bill of indictment**; or
- **committed for sentence** or been subject to section 70 committal, see ch. 5, pp. 64 and 73.

→ see ch. 4 for details of these procedures

▌ Arraignment

A defendant whose case is sent for trial or committed for trial or transferred to Crown court is asked, when he/she appears there, to state for each charge listed on the **indictment** whether he/she pleads guilty or not guilty. These pleas are recorded. This process is known as the arraignment. At Crown court charges are referred to as 'counts'. See also, below, p. 82 on reporting arraignments.

→ glossary

▦ Point for consideration

The details within charges in the indictment may differ from those listed originally in the magistrates court, and so a reporter at Crown court should not for such details rely on cuttings of or a print-out of any earlier report of the case.

▌ Hearings prior to jury involvement: automatic reporting restrictions

In cases in which a defendant is denying guilt, there is likely to be at least one hearing at Crown court before the jury is involved. There are specific and automatic restrictions which limit what the media can contemporaneously publish from three types of hearing held prior to trial:

Applications for a case to be dismissed, prior to arraignment A defendant at Crown court may choose to apply to a judge there for a charge or charges to be dismissed for insufficient evidence. There is statutory provision for such hearings to occur prior to the arraignment.

'Pre-trial' hearings The term 'pre-trial hearing' is used specifically in the Criminal Procedure and Investigations Act 1996 of any hearing which occurs at Crown court before a guilty plea is accepted (i.e. in such cases, before it becomes clear there will be no trial) or – in cases which remain contested – of all hearings which occur before a jury is sworn in or before the beginning of any 'preparatory' hearing in the case.

see p. 84 for jury procedure

'Preparatory hearings' A 'preparatory hearing' may be held for the longer and more complex cases, and must be held in terrorism cases, to enable the judge to make rulings and to approve arrangements for the trial to proceed efficiently. Such a hearing, if it occurs, technically marks the start of the trial, and takes place shortly before the jury is sworn. The arraignment,

see above, if it has not yet occurred, must take place at the start of the 'preparatory hearing'.

These three types of hearings share the common feature that no potential jurors should be present. The jury has yet to be chosen and a primary purpose of many such hearings is for the judge to rule on matters of law and/or on the admissibility of evidence – rulings which determine what a jury, if the case proceeds to trial, will be told in it. The hearings may include the judge making decisions on **bail**. The purpose of the automatic reporting restrictions is to prevent prejudicial matter aired or decided in these hearings being published in advance of the jury trial. The kinds of matter which could cause prejudice are discussed in ch. 4, pp. 51–52, in relation to the similar restrictions in section 8 of the Magistrates' Courts Act 1980 which apply – for the same reason – to media reports of **preliminary hearings** in magistrates courts of cases with potential for jury trial.

 see below, p. 84, on trial procedure

→ glossary

In respect of Crown court hearings occurring prior to trial, the reporting restrictions – the scope of which is described below – place such constraint on contemporaneous (i.e. immediate) reports of these hearings that such media coverage tends to occur only for a particularly newsworthy case, to inform the public of the case's progress towards a trial date. However, other reasons for reporters to attend such hearings are to know immediately about any sudden development, e.g. that the case is dismissed and to glean detail about the case to prepare background features for whom the restrictions cease to apply, see below.

The scope of the automatic reporting restrictions

Reporting restrictions in the Crime and Disorder Act 1998, the Criminal Justice Acts of 1987 and 1991, and the Criminal Procedure and Investigations Act 1996 apply to media reports of hearings for applications for charges to be dismissed and of 'preparatory hearings', see above.

When in force, these restrictions limit such reports to the following seven categories of information:

- the name of the Crown court and the judge's name;
- the names, ages, home addresses, and occupations of the defendant(s) and witnesses;
- the charge(s), or a summary of it/them;
- the names of solicitors or barristers acting in the case;
- if proceedings are adjourned, the date and place to which they are adjourned;

→ glossary

→ glossary

- arrangements as to bail, i.e. whether bail was granted or refused, and, if it was granted, any bail conditions and **surety** arrangement;

- whether **legal aid** was granted.

Witnesses are unlikely to take part in any such hearing held prior to trial. But if they do, or if they are mentioned in court, under these restrictions they can be identified as witnessess in contemporaneous media reports – though in some instances other law may require such media reports to provide anonymity for the alleged victim of the crime or for someone else who is a witness.

→
see chs 7,
8, and 9
for such
other law

As regards cases in which bail is refused, the usual interpretation of the restrictions is that the media should not report why the prosecution opposed bail or reasons the judge gave for refusing it – because such matter could be prejudicial.

The same restrictions apply to any application to a Crown court judge for leave to appeal against his/her rulings as made in a 'preparatory hearing', and to any appeal hearing, i.e. in the Court of Appeal or House of Lords/Supreme Court concerning such rulings (see below for descriptions of these highters Courts).

→
see ch, 5,
p. 67

As regards what home addresses may be published, the relevant legislation is identical to that in section 8C of the Magistrates' Courts Act 1980.

If there is an application at Crown court to dismiss transferred fraud charges, the media can, even when the automatic reporting restrictions apply, report – in addition to the seven categories of information listed above – the following 'relevant business information':

- any address used by the defendant for carrying on business on his/her own account;

- the name of any such business at 'any relevant time' i.e. a time when events which gave rise to the charge(s) occurred;

- the name and address of any firm in which he/she was a partner, or by which he/she was engaged, at any such time;

- the name of any company of which he/she was a director, or by which he/she was otherwise engaged, at any such time, and the address of its registered or principal office;

- any working address of the defendant in his/her capacity as a person engaged by any such company.

'Engaged' here means under a contract of service or a contract for services.

Restricted reports of hearings for applications for charges to be dismissed and of 'preparatory hearings' can safely include neutral descriptions of the court scene, and some non-prejudicial, background facts about the case, of the type referred to in ch. 4 in relation to preliminary hearings before magistrates, see pp. 55–56. It should be noted, though, that any mis-judgement by the media, when deciding what is non-prejudicial material, is more likely to be regarded as breach of statutory reporting restrictions (as regards matter aired in such a hearing) or contempt of court (as regards matter added from other sources) when a case is in the Crown court stages. This is because the protection of any 'fade factor' diminishes as the start date of any relevant jury trial draws nearer.

See also, p. 82, on reporting from arraignments. See below for when the automatic reporting restrictions cease to apply.

see ch. 16, p. 281 on fade factor

Automatic restrictions on reporting of pre-trial rulings

There is also a specific set of restrictions applying to media reports of 'pre-trial hearings', see above p. 78. These restrictions are set out in the Criminal Procedure and Investigations Act 1996, and prohibit any publication, before the conclusion of all Crown court proceedings in the case, of what is said in such hearings in:

- an application for any ruling on the admissibility of evidence or any other question of law, including any such ruling made by the judge
- an application for such a ruling to be varied or discharged, including any such order made by the judge.

The purpose of these restrictions, too, is to prevent prejudicial matter being published. The law on what *can* be reported contemporaeously from such 'pre-trial hearings' is not particularly clear. However, a journalist's safest course – to ensure there is no breach of contempt law – is for a contemporaneous report of any Crown court hearing held prior to jury involvement (i.e. in a contested case) to include only the seven categories of information listed under the heading: 'The scope of the automatic reporting restrictions', p. 79 above, and other non-prejudicial matter, as indicated there. See also guidance on reporting the arraignment, below.

see ch. 16 on contempt law

 See the Online Resources Centre, ch. 6, for discussion of why the scope of the 1996 Act restrictions is unclear.

Lifting or cessation of the automatic reporting restrictions

As regards hearings of applications for charges to be dismissed, pre-trial hearings, and preparatory hearings, the Crown court judge can lift the automatic reporting restrictions, or lift them in part, to allow the media to publish contemporaneously fuller reports of such hearings. If any defendant objects to lifting of the restrictions, the judge may lift them only if satisfied that lifting is in the interests of justice. If there are such objections, argument in court about whether the restrictions should be lifted cannot be reported until the conclusion of all relevant trials, even if restrictions are lifted in other respects.

If not lifted by the judge, the point at which these reporting restrictions automatically cease to apply is at the 'conclusion' of the relevant proceedings. This 'conclusion' under the relevant legislation either is stated to be, or can safely be construed to be, the acquittal or conviction of the sole defendant or, if there are more than one, all defendants in the case in respect of all charges in all trials in the case – or when it becomes clear that, for some other reason, no relevant trial remains pending. This might be when the prosecutor decides not to proceed with the case, or when all charges against all defendants are dismissed by the judge for insufficient evidence. Again, reporting restrictions under other law may still apply – see chs 7, 8, and 9.

Reporting the arraignment

A defendant can be arraigned either in a 'pre-trial hearing' or, in cases in which a 'preparatory hearing' is held, at the start of that hearing.

Whenever the arraignment occurs, if all defendants in the case plead guilty to all charges, they are thereby convicted of all charges, and therefore the restrictions set out on pp. 79 and 81 automatically cease to apply, because there will be no trial. Sentencing procedures are described later in this chapter.

If when arraigned the sole defendant, or all defendants, in the case deny all charges faced, the media can safely report those pleas contemporaneously if there is only to be one trial in the case, and if all such denied charges are definitely going to be made known to the jury.

But if a defendant or co-defendants enter a mixture of guilty and not guilty pleas, or if denied charges are to be dealt with in more than one trial, a judge may – to avoid what he/she considers a substantial risk of prejudice – make an order under section 4(2) of the Contempt of Court Act 1981 prohibiting media reports of an arraignment from mentioning, until the trial ends, any charge which has been admitted (if the jury is not to be told about it) or – if the case is due to involve more than one trial – any charge not due to be dealt with in the first trial.

 For further detail on use of a section 4(2) order in such circumstances, and for considerations to be borne in mind even if a judge does not make such an order, see ch. 16, pp. 289–293

Liability and penalty for breach of the automatic reporting restrictions

Liability and penalty, for breach of the automatic reporting restrictions under the various Acts cited above, are the same as for breach of restrictions under the Magistrates' Courts Act. And if a breach occurs after a trial has begun, and causes it to be aborted, a media organisation may be also liable for costs under the Courts Act 2003, see ch. 16, p. 284.

see ch 4, p. 53

▌ Appeals by prosecution against rulings by judge: reporting restrictions

If a Crown court judge, either in a hearing prior to a trial or after it begins, makes a ruling which would terminate all or part of the case, e.g. a ruling that there is no case to answer in respect of one or more charge, the prosecution may under the Criminal Justice Act 2003 appeal to the Court of Appeal against this ruling. Under the Act, automatic restrictions – to prevent prejudice to the trial, should it proceed, or to any linked trial – prohibit the reporting of any discussion (which would be in the absence of the jury) in the Crown court proceedings about such an appeal and in the relevant Court of Appeal hearing. The restrictions limit reports of such appeal proceedings to the same seven categories of information listed above under the heading: 'The scope of the automatic reporting restrictions', pp. 79–80. These 2003 Act restrictions apply until the conclusion of all trials in the case, if not lifted earlier.

▌ Procedure in Crown court trials

When a Crown court trial begins, the media are free to publish immediately (i.e. contemporaneously) and fully what occurs in it <u>when the jury is present in the courtroom</u>, unless – see ch. 16 – a section 4(2) order postpones reporting of it and with the exception of the various actual and potential limitations on reporting explained in chs 7, 8, and 9.

see ch. 16, pp. 291–293 on absence of jury

Until the jury has returned all verdicts in the trial, no report should publish any matter discussed in court, or rulings made, while the jury was not in the courtroom.

→
see also
p. 76 on
jurors

A Crown court trial can be regarded as under way when the process begins to 'empanel' a jury for it, i.e. a group of potential jurors is brought into the courtroom, and from them the court clerk, usually by shuffling pieces of paper or card bearing their names, selects 12 at random. These 12 will then be ushered into the jury box and 'sworn', i.e. required to swear a legal oath to try the case according to the evidence.

→ glossary

After the jury is sworn, **counsel** for the prosecution will normally 'open the case' in a speech, i.e. outline the evidence, and state the relevant law. Then prosecution witnesses will give evidence. The sequence of a Crown court trial, as regards speeches by lawyers, and questioning, cross-examination, and re-examination of prosecution and defence witnesses, is usually the same as occurs in trials conducted by magistrates (and there are the same rules requiring pre-trial disclosure of information between prosecution and defence). Hence, at Crown court, too, the defence may choose to make a speech 'opening' the defence case prior to calling the defence witnesses, and after all these have been heard, prosecuting counsel in most cases makes a closing speech to the jury, and this is followed by the defence's closing speech.

→
see ch. 5,
pp. 68–70
on trials
in mag-
istrates
courts

The judge then sums up the case, to remind the jury of evidence heard. He/she directs the jury as to the law, but verdicts are the province of the jury alone. The judge should, however, if he/she decides in the course of the trial that the evidence is not sufficient to support a charge, direct the jury to bring in a verdict of not guilty on that charge.

The jury, which will have been directed to elect a foreman or forewoman to be its spokesperson, 'retires' – i.e. withdraws – to a jury room to decide its verdict(s), with one of the court staff (probably one who has already acted as an usher in the case), acting as jury **bailiff**. The bailiff escorts jurors to and from their room and is the only official permitted to have contact with them in it.

→ glossary

Majority verdicts

A judge will initially advise a jury to arrive at a unanimous verdict on each charge, i.e. a unanimous vote either to acquit or convict.

- However, if the jury has 'retired' – i.e. has discussed the case – for at least two hours and ten minutes and has failed to reach a verdict, the judge can then recall it to the courtroom to tell it that a majority verdict is acceptable (for each charge).
- For a full jury of 12, majority verdicts of the ratios 11–1 or 10–2 are acceptable.

- If a jury is reduced in number for any reason, e.g. because one or two jurors have fallen ill during the trial, a majority of 10–1 or 9–1 is permitted.

- If a defendant is convicted by a majority of the jury, rather than by a unanimous vote, it is unproblematic for the media to refer to the fact that it was by a majority decision, because this indicates that one or two people in the jury disagreed with the 'guilty' verdict, and to report this is regarded as fair to the defendant.

- But if a defendant is acquitted by a majority vote, it is by convention regarded as undesirable to publish the fact that it was by a majority verdict, as this indicates that at least one juror thought the defendant guilty. Such a suggestion if reported leaves a stain on the defendant's character even though he/she was cleared of the charge.

For the same reason, the format of words used in court to ask a jury for its verdict on each charge is phrased to minimise the chance of the foreman/forewoman disclosing that an acquittal is by a majority rather than unanimous. But if the verdict is 'guilty', the foreman/forewoman will be asked if this was unanimous or not, and if not how many jurors agreed with this verdict and how many dissented.

If a jury is unable to reach a verdict by a sufficient majority, then this is the unresolved situation known as a 'hung jury' for any such charge. The prosecution then has to decide if it wants to seek a retrial. The more serious the alleged crime, e.g. murder, the more likely it is that there will be a retrial, because of the high public interest in justice being done.

Journalists or a media organisation could be prosecuted for contempt of court if they reveal jurors' identities, or seek to interview them about their discussions about the verdict deliberations or publish such discussions.

see ch. 9, pp. 146–148

▌ Sentencing at Crown court

If a defendant pleads guilty at Crown court to the sole charge or all charges faced, the judge in that same hearing, or in one held after an adjournment, will sentence after a procedure similar to that used for defendants sentenced in the magistrates court. That is, the prosecution summarises the evidence; the judge will be told of any relevant previous convictions the defendant has, and of any offences to be taken into consideration, and will consider, in

see ch 5, p. 63

cases where relevant, any formal statement made by the crime's victim(s), or – in a homicide case – an 'impact' statement by relatives of the victim, on how it has affected them; and the defence will make a speech of mitigation.

 → glossary There may be a **Newton hearing**.

A defendant who, after conviction in the magistrates court, is committed for sentence to the Crown court will be subject to the same sentencing procedure.

Sentencing at Crown court after conviction in a trial there follows similar procedure, though the judge, having presided over the trial, will not normally need to hear again detail of the proved offence(s). Again, there may well be an adjournment before sentencing. Crown courts, in that they deal with the most serious offences, frequently impose jail terms, but do have the same range of sentencing options as magistrates.

→
see ch 5, p. 71–72 on sentence options

Life sentences, 'dangerous' offenders, and indeterminate sentences

The death penalty was abolished in 1965 for murder. Now the only sentence provided by law for murder is one of life imprisonment if the offender is aged 21 or over. Sentences of life imprisonment may also be imposed for other

 → glossary offences (e.g. arson, **robbery**, rape). The judge may state, when sentencing, a minimum term of the life sentence which the defendant should actually serve. Sometimes the judge may recommend that it should actually be for life.

Each life prisoner will normally at various times during their time in jail, e.g. as the end of any stated minimum term approaches, have their case reviewed by the Parole Board, including assessment of the risk of them

→
see Useful Websites, below reoffending, and may then be released on 'licence', supervised by a probation officer.

A defendant convicted of specified sexual and violent offences committed on or after 4 April 2005 can be categorised by the judge as a 'dangerous offender', if the Crown court judge considers there is significant risk of the defendant committing further such offences, and such risk of serious harm to members of the public if he/she does reoffend. This means he/she must be given a life sentence if the circumstances of the offence of which he/she is convicted are deemed particularly serious, and the law allows such penalty. Otherwise, a 'dangerous offender' can be given an 'indeterminate sentence for public protection'. This means he/she will not be released from prison until a stated minimum term is served <u>and</u> until and unless the Parole Board decides the level of risk he/she poses to the public is deemed as manageable in the community, e.g. through contact with probation officers. If the risk is deemed too high, and the Board continues to take this view, such a prisoner will remain in jail indefinitely, even though the sentence imposed was not a life sentence.

A prisoner released on licence can be returned to prison to serve the remainder of the jail term if when at liberty he/she breaks any condition of the licence, e.g. by committing further crime.

Both legislation and the Consolidated Criminal Practice Direction encourage Crown court judges (and magistrates, in their courts) to explain when sentencing the reasons which led them to decide on the punishment imposed, and – if it is a prison term – its actual effect in terms of time due to be spent in jail.

→ see ch 12, p. 205

If no other legal factors apply, e.g. the defendant is not sentenced to life or deemed 'dangerous', see above, he/she can be expect, if he/she behaves well in prison, to be released on licence, see above, at the halfway point of any jail term of 12 months or more imposed by the court. He/she will, unless convicted of further crime, be released when the term ends, if not already released, i.e. the sentence is <u>not</u> indeterminate.

▶ Protocol for the media to have prosecution material

Journalists often have, when covering court cases and preparing background features for when they end, assistance from the investigating police force and the prosecuting agency, because it is in the public interest for cases to be fully aired and explained in media reports. The media may need copies of or access to items which formed part of the prosecution evidence, e.g. film, video footage, or photos. In 2005 the Crown Prosecution Service issued a national protocol, agreed after discussions with media representatives and the police, stating that material which has been relied upon by the prosecution in a trial (including a trial at a magistrates court), and which *should* normally be released to the media includes:

- maps and photographs, including custody photos of defendants, and other diagrams produced in court;
- videos showing scenes of crime;
- videos of property seized, e.g. weapons, drug hauls, or stolen goods;

- sections of transcripts of interviews that have been read to the court;
- videos or photographs showing reconstructions of the crime;
- CCTV footage of the defendant, subject to copyright issues.

The protocol also says that material which *might* be released following consideration by the CPS, in consultation with the police, victims, witnesses, and other people directly affected by the case, such as family members, includes:

- CCTV footage showing the defendant and victim, or the victim alone, which has been viewed by the jury and public in court, subject to copyright;
- video and audio tapes of police interviews with defendants, victims, and witnesses;
- victim and witness statements.

see Useful Websites, below for the protocol

The protocol also enables the media to ask the CPS head of strategic communications to become involved in the event of a dispute over disclosure.

See also ch. 16, p. 298, for the risk of contempt of court being committed by journalists who interview witnesses too soon.

▌ The Court of Appeal

see Figure 1, ch. 1, p. 8 on hierarchy of courts

A defendant who wishes to appeal against a conviction in, or the severity of sentence imposed in, a Crown court can seek permission to appeal to the Criminal Division of the Court of Appeal, based at the Royal Courts of Justice in London. Permission to make such an appeal can be granted by the Crown court trial judge or the Court of Appeal itself. However, a defendant's right to appeal on a point of law from Crown court to this higher court is automatic.

The Court of Appeal may, if it allows the appeal, quash a conviction. It may order a new trial – i.e. a retrial – at Crown court. Such an order by the Court of Appeal has resulted in at least one case of a man charged with murder being tried twice, and acquitted at the second trial.

The Court of Appeal can decide, in appeals against sentence, to reduce the severity of punishment imposed by a Crown court. Under other law, the Attorney General can ask the Court of Appeal to review what the prosecution considers an unduly lenient Crown court sentence for any indictable-only offence and certain others. In this procedure, the Court of Appeal may increase the sentence to any other sentence which was within the Crown court's power.

The Lord Chief Justice is president of the Court of Appeal's Criminal Division. Appeals are usually heard by three judges, e.g. the Lord Chief Justice or the president of the High Court's Queen's Bench Division or one of the Lords Justice of Appeal, plus either two High Court judges or one High Court judge and a senior circuit judge specially nominated for Court of Appeal duty. Lords Justices of Appeal have the title Lord/Lady Justice, e.g. Lord Justice Smith.

A reporter covering a Court of Appeal hearing in which its judgment is delivered may, in cases decided by a majority rather than a unanimous decision, have to wait until each of the three judges has in turn announced his/her own decision before that majority, and therefore the case result, is clear. Some appeal matters can be heard by only two judges, but if they cannot agree the matter must be reheard by three.

The Criminal Cases Review Commission, created by statute in 1995 to investigate alleged miscarriages of justice, has power to refer to the Court of Appeal any conviction or sentence if the Commission considers there is a real possibility it will be quashed.

→ see Useful websites, below

The right of a convicted prisoner to be visited in jail by a journalist investigating whether there had been a miscarriage of justice was upheld in *R v Secretary of State for the Home Department, ex p Simms* [1999] 3 All ER 400.

Appeals beyond the Court of Appeal go to the House of Lords/the Supreme Court.

▌ The House of Lords/the Supreme Court

The House of Lords is the highest court in the hierarchy of both the criminal and civil courts. It usually hears no more than 40 to 50 cases a year. The court is not a sitting of the full Parliamentary House of Lords. The Court's formal title is the House of Lords Appellate Committee. Its 12 judges are commonly known as law lords and they hold life peerages. Their official title is **Lords of Appeal** in Ordinary. The court consents to hear only cases of high significance. Such appeals are normally heard by five law lords. Majority decisions, e.g. four to one or even three to two, are binding. In cases

→ glossary

of exceptional importance the number of judges sitting may be increased. For example, in a case in 2004, nine law lords presided over appeals against the detention of foreign terrorism suspects without trial.

From October 2009 the name of this highest court in the land is due to change to the Supreme Court, under the terms of the Constitutional Reform Act 2005, and as part of these changes – designed to distance it from the House of Lords as a legislature – it is due to have a new venue in Middlesex Guildhall. Its procedures will be largely unchanged, but the senior Lord of Appeal in Ordinary will thereafter have the title President of the Supreme Court. All new judges appointed to the Supreme Court after it begins operation will not be members of the House of Lords, but will be known as Justices of the Supreme Court.

▌ Retrials after 'tainted acquittal' or after compelling new evidence emerges: reporting restrictions

Under what is generally known as the 'double jeopardy rule', the law usually – as a protection of civil liberties – prevents someone who has been acquitted of an offence being tried for it again. But there are now two major exceptions to this rule:

- Under the Criminal Procedure and Investigations Act 1996, when a Crown court convicts a person of interference with or intimidation of a juror, witness, or potential witness in an earlier trial in which the same or another defendant has been acquitted, application may be made to the High Court, see below, for an order quashing that acquittal, thus allowing a retrial.

- Under the Criminal Justice Act 2003, if after a defendant is acquitted at Crown court of a serious charge as defined by the Act (including, for example, any murder or rape charge, and certain Class A drug offences) 'new and compelling evidence' emerges, the prosecution, if so authorised by the Director of Public Prosecutions, can apply to the Court of Appeal for it to quash that acquittal and to order that a Crown court retrial takes place. The Court of Appeal can make an order

see ch. 2, p. 24 on DPP

imposing reporting restrictions, so making it an offence to publish any matter which would create a substantial risk of prejudice to any such retrial. The court can thereby ban media reports of the application itself, or of anything in connection with it, including any ongoing investigations into the alleged offence, and matter from the original case, until the end of any retrial, or until the matter is otherwise dropped. In the case of *R v D (acquitted person: retrial)* [2006] All ER (D) 387 (Feb) the Court of Appeal granted such a reporting restriction order, but said that in future the media should be given notice of such an application, and suggested that the notice should be of 14 days.

◗ The Crown court as an appeal court

Defendants can appeal to a Crown court judge against refusal by magistrates to grant bail.

→

see also
ch. 12,
p. 198

Defendants can appeal to the Crown court against conviction by magistrates, including in youth courts (which are explained in ch. 6). The appeal will take the form of a complete rehearing at Crown court but there will be no jury. A judge will sit normally with two lay magistrates (not those previously involved in the case being appealed). The court may confirm, reverse, or vary the magistrates' decision or send the case back to them for a retrial.

The Crown court also hears appeals against the severity of sentence imposed by magistrates, and may confirm the sentence, substitute a lesser penalty, or increase the sentence, but not to more than the highest sentence magistrates could have imposed.

◗ The High Court

The High Court Queen's Bench Division, which deals with criminal and other matters, has about 60 judges, headed by the Lord Chief Justice. It hears cases in London and Cardiff and major regional cities.

A defendant convicted by magistrates, or who has appealed unsuccessfully from them to the Crown court, may appeal on a point of law to the Queen's Bench Division on the grounds that a decision, whether taken by magistrates or by a Crown court judge, was wrong in law. This procedure is known as appeal by way of 'case stated', in that no evidence is given verbally to the High Court, which considers – in a hearing involving two or three judges – a written record of the case, and submissions about it. The prosecution can also use this appeal procedure to challenge an acquittal by magistrates. The High Court has wide power in this procedure to reverse, affirm, or amend decisions by magistrates including those taken in youth courts. For example it can order the case to be retried again summarily, or quash an acquittal and make a direction that the magistrates court or youth court convicts and sentences.

→ glossary

Part of the High Court's work involves **judicial reviews**, hearings which can consider other types of challenges to decisions made by magistrates, e.g. allegations of breach of natural justice. Also, the judicial review procedure can be used by the media to challenge discretionary reporting restrictions imposed by magistrates.

→
see ch. 13, p. 211 on challenges

◗ Courts martial

→
see Useful Websites, below

Men and women serving in the British armed forces, wherever they may be stationed around the globe, are subject to UK law and that is enforced through the courts martial system. This allows for service personnel to be tried under UK law even though the offence may have been committed in a foreign jurisdiction. Courts martial have become more frequent in recent years, especially in relation to the conflict in Iraq, which saw the first conviction of a UK soldier for a war crime. The court is presided over by a

→
see also ch. 13, p. 211

civilian judge advocate sitting with three to seven service personnel, the number depending on the seriousness of the offence.

Courts martial are usually open to the public and the media.

▦ Recap of major points

- Crown courts deal with the most serious criminal cases, including all indictable-only charges, such as murder, rape, and robbery.
- At Crown court judges rule on law and decide on punishment, and in trials juries decide whether each charge is proved.

- Automatic reporting restrictions limit what the media can report from most Crown court hearings prior to trial. These restrictions cease to operate when all trials in the case are over.

- Juries can reach a verdict by a majority, but the media should not report the fact that an acquittal was by a majority decision.

- The Crown Prosecution Service has issued guidelines about what material held by the police and/or prosecutors can be released to the media to help it report court cases.

- A defendant convicted in Crown court can seek to appeal to the Court of Appeal, and thereafter possibly to the House of Lords/Supreme Court.

- The Crown court can act as a court of appeal from magistrates courts, as regards conviction or sentence.

- The High Court is also an appeal court, for certain matters.

🌐 Useful Websites

http://juror.cjsonline.gov.uk/
Government guidance on jury service

www.judiciary.gov.uk/
Judiciary website

www.judicialappointments.gov.uk/
Judicial Appointments Commission

www.probation.homeoffice.gov.uk/
National Probation Service

www.paroleboard.gov.uk/
Parole Board

www.cps.gov.uk/Publications/agencies/mediaprotocol.html
Protocol for working together: Chief Police Officers, Chief Crown Prosecutors and the Media

www.ccrc.gov.uk/
Criminal Cases Review Commission

www.judiciary.gov.uk/about_judiciary/roles_types_jurisdiction/military_justice/index.htm
Judiciary website on courts martial

7

Juveniles in criminal, ASBO, and drink ban proceedings

Chapter summary

Most children and young people prosecuted for criminal offences appear in youth courts, where specially trained magistrates preside. **Automatic** reporting restrictions usually ensure that media reports of youth court cases do not identify juveniles involved in them, including witnesses – to protect their welfare. The term 'juvenile' describes anyone aged under 18. This chapter explains how some juveniles are tried in adult criminal courts (the magistrates courts and Crown courts) if co-accused with adults. The case of a juvenile accused of a very serious offence must be dealt with by the Crown court. When a juvenile is involved, adult courts have discretion to restrict media reports of such cases from identifying him/her. Juveniles made the subject of anti-social behaviour orders, including those prosecuted for allegedly breaching them, can be identified in reports of such ASBO cases, subject to the court's discretion. See also ch. 9 for other reporting restrictions, some of which could apply in court cases concerning juveniles. Anonymity provision for children in family law cases is explained in ch. 11.

▌ The term 'juvenile', and the age of criminal responsibility

In the criminal law most relevant to this chapter, a 'child' is defined as being under 14 years and a 'young person' as being aged 14 or over but under 18. A child under 10 cannot be prosecuted for a criminal offence, because he/she is considered too young to distinguish between right and wrong, i.e. not to have reached the **age of criminality**. But if his/her behaviour seems beyond parental control he/she can be made subject to supervision by a social worker. The distinction between a 'child' aged 10 and over and a 'young person' is less important in law than it used to be, but relates to the degree of knowledge of right and wrong which could be assumed to exist in each age group. Lawyers use the term 'juvenile' to describe defendants aged from 10 up to, but not including, the age of 18, and for child and youth witnesses under the age of 18.

→ glossary

→
see ch. 11, p. 168 on social workers

▶ Juveniles in youth courts

A juvenile accused of a crime may not necessarily, particularly for a first and minor offence, be prosecuted. Instead, the police may issue a reprimand or warning. In most instances, prosecuted juveniles are dealt with by a youth court. Magistrates (including **district judges**) preside in them. But youth courts – though usually in the same building as magistrates courts (i.e. where adult defendants appear) – are usually smaller courtrooms with a less formal layout, designed to make juveniles feel less nervous than they might be in an adult courtroom. Magistrates who sit in youth courts receive special training, geared to helping juveniles understand proceedings. But hearings there, including trials, use procedures similar to those in the (adult) magistrates courts, as described in chs 4 and 5. A juvenile denied **bail** while awaiting trial at a youth court will be sent either to non-secure accommodation run by the local authority, e.g. a children's home or – for example, if the alleged offending is persistent or particularly serious – to custody, as explained below.

→
see ch. 4, pp. 42–43 on magis- trates

Youth courts' powers to sentence

The categorisation of charges – i.e. as **indictable-only**, **either-way**, or **summary** – used for adult defendants does not apply in youth courts. A youth court, because its sentencing powers are limited, cannot try extremely serious cases, e.g. homicide. It therefore must commit juvenile defendants in such cases to a Crown court. But a youth court has discretion, if it considers its punishment powers sufficient for a particular case, to try other offences, e.g. **robbery**, which, had the defendant been an adult, would have been indictable-only.

→ glossary
→ glossary

→
see p. 34 for this categor- isation

see ch. 5,
pp. 71–72
on such
sentences

Most of a youth court's work involves less serious crime. Its sentencing powers include community punishment, absolute and conditional discharges, orders for offenders to pay compensation to their victims, and fines (which parents must pay if the offender is aged under 16). Recent law has introduced the term 'youth rehabilitation order' to describe a 'menu' of community punishments and requirements, e.g. a curfew, from which a youth court can choose several for an offender. Many young offenders pleading guilty at a youth court to a first offence are dealt with by being made subject to a referral order. This means he/she must co-operate with a referral to a youth offender panel, comprising of trained youth workers, and agree with it a 'contract' which seeks to prevent reoffending. This includes unpaid work in the community. If the offender fails to co-operate, he/she can be re-sentenced, i.e. incur heavier, court punishment.

Youth courts, in the most serious cases they can deal with, can make a detention and training order. These can be imposed for a range of time spans, from a minimum of four months to a maximum of two years. Normally this means that the offender spends half the period in custody, see below, with training, and the rest under supervision in his/her community.

The court can make a parenting order. This requires a parent, or any other specified adult responsible for the child, to attend counselling and guidance sessions, and to co-operate with other steps to help the juvenile avoid involvement in crime or behaving antisocially in other ways. If the adult breaches the order, he/she will be liable to court punishment, e.g. a fine of up to £1,000.

Juveniles in custody

A juvenile who in a youth court has been remanded to custody after being refused bail or who, after conviction, has been sentenced to detention and glossary training, see above, can be held during that **remand**, or to serve that sentence, in a secure children's home, a secure training centre, or a young offenders' institute. The choice of appropriate custody venue depends on criteria related to age, gender, and whether the juvenile is considered 'vulnerable', e.g. at risk of self-harm.

→ For more detail, see the Youth Justice Board's website, listed at the end of this chapter.

Committal for trial of 'grave' and other cases

A juvenile charged with a homicide offence, e.g. murder or manslaughter, and certain firearms offences, cannot by law be tried or sentenced by a youth court, because of the extreme seriousness of the charge. In most such cases defendants make initial appearances there, for decisions on bail and procedural matters. But then the youth court will commit the case for trial to a Crown court where, if there is a conviction, a judge will sentence. In respect of other offences categorised as 'grave', e.g. causing death by dangerous driving, and certain sexual offences, the youth court considers in mode of trial proceedings if its maximum power of punishment – i.e. a two-year detention and training order – would be sufficient in the event of conviction in a youth court trial. If the court considers this power insufficient, the case will be committed to Crown court for trial. These **mode of trial hearings** and **committal hearings** differ from those in the magistrates court, in that in the youth court the juvenile has no right to choose jury trial, and the court does not consider if there is sufficient evidence, but considers the nature of the alleged offence. Also, a case will be sent for Crown court trial if the youth court considers the defendant would, in the event of conviction, meet the 'dangerous' offender criteria, explained on p. 86.

→ glossary

→
see ch, 4,
for these
proce-
dures in
magis-
trates
court

Section 8 reporting restrictions

- Because a youth court case of the type subject to such committal or sending procedure has the potential of jury trial, the automatic reporting restrictions of section 8 of the Magistrates' Courts Act 1980 apply to all **preliminary hearings** of such a case in the youth court for as long as that potential exists, and, if there is a jury trial, will continue in force in respect of those preliminary hearings until the trial ends.

→ glossary

Therefore in such cases the media must only report certain categories of information contemporaneously from the cases' hearings in the youth court, because they are preliminary proceedings. See ch. 4, pp. 51–59 for full details of the restrictions, explained there in relation to cases in the (adult) magistrates courts, but they apply identically in respect of such youth court hearings.

If a youth court convicts a juvenile itself, it can again consider whether the juvenile can be regarded a 'dangerous offender'. If it considers he/she meets the 'dangerous' criteria, it can commit him/her to Crown court for sentence. The section 8 restrictions will not apply in respect of a trial at the youth court or a **committal for sentence** because any potential for jury trial in such a case will have already been extinguished, or – as regards many cases tried in the youth court – will not have existed because the charge is relatively minor.

→ glossary

▶ Admission to youth courts

Many juveniles convicted of crime grow up to be law-abiding citizens. Some accused of crimes are found not guilty. Parliament has decided that to avoid juveniles being stigmatised in their communities by allegations of or conviction for immature law-breaking, the public should not be permitted to attend youth courts. The court may make exceptions, e.g. a victim of an offence may be allowed to see sentencing done. Another reason for these courts being closed to the public is to help prevent juvenile witnesses feeling nervous.

- Though the public is barred from youth courts, journalists are entitled to attend and report cases there, because section 47 of the Children and Young Persons Act 1933 states that 'bona fide representatives of newspapers or news agencies' can attend.

However, reporters attend so rarely that some court ushers may, unaware of section 47, challenge their right to be there.

▶ Automatic restrictions on identifying juveniles in youth court cases

Parliament decided – again, to stop juveniles being stigmatised – that defendants in youth courts should not usually be identified in media reports of such cases. This anonymity also applies to juvenile witnesses in them, and so helps make giving evidence less of an ordeal and protects their reputation, in that their character may be scrutinised in cross-examination. The anonymity is provided by automatic reporting restrictions under section 49 of the Children and Young Persons Act 1933 (as amended by section 49 of the Criminal Justice and Public Order Act 1994).

Section 49 states that reports of youth court proceedings must not reveal:

- the name,
- or address,
- or school

of a person aged under 18 who is 'concerned in the proceedings', either as a defendant or witness. Nor must they include:

- any particulars likely to lead to his/her identification

- or any picture (including in any TV programme) of, or including, any such juvenile.

In the Act, the definition 'concerned in the proceedings' also covers a juvenile 'in respect of whom the proceedings are taken'.

- So, the section 49 anonymity also applies, in media reports of a youth court case, to a juvenile who is the victim/alleged victim in the case, as stated in the charge, even if such a person is not a witness, e.g. because he/she is a baby or toddler, too young to give evidence.

But, as can be construed from precedent judgments about Court orders made under the Act's section 39 which is explained below, a juvenile victim who is dead, e.g. of a homicide offence, would not be covered by the section 49 anonymity. Such a case would be committed to Crown court – see above, p. 95.

→ see ch. 13, p. 235 on these precedents concerned in proceedings

To comply with section 49, reporters must not include in a youth court story *anything* that could identify a juvenile concerned in the proceedings. To say 'a 14-year-old Bristol boy' would not identify him. But to use the name of a small village, or his nickname among friends, might, as would a statement that a boy was the 12-year-old twin son of a policeman. The test must always be whether any member of the public could realise, as a result of information in the media report, who the juvenile is. There is nothing to stop the naming of adults, e.g. witnesses, concerned in youth court proceedings, provided this does not identify a juvenile. A father cannot be named as giving evidence about his son, the defendant. Under section 49 there is a complete ban on identifying the juvenile's school, however large.

These section 49 restrictions also apply to reports of Crown court hearings of appeals from the youth court against conviction or severity of sentence, and to reports of High Court hearings of appeals from the youth court (or from the Crown court appeal hearings described above) on a point of law.

→ see ch. 6, pp. 91–92 on these appeal routes

The section 49 restrictions also apply to appeal proceedings in any court (for example, a Crown court) for varying or revoking a supervision order against a juvenile, provided the restriction is announced in open court.

- So, the section 49 restrictions automatically travel up with the youth court case when a higher court hears any appeal originating in the youth court.

However, the section 49 restrictions do *not* apply to reports of proceedings at Crown court where a juvenile has been committed for trial or for sentence. But a discretionary order providing anonymity for him/her at Crown court may be made there under section 39 of the Children and Young Persons Act – see below, p. 103.

Recent breaches of section 49

Under the Criminal Justice and Public Order Act 1994, if a media organisation breaches section 49, i.e. publishes matter which identifies a juvenile covered by it, the proprietor, editor, or publisher can be prosecuted and in the case of a TV or radio programme, 'the body corporate which provides the service' and any person whose 'functions in relation to the programme correspond to those of an editor of a newspaper'. The maximum fine is currently £5,000. The Attorney General has to consent to such prosecutions.

A production editor of a weekly newspaper was fined £1,000 in 2007 after being convicted of such a breach, which he had denied. The offence arose from a picture being published of a juvenile whose eyes and nose had been blacked out, but his mouth and hair were visible, and this identification of him led to the fine (*Media Lawyer*, 18 December 2007). A district judge at Plymouth magistrates court fined the *Plymouth Evening Herald* £1,500 in 2003 for publishing a photograph of a 15-year-old boy who had been convicted at youth court of stabbing a fellow pupil. The district judge said evidence by friends and relatives that they had recognised the boy, even though the face was pixellated, meant that the paper was guilty of breaching section 49. An appeal by the paper was rejected (*Media Lawyer*, 4 March 2004).

When section 49 anonymity ceases to apply

A youth court can, under section 49, remove a juvenile's anonymity 'to any specified extent' in three types of circumstance, thus allowing the media to identify such a juvenile in a report of the case.

1) *To avoid injustice* – A youth court can remove the section 49 anonymity 'for the purpose of avoiding injustice' to a juvenile.

This power is rarely exercised. But the court could use it to permit the media to identify, prior to a trial there, a juvenile defendant who needs the public to know who he/she is because he/she needs witnesses to come forward, for example, to support an **alibi**. Parliament also envisaged that under

→ glossary

this power the court could permit a media report to identify a juvenile to correct, via the media, false rumour in a community confusing a juvenile witness with a juvenile defendant.

2) *Unlawfully at large* – A youth court, if asked to do so by or on behalf of the Director of Public Prosecutions (e.g. by a Crown Prosecution Service lawyer), can remove the section 49 anonymity to help to trace a juvenile who is 'unlawfully at large' after being charged with or convicted of
   - a violent offence
   - a sexual offence
   - or any offence for which a person aged 21 or over could be jailed for 14 years or more.

This power can therefore be used to allow the media to name – and publish a photograph and other details of – a juvenile who has absconded while on bail or escaped from secure accommodation, and who is deemed to pose a potential threat to public safety.

3) *In the public interest* – If a juvenile is convicted at a youth court, the court can, whatever the offence, remove his/her section 49 anonymity if it is satisfied this is 'in the public interest'.
   - But before taking this decision it must give the prosecution and defence representatives, and any other 'parties' to the case, the opportunity to argue for or against lifting the anonymity, and must take such argument into account.

This power, granted by section 45 of the Crime (Sentences) Act 1997, can, for example, be used when the court feels that a juvenile who persistently offends, or who is responsible for a particularly newsworthy crime, should be identified by the media, as a deterrent to other potential offenders or to enable the community to be alert to the possibility of him/her committing further crime, or to reassure the local community that justice has been done. See also ch. 13, p. 230, for the media's ability to make representations that the court should use this power to lift a juvenile's anonymity.

The ability of youth courts, in the three types of circumstance outlined above, to decide whether to lift the section 49 anonymity wholly or partially, i.e. 'to any specified extent', is illustrated by the decision of a youth court in Newbury, Berkshire, in 2006 to allow the media to identify a 14-year-old girl convicted of **drink driving**, while refusing to permit publication of photo- →glossary
graphs of her or to allow her school to be named.

Youth court defendants who attain their 18th birthday

If part of Schedule 2 to the Youth Justice and Criminal Evidence Act 1999 is implemented, there will be clear statute that anonymity for juveniles involved in youth court proceedings ceases to have effect as soon as they reach the age of 18. The Act would specifically ban publication of the juvenile's name 'while he is under 18'.

But even without the implementation of this part of the 1999 Act, the anonymity for young people in the youth courts appears to end on their attaining the age of 18. In 2003 the High Court ruled, in *Todd v Director of Public Prosecutions* [2003] All ER (D) 92 (Oct), that the purpose of the Children and Young Persons Act 1933 was not to protect the interests of 'young persons' after they had ceased to be 'young persons' (see above, p. 94) and that therefore reporting restrictions applied only as long as the individual concerned remained under 18. In this case, the court dismissed an appeal against the decision of South Shields youth court that a defendant who was 17 when proceedings against him began no longer had anonymity when the case resumed after his 18th birthday.

> See also the Online Resource Centre, ch. 7, for detail of amendments to the law on anonymity for juveniles, including to definitions in sections 39 (see below) and 49 of the Children and Young Persons Act 1993, which would take effect if and when relevant parts of the 1999 Act are brought into force.

▌ Juveniles in adult courts

A juvenile may appear in the (adult) magistrates court if he/she is jointly charged with an adult appearing there, or faces a charge linked by the same alleged events to a charge an adult is facing. Whether the juvenile is tried there depends on each such case's circumstances. But the magistrates court has discretion to remit the juvenile to the youth court for trial, or for sentencing if the juvenile admits the offence. If an adult in a case involving a juvenile defendant is, by the magistrates court, committed or sent for trial to the Crown court, the juvenile may be sent there too for trial if the magistrates think a joint trial there is in the interests of justice, e.g. to avoid witnesses having to testify in more than one trial of the same events.

Furthermore, as described above (see pp. 96 and 97), a juvenile defendant can also end up at Crown court by being committed or sent there by a youth court.

→ see ch. 4, on sendings, committals

Section 39 reporting restrictions on identifying juveniles in adult courts

When a juvenile appears as defendant or witness in any criminal court other than a youth court, other than in an appeal from a youth court (see above, page 99) there is no automatic ban on the media identifying him/her in a report of the proceedings.

- But the adult court, e.g. a magistrates court or a Crown court, has discretion to impose such a ban under section 39 of the Children and Young Persons Act 1933.
- If a section 39 order is made, its scope normally is that, in respect of a person aged under 18 'concerned in the proceedings', no report of the case shall reveal his/her:
  - name
  - or address
  - or school

  or include:

- any particulars 'calculated' to lead to his/her identification
- or any picture of him/her.

The word 'calculated' is best construed as 'likely'. The phrase 'concerned in the proceedings' means that the order can be made in respect of

NB: 'calculated' survives from the Act's original wording

- a juvenile defendant, or juvenile witness or any other juvenile who is the victim/alleged victim named in the charge.

Because a section 39 order can apply to a juvenile 'in respect of whom the proceedings are taken' it can also be used to bestow anonymity, in media reports of the case, on a child whose parent is prosecuted in the (adult) magistrates court for allowing the child to play truant, and the effect of such an order would be that the reports could not identify the parent either.

As with the section 49 restriction, a journalist must take care not to breach a section 39 order by including too much detail about a juvenile protected by it. As in section 49, the ban on identifying a juvenile's school is a blanket ban unless the court decides the school can be identified.

see p. 99 on care needed

The courts, in order to pay proper heed to the principle of open justice, should not make a section 39 order merely because of the juvenile's age, or as an order arbitrarily covering all such juveniles in the case, but must consider in respect of each juvenile whether there is good reason to bestow such anonymity. See ch. 13, pp. 231–237 on challenging these orders.

see Ch.
13,
p. 236

Although a section 39 order cannot validly specify that an adult, rather than a juvenile, have anonymity the effect of section 39 anonymity bestowed on a juvenile may be that an adult defendant or adult witness related to the juvenile cannot be identified either. For example, if a father is charged with an offence of violence to his own child, and if the child's identity is protected by a section 39 order, this family relationship cannot be included in media reports if the father is named as the defendant, because specifying the relationship would identify the child. Indeed, it may be impossible to report such a case in any meaningful detail if media reports identify the father, because mere mention of the child's age could suggest a familial relationship.

> ➔ See also pp. 105–107 for discussion of such familial abuse cases.

Section 39 orders can also be made in civil courts and by coroners, see chs 10 and 14.

Recent breaches of section 39 orders

Under the Children and Young Persons Act 1993, 'any person' who publishes matter breaching a section 39 order can be fined up to £ 5,000. The term 'person' here includes companies. The *Glamorgan Gem* newspaper was fined £2,000 in 2008 after breaching a section 39 order by naming a child witness in a murder case. It volunteered to pay her compensation of £5,000 after it admitted the breach to magistrates in Barry (*Media Lawyer*, 31 December 2008).

The *Sun*, *Daily Mirror*, and the *Wigan Evening Post* apologised to a judge at Chester Crown court in 2008 after each breached, to some extent, a section 39 order made in a murder case. The *Sun* published details of a disability condition of one of the convicted juvenile defendants, and the *Evening Post* published an address for him, yet both matters were covered by the order. Under it, the judge had also specified that only one particular photograph could be published of two juvenile witnesses (the teenage daughters of the murder victim). But the *Mirror* published a different photograph. The judge said that, in view of the apologies, he would not refer the breaches to the Attorney General for possible prosecution. The judge also said: 'The common theme of these things is that it almost always seems to be a sub editor or features editor who is not aware of something which the news department are' (*Media Lawyer*, 12 February 2008).

When does section 39 cease to apply to a juvenile?

The 1933 Children and Young Persons Act does not make clear when section 39 anonymity lapses for a juvenile. But from the decision on the scope of section 49 in *Todd v Director of Public Prosecutions* (see above, page 102), and from what is becoming a recognised legal principle that Article 10 of the European Convention on Human Rights requires any statutory restriction on reporting to be construed as narrowly as possible to comply with Article 10, it can be strongly argued that the section 39 anonymity automatically lapses when a juvenile reaches the age of 18.

 See ch. 9, pp. 136–137 for detail of rare cases when the High Court bestowed indefinite anonymity, in respect of media reports, on two defendants convicted as juveniles of homicides.

▌ Jigsaw identification

The term 'jigsaw identification' describes the effect when someone to whom the law has given anonymity is nevertheless identified to the public when two or more media organisations are covering the same case. Jigsaw identification occurs because, though each media organisation publishes a report which in itself preserves such anonymity, a member of the public who reads, views or hears the reports of more than one organisation acquires, from the different detail in each, a combination of detail which destroys the anonymity. The examples given below relate to anonymity for juveniles. But jigsaw identification can also destroy anonymity granted to other categories of people under other law, e.g. to alleged victims of sexual offences.

Example 1 A juvenile defendant in the youth court, who has anonymity under section 49 of the Children and Young Persons Act 1933, admits causing criminal damage to a sports car owned by local millionaire John Doe. One local paper states: 'A 15-year-old boy vandalised a sports car owned by London tycoon John Doe, costing him £5,000 in repairs.' Another local paper reports the same day: 'A 15-year-old boy vandalised his rich neighbour's sports car, causing £5,000 damage.' Neither paper names the boy. The second paper does not name Doe. But anyone reading both papers will know the boy is a neighbour of Mr Doe, which identifies the boy locally.

Example 2 A juvenile, subject to the section 39 order made under the 1933 Act, is giving evidence at Crown court in a murder trial. One local radio station describes her as 'a 16-year-old who works as a shop assistant in London'. Another radio station does not mention her job but describes her routine as 'commuting each morning to work in Charing Cross'. A newspaper gives the detail that she lives in Islington. This kind of accumulation of detail could lead to those who know her, and who listen to both stations and read that newspaper, to realise that she is the witness.

▌ Cases of abuse within a family

There is a particular danger of jigsaw identification, see above in media coverage of cases of violence or other types of physical abuse allegedly inflicted on a child by a relative, e.g. when a father or stepfather is the adult defendant. In such cases it will be standard practice for magistrates and the Crown court judge to make a section 39 order to forbid media reports from identifying the alleged, child victim. In cases of alleged sexual abuse, the child will have automatic anonymity under other law, see ch. 8.

In such abuse cases, media organisations can either:

a) *name the adult defendant*, but, if the defendant is a relative, this means they must not, in order to protect the child's anonymity, publish any detail of the defendant's relationship to the child, and this can severely restrict what evidence is published, e.g. about how the defendant had access to the child or even the child's age. Lord Justice Maurice Kay warned in the Court of Appeal in 2005, alluding to a case in which a father was convicted of distributing indecent photographs of a child and of conspiracy to rape her: 'Offences of the kind established in this case are frequently committed by fathers and step-fathers.... If the offender is named and the victim is described as "an 11-year old schoolgirl", in circumstances in which the offender has an 11-year old daughter, it is at least arguable that the composite picture presented embraces "particulars calculated to lead to the identification" of the victim.' (*R v Teesside Crown Court, ex p Gazette Media Company Ltd and others*, [2005] All ER (D) 367 (Jul).

see p. 103 on 'calcu- lated'

b) *choose not to identify the adult defendant in any way*, and therefore the report can refer to the familial relationship between the defendant and child, can refer to the child's age, and can include greater detail of evidence, while preserving the child's anonymity.

An editor's instinct is usually that it is in the public's best interests for people accused of crime to be named, as a deterrent and so that a community can be wary of such an individual. This is achieved by the approach in (a), if it is possible to construct a meaningful report without revealing the family relationship. But another editor may feel that the public interest is best served by the approach in (b) which makes clear the alleged abuse was by a relative of the child. Approach (b) allows more evidence to be published and therefore more questions to be raised, e.g. about why the community, social services, or the police remained unaware of such abuse within that family.

Jigsaw identification would arise if two media organisations covering the case adopted different approaches. If one media organisation followed policy (a), naming the adult defendant but obscuring his relationship to the child victim, and the other organisation followed approach (b), not identifying the defendant but reporting, for example, that he was the child's father, anyone reading both organisations' reports would be able to identify the child. In coverage of such a case, local and regional media may prefer to name the adult defendant, because local readers may know this person or know the community where he lives. National media have less interest in identifying the defendant, so may prefer approach (b), which allows more evidence to be aired, to make a report more interesting for national readership. But to avoid jigsaw identification of the child, all the newsrooms involved in covering the case need to adopt the same approach. The reporters must realise this.

▶ Anti-social behaviour orders on juveniles

A court can make an anti-social behaviour order against a person to prohibit the repetition of behaviour, whether itself criminal or not, which causes harassment, alarm, or distress to one or more other people not in the person's household. Such orders – known as ASBOs – were introduced by the Crime and Disorder Act 1998. They can be made against an adult or a juvenile if he/she is aged at least 10.

An ASBO may follow a previous, but unsuccessful, attempt to amend a juvenile's behaviour by means of an 'acceptable behaviour contract' (e.g. an agreement made between the juvenile and the local authority, housing landlord, or the police). The order may seek to prevent the person engaging in

see ch. 3,
p. 39 on
'twockers'

activity which may lead to crime, e.g. a persistent shoplifter can, by means of an ASBO, be banned from going into any shop, or a juvenile known to take cars without their owners' consent can be banned from getting into any car. In some cases, juveniles have been banned by an ASBO from entering an area or a street where they have habitually been creating a nuisance, or from associating with other named juveniles with whom they have misbehaved.

An ABSO is an order made in civil law, but breach of it is a criminal offence. So, for example, if a person banned from entering shops ignores the ban, this is an offence even if he/she cannot be proved to have indulged in further shoplifting. The minimum term for which an ABSO can be made to apply is two years.

The Labour Government's determination to establish the use of ASBOs, and to encourage media identification of juveniles subject to them, has led to statutes amending the 1998 Act, making this a complex topic.

There are two main types of court hearing which can result in an ASBO for a juvenile – applications made in civil proceedings to the magistrates courts, and 'bolt-on' hearings in the youth courts (which are criminal courts, though ASBOs imposed there remain part of civil law).

ASBO applications in civil proceedings in magistrates courts

An (adult) magistrates court, sitting in civil proceedings, can make an ASBO against an adult or juvenile, if persuaded to do so by an application by a local authority, a registered social landlord (e.g. a housing association), the Environment Agency, or the police.

- There is no automatic restriction on the media identifying a juvenile in a report of such an ASBO application hearing in a magistrates court, whether or not it results in an ASBO.

- But the magistrates have discretion to make an order under section 39 of the Children and Young Persons Act 1933 to grant a juvenile anonymity, if he/she is 'concerned in the proceedings', e.g. the juvenile against whom the order is sought, or a witness (see above, p. 103).

Such applications for ASBOs are often adjourned, especially if the juvenile objects to the order being made. Sometimes an interim, i.e. temporary ASBO to restrain objectionable conduct may be made at this point. In 2004 the High Court (Queen's Bench Administrative Court) in *Keating v Knowsley Metropolitan Borough Council* [2004] EWHC 1933 (Admin) gave guidance on whether a section 39 order should be made at this interim stage. In that case Mr Justice Harrison said the fact that no allegations had been proved and the defendant had not had the opportunity to put his case were weighty matters to consider. He allowed an appeal by a juvenile against the magistrates' decision to refuse a section 39 order, because there had been no consideration by that bench of the interim nature of the proceedings.

A county court has similar power to make an ASBO, e.g. when resolving disputes between landlord and tenant. See ch. 10 on county courts.

> For arguments a journalist can use in court to challenge a juvenile being given section 39 anonymity in an ASBO case, see ch 13, pp. 237–239.

'Bolt-on' ASBO hearings

The criminal courts, including youth courts, can make an ASBO against a defendant *after* he/she has been convicted there of a criminal offence, whether or not any agency makes an application for such an ASBO. Because, if it occurs, such a hearing – on whether an ASBO is needed – is a consequence of a preceding conviction (e.g. for **theft** or taking cars), and may ➔glossary proceed immediately after that criminal case concludes, this type of ASBO hearing has become known as a 'bolt-on' hearing.

- As regards youth courts, the usual ban under section 49 of the 1933 Act will prevent the media identifying the juvenile defendant, and any juvenile witnesses, in any report of the actual criminal case (e.g. for theft or taking cars) which precedes the 'bolt-on' ASBO hearing – unless the court specifically waives the section 49 restrictions in that criminal case, e.g. 'in the public interest' as regards a persistent offender.

➔
see above, pp. 100–101 on such waiving

- When a 'bolt-on' hearing follows, for the youth court to consider making an ASBO against such a convicted juvenile, then if (and only if) the court *does* impose an ASBO on him/her, the section 49 anonymity automatically ceases to apply, as regards that juvenile, to media reports of the 'bolt-on' hearing, thus permitting the media to identify him/her as the subject of an ASBO, unless...

- the youth court in that 'bolt-on' hearing decides to preserve the juvenile's anonymity by using its discretion to make a section 39 order.

- Whether or not an ASBO is imposed, the section 49 anonymity automatically continues to apply as regards any other juvenile concerned in the 'bolt-on' proceedings, e.g. a witness.

> see also ch. 13 pp. 237–239 on challenges to anonymity in ASBO cases.

As is set out above, as regards these 'bolt-on' hearings Parliament has, in section 86 of the Anti-Social Behaviour Act 2003, made the 'default' position in law to be that, unless a section 39 order is made, the media <u>can</u> identify the juvenile on whom an ABSO is imposed. However, that juvenile may well still enjoy anonymity, under section 49, in respect of the earlier hearing in which he/she was convicted (e.g. of theft or taking cars). In this situation, a media organisation has the choice of:

a) identifying the juvenile in a report of the 'bolt-on' ASBO hearing, without reporting, from the earlier hearing, details of the conviction which led to the ASBO, even though lack of such of detail may make published explanation of why an ASBO was needed less meaningful, or

b) reporting both hearings without identifying the juvenile, an approach which may produce detailed coverage of his/her offending, yet which will lack the impact of revealing who is subject to the ASBO.

The Justices' Clerks Society has given guidance to its members that when a magistrates court draws up an ASBO it should include details of the anti-social behaviour which led to the order being made. A reporter can point out this guidance to the court clerk. A reporter can argue against the section 49 anonymity, see pp. 239–241.

→

see
Useful
Websites,
below

Alleged breach of an ASBO by a juvenile

If a juvenile is alleged to have breached an ABSO, he/she will face a criminal charge making that accusation, because such a breach is a criminal offence. Such a charge will normally be dealt with at a youth court.

- The usual anonymity – under section 49 of the 1933 Act – for juveniles accused in a youth court of crime does **not** apply to a juvenile accused of a breach of an ASBO, whether or not that charge is proved. Therefore the media can identify such a juvenile when reporting such a case in a youth court, unless…

- the youth court decides to preserve the juvenile defendant's anonymity by using its discretion to make a section 39 order under the 1933 Act.

- If the youth court does make such a section 39 order, the court must give its reasons for preserving the anonymity of the juvenile.

The law which removed the section 49 anonymity for defendants, if accused of breaching an ASBO, and which imposed the requirement for the youth court to state why in such a case a section 39 order is being made, if it is, is contained in section 141 of the Serious Organised Crime and Police Act 2005.

 see also ch. 13, pp. 237–239 on challenging section 39 orders in ASBO cases.

▌ Drinking banning orders

In the Violent Crime Reduction Act 2006, Parliament passed law to create a new civil order – a drinking banning order (DBO). When this book went to press in 2009, this law had not been put into effect. But when it is put into force, the police or a local authority will be able, if an adult or a juvenile aged 16 or over has engaged in criminal or disorderly conduct while under the influence of alcohol, to apply to magistrates or to a county court for such a person to be subjected to such an order. Also, a criminal court (including, in respect of such a juvenile, the youth court) will be able to impose such an order in a 'bolt-on' hearing after he/she is convicted of an offence. The order would prohibit the person from entering premises which sell alcohol, and could include other prohibitions which the court considers will prevent him/her engaging in such alcohol-influenced conduct in future. Under the 2006 Act, anonymity under section 49 of the Children and Young Persons Act 1933 will not apply to a media report of a youth court 'bolt-on' hearing in respect of any juvenile who is made subject in it to a DBO. Nor will section 49 anonmity apply to youth court proceedings if he/she is subsequently accused of breaching it, whether or not he/she is convicted of such a breach. But any court, including the youth court, will have discretion to use the 1933 Act's section 39 to grant such a juvenile anonymity in media reports of the DBO's imposition or of criminal proceedings for alleged breach of it. Under the 2006 Act a youth court must state its reasons if it makes a section 39 order to bestow such anonymity on a juvenile accused of breaching a DBO. The law on whether media reports can identify juveniles as regards DBO proceedings will, then, be in essence the same as for ASBO proceedings. A juvenile will, unless the youth court lifts it, have section 49 anonymity in respect of the criminal case (e.g. for disorderly conduct) which precedes a 'bolt-on' hearing to decide whether a DBO should be imposed.

⠿ Recap of major points

- A defendant or witness under 18 cannot be identified in a report of youth court proceedings if reporting restrictions apply under section 49 of the Children and Young Persons Act 1933, as they usually do.

- The section 49 anonymity can be lifted to any specified extent to avoid injustice to a juvenile, or to trace a juvenile unlawfully at large who is charged or convicted of a serious offence or in the public interest in the case of any convicted juvenile. It lapses anyway when the juvenile reaches the age of 18.

- There is no automatic anonymity for juveniles as regards reports of adult court proceedings but the court has discretion to impose anonymity by making an order under section 39 of the 1933 Act.

- A section 39 order cannot be imposed for a person over 18, or for a dead person.

- Anti-social behaviour orders can be imposed either by magistrates sitting in civil proceedings (an adult court) or by a youth court as regards a juvenile convicted there of a crime. The default position in law is that a juvenile made subject to an ASBO, or accused of breaching one, can be identified, unless a section 39 order is made.

🌐 Useful Websites

www.yjb.gov.uk/en-gb/yjb/
Youth Justice Board

www.jc-society.com/File/ASBO_updated_GPG_May_2006.pdf
Justices' Clerks' Society Good Practice Guide on ASBOs

Sexual offences

Chapter summary

The law bestows lifelong anonymity on the victims and alleged victims of the majority of sexual offences, including rape, as regards any media report about or referring to such crime. The anonymity is provided by **automatic** reporting restrictions →glossary which make it illegal to publish any detail likely to identify someone as being such a victim/alleged victim. In recent years several newspapers have been fined and ordered to pay compensation for inadvertently publishing matter which breached this anonymity, thereby causing distress to people who should have been shielded from such publicity. This chapter explains these restrictions and how the anonymity can be lifted in certain circumstances. Even when the law permits the media to identify such a person, a journalist should consider whether this would be ethical, particularly in respect of a sexually abused child. The range of sexual offences involved has been extended by recent law. It includes the trafficking of women (and men) for prostitution, so such people are entitled to anonymity in media reports of alleged trafficking. The anonymity also applies to people allegedly secretly filmed by voyeurs, and to children alleged to have been the target of internet 'grooming' by paedophiles. Chapter 11 explains anonymity provision in family law cases, some of which concern children allegedly sexually abused.

▌ Automatic anonymity for complainants of sexual offences

In respect of the vast majority of sexual offences, when an allegation is made that such a crime has been committed, the person said to be the victim has by law lifetime anonymity as regards any media report of that allegation or which refers to it in any way. The anonymity is automatic and unconditional, in that it applies:

- immediately, from the time the allegation is made, whether made by the alleged victim or anyone else;

- whether or not the allegation is subsequently withdrawn;

- whether or not anyone has told the police about it;

- whether or not the alleged perpetrator is prosecuted for it;

- whether, if there is a prosecution, there is a conviction or an acquittal.

The anonymity also applies to anyone who allegedly was intended to be such a victim, e.g. the target of a conspiracy to commit a sex offence or of an incitement to commit one.

So, for example, the anonymity applies in respect of any initial report in the media that a rape may have or has occurred (e.g. 'Police in Southampton are investigating a rape') and to a report of any subsequent rape trial.

As regards those unable to state that they are the victim of a sex offence, e.g. a baby or young child, or someone with a mental incapacity, the anonymity applies as soon as someone else makes the allegation in respect of them, e.g. when a parent or doctor tells police, or a journalist, of suspicion that a child is a sex offence victim.

This anonymity for rape victims dates from statute passed in 1976. Parliament decided that the violation of rape, and the potential for victims to suffer embarrassment and further trauma when testifying in court, justified them being given such anonymity. It has since been extended to the victims/alleged victims of other sexual offences, and is currently defined by the Sexual Offences (Amendment) Act 1992, as amended by the Youth Justice and Criminal Evidence Act 1999 and the Sexual Offences Act 2003.

The anonymity applies to reports of civil law matters, as well as to crime stories and reports of criminal trials and of courts martial. Hence, if a woman who alleges she was raped sues in the civil courts the alleged perpetrator, the woman by law must be anonymous in media reports of that case, irrespective of whether she wins damages.

→

see ch. 15, p. 266

Similarly, if someone making a claim at an employment tribunal alleges he/she was the victim of a sexual offence, that person should have anonymity in reports of the tribunal case.

The anonymity also applies in contexts other than contemporaneous reporting of crimes or court cases. For example, if a journalist is interviewing someone for a biographical feature, and that person says that as a child he/she was sexually molested, then the anonymity applies, making it illegal for the feature to identify that person as such a victim/alleged victim – unless the person gives valid, written consent to such identification, as explained below. The lifetime anonymity also ceases to apply in other, rare, circumstances, e.g. if a court lifts it.

- The anonymity does not apply to dead people. So, it will not apply to someone who is raped and murdered.

 see below, p. 121–124, for details of when the anonymity ceases to apply

The scope of the anonymity restriction

Section 1 of the Sexual Offences (Amendment) Act 1992 states that after an allegation of a sex offence is made, it is illegal to include in any publication:

- any matter which is likely to lead members of the public to identify the person during his/her lifetime as the victim/alleged victim of that offence, including in particular:
  - his/her name,
  - his/her address,
  - the identity of any school or other educational establishment attended by him/her,
  - the identity of his/her place of work,
  - any still or moving picture of him/her.

Publication includes any speech, writing, relevant programme, or other communication in whatever form addressed to the public at large or to any section of the public. A picture means 'a likeness however produced'. The section prohibits publication of matter when it is 'likely to lead' to such identification. A media report referring to someone's school or workplace, particularly if their age is published, could prompt speculation likely to lead to identification. But in some instances naming a large educational establishment, e.g. a university, when stating that the victim/alleged victim is a student there, will not in itself be likely to identify him/her. However, inclusion of further detail could breach his/her anonymity. A report which describes a woman victim of rape as aged 25 and as studying music at a particular university could well identify her. The then Solicitor General said in 1983 that a report of a rape case could be illegal if no names or specific addresses were published but nevertheless the detail included was sufficient to identify the victim/alleged victim in the minds of some people even though not in the minds of the community generally.

When the victim/alleged victim of a sexual offence is aged under 18, courts sometimes impose an order under section 39 of the Children and Young Persons Act 1933 to protect his/her identity. This is unnecessary because of the automatic effect of the 1992 Act. However, a section 39 order usually includes a blanket prohibition as regards identifying the juvenile's school, i.e. irrespective of whether naming the school is 'likely' to breach anonymity.

→
see ch. 7,
on sec-
tion 39

Jigsaw identification

For a definition of jigsaw identification, see ch. 7, p. 105. Jigsaw identification could occur – for example – if in reports of a rape trial a town's newspaper describes the alleged victim as 'a mother of three' who lives and works locally, a TV station states that she is 'a nurse', and a radio station says she is 'a woman in her thirties' and also reports that the alleged rape occurred when she was working at night. A member of the public could then know she is a local nurse in her thirties, who has three children and has worked locally at night, detail which could identify her to colleagues and acquaintances.

When a court case involves sexual abuse of a child or children within a family, all media organisations covering it should agree whether their reports (a) name the adult defendant, but omit any detail of his/her relationship to the children, or (b) do not identify the adult defendant, and can therefore reveal that the alleged abuse was of children in the same household. See also ch. 7, p. 106 and below, p. 125 as regards the Press Complaints Commission Code of Practice and the Ofcom Broadcasting Code.

Invalid orders purporting to give an adult defendant anonymity

As indicated above, the media may decide, when covering a court case involving alleged sexual abuse within a family, that the only possible approach to preserve anonymity for the alleged victim(s) is not to publish anything to identify the adult defendant. But occasionally a magistrates court or a Crown court judge has sought to make that choice for the media by passing an order, purportedly under the Sexual Offences (Amendment) Act 1992, stating that the adult defendant should not be identified. The reason usually stated for such a prohibition is that it is an extra measure to protect the anonymity of the alleged victim(s). But the Act gives no power to courts to impose such an order. And there is no power in section 39 of the Children and Young Persons Act 1933 to specify that an adult should have such anonymity, though courts sometimes claim there is. Either such order can be challenged as invalid. See ch. 13, pp. 222, and 236–237.

▌ Sexual offences for which alleged victims have anonymity

The anonymity for victims/alleged victims applies for almost all offences with any kind of sexual element. The most serious sexual offences are **indictable-only** with a maximum sentence of life imprisonment. These →glossary include (and definitions here are simplified):

- rape, defined as penetration of vagina, anus, or mouth without consent, by penis. If the victim is aged under 13, any such conduct is defined as rape, even if the victim says there was no compulsion, because a victim so young cannot be deemed in any circumstance to have given consent. Males and females can be victims of rape, but only males can be rapists; females can be guilty of rape-related crime, e. g. inciting rape.

- assault by penetration of vagina or anus, without consent and otherwise than by penis, e.g. by finger or object. See also 'indecent assault', below;

- causing or inciting a child under 13 or a person who has 'a mental disorder impeding choice' to engage in sexual activity in which the activity caused or incited involves penetration by penis or otherwise;

- an attempt, conspiracy, or incitement to commit any of the above offences;

- aiding, abetting, counselling, or procuring the commission of any of the above offences, or of an attempt to commit one.

It apparently follows, from the fact that no girl aged under 13 can give legal consent to sexual intercourse, that for the media to identify any such girl as having been made pregnant is to identify her, in breach of her anonymity, as a victim of rape, even though if she has given birth and kept the baby her parenthood will in most cases be obvious in her local community. (Any such girl may be subject to ongoing proceedings involving social workers, and so may have related anonymity too under the Children Act 1989 – see ch. 11, pp. 174–175.)

Some sexual crimes which are **either-way charges** can incur severe pun- →glossary ishment for the worst offenders, e.g. maximum sentences of 10 or 14 years. These either-way charges include (again, definitions are simplified):

- sexual assault, i.e. intentional sexual touching, without consent. See also 'indecent assault', below;

- causing a person to engage in sexual activity without consent;

- administering a substance (e.g. spiking someone's drink with a drug) with intent to stupefy or overpower him/her to enable the perpetrator to engage him/her in sexual activity;

- trespass with intent to commit a sexual offence (a replacement for the offence of burglary with intent to rape);

- sexual intercourse with a girl who has reached the age of 13 but who is under 16 – this offending is not classed as rape if there is no compulsion, though it could well be regarded as a very serious, exploitative offence if the perpetrator is a much older adult;

- abuse of a position of trust, through sexual activity with someone aged under 18 – so, for example, if a male teacher has consensual sex with a 17-year-old girl, this would – because she is over 16, the age of sexual consent – not be a crime unless she was a pupil at the school where he works, in which case by having sex with her he has criminally abused his position of trust as a teacher;

- sexual activity by a care worker, e.g. in a hospital, if it involved such activity with a person in his/her care who has a mental disorder;

- engaging in sexual activity in the presence of a child, or causing a child to watch a sexual act, for the perpetrator's sexual gratification;

- arranging or facilitating commission of a child sex offence, anywhere in the world;

- meeting or intending to meet a child following sexual grooming;

- sexual activity by an adult with a child family member;

- abduction of a woman with the intention that she shall marry or have unlawful sexual intercourse;

- indecent conduct towards a child;

- taking an indecent photograph of a child;

- causing or inciting child prostitution;

- procurement of a woman by threats or false pretences;

- causing or inciting an adult to be a prostitute, or controlling such a prostitute, for gain;

- trafficking a person into or within the UK for sexual exploitation, e.g. prostitution;

- exposure (colloquially called 'flashing') of genitals, intending to thereby cause someone alarm or distress;

- voyeurism, i.e. observing for sexual gratification someone else or people doing something private (e.g. taking a shower, or having sex), when knowing the person/people did not consent to be observed.

Again, it can be seen from this list that, because anonymity applies to victims/alleged victims of all these offences, it does not depend on the accusation being that there was a physical, sexual assault. A child allegedly being groomed for sex by a man chatting to him/her on the Internet, but who never met him, has lifetime anonymity in respect of any media report of that allegation. A victim of a man who exposes himself in a park cannot be identified in a media report of the case. Someone who has actually or allegedly been secretly filmed in their bathroom by a voyeur has such lifetime anonymity too, and so does someone who has been, or is intended to be, involved in prostitution as a result of a crime under the Act, e.g. trafficking.

The Sexual Offences Act 2003 came into force on 1 May 2004, introducing new sexual offences, some listed above, and changing the definitions of others. Some journalists may not be familiar with all of these new offences, but need to realise the anonymity provision applies in respect of both new and older offences. A sexual offence which allegedly occurred before 1 May 2004 will be charged according to the older definition. For example, one such older offence is 'indecent assault', which covers a range of conduct, the most serious of which would, if the offence occurred after that date, meet the definition of assault by penetration, while less serious sexual touching would, if it occurred after that date, be charged as sexual assault.

If two adults are both charged with a consensual, illegal sexual activity with the other, i.e. sex between adult relatives (which could be charged as 'incest' under the older law) or sexual activity in a public lavatory, the anonymity does not apply to either of them. But if only one of them is charged, the other retains anonymity. Buggery is no longer illegal between consenting adults, but is an offence if perpetrated on someone aged under 16 – a victim who should therefore have anonymity.

Liability for breach of the anonymity provision

The Attorney General must approve any prosecution for breach of the anonymity of a victim/alleged victim of a sexual offence. Those who can be prosecuted are any proprietor, any editor, and any publisher of the relevant newspaper or periodical; or, as regards a broadcast programme, any body corporate providing the programme service and any person whose functions in relation to the programme correspond to those of an editor of a newspaper; or as regards any other form of publication, any person publishing it. When such a breach is proved to have been committed with the consent or connivance of, or to be attributable to any neglect on the part of, a director, manager, secretary, or other similar officer of a body corporate, or any person purporting to act in such capacity, he/she too shall be guilty of the offence.

It is a defence if the person accused of such a breach can prove that he/she was not aware, and neither suspected nor had reason to suspect, that the matter published would be likely to identify the victim/alleged victim of a sexual offence. The maximum fine for a breach is £5,000.

Examples of recent breaches of the anonymity

In 2007 the *Lancashire Evening Post's* parent company was fined £3,000 and ordered to pay £4,000 compensation to two women victims of trafficking, whose anonymity was breached in a report. Editorial director Simon Reynolds denied responsibility for the breach. The case against him was withdrawn (*Media Lawyer*, 14 December 2007). In 2007 MEN Media, owner of the *Macclesfield Express*, was fined £1,500 after the paper accidentally named a sexual assault victim. Its editor David Lafferty denied responsibility, and was acquitted.

In 2006 the *Sunderland Echo's* parent company was fined £2,500, and ordered to pay £2,500 in compensation, after the paper mistakenly published matter identifying a rape victim. In the same year the *Daily Telegraph* was fined £2,000, and ordered to pay £5,000 compensation and the *Daily Express* was fined £2,700 and ordered to pay £10,000 compensation for publishing photographs of a servicewoman who was a complainant at a court martial at which a serviceman was cleared of a serious sexual assault. The photos pictured her from behind, so her face was not shown. After being prosecuted, the newspapers admitted the photos identified her, but said at the time they were published it had been genuinely believed her anonymity was preserved. The *Daily Mail*, which had also used a similar photo of the woman but had changed the colour of her hair, was not prosecuted.

The compensation paid to those whose anonymity was breached was awarded under the Powers of the Criminal Courts (Sentencing) Act 2000, at the request of the Crown Prosecution Service.

In 2005 Marie O'Riordan, as editor of *Marie Claire* magazine, was fined £2,500 after it mistakenly published matter identifying a 12-year-old girl who had been sexually assaulted by a 30-year-old man who befriended her over the Internet. The hunt for the girl, after she disappeared with him, had been a national story, in which she was initially named and pictured. But after she returned home she told police he had sexually touched her. This meant she could no longer be identified in reports alluding to the case, in which he was subsequently convicted. But *Marie Claire*, when it re-aired the disappearance story in an 'end-of-year' review, named her from the earlier reports. At the High Court, Lord Justice Rose, dismissing an appeal by Ms O'Riordan, said: 'It seems to me very little to ask of the media that they take precautions to prevent publications which might affect a 12-year-old victim in circumstances such as these.'

See also Ethical considerations, below, p. 125.

When does the anonymity cease to apply?

The requirement for media reports not to identify a victim/alleged victim of a sexual offence lapses on the person's death. During their lifetime the anonymity will cease to apply if any of the following four circumstances occurs.

By court order, at the request of a defendant

- A court due to try someone for a sexual offence can make a direction (an order), if that defendant or a co-defendant applies for it, to remove the anonymity for the alleged victim if the court is satisfied that:
  - this direction is required to induce people likely to be needed as witnesses to come forward, <u>and</u> that
  - otherwise the conduct of the applicant's defence at the trial is likely to be substantially prejudiced.

For example, a defendant may argue that he needs witnesses to come forward to support an **alibi**, if his defence is that he could not have raped the alleged victim because he was not in the same location as her when the alleged rape occurred. If the media are permitted to identify the alleged victim when reporting the alibi defence, relevant members of the public can remember where and when they saw her, and who, if anyone, was with her at the time of the alleged offence. → glossary

A court due to consider an appeal against a conviction for a sexual offence can make the same order, if satisfied that the alleged victim's anonymity should be waived to help obtain evidence for the appeal, and that otherwise the appellant is likely to suffer substantial injustice.

By court order, to lift 'a substantial and unreasonable' restriction on reporting

- At a trial of a sexual offence, the court can order that the alleged victim's anonymity should be waived if it is satisfied that:
  - otherwise the anonymity would impose a substantial and unreasonable restriction on the reporting of the trial, <u>and</u> that
  - it is in the public interest to remove or relax that restriction.

For example, this happened in the case of *R v Arthur Hutchinson* (1985) 129 SJ 700; (1985) 82 CrApp 51. He had been hunted by police after three members of the same family were murdered in Sheffield after a wedding party at their home. To get information to help trace Hutchinson, police had publicly named him as the suspect. The media had by then also published the names of those murdered. Some time after being charged with the murders, Hutchinson was also charged with raping a teenage girl from the same family as those murdered, in the same terrible attack. The media had not previously been told of the rape allegation. At Hutchinson's trial he faced the murder and rape charges. There lawyers acting for newspapers argued that it would be impossible for them to report it at all if they could not identify the family involved, including the girl as the alleged rape victim. It was pointed out that publishing Hutchinson's name or that he was charged with three murders would in itself be enough for the Sheffield public to remember who the victim family was, and that the evidence concerning the rape and murders was inextricably linked. The judge agreed that the media could identify the girl, and thereby the family, because anonymity would otherwise impose a substantial and unreasonable restriction on the reporting of the trial, and that it was in the public interest for the trial to be fully reported. Hutchinson was convicted of the rape and murders.

In a circumstance such as this, the court can decide the extent of the identifying detail permitted to be published, e.g. it could permit the name of an alleged victim to be published, but – to retain some privacy for him/her – not his/her photograph.

⠿ Points for consideration

Neither of the two circumstances cited above occur with any frequency. If the alleged offence is indictable-only, e.g. rape or assault by penetration, a Crown court has power to waive the anonymity in these circumstances, but a magistrates court – i.e. in a **preliminary hearing** there – does not.

→ glossary

Thus the law ensures that only a judge with considerable legal experience will decide, in these most serious of cases, whether it is necessary, for the reasons set out above, for the alleged victim to be exposed to the trauma of being publicly identified.

In 2006 the then Attorney General told the House of Lords that the 1992 Act gave no power to the Court of Appeal to allow the media to identify 'in the public interest' a woman who was revealed to have made serial, false accusations of rape. The power to lift 'in the public interest' the anonymity of an alleged rape victim lies only with the trial judge [to enable unrestricted reporting of the trial], not in an appeal, he said.

If the victim/alleged victim gives written consent

The media can identify someone as being the victim/alleged victim of a sexual offence if he/she agrees to this. But the Sexual Offences (Amendment) Act 1992 specifies that to be valid the agreement must be:

- written consent, not merely a verbal agreement, and
- the person thus waiving his/her anonymity must be aged 16 or over.
- Also, the consent will not be valid if it is proved that anyone 'interfered unreasonably with the peace and comfort' of that person, with intent to obtain the consent.

No permission is needed from a court for a person to give consent. But, as can be seen above, the law guards against someone being pressurised by a journalist into giving consent, and makes clear that any child under 16 is regarded as too immature to understand the consequences of being publicly identified in this context.

Instances occur fairly regularly of victims/alleged victims of sexual offences giving written consent to be identified by the media, particularly after a perpetrator is jailed. For example, a woman who has suffered rape may feel that, by permitting the media to identify her, she is sending a powerful signal to other rape victims that they can find the courage to seek justice, and that there is no stigma in being a victim. Other victims may feel they need the anonymity to last for life.

If someone is prosecuted for making a false allegation

As stated above, anonymity for anyone alleged to be the victim of a sexual offence continues to apply in respect of media reports even if no one is prosecuted or convicted for that offence, and even if the allegation is withdrawn. However, occasionally someone believed to have falsely accused another of a sexual offence is prosecuted in respect of that alleged falsity. So, for example, a woman who has told police she was raped may, if evidence emerges that she knows her allegation is false, be prosecuted for wasting police time or for perjury or for perverting the course of justice – the charge she faces depends on the circumstances of her alleged lying.

→ see ch. 3, p. 40 on these offences

- When such a person appears in court facing such a charge, e.g. proceedings for alleged wasting of police time or alleged perjury, he/she <u>can</u> be identified in a report of those proceedings as someone who was alleged to be the victim of a sexual offence.

It is legal to identify such a person in such a court report because the 1992 Act states that matter identifying an alleged victim of a sexual offence can be published if it consists 'only of a report of criminal proceedings other than' proceedings for the alleged sexual offence. This wording in the Act would also permit, for example, the identification in a court report of a burglary trial of a witness who states in it that he/she was sexually assaulted by the alleged burglar, if that defendant is <u>not</u> charged in that trial of that alleged sexual offence and if no reporting restriction applies under other law.

→ see ch. 9, for other restrictions

▌ Sexual offences prevention orders

Under the Sexual Offences Act 2003, courts can make a sexual offences prevention order (SOPO), under civil law, placing restrictions on the behaviour and actions of a sexual offender – whether an adult or a juvenile – to protect the public from the risk of 'serious sexual harm'. For example, an offender can be banned from loitering around schools or inviting children back to his house, or from making unsolicited approaches to women. The court can make a SOPO when sentencing for a sexual offence. Also, police can apply to magistrates for such an order at a later stage if an offender's behaviour causes concern – for example, after he or she has been released from jail for the offence. Breach of such an order is a criminal offence. An interim order can be made before a full hearing into such a police application. The minimum term of a finalised order is five years.

see also ch. 13, p. 219 on SOPOs

▶ Ethical considerations

The code of practice used by the Press Complaints Commission (PCC) to adjudicate on complaints made against newspapers, magazines, and their websites has two clauses specifically about sex offences. These make clear that, even if the law permits a victim/alleged victim of a sex offence to be identified in a media report, there is an ethical decision to be made on whether this should be done.

see ch. 1, pp. 16–17 on PCC and Ofcom

- Clause 11, headed 'Victims of sexual assault', states: 'The press must not identify victims of sexual assault or publish material likely to contribute to such identification unless there is adequate justification and they are legally free to do so.'

The term 'sexual assault' here includes all sexual attacks, e.g. rape.

- Clause 7, headed 'Children in sex cases', states: 'The press must not, even if legally free to do so, identify children under 16 who are victims or witnesses in cases involving sex offences.' It adds that:
- In any press report of a case involving a sexual offence against a child:
  - The child must not be identified;
  - The adult may be identified;
  - The word 'incest' must not be used where a child victim might be identified;
  - Care must be taken that nothing in the report implies the relationship between the accused and the child.

Clause 7 is subject to the Code's public interest exceptions, but Clause 11 is not, though the term 'adequate justification' arguably embraces the idea of the public interest. As regards Clause 7 the Code notes that there would have to be 'exceptional public interest' to override the normally paramount interests of a child under 16.

Ofcom's Broadcasting Code warns against jigsaw identification and inadvertent use of the term 'incest'.

see Useful websites below

The PCC has in several adjudications condemned newspapers for unintentionally publishing matter likely to identify a sexual offence victim. In 2007, the PCC, referring to a newspaper report of a man being convicted for sexual offences against under-age girls, said that a reference in it to an injury previously suffered by one of the girls was in itself 'sufficient to identify her, or confirm the suspicions of those who already knew something about the case'. The PCC guidance says that in such cases 'editors should err on the side of caution' on what detail is published.

In guidance on reporting cases involving paedophiles, the PCC has drawn attention to the rights of relatives and friends of people who have been accused of sex crimes: 'Not only do they also have a right to respect for their private lives under Clause 3, but the Code also makes clear under Clause 10 that the "press must avoid identifying [them] without their consent" – or unless there is a public interest in doing so.'

→
see
Useful
websites,
below

⬚ Recap of major points

- People who are victims or alleged victims of sexual offences must not be identified in media reports about or alluding to those offences.
- The offences involved include rape, assault by penetration, sexual assault, indecent assault, sexual activity with children, and what may be charged under older law as incest.
- The victims/alleged victims of voyeurs and 'flashing' also have such anonymity, as do people allegedly or actually trafficked to be prostitutes.
- The anonymity can be waived by a court if a defendant requests this, and the court is satisfied that the identity of an alleged victim should be published to induce witnesses to come forward for a trial, and that otherwise the defence is likely to be substantially prejudiced.
- There is a danger of 'jigsaw identification', particularly when several media organisations are covering a case of alleged sex abuse within a family, if newsdesks fail to agree a common policy on what details are published.
- At a trial of a sexual offence, the court can waive the anonymity of the alleged victim to remove a substantial and unreasonable restriction on the reporting of the trial, if it is satisfied it is in the public interest to do this.
- A victim/alleged victim can waive the anonymity, by giving a media organisation written consent to identify him/her, if aged 16 or over. But if it is proved the person has been pressurised to do this, the consent will not be legally valid.

- If someone is charged with making a false claim that he/she is the victim of a sexual offence, that person can be identified in a report of criminal court proceedings arising from the charge that the claim was false.

- The Press Complaints Commission code of practice warns that even when the law permits a media report to identify the victim/alleged victim of a sexual offence, journalists should still consider whether there is adequate, ethical justification to do this.

- Ofcom's Broadcasting Code gives similar guidance.

☻ Useful Websites

www.cps.gov.uk/legal/s_to_u/sexual_offences_act/
  Crown Prosecution Service guidance on the Sexual Offences Act 2003

www.ofcom.org.uk/tv/ifi/codes/bcode/
  Ofcom Broadcasting Code

www.pcc.org.uk/news/index.html?article=OTQ/
  Press Complaints Commission guidance to editors on the reporting of cases involving paedophiles

9

Other court reporting restrictions

Chapter summary

→glossary As earlier chapters have shown, a journalist covering court cases must know what can legally be reported from them, and when. There are **automatic** reporting restrictions, and courts have discretionary powers to lift them. Courts also have discretionary powers to ban publication of various matters. This chapter gives details of more of these powers. It explains that courts can grant lifelong anonymity to certain adult witnesses. The High Court also has power to ban the media from revealing the new identities and whereabouts of defendants convicted in notorious →glossary cases. The chapter also explains that reporting what a court has heard **in private** can, depending on the case's category, be punishable as contempt of court. This chapter also sets out the automatic and general bans on photography, filming, and audio-recording in courts; on anyone seeking to discover or publishing what jurors discussed in reaching verdicts or how an individual juror voted; and on publishing, while a trial is ongoing, that there has been a 'special measure' made in respect of a witness. Chapter 13 explains how some restrictions can be challenged.

▌ Section 11 orders

Section 11 of the Contempt of Court Act 1981 states that:

- if a court allows a name, or other matter, to be withheld from the public during its proceedings it may prohibit the publication of that name or matter in connection with the proceedings.

A section 11 order, then, is the second step in a two-stage process. First the court decides that a name or matter should not be aired in its sessions held in public. It may, for example, hold all or part of a case in private to hear such matter, excluding the public and reporters, and/or rule that a name or matter should not be mentioned in its public sessions by parties to the case, witnesses, and lawyers. Then it can impose a section 11 order, which means that if the name or matter slips out through mistake in a public session, or the media have found out by other means what the name or matter is, that information cannot be published in any report of the case (including in any context which relates it to the case). The section states that the scope of the prohibition can be as 'necessary for the purpose' for which the name or matter was withheld from the public. A section 11 order remains in force indefinitely, unless a court revokes it.

Typical usage of section 11 orders

Section 11 orders are typically used in cases concerning:

- *Blackmail* – the allegation may be, for example, that a blackmailer threatened to reveal to others a secret or material, the revealing of which would prove damaging or distressing for the blackmailed victim. If someone is the target of such blackmail, clearly he/she will be less likely to report the threat to police, and thereafter to be a witness, if there is a prospect that his/her identity will be revealed in an open court, and by the media, when this secret or material figures in evidence. In blackmail trials, the alleged victim is usually referred to in open court not by name but by means of a letter of the alphabet, e.g. Ms X or Mr A.

  see also ch 3, p. 39 on blackmail

- *National security, state secrets* – for example, in a prosecution under the Official Secrets Act 1911 of someone accused of betraying UK military secrets to a foreign power, the court may well go into private session – in camera – to hear evidence about those secrets, and the alleged betrayal, from UK intelligence officers. A section 11 order could be used to specifically forbid publication of such matter, in case it leaks out, and also to prohibit publication of the identities of those officers, because if their identities were published their usefulness as undercover agents would be destroyed, or personal safety may be imperilled by the UK's enemies. If such officers give evidence in public, they may well be referred to in court only as Officer A or B, etc.

  see ch. 31

  → glossary

- *Commercially sensitive information, secret processes* – for example, if a company is suing another for damages over alleged breach of confidence as regards valuable technical data, or a new manufacturing process, the court may decide to hear evidence about it in camera, to preserve its confidentiality. A section 11 order could be made to specifically forbid reports of the case publishing the data or process details.

→

see ch. 7, p. 105

When several media organisations cover a court case in which a section 11 order bestows anonymity on someone, journalists need to guard against 'jigsaw identification'.

Anyone, including a journalist, proved to have committed contempt of court by disobeying a section 11 order can be jailed – the maximum term being two years – and/or be fined a sum unlimited by statute.

→

see ch. 13, 212–219

The media have successfully challenged invalid or unnecessary use of section 11 orders by courts.

▌ Contempt risk of reporting matter from a court's private hearing

Section 12 of the Administration of Justice Act 1960 makes it an offence of contempt of court to publish, without the permission of a court, a report of

→ glossary

proceedings it has heard in private, i.e. in chambers or in camera, if the case falls into certain categories listed in the Act.

These categories are:

→ glossary

- proceedings which relate to the exercise of the inherent jurisdiction of the High Court with respect to children;

- proceedings under the Children Act 1989 or the Adoption and Children Act 2002 or which otherwise relate wholly or mainly to the maintenance or upbringing of a child;

- proceedings brought under the Mental Capacity Act 2005, or under any provision of the Mental Health Act 1983 authorising an application or reference to be made to the First-Tier Tribunal, the Mental Health Review Tribunal for Wales, or a county court;

- national security;

- proceedings about a secret process, discovery, or invention which is in issue in the case;

- any case where the court (having power to do so) expressly prohibits the publication of all information or specified information relating to the private hearing.

Chapter 11 explains family law, which includes some categories of case listed in section 12. Chapter 15 refers to the mental health tribunal system. Chapter 31 covers national security matters.

A reporter may be told what has happened in a private hearing by one of the parties in it. But section 12 automatically prohibits the publication, as specified in it, of matter which has been heard by a court in private to protect the welfare, including the privacy, of children, of the mentally ill, and of the mentally incapacitated; or to protect national security or commercial secrets. Also, if a court decides to hear matter in private for any other reason, and orders that those proceedings should not be reported, a breach of that order will be punishable under section 12 if proved as contempt.

If a breach of section 12 is ruled to be contempt, the maximum jail term is two years, and there can be a fine which has no statutory limit.

- Any document 'prepared for use' in a court's private hearing is deemed part of those proceedings, so – if the case falls into the 1960 Act's section 12 categories – it may well be regarded by the court as contempt if material in the document is quoted by the media, e.g. a social worker's report on a child.

Some matters *can* be published about a private hearing in these types of case. Section 12 itself makes clear that publication of the text or summary of any order made in such a private hearing is not contempt, unless the court has specifically prohibited its publication. In *Re B (A Child)* [2004] EWHC 411 (Fam), Mr Justice Munby stated that section 12 did not of itself prohibit published reference to 'the nature of the dispute' being heard in the private proceedings. He added that matter which *can* be published without breaching section 12 included: see also ch. 11 pp. 179–182

- the names, addresses, or photographs of parties involved in the private proceedings;

- and of witnesses involved;

- the date, time, or place of hearings in the case;

- and 'anything which has been seen or heard by a person conducting himself lawfully in the public corridor or other public precincts outside the court.'

It is possible, though, as Mr Justice Munby added, that a court will under other law specifically prohibit such details being published, or that automatic restrictions under other law will apply (e.g. the Children Act 1989 bestows anonymity on children involved in ongoing cases concerning the Act – see also ch. 11, p. 174).

If the court hearing in private does not fall into the section 12 categories, a media organisation may be able to publish safely an account of it, e.g. if guided by a person who was in it. For example, section 12 does not necessarily cover applications made to a judge in chambers for bail. But a report of a case heard in private will not be protected by any statutory privilege as regards libel law, and will not be protected by section 4 of the Contempt of Court Act 1981 if it creates a substantial risk of serious prejudice to an 'active' case.

In 2006 the High Court ruled that it was not contempt under the 1960 Act to report matter from a hearing held in private in a county court, other than where the case concerned those matters listed in section 12, in the absence of an express prohibition (*AF Noonan v Bournemouth and Boscombe Athletic Community Football Club* [2006] EWHC 2113 (Ch)).

→ glossary

→

see also
ch. 16, p.
288. and
ch. 19. pp.
337–345
on
privilege

▶ Contempt in publishing matter from court documents

As stated above, it could be proved to be contempt under the Administration of Justice Act 1960 if a media organisation publishes matter from a document prepared for proceedings of the type listed in the Act's section 12, heard in private .

Even if a case is heard in public, a journalist should exercise care before quoting from a document used in the case if the material has not been read out in court.

→

see ch.
11, pp.
201–204

In a civil case, it will be safe to quote from any document provided by the court to the journalist, or from matter in it read out in open court as being evidence. Similarly, it will be safe for a journalist to quote from any case document which he/she is able to inspect by right or with the court's permission. And if the case is heard in public, it will be safe to quote from any skeleton argument provided to a journalist by lawyers involved, unless the court forbids this or an automatic reporting restriction applies to the material, e.g. one protecting the identity of a child or alleged victim of a sexual offence. Civil cases are conducted mainly by reference to documents. See ch. 10.

But in either a criminal or civil case, if one side provides to a journalist a document the other side was compelled or knew it had a duty to produce under the 'disclosure' process – the pre-trial swapping of evidential material – then, if the material has not been aired in open court, there is a risk of the journalist or his/her editor being deemed in contempt of court if matter from it is published. Contempt law applies because if parties feared that material they provide to the other side could end up published, despite it not being aired in open court, people might be less willing to fully co-operate with the disclosure process.

Also, as stated above, p. 132, publication of matter not aired in open court will not be protected by statutory privilege as regards libel law, or by section 4 of the Contempt of Court Act 1981 if that Act's strict liability rule is breached.

▶ Section 46 lifetime anonymity for adult witnesses

- Section 46 of the Youth Justice and Criminal Evidence Act 1999 gives courts a discretionary power to forbid publication, in a report of a court case, of the identity of an adult witness in his/her lifetime, if the witness is deemed eligible for such anonymity.

This law was passed as part of Parliament's intention to provide better protection for witnesses deemed 'intimidated' – including those who fear retaliation from defendants they testify against, or from defendants' relatives or associates.

Under the Act, in any criminal court 'a party in the proceedings' – including the defence, though it will usually be the prosecution – can ask the court to make such an anonymity order, called a reporting direction, in respect of a witness aged 18 or over. An application for a section 46 order may be heard in camera.

- If a section 46 order is made, it is illegal to include in any publication during the witness's lifetime any matter likely to lead members of the public to identify him/her as a witness in those court proceedings.

The Act says that the matter which cannot be published, if likely to identify such a witness, includes in particular:

- the witness's name;
- the witness's address;
- the identity of any educational establishment attended by him/her;
- the identity of any place where he/she works; and
- any still or moving picture of the witness.

But such a section 46 order cannot be used to provide anonymity for a defendant.

The witness concerned may be the alleged victim of the offence(s) the relevant trial is due to consider. The section 46 order will in such circumstances affect greatly what can be published about the trial, and that effect will be similar to that of the lifetime anonymity which other law bestows on the victims/alleged victims of sexual offences – they, therefore, do not need section 46 anonymity. When a section 46 order is made, journalists should ensure they avoid jigsaw identification, see p. 105.

→

see also
ch. 8 on
sexual
offences

In deciding whether a witness is eligible for section 46 anonymity the court must be satisfied that the quality of the witness's evidence or his/her level of co-operation in connection with preparations for the case is likely to be diminished by reason of fear or distress on the part of the witness in connection with being identified by members of the public as a witness in the proceedings. The court must also be satisfied that the granting of such anonymity is likely to improve the quality of the witness's evidence or the level of his/her co-operation.

The court, in deciding on such eligibility, must take into account the view of the witness about such anonymity; the nature and circumstances of the alleged offence in the trial; the witness's age; his/her social and cultural background, and ethnic origins; his/her domestic and employment circumstances, religious beliefs, or political opinions; and any behaviour towards the witness on the part of the defendant, or the defendant's family or associates, or anyone else likely to be a defendant or witness in the proceedings.

When deciding whether to grant section 46 anonymity, the court must also consider whether:

- it would be in the interests of justice to do so, and
- the public interest in avoiding the imposition of a substantial and unreasonable restriction on the reporting of proceedings.

If matter is published which breaches the anonymity, liability is the same as for breach of section 1 of the Sexual Offences (Amendment) Act 1992, with the same maximum fine.

see ch. 8, p. 119

Anyone prosecuted for breach of section 46 has a defence if he/she can prove that:

- he/she was not aware, and neither suspected nor had reason to suspect, that the publication included the matter or report in question, or that

- the witness concerned gave written consent for the matter to be published, but

- this 'written consent' defence will fail if it is proved that a person 'interfered with the peace or comfort' of such a witness with intent to obtain that consent.

The court which bestowed the section 46 anonymity, or a higher court, can make 'an excepting direction' to remove the anonymity entirely or to relax it to some extent. However, a court can only lift or vary the restriction if:

- it is satisfied that this is necessary in the interests of justice; or

- it is satisfied that the restriction imposes a substantial and unreasonable restriction on the reporting of the proceedings, and that it is in the public interest to remove or relax the restriction.

See ch. 13, pp. 220–222, on challenging section 46 orders; see ch. 2, p. 30 for anonymity provided by the Serious Organised Crime and Police Act 2005 for informants and witnesses given a new identity, and for details of the 'investigation anonymity order', a power proposed in the Coroners and Justice Bill 2009. See also p. 194 on sentence reviews for informants.

▶ Other orders bestowing anonymity

The High Court has power to forbid publication of the identities of people concerned in cases it deals with. It is established and routine practice for the High Court to use this power if necessary to ensure that children involved in family law cases have anonymity in media reports of them. The High Court has similar powers to bestow anonymity, as regards reports of its civil cases, on adults to keep private matters concerning their health, e.g. in cases where it is protecting the interests of the mentally incapacitated.

for further detail, see ch 11, p. 178

A media organisation which publishes matter identifying such people, in breach of such an order, could be punished for contempt of court, if made aware of the order. The High Court's powers in this area derive from its **common law** inherent jurisdiction and, in recent years, from Article 8 of the European Convention on Human Rights, which protects privacy. The anonymity can last for the lifetime of those it protects, depending on the circumstances of each case.

The Civil Procedure Rules which govern how civil cases are processed in the county courts and High Court state: 'The court may order that the identity of any party or witness must not be disclosed if it considers non-disclosure necessary in order to protect the interests of that party or witness' – see also ch. 12, p. 196.

> → For information on anonymity for persons subject, as suspected terrorists, to 'control orders', see ch. 33, p. 535.

High Court injunctions giving indefinite anonymity to convicted defendants

→ glossary In a few, exceptional instances, the High Court has – by use of **injunctions**, i.e. court orders – forbidden the media to publish the new identities and whereabouts of people who became infamous as defendants in criminal cases.

Mary Bell – The first such case concerned Mary Bell who in 1968, when she was 11, was convicted of the manslaughter of two boys, aged 4 and 3. She was sentenced to detention for life. When released on licence in 1980, she was provided by the Home Office with a new identity, to help her rehabilitation, because those killings remained notorious. In 1984 the High Court made an order forbidding any publication of her new name, or any matter which could identify her new-born daughter as being 'the child of Mary Bell', or which could identify the child's father (*X County Council v A and another* [1985] 1 All ER 53). This order was made for the welfare of the daughter, to ensure a stable home environment for her, and was based in the court's inherent jurisdiction to protect the child as a ward of court.

→ for information on wardship, see ch 11, p. 177

By 2003 the daughter had ceased to be a ward, having reached the age of 18. But that year the High Court made a fresh order to protect the anonymity of Bell and her daughter for their lifetimes, thereby preventing any publication of where both live. The judge, Dame Butler-Sloss, had heard evidence that Bell had been paid a substantial sum to collaborate with a journalist producing a biographical book about her, but that she suffered from anxiety and depression, and that she and her daughter had, because of press intrusion and hostility from members of the public, been forced to move home five times. Dame Butler-Sloss said the order was based on the law of confidence having developed to protect privacy (see also ch. 24) and that the women's privacy rights under Article 8 overrode the media's rights to freedom of expression under Article 10 (X *(a woman formerly known as Mary Bell) and another v O'Brien and others* [2003] All ER (D) 282 (May)).

Venables and Thompson – Dame Butler-Sloss used a similar legal analysis in 2001 when in the High Court she granted indefinite anonymity to Jon Venables and Robert Thompson, at their request. In 1993 when they were aged 11, they had been convicted of the murder, earlier that year, of James Bulger, aged two. Both had been sentenced to indefinite detention 'during Her Majesty's pleasure' (the equivalent, for a juvenile, of a life sentence). In 2001 the Parole Board was due to make a decision about when the pair, then both 18, should be released and reintegrated into the outside world – see also ch. 6, p. 86. Dame Butler-Sloss agreed to make an injunction forbidding publication of new identities being planned for them, of recent photos of them, and of any matter likely to identify their 'present or future whereabouts'. She said that – because their crime had led to threats of vengeance against them – Venables and Thompson had a right to such anonymity under Article 2, which protects the right to life itself and under Article 3, which prohibits torture – see Appendix 1, p. 565. Later in 2001 the *Manchester Evening News* was fined £30,000 for contempt of court after it published material which – the High Court ruled – included detail likely to identify, to someone with local knowledge, the secure units in which Venables and Thompson were then held. The court accepted that the material, which neither named the units nor gave their precise location, was not aired deliberately to identify them (*Attorney General v Greater Manchester Newspapers Ltd* [2001] All ER (D) 32 (Dec)).

Maxine Carr – Similar anonymity has been granted to Maxine Carr, former girlfriend of Ian Huntley. In 2003 Huntley was convicted of murdering two schoolgirls in Soham. Carr was convicted at the same trial of conspiring to pervert the course of justice, in that she had provided a false **alibi** for him →glossary during the police investigation of the murders (though she was acquitted of knowing, when she gave the alibi, that he had murdered them). In 2005 at the High Court Mr Justice Eady granted an injunction, forbidding indefinitely publication of her new identity and whereabouts, and the nature of her employment, after hearing how death threats and harassment by members of the public had occurred after she had been released from her jail sentence (*Media Lawyer*, 25 February 2005).

Kenneth Callaghan – In 2009 Mr Justice Stephen in Belfast High Court banned Independent News and Media Ltd, publishers of *Sunday Life* newspaper – and thereby banned all the media – from publishing any photograph which would identify Kenneth Henry Callaghan, aged 39, and any information identifying his address, place of work, or any location where he stays or frequents. He had become eligible for parole after serving 21 years for the murder of a 21-year-old woman in 1987, whom he had raped as or after she died. The newspaper had taken photographs of him in 2008 when he was on temporary release from a prisoner assessment unit, being considered for permanent release back into the community. The judge found that the newspaper's articles about Callaghan's possible release, which described him as an ongoing risk to the public, were likely to incite hatred for him, and were counter-productive in that such hatred and the revelation through such photographs of his future whereabouts would increase the risk of him reoffending. The newspaper had argued it should be allowed to continue to take and publish photographs of him. The judge said that overall such conduct was capable of amounting to harassment. He granted the injunction on the grounds of Callaghan's privacy rights under Article 8 and to protect him from harassment. In the same judgment, the judge – at the request of the Northern Ireland Office – ordered, to protect the NIO's statutory responsibility with regard to prisoners, that no photograph should be published identifying any serving prisoner being assessed at the unit without giving the NIO 48 hours' notice of intention to publish it (*Callaghan v Independent News and Media Ltd* [2009] NIQB 1).

- It has been ruled that Crown courts and magistrates courts do *not* have a general, inherent jurisdiction powers to ban the media from publishing the identities of defendants – see ch. 13, p. 212.

▶ Section 4(2) of the Contempt of Court Act 1981

A court has power, under section 4(2) of the Contempt of Court Act 1981, to order the postponement of the reporting of a court case, or of any part of a case, where this appears necessary for avoiding a substantial risk of prejudice to the administration of justice in those proceedings, or any other proceedings pending or imminent. The postponement can be for such period as the court thinks necessary for this purpose.

This reporting restriction is best understood in the general context of contempt law, and so is explained in ch. 16, see p. 289. See also ch. 13, pp. 223–229 for grounds on which a section 4(2) order may be challenged.

❿ Postponed publication of 'special measures' and section 36 orders

Section 19 of the Youth Justice and Criminal Evidence Act 1999 has given courts the discretionary power to make a 'special measures direction' (i.e. an order) to assist 'vulnerable' or 'intimidated' witnesses to give evidence. Special measures which can be introduced include permitting such a witness to give evidence behind a screen so he/she cannot see the defendant; permitting such a witness to give evidence by live television link or (for example, in the case of a young child alleged to be the victim of sex abuse) in a video recording; excluding the public and some reporters from the court while a witness gives evidence; lawyers and the judge taking off wigs and gowns to make proceedings seem less strange to a child witness. The definition of 'vulnerable' can include the following categories of witness (other than the defendant): any witness aged under 17; a witness whose quality of evidence, in the court's view, is likely to be diminished by reason of mental disorder or significant impairment of intelligence or social functioning, or physical disability or physical disorder. The definition of 'intimidated' can include the following categories of witness (other than the defendant): an alleged victim in a sex offence case; any other witness whose quality of evidence, in the court's view, is likely to be diminished by reason of fear or distress in connection with testifying in the proceedings.

see also ch. 12, p. 193 on exclusion of reporters

A special measures direction is not automatic. So, for example, a witness aged under 17 or the alleged victim of a sexual offence will not necessarily be deemed to need a special measure. Courts retain other discretionary powers under common law or other Acts to assist any witness.

⸬ Point for consideration

In the Coroners and Justice Bill 2009, it is proposed to make a witness aged up to, but not yet, 18 eligible on grounds of age alone to be considered vulnerable.

The Bill also, as part of the Government's plans to counter the intimidating effect of street gang culture, proposes that any witness should, if the defendant(s) in the case are charged with knife or firearms offences listed in the Bill, be automatically eligible for special measures protection without the need for the court to consider if the quality of their evidence is likely to be diminished by fear or distress. See Preface, p. ix.

Section 36 orders banning cross-examination by defendants

In the 1999 Act, Parliament also – in another provision to reduce intimidation of witnesses – set limits on a defendant's right in a trial to personally question prosecution witnesses. Historically a defendant has the right to conduct his/her own defence in court, including cross-examining such witnesses, if he/she chooses not to employ a lawyer. But, after some notorious incidents in which defendants used this right to intimidate those testifying against them, the 1999 Act prohibited defendants in certain types of trials, e.g. concerning allegations of sexual offences or of violence against children, from personally cross-examining witnesses. The Act enables courts to arrange for a lawyer to conduct such cross-examination if the defendant fails to appoint one. Thus a man accused of rape can no longer personally cross-examine his alleged victim. The Act also gives courts the discretion, in certain circumstances, to pass an order under its section 36 prohibiting a defendant in any type of case from personally cross-examining a witness.

Restrictions on reporting special measures and section 36 orders

Under section 47 of the Act, automatic reporting restrictions temporarily prohibit the media from publishing the fact that a section 19 (special measures) order or section 36 order has been made, varied, or discharged; or anything from discussion or argument in court about whether such orders should be made, varied, or discharged. These restrictions apply to proceedings in magistrates courts as well as to jury trials, but their apparent primary purpose is to prevent jurors (who would not be present in court when such an order was made or discussed) being prejudiced against the defendant or a witness by learning, before they reach all verdicts in the case, why a court considered making or made such an order. It will be safe to report, during a trial, anything the jury can see anyway, i.e. that a witness is giving evidence by video, and anything the judge says to the jury to explain the effect of a section 19 or section 36 order, e.g. why a witness is giving evidence by video or why a lawyer suddenly appears to act for a defendant in cross-examination of a witness. But it would, for example, be illegal to publish the fact, beyond any explanation the judge gives to the jury, that most reporters had been ordered to leave the courtroom. These reporting restrictions with regard to section 19 and section 36 orders cease to have effect when the relevant proceedings, against all defendants involved, are determined by acquittal, conviction, or otherwise, or are abandoned, or if the court lifts the restrictions during the trial itself. Under the Act, the court must state in open court its reasons for granting, refusing, or lifting a section 19 or section 36 order, so these reasons can be published when jury involvement ceases. Liability for breach of these section 47 reporting restrictions is the same as for breach of an order made under the Act's section 46. It is a defence for a person charged with a breach of section 47 to prove he/she was not aware and neither suspected nor had reason to suspect that such matter was included in what was published. An adult witness subject to a special measures direction under section 19 of the Act may also have been granted lifetime anonymity, in respect of media reports of the trial, under section 46.

 see ch. 12, p. 193

 For details on section 46 orders, see above p. 133.

▶ Derogatory assertions in mitigation

If a defendant is convicted, the court will hear a 'speech in mitigation', either from the defendant or from his/her lawyer, before deciding what punishment to impose or, if it is an **either-way** case in a magistrates court, whether to commit the defendant to Crown court for sentence. Such a speech is a plea for the court to show leniency. There is occasionally controversy over defendants using such mitigation pleas to besmirch the reputations of other people, e.g. the victim of the crime. For example, a defendant who admits attacking another man could claim that the assault victim provoked the violence by making an improper remark to the defendant's girlfriend. The person thus derogatively referred to cannot sue for defamation, because what is said during court proceedings, and what the media properly publishes in court reports, is 'privileged'. Reacting to such controversy, Parliament, in section 58 of the Criminal Procedure and Investigations Act 1996, gave

 → glossary

→ see ch. 5, pp. 63–64 on mitigation

→ see ch. 19 on privilege

courts a discretionary power to impose a temporary reporting restriction on the media, namely:

- the postponement for 12 months of the reporting of an assertion made in a speech of mitigation,
- if the assertion is derogatory to a person's character,
- such as where it is suggested that the person's conduct has been criminal, immoral, or improper.

The Act allows the court to order such a postponement:

- if there are substantial grounds for believing that the assertion is false,
- or that it is irrelevant to the sentence.

A section 58 order makes it an offence to publish the assertion during the 12 months if the report contains enough information to make it likely that a member of the public will identify the person whose character was thus besmirched.

- Such an order cannot validly be made if it appears to the court that the derogatory assertion made in mitigation has previously been made in evidence in the relevant trial or 'during any other proceedings relating to the offence'.

A journalist who is aware that the assertion has already been aired in trial evidence can therefore challenge the court to lift, as invalid, a section 58 order made in respect of the same assertion when repeated in a speech of mitigation.

→

see also
ch. 13,
p. 229

A court can make, before its sentencing decision, an interim order postponing publication of the assertion. An interim order automatically lapses when the sentence is determined, but the court can then make a full order of postponement of publication for 12 months, irrespective of whether an interim order was made. It can revoke such an order at any time before its automatic expiry when the 12 months have passed. As Parliament realised when it passed the law, the news value of a derogatory assertion would, in most cases, be non-existent after 12 months, making it unlikely in such cases that the assertion would be published at all. This section 58 reporting restriction seems to have been rarely used by the courts. Defence lawyers are required to give notice of any intention to make a derogatory assertion in mitigation, in case the prosecution choose to require the assertion to be

→ glossary proved as true in a **Newton hearing**. The making of untrue assertions is thereby generally discouraged.

Liability for any breach of a section 58 order is the same as for breach of section 1 of the Sexual Offences (Amendment) Act 1992, with the same maximum fine. It is a defence for anyone accused of breaching a section 58 order to prove that he/she was not aware of the order or, otherwise, that he/she did not know and had no reason to suspect what was published contained the relevant assertion.

 see ch.8, p. 119

▶ Ban on publication of 'indecent' matter

The Judicial Proceedings (Regulation of Reports) Act 1926 prohibits publication in any court report of any 'indecent medical, surgical, or physiological details which would be calculated to injure public morals'.

It is unlikely that mainstream media organisations would be prosecuted today under this law. Their journalists do not usually include in court reports material likely to revolt or offend readers, and – in any event – the test of what would 'injure public morals' would be hard to frame in an age more relaxed about what is published. This 1926 Act arose from politicians deciding to curb salacious reporting of divorce cases – see ch. 11, p. 172.

▶ Ban on photography, filming, and sketching in courts and precincts

More than eighty years ago, Parliament passed law forbidding photographs being taken of court proceedings. A primary objection to such photography, or of allowing TV cameras into trials, remains that added strain would be put on witnesses and defendants.

Under Section 41 of the Criminal Justice Act 1925, it is illegal:

- to take or attempt to take any photograph of
- or make or attempt to make – with a view to publishing it – any portrait or sketch of
- any person in any court, its building, or its precincts,
- or of any person while they are 'entering or leaving' a court building or its precincts.

→ glossary **Case law** has made clear that filming (including videoing), or attempting to film, are also thus prohibited by section 41.

Under section 41:

- the publication of any such photo (or film), portrait, or sketch is also prohibited, as an offence in itself.

Section 41 applies to criminal and civil courts, and inquests. It specifies that the term 'any person' includes judges, magistrates, coroners, jurors, witnesses, and parties (e.g. defendants). The bullet points above seek to summarise section 41. However, the Act's wording is not in all respects clear.

- The Act does not define what 'precincts' are, and this has caused practical difficulties of interpretation.

The term 'precincts' includes areas, e.g. a foyer or corridors, within the walls of the courthouse property. It is unclear to what extent the term refers to areas immediately outside which are not part of the courthouse property. Media photographers covering a specific court building should find out what the court authorities consider to be its precincts. As regards people 'entering or leaving', journalists standing on the public pavement frequently photograph and film judges, lawyers, defendants, and witnesses as they enter and/or emerge from court buildings, e.g. the Royal Courts of Justice in London. Where this has become customary, it is rare for such a court to object to this practice, though it would seem to breach section 41. However, jurors should not be thus photographed, because this may well be regarded as a contempt in common law (see below, p. 147).

If a judge or coroner decides that a jury should visit a location outside a court, e.g. a crime or accident scene, to help the jurors understand the evidence, then the making of this visit at that location should not be filmed, photographed or sketched there without the court's permission.

To illustrate newsworthy cases, the media publish artists' sketches of the scene in court, including the faces of those there, e.g. the defendant, witnesses, judge, lawyers.

To comply with section 41, these artists, having visited the court's public gallery or press bench to memorise the scene and faces, then do the actual sketching elsewhere, either in another building or in the courthouse press room. The latter is within the court's precincts. But a Government consultation paper has made no objection to sketching being done in the press room.

Breaches of the 1925 Act can be punished with fines up to £1,000.

- Irrespective of the 1925 Act, a court may deem the taking of a photograph or filming in court or in its precincts, or even elsewhere, e.g. on the pavement outside, as contempt of court, in common law (see below, and see also ch. 16, p. 298).

Such activity by a photographer could, for example, be regarded as contempt if it amounted to 'molestation', i.e. interference with the administration of justice. Case law suggests that chasing down a pavement after a defendant for a short while in order to photograph him/her would not usually be seen as molestation, even though he/she may not want to be photographed. But stalking a defendant or witness further, or pushing or jostling them, could be regarded as contempt, in that this may deter them or other witnesses from giving evidence.

If any photography or filming or sketching is held to be contempt under common law, the punishment in terms of fine or imprisonment is at the discretion of the judge. Members of the public have been swiftly punished for such contempt, particularly when it was regarded as an attempt to intimidate a witness. In 2004 a teenager who used a mobile phone to take pictures in Bristol Crown Court was sentenced to six months in a young offenders' institution. The same year a man received a nine-month sentence for taking similar pictures in Birmingham Crown Court, and here the judge said he believed there was a 'sinister motive' to the taking of the images. In 2003 a man who took a picture of his brother in the dock at Liverpool Crown Court was jailed for a year, a sentence that was upheld on appeal.

In 2005 a pilot scheme was undertaken in the Court of Appeal to allow cameras into it, being a court which rarely hears evidence from witnesses in person. In 2005 Parliament amended section 41 to ensure that the new **Supreme Court** – which is replacing the House of Lords – can permit broadcasting of its proceedings which, too, being concerned with points of law, are argued from documentary evidence, and are rarely likely to involve witnesses in person.

 glossary

→

see
p. 89 on
Supreme
Court

◗ Ban on audio-recording in court

It is illegal to use a tape-recorder or any other audio-recording device (e.g. to record on a mobile phone) in a court, without the court's permission. One aim of this prohibition is to prevent witness testimony being broadcast, which would for some witnesses increase the strain of giving evidence. The ban on audio-recording is also to deter surreptitious recording in the public gallery by, for example, associates of a defendant, who could use such a recording to intimidate or humiliate a prosecution witness. Also, such a recording could be used by dishonest witnesses to collude, if one – after listening to the recording of the other's evidence – sought subsequently to state in evidence the same detail, when purporting to have recollected it independently.

Under section 9 of the Contempt of Court Act 1981:

- it is contempt of court to use in court a tape-recorder or any other audio-recording device or to bring one into court for use, unless the court permits this;

- it is contempt to broadcast any audio-recording of court proceedings, including any playing of it in the hearing of any section of the public;

- it is contempt, if recording is permitted, to make any unauthorised use of the recording.

→

see ch. 12, p. 205 for Direction

Section 9, as can be seen, gives scope for a court to permit audio-recording for the purpose of an individual, including a journalist, making notes for himself/herself. Part I.2 of the Consolidated Criminal Practice Direction states that a court hearing an application for leave to record should consider 'the existence of any reasonable need on the part of the applicant... whether a litigant or a person connected with the press or broadcasting' and whether use of a recorder 'would disturb the proceedings or distract or worry witnesses or other participants'. The penalty for a contempt arising from breach of section 9 is a jail term – the maximum being two years – and/or an unlimited fine.

▌ Confidentiality of jury deliberations

The law prohibits journalists or anyone else from infringing on the confidentiality of a jury's deliberations, whether it is a Crown court jury, an inquest jury, or one in a civil case.

 For the role of juries in criminal trials, inquests, and civil cases, see ch 6, ch 10, and ch 14.

Section 8 of the Contempt of Court Act 1981 says:

- it is contempt of the court to obtain, solicit, or disclose any detail of:
  - statements made,
  - opinions expressed,
  - arguments advanced,
  - or votes cast
  - by members of a jury in the course of its deliberations.

The members of the public selected to serve on a jury should not need to fear, for example, that a man or woman convicted by a majority verdict at Crown court can discover vengefully from a media report who voted to convict and who in the jury argued for this. This section 8 prohibition applies even if neither an individual juror nor a particular trial is identified in what is published. There is criticism that this prevents worthwhile research into how juries reach decisions.

The penalty for a contempt arising from breach of section 8 is a jail term – the maximum being two years – and/or an unlimited fine. In 1994 the *Mail on Sunday*, its editor Stewart Steven, and a journalist were fined a total of £60,000 for such a breach (*Attorney General v Associated Newspapers Ltd* [1994] 2 AC 238).

See also Late News, p. xxxi

It is permissible to publish, when a trial is over, a juror's general impressions of the experience of serving on a jury, provided the juror is willing to volunteer these, and is not asked about statements made, opinions expressed or arguments advanced, or votes cast in the course of the jury's deliberations, and he/she does not refer to such matters in what is published. A juror could thus be interviewed, for example, on whether he/she felt that evidence was clearly presented, and on how the jury was treated generally in the court's handling of the case. For example, there is an ongoing debate about whether juries should continue to be used in complex fraud cases.

When journalists probe alleged miscarriages of justice, e.g. a controversial conviction for murder, jurors from the trial sometimes make their voices heard months or years later, e.g. by writing to a newspaper, on what influenced their verdict at the time. Sometimes, in the light of new evidence, these jurors say they are no longer certain of the guilt of the accused. Some such former jurors have been identified by the media. There remains a danger that for a journalist to interview such a juror about jury deliberations could be seen as breach of section 8. Because of this danger, the safest course is for a journalist to seek legal advice before conducting or publishing such an interview.

Also, there is a risk of a media organisation being accused of common law contempt if it publishes the identity of a juror against his/her wishes, even after a trial is concluded, because this could be ruled to be an interference with the judicial process by putting the juror at risk of vengeance from anyone unhappy with a verdict, or because identifying jurors in some contexts, or being held to have harassed them for an interview, might be seen as generally discouraging people from serving as jurors.

 For more information about common law contempt, see ch. 16. See also ch. 36, p. 563 as regards the ban on identifying jurors who have served in trials in Northern Ireland.

If a juror is discharged in the middle of a case for late attendance or drunkenness, then he/she may well be named in court, and could be punished by the judge for such misbehaviour. In the absence of any court order to the contrary, the media can safely publish how the court deals with such a juror. If a trial is abandoned before the jury retires to discuss any verdict, a juror can be safely interviewed, if he/she is willing to be interviewed, because he/she has played no part in any deliberations covered by section 8.

⠿ Recap of major points

- An order made under section 11 of the Contempt of Court Act 1981 prohibits publication, in a media report of a court case, of a name or matter withheld from the public proceedings of the court, e.g. the name of an alleged victim of blackmail.

- Under the Administration of Justice Act 1960, it is contempt of court to publish matter heard by a court in private, in certain categories of case.

- Under section 46 of the Youth Justice and Criminal Evidence Act 1999, an adult witness in a criminal case can be granted lifelong anonymity as regards media reports of that case.

- The media can identify such a witness in such reports if the witness has given valid, written consent for this.

- If a court under the 1999 Act makes a 'special measures direction' to assist a vulnerable or intimidated witness to give evidence, or makes an order preventing a defendant from cross-examining a witness, or considers making either such order, the media are automatically restricted until the trial is concluded from publishing that such an order was made or discussed.

- In some exceptional cases, the High Court has given defendants indefinite anonymity, so the media cannot reveal their whereabouts after they have served their sentence.

- A court can order the media to postpone, for 12 months, publication of a derogatory assertion made in mitigation, if the assertion meets certain criteria.

- It is illegal under the Criminal Justice Act 1925 to take photographs of, to film, or to sketch people in a court or its precincts, and may be adjudged to be contempt in common law.

- It is illegal under the Contempt of Court Act 1981 to make an audio-recording of a court case without the court's permission.

- It is illegal under the Contempt of Court Act 1981 to seek to discover, or to publish, what a jury discussed in deliberating on a verdict, or how an individual juror voted in the verdict.

10

Civil courts

Chapter summary

Civil law cases are a rich source of news stories. Civil law deals with the resolution of private disputes and the redress of private wrongs. Some civil cases involve companies or individuals suing each other. Some civil lawsuits are brought against the State and public bodies, e.g. a hospital trust can be sued for medical negligence by an aggrieved patient. As this chapter explains, most civil litigation is dealt with in the county courts. The High Court deals with more complex or high-value claims. Juries are not generally used in civil cases, but do decide some. Bankruptcy cases and company liquidations are also matters dealt with in civil law. Magistrates courts have some civil functions. There are some particular defamation and contempt of court dangers for journalists who cover civil cases, as this chapter explains. See ch. 12 for rights of admission to civil courts.

▌ Types of civil litigation

Most civil litigation is concerned with:

- breaches of contract, including the recovery of debts;
- torts – that is, civil wrongs for which monetary damages are recoverable, such as negligence, trespass, and defamation;
- breach of statutory duty, where a statute creates an actionable duty;
- possession proceedings against mortgagors and tenants, usually for failure to pay mortgage instalments or rent;

- 'Chancery' matters (see below), such as disputes relating to properties, business partnerships, trusts, and the administration of estates;
- insolvency, including bankruptcy and the winding up of companies;
- family law cases, including divorce; associated disputes over matrimonial assets and between estranged parents over residence arrangements for and contact with their children; applications by local authorities to take children considered at risk into care.

→ Family law is primarily dealt with in ch. 11

▌ County courts

County courts deal with the bulk of civil cases. They cover areas which are no longer based on counties. There are more than 200 of them, situated to be convenient to the centres of population. Some are designated as civil trial centres or family hearing centres, where the longer trials take place.

▌ The High Court

The High Court deals with the most complex or serious civil cases, and those of highest value. The administrative centre of the High Court is at the Royal Courts of Justice in The Strand, London, but its district registries are located in the larger county courts. Cases are heard both in London and 'on circuit' when High Court judges travel to the larger cities, although a **circuit judge**, see below, may be authorised to try a High Court case.

→ glossary

The High Court is made up of three divisions:

- *the Queen's Bench Division* (QBD), within which there are also specialist courts: the Admiralty Court, the Commercial Court, and the Technology and Construction Court;
- *the Chancery Division* which deals primarily with company work, trusts, estates, insolvency, and intellectual property. County courts also have limited jurisdiction in this area;
- *the Family Division*, see ch. 11.

High Court judges normally sit singly to try cases. The High Court is also an appeal court, both in civil law and criminal law (for its role in criminal law, see ch. 6). When it hears appeals and for some other functions there are two and sometimes three judges, and it is then known as the Divisional Court. Within the QBD, when the High Court carries out certain functions it is referred to as the Administrative Court, and these functions include glossary **judicial review** of the administrative actions of government departments and of other public authorities, and of the decisions of tribunals (see ch. 15).

▌Court of Appeal

The Court of Appeal, presided over by the Master of the Rolls, is for most cases the court of final appeal in civil law. It hears appeals from the county courts and the High Court. Some appeals are heard by three judges, but usually there are two. When there are three, each may give a judgment but the decision is that of the majority. A newspaper can make itself look foolish if it gives great prominence to the outspoken opinion of one judge without pointing out that this was overruled by a majority of his/her colleagues.

In a very limited number of cases, appeals can be made to the House of →glossary Lords, due to be known from October 2009 as the **Supreme Court**. Its procedures in civil cases are similar to those in its criminal cases, see ch. 6, p. 89.

> → See ch. 1, p. 8, where Figure 1 shows the hierarchy of the civil and criminal courts.

▌Types of judge in civil courts

Three types of judge preside in the county courts and High Court.

- *District judges* – each county court has one or more district judges, who are appointed from among practising solicitors and barristers. They deal in open court with many of the fast track and small claims track cases, see below, and also deal privately in their own chambers with claims for possession of land and many family disputes, insolvency matters, and procedural matters. They may be referred to in reports as District Judge John Smith, but are increasingly being referred to in newspapers as Judge John Smith. They 'case manage' High Court cases, e.g. ensure preliminary stages are completed.

A district judge also acts as the 'costs judge' on the detailed assessment of costs. Deputy district judges are part-time appointments.

- *Circuit judges* – In the busier county courts there may be two or more senior judges known as circuit judges; in other court groups the circuit judges may travel between several towns. Circuit judges may also sit in the Crown court to deal with criminal cases – see ch. 6, p. 76 for more information. **Recorders** are barristers and solicitors who sit part-time with the jurisdiction of a circuit judge. Retired circuit judges who continue to sit part-time are known as deputies. Circuit judges hear some fast track and most multi-track trials, see below. They may also hear appeals against the decisions of district judges. Appeals from a circuit judge lie direct to the Court of Appeal. → glossary

- *High Court judges* are the most senior – before they can be appointed they must have appeared as lawyers in all proceedings in the High Court for at least ten years, or have been a circuit judge for at least two years.

Legal terms for parties in civil cases

In many civil actions, the party initiating the action, e.g. suing for damages, is in law termed the 'claimant' (this party was formerly termed the 'plaintiff') and the term for the party against whom/which the action is taken is the 'defendant'. In some civil actions, e.g. a divorce case, the party initiating the action is termed the 'petitioner' and the other party is termed the 'respondent'. Divorce law is explained in ch. 11.

Media coverage of civil cases

The media have privilege against libel actions for their reports of judicial proceedings, including civil cases, as regards coverage of what is aired in open court and what can be reported from case documents made available by the court, see below – if the requirements of the privilege defences are met.

→ see ch. 19, pp. 337–348 on privilege

Settlements – If one party is suing the other for damages, the case may well be settled before a full trial of the issue, with one side paying the other a sum of money, which – e.g. if medical negligence is alleged – may be very large. Because of the settlement, there will be no court judgment on the facts. A media report of the settlement should therefore not suggest that the side paying the money has admitted liability for the wrong allegedly suffered by the other party, because this suggestion may be defamatory – unless liability *is* clearly admitted. For example, a private health clinic may sue for libel if a report wrongly suggests it has admitted liability for medical negligence.

Judges in civil cases have some of the same powers used by criminal courts as regards reporting restrictions. For example, in a civil court an order can be made under section 39 of the Children and Young Persons Act 1933 to prohibit the media from identifying a juvenile concerned in the case. Judges in civil cases, particularly in family law cases, may use their **inherent jurisdiction** to order that certain people, especially children, are protected by anonymity in reports of their cases.

→
see ch. 7

→ glossary

→
see ch.
9, p. 135,
and ch.
11, p. 178

The Contempt of Court Act 1981 applies to media reports of civil cases, in that once a case is 'active' nothing must be published which creates a substantial risk of serious prejudice to it. However, because juries are rarely used in civil cases, the Act is generally much less restrictive, as regards pre-trial media coverage, than it is for criminal cases. The bans on taking photographs, sketching, filming, or audio-recording in court apply to civil cases, as do other statutory and **common law** protections of the confidentiality of jury deliberations, and of jurors and witnesses generally – see chs 9 and 16.

→
see ch.
16, p. 295
for when
a civil
case is
active

'Payments into court' – the defendant being sued in certain types of civil action, e.g. a contract dispute or in a defamation case, may make a 'payment into court' before trial of the issue. This is a formal offer of payment in an attempt to put an end to the case, because such a defendant hopes that the **claimant**, who will be told of the sum offered – will accept it as a settlement. If the media discover that such an offer has been made, they should not report this fact unless and until it is referred to in open court at the end of the trial, if the case proceeds to trial. Publishing at any earlier stage that such an offer has been made may well be regarded as contempt of court because the revelation would be seen as potentially prejudicing the court's decision in the trial. The judge in the case, or the jury, if there is to be one, will not be told, before making a judgment/verdict in it, of this pre-trial offer. If at the end of trial the court finds for the claimant, but awards a lesser sum than that formally offered pre-trial by the defendant, the claimant will have

→ glossary

to pay that part of his/her own costs which was incurred after the date of the offer.

Starting civil proceedings

Most civil law actions in both the High Court and the county courts are begun by the issue by the court of a **claim form** (the modernised version of →glossary the document which was formerly called a writ). The claim form is prepared by the claimant and sets out the nature of the claim against the defendant and the remedies sought from the court. The remedy sought may be an **injunction** (a court order compelling the other party to do something, or →glossary refrain from doing something), or an order for the defendant to pay a debt or damages. When the claim is for money, the claim form will specify the amount (e.g. for a debt owed) or may, if damages are sought, ask for the sum to be decided by the court. The claim form is served on the defendant.

The vast majority of money claims – e.g. over debts – do not proceed to a trial, because the defendant usually does not file any defence, and if so the claimant simply writes to the court asking for judgment to be entered 'in default'. If damages are claimed there may need to be a hearing to assess what sum is appropriate. As soon as judgment is entered, the claimant may enforce it, seeking to get the money from the defendant. The court's enforcement procedures can could include **bailiffs** taking goods from the defendant →glossary to sell to pay off the money owed.

> See Useful Websites, below, for the Courts Service site, which offers guidance on procedures in civil cases.

Trials in civil cases

If the defendant in a civil case disputes what is said in the claim he/she must file either a defence or an acknowledgement of service within 14 days of service of the claim form and in any case must file his/her defence within 28 days of that date.

A civil trial is confined to issues that the parties set out in their **statements** →glossary **of case** (previously known as **pleadings**), these being the particulars of →glossary claim, see above, the defence, any counterclaims or reply to the defence, and 'further information documents'.

 See also ch. 12, pp. 201–204, for the rights of other people, including journalists, to see these documents.

The court can permit the parties to amend their statements of case, exceptionally even during the trial.

Each case is allocated to an appropriate 'track' based upon various factors including the financial value, complexity, the amount of oral evidence, the nature of the remedies sought, and the circumstances of the parties.

There are three tracks:

- the small claims track;
- the fast track;
- the multi-track.

While the money value of the claim is not necessarily the most important factor, the general approach is that where the claim exceeds £5,000 (or £1,000 for personal injuries) but not £15,000 it will be allocated to the fast track. Those below these levels are allocated to the small claims track (but possession claims are excluded from this track).

Cases allocated to the fast track are intended to be heard within 30 weeks and to be concluded within a hearing lasting no more than one day.

The multi-track covers a very wide range of claims. Many are little more complicated than those on the fast track. Others will require more care and the judge will normally arrange a case-management conference (which sometimes he/she will conduct by telephone) at which the issues in the claim will be clarified, and efforts made to encourage a negotiated (or mediated) settlement.

Small claims hearings

On the small claims track cases are decided at a county court by the district judge and are intended to be heard within three months. The procedure is designed to allow litigants to present their own case without the need for a lawyer, but they have the right to be represented in their presence by a friend (known as a 'lay representative'). Proceedings are informal and strict rules of evidence do not apply. The judge must give reasons for the final decision. These cases are now heard in public, though this will often be in the district judge's 'chambers' (i.e. a private room) with access allowed.

Full trials

In fast track and multi-track claims there is a formal trial by a judge with no jury, unless the case falls into a limited number of categories where there may be a jury, see below, p. 158.

For civil trials at county courts and the High Court, most parties instruct a solicitor to prepare their case. In consultation with their clients the solicitors will either brief **counsel** (i.e. instruct a barrister to provide further advice and to argue the case in court) or represent the client themselves if the trial is in the county court. As a noun, the term 'brief' is the name given to the bundle or file of documents prepared for each case, comprising the solicitor's narrative of it, the statements of case, the statements of the parties and of their witnesses and copies of all relevant disclosed documents. By extension, a 'brief' is also slang term for a lawyer. Some solicitors now have right of audience in the High Court, i.e. they can appear for their clients without needing to brief a barrister.

→ glossary

→ see ch. 1, p. 14, on the legal profession

Full trial procedure

A claimant or defendant can represent himself/herself in court and can generally be assisted by some other person (often called a 'McKenzie friend') although the judge may refuse to allow this for specified reasons.

Unless there is a jury, civil trials are now largely paper based. The claimant files a set of papers for the judge to read before the trial. The set will include witness statements, relevant documents, and the parties' respective 'skeleton arguments', setting out their case in law. With a few exceptions each party must serve his/her opponent with copies of all his/her proposed witness statements before the trial. The claimant or his/her advocate will call his/her witnesses, who may be asked in examination to do no more than confirm that the content of their statements is true, although usually the judge will allow some supplementary questions. There will then be cross-examination by the defendant or his/her advocate and the judge may ask further questions. If the defendant calls witnesses there will be the same process of (a short) examination and cross-examination. Expert evidence may be admitted only with the permission of the court – to which any expert owes a duty of impartiality. Unless the expert evidence is likely to be strongly contested the court will appoint a single expert who will be jointly instructed by the parties.

After all evidence is given, the respective advocates make their submissions on the evidence and law. Finally, the judge delivers judgment, giving his/her decision and the grounds on which it is based. In civil law, the standard of proof is 'on the balance of probabilities'. This is the test used by a judge (or jury, see below) to decide which of any competing pieces of evidence will be accepted as the truth. This is a lower standard of proof than that needed for criminal convictions – see ch. 2, p. 21. In more difficult cases a judge may reserve judgment so that he/she has more time to weigh the evidence and consult law books. He/she will then write out his/her judgment, referred to as a 'reserved judgment' and may read it out in court at a later date or have the judgment typed and 'handed down' at a subsequent hearing. Court reporters as well as lawyers are usually provided with a copy of the judgment. After the judgment (or, in jury trials, the verdict, see below) there will usually be argument about costs, and the judge must make an appropriate order – although more discretion is now allowed and it is not simply a question of the loser paying the winner's costs.

 See ch. 12, p. 203, for information on access to judgments in civil cases.

Trials with juries

In a civil law, there is a right to apply for trial by a jury if the claim:

- involves an allegation of fraud, or
- is for defamation – see ch. 17,
- or false imprisonment,
- or malicious prosecution.

The reasons why juries can be used in these categories of case have been described in a House of Lords judgment as 'historical rather than logical'. However, among those historical reasons are: that defamation cases and those involving a fraud allegation particularly concern allegations against someone's integrity and honour; that in a defamation case, a jury may understand nuances in current meanings of words which a judge – who may be remote from everyday 'street language' – may not; that false imprisonment or malicious prosecution cases usually involve allegations against an arm of the State (e.g. the police), and therefore, because a judge is within the court system which could be seen as another arm of the State, a jury is needed to ensure that the public has confidence that there has been independent decision-making in the case. A judge has discretion to allow jury trial in other types of civil case, but it is exceptional for a judge to agree to this. If there is a jury in a civil case, after each side has made final submissions at the end of the trial procedure outlined above, the judge will sum up the case, to help the jury. In some cases he/she may ask the jury for a general verdict,

 see ch. 17, p. 306 on meanings

but in the more complicated cases he/she will put a series of questions to them. Juries decide the level of damages if the verdict is for the claimant. Juries in civil cases are selected from the electoral role, in the same way as juries in criminal trials. A county court jury is of eight people and a High Court jury is of 12.

→ see ch. 6, p. 76 on jury summons

▌ Civil functions of magistrates

Magistrates have various civil powers, including those to impose anti-social behaviour orders (ASBOs), and sexual offences prevention orders (SOPOs), and – under law not in effect when this book went to press – are due to be given power to make 'drinking banning orders'.

The role of magistrates courts in family law cases, e.g. in maintenance matters and care proceedings, is outlined in ch. 11.

Magistrates courts became responsible from 2005 for hearing appeals from decisions of licensing committees of local authorities on public houses, hotels, off-licences and betting shops, and on licence holders. Previously magistrates themselves exercised control over such licensing in the first instance.

→ see ch. 7, pp. 107 and 111, and ch. 8, p. 124 on these powers

▌ Bankruptcy

Many bankruptcies are small affairs of limited news value, dealt with routinely by the county courts. Others, however, are stories of wild extravagance at the expense of creditors or the accumulation of large bills for unpaid tax. Some may involve criminal conduct, although there can be no prosecution for debt alone.

The Enterprise Act 2002 introduced a more lenient regime for those facing bankruptcy and insolvency. These changes came into effect on 1 April 2004. The issue of personal debt has become increasingly newsworthy due to the rising numbers of people becoming insolvent.

Questions put in the public examination in bankruptcy of John Poulson in 1972 led to the first substantial disclosures of corruption in the affairs of local councils and other public bodies, eventually leading to jail sentences for several men.

Now, a public examination in bankruptcy is not held automatically, see below.

Reporters should note the different procedures for companies and for individuals who are insolvent. Companies go into liquidation (see later in this chapter) while individuals become bankrupt.

For journalists, a useful source of information on bankruptcy and insolvency is the website of the Government's Insolvency Service.

see
Useful
Websites,
below

Bankruptcy petitions

A petition can be filed at the county court for a bankruptcy order to be made by a district judge against an individual who owes at least £750 in unsecured debts. A creditor will file a petition if this is regarded as the best way to get the debt – or some of it – repaid. Even if the creditor realises that the debtor has little money to offer, he/she may file a petition because he/she believes that the debtor deserves bankruptcy and will otherwise run up more debt. A debtor may file for his/her own bankruptcy to stop the hassle of bailiffs and creditors calling at his/her home, because after bankruptcy he/she can refer them to a trustee or official receiver, see below. Another reason a debtor may file for their own bankruptcy is that it seems to offer the prospect of starting life afresh when its term ends, with debt wiped out.

A bankruptcy order will be granted by the district judge unless, if the petition is from a creditor, the debtor has made an offer to repay the debt, but this has been unreasonably refused. In place of a bankruptcy order, an 'individual voluntary arrangement' may be made. In this case, the district judge may make only an interim bankruptcy order and may refer the matter to a licensed insolvency practitioner from a firm of accountants. This would be done in the hope that the debtor would be able to avoid bankruptcy through voluntary arrangements for a schedule for payment, if the creditors agree.

Otherwise, after a bankruptcy order the official receiver (a civil servant in the Insolvency Service, who is not a court official) takes over the legal control of all the debtor's property, apart from basic domestic necessities, tools, and other items necessary for the bankrupt to work. The debtor must within 21 days submit a statement of affairs setting out his/her assets, liabilities, and the deficiency. When the prospects of the creditors getting a substantial proportion of what is owed to them are fairly bright, the creditors will appoint a licensed accountant as the trustee in bankruptcy who is responsible to the court for the management of the debtor's affairs. In this case, the trustee and not the official receiver supervises the sale of any assets and the process of repayment.

Libel danger in wrongly stating someone is bankrupt

- Imputations of insolvency may well be regarded as defamatory.
- Therefore it may not be safe, as regards the danger of a libel action, for a media organisation to report – until and unless a bankruptcy order is made – the filing of a petition by a creditor for such an order, because the alleged debtor may be found by the county court to be solvent.
- But if the debtor files his/her own petition, he/she is admitting insolvency, so it is safe to report this.
- When a bankruptcy order has been made and is therefore open to public inspection at the court, or is disclosed on the Insolvency Service website – see below – or when a media organisation can quote from an announcement in the *London Gazette* (a government newsletter) that a bankruptcy order has been made, or can quote this from a notice for the public issued by the Official Receiver, there is no libel risk in reporting the information, because such a report will be protected by qualified privilege under the 1996 Defamation Act if that defence's requirements are met.

→
see ch.
17, p.
304–305
on
defama-
tory
state-
ments

→
see ch.
19, p.
340–346
on
qualified
privilege

Creditors meetings and public examinations

A meeting of the bankrupt's creditors may be held. There is no statutory right for the press to attend (though if the bankrupt owes money to his/her local paper, one of its journalists can offer to be there for his/her employer). The press can be formally admitted if the official receiver so rules. But the meeting can be a tricky one to report because a published account of it will not be privileged in libel law. A public examination in bankruptcy – which, as its name implies, can be attended by anyone – may be held next, though for one to be held is rare. This is a form of court hearing, so a media report of it will be protected by absolute or qualified privilege if the respective requirements of these libel defences are met – see ch. 19. The purpose of such a hearing is to satisfy the county court that the full extent of the debtor's assets and liabilities are known, to establish the causes of his/her financial failure, to probe the bankrupt's financial affairs to discover whether any criminal offence has been committed, and to establish whether any assets transferred to another person ought to be recovered.

Such an examination usually takes place before a district judge. The debtor is examined by the official receiver or his/her assistant. If there is a trustee in a bankruptcy, he/she, or a lawyer representing him/her, may also ask questions. Otherwise any proven creditor may question the debtor.

Figures reflecting the size of the bankruptcy will emerge during the hearing – the liabilities, the assets, and, most important of all, the deficiency.

A public examination in bankruptcy may also take place after a judge has made an order following the conviction of a criminal. The purpose of this is to distribute the criminal's assets fairly among the victims of his/her **theft** or fraud. Examinations after such criminal bankruptcy orders may take place in prison for security reasons.

→ glossary

Effects of bankruptcy

A bankrupt cannot obtain credit of £500 or more without disclosing his/her bankruptcy, nor trade under any name other than that in which he/she went into bankruptcy without disclosing the former name and the bankruptcy. A bankrupt is not allowed to open new bank accounts. He/she cannot act as a company director nor take part in the management of any company without the leave of the court.

He/she cannot sit in Parliament or on a local authority, nor take any public office. Most credit card companies will blacklist all bankrupts for six years.

Bankruptcy documents open to public inspection

Rules 7.28 and 7.31 of the Insolvency Proceedings Rules 1986 allows for public inspection of the court's record of bankruptcy proceedings, including bankruptcy orders, but if the district judge is not satisfied with the propriety of a request to inspect the record, he/she may disallow the request. Online searches for court orders still in force for bankruptcy or for individual voluntary arrangements, or for bankruptcies which have ended in the preceding three months, may be made through the Insolvency Service's website, see below. A search can reveal, for example, which insolvency practitioner is dealing with a bankrupt's affairs, and the bankrupt's date of birth and address.

Discharge from bankruptcy

One of the aims of the Enterprise Act 2002 was to reduce the stigma attached to bankruptcy for those who were making a genuine effort to clear their debts.

Whereas in the past a bankruptcy would not be discharged until at least three years, under the Act that period was reduced to 12 months. The effects of bankruptcy, listed above, remain the same. They end with the automatic discharge of the bankruptcy.

The new regime also relaxes the obligations placed on the official receiver to investigate a bankrupt's behaviour. A bankrupt can in some circumstances be discharged earlier than 12 months.

One side-effect of the Act was that heavily indebted students were able to use bankruptcy as a means of avoiding repayment of their student loans, including those owed to the Student Loans Company. But this loophole was closed by the Higher Education Act 2004, so now bankruptcy does not cancel an obligation to repay a student loan.

An official receiver, if he/she considers that a bankrupt has been dishonest or otherwise blameworthy as regards debt incurred, can ask the court to impose a Bankruptcy Restrictions Order. The effect of a BRO is to increase the duration of the restrictions on the bankrupt to a term of between two and fifteen years, depending on the court's decision.

▶ Company liquidation

In reporting that a limited company has gone into liquidation, care should be taken to make the circumstances clear. Otherwise, misuse of terms in a report could create a libel problem.

(1) A *members' voluntary liquidation* takes place where the company is solvent, but the directors and shareholders decide to close it down, possibly in the case of a small firm because of impending retirement, or because of a merger. To imply that such a company is in financial difficulties in this case is defamatory.

(2) A *creditors' voluntary liquidation* takes place for a voluntary winding up to proceed under the supervision of a liquidator.

(3) A *compulsory liquidation* follows a hearing in public in the High Court or county court of a petition to wind up the company. This is usually because a creditor claims that the company is insolvent, but technically can also arise where a company fails to file its statutory report or hold its statutory meeting on being set up; where it does not start, or suspends, business; or where members of the company are reduced to below the number required in law. Once a winding-up order is made, a liquidator is appointed to collect the assets and pay off the creditors.

As stated above, in law the term bankrupt applies only to individuals, not to companies.

▦ Recap of major points

- County courts handle most civil litigation, but the High Court deals with the more serious or high-value claims.
- Civil case hearings are largely conducted by reference to documents. A journalist has rights of access to key documents of cases heard in public.
- Civil courts can impose reporting restrictions. Contempt law applies to media coverage reports of their cases, but is less restrictive if no jury is involved.
- Magistrates handle some types of civil case.
- The county courts deal with bankruptcy cases. Individuals go bankrupt when they are financially insolvent.
- The Enterprise Act 2002 introduced a more lenient regime for bankrupts.
- Care must be taken with imputations of insolvency as they can have a defamatory meaning.
- Until a bankruptcy order is made the media, to avoid a potential libel problem, should be wary of reporting that someone is 'going bankrupt', unless that person has filed for his/her own bankruptcy.
- There are three ways in which companies can go into liquidation – a members' voluntary liquidation, a creditors' voluntary liquidation, and a compulsory liquidation.
- Because of libel dangers, care must be taken to distinguish between these types of liquidation.

🌐 Useful Websites

www.hmcourts-service.gov.uk/
  Her Majesty's Courts Service

www.judiciary.gov.uk/
  The Judiciary website

www.insolvency.gov.uk/
  The Insolvency Service website

11

Family courts

Chapter summary

Family law is a branch of civil law, dealt with in the magistrates courts, county courts, and the High Court. Many family cases arise from broken relationships, including disputes between couples – e.g. over divorce, separation, maintenance, and the upbringing of children. They include applications for court orders to prevent domestic violence. These courts also deal with applications by local authorities seeking through social workers to protect children considered at significant risk within families, e.g. from abuse or neglect. Because of the need to protect the privacy of those involved, and to safeguard children's welfare, there are – for most types of family court proceedings – restrictions on who can attend such hearings. In many cases there are also restrictions on what the media (and the parties involved) can disclose from them. This chapter sets out these restrictions. It notes how they have led to controversy about whether family courts sufficiently benefit from the principle of open justice. See ch. 12 for further explanation of the open justice principle.

▶ Types of case in family courts

The term 'family cases' covers a range of matters dealt with in civil law. These cases are heard in the magistrates courts, the county courts, or the Family Division of the High Court, depending on the nature of each case and its complexity. Cases may be transferred within these three tiers. The High

Court, the Court of Appeal, and thereafter the House of Lords (soon to be known as the **Supreme Court**), hear appeals.

 → glossary

 → see ch. 11 for an overview of the civil court system

Many family cases are heard **in private**, although there is a presumption in →glossary relevant court rules that if someone faces being jailed, e.g. for disobeying a court order in such a case, this part of the proceedings will usually be in public. In addition to restrictions on admission to the court, there are several sets of statutory reporting restrictions on what can be published from such cases – see below.

Family cases fall into two main categories. One is referred to as 'private law'. This includes:

- Proceedings for the dissolution of a marriage, i.e. for divorce, judicial → separation, or nullity, or to end a civil partnership. Judicial separation see also is legal recognition that though no divorce has occurred a couple will p. 170 no longer cohabit. It may be sought, for example, by those whose religious beliefs forbid divorce. Nullity proceedings are taken when someone wants their marriage annulled – i.e. declared invalid – because, for example, it has not been sexually consummated or their spouse turned out to be already married, i.e. bigamous. Civil partnerships are legally recognised relationships between gay people, and can be legally dissolved, or subject to judicial separation. In all the types of case listed in this paragraph, the courts can also rule on 'ancillary relief', i.e. financial arrangements and division of property between the estranged couple.

- Enforcement of financial arrangements between estranged couples, including unmarried couples. The Child Support Agency, created in 1991, has a key role in securing maintenance for children, usually a father paying money to the mother. But the courts still hear some such cases and can enforce co-operation with CSA decisions.

- Other disputes between estranged parents about their children, e.g. over which parent the children will live with – leading to the court making a residence order; or over the other parent's rights to contact with the children – leading to the court making a contact order. Such orders are made under the Children Act 1989. NB: as regards parental arrangements, the term 'custody' of children is no longer used in law.

- Applications for court orders seeking to ensure the return of a child abducted by one partner after a relationship breaks down.

→ glossary

- Domestic violence applications, e.g. a woman seeking an **injunction** to forbid a former partner from continuing to threaten her and/or from entering her home.

- Applications to protect a person from being coerced to marry, i.e. a forced marriage.

- Disputes over paternity, i.e. if a man claims he is not a child's father, or that he is.

- Adoption cases: these may formalise family-made arrangements, e.g. a step-father becoming adoptive father, or the court can sanction adoption by non-relatives, e.g. an approved couple adopting a child previously removed from his/her natural parents by a local authority in its child protection role (see below).

- Non-contentious probate business, e.g. concerned with release of assets bequeathed in wills.

The other category of family cases is referred to as 'public law'. These are applications, mainly by local authorities, for court orders to authorise social workers to intervene to protect a child, e.g. if there is suspected neglect or abuse within a family or if a child's misbehaviour seems beyond parental control. Such orders are made under the Children Act 1989, mainly in magistrates courts.

For example:

- an assessment order requires parents to co-operate with assessment of their child;

- a care order enables social workers to remove a child from parents, for placement in a foster home or children's home run by the local authority;

- if there is concern for a child's immediate safety, such removal can be rapidly sanctioned by an emergency protection order.

Staff employed by the Children and Family Court Advisory and Support Service (CAFCASS) assist the courts in 'private law' and 'public law' cases involving children. CAFCASS staff can advise the adults involved, e.g. seek to resolve parental disputes, and can ensure if necessary that a Children's Guardian (someone experienced in social work) is appointed by the court to independently prepare a report on a child, e.g. taking into account a child's wishes for his/her future, and that the child has his/her own legal representation in court. It is unusual for children themselves to attend family cases.

see
Useful
Websites,
below

❚ Admission to family proceedings in magistrates courts

- Family proceedings in magistrates courts are not open to the public, but section 69 of the Magistrates' Courts Act 1980 permits 'representatives of newspapers and news agencies' to attend, with the exception of adoption cases – see below.

- However, magistrates have discretion to exclude reporters from any family proceedings case when exercising powers under the Children Act 1989 in relation to a child, if such exclusion is 'expedient in the interests of the child'. For most parts of the Act, a child is defined as someone aged under 18.

A consultation paper prepared for the Lord Chancellor's Department said in 1993 that it seemed that a magistrates court must not have a general policy in such cases of excluding the press, but must make a specific decision in each case based on the interests of the particular child involved. The 1989 Act's definition of a child includes someone who has reached the age of 18 if the case concerns funding for him/her to benefit from education or training.

- Magistrates must exclude the press (as well as the public) when dealing with adoption cases.

- Magistrates also have discretionary power, under section 69 of the Magistrates' Courts Act 1980, to exclude the press during the taking of indecent evidence, if satisfied this is necessary in the interests of the administration of justice or of public decency.

 Magistrates also have common law powers to exclude the press and public – see ch. 12, pp. 190–191. Restrictions apply to media reports of family proceedings at magistrates courts, see below, page 173.

❚ Admission to family cases in county courts and higher courts

Most family law cases in the county courts and High Court have, until recently, been heard in private – but see also Late News, p. xxix. A journalist

see
below,
p. 179,
and ch. 9,
p. 130

should be aware that reporting on a court case heard in private has particular dangers in libel law and, for certain types of cases and in some circumstances, particular dangers as regards contempt of court. As regards contempt law, the media's ability to legally report the outcome of a court case heard in private may well depend on whether a judgment or order is made public by the court.

Matrimonial dissolution cases

Proceedings for divorce, judicial separation, or nullity, or to end a civil partnership, are dealt with by the county courts, with a small proportion being transferred to the High Court.

Divorce proceedings, the most common action in this type of case, begin with either the wife or the husband lodging a petition for a divorce at a county court. The spouse starting the proceedings is known as the petitioner. The petition is served on the other spouse, known as the respondent, who is required to state whether he/she intends to contest the petition, i.e. whether he/she wants to stay married. In cases which are uncontested, which are by far the majority, the judge considers evidence about the marital breakdown in private. But if any matrimonial case is contested, evidence is given in open court, under the Family Proceedings Rules (FPR), rule 2.28, except that in a nullity case, evidence of sexual incapacity will usually be heard in private.

Lists of petitioners granted a decree nisi – the first stage of a divorce – are read out in open court, a requirement of rule 2.36(2) of the FPR 1991. A decree nisi does not allow the parties to remarry. They can do this after the decree is made absolute (usually after six weeks). Any person may within 14 days of a decree nisi being pronounced inspect at the court the relevant certificate and any evidence filed in support of the petition (rule 2.36(4)). However, reporting restrictions apply to divorce and other types of matrimonial dissolution proceedings, see below, p. 172. Hearings about 'ancillary relief' – see above, p. 167 – are also normally heard in private (rule 2.66(2)). However, a judgment determining the financial settlement in a divorce case can be made public if the judge considers there is a particular public interest in it being reported. This is normally seen to be the case in large awards. For example, in 2008 Mr Justice Bennett made public his award of £24.3 million to Heather Mills in her settlement with her ex-husband Paul McCartney, after she failed to persuade the Court of Appeal that this High Court judgment, which contained criticism of her, should be kept private (*Media Lawyer*, 25 March 2008).

Other cases in county courts and the High Court

In other types of family case dealt with by county courts and the High Court, whether private or public law, contested or not, judges have discretion under various provisions to decide whether the proceedings should be in open court. The norm has been for family cases to be held in private, with the judge(s) exercising discretion on whether a judgment is made public. But see Late News, p. xxix. The Adoption and Children Act 2002 gives these courts power to hear and determine adoption cases in private.

Various reporting restrictions can apply to cases involving the upbringing of children, see the rest of this chapter.

In county courts and the High Court the text of a judgment, if made public, will be anonymised if statute requires this to prevent a child or adult being identified, or if the judge uses the court's **inherent jurisdiction** – see below, p. 178 – to bestow such anonymity on privacy or other grounds. A media organisation would commit an offence, understatute or as contempt of court, if it reported an anonymised judgment in such a way as to identify the protected person, e.g. by adding their name.

The Court of Appeal and the House of Lords almost invariably hear appeals in family cases in open court, but evidence is almost always considered in documents, not orally from witnesses. They deliver judgments in public, but usually use their inherent jurisdiction to bestow anonymity if a family case involves a child.

▶ Restrictions on reports of family cases

Several statutes **automatically** restrict what the media can report about family cases. In particular, a journalist should know that: → glossary

- if a case does or may involve use of powers under the Children Act 1989 any child involved cannot be identified in any way in respect of an ongoing case – see below, p. 174.

- a media organisation could be prosecuted for contempt of court if matter aired in a court hearing held in private, i.e. one closed to both press and public, is published in any report of the case or within a more general feature about a family, even if the anonymity of any child in the case is honoured in such coverage – see below, p. 179.

Reporting restrictions in divorce, judicial separation, and nullity cases

Reporting restrictions automatically apply to any published report of matrimonial dissolution proceedings, e.g. divorce or dissolution of a civil partnership – see above, pp. 167 and 170. These restrictions, under section 1(1)(b) of the Judicial Proceedings (Regulation of Reports) Act 1926, limit reports of these proceedings to the following information:

- the names, addresses, and occupations of parties and witnesses;
- the grounds of the application and a concise statement of the charges, defences, and counter-charges in support of which evidence has been given;
- submissions on any point of law arising in the proceedings and the decision of the court on the submissions;
- the summing up of the judge, the judgment, and any observations made by the judge in giving it.

This legislation was enacted by Parliament in 1926 because it wanted to curb the established practice of some newspapers to report at length salacious evidence from divorce cases – the most newsworthy of which involved the upper classes. In a divorce case, the 'charges' made by the petitioner are the grounds for seeking a divorce, e.g. that their spouse has been adulterous or behaved unreasonably in another way. The restrictions mean that media reports of the few contested divorce actions which occur are primarily based on what is said by the judge in judgment, though this may well provide a lengthy account of the case's issues. To comply with these restrictions, the safest course for a journalist at a court hearing of a contested divorce is to wait until all evidence in the case has been given, to guard against key elements in it being withdrawn – because of the stipulation that charges, defences, and counter-charges can only be reported if evidence has been given in support of them. The only known prosecution for alleged breach of the restrictions halted on a technicality, so its result did not aid precise interpretation of the restrictions. If these restrictions are breached, 'a proprietor, editor, master printer or publisher' is liable for a jail term of four months and/or a fine of up to £5,000. The Attorney General must give consent for a prosecution for breach of the restrictions.

If there is any legal dispute, before or after divorce proceedings, between a couple about a child, and it involves proceedings under the Children Act 1989, a reporting restriction under that Act prohibits identification of any such child (and therefore also of his/her parents) in media reports of such proceedings, while they are ongoing – see below, p. 174.

There are also restrictions on what can be reported from a private hearing. See p. 179.

Section 71 restrictions on magistrates' family proceedings

Section 71 of the Magistrates' Courts Act 1980 says that a published report of 'family proceedings' in a magistrates court must only contain the following information:

- the names, addresses, and occupations of parties and witnesses;
- the grounds of the application and a concise statement of the charges, defences, and counter-charges in support of which evidence has been given;
- submissions on any point of law arising in the proceedings and the decision of the court on the submissions;
- the decision of the court, and any observations made by the court in giving it.

The section 71 restrictions are automatic, and – as can be seen – are configured in essentially the same form as the restrictions for matrimonial dissolution hearings. Thus, they have the same effect of limiting the reporting of evidence – the element of proceedings in which personal matters figure in most detail. Under section 71, evidence can only be published in the form of quotations from magistrates' decisions and their observations.

The definition of 'family proceedings' in the 1980 Act includes cases concerning maintenance – e.g. payments by a man to his ex-wife to support her and any child of theirs; applications for consents to marry – someone aged 16 or 17 needs parental consent to marry, and a court may give consent if parents refuse it; declarations of parentage – to decide if an adult is a child's parent, e.g. thereby making a father liable to support that child; disputes, after allegations of domestic violence, about who can continue to live in the couple's home; applications for 'non-molestation orders' to prevent such violence; applications under the Children Act 1989, including for intervention by social workers. If any ongoing case involves use or potential use of powers under the 1989 Act, anonymity provisions apply under that Act in addition to the section 71 restrictions under the 1980 Act which limit the reporting of evidence (see below, p. 174).

Family proceedings are a branch of civil law, so the reference to 'charges' in section 71 is to the nature of the reason(s) asserted for the application being made (e.g. that maintenance has not been paid), not to criminal charges. To be sure of complying with section 71 a media organisation should wait until all evidence in the case has been given before publishing a charge, defence, or counter-charge, to ensure that each is supported by evidence and to know if any such evidence has been withdrawn – assuming that its journalist *is* allowed into the court to hear the case – see above, p. 169. Liability for breach of section 71 is the same as for breach of the 1980 Act's section 8 except that the maximum fine is £2,500.

→

see ch. 4,
p. 53

Other reporting restrictions in family cases

Some types of family case – e.g. over neglect to pay maintenance, or for declarations about legitimacy or marital status – are covered by automatic reporting restrictions under the Domestic and Appellate Proceedings (Restriction of Publicity) Act 1968 in respect of any court which hears such a case. This Act applies to such cases the restrictions set out in section 1(1)(b) of the Judicial Proceedings (Regulation of Reports) Act 1926 – see above, p. 172 – with the same liability in the event of breach. In relevant cases 'the particulars of the declaration sought' can be published, instead of a 'concise statement of charges, defences, and counter-charges in support of which evidence has been given'. Again, the Attorney General's consent is needed for any prosecution for breach of the reporting restrictions.

Section 39 orders

→

see ch. 7,
p. 103 and
ch. 13,
p. 231

As a general provision, all courts – including family courts – have discretion to make an order under section 39 of the Children and Young Persons Act 1933 to prevent media reports of a case identifying a child aged under 18. But there must be a good reason to make a section 39 order, and the child must be 'concerned in the proceedings'.

Anonymity for children under the Children Act 1989

Section 97 of the Children Act 1989 makes it an offence to publish:

- a name or other material which is intended or likely to identify any child as being involved in any ongoing proceedings in magistrates courts, the county courts, or the High Court in which any power under the Act may be exercised with respect to that or any other child;

- or to publish an address, or school, as being that of a child involved in any such ongoing proceedings.

The term 'ongoing' is not in the Act, but this is the effect of the judgment in *Clayton v Clayton* [2006] EWCA Civ 878, see below. A child is usually defined in the Act as aged under 18. The section 97 anonymity therefore automatically applies, for example, to children in unresolved disputes between parents about residence and contact, and to children who are the subject of applications for intervention by social workers. This anonymity applies, in an ongoing case, not only to a report of what is said in court or of any written judgment but also to any wider feature on the family which makes any reference to the child's involvement in such a case. Consequentially, to protect the child's anonymity under the 1989 Act, the family cannot be identified either by any published detail within any such coverage, and jigsaw identification must also be avoided – see ch. 7, p. 105. In an ongoing family case brought under other statute, e.g. domestic violence or maintenance proceedings, section 97 will also bestow such anonymity to a child concerned in it if any power under the 1989 Act may be exercised in it in respect of the child. This is true even if, under other statute – e.g. section 71 of the Magistrates' Courts Act 1980, see above, p. 173 – the parents could otherwise be named as the 'parties'. A reporter unsure if the 1989 Act applies to the case should check with the court clerk. If 'any person' breaches section 97, i.e. publishes material identifying a child covered by it, the person can be fined up to £2,500. It is a defence if anyone accused of such breach proves that he/she did not know, and had no reason to suspect, that the published matter was intended or likely to identify such a child. To avoid breaching section 97, the media – if considering publishing a story about estranged parents warring over a child – should check if a court case is ongoing.

see p. 169

see p. 176 on when section 97 ceases to apply

Adoption cases

The 1989 Act's section 97, see above, also automatically forbids reports of adoption cases from identifying the child concerned.

⠿ Point for consideration

Also, the Adoption and Children Act 2002 makes it an offence for anyone other than an officially recognised adoption agency, or someone acting on its behalf, to publish (including internet publication) information indicating that a particular child is available for adoption or information about how to do anything which would be an offence under the Act as regards arranging an adoption without legal authority; or any advertisement that a parent or guardian of a child wants the child to be adopted or any advertisement that a person other than such an adoption agency is willing to arrange an adoption, or is willing to receive a child handed over to him/her with a view to adoption, or is willing to remove a child from the UK for the purposes of adoption.

When does a child's anonymity under the Children Act 1989 cease to apply?

- If the welfare of a child requires it, under section 97(4) of the Children Act 1989, a magistrates court, a county court, or the High Court, or the Lord Chancellor with the agreement of the Lord Chief Justice, can waive to any specified extent the anonymity which would otherwise be automatically bestowed by the Act on a child.

The courts in ongoing cases have used this discretionary power to enable the media to help trace missing children by publishing their names, photos, and other details, in the hope that the public may then provide information about the children's whereabouts. The courts have thus waived anonymity in respect of children abducted from their home, e.g. by a parent refusing to co-operate with social workers or with a residence or contact order obtained under the Act by an ex-partner.

- But in any event, the section 97 anonymity is not permanent for any child. It only applies while the relevant court proceedings are ongoing, i.e. it ceases to apply when the case has concluded.

This was made clear by the Court of Appeal in 2006 in *Clayton v Clayton* (2006), which set precedent for the interpretation of the wording of section 97. In that judgment, Sir Mark Potter, president of the Family Division, said that if a court felt that, to protect a child's welfare or to otherwise protect his/her privacy under Article 8 of the European Convention on Human Rights, anonymity in relation to those proceedings should continue beyond their conclusion, e.g. until the child was 18, it would have to make an order to that effect. This could be done under its inherent jurisdiction, see below, p. 178. Sir Mark said that, as a practical consequence of this judgment, it will be appropriate for a court, when it believes that it has concluded a case involving the 1989 Act, to consider if there is an outstanding welfare issue which needs the child's anonymity to be continued in the longer term by such an order being made. In the same judgment, Lord Justice Wall added: 'My

see ch. 1, p. 9 on Convention

impression is that there are unlikely to be many cases in which the continuation of that protection will be required.' A consequence of the 2006 *Clayton v Clayton* judgment is that a journalist seeking to refer to a child's involvement in proceedings under the 1989 Act – e.g. in a dispute between estranged parents over contact, or concerning intervention by social workers – should be sure, before publishing anything likely to compromise the child's anonymity, that the proceedings *are* concluded *and* that no order has been made to continue that anonymity beyond the case's conclusion. Long adjournments can occur in such cases, e.g. a local authority may seek several interim care orders before a case is concluded.

In *Re Brandon Webster, Norfolk County Council v Webster* [2006] EWHC 2733 (Fam) and [2006] EWHC 2898 (Fam) the High Court ruled that a child's anonymity under section 97 can be waived by a court on grounds other than his/her welfare, if this is necessary to protect the rights of others under the European Convention, including those of freedom of expression under Article 10.

see below, p. 184, for further discussion of this case

Journalists should remember that section 12 of the Administration of Justice Act 1960 (see below, p. 179) forbidding disclosure of matter aired in private hearings, will – unless a judge orders otherwise – apply permanently, even though section 97 anonymity may have ceased.

The Ministry of Justice announced in 2008 that it intended to 'reverse' the effect of the *Clayton v Clayton* (2006) ruling, by passing law which would automatically give a child anonymity lasting beyond the conclusion of a case. The Ministry's intention was apparently that the default position in law will be that the anonymity stays in place until the child is 18, unless a judge makes an order to lift the anonymity before that time.

 However, see late News p. xxx and check the legal updates posted on the Online Resource Centre.

Wards of court and other children in 'parens patriae' cases

A child who has been made a ward of court by the High Court, or who is subject to proceedings seeking to make him/her a ward, or who is involved in any other form of 'parens patriae' case there, is automatically protected by the 1989 Act's section 97 anonymity in respect of published reports of such proceedings, while they are ongoing (and the court can extend the duration of the anonymity). See *Kelly v British Broadcasting Corporation* [2001] Fam 59. In wardship and other 'parens patriae' cases, the High Court

→glossary uses its inherent jurisdiction in **common law** to act in a parental capacity to approve important decisions made about the child, e.g. about education or medical treatment. These High Court powers to protect a child are based
→glossary on centuries-old **case law** originally derived from the role of monarch, who was regarded as the 'parent' of the whole nation (in Latin, parens patriae). A child may be made a ward if, for example, his/her parents are dead or deemed to be unfit to raise him/her or to be otherwise acting against the best interests of the child. But a child can also be made a ward at the request of his/her family e.g. if he/she runs away or is abducted. Wardship means the High Court can order anyone to tell it of the child's whereabouts. To disobey will be punishable as contempt of court.

In *Kelly v British Broadcasting Corporation* Mr Justice Munby ruled in the Family Division that the media did not require the leave of the court either to interview a ward of court or to publish such an interview. But he warned that in publishing the media would have to take care to avoid any breach of reporting restrictions (e.g. anonymity may apply in respect of the ward, and a published interview should not breach contempt law in respect of matter heard by a court in private, see p. 179).

Anti-publicity injunctions

The High Court, Court of Appeal, and House of Lords can use their inherent jurisdiction to order that a person, whether a child or adult, ward or not, must
→

see also
p. 171 on
judg-
ments

be anonymous in published reports of their proceedings and judgments, if, for example, statute does not already provide such anonymity and if the court wishes thus to protect the person's welfare from the effect of publicity. In such injunctions, the High Court can also – e.g. at the request of a local authority or a lawyer appointed to act for a child – forbid news-gathering or other actions which, irrespective of what has been or may be published, are deemed in themselves likely to jeopardise such anonymity or harm in other ways the welfare of the person granted it. For example, in 2008 Mr Justice McKinnon made an order forbidding media organisations from approaching two women whose father had been jailed at Sheffield Crown Court for life for repeatedly raping them in their childhood and subsequently, causing them to have children by him. This High Court order also forbade the media from 'attending at or remaining in the vicinity' of any address at which the daughters and/or any of their children were or had been living, in circumstances in which such media activity would create a likelihood of the daughters or their children being identified 'directly or indirectly' to the public in connection with the rape case. To comply with the automatic statu-
→

see ch. 8
tory anonymity for rape victims the media, in reporting that rape case, had

not named the father, the daughters, or their children. But lawyers acting for the daughters argued that detail in some reports and such media activity could identify them and their children in local communities.

The House of Lords judgment in *Re S (A Child) (Identification: Restrictions on Publication)* [2004] UKHL 47 – see below, p. 185 – made clear in 2004 that the scope of the High Court's inherent jurisdiction to restrain the discussion of and reporting of cases involving children derives, since the Human Rights Act 1998 incorporated European Convention on Human Rights fully into UK law, from the protection of privacy in the Convention's Article 8, and no longer relies on earlier case law. In the Court of Appeal judgment in *Clayton v Clayton* – see above, p. 176 – Sir Mark Potter, President of the Family Division, said that this Convention-based approach meant that the power to grant such anti-publicity injunctions to protect the welfare of children applied to county court proceedings as well as to those in the High Court.

 See below, p. 183–186, for other cases in which the High Court has used, or refused to use, its inherent jurisdiction to restrict media coverage of children.

To enable media organisations to have warning of such an injunction being sought, e.g. by a local authority, and therefore to decide whether to oppose it, the Family Division issued a practice direction in 2005 that a party applying for such an injunction should circulate advance notice to media organisations. The direction said this should be done, as regards alerting national media organisations, through the Press Association's CopyDirect service, and that such advance notice will help the applicant comply with section 12 of the 1998 Act. (*President's Practice Direction Application for Reporting Restriction Orders* [2005] 2 FLR 120 and *Practice Note: Official Solicitor: Deputy Director of Legal Services: CAFCASS: Applications for Reporting Restriction Orders* [2005] 2 FLR 111). see ch. 1, p. 5 on 1998 Act

 See the Online Resource Centre, ch. 11, for more detail on this alert procedure.

▶ Contempt danger in reporting matter from family cases held in private

Section 12 of the Administration of Justice Act 1960 makes it an offence of contempt of court to publish, without the permission of a court, a report of

→ glossary

→
see also
ch. 9,
pp.
130–132

proceedings it has heard in private, i.e. in chambers or in camera, if the case falls into certain categories listed in the Act. The categories include:

- proceedings which relate to the exercise of the inherent jurisdiction of the High Court with respect to children (see above pp. 177–179);

- proceedings under the Children Act 1989 or the Adoption and Children Act 2002 (see earlier in this chapter);

- or which otherwise relate wholly or mainly to the maintenance or upbringing of a child;

- any case in which the court has specifically forbidden publication of matter it has heard in private.

Therefore, the section 12 prohibition applies broadly across family cases, in that many such proceedings in these categories can be heard in private. It is also regarded as contempt if information is published from a document prepared for use in such a private hearing (*Re F (A Minor) (Publication of Information)* [1977] Fam 58; [1977] 1 All ER 114). Such a document could be a witness statement in a dispute between parents over contact arrangements regarding their children, or a social worker's report concerning a child taken into local authority care. Mr Justice Munby said in 2004 that the prohibition on publication of documents such as witness statements, reports, transcripts or notes made of the judgment, or quotations extracted from them, applied equally to documents that had been anonymised (*Re B (A Child)* [2004] EWHC 411 (Fam)). Reflecting section 12, the Family Proceedings (Amendment Number 4) Rules 2005 (SI 2005/1976) make it a contempt, except with the court's permission, for the parties to a case to communicate information from private proceedings relating wholly or mainly to the maintenance or upbringing of a child, unless the communication is to a legal adviser or other categories of people specified in the rules, e.g. those with official duties involving children. The rules therefore implicitly seek to forbid, for example, a parent of a child taken into local authority care communicating to a journalist information from such proceedings held in private.

- However section 12 permits the publication of any order a court makes in private proceedings, unless the court specifically prohibits the order from being published.

Also, section 12 does not prohibit the media from making basic reference to a case being heard in private, nor does the section, in itself, prevent the media identifying those involved. In *Re B (A Child)*, see above, Mr Justice Munby stated in 2004 that section 12 did not of itself prohibit publication of 'the nature of the dispute' being heard in the private proceedings, or that it concerned a ward of court or wardship proceedings or proceedings under the Children Act 1989 or was otherwise concerned with a child's maintenance or upbringing. He said that, concerning such a private hearing, matter which *can* be published without breaching section 12 included:

- the names, addresses, or photographs of the child and of adult parties involved in the private proceedings;
- and of witnesses involved;
- the date, time, or place of hearings in the case;
- and 'anything which has been seen or heard by a person conducting himself lawfully in the public corridor or other public precincts outside the court';
- the text or summary of any order made in such a private hearing (unless the court has specifically prohibited its publication).

As an example of what information could be legally published under section 12 as regards 'the nature of the dispute', he said it would not prohibit publication that such private proceedings concerned an issue of whether a mother had attempted to smother or poison her children. He noted though that if anonymity was in place for a child under the 1989 Children Act or there was another restriction, imposed by the court, this would limit what could otherwise be published from the matter he listed.

- As this chapter has already stated, a journalist should realise that there is a particular risk in defamation law when publishing a report of court proceedings held in private, because no privilege applies.

→ see also ch. 19 on privilege

In *Clibbery v Allan* [2002] EWCA Civ 45; [2002] Fam 261; [2002] 1 FLR 565 the Court of Appeal ruled that it was not contempt for one of the parties in a Family Division case to disclose to a newspaper matter from proceedings held in chambers when the matter related to a dispute between adults over money or property (rather than a dispute concerning children). Public disclosure could be made lawfully in the absence of: (1) a specific statutory restraint; (2) a lawfully imposed order of the court; (3) an implied undertaking not to make use of material compulsorily disclosed for the hearing; or (4) any restrictions imposed by the duty of confidentiality. This Court of Appeal case concerned a woman disclosing to the *Daily Mail* material placed before a court during her attempt to obtain an occupation order for the flat she had shared with a millionaire businessman for 15 years.

It was established in the Court of Appeal in 1977 that for there to be a contempt in reporting child cases heard in private, it has to be shown that the publisher knew that he/she was publishing information relating to private proceedings, or published the information recklessly, not caring whether or not publication was prohibited (*Re F (A Minor) (Publication of Information)*).

Those who publish material found to be in contempt through breach of the 1960 Act's section 12 can, under section 14 of the Contempt of Court Act 1981, if punished by a superior court (i.e. not by magistrates), be fined an unlimited amount and/or be jailed for up to two years.

Examples of breaches of section 12

In 1994, the *Sun* newspaper was fined £5,000 and its editor £1,000 for contempt arising from the publication of extracts from a doctor's report which had been presented at proceedings before a judge in chambers about a child. In 1998 Mr Justice Wilson in *X v Dempster* [1999] 1 FLR 894 fined the *Daily Mail* £10,000 and the columnist Nigel Dempster £1,000 for contempt after an article revealed that a woman had been portrayed as a bad mother in child proceedings before a judge in chambers. In 2007 the Attorney General considered, but decided not to initiate, a prosecution for contempt after the *Coventry Times* published quotations from a CAFCASS report, prepared for a family court hearing, held in private, which considered claims that a father had sexually assaulted a child. The published story, which aired the mother's complaint that the claims were not properly investigated, preserved anonymity for the child and the adults. But CAFCASS said that the publication of matter from its document could still be considered contempt under section 12. *Media Lawyer* (18 June 2007) reported that the Attorney General had decided that, rather than prosecute for contempt, the public interest would be served by giving the newspaper a chance to highlight in the trade press the contempt danger in such circumstances.

→
see
p. 168
about
CAFCASS

◗ Controversy about family courts

There has been criticism and concern that the family law system is, or is unfairly perceived to be, secretive with hidden flaws, and that this perception arises from its multi-layered restrictions on what information can be disclosed – by the media or parties involved – from its workings, in particular from proceedings heard in private. Its critics include those parents aggrieved by court decisions made against them in highly polarised disputes with ex-partners. One high-profile, critical campaigning group is Fathers For Justice. Other critics, including some journalists, say the current system permits insufficient public scrutiny of the actions of local authorities when children are removed by social workers, sometimes permanently, from their parents in care proceedings. Other groups say the courts sometimes fail to adequately protect women and their children from male ex-partners, some of whom are violent. Leading judges, some of whom want the system to be more open, have expressed frustration that some media reports based on partial, unofficial accounts of court decisions, unfairly represent the difficult work of the family courts, and of social workers.

In December 2008 the Ministry of Justice published a report, 'Family Justice in View', following consultations about how to improve the transparency of, and public confidence, in the family courts. The report said that family courts should make public more of their judgments, anonymised as necessary. It added that legislation would be introduced to give journalists an automatic right of admission to all family courts. But, it said, under any such new law the courts will retain a limited discretion to exclude journalists if this was necessary 'in the interests of children, or for the safety or protection of parties and witnesses'. The report described the several sets of reporting restrictions – described above in this chapter – which apply in the family law system as not comprehensive 'or particularly comprehensible'. It added that the law on reporting restrictions would be revised 'as soon as parliamentary time allows', and that in these revised restrictions, anonymity for children 'will be automatically protected beyond the conclusion of a case, unless the court decides otherwise'. But see Late News, p. xxx.

see
Useful
Websites
below

 Check the Online Resource Centre, where any such change in the law will be posted.

Legal disputes about lifting of children's anonymity

In recent years the courts have increasingly been asked to resolve disputes about whether a child should be the subject of media coverage.

In 1995 the Court of Appeal upheld a High Court injunction, made on child welfare grounds, prohibiting a mother from involving her daughter in a television documentary about treatment she was receiving for her special educational needs (*Re Z (a minor) (Identification: Restriction on Publication)* [1997] Fam 1).

In 2002 a woman wrongly accused of harming her twin babies, who were then placed in foster care, successfully applied, with the support of the *Daily Express*, to the High Court for the anonymity under section 97 of the Children Act to be lifted so that she could be publicly exonerated after her babies were returned to her (*Daily Express*, 17 December 2002).

In 2003 Mr Justice Munby ruled in the High Court that a girl, then shortly to be 17, who had given birth when she was 12, should be allowed to have her story published in a newspaper and be identified in it. The story included her account of how when she was 14 she had unsuccessfully opposed a court order that her baby should be adopted by another family. Mr Justice Munby said he emphatically agreed with the newspaper's assertion that it was in the public interest that the girl should be able to tell her story. Torbay Borough Council had previously secured an injunction which had prevented identification of the girl, her child, or the child's father. The judge varied it to allow the girl to be identified (*Re Roddy (A Child); Torbay Borough Council v News Group Newspapers* [2003] EWHC 2927 (Fam)).

In 2006 Mr Justice Munby, after an application by Nicola and Mark Webster, the BBC, and the Associated Newspapers and Archant newspaper groups, permitted the media to identify the Websters, and their five-month-old son Brandon, despite ongoing care proceedings concerning the child. The couple's three older children had in 2004 been removed from them by Norfolk County Council, and were later permanently adopted by other families, after one of the children was found to have suffered several fractured bones. The Websters had denied this was the result of physical abuse. The media aired their assertion that the removal of their older children had been a miscarriage of justice.

→

see pp.
174–177
on
section 97

In the High Court, Mr Justice Munby waived the anonymity which section 97 of the Children Act 1989 would otherwise have bestowed on Brandon (and therefore on his parents) although a barrister appointed to represent Brandon had argued for it to remain. The judge noted argument by the media that Brandon was too young to be affected by publicity over the case. The judge said that he himself was not in a position to assess whether the Websters 'may not be the martyrs they claim to be'. But, he added, that was not of itself any reason for denying them the right to speak to and be identified by the media. 'It is, after all, the underdog who is often most in need of the help afforded by a fearless, questioning and sceptical press.' The judge made clear that, apart from his acknowledgement of the rights of the Websters and the media under the European Convention's Article 10, he had authorised such publicity about the case for the following reason. After the Websters had alleged that the removal of their three oldest children had been a miscarriage of justice, there was a pressing need for public confidence in the courts system to be restored by a 'public and convincing demonstration' either that no such miscarriage had occurred or by acknowledgement that it had (*Re Brandon Webster, Norfolk County Council v Webster* (2006)). Subsequently Norfolk County Council withdrew care order proceedings in respect of Brandon, being satisfied that the Websters were 'fit and able' to care for him. He continues to live with them. In late 2008 the Court of Appeal heard that, since the Websters' oldest children had been removed from them in 2004, further medical evidence had been obtained. It was argued for the Websters that the child who had been diagnosed in 2004 as having bone fractures had suffered them because of scurvy and/or iron deficiency, and not from any abuse. But the Court of Appeal ruled in 2009 that it was too late to consider returning these children from the adoptive parents (*Nicola and Mark Webster v Norfolk County Council* [2009] EWCA Civ 59).

→ Article 10 protects freedom of expression, see ch. 1, p. 11

The lifting of a child's anonymity need not involve the expense of hiring barristers. In 2008 Mr Justice Munby agreed with a mother's request, which she made to him in emails, that she and two of her children could consent to being identified in media reports of how these children had previously been taken from her and her husband in care proceedings by a local authority. The children had been returned to the couple 10 months later, after the authority agreed this was best for them. The children, aged 10 and 15, had also written to the judge, asking to be allowed to speak out publicly about that case. Mr Justice Munby noted that since the care proceedings were concluded, no anonymity applied to the children under section 97 of the Children Act 1989, and that section 12 of the Administration of Justice Act 1960 – see above, p. 179 – permitted, within certain bounds, reference to the nature of the dispute with the local authority in the care proceedings (*Re B: X Council v B (No 2)* [2008] EWHC 270 (Fam)).

▶ Family law injunctions restricting reports of criminal and inquest proceedings

In the 2004 case of *Re S (A Child) (Identification: Restrictions on Publication)*, the House of Lords ruled that the freedom of the media to report a criminal

→ see p. 179

trial should not be restricted to protect the privacy of the child not involved in that trial, in which a mother was accused of murdering her nine-year-old son by poisoning him with salt. Her younger son, aged eight, was made subject to care proceedings by a local authority. His legal guardian had later applied to the High Court for an injunction designed to prohibit the media from naming the mother or the dead son in reports of the pending murder trial, or publishing photographs of them, or identifying the surviving son. In the House of Lords, Lord Steyn said the publicity impact on the surviving son would be essentially indirect. He added that if such an injunction was granted the process of piling exception upon exception to the principle of open justice would thus be encouraged and would gain momentum, to the detriment of the media's role in reporting criminal cases. He noted that for local newspapers, which did not have the financial resources of national newspapers, the spectre of being involved in such costly legal proceedings to oppose such injunctions was bound to have 'a chilling effect'.

However subsequently, in 2005, the High Court Family Division banned the media from identifying a defendant in a criminal trial, in order to protect her children from publicity, even though they were not involved in that criminal case. The mother was awaiting sentence after admitting knowingly infecting with the HIV virus the father of one of the children. The local authority submitted that if media reports identified the mother as this defendant, placement of her children with foster parents would be prejudiced because of the stigma of HIV, and that it was likely the children would face continued ostracism in the community (*Re W (Children) (Identification: Restrictions on Publication)* [2005] EWHC 1564 (Fam)).

In *Re LM (Reporting Restrictions: Coroner's Inquest)* [2008] 1 FLR 1360, the High Court in 2007 by means of an injunction prohibited the media from referring, in coverage of an inquest, to the existence of a five-year-old girl whose older sister – having been found dead in suspicious circumstances – was the subject of the inquest. The surviving girl had been removed from their parents after a family court concluded the mother had caused her sister's death through ill-treatment. But the High Court refused an application by the legal guardian of the five-year-old that media reports of the inquest should not be permitted to identify the parents or dead girl. It had been argued that publicity naming them would undermine therapy the surviving girl was receiving and jeopardise efforts for her to be adopted.

⠿ Recap of major points

- Family courts are difficult to report, because many of their hearings are in private and because various reporting restrictions apply in many cases.

- But the cases in these courts contain newsworthy stories, some of great public interest.

- It will usually be contempt of court to publish reports of court proceedings held in private concerning a child's upbringing, but it is usually possible to publish other information about such a case and may be possible to publish the court's order or judgment.

- A child involved in ongoing proceedings under the Children Act 1989 should not be identified in media reports of such cases, unless the court authorises it.

- When such a case concludes, it may be possible for the media to identify the child in reports of it.

- The High Court has wide-ranging powers to protect the welfare of children and others, including anonymity orders.

🌐 Useful Websites

www.family-solicitors.co.uk/
  Online guide to family law

www.csa.gov.uk/
  Child Support Agency

www.cafcass.gov.uk/
  Children and Family Court Advisory and Support Service

www.womensaid.org.uk/
  Women's Aid

www.justice.gov.uk/publications/cp1007.htm
  Ministry of Justice (2008) 'Family Justice in View', Cm 7502

www.dca.gov.uk/consult/courttransparencey1106/consultation1106.pdf
  Department for Constitutional Affairs (2006) 'Confidence and confidentiality: Improving transparency and privacy in family courts', Cm 6886

12

Open justice and access to court information

Chapter summary

This chapter explains why the principle of open justice is vital to society. The journalist is the public's eyes and ears in courtrooms. Journalists need to know their rights as regards admission to courts. The law does authorise courts to sit →glossary **in private** for some matters. This chapter explains these rights of admission in criminal and civil courts generally. Other chapters refer to these rights for specific types of court – youth courts in ch. 7, family courts in ch. 11, coroners courts in ch. 14, and employment tribunals in ch. 15. This chapter also explains what rights citizens, and therefore journalists, have to see court documents in civil cases. It also explains the assistance that criminal courts are required to give to reporters covering cases. Chapter 13 explains how a journalist, if told by a court that he/she is not allowed in the courtroom, can challenge that decision.

▶ A fundamental rule in common law

On occasion, courts seek to exclude the public and journalists when the law does not permit them to do so. There are certain limited circumstances →glossary when statute or **common law** requires a court to sit in private, either *in cam-* →glossary *era* or *in chambers* – see below.

But as long ago as 1913, the House of Lords in *Scott v Scott* [1913] AC 417 affirmed the general rule in common law that courts must administer justice in public. One of the law lords in that case, Lord Atkinson said:

> The hearing of a case in public may be, and often is, no doubt, painful, humiliating, or deterrent both to parties and witnesses, and in many cases, especially those of a criminal nature, the details may be so indecent as to tend to injure public morals, but all this is tolerated and endured, because it is felt that in public trial is to found, on the whole, the best security for the pure, impartial, and efficient administration of justice, the best means for winning for it public confidence and respect.

 See the Online Resource Centre, ch. 12, for background to the case of Scott v Scott.

A major benefit of open justice is that if a witness testifies in public proceedings he/she is less likely to lie, because a lie told in public is more likely to be exposed than one made behind closed doors. Other benefits of open justice were categorised by Lord Woolf, when Master of the Rolls, in the Court of Appeal judgment in *R v Legal Aid Board ex p Kaim Todner* [1998] 3 All ER 541:

> It is necessary because the public nature of proceedings deters inappropriate behaviour on the part of the court. It also maintains the public's confidence in the administration of justice. It enables the public to know that justice is being administered impartially. It can result in evidence becoming available which would not become available if the proceedings were conducted behind closed doors or with one or more of the parties' or witnesses' identity concealed. It makes uninformed and inaccurate comment about the proceedings less likely.

As Lord Woolf noted, any reporting restriction imposed is a departure from the open justice principle. Such restrictions must have an overriding justification in law. Chapter 13 deals with specific grounds on which reporting restrictions can be challenged by journalists, and explains the procedures by which a journalist can challenge a restriction or a court's decision to refuse him/her admission to a court hearing. The foundation of either such challenge is that general benefits always flow from open justice.

- The term in chambers refers to occasions when a judge holds a hearing at a courthouse in a room allocated for his/her use which is not a large, formal courtroom. This may well be a **preliminary hearing** in the case. → glossary

- The term in camera tends to be used when the public and media are excluded from all or part of the main hearing in a case – e.g. a criminal trial – which is being held in a courtroom.

- The term 'in private' is used to cover both the above terms, although a hearing may be held in chambers for administrative convenience rather than because of a decision or rule that it should be private – see below, p. 197.

Role of the media

The vital role of the court reporter as trustee for the wider public has been recognised in many judgments. For example, Lord Justice Watkins said in *R v Felixstowe Justices ex p Leigh* [1987] QB 582; [1987] 1 All ER 551:

→

see more about this case, below, p. 199

66 The role of the journalist and his importance for the public interest in the administration of justice has been commented upon on many occasions. No-one nowadays surely can doubt that his presence in court for the purpose of reporting proceedings conducted therein is indispensable. Without him, how is the public to be informed of how justice is being administered in our courts? The journalist has been engaged upon this task in much the same way as he performs it today for well over 150 years. 99

Common law exceptions to open justice

It is generally acknowledged that exclusion of the press and public from a court case is only justified in common law in three types of circumstance:

- *when their presence would frustrate the process of justice* – for example, when a woman or child cannot be persuaded to give evidence of intimate sexual matters in the presence of many strangers;
- *when unchecked publicity would defeat the whole object of the proceedings*, e.g.
  - when a civil case concerns ownership of a trade secret, and publicity would reveal the secret to commercial rivals; or
  - when either a civil case or a criminal prosecution concerns a matter relating to the security of the State (national security), and publicity

could damage that security if, for instance, military or intelligence secrets were revealed;

- *when the court is exercising a parental role to protect the interests of vulnerable people, mainly,*
  - *children,* for example, wardship and other family law cases, *or*
  - *people with mental incapacity or mental illness* (what used to be referred to as lunacy cases); and unchecked publicity could harm the welfare of such vulnerable people.

→ see, ch. 9 p. 135 and ch. 11

Emphasising that there is only limited scope in common law to override the open justice rule, Lord Diplock indicated in 1979, in a House of Lords judgment often quoted by judges, that the rule should only be departed from:

❝ where the nature or circumstances of the particular proceeding are such that the application of the general rule in its entirety would frustrate or render impracticable the administration of justice or would damage some other public interest for whose protection Parliament has made some statutory **derogation** from the rule (*Attorney General v Leveller Magazine Ltd* [1979] AC 440 at 449, 450). ❞

→glossary

> See the Online Resource Centre, ch. 12, for background to the case of *Attorney General v Leveller Magazine Ltd.*

As this chapter explains, statutes and procedural rules created by **statutory instruments** give courts powers in specific circumstances to exclude the public and, in some instances, the press too. These statutory powers cover, to an extent, the same kinds of occasions which justify such exclusion in common law. If no such statutory power applies to a particular case, a court which believes such exclusion is justified can use common law powers.

→glossary

▶ Other landmark decisions in common law on open justice

In 1983 magistrates in Surrey were persuaded to exclude press and public when the court heard a speech in mitigation made on behalf of a defendant who had given assistance to the police. Subsequently, the magistrates were strongly criticised in the High Court, when this exclusion was challenged.

→ see ch. 5, p. 63 on mitigation

Lord Justice Ackner said hearing a matter in private was a course of last resort to be adopted only if the proceedings in open court would frustrate the process of justice (*R v Reigate Justices, ex p Argus Newspapers* (1983) 5 Cr App R (S) 181).

In another case, in 1987 Malvern magistrates excluded press and public during a speech in mitigation about the personal circumstances of a woman who admitted driving with excess alcohol. The High Court later ruled that although magistrates were entitled to use their discretion to sit in camera, it was undesirable that they should do so unless there were rare, compelling reasons (*R v Malvern Justices, ex p Evans* [1988] QB 540; [1988] 1 All ER 371, QBD).

Exclusion of public and press should be no longer than is necessary Lord Lane, Lord Chief Justice, said in the Court of Appeal in 1989 that a judge should be alive to the importance of adjourning into open court as soon as exclusion of the public was not plainly necessary (*Re Crook (Tim)* (1991) 93 Cr App R 17, CA).

Journalists can sometimes stay when public excluded If the public are lawfully excluded, it does not follow that journalists must necessarily go too. In 1989 in the Court of Appeal Lord Lane said it would not be right generally to distinguish between excluding the press and excluding the public. There might be cases, however, during which the press should not be excluded with the other members of the public, such as a prosecution for importing an indecent film, where the film was shown to the jury and some members of the public might gasp or giggle and make the jury's task more difficult (*R v Crook (Tim)* (1989) 139 NLJ 1633 CA).

▌ Articles 6 and 10

see ch. 1, on Conventions and Appendix 1, p. 565

Article 6 of the European Convention on Human Rights states that everyone is entitled to a fair and *public* hearing within a reasonable time by an independent and impartial tribunal established by law. However, the rights which the Article primarily protects are not those of the media or of the wider public, as regards the need for justice to be transparent, but those of the parties in civil litigation or someone being prosecuted in criminal law. Geoffrey Robertson and Andrew Nicol, in their book *Media Law*, state that the common law protects open justice more than Article 6 does (see Book list p. 579). They suggest that if those involved in a court case use the exceptions in Article 6 to argue against it being heard in public, counter-argument should include reference to section 11 of the Human Rights Act 1998. This states that the Convention does not restrict existing rights in a nation's law, i.e. in this context, the UK common law's protection of open justice for the benefit of society.

Article 10, which protects the right to freedom of expression and to impart information should be cited by any journalist challenging his/her exclusion from a court.

▌ Statute on open and private hearings

Requirement of magistrates Section 121 of the Magistrates' Courts Act 1980 stipulates that, other than in a circumstance in which another statute permits them to sit in private, magistrates must sit in open court when trying a case or imposing prison sentences or inquiring into an offender's financial circumstances or hearing a complaint in civil law (see ch. 11 for statute governing magistrates' family proceedings). Also, when magistrates are sitting as examining justices at a **committal hearing**, and in hearings leading up to it, they are required by the 1980 Act's section 4 to sit in open court except when 'the ends of justice' would not be served by an open hearing.

→ see ch. 4, p. 48 on committal hearings

Indecent evidence When a witness aged under 18 is giving evidence in a case involving indecency, any court can exclude the public, under section 37 of the Children and Young Persons Act 1933, but cannot under this section exclude journalists.

Sexual history When a court is hearing an application to introduce evidence or questions about a complainant's sexual history, e.g. in a rape case, the court must sit in private – to comply with section 43 of the Youth Justice and Criminal Evidence Act 1999. The court must give its decision and the reasons for it in open court but in the absence of the jury (if there is one).

Vulnerable or intimidated witnesses Under section 25 of the 1999 Act, a court can make a 'special measures direction' to exclude the public and some journalists when a witness deemed 'vulnerable' or 'intimidated' is due to give evidence in a sexual offence case or when it appears to the court that there are reasonable grounds for believing that any person other than the defendant has sought, or will seek, to intimidate the witness. However, the Act states that one journalist must be allowed to remain in court. The Act defines journalists as 'representatives of news gathering or reporting organisations'.

→ see ch. 9, p. 139 on special measures generally

Lord Williams of Mostyn QC, then a Home Office Minister, said of section 25: 'We believe the court will rarely want to exclude the press.'

The 1999 Act says that even if, under this provision, some journalists and the public are excluded from a courtroom, these proceedings shall still legally be deemed to be held in public 'for the purposes of any privilege or exemption from liability available in respect of fair, accurate and contemporaneous reports', a reference to contempt and libel law.

→
see
ch. 16,
p. 288 and
ch. 19 on
privilege

Sentence review for informants Under section 75 of the Serious Organised Crime and Police Act 2005, a Crown court can exclude the public and press when it is reviewing a sentence previously imposed on a defendant who pleaded guilty, and who has given or offered assistance – e.g. information – about a criminal offence to a prosecuting or investigating agency, such as the police. In the review, the original sentence could be reduced as a reward for the assistance. Or if the original sentence was lenient because the defendant had already offered such assistance, the review can increase the sentence if he/she knowingly failed to provide the assistance. But the public and press can only be excluded if the judge considers that exclusion is in the interests of justice and is necessary to protect someone's safety. This might be, for example, because the informant would be at risk of retaliation from other criminals if the fact that assistance was given were to be publicised. In a case where a defendant has failed to honour a pledge of assistance, a journalist has particularly strong grounds to argue that the review of the leniency of the previous sentence should be in open court. The wider public would want to be confident that such a defendant serves a sentence fully reflecting the nature of his/her crime. However, the Act empowers the court to prohibit 'as it thinks appropriate' the publication of 'any matter relating to the proceedings.' The judge may, then, seek to ban the media from referring to the review at all.

Official secrets trials Press and public can be excluded, see ch.31, p. 502

◗ Procedural rules on open justice

Rules of procedure set out in statutory instruments govern how courts operate. Though these are drawn up to reflect the position in common law, see above, or in statute, the wording of some rules gives courts a wide discretion on whether to sit in private. If a court considers excluding a journalist because of a procedural rule, he/she can make representations that it must be interpreted to fully comply with the common law protection of open justice and Article 10. He/she could point to the comment made by Lord Shaw in *Scott v Scott*, stressing that judges must be vigilant that the open justice principle should not be usurped: 'There is no greater danger of usurpation than that which proceeds little by little, under cover of rules of procedure, and at the instance of judges themselves.'

 see above, p. 188

 Courts must construe their rules to be compatible with the Convention, see pp. 10–11.

Criminal cases: rules on open and private hearings

Procedure for criminal cases in magistrates courts, the Crown courts, and the Court of Appeal (Criminal Division) is governed by the Criminal Procedure Rules, as supplemented by the Consolidated Criminal Practice Direction. Rule 16.10 states that when a prosecutor or the defence intends to apply for all or part of a trial to be held in camera for reasons of national security or for the protection of the identity of a witness or of any other person, notice of the intention should be served on the court not less than seven days before the trial is due to begin. The rule also states that the notice shall be displayed in a prominent place within the court precincts. The rule further states that the application itself shall be heard before the jury is sworn and be heard in camera unless the court orders otherwise. The rule adds that if a Court makes an order for a trial to be heard wholly or in part in camera the trial will then be adjourned for 24 hours (which gives the media some time to challenge the order) or, if leave is given to appeal against a decision not to hold the trial in camera, until after the determination of the appeal.

 see Useful Websites below

 see ch. 6, p. 84 on jury procedure

Civil cases: rules on open and private hearings

The Civil Procedure Rules (CPR) govern civil proceedings in the Queen's Bench and Chancery divisions of the High Court and the county courts.

 see Useful Websites, below

 For general information on civil courts, see ch. 10. Other procedural rules apply to the family courts – see ch. 11.

Part 39(2) of the CPR says that the general rule is that a hearing is to be in public but that a hearing, or part of it, may be in private if it falls into any of the following categories:

- publicity would defeat the object of the hearing;

- it involves matters relating to national security;

- it involves confidential information (including information relating to personal financial matters) and publicity would damage that confidentiality;

- it is necessary to protect the interest of any child or protected party;

→ glossary

- it is an application **without notice** and it would be unjust to any respondent for there to be a public hearing i.e. one party to the case is not yet aware of the proceedings;

- it involves uncontentious matters arising in the administration of trusts or of a deceased's estate;

- the court considers it to be necessary in the interests of justice.

The practice direction which supplements this rule lists types of case which shall, 'in the first instance', be listed as private. These include a claim by a mortgagee for possession of land; landlords' applications for possession of residential property because rent is allegedly owed; and proceedings brought under the Consumer Credit Act 1974 and the Protection from Harassment Act 1997 (the latter would include some domestic violence cases). A journalist can make representations to the judge that a case in these categories should be heard in public. The practice direction states that the judge should have regard to 'any representations' made and to Article 6. If one of the parties also wants the hearing to be in public, this strengthens the journalist's arguments.

→

see above, p. 192 on Article 6

Part 39.2 also states: 'The court may order that the identity of any party or witness must not be disclosed if it considers non-disclosure necessary in order to protect the interests of that party or witness.'

Professor CJ Miller, author of *Contempt of Court*, has written that the problem with this rule is that the focal point is the interests of parties and witnesses, and it does not address the competing requirement of freedom of expression under Article 10 of the European Convention on Human Rights. 'In any event section 3 of the Human Rights Act will require all such delegated legislation to be construed so far as is possible in a way compatible with the Convention rights'. The courts must interpret the rule with this requirement in mind.

There is provision in the CPR for other types of hearing to be held in private. A journalist excluded from a civil court should ask what rule applies.

→

see ch. 13 on challenging court decisions

A judge may decide to have a small claims hearing in private. Judges also deal in private with arbitration, many family disputes, and routine matters. When dealing with arbitration, they can give leave for other people to attend, although this is exceptional.

The practice direction says that, where there is no sign on the door of the court or of the judge's room (if a case is heard there), indicating that proceedings are in private, members of the public will be admitted where practicable. A judge may adjourn the proceedings to a larger room or court if he/she thinks it appropriate.

▶ Contempt and libel issues in reports of private hearings

If a journalist discovers what has been said within a court hearing held in private, then to publish such material, and matter from documents prepared for use in the case, could in respect of some types of case be an offence of contempt of court. Also publication of matter from a private hearing in any court case:

see ch. 9, p. 130

- is not protected by section 4 of the Contempt of Court Act 1981 should such publication create a substantial risk of serious prejudice to later stages of the same case or to another 'active' case;

see p. 288

- and is not protected by **privilege**, even if the report is a fair and accurate account of the court hearing, if someone defamed by what is published sues for libel.

→ glossary

see ch. 19 on privilege

Non-private hearings in chambers in criminal and civil cases

In various circumstances in criminal and civil law, a hearing will be held in chambers – that is, in the judge's room. For example, in civil cases pretrial, case management decisions to expedite progress towards a trial are sometimes made by a judge in chambers. A hearing may be held in chambers, rather than in public in a courtroom, merely because of routine, administrative convenience. The matter being discussed may not be of the type recognised in common law or statute as requiring a private hearing.

The Master of the Rolls, Lord Woolf (later Lord Chief Justice), said in the Court of Appeal in February 1998 that the public had no right to attend hearings in chambers but, if requested, permission should be granted for them, and journalists, to attend if this was practical and the case was not within the categories listed in section 12 of the Administration of Justice

→
see p.
130 on
1960 Act

Act 1960. He added that if those who sought to attend a non-private hearing in chambers could not be accommodated in the room, the judge should consider adjourning the whole or the part or the proceedings into open court or allowing one or more representatives of the press to attend the hearing in chambers (*Hodgson v Imperial Tobacco* [1998] 2 All ER 673; [1998] 1 WLR 1056). Lord Woolf added that a judgment or order made in a case in chambers was normally a public document even though there was no right to inspect it without leave. He said that such a judgment or order could and should be made available when requested.

→
see also
below,
p. 203 on
civil judg-
ments

Bail applications at Crown court

→ glossary

Mr Justice Gray said in the Queen's Bench Division in 2006 that bail applications in the Crown court, including those in which a defendant is seeking to overturn a refusal by magistrates to grant bail, should normally be held in public (*Malik v Central Criminal Court* [2006] EWHC 1539 (Admin)). The Criminal Procedure Rules (rule 16.11), he said, allowed that applications *may* be dealt with by a judge in chambers but this was not to be taken as a presumption in favour of their being held in private.

Court of Appeal and House of Lords/Supreme Court

The Court of Appeal rarely sits in private in either its Criminal or Civil Divisions. It is rare for witnesses to give evidence in person at either that court or the House of Lords (due to be known from October 2009 as the **Supreme Court**) because cases are decided on the basis of legal argument and by reference to case documents.

→ glossary

◗ What information and assistance must criminal courts provide to journalists?

→
see
Useful
Websites,
below

Part III.30.16–18 of the Consolidated Criminal Practice Direction, which applies to criminal courts, states:

❝ Facilities for reporting the proceedings...must be provided. But the court may restrict the number of reporters attending in the courtroom to such number as is judged practicable and desirable. In ruling on any challenged claim to attend in the courtroom for the purpose of reporting the court should be mindful of the public's general right to be informed about the administration of justice. ❞

The direction adds that if it is decided to limit access to a courtroom, arrangements should be made for the proceedings to be relayed, audibly and if possible visually, to another room in the same court complex to which the media and the public have access if it appears there is need for this.

 See also below, p. 200, on journalistic access to documents used in court cases.

Names of magistrates

The High Court ruled in 1987 in *R v Felixstowe Justices, ex p Leigh*, that the names of magistrates dealing with a case must be made known to press and public.

In that judgment, Lord Justice Watkins said any attempt to preserve anonymity was inimical to the proper administration of justice, adding: 'There is, in my view, no such person known to the law as the anonymous JP'. This case was a **judicial review** of the policy of magistrates in the Felixstowe →glossary area not to disclose their names. Their justices' clerk had refused a request made by journalist David Leigh, then chief reporter with the *Observer*, for the names of magistrates who had heard a particular case.

Names, charges, and other details of defendants

The Ministry of Justice commends the practice of magistrates courts making their daily lists, of defendants due in court, available to journalists. A Home Office circular (number 80/1989) said that these court lists should contain each defendant's name, age, address, the charge he/she faces and, where known, his/her occupation. But it is unclear whether any form of qualified privilege protects a fair and accurate, media report of information from a court list, should anyone sue for libel because of error in the list. A journalist at a court hearing should quote the defendant's details and charge(s) in the form these were stated in the hearing, and not rely on the list. A report of the hearing *will* be protected by privilege, if the relevant defence's requirements are met, see ch. 19.

The Ministry also approves of magistrates courts supplying to local media copies of court 'registers'. By law the courts keep these to briefly record each day's proceedings, with details of convicted defendants and punishments. It is unclear whether privilege protects a media report based on these registers, should any register be inaccurate. But it is common for newspapers to publish reports based on them. In 2008 the Government announced that magistrates courts will provide to the media lists and registers without making a charge. Previously the courts had discretion to levy charges.

The Judicial Studies Board's publication 'Reporting Restrictions: Magistrates Courts' states that justices' clerks can, without breaching data protection law, assist reporters' checks on the progress of cases and on defendants' names, charges and 'or other matters'. See Useful Websites, below. See also p. 431 on court clerks' discretion to provide information to reporters.

The Home Office, in circular no. 78/1967 and in a similar circular in 1969, recommended that the names and addresses of defendants should be stated orally in magistrates courts. The 1967 circular stated: 'A person's address is as much part of his description as his name. There is, therefore, a strong public interest in facilitating press reports that correctly describe persons involved.' See also ch. 18, p. 320, on good practice to avoid libel actions.

→
see also
ch. 13,
p. 214–215

The High Court ruled in 1988 that a defendant's address should normally be stated in court (*R v Evesham Justices, ex p McDonagh* [1988] QB 553; [1988] 1 All ER 371).

The guide to reporting restrictions in the magistrates courts, issued by the Judicial Studies Board, says: 'Announcement in open court of names and addresses enables the precise identification vital to distinguish a defendant from someone in the locality who bears the same name and avoids inadvertent defamation.' See also below, p. 204 for detail of a public register which shows if an individual has not paid a fine imposed by magistrates or by a Crown court.

Facts of an admitted case

→
see
above,
p. 195

Part III.26 of the Consolidated Criminal Practice Direction requires the facts relating to any charge to which a defendant has pleaded guilty to be stated in open court before sentence is imposed, to enable the public and press to know the circumstances of the offence.

Details of witnesses in criminal cases

A Home Office statement on standards of witness care, issued in 1998, said that unless it was necessary for evidential purposes, defence and prosecution witnesses should not be required to disclose their addresses in open court.

▌ Journalistic access to documents used in court cases

As regards contempt law, journalists can safely report information from documents used in court cases if read out in open court or officially provided to them by the court.

However, if any other document is given to a journalist by one party in a case, e.g. the defendant, but it is a document originally submitted in the proceedings by the other side, there is a risk as regards some types of document that publication of matter from it will be regarded as an offence of contempt of court. See ch. 9, p. 132.

A media organisation may face a libel action if it publishes from a document defamatory matter which was not read out in open court, because no privilege protects such publication unless the document was officially made available by a court as being part of its proceedings or by law is open to public inspection.

see
ch. 19, on
privilege

Access to documents in criminal cases

See ch. 6, p. 87, for details of a protocol agreed by the Crown Prosecution Service about what material can be released to the media for use in background features after a case ends.

Access to documents in civil cases

The Civil Procedure Rules 1998 (CPR) were amended in 2006 to allow non-parties to civil cases, such as journalists, greater access to documents filed with the court, as regards a claim lodged with it after 2 October 2006.

see
above, p.
195 and
Useful
Websites
below

This access is particularly important in view of the modern practice of civil cases being largely conducted by reference to documents rather than by the systematic taking of oral evidence. As chapter 10 explains, if a reporter has not read key documents, a civil trial may be impossible to report meaningfully.

Pending and ongoing civil trials Under Part 5.4C of the CPR the general position is that a non-party, e.g. a journalist, who pays the prescribed fee may obtain from the central office or at a district registry of the High Court, or from a county court, a copy of any 'statement of case' if the relevant claim has been listed for a hearing and all defendants have filed acknowledgements of service or defences.

Statement of case, which is defined in Part 2.3, means the **claim form**, particulars of claim (if not in the claim form), defence, and also any counterclaim or reply to the defence. For further detail, see Part 16 of the CPR. 'Further information documents' supplied in response to a request under Part 18 of the rules are also included in a statement of case. Court staff are responsible for administering the rule in the first instance, and they will ask a judge if unsure. A statement of case does not include witness statements. However, Part 32.13 provides that: 'A witness statement which stands as

see pp.
155–156
on such
docu-
ments

evidence-in-chief is open to inspection during the course of the trial unless the court otherwise directs.' This enables public access during the course of the trial to written evidence relied on in court but not read out. However, the court may direct that, because of the interests of justice, the public interest, or the nature of any medical evidence or confidential information, or because of the need to protect the interests of any child or protected party, a witness statement should not be made available (see also below, p. 203, on access to documents in a civil case after it is concluded). A non-party may obtain a copy of any other document filed with the court if the court gives permission. But a party or any person identified in a statement of case may apply to the court for availability of such documents to be restricted, and/or for them to be edited before non-parties are allowed to see them.

⠿ Point for consideration

The Court of Appeal has ruled that if a party to a civil court case objects to a document being made available for publication, a court will require 'specific reasons' why the party will be damaged by its publication, and that 'simple assertions of confidentiality', even if supported by both parties in the case, should not prevail (*Lilly Icos Ltd v Pfizer Ltd* [2002] EWCA Civ 02).

see ch. 19, p. 345

Qualified privilege will protect media reports of documents made available to the media as copies, or for public inspection, by a court, if the defence's requirements are met.

> Again, remember that family courts have their own procedural rules, which stipulate that no document shall be disclosed other than to a limited range of people – see ch. 10.

Skeleton arguments The judge in the *Chan* case, see below, made clear he had no objection to Mr Chan or his legal team having already provided the *Guardian* with a copy of their skeleton argument – i.e. the document summarising their arguments in law. Lord Justice Judge said in the Court of Appeal in 2003 that barristers should give journalists copies of the skeleton arguments they prepare for court hearings if they were asked to do so. He said it would be a waste of time for the skeletons to be repeated in court. The court had concluded that the principle of open justice led inexorably to the conclusion that written skeleton arguments, or those parts of skeleton arguments adopted by **counsel** and treated by the court as forming part of an oral submission, should be disclosed when a request to do so was received.

→ glossary

Judgments and orders The practice direction which supplements Part 39 of the Civil Procedure Rules states that when a hearing takes place in open court members of the public can obtain a transcript of any judgment given or a copy of any order made, subject to payment of the appropriate fee. When a judgment is given or an order is made in a private hearing, a non-party wanting a copy will need permission from the judge involved. Mr Justice Jacob said in the Chancery Division in January 1998 that, with very rare exceptions, and even when a hearing had been in private, no judgment could be regarded as a secret document. The best way to avoid ill-informed comments in the media in a case of high public interest was for the court to be as open as possible (*Forbes v Smith* [1998] 1 All ER 973).

 See ch. 10, p. 162 for information about bankruptcy records and ch. 11, p. 170 for divorce records. See below, p. 204, for details of the public register of monetary judgments.

Access to statements of case and witness statements after a civil case concludes

A High Court case in 2004 resolved the question whether a journalist could obtain access to witness statements relating to a case which had concluded – including from cases which had been settled, i.e. there had been no judgment.

The *Guardian* applied to the court for access to witness statements in a case involving Alvis Vehicles Ltd, a subsidiary of BAE Systems, an armaments company. Alvis was being sued by a businessman Chan U Seek, who said he was entitled to a commission arising from sales of military vehicles to an overseas government. The newspaper has for several years investigated BAE's paying of commissions (see the *Guardian*'s website). A *Guardian* reporter attended some hearings of the case, but then it was unexpectedly settled. Alvis opposed the newspaper seeing witness statements. But the judge Mr Justice Park, equating the press with the public, said: 'The public should not, by reason of modern practice, lose the ability to know the contents of witness statement evidence-in-chief which they would have had under the earlier practice when evidence-in-chief was given orally.' In the judge's view, a successful application to inspect witness statements, as well as for a statement of case, see above, could be made after a case had ended. The judge also said: 'The fact that The *Guardian* did not have a reporter permanently in court does not in my view make any difference.' (Note, however, that because Alvis objected to the witness statements being provided to the *Guardian*, the judge held a hearing to decide this issue, and that therefore the newspaper, had it not succeeded in its application, could have been held liable for Alvis's costs for the hearing (*Chan U Seek v Alvis Vehicles Ltd and Guardian Newspapers*, [2004] EWHC 3092 (Ch)).

Public register of monetary judgments and fines

A public register, under the control of the Ministry of Justice, shows the names and addresses of people and businesses with county court and High Court monetary judgments against them, if these sums were not paid within a required timescale. The register also shows if these are recorded as being paid later or as still unpaid. This information stays on the register for six years. It is run by the Registry Trust and can be searched online. Not all categories of High Court judgments are shown.

→ see Useful Websites, below

In recent years, the register has been extended to include similar records in respect of:

- fines which were not paid quickly, or which remain unpaid, after being imposed in criminal cases by magistrates courts or Crown courts
- Child Support Agency liability orders (see ch. 11, p. 167).

There is a small fee to search the register. Any person wishing to search it needs to input both the name and address of the person/business he/she is interested in. A fair and accurate report of matter on the register is protected, as regards a libel action, by qualified privilege if all requirements of that defence are met – see ch. 19, p. 345. Care should be taken to understand what the register shows.

Recap of major points

- The benefits of open justice protect both the individuals on trial and society as a whole.
- Common law, statute, and courts' procedural rules enshrine the open justice principle, but do permit courts to sit in private in some circumstances.

- If the court has discretion under procedural rules on whether to exclude a journalist, he/she can argue that the rules must be interpreted in compliance with Article 10 of the European Convention on Human Rights.

- Precedent cases make clear that courts must provide reporters with the names of magistrates, and that defendants' addresses should normally be given in open court.

- The Civil Procedure Rules enable journalists to get copies of and inspect documents in civil cases.

- There is a public register of monetary judgments in civil cases, and of fines imposed in criminal cases by magistrates and Crown courts which were not paid as required.

🌍 Useful Websites

www.justice.gov.uk/criminal/procrules_fin/contents/practice_direction/pd_consolidated.htm

Consolidated Criminal Practice Direction

www.justice.gov.uk/criminal/procrules_fin/

Criminal Procedure Rules

www.justice.gov.uk/civil/procrules _fin/index.htm

Civil Procedure Rules

www.jsboard.co.uk/publications.htm

Judicial Studies Board publications

www.trustonline.org.uk/about-us/

Registry Trust public register

13

Challenging the courts

Chapter summary

A journalist needs to be able to recognise when a court has imposed, or is considering imposing, a reporting restriction which is not justified by the case's circumstances or which is legally invalid. A journalist must be prepared to challenge such a restriction, because he or she may be the only person in court arguing for the open justice principle. This chapter provides details of precedent cases which a journalist can cite in court in these challenges. The chapter also explains the methods for making such challenges, and for a journalist to contest a court's decision to deny him/her admission to the courtroom. A court which imposes constraints on media coverage of a case should listen to journalists who oppose or query these. This chapter also outlines the legal routes for the media to take a challenge to a higher court, if argument fails to persuade the lower court.

▎ The necessity of challenges

The court reporter of today needs to know considerably more law on reporting restrictions than his/her predecessors knew. Year by year Parliament has passed new Acts which include restrictions, as other chapters explain, in particular ch. 9. There is also an enduring tendency for courts to seek to restrict the reporting of some cases to a greater extent than statute or legal precedent permit or without fully realising the overall effect on what can be published. Chapter 12 sets out the general benefits to society of open justice. These accrue most fully from unrestricted reporting. A journalist, when challenging grounds on which a reporting restriction has been imposed or is proposed, should – in addition to specific points made about the particular case – allude to those general benefits. Also, as ch. 12 makes clear, it is only in highly exceptional cases that a court should sit in private. A journalist glossary wanting to challenge being shut out of a court case should refer to ch. 12 as well as to this chapter.

> → Chapter 11 explains that, compared to other types of court, family courts have greater authority to sit in private and to impose restrictions.

▶ An invalid restriction has to be obeyed, until a court rescinds it

When a court makes an order, those subject to it, including journalists, are under a duty to obey it unless the court can be persuaded to lift or relax it. Mr Justice Eady said in 2002 that it was the obligation of every person against, or in respect of, whom an order was made by a court of competent jurisdiction to obey it unless and until that order was discharged. The obligation extended, he said, even to cases where the person affected believed the order to be irregular, or even void. The person should come to the court and not take it upon himself to determine such a question (*Lakah Group and Ramy Lakah v Al Jazeera Satellite Channel* [2002] EWHC 2500; [2002] All ER (D) 383 (Nov) (QB)).

▶ The media's right to be heard in court

It is well established that a court which proposes to sit in private or which has imposed a reporting restriction, or which is considering imposing one, should consider representations made by the media about this.

For example, Lord Bingham, then Lord Chief Justice, said in the High Court in 2000 that there was nothing which precluded magistrates from hearing a representative of the press, either orally or in writing:

❝ Of course, a reporter in that position does not enjoy formal rights of audience, but it is within the experience of this court, and of other judges in other courts, that on occasion the observations of the press are invited, and that can be a valuable process since a reporter may well have a legitimate point to make and one which will save the court from falling into error (*McKerry v Teesdale and Wear Valley Justices* (2000) 164 JP 355; [2000] Crim LR 594). 🙰

→
see
Useful
Websites,
below

Referring to orders made under the Contempt of Court Act 1981, the Consolidated Criminal Practice Direction, which supplements procedural rules in criminal cases, states in Part 1.3.2: 'When considering whether to make such an order there is nothing which precludes the court from hearing a representative of the press. Indeed it is likely that the court will wish to do so.' The direction adds that courts will normally give notice to the press that such an order has been made, that a permanent record of such orders should be kept, and that court staff should be prepared to answer any inquiry about any such order.

→
see
Useful
Websites,
below

Guidance material is issued by the Judicial Studies Board on reporting restrictions in the Crown courts and magistrates courts. This states:

🙰 There will be cases where the court will be assisted before making an order by receiving either written or oral representations from the media. Factors known to the media may not be apparent from the [case] papers and neither the prosecution nor the defence may be aware of them or have any particular interest in advancing them. It is sensible always to consider inviting such representations. 🙰

The guidance also advises courts to allow the media to make representations about orders already made.

▌ Methods of challenge

Later in this chapter detail is given of specific grounds on which various reporting restrictions can be opposed. As regards the raising of such an issue, a reporter in court should, obviously, not disrupt the court's proceedings to do so. But the earlier the issue is raised, the better – see below, p. 210, about the risk of adverse costs being awarded.

An approach to the court by a reporter or editor

In any type of court, the reporter – ideally after having checked, if necessary, what relevant law says – should approach the court clerk as the first step to raising a query about or to challenge a reporting restriction. This approach should be made either before a hearing gets under way, or in an adjournment, or if necessary by asking an usher to pass the clerk a note. This approach can also be used to query why a court is in closed session, if this has not been made clear.

In respect of an order already made to impose a restriction, or to exclude a reporter from the courtroom, the clerk can be asked to:

- provide it in written form, if it has not already been provided or displayed;
- specify in writing why it was made, if the order does not make this clear;
- state in writing under what statute it was made, and which section of the statute, if the order itself does not make this clear.

It is possible that a court has used, or has purported to have used, **common law** power to make the order, rather than statute, but such a request should discover if this is so.

 → glossary

Any such request to the clerk may prompt the court to reconsider the order's validity, especially if a reporter – or an editor by fax, letter, or email – quotes case references which suggest the order is invalid.

→ see also p. 212 and ch. 12, p. 190 on common law powers

- The Court of Appeal has said that when an oral order is made restricting reporting, a written copy of it should be drawn up as soon as possible and be made available for inspection at the relevant court's office. The Court of Appeal also suggested that each court's daily list should make clear for any relevant case that such an order applied to it (*R v Central Criminal Court, ex p Crook and Godwin* [1995] 2 FCR 153).

Under Article 10 of the European Convention on Human Rights, all citizens, including the media, have rights to freedom of expression and to receive and impart information.

- When a journalist opposes a reporting restriction, or being excluded from a court, the court should be asked to take into account the media's, and the public's, rights under Article 10.

Article 10 does qualify rights in various ways.

Once alerted that a reporter wants to raise an issue, the magistrates or judge may ask him/her to address the court. An inexperienced reporter may feel some trepidation in doing this, but should be confident that he/she may well have a chance of success. He/she can cite cases from this chapter.

 → see Appendix 1, p. 566

The advantages of a reporter raising a query or challenge in person or of an editor writing to the court, are:

- this method can resolve the matter quickly;
- it is the cheapest method of query or challenge – because there is no need to involve a lawyer.

A challenge to a reporting restriction does not necessarily have to demand that it be completely rescinded, but can suggest it be changed in some respect.

Costs in this approach

Normally if a journalist adopts this direct but relatively informal approach the court will not make a costs order against him/her or any media employer, even if the challenge fails. But it is important to make a challenge as early as possible. In 2006 Brighton magistrates refused a defence application for a costs order against *The Argus* after one of its reporters challenged a reporting restriction imposed at an earlier hearing when no reporter was present. The restriction banned the identification of four juveniles in reports of ASBO proceedings. Defence lawyers said the restriction should have been challenged when it was imposed. But the reporter, Claire Truscott, said it would be disproportionate for the newspaper to have to pay costs for making a legitimate representation (*Media Lawyer*, 3 August 2006).

→
see also
below, p.
237 on
ASBOs

After a barrister, on behalf of media organisations, applied unsuccessfully to a family court for a case it was hearing to be in public, Mr Justice Sumner said in *A v Times Newspapers* [2002] EWHC 2444 (Fam); [2003] 1 All ER 587 that if the media knew in advance that a hearing would be subject to restrictions but delayed, until after the hearing began, in applying for the restrictions to be lifted, and thereby caused disruption to its progress, they risked an order for costs being made against them – whether the application was successful or not. He said that they were unlikely to incur the risk of adverse costs if they made an application before a family court hearing began if they presented an arguable, though unsuccessful, case.

Challenges taken to a higher court

If an approach by a reporter, or by an editor in correspondence, does not persuade a court to lift, or not to impose, a reporting restriction, or that a hearing should not be held in private, its decision can be challenged in a higher court.

Judicial review of restrictions imposed by magistrates

- A journalist or media organisation can apply to the Queen's Bench Divisional Court, a part of the High Court, for a **judicial review** of the legality of a decision by a magistrates court.

→glossary

The disadvantages are that:

- this will normally involve hiring lawyers, and there will be a court fee;
- if this challenge fails, some or all of the costs of any party which opposed the application may well have to be met by the journalist or media organisation.

An applicant may have to bear costs even when successful. For example, when the High Court ruled in 1995 that an employment tribunal had exceeded its powers in excluding reporters from a sexual harassment case, the INS agency and Express Newspapers, the applicants in the review, were not awarded their costs, estimated at £10,000.

see ch. 15, p. 263

Crown court restrictions can be challenged at the Court of Appeal

- Reporting restrictions imposed by a Crown court judge, or a decision made by such a judge that a Crown court hearing shall be in private, can be challenged by using section 159 of the Criminal Justice Act 1988, which gives the media a route of appeal to the Court of Appeal.

see ch. 6, p. 88 for Court of Appeal

The disadvantages are:

- the Court of Appeal may not consider the appeal very quickly, and so a story's news value may have perished by the time it considers the case;
- the appeal will normally involve hiring lawyers, paying a court fee, and, even if the appeal is successful, legal costs (there is no right to recover costs from any other party).
- The appeal can only be made in writing. There is no right for an appellant using section 159 to appear in person before the Court of Appeal to argue the case.

A similar provision to section 159 was included in the Armed Forces Act 2006 to allow the media to appeal against orders restricting the reporting of, or banning the press and the public from courts martial. This followed objections by the media that they were not allowed to appeal against a

see ch. 6, p. 92 on courts martial

judge's banning of all reporting of the court martial of a soldier accused of abusing Iraqi civilians being held as looters.

▶ Limits of common law power to ban publication of defendants' identities

→glossary

It has been ruled that Crown courts or magistrates – unlike the High Court – do *not* have a general, common law **inherent jurisdiction** to ban the media from publishing the identities of defendants in criminal cases (*R v Newtownabbey Magistrates' Court, ex p Belfast Telegraph Newspapers Ltd* (1997) *The Times*, 27 August and [1997] NI 309; *Re Trinity Mirror plc and others* [2008] QB 770 [2008] EWCA Crim 50). In the latter ruling, the Court →glossary of Appeal ruled that an **injunction** issued by a Crown Court, unless directly linked 'to the proper dispatch of the business before it' – a defendant's trial, and in the event of conviction, sentencing – lacked the appropriate jurisdiction. See detail about this case on p. 215.

> See also ch. 11, p. 186, for an example of the High Court using inherent jurisdiction powers to ban media reports from identifying a defendant.

▶ Section 11 anonymity for defendants and witnesses: grounds of challenge

Courts have power under common law to permit a name or other matter to be withheld from the public during their proceedings, either by holding a hearing in private and/or by forbidding the mention of such information in open court. If a court uses either such power, it can then make an order under section 11 of the Contempt of Court Act 1981 to ban indefinitely the publication of that name or matter in connection with the proceedings.

→ for more detail about such orders, see ch. 9, p. 128

Section 11 orders have been used to ban media reports from identifying a defendant or witness, or to prevent publication of a defendant's address. But in numerous instances such orders have been made invalidly, and/or with insufficient justification to use section 11 to override the open justice principle.

The terms of section 11 orders must be precise The Consolidated Criminal Practice Direction – see above, p. 208 – states in its Part 1.3.3 that a section 11 order must be put in writing either by the judge personally or by the clerk of the court under the judge's directions, and it must state its precise scope and the specific purpose of making the order.

Has the name or matter been withheld from the public in the proceedings?

- The High Court has ruled that a section 11 order should not be made if the name or matter *has already* been mentioned in public in the case (*R v Arundel Justices, ex p Westminster Press* [1985] 2 All ER 390; [1985] 1 WLR 708).

R v Arundel Justices concerned a section 11 order made at Arundel magistrates court banning the publication of the name and address of a man charged with burglary offences, which he later admitted. His solicitor asked for the order, supported by the prosecutor. After a newspaper group sought judicial review of it, the Queen's Bench Divisional Court ruling in 1985, cited above, was that the magistrates had no power to make the order because, before they made it, the defendant's details had already been aired in public in the burglary case – apparently when the clerk routinely checked these details with the defendant in the case's first hearing.

The Court of Appeal made clear in 2008 that for a section 11 order to be valid the court which made it must have already 'deliberately' decided to withhold the relevant name or matter from the public (*Re Trinity Mirror plc and others* (2008), see above, p. 212). In another case, the Court of Appeal ruled in 2007 that if a court *has* taken action to withhold a name or matter from the public, it can pass a section 11 order to forbid its publication if it is subsequently mentioned by mistake during its public proceedings (*Re Times Newspapers Ltd* [2007] EWCA Crim 1925).

Is section 11 anonymity necessary for justice to be done?

A journalist may need to remind a court that Lord Diplock said in 1979, in the House of Lords judgment in *Attorney General v Leveller Magazine Ltd*, that departure from the open justice rule is only justified:

❝ where the nature or circumstances of the particular proceeding are such that the application of the general rule in its entirety would frustrate or render impracticable the administration of justice or would damage some other public interest for whose protection Parliament has made some statutory **derogation** from the rule. 🟊🟊

 →glossary

→

see also
ch. 12,
p. 191 on
Leveller
case

It follows from the *Leveller* judgment that, before making a section 11 order bestowing anonymity, a key question any court should consider is: if this person does *not* have such anonymity in media reports, will this case be able to proceed to a just conclusion? If the answer is 'yes, it will' the order is not needed for the administration of justice in that particular case. A defendant in a criminal case cannot usually be said to need such anonymity for it to reach a just conclusion, because he/she has no choice but to be involved in it.

Lord Justice McCollom and Mr Justice Pringle stated in a High Court judgment in 1997: 'The use of the words "some other public interest" indicates that Lord Diplock had in mind the protection of the public interest in the administration of justice rather than the private welfare of those caught up in that administration' (*R v Newtownabbey Magistrates' Court, ex p Belfast Telegraph Newspapers Ltd*, see p. 212, above).

> → See also p. 217 on whether anonymity is needed to prevent risk of attack to a defendant or witness.

Section 11 is not to protect the 'comfort and feelings' of defendants

- The High Court ruled in 1988 that a section 11 order should not be made for the 'comfort and feelings' of a defendant. This ruling was in *R v Evesham Justices, ex p McDonagh* [1988] QB 553; [1988] 1 All ER 371.

Evesham magistrates had allowed a defendant not to have his address read out in court because he feared harassment from his ex-wife. The magistrates had then made a section 11 order forbidding the media to publish the address. In a judicial review of their decision, at the High Court Lord Justice Watkins said that while no statutory provision lays down that a defendant's address has publicly to be given in court, 'it is well established practice that, save for a justifiable reason, it must be'. He added that there were many defendants – probably the vast majority – who would like their identities and addresses not to be revealed, and who would be capable of advancing 'seemingly plausible' reasons for this. But, he said, it was only in rare circumstances, conforming to those set out in *Attorney General v Leveller* (see above), that a court would protect a defendant from publicity.

Section 11 is not to protect a defendant's business interests

The High Court ruled in 1991 that section 11 could not be used to protect a defendant from financial damage. Dover magistrates had acted wrongly in making a section 11 order banning publication of the identity of a restaurateur awaiting trial on food hygiene offences (*R v Dover Justices, ex p Dover District Council and Wells* (1991) 156 JP 433).

Someone else may be wrongly perceived as the defendant

A journalist opposing section 11 being used to ban publication of a defendant's address should point out that if it cannot be published there is a danger that someone else entirely unconnected with the case, but with the same or a similar name, may be wrongly thought by the public to be the defendant.

 see also ch. 12, p. 199 on defendants' addresses

Judge David Clarke, Honorary Recorder of Liverpool, said in *R v Thomas Carroll* (*Media Lawyer*, January 2001): 'It is important to remember that if a name is published without an address, a reader might be misled in the belief that another person with same name is involved rather than the true defendant. This is a real danger, particularly where the defendants bear common names such as my own.'

This danger could also occur when there is a total ban on identifying a defendant.

Section 11 anonymity is not to protect a defendant's children

The Court of Appeal in 2008 ruled that Judge McKinnon at Croydon Crown court had been wrong to use section 11 to ban the media from publishing the identity of a man who had admitted 20 charges of downloading pornographic pictures of children from the internet. His name had been used in open court throughout the sentencing hearing. Judge McKinnon had made the order on the basis that the man's two daughters, aged six and eight, who were neither victims nor witnesses in the case, would be likely to suffer significant harm if their father was identified publicly as guilty of such crime. The Court of Appeal, allowing the media to identify the man, said the judge had been wrong to conclude that the children's rights under Article 8 of the European Convention outweighed those of the media and the public under Article 10. Giving the Court of Appeal's judgment, Sir Igor Judge, president of the Queen's Bench Division, who later in 2008 became Lord Chief Justice, said:

 see also ch. 1, p. 12 on weighing rights

❝ Everyone appreciates the risk that innocent children may suffer prejudice and damage when a parent is convicted of a serious offence....However

> we accept the validity of the simple but telling proposition put by the court
> reporter to Judge McKinnon on 2 April 2007, that there is nothing in this
> case to distinguish the plight of the defendant's children from that of a
> massive group of children of persons convicted of offences relating to child
> pornography. **""**

Sir Igor said that to allow the defendant such anonymity on the basis of his
children's Article 8 rights would be 'to the overwhelming disadvantage of
public confidence in the criminal justice system'. He also said that any such
reporting restriction had to depend 'on express legislation' and on the basis
of 'absolute necessity' *Re Trinity Mirror plc and others* – see p. 212.

> See also ch. 11, p. 185, on instances of injunctions in family law restricting coverage of criminal
> trials and inquest proceedings.

Section 11 anonymity for witnesses in criminal cases

It is routine for courts to use section 11 to provide anonymity in media
reports for an alleged victim of blackmail when the allegation is that a threat
was made to reveal embarrassing or compromising information about him/
her. The rationale for such anonymity is that: (a) it encourages the alleged
victim to give evidence, and (b) it protects the administration of justice as a
continuing process, because if *any* alleged victim of such blackmail is identified publicly in court reporting, this makes it less likely in the future that
other victims of similar blackmail will report it to the police.

see ch. 9,
p. 129 on
blackmail

Lord Woolf, then Master of the Rolls, said in 1998 that it was well established in blackmail and rape cases that the alleged victim can be entitled to
the protection of anonymity, but outside such well-established cases there
had to be 'some objective foundation' to the claim for entitlement to section
11 anonymity (*R v Legal Aid Board, ex p Kaim Todner* [1999] QB 966; [1998]
3 All ER 541, CA).

> See also ch. 8, which explains the automatic anonymity provided for alleged victims of rape.

In the High Court in 1984 Lord Justice Brown expressed disapproval of a
section 11 order made by a Crown court judge to give anonymity to a witness
on the grounds that the stress of publicity might cause her to relapse into
heroin addiction, for which she was being treated. Lord Justice Brown said:

> **""** There must be many occasions when witnesses in criminal cases are faced
> with embarrassment as a result of facts which are elicited in the course of

proceedings and of allegations made which are often without any real substance. It is, however, part of the essential nature of British criminal justice that cases shall be tried in public and reported and this consideration must outweigh the individual interests of particular persons (*R v Central Criminal Court, ex p Crook* (1984) *The Times*, 8 November). 🗩🗩

 See ch. 12, p. 200 for Home Office guidance that in criminal cases witnesses' addresses should normally not be aired in court.

Section 11 anonymity in civil cases

In *R v Legal Aid Board, ex p Kaim Todner*, cited above, Lord Woolf said in 1998 that, in general, parties and witnesses in civil cases have to accept the embarrassment, damage to their reputation, and possible consequential loss which can be inherent in being involved in litigation, and that their protection was that normally a public judgment would refute unfounded allegations.

In a few civil cases the courts have ruled that the potential harm to a claimant of his/her medical condition being reported from proceedings justified an anonymity order. In *H v Ministry of Defence* [1991] 2 QB 103; [1991] 2 All ER 834 the then Master of the Rolls, Lord Donaldson, said such anonymity was justified so that citizens would not be deterred from seeking access to justice by public scrutiny of evidence which would prove not only embarrassing but positively damaging.

→ glossary

▌ Is anonymity justified because of risk of attack?

In 1997 the High Court in Belfast overturned a magistrate's order preventing the publication of the name and address of a man charged with indecent assault. The order had been made on the grounds that publication of his identity might put him at risk. However, Lord McCollum's and Mr Justice Pringle's judgment stated that 'an attack upon the accused by ill-intentioned persons cannot be regarded as a natural consequence of the publication of the proceedings of the court and the danger of its occurence should not cause the court to depart from well-established principles.' (*R v Newtownabbey Magistrates' Court*), see p. 212, above.

Judge David Clarke, Honorary Recorder of Liverpool, in 2000 rejected an application for an order banning publication of the addresses of three defendants on child abuse charges. The application was made on the grounds that publicity would put them at risk of attack. Their lawyers cited Article 8 (right to privacy) of the European Convention on Human Rights. But Judge Clarke said he was not able to find any special factors justifying an exception to the open justice rule, adding: 'their position in this respect is no different from that of anyone facing any criminal charge.' The judge said that overall the Convention did not increase the number of situations in which a reporting restriction was appropriate (*R v Thomas Carroll*, see p. 215 above).

Journalists should know that:

- various judgments have established that for a defendant or witness to be granted anonymity by a court on safety grounds the risk to their safety must be 'real and immediate' and therefore that the concern about their safety must have an objective basis and not be based merely on the person's subjective fears.

See for example, *Re Times Newspapers Ltd and another* [2008] *The Times* 31 October and cases alluded to below.

Police and prison officers as defendants – risk of attack

On numerous occasions, defence lawyers in cases in which the defendant is a police or prison officer have argued for the court to grant that defendant anonymity, by use of section 11 of the Contempt of Court Act. The argument made is that if such a defendant's name and address is included in a media report of the case, the nature of his/her job puts him/her at particular risk of attack or harassment.

→ glossary   A **district judge** at Birmingham lifted a section 11 order made by lay magistrates in 2004, which had been intended to prevent reporting of the case of a police constable accused of careless driving in an unmarked police car on his way to the scene of an armed robbery. A 12-year-old girl was knocked down and lost a leg in the accident. Lawyers defending the constable said that reporting of the case would put his life in danger because he was due to be a witness in a murder trial. It also would prejudice the administration of justice in that trial. District Judge Robert Zara rejected these arguments. He said although the constable might have some subjective fear for his life, he had not established an objective basis for that fear. The district judge said there was no connection between the careless driving proceedings and the murder trial.

Police officers as witnesses: risk of attack

In 2007 the House of Lords approved the approach taken by a tribunal of inquiry when it had decided not to allow some police witnesses anonymity when they gave evidence to it, despite them arguing that they feared for their lives. The tribunal was established to investigate the murder of a Catholic in Northern Ireland. An allegation it was due to consider was that police could have prevented the murder. In the Lords judgment, Lord Carswell referred to the established criterion that, to justify such anonymity, there should be 'a real and immediate risk' to life. This, he said, is a test 'not readily satisfied: in other words, the threshold is high'. The fear had to be objectively founded (*Re Officer L* [2007] UKHL 36, [2007] 4 All ER 965, [2007] All ER (D) 484 (Jul)).

Police firearms officers involved in fatal shootings while on duty have been given anonymity at inquests. See for example the judgment in *R (on the application of Officer A and another) v HM Coroner for Inner South London* [2004] All ER (D) 288 (Jun). Coroners have inherent jurisdiction in common law to grant anonymity to inquest witnesses – see ch. 14, p. 249.

Sexual offences prevention orders

Police can apply in civil law for a 'sexual offences prevention order' (SOPO) to be made against a convicted sexual offender if he exhibits behaviour in his community – e.g. after release from a jail sentence – which suggests he may reoffend. Home Office guidance issued in 2004 states that police should consider asking magistrates, at the outset of the application hearing, to make an order under section 11 of the Contempt of Court Act 1981 to prevent the offender being identified in reports of it. The guidance states that any public disorder arising from such identification would encourage and allow such a person to abscond from arrangements to monitor him, but adds: 'It is, of course, for the court to decide whether such a [section 11] prohibition is necessary.'

see also ch. 8, p. 124 on SOPOs

In 2008 a 72-year-old paedophile with a history of sexual offences was sent back to jail, convicted of breaching a SOPO. This conviction was the result of a three-year-old boy recognising the man's picture on the *Essex Chronicle*'s website and exclaiming: 'It's George!' It transpired that the man had approached the boy to give him a toy when the man saw the boy out with his family. The photo had been published with an unrestricted report of an earlier breach of the SOPO, which forbade the man from associating with children (Holdthefrontpage website, 30 December 2008).

▌ Challenging section 46 anonymity for adult witnesses in 'fear or distress'

Section 46 of the Youth Justice and Criminal Evidence Act 1999 has since 2004 given courts a discretionary power to ban publication, in a report of a court case, of the identity of an adult witness in his/her lifetime. For a witness to be eligible for such anonymity, the court must be satisfied that the quality of the witness's evidence or his/her level of co-operation in connection with preparations for the case is likely to be diminished by reason of his/her fear or distress in connection with being identified by members of the public as a witness in the proceedings. The court must also be satisfied that the granting of such anonymity is likely to improve the quality of the witness's evidence or the level of his/her co-operation. For more details about such orders, see ch. 9, pp. 133–135.

The Criminal Procedure Rules state, in rule 16.4, that an application for a section 46 order to be lifted or varied can be made by any person 'directly affected' by the order – a definition which would include a journalist covering such a case. The application may be made orally, or in writing on an official form, at any time after proceedings start, and must state why the order places a substantial and unreasonable restriction on reporting the case and why it is in the public interest for it to be removed or relaxed.

see Useful Websites, below

Would the quality of evidence be improved?

The Home Office explanatory notes to the 1999 Act state: 'Neither "fear" nor "distress" is seen as covering a disinclination to give evidence on account of simple embarrassment.' The notes also state that a witness eligible under the Act for 'special measures' protection (e.g. the giving of evidence from behind a screen or by video link – see ch. 9, p. 139) is not necessarily eligible too for section 46 anonymity.

Some courts have made section 46 orders to ban media reports from identifying witnesses who – in the view of journalists – were *not* obviously people whose 'quality of evidence' or 'level of co-operation' would be likely to be diminished as a result of such identification.

see Late News, p. xxx

In 2005 in a case at Northampton Crown court, in which two people were accused of harassment of a clergyman, the **recorder** made a section 46 order to ban the media from identifying the clergyman. The harassment included accusations of sexual impropriety being made against the clergyman, which he strongly denied. A barrister for the *Sun* argued that as the clergyman had already publicly referred to the harassment in a church newsletter, he had nothing further to fear from the community knowing details of it. But the recorder declined to lift the order. The pair accused of harassment eventually pleaded guilty (*Media Lawyer*, 3 May 2005).

In 2006 magistrates in Gloucester made a section 46 order in respect of a woman witness after being told that her job was of 'a highly sensitive nature' and that therefore it was necessary to ban the media from reporting where she worked. The male defendant in the case was accused of sending indecent or obscene photographs to her employer. *Media Lawyer* (20 October 2006) commented that it seemed the order was sought to protect 'national security' rather than to protect the quality of her testimony.

Does the section 46 order serve much purpose?

Courts have recently been given a (controversial) statutory power to make 'a witness anonymity order' to prevent a defendant knowing the identity of a witness testifying for the prosecution or for another defendant in certain cases. These are cases where the witness is alleged to be at risk of intimidation or retaliation by a defendant, or by a defendant's associates or supporters, e.g. a violent gang. This means that the name of such a witness will not be aired in court and not be included in documents used in the case. The witness will also be given protection under the Youth Justice and Criminal Evidence Act's 'special measures', e.g. the witness will give evidence from behind a screen. Technology may be used to disguise the witness's voice.
But if a 'witness anonymity order' is not needed or is not appropriate for a witness – for example, because the defendant already knows the witness's identity – then use of section 46 to ban the media from identifying that witness in its reports of the case must be justified, within the Act's scope, for a purpose other than keeping his/her identity from the defendant.

see also Preface, p. ix

In 2007 a judge at Kingston Crown court imposed a section 46 order preventing media reports identifying witnesses due to give evidence as the alleged victims of an attempted robbery. But she lifted it after the Newsquest newspaper group and local reporters pointed out that the defendants knew the witnesses, that their identities were already in the public domain because they had previously been named in the case in open court, and that if the order stayed in place the media would no longer be able to state who the alleged crime victims were or where the alleged offence occurred (Holdthefrontpage website and *Media Lawyer*, 19 and 20 September 2007 respectively).

Is the person due to testify as a witness?

The 1999 Act gives no power for section 46 anonymity to be bestowed on defendants, or on people *not* due to testify as witnesses. In 2005 a barrister representing media organisations persuaded a judge at Guildford Crown court to lift a section 46 order which prevented their reports of a paedophile's sentencing identifying 19-year-old Gemma Dowler, sister of the murdered schoolgirl Milly Dowler. The paedophile was given a jail term for sending sexually explicit hate mail to her family, including a letter Gemma had opened. He had pleaded guilty. The media argued that because the case therefore did not need any witness testimony, a section 46 order could not be imposed after that plea (*Media Lawyer*, 23 May 2005).

▶ No right of anonymity for defendant under sexual offence law

→ glossary As ch. 8 explains, the Sexual Offences (Amendment) Act 1992 **automatically prohibits** the identification in media reports of victims or alleged victims of most sexual offences during their lifetime. That Act gives courts no power to ban media reports from identifying a defendant. Occasionally magistrates and judges have asserted that it does, when insisting that such anonymity for a defendant is necessary as an extra precaution to prevent media reports including detail likely to identify a victim/alleged victim.

But Mr Justice Aikens stressed at Maidstone Crown court in 2004 that defendants accused of sexual offences have no right of anonymity under the Act (*R v Praill* (2004) *Media Lawyer*, 19 November 2004). The judge overturned an order by West Kent magistrates, which had been confirmed by Judge Anthony Balston at Crown court. The order purported to give such anonymity to the chief executive of a charity who appeared on one charge of rape and eight of indecent assault. Mr Justice Aikens praised representations made by Keith Hunt, a reporter with the *Kent Messenger* group who objected to the order. The judge said he was satisfied the alleged victims' anonymity could be protected without such an order being made.

Also in 2004, a **district judge** at Cardiff magistrates court rejected a defence solicitor's attempt to get such anonymity for a teacher charged with sexual offences against girls. The solicitor argued that otherwise the girls would inevitably be identified in media reports of the case. But district judge Richard Williams said it was a matter of judgement for an editor as regards what details of such a defendant could be published.

> See also pp. 215, 217 and 218 for arguments against anonymity for those accused or convicted of sexual offences.

▌ Section 4(2) orders: grounds of challenge

Section 4(2) of the Contempt of Court Act 1981 gives courts power to order the postponement of publication of media reports of a court case, or of part of one. Under the Act, this power can be exercised to 'avoid a substantial risk of prejudice' to later stages of the same case or to other cases pending or imminent. For more detail on such orders, see ch. 16, p. 289.

Compelling the media to postpone reports of a court case may well mean that eventual coverage of it, when the restriction no longer applies, is substantially less – and therefore of less benefit for the public – than would have been achieved by contemporaneous daily reports, which also have the advantage of helping the public understand evidence by gradually unfolding it. This reduction in overall coverage may occur in particular if a section 4(2) order postpones coverage of two or more major trials which form a series involving the same defendants and/or related events. By ordering such postponement of publication a judge may have thus prevented any reporting of the earlier trial(s) until the final trial is concluded. The media, at that conclusion, then have the practical problem of finding space or air time, within the limitations of a single day's news output, to report the verdicts in and background material about each trial in the series. The necessarily tight editing may mean that some details cannot be published, and therefore that the impact on the public consciousness of each verdict is diminished. Public knowledge and understanding of such cases, and other benefits of open justice, may well thereby be substantially reduced.

see ch. 12 on open justice

In 2006 the head of the Metropolitan police's counter-terrorism branch Peter Clarke expressed frustration that section 4(2) orders were delaying publication of reports of concluded terrorism trials in cases which had already taken two years to reach the trial stage, and with each trial averaging several months in length. He said that as a result myths were being peddled that the terrorism threat had been exaggerated to justify the government's foreign policy, adding: 'I do not see the public being well-served by this. It skews the debate if they do not know about things.'

In the view of some legal experts, a recognition of such concerns has led to senior members of the judiciary being willing to give more weight to arguments that juries can be trusted, even in a series of related trials, to consider each charge on its own merits, whatever has been published previously.

 See also below, p. 226, for reference to the Court of Appeal's decision in the Dhiran Barot case.

A court should hear media representations on section 4(2) orders

The High Court ruled in 1992 that any court, including a magistrates court, has discretionary power to hear representations from the press when the court is considering making or continuing a section 4(2) order. The High Court said the media are the best qualified to represent the public interest in publicity (*R v Clerkenwell Metropolitan Stipendiary Magistrates, ex p Telegraph plc* [1993] QB 462; [1993] 2 All ER 183). In another case, Lord Justice Farquharson said the best course was for the judge to make a limited order under section 4(2) for, say, two days, and thus give the press time to make representations (*R v Beck, ex p Daily Telegraph* [1993] 2 All ER 177, 181).

The terms of section 4(2) orders must be precise

- The Consolidated Criminal Practice Direction – see above, p. 208 – states that a section 4(2) order must be put in writing either by the judge personally or by the clerk of the court under the judge's directions, and must include:
  - its precise scope,
  - the time at which it shall cease to have effect, and
  - the specific purpose of making the order.

The risk of prejudice must be substantial

The risk of prejudice to a future trial must be substantial to justify a section 4(2) order being made to postpone a media report.

In 1982 Lord Denning, Master of the Rolls, gave this guidance:

66 At a trial judges are not influenced by what they may read in newspapers nor are the ordinary folk who sit on juries. They are good sensible people. They go by the evidence that is adduced before them and not by what they may have read in newspapers. The risk of their being influenced is so slight that it can usually be disregarded as insubstantial and therefore not the subject of an order. (*R v Horsham Justices, ex p Farquharson* [1982] QB 762, 794) 99

In 1993 in the Court of Appeal the Lord Chief Justice, Lord Taylor, said that in determining whether publication of matter would cause a substantial risk of prejudice to a future trial, a court should credit the jury with the will and ability to abide by the judge's direction to decide the case only on the evidence before it. The court should also bear in mind that the staying power and detail of publicity, even in cases of notoriety, were limited and that the nature of a trial was to focus the jury's minds on the evidence put before them rather than on matters outside the courtroom (*R v Beck, ex p Telegraph plc* [1993] 2 All ER 971).

Lord Bingham said in the Court of Appeal in 1999, when he was Lord Chief Justice:

66 **Counsel** has drawn attention to what the court accepts is a serious problem in some parts of the country: that orders restricting publication are made in situations where they should not be made. The problem is exacerbated in the ordinary run of cases where the story itself, although something which a local newspaper would wish to publish, is not the sort of story of the highest public interest such as to justify the expense by the newspaper of seeking to have the order rectified. (*Ex p News Group Newspapers* (1999) *The Times*, 21 May) 99

→ glossary

Principles for decisions on section 4(2) orders

The Court of Appeal set out three principles on section 4(2) orders, in *R v Sherwood, ex p Telegraph Group* [2001] EWCA Crim 1075; [2001] 1 WLR 1983:

(1) Unless the perceived risk of prejudice is demonstrated no order should be made.

(2) The question has to be addressed of whether an order is necessary under the European Convention on Human Rights. Sometimes wider considerations of public policy will come into play to justify the refusal of a section 4(2) order even though there is no other way of eliminating the prejudice anticipated.

(3) Applications for postponement orders should be approached as follows: (i) whether reporting would give rise to a not insubstantial risk of prejudice. If not, that will be the end of the matter; (ii) if such a risk is perceived to exist, would an order eliminate it? If not, obviously there can be no necessity to impose such a postponement. However, even if the judge is satisfied that an order would achieve the objective, he will have to consider whether the risk can satisfactorily be overcome by less restrictive means; (iii) the judge might still have to ask whether the degree of risk contemplated should be regarded as tolerable in the sense of being the lesser of two evils.

Risk of prejudice in sequential cases

→ glossary

Lord Justice Farquharson said in 1991 that the fact that an accused expected to face a second **indictment** after a trial of the first one did not in itself justify the making of a section 4(2) order. It depended on all the circumstances, including the nature of the charges, the timing of the second trial, and the place where that second trial was to be heard. If by an extension of the period between trials, or by the transfer to another court, substantial prejudice to the accused could be avoided then that course should be taken (*R v Beck, ex p Daily Telegraph* – see p. 225, above).

In 2008 Judge Henry Globe QC, the Recorder of Liverpool, lifted a section 4(2) order to permit the media 'in light of the interests of open justice' to report the sentencing of footballer Joey Barton for admitted charges of affray and assault causing actual bodily harm (ABH), though Barton was due within weeks to face a trial by magistrates of a criminal damage charge and a trial by jury for an assault charge – allegations which arose from unrelated incidents. Judge Globe was made aware that the jury in the pending assault trial would be told during it of Barton's ABH offence. The judge said the allegations due to be tried were 'distinct' from Barton's admitted offences. Judge Globe also said he was not satisfied that media reports of Barton being sentenced for the admitted charges would create a substantial risk of prejudice to his pending trial by jury. The judge was also not satisfied that the risk of prejudice to Barton's pending trial by magistrates was sufficient to displace the public interest in the media being able to contemporaneously report Barton being sentenced on the admitted charges (*Media Lawyer*, 22 May 2008).

Risk of prejudice if one defendant is sentenced before others tried

In 2006 the Court of Appeal overturned a judge's section 4(2) order which had postponed reporting of the sentencing of a terrorist, Dhiran Barot. The order had been made on the grounds that such media reports would prejudice the forthcoming trial of remaining defendants in the case. It was submitted on behalf of the media that five months would elapse before that new trial and that therefore the 'fade factor' would mean that contemporaneous reporting of Barot's sentencing would not create serious prejudice. Giving the Court of Appeal's ruling, Sir Igor Judge, president of the Queen's Bench Division, said that although there was a primacy in the right to a fair trial it did not follow that a section 4(2) order ought to have been made, as contemporaneous reporting could be the lesser of the two evils. The right of a fair trial had to be balanced with the hallowed principle that the media had the freedom to act as the eyes and ears of the public at large. Sir Igor said that juries had:

see
ch. 16,
p. 281
on fade
factor

" passionate and profound belief in, and a commitment to, the right of a Defendant to be given a fair trial....They know that it is integral to their responsibility. It is, when all is said and done, their birthright; it is shared by each one of them with the Defendant. They guard it faithfully. The integrity of the jury is an essential feature of our trial process. Juries follow the directions which the judge will give them to focus exclusively on the evidence and to ignore anything they may have heard or read out of court.' (*R v B* [2006] EWCA Crim 2692). "

see also
ch. 16,
p. 280 on
juries

The possibility of retrial does not mean a hearing is 'pending or imminent'

In 2006 in Scotland Lord Macfadyen, giving the opinion of the Extra Division of the Inner House of the Court of Session, rejected the arguments of a convicted murderer William Beggs that section 4(2) should be used to compel postponement of media reports of a legal hearing in which he was arguing to be moved to a different jail. Beggs had by then appealed against his murder conviction. He argued that publicity about the prison case might cause a substantial risk of prejudice to any eventual retrial of the murder case, if the appeal led to a retrial. Lord Macfadyen said that any such retrial 'cannot at this stage be said to be "pending or imminent"'.

see also
ch. 16,
p. 285 on
appeals

Risk of reports of a civil case prejudicing a criminal case

In 1994 Mr Justice Lindsay refused to make a section 4(2) order postponing reporting of civil cases involving Maxwell pension funds, despite there being criminal proceedings pending. He said: 'By framing [section 4(2)] as it did, the legislature contemplated that a risk of prejudice which could not be described as substantial had to be tolerated as the price of an open press and that if the risk was properly to be described as substantial, a postponement order did not automatically follow' (*MGN Pension Trustees Ltd v Bank of America* [1995] 2 All ER 355, Ch D).

Section 4(2) cannot be used for other types of ban

Magistrates and Crown court judges have on occasion when imposing orders under section 4(2) rendered them invalid by seeking to use them for a purpose other than to avoid a substantial risk of prejudice to a future hearing. For example, a section 4(2) order cannot validly be used to ban publication of a name or matter to encourage a witness to give evidence, or to protect anybody's general welfare or safety, whether its purported duration is temporary or indefinite. The media have successfully challenged section 4(2) orders being thus used invalidly. If the court then seeks to make the reporting restriction valid by converting it to a section 11 order, it may be that this too can be challenged as invalid or unnecessary – see pp. 212–219, above. The Court of Appeal judgments in 2008 in *Re Trinity Mirror plc and others* and in *Re Times Newspapers Ltd*, cited above on pp. 212 and 213, are among those which make clear that section 4(2) orders are invalid unless they are intended to be temporary *and* are made to avoid a substantial risk of prejudice.

Use of section 4(2) orders to restrict reports of events outside the courtroom

The wording of section 4(2) refers only to postponement of reports of a court's proceedings. But in some cases courts have made section 4(2) orders purporting to temporarily ban reporting of an event which has occurred outside the courtroom. Any such order would seem to be beyond the section's scope, and is unnecessary because the legal position is, anyway, that a media organisation can be prosecuted under the Contempt of Court Act's strict liability rule if extraneous matter published creates a substantial risk of serious prejudice to an 'active case'.

see ch. 16, pp. 274–279

The High Court ruled in 1985 in *R v Rhuddlan Justices, ex p HTV Ltd* [1986] Crim LR 329 that magistrates had acted outside their jurisdiction in making a section 4(2) order which sought to postpone the broadcasting of a television programme on drug trafficking because it was due to show the arrest of a man who had appeared before them on admitted drugs charges. Lord Justice Watkins, having noted that the programme would create no risk of prejudice in that case's circumstances, said that section 4(2) only referred to reports of a court's proceedings. He went on to say that if in any case breach of the strict liability rule was anticipated the appropriate procedure was for the person aggrieved to seek a High Court injunction to restrain the matter from being published.

see also ch. 16, p. 278 on instructions

In 2008 Mr Justice Mackay at Woolwich Crown Court lifted a section 4(2) order he had made which purported to ban publication of 'material of any kind relating to this trial, unless and until it has been put to the jury in court, until after verdicts have been reached'. Media organisations had protested to him that the terms of the order went beyond the scope of section 4(2), and that editors should be free to make their own decisions, paying heed to the strict liability rule, on what extraneous material might create a substantial risk of serious prejudice (*Media Lawyer*, 14 October 2008).

For example, the media would argue that even after a trial begins a re-broadcasting of original footage of the crime – for example, of a terrorist bomb exploding – will not necessarily create any risk of prejudice if no alleged perpetrator is shown in it, or if the visual identification of a defendant is not an evidential issue, or if the jury is due to be shown this footage anyway.

▶ Challenges to postponement of reports of derogatory mitigation

Section 58 of the Criminal Procedure and Investigations Act 1996 gives courts a discretionary power to order the postponement, for 12 months, of publication of an assertion made in a speech of mitigation if the assertion is derogatory to a person's character. The use of this restriction seems rare. A journalist confronted with it should remember that it cannot validly prohibit contemporaneous reporting of an assertion already been made during trial evidence, i.e. prior to it being included in a mitigation speech.

→ for more details on this restriction, see ch. 9, pp. 141–143

In 2007 Judge John Machin at Lincoln Crown court refused a prosecution request for such an order in respect of a defendant who admitted affray and other offences, and whose mitigation was that she was the victim of domestic violence inflicted by her former partner. The judge said: 'There has to come a time when the press is able to make a balanced report' (*Media Lawyer*, 2 October 2007).

▶ Challenges to section 49 anonymity in youth court cases

Juveniles concerned in youth court proceedings, and in appeals from that court, have by law *automatic* anonymity in media reports of such cases. See ch. 7 for more details of this anonymity, imposed by section 49 of the

Children and Young Persons Act 1933. A juvenile, under the Act, is someone aged under 18.

If a juvenile is convicted at a youth court, it can – by virtue of section 45 of the Crime (Sentences) Act 1997 – make an order that such anonymity should be lifted, thereby allowing media reports of the case to identify him/her. The Act permits the court to do this if it is satisfied that the removal of the anonymity is 'in the public interest'.

→

See ch. 7,
p. 101 on
1997 Act

In 1998 the Home Office and Lord Chancellor's Department issued a joint circular 'Opening up youth court proceedings' which said that the lifting of section 49 anonymity would be particularly appropriate in respect of a juvenile defendant:

- whose offending was persistent or serious, or
- whose offending had had an impact on a number of people, or
- in circumstances when alerting people to his/her behaviour would help prevent further offending.

The guidance said that occasions when it would not be in the best interests of justice to lift the section 49 restriction would include:

- when publicity might put the offender or his/her family at risk of harassment or harm;
- when the offender was particularly young or vulnerable;
- when the offender was contrite and ready to accept responsibility for his/her actions;
- when public identification of the offender would reveal the identity of a vulnerable victim and lead to unwelcome publicity for that victim.

In 2001 in *McKerry v Teesdale and Wear Valley Justices* – see above, p. 208 – the High Court made clear that youth courts have discretion to consider applications from journalists for section 49 anonymity to be lifted.

In that judgment Lord Bingham, then Lord Chief Justice, said that a court's power to dispense with section 49 anonymity had to be exercised with great care. It would be wholly wrong for anonymity to be removed as an additional punishment for the juvenile. He said it was extremely difficult to see any place for naming and shaming (a view contrary to that expressed by Home Office Ministers previously). He added that it would rarely be in the public interest for the anonymity to be removed, and that magistrates had to be clear in their minds why it would be in the public interest. In that case, however, the High Court upheld the decision of Teesdale and Wear Valley magistrates who, on the application of the editor of the *Northern Echo*, had lifted the anonymity of a 15-year-old offender, giving as their reasons that he constituted a serious danger to the public and had shown a complete disregard for the law.

Other examples of the media asking youth courts to lift a convicted juvenile's section 49 anonymity can be read on the Holdthefrontpage website. These include the *Manchester Evenings News* persuading a youth court in 2003 that the media should be able to name a 17-year-old youth whose dangerous, hit-and-run driving left a boy paralysed and almost killed a lollipop lady; *Bolton Evening News* successfully arguing in 2005 that its report should be able to identify a 17-year-old gang leader whose serious offences including attacking a policeman; the *Uxbridge Gazette* in 2008 being able to name a 16-year-old who was a persistent graffiti vandal.

 see Useful Websites, below

Section 39 orders: challenging their imposition or continuation

Under section 39 of the Children and Young Persons Act 1933, a court has discretion to order that media reports of a case should not identify any specified juvenile – i.e. a person aged under 18 – 'concerned in the proceedings'.

> See ch. 7, pp. 103–105 for more details on such anonymity orders.

It is not unusual for section 39 orders to be challenged by journalists. Courts frequently impose these orders without any or much consideration of whether they are necessary – and on occasion make them invalidly.

Courts should listen to what journalists say about section 39 orders

In 1994 Lord Justice Glidewell said that a judge had complete discretion to hear representations from parties – including the press – with a legitimate interest in the making of, or in opposing the making of, a section 39 order (*R v Central Criminal Court, ex p Godwin and Crook* [1995] 1 FLR 132). Magistrates have sometimes said they do not have power to lift a section 39 order once it has been imposed. But the legality of lifting such an order has been implicitly recognised by the higher courts, e.g. in 1998 in *R v Central Criminal Court, ex p Simpkins* (1998) *The Times*, 26 October and in 1999 in *R v Crown Court at Manchester, ex p H* [2000] 2 All ER 166.

A section 39 order must be clear about whom it protects

Lord Justice Glidewell said in 1995 in *R v Central Criminal Court, ex p Godwin and Crook* – see above – that if there is any possible doubt as to which child or children a section 39 order relates to, the judge or magistrate should identify the relevant child or children with clarity. Lord Justice Laws said in the Queen's Bench Divisional Court in 2001: 'Such orders constitute a significant curtailment of press freedom and courts have to be vigilant to see that they are justified and if made are clear and unambiguous.' Mr Justice Newman, concurring, said in the same case: 'A draft should be available for the court in every case. There will then be an opportunity to consider the ambit of the application, the terms of the order and whether "a pressing social need" exists' (*(1) Briffett and another v DPP* [2001] EWHC Admin 841; (2001) 166 JP 66).

There must be a good reason for a section 39 order

The courts should not make a section 39 order merely because of the juvenile's age, or unthinkingly as a 'blanket' order covering all juveniles in the case.

Guidelines for Crown court judges and magistrates issued by the Judicial Studies Board state that these orders should not be made as a matter of routine.

→

see
Useful
Websites,
below

- In 1993 Lord Justice Lloyd in the Court of Appeal said in *R v Lee* 'There must be a good reason for making an order under section 39.' – [1993] 2 All ER 170; [1993] 1 WLR 103, CA.

In this judgment, Lord Justice Lloyd said such orders should not be made automatically, and added: 'If the discretion under section 39 is too narrowly confined, we will be in danger of blurring the distinction between proceedings in the juvenile [now youth] court and proceedings in the Crown court, a distinction which Parliament clearly intended to preserve.' In this case the Court of Appeal gave its approval to the refusal of Judge Michael Coombe at the Old Bailey to extend section 39 anonymity for a 14-year-old boy who

→ glossary

took part in a **robbery** while on **bail** on a rape charge. Judge Coombe had said he could see no harm to the boy, and a powerful deterrent effect on his contemporaries, if his name and photograph were published. A similar ruling was made by the High Court in *R v Central Criminal Court ex p W, B and C* [2001] 1 Cr App R 7.

Principles to guide a court about section 39 orders

Lord Justice Simon Brown in *R v Crown Court at Winchester, ex p B* [2000] 1 Cr App R 11 identified seven principles to be considered by a court when deciding whether to make a section 39 order. He said, drawing on wordings of earlier judgments:

> (1) In deciding whether to impose or to lift reporting restrictions, the court will consider whether there are good reasons for naming the defendant.
>
> (2) In reaching that decision, the court will give considerable weight to the age of the offender and the potential damage to the child or young person of public identification as a criminal before the offender has the benefit or burden of adulthood.
>
> (3) The court must have regard to the welfare of the child or young person.
>
> (4) The prospect of being named in court with the accompanying disgrace is a powerful deterrent and the naming of the defendant in the context of his punishment serves as a deterrent to others. These deterrents are proper objectives for the court to seek.
>
> (5) There is a strong public interest in open justice and in the public knowing as much as possible about what has happened in court, including the identity of those who have committed crime.
>
> (6) The weight to be attributed to the different factors may shift at different stages of the proceedings, and, in particular, after the defendant has been found, or pleads, guilty and is sentenced. It may then be appropriate to place greater weight on the interest of the public in knowing the identity of those who have committed crimes, particularly serious and detestable crimes.
>
> (7) The fact that an appeal has been made may be a material consideration.

Effect on a juvenile defendant's family

In 2000 Mr Justice Elias in the High Court said that normally there was no justification for making a section 39 anonymity order in respect of a juvenile offender simply to spare his/her relatives from being identified in publicity about the relevant case. He said:

> Sadly, in any case where someone is caught up in the criminal process other members of the family who are wholly innocent of wrongdoing will be innocent casualties in the drama. They may suffer in all sorts of ways from the publicity given to another family member. But I do not consider that in the normal case that is a relevant factor or a good reason for granting a direction under section 39 (*Chief Constable of Surrey v JHG and DHG* [2002] EWHC 1129 (Admin); [2002] All ER (D) 308 (May)).

see also p. 234, 'Concerned in the proceedings'

The Judicial Studies Board's guidance states: 'There is no power to impose restrictions to prevent identification of children other than the defendant, a victim or a witness, e.g. the siblings of the defendant or a victim.'

see Useful Websites, below

The identity of the juvenile is already in the public domain

In *R v Cardiff Crown Court, ex p M (a minor)* (1998) 162 JP 527, DC, the High Court ruled that if a section 39 order was not made when the case was first listed, publicity identifying the relevant juvenile might make it inappropriate to make an order at a later stage. In 2005 a magistrates court at Liverpool, **sending for trial** at Crown court two youths aged 18 and 17 charged with murdering a teenager, made a section 39 order banning identification of the 17-year-old. It was rescinded later that day at Crown court on the application of a solicitor for BSkyB and Independent Television News on the grounds that the name of the 17-year-old was already in the public domain in that his brother, a Premier League footballer, had appealed on television for him to give himself up. Also, he would be 18 by the time he came to trial. Judge Henry Globe QC accepted the arguments.

→ glossary

Victim is too young to need section 39 anonymity

→
see
Useful
Websites,
below

The guidelines 'Reporting Restrictions in the Crown courts' issued by the Judicial Studies Board state that in a number of cases courts have considered that: 'it is a very relevant consideration that a child victim was a baby or very young so that any adverse publicity was likely to have been a thing of the past before the child would even be aware of it.'

Judge Suzan Matthews in 2004 rescinded an order she had made at Reading Crown court banning the naming of an 18-month-old girl left blind and disabled by her father and said the order had been wrong in principle. The order had been challenged by Anita Howells, a reporter for the INS News Group, who had argued that the baby could not be affected by publicity at her age and that the order was effectively giving anonymity to the father. Judge Peter Jacobs at Norwich Crown Court in 2006 lifted an order banning the identification of an 11-month-old baby in a cruelty case which had prevented the naming of the defendant, the child's stepfather. The *Eastern Daily Press* had submitted that the child was too young to be affected by publicity. Judge Jacobs agreed and said: 'It is highly unlikely that anybody is going to say to this child "Oh by the way, didn't I see you in the EDP six years ago?" People in six years time are more likely to raise this if they knew the child in the first place. I cannot see any reason to uphold the order.'

A section 39 order can only protect a juvenile 'concerned in the proceedings'

→
see
p. 103

Some courts have made section 39 orders purporting to ban the identification of children who were not 'concerned in the proceedings', i.e. they were not a defendant, a witness, or a victim/alleged victim. In 1998 magistrates at Bingley, West Yorkshire, imposed a ban on the naming of a 14-year-old boy who was referred to in court merely because he was the subject of a row between his mother and his father's girlfriend. During the row the girlfriend (the defendant) punched the mother in the face. Magistrates rescinded the order when the editor of the *Bingley News*, Malcolm Hoddy, contacted the chief clerk.

Which proceedings are covered by a section 39 order?

In *R v Lee* (see p. 232) Lord Justice Lloyd said that the word 'proceedings' in section 39 must mean the proceedings in the court making the order and not any proceedings anywhere. His statement indicates that a section 39 order made in the magistrates court does not apply to reports of the case when it reaches Crown court. However, a judge at Crown court can make a section 39 order there.

 See ch. 11, pp. 185–186, for rare examples of the High Court using its inherent jurisdiction to bestow anonymity on a child even though the child is not 'concerned in the proceedings'.

Section 39 cannot be used to spare a defendant's children from embarrassment

In 2008 the High Court lifted section 39 orders imposed by Highbury Corner magistrates and the Inner London Crown Court in respect of the children of a barrister. He had been convicted summarily of harassing his former wife, and had then lost an appeal to the Crown court against the conviction. The section 39 orders had prevented the media from identifying the barrister in reports of those proceedings. In the High Court Lord Justice Thomas said: 'There was no evidence of any particular harm to his children other than the obvious embarrassment of their father having been convicted of a criminal offence' (*Crawford v Director of Public Prosecutions* (2008) *The Times*, 20 February). Lord Justice Thomas made clear that in making this judgment the High Court had followed the decision in *Re Trinity Mirror plc and others* made earlier that year in respect of a section 11 order, see p. 215, above.

A section 39 order cannot validly be made in respect of a dead juvenile

Courts sometimes make section 39 orders attempting to ban the identification of dead children, usually because of sympathy for bereaved relatives.

But over the years several High Court judges have said the courts do not have this power. For example:

- Mr Justice Bristow said at Warwick Crown Court in 1973 that when a child who is a victim of an attack is dead section 39 does not apply.

→
see
Useful
Websites,
below

The guidelines issued to magistrates courts by the Judicial Studies Board state: 'Orders cannot be made in respect of dead children.'

Judge Grigson, imposing a section 39 order at the Old Bailey in 1994, said: 'The order I have made refers specifically to those children who are alive. I have no power to protect the dead and no power to prevent the publication of names of defendants.'

Sarah Leese, a reporter on the *Evening Chronicle*, Newcastle, in 2002 successfully challenged a section 39 order imposed by the North Tyneside coroner in respect of a 13-month-old baby who had died, allegedly through neglect. The coroner had made the order in respect of the baby to protect the identity of a surviving child in the family.

A court, however, may give *guidance* that publication of the name of a dead child could infringe a section 39 order made to protect living siblings, such as where parents are accused of charges of cruelty.

A section 39 order cannot be imposed if the juvenile has turned 18

→
see also
ch. 7,
p. 105

A section 39 order can only be imposed in respect of a person aged under 18. It is significant that section 45 of the Youth Justice and Criminal Evidence Act 1999, not yet implemented, but which was designed to replace section 39 of the 1933 Act in criminal cases, provides that no matter relating to any person involved in the offence shall *while he is under 18* be included in any publication.

Section 39 orders cannot specifically give adults anonymity

Section 39 was enacted to protect juveniles aged under 18, not adults.

- In 1991 the Court of Appeal ruled that section 39 orders could not be used to ban the publication of the identity of an adult defendant (*R v Southwark Crown Court, ex p Godwin* [1992] QB 190; [1991] 3 All ER 818).

Magistrates and Crown court judges occasionally make such invalid orders, particularly in cases of alleged child abuse within a family, when seeking to provide extra protection against any alleged child victim being identified in media reports. But to use section 39 to specifically ban identification of an adult defendant – i.e. someone aged 18 or over – is not only invalid but in such cases unnecessary if the alleged child victims are themselves covered by a section 39 order or have automatic anonymity under the Sexual Offences (Amendment) Act 1992. In these circumstances, it is for editors to decide what detail can be published about the adult defendant without identifying the children.

In the Court of Appeal judgment cited above Lord Justice Glidewell said:

→ see pp. 106 and 116 on abuse cases

❝ In our view, section 39 as a matter of law does not empower a court to order in terms that the names of [adult] defendants should not be published. It may be that on occasions judges will think it helpful to have some discussion about the identification of particular details and give advice...If the inevitable effect of making an order is that it is apparent that some details, including names of [adult] defendants, may not be published because publication would breach the order, that is the practical application of the order; it is not a part of the terms of the order itself. ❞

In 2005 the Court of Appeal held that there was no power under section 39 to prohibit identification of adults charged with sexual offences against children but warned of the danger of publication of material which might lead to the identification of the children. In that case the *Evening Gazette*, Middlesbrough, and others, successfully appealed against an order made at Teesside Crown Court under section 39 banning identification of two men charged with making or distributing indecent photographs and conspiracy to rape (*R v Teesside Crown Court, ex p Gazette Media Co* [2005] EWCA Crim 1983).

▌ ASBOs: arguments for the identification of juveniles

Courts have power to make anti-social behaviour orders in civil law to prohibit repetition of criminal or otherwise objectionable conduct. An ASBO can be made against anyone who is aged 10 or over. When the order is imposed by a magistrates court sitting in civil proceedings there is no automatic ban on media reports identifying any juvenile involved in the proceedings, either as the subject of the application for an ASBO or as a witness. But the magistrates can choose to bestow such anonymity by making an order under section 39 of the Children and Young Persons Act 1933. If an ASBO is imposed by a youth court, it will be as a consequence of the juvenile on whom it is imposed having been convicted there, in a concluded hearing, on → glossary a criminal charge (e.g. for theft) for which section 49 anonmity may well apply. If an ASBO is imposed on him/her, that juvenile will have no automatic anonymity in respect of media reports of those ASBO proceedings, but the youth court can choose to make a section 39 order to bestow anonymity. If a juvenile appears in the youth court accused of the criminal offence of breaching an ASBO he/she will only have such anonymity in respect of that hearing if the court makes a section 39 order.

> → For more details on section 39 orders, youth courts, and ASBO proceedings, see ch. 7, and pp. 231–237, above.

As explained above, pp. 207 and 231, courts are expected to listen to journalists who argue against reporting restrictions. If journalists want a court to

→

see also
p. 230
on lifting
sec-
tion 49
anonmity

permit their reports to identify a juvenile in an ASBO case, they can cite Home Office guidance, 'Publicising anti-social behaviour orders', issued to local authorities in 2005. See Useful Websites, below. This states that:

❝ ASBOs protect local communities: Obtaining the [ASBO] order is only part of the process; its effectiveness will normally depend on people knowing about the order.

Publicity should be expected in most cases. It is necessary to balance the human rights of individuals subject to an ASBO against those of the community as a whole when considering publicising ASBOs. ❞

The guidance added that the benefits of publicity include:

- public reassurance that action has been taken to protect the community's human rights;

- enforcement – local people have the information to identify individuals who breach ASBOs;

- deterrence, in that if a person subject to an ASBO knows he/she may be identified by citizens as being in breach of it, a breach is less likely, and in that others who see publicity about ASBOs may be deterred from causing a nuisance.

Mr Justice Elias said in 2002 in *Chief Constable of Surrey v JHG and DHG* (see above, p. 233) that when a court is considering whether to impose or lift a section 39 order the general public interest in the public disclosure of court proceedings is reinforced, in some cases strongly, by the fact that the juvenile has been made subject to an ASBO.

- Mr Justice Wilson said in the High Court's Family Division in 2001 that in most cases it would be inappropriate for magistrates to ban identification by the press of a child as being the subject to an ASBO, as the efficacy of such orders would often depend on the local community knowing that that child was subject to an ASBO (*Medway Council v BBC* [2002] 1 FLR 104).

The guidelines issued by the Judicial Studies Board on reporting restrictions in magistrates courts state, referring to *R v Lee* – see above, p. 232 – that magistrates must have good reason, aside from the juvenile's age alone, to make a section 39 order in applications for ASBOs.

The High Court in 2004 dismissed applications for a judicial review brought by six youths who claimed their rights to privacy had been breached by their identities being published when ASBOs were made against them (*R (Stanley) v Metropolitan Police Commissioner* (2004) *The Times*, 22 October).

▦ Recap of major points

- Challenges to reporting restrictions can be made by a reporter or by an editor contacting the court. If this fails, the challenge can be taken to a higher court.

- An order under section 11 of the Contempt of Court Act 1981 should only be made if the relevant name or matter has already been deliberately withheld by the court from its public proceedings.

- An order under section 11 can be validly made if otherwise the administration of justice would be frustrated or rendered impracticable, but in most other circumstances is not valid.

- An anonymity order under section 46 of the Youth Justice and Criminal Evidence Act 1999 should only be made if the witness is eligible for this protection and if the order is likely to achieve one of the section's purposes.

- The making of an order under section 4(2) of the Contempt of Court Act to postpone media reporting of a case is only justified to avoid a substantial risk of prejudice to a pending or imminent hearing.

- Journalists can under the Crime (Sentences) Act 1997 request a youth court to remove, after a juvenile is convicted, the anonymity provided by section 49 of the Children and Young Persons Act 1933, and can cite Home Office guidance on this.

■ There must be a good reason for a court to make an order under section 39 of the Children and Young Persons Act 1933 to provide anonymity for a juvenile in media reports of a court case.

■ A section 39 order cannot be made in respect of an adult or a dead juvenile. It can be argued that a baby or toddler is too young to need section 39 anonymity.

■ Journalists arguing that a juvenile subject to an ASBO should be identified in their reports can point to Home Office guidance on when such identification is justified.

🌐 Useful Websites

www.justice.gov.uk/criminal/procrules_fin/
Criminal Procedure Rules

www.jsboard.co.uk/
Judicial Studies Board guidance on reporting restrictions in magistrates and Crown courts

www.holdthefrontpage.co.uk/
Holdthefrontpage

www.respect.gov.uk/members/article.aspx?id=11490/
Home Office guidance: 'Publicising anti-social behaviour orders'

Coroners courts

Chapter summary

Coroners have a duty to investigate certain types of death. The inquests they hold often produce newsworthy stories. These are court hearings, so – as this chapter explains – the media can safely report defamatory matter stated in them. The law of contempt also applies to media coverage of inquest cases. This chapter provides an outline of coroners' duties. It explains why some inquests have juries. Coroners may impose reporting restrictions to provide anonymity for a juvenile or adult witness. Coroners courts also decide when a found object should be classed as historical 'treasure'. The Government plans to reform the coroner system.

▶ Changes planned to the coroner system

The office of coroner is one of the most ancient in English and Welsh law, originating in the twelfth century. A coroner must be a barrister, solicitor, or doctor of at least five years' standing. There are more than 120, each covering a district, aided by deputy and assistant coroners. Coroners in their courts investigate the causes and circumstances of certain types of death. In another role, they investigate whether found items can be legally classed as historical 'treasure', see below, p. 250. Either type of hearing is called an inquest. As this edition of McNae went to press, coroners' duties remained those set out in the Coroners Act 1988 and in a **statutory instrument**, the →glossary

Coroners Rules 1984. However, the Coroners and Justice Bill 2009, if it becomes law, will implement Government plans to 'modernise' the coroners' system, and will redefine coroners' duties. These plans include the reorganisation of some existing coroners' districts into larger ones, and for the existing offices of coroner, deputy coroner, and assistant deputy coroner to become known, respectively, as senior coroner, area coroner, and assistant coroner.

> ➔ See further references to the Coroners and Justice Bill.

▶ Inquests into deaths

Coroners' inquiries into deaths are to help communities and institutions be vigilant about fatal dangers. Such inquests provide explanations for deaths where cause is unclear. Their findings are included in national statistics on mortality. Anyone concerned about the circumstances of a death can report it to the local coroner. But usually a death is reported to him/her by police or by local doctors, professionals who have guidelines on what types of death they must tell the coroner about. Under the 1988 Act, a coroner has a duty to hold an inquest if he/she has reason to suspect that the fatality is 'a sudden death of which the cause is unknown' or 'a violent or unnatural death', or if someone has died in prison, or if a death has occurred in any other place or circumstance where the death triggers, under other legislation, a requirement for an inquest to take place. These definitions include deaths caused by accidents, suicide, excessive alcohol, or drug abuse; deaths which occurred during a surgical operation, or before recovery from an anaesthetic; and other types of death which by law require an inquest to have a jury, see below. Also, if the deceased person was not seen, during the 14 days before death, by the doctor who issued the medical certificate of death, or the doctor did not see the body after death, the death should be investigated by the coroner.

 →glossary   A coroner has the right at **common law** to take possession of a body until after his/her inquiries have been completed. The coroner decides, after an initial investigation, including an autopsy, whether an inquest should be held, and which witnesses are to appear. He/she may see no need for an inquest if an autopsy shows conclusively that a sudden death was due to natural causes. In 2007, 234,500 deaths were reported to coroners, and inquests were held into 30,800 of them. The jurisdiction of a coroner to hold an inquest arises from the fact that the body is in his/her district. The Court of Appeal ruled in 1983 that a coroner must hold an inquest if a body has been brought from abroad into his/her district and it is believed the death was violent or unnatural. This is why, for example, the deaths of British soldiers killed in Afghanistan give rise to inquests in the UK.

- The purpose of a coroner's investigation, and therefore an inquest if one is held, is to find out:
  - who the deceased was,
  - how, when, and where he/she met his/her death,
  - the particulars about the death which have to be registered according to statute.

Establishing the deceased's identity is usually straightforward, but may require lengthy investigation if, for example, a decomposed body is found in countryside and the person has not been reported missing. The particulars which have to be registered include the date and place of death, and the dead person's name, age, address, occupation, and gender. In most inquests the 'findings' are made by a coroner alone, after he/she considers evidence from witnesses. But juries figure in some inquests.

Inquests which have juries

Under current law, a jury must be summoned for an inquest to make its findings if there is reason to suspect that the death is one which under statute has to be notified to a government department, e.g. a death in a workplace, or by poisoning, or from certain diseases; or that the person died when in prison or in police custody; or that the death resulted from an injury caused by a police officer in the purported execution of his/her duty. A jury must also be summoned if the coroner feels there is reason to suspect the death 'occurred in circumstances the continuance or possible recurrence of which is prejudicial to the health and safety of the public'. This wording, in the 1988 Act, gives the coroner scope to summon a jury when inquiring into a local hazard. For example, if there has been a series of fatal crashes on the same section of road he/she may feel there may be an underlying cause to be addressed, perhaps bad design of the road. An inquest jury is currently of at least seven and not more than 11 people. The 2009 Bill proposes it should be smaller, no less than six and no more than nine people. Jurors are selected randomly from the electoral rolls, in the process used by the local Crown court.

see also
ch. 6, p. 76

The 2009 Bill does not propose great change in what coroners initially investigate. It proposes that an inquest must be held with a jury if there is reason to suspect that the death falls into the following categories:

- the death was in 'custody or otherwise in state detention', and that either this death was a violent or unnatural one, or the cause of this death is unknown;

- the death resulted from an act or omission of a police officer or member of a police force of the armed services, in the purported execution of the officer's or member's duty;

- the death was caused by any accident, poisoning, or disease which under other law (e.g. health and safety legislation) must be notified to a government department.

Also, the Bill proposes that an inquest into any other type of death can be held with a jury if the district's senior coroner thinks there is 'sufficient reason' for this. The full scope of changes arising from the Bill will not be clear until, if it becomes law, subsequent regulations empowered by it are finalised. For example, the Bill has provision for the Lord Chancellor to make regulations setting out the circumstances in which a doctor must report a death to a coroner.

Information about inquests

A Home Office circular in May 1980 urged coroners to make arrangements to ensure that the media were properly informed of all inquests. A reminder was sent out in 1987. This duty often falls to the coroner's officer – a police officer attached to the coroner's office on a full or, occasionally, part-time basis.

An exemplar of assistance to the media was the Lincolnshire county coroner, Stuart Fisher, when he was rung by a Press Association reporter in 2006 concerning an inquest he had held the previous day into the death of a baby. Mr Fisher fetched the file on the hearing from the boot of his car, and →glossary proceeded to read his **narrative verdict** – see below, p. 246 – as well as evidence from witnesses.

Though the Home Office circular is clear, it is advisable for journalists interested in a particular death to make regular calls to the coroner's officer to check if there will be an inquest, and if so, when it will take place.

Procedure at inquests into deaths

- Under rule 17 of the Coroners Rules 1984, every inquest shall be held in public, with the only exception being that the coroner can exclude the public (and reporters) from an inquest on grounds of national security.

For example, if some evidence about the death of a soldier in a military operation could prove useful to the State's enemies, that part of the inquest could legally be held **in private**. Controversially, the 2009 Bill contained proposals to extend the circumstances in which inquests can be held in private.

→ glossary

> See details on these proposals below, p. 247, and see also pp. 249–250 on legal considerations

In respect of most inquests, there is usually an initial, brief hearing in public at the coroners court to ascertain who the deceased was. This is called the 'opening' of the inquest. It is then adjourned to permit burial or cremation of the body, there having already been an autopsy. Then, after some weeks or months, the inquest is usually resumed to hear, in public, fuller evidence about the circumstances of the death. An inquest is inquisitorial in its procedure – unlike the criminal courts, where the process is accusatorial and adversarial, and consequently subject to strict procedural rules in the interests of justice. The coroner will lead witnesses through their evidence. Coroners often allow family members and other interested parties, although not reporters, to ask questions of witnesses at the end of their evidence.

- Rule 37 of the Coroners Rules 1984 allows a coroner to take documentary rather than oral evidence from any witness where such evidence is unlikely to be disputed – so, for example, a busy hospital doctor may not need to attend an inquest to give evidence in person.
- But rule 37 also says that the coroner:
  - must announce publicly at the inquest the name of anyone whose evidence is accepted in documentary form; and
  - must read aloud at the inquest this documentary evidence, unless the coroner otherwise 'directs' (i.e. makes a formal decision) that this evidence will not be read out.

The rule therefore gives some prospect of a reporter at an inquest hearing evidence submitted by someone not there.

It is the custom of coroners not to read out suicide notes and psychiatric reports.

Findings and verdicts

An inquest into a death produces a finding or findings on the circumstance of the death, determined by the coroner sitting alone or by a jury if one is involved, see above. The finding/findings may be expressed in a succinct form at the inquest and if so this is commonly referred to as a verdict. Verdicts include that death was by 'natural causes', i.e. a naturally occurring illness/ disease; by dependence on drugs; by non-dependent drug abuse; or that the person killed himself/herself. Two other verdicts, frequently used, are 'accidental death' and 'misadventure'. Some argue there is no clear distinction in law between these. But the latter is sometimes used if an action which has risk leads to a fatal accident, e.g. speeding in a car. A verdict of 'unlawful killing' is rare, but can be used if the conclusion is that the death was caused by homicide, e.g. murder, and inquest juries also sometimes decide to use this verdict if they consider a death was caused by gross negligence by someone other than the deceased. An 'open verdict' is used when an inquest decides there is insufficient evidence for any other verdict. A recent development is increasing use of 'narrative verdicts'. A narrative verdict is a brief statement summing up the findings of how the deceased came to die. A coroner or a jury may choose to deliver a narrative verdict rather than one of the 'short-form' verdicts referred to above, though the narrative can contain such a verdict term. The types of verdict recognised in law are currently set out in the Coroners Rules 1984, and may be changed if the 2009 Bill becomes law. It has become the journalistic convention to report that a coroner's jury *returns* a verdict and that a coroner sitting without a jury *records* a verdict.

It is not the job of an inquest to decide who, if anyone, is liable in civil or criminal law for the death. That is the function of other types of court. For example, a coroner's jury is not permitted in a verdict of unlawful killing as regards a murder to state who it believes the murderer is. To do so would be unfair to those who might face criminal proceedings. But in 2002 the Court of Appeal held that the rules did not prevent a jury making a finding of 'neglect' – e.g. if it decides that neglect contributed to the death of an elderly person in a nursing home – if that finding identified a failure in the system and reduced the risk of repetition. It has also been ruled in case law that a coroner should allow a jury to express a brief conclusion about the disputed facts at the centre of the case. This change of interpretation of inquest rules was required to comply with Article 2 of the European Convention on Human Rights, which protects the right to life.

When a person is suspected of crime in connection with a death, an inquest is usually opened and is then adjourned until after any criminal proceedings

→ glossary

→
see
Appendix
1, p. 565)

have been completed. The inquest may then be resumed if there is sufficient cause, e.g. if someone accused of a murder is acquitted, an inquest may subsequently return a verdict of unlawful killing, while not attributing blame. If a public inquiry is instigated to consider why a person or people died (e.g. in a train crash, or in crowd crush at a football stadium) the Lord Chancellor may direct under the Access to Justice Act 1999 that any inquest should be adjourned. It will not be reopened unless there is an exceptional reason.

see ch. 15 on public inquiries

Appeals against inquest decisions

- There is no direct right of appeal against a verdict at an inquest, but an application can under current law be made to the High Court for **judicial review**, which could result in that court making an order to quash a verdict and to order a fresh inquest to be held in the interests of justice.

→ glossary

Such applications have been made by relatives of the deceased, when aggrieved by an inquest's findings.

Under the proposals in the Coroners and Justice Bill 2009, an 'interested person' would be able to appeal to the Chief Coroner for England and Wales – which would be a newly created post – if aggrieved by an inquest verdict or by a decision taken earlier by a senior coroner in an investigation, e.g. on whether an autopsy or jury is needed. The Chief Coroner, who would be someone who had served as a High Court judge, would have power to amend or quash the verdict or to change a challenged decision. The definition of 'interested person' includes relatives of the deceased, and 'any other person who the senior coroner thinks has sufficient interest'. The Chief Coroner would also have duties concerning the training of coroners and the setting of standards for them.

Inquests to be held in private: the proposals

The Coroners and Justice Bill 2009 controversially proposed new law to extend the grounds on which inquests can be held in private, i.e. with the press and public barred from entry. Under this proposal the Home Secretary would have been empowered, if he/she considered that a matter relevant to an investigation into a death should not be made public, to 'certify' – i.e. to order – that the investigation be carried out by a High Court judge, rather than by a coroner. The Bill proposed that the Home Secretary could order this in the interests of national security, or of the relationship between the United

Kingdom and another country, or of preventing or detecting crime; or to protect the safety of a witness or another person; or to protect 'real harm to the public interest'. The Home Secretary's decision to 'certify' could have been challenged by a party seeking judicial review. If this part of the Bill had become law, any inquest held as a result of such a 'certified' investigation would have been conducted by the appointed judge, rather than by any coroner, and would not have had a jury – even if the death would otherwise qualify for a jury inquest, see above. Also, the judge would have had power to conduct all or part of such an inquest in private, excluding even the relatives of the dead person. Similar provisions were proposed for, but were later dropped from, law enacted in the Counter-Terrorist Act 2008. Part of the Government's argument for such proposals was that inquests without juries and held in private would give greater scope for consideration of sensitive evidence from secret operations by the police and intelligence services, e.g. evidence from interception of phone or email messages. Critics of the proposals felt such law could, conveniently for state agencies, prevent jury – and full public – scrutiny of:

- deaths in which people suspected, perhaps wrongly, of being terrorists or criminals have been killed by armed police; or
- the deaths of British military personnel in controversial warfare, e.g. those killed in Afghanistan.

➜

see Preface, p. ix, and Late News, p. xxix

In May 2009 the Government abandoned these 'non-jury inquest' proposals. In the 2009 Bill's proposals, coroners will retain their own discretion, i.e. in cases which are not 'certified', to hold all or part of an inquest in private on grounds of national security, and be able in any inquest to exclude 'specified persons' during the giving of evidence by a witness under 18, if the coroner feels this is likely to improve the quality of the witness's evidence.

▶ Legal considerations in media coverage of inquest cases

➜

see ch. 19, pp. 337–345

A inquest is a type of court proceeding, and therefore fair, accurate, and contemporaneous reports of an inquest (whether into a death or concerning treasure, see below) held in public are protected by absolute privilege from libel actions, and non-contemporaneous reports are protected by qualified privilege if the requirements of that defence are met.

A coroners court is covered by the provisions of the Contempt of Court Act 1981.

→ see ch. 16 for detail of the Act

- The Court of Appeal has ruled that an inquest becomes 'active' under the 1981 Act when it is opened, see p. 245.

This ruling was given in *Peacock v London Weekend Television* (1986) 150 JP 71.

It seems unlikely that a coroner could be influenced by media coverage as regards his/her verdict. But the media should take care, in a case where an inquest jury could be or is involved, not to publish matter which could be ruled under the 1981 Act to create a substantial risk of serious prejudice to the jury's deliberations. Similar care should be exercised by the media in respect of publishing matter which could influence the evidence of any witness.

An inquest may precede a hearing in a criminal court into the same or related events, e.g. an inquest may open but be adjourned because someone is charged with murder. In such a circumstance the media can nevertheless report that inquest opening contemporaneously, if it is held in public. This is because, provided the report is fair and accurate, it will be protected by section 4 of the 1981 Act unless the coroner has made an order under the Act's section 4(2) to postpone reporting of the inquest hearing. Coroners can make orders under other statute to restrict reporting, e.g. for a juvenile witness to have anonymity under section 39 of the Children and Young Persons Act 1933 – see ch. 7. Also, coroners have **inherent jurisdiction** in common law to order that a witness should have anonymity in media reports of inquests. At the 2008 inquest into the death of Jean Charles De Menezes, the innocent Brazilian shot dead by police in London after he was mistaken for a terrorist, the coroner Sir Michael Wright granted anonymity to the police firearms officers involved. He warned that any attempt to take photographs of anonymised witnesses would be punished as a contempt of court.

→ see ch. 16, pp. 288–289

 → glossary

Under current law, any challenge to a coroner's refusal to reconsider such a reporting restriction must be made to the High Court for judicial review. In the 2009 Bill, it is proposed to give coroners the power, in future procedural rules for inquest proceedings, to direct that a name or matter should not be disclosed except to specified persons.

→ see ch. 13, p. 219 on firearms officers

Publication of matter heard at an inquest in private, e.g. if the case concerns national security, could be deemed contempt of court. The proposals to extend the grounds for private hearings at inquests would have meant, had these proposals become law, that publication of matter from a wider range of cases thus heard could be deemed illegal, punishable either as contempt – ch. 9, p. 130 – or under any specific provision enacted. Publication of matter heard by an inquest in private will not be protected by privilege in libel law – see ch. 19.

Coroners have power to punish certain types of contempt themselves, in common law, e.g. a refusal by a witness to turn up to give evidence. Common law and statutory protections of witnesses and jurors also apply to inquest proceedings as does the ban on photography, filming and audio-recording in courts.

→ See ch. 9 and ch. 16, pp. 297–298. See also ch. 11, p. 186 for an example of a High Court family law injunction restricting media reports of an inquest.

Ethical considerations in reporting death inquests

In 2006 the Press Complaints Commission (PCC) code of practice was expanded, in its Clause 5 (Intrusion into grief or shock), to minimise the risk of copycat suicides. The relevant sub-clause reads: 'When reporting suicide, care should be taken to avoid excessive detail about the method used.' In 2009 the PCC censured 12 publications, including several national newspapers, for breach of this clause in their reports of an inquest about the death of a man who decapitated himself using a chainsaw.

→ see ch. 1, p. 17, on PCC

In 2008 the Ministry of Justice dropped a controversial proposal for coroners, in their investigations into suicide and child death cases, to be given discretionary power to forbid publication of the identity of the deceased person. It had been argued that the proposed power was necessary to protect the privacy of the bereaved. The Ministry then published a discussion paper, 'Sensitive Reporting in Coroners' Courts'. This alludes to instances of bereaved people being upset by media coverage of inquests.

→ See Useful Websites, below

Treasure inquests

Coroners courts decide whether historical objects found on or buried in the ground should be classed as 'treasure'. This function dates from coroners' original role as district representatives of the Crown. The monarch had legal rights in some circumstances to take possession of gold and silver objects deemed to have been deliberately hidden by a past generation – e.g. buried to keep them safe during warfare. The Treasure Act 1996 made changes to this law, a main Parliamentary aim being to encourage those who use metal-detectors as a hobby to declare discoveries so museums can decide if they want the objects found. The Act has various definitions of treasure, one being:

- a found object which is not a single coin and which contains at least 10 per cent of gold or silver, and which is at least 300 years old, and any other object found with it.

If 10 or more coins are found together, whatever their metallic content, and are at least 300 years old, this find is also classed as treasure. Broadly speaking, the law now states that anyone realising that something they have found might be classed as treasure must notify the district's coroner of the find within 14 days. Failure to notify is punishable by a fine, or a jail term of up to three months. The coroner, if he/she considers the find might be treasure, will hold an inquest, with or without a jury, to determine this.

- If the find is ruled to be treasure, public museums, e.g. the British Museum or National Museum of Wales, are given the opportunity to take ownership, and if a museum wants to acquire the find there is a system for a reward – based on the treasure's market value – to be paid from public money to the finder; it is also possible for some of this money to be awarded to the owner or occupier of the land where the treasure was found.

The reward may be reduced, or not be offered, if the finder was trespassing or illegally disturbing an archaeological site. If the object is not classed as treasure or no museum wants it, the finder keeps it, and can sell it, subject to any rights the land's owner or occupier has.

Under the proposed changes to the coroner system, an 'interested person', e.g. the finder, aggrieved by a coroner's investigatory decision in a treasure case, or by an inquest finding in it, would be able to appeal to the Chief Coroner, see above, p. 247.

::::: Recap of major points

- The purpose of an inquest is to find out who the deceased was; how he/she met his/her death; and for the particulars to be registered.

- Under rule 17 of the Coroners Rules, every inquest shall be held in public, though the coroner can exclude the public (and reporters) from an inquest on grounds of national security.

- There is no direct right of appeal against a verdict at an inquest into a death, but an application may be made to the High Court for judicial review, which could result in that court making an order to quash a verdict and to order a fresh inquest to be held in the interests of justice.

- A judicial review is also the route to challenge a reporting restriction made by a coroner, e.g. one under section 39 of the Children and Young Persons Act 1933.

- Evidence at an inquest can be accepted in documentary form if it is unlikely to be disputed, but the coroner should usually read it aloud and state who the witness is.

- Under the Contempt of Court Act 1981, an inquest becomes 'active' when it is opened.

- Inquests also decide if found, historical objects are 'treasure'.

- In 2009 the Government published a Bill to 'modernise' the coroner system.

🌐 Useful Websites

www.direct.gov.uk/en/Governmentcitizensandrights/Death/WhatToDoAfterADeath/ DG_066713/
Government guidance on inquests into deaths

www.coronersociety.org.uk/index.aspx/
The Coroners Society

www.justice.gov.uk/publications/sensitive-reporting-coroners.htm
Government Discussion Paper: 'Sensitive Reporting in Coroners' Courts'

www.yourrights.org.uk/yourrights/rights-of-the-bereaved/investigations-into-deaths/ inquests.html
Liberty guide to rights of the bereaved

www.culture.gov.uk/images/publications/TreasureAct1996CodeofPractice2ndRevision.pdf
The Treasure Act code of practice

Tribunals and public inquiries

Chapter summary

Tribunals and public inquiries are terms which have some overlap, e.g. 'a tribunal of inquiry'. Some such bodies are known by other names, such as a 'commission' or 'panel'. The majority of tribunals, whatever their titles, are bodies with routine, statutory duties to decide on legal matters in specialised areas. For example, many rule on the validity of decisions made by civil servants. These tribunals have a huge annual caseload. Other tribunals are disciplinary, convened to adjudicate on someone's fitness to practise in a regulated profession, e.g. as a lawyer. The term 'public inquiry' denotes another kind of process. A public inquiry can be one held routinely, as required by statute, to resolve a contested matter, e.g. a local planning inquiry. But a public inquiry can also be set up ad hoc by a Minister to examine the causes of an event which has prompted national concern.

This chapter examines how the law, including that of defamation and contempt of court, affects media coverage of tribunal and inquiry hearings.

▌ Tribunals in the administrative justice system

Most tribunals are official bodies, other than the courts, which make decisions determining someone's legal rights, e.g. regarding entitlement to money or to a particular legal status. There are more than 70 types of such tribunals. The majority rule on disputes between an individual or private organisation and state agencies (e.g. about tax obligations, entitlement to benefits, immigration status, or transport and traffic regulation). Some tribunals – e.g. employment tribunals – adjudicate on disputes between individuals and private organisations. In total, the annual workload of tribunals in this 'administrative justice' system can exceed 500,000 cases. For examples of individual tribunals and description of their work, see below. Courts often do not have the specialised experience to deal adequately with disputes dealt with by tribunals. However, appeals from tribunal decisions can in some instances be made to the courts in the civil law system – see ch. 11 – and in some tribunals decision-makers are or include judges.

→
see figure
1, p. 8

Reforms in the Tribunals, Courts and Enforcement Act 2007 have created a unified organisational framework to include most 'administrative justice' tribunals relating to departments and agencies in central government. The Act created the First-Tier Tribunal, an over-arching body to assimilate most existing tribunals which deal with appeals against decisions made by officials. Under the Act a decision of the First-Tier Tribunal may, in some instances, be appealed further to, or be reviewed by, another newly created body, the Upper Tribunal. The Upper Tribunal can rule on some matters formerly dealt with by the High Court in **judicial review**, and is gradually, as the new framework is implemented, encompassing the functions of various pre-existing appeal tribunals. It already includes the functions of the Social Security and Child Support Commissioners. The Upper Tribunal is a 'superior court of record', so its rulings are binding as precedents on the First-Tier Tribunal. Appeals on a point of law from Upper Tribunal decisions may in some instances be made to the Court of Appeal, or the tribunal can transfer some types of application to the High Court. In exceptional circumstances, Court of Appeal decisions on tribunal cases may be challenged in the House of Lords.

→glossary

The First-Tier Tribunal is organised administratively into several sections, called 'chambers', in which pre-existing tribunals are grouped according to their field of work, e.g. the mental health review tribunals for England are now subsumed in the Health, Education and Social Care Chamber. The Upper Tribunal's own chamber structure reflects these groupings.

→
see also
below, p.
256 on
mental
health
tribunals

The Act creates a new judicial post, the holder of which will be known as the Senior President of Tribunals, to lead the tribunal judiciary in this new framework. Some tribunals consist of a lawyer sitting alone. Others include experts in the relevant field, e.g. doctors or accountants. Legally qualified members of First-Tier and Upper tribunals are now all to be called judges. **Circuit judges** will automatically be eligible to serve on tribunals.

→glossary

The Tribunals Service, an executive agency of the Ministry of Justice, was launched in 2006 to provide administrative support for most tribunals which are the responsibility of central government. The Asylum and Immigration Tribunal, employment tribunals, and the Employment Appeals Tribunal (for more information on these, see below) will not be part of the First-Tier/Upper Tribunal system and will retain their existing appeal routes, though their judiciary will be led by the Senior President. The Special Immigration Appeals Commission, see below, will also not be part of the new framework. Tribunals run by local government are not part of it either.

Under the Act, a new body, the Administrative Justice and Tribunals Council, has replaced the former Council on Tribunals, to oversee and review the tribunals system.

→ see Useful Websites, below

▶ Examples of administrative justice tribunals

The tribunals listed here are some which may be of particular interest to journalists. Those marked with an asterisk will remain outside the new First-Tier/Upper Tribunals structure referred to above, and therefore have their own procedural rules on, for example, when cases are heard in public.

→ for employment tribunals, see below, p. 262

Asylum and Immigration Tribunal This hears appeals against decisions made by the Home Secretary and his/her officials in asylum, immigration and nationality matters. See www.ait.gov.uk/.

Special Immigration Appeals Commission This hears appeals against decisions made by the Home Office to deport, or exclude, someone from the UK on national security grounds or for other public interest reasons, and appeals against decisions to deprive someone of UK citizenship. The SIAC is a 'superior court of record'. It can hear evidence **in private**, e.g. when hearing evidence from the intelligence services. In most of its cases, the person appealing is protected by an anonymity order as regards media reports, but he/she can waive this. It has been criticised as the UK's 'most secretive court', e.g. as regards its consideration in 2008 of the case of a radical Islamist cleric. See www.siac.tribunals.gov.uk/.

Family Health Services Appeal Authority This hears appeals by primary care practitioners, e.g. against decisions to remove them from, or not to let them join, the lists of such practitioners permitted to work in the National Health Service. It may be encompassed within the First-Tier Tribunal at some stage in 2009. See www.fhsaa.org.uk/.

Lands Tribunal This is an independent judicial body which rules on disputes concerning land, e.g. about compensation arising from compulsory purchase of land. Appeals against its decisions are to the Court of Appeal. This tribunal was due to be integrated into the Upper Tribunal in 2009. See www.landstribunal.gov.uk/.

The Social Entitlement Chamber of the First-Tier Tribunal hears appeals from disputes about social security and child support payments, criminal injuries compensation, and asylum support. See www.tribunals.gov.uk/Tribunals/firsttier/socialentitlement.htm.

War Pensions and Armed Forces Compensation Chamber of the First-Tier Tribunal This hears appeals from ex-servicemen or women who have had their claims for a war pension rejected and, for injuries after 5 April 2005, armed forces compensation rejected. See www.tribunals.gov.uk/Tribunals/firsttier/warpensionsarmedforces.htm.

The Health, Education and Social Care Chamber of the First-Tier Tribunal hears appeals from people who have, for example, been banned from working for organisations concerned with children and vulnerable adults, or in schools. See www.tribunals.gov.uk/Tribunals/Firsttier/healtheducation.htm. This chamber includes the First-Tier tribunal (mental health) for England (formerly the mental health review tribunals) which hears applications for discharge from patients detained under the Mental Health Act 1983. See www.mhrt.org.uk/. There is a separate mental health review tribunal for Wales: www.wales.nhs.uk/sites3/page.cfm?orgid=816&pid=34216/.

→
see p. 258 on prohibitions on publicity

Rent assessment panels These hear appeals against rent levels fixed by a rent officer for regulated tenancies and can determine a market rent in certain circumstances for assured and assured short-hold tenancies. Hearings are open to the public unless held in private for 'special reasons' – which are not defined.

Valuation tribunals These hear appeals against the valuation of non-domestic property assessed by valuation officers and against the valuation of domestic property by listing officers – the same people wearing different hats. Upon these valuations are based tax payments due to local authorities. These tribunals must sit in public unless satisfied that a party's interests would thereby be prejudiced.

▶ Admission to tribunals

Under the new framework of the 2007 Act – see above, p. 254 – each chamber of the First-Tier Tribunal has its own procedural rules, as does the Upper Tribunal. These rules are intended to harmonise the procedural rules used by relevant pre-existing tribunals, and therefore to some extent reflect them. The First-Tier rules (which came into effect in November 2008 for those chambers which began operation then) state that hearings must be in public subject to certain exceptions. For example, hearings in cases concerning disability discrimination in schools, mental health or special needs must be held in private unless the tribunal considers that it is in the interests of justice for them to be public. An appellant in a criminal injuries compensation case must consent that the hearing should be public. Upper Tribunal rules state that its hearings must be in public unless it directs otherwise. The various **statutory instruments** which specify these rules can be accessed through the website of the Tribunal Procedure Committee.

Other types of tribunal will continue to operate under rules made specifically for them.

→ see Useful Websites, below

- A journalist excluded from a tribunal hearing should ask under what rule the decision was made, in case he/she chooses to challenge the exclusion.

See below, p. 263, as regards admission to employment tribunals.

▶ Tribunal prohibitions on disclosure and publication

Procedural rules for the First-Tier Tribunal and the Upper Tribunal say each may make an order to prohibit the disclosure or publication of specified documents, or information, relating to their proceedings, or of any matter likely to lead members of the public to identify any person these tribunals consider should not be identified. As regards any directive that such a document or information should not be disclosed to another person, the rules state that the tribunal must be satisfied that otherwise disclosure would be likely to cause some person serious harm and that having regard to the interests of justice the directive is proportionate. The term 'document' embraces anything in which information is recorded in any form. The rules also state that unless the tribunal gives a direction to the contrary, information about mental health cases and the names of any persons concerned in such cases must not be made public. These rules are primarily directed to the parties and legal representatives in cases at these tribunals. But the Upper Tribunal has High Court powers, in all matters incidental to its functions, to protect those functions.

→ See also below, p. 260 as regards contempt of court issues concerning tribunals including mental health tribunals. For temporary reporting restrictions which can be imposed by employment tribunals and the Employment Appeals Tribunal, see below, pp. 263–267.

Examples of disciplinary tribunals

The disciplinary tribunals below, being those of regulated professions, are not part of the 'administrative justice' system reformed under the 2007 Act – see above, p. 254.

The General Medical Council hears complaints against doctors in its professional conduct committee. This sits in public but can exclude the public if it considers this is in the interest of justice or desirable having regard to the nature of the case or the evidence. It must, however, give its decision in public.

Solicitors' disciplinary tribunals must, in general, hear allegations of professional misconduct in public. But these tribunals may exclude the public from all or any part of the hearing if it appears that 'any person would suffer undue prejudice from a public hearing or that for any reason the circumstances and nature of the case make a public hearing undesirable'.

The Bar Council's disciplinary tribunal hears complaints against barristers in private unless the barrister asks for a public hearing. The decision must be announced publicly.

Defamation issues in reporting tribunals

Most tribunals, including the disciplinary tribunals of professions regulated by statute, derive their powers from an Act of Parliament. Consequently, as specified by paragraph 11 of Part 2 of Schedule 1 to the Defamation Act 1996, fair and accurate published reports of the public proceedings of these tribunals are protected by qualified privilege if the requirements of that libel defence are met. The requirements are that the report is:

- fair and accurate, and
- published without **malice**, and →glossary
- about a matter of public concern, and its publication is for the public benefit.
- Also, a requirement is that, at the request of anyone defamed by the published report, a reasonable letter or statement of explanation or contradiction must be published.

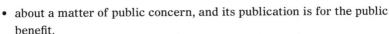

→ See also ch. 19, pp. 340–348 for more detail of this defence.

The proceedings of most tribunals are not as formal as those in an ordinary court of law. The parties might not be represented by lawyers. These factors mean that extra care must be exercised in what is reported from tribunal hearings. Defamatory things might be said during exchanges which are not relevant to the tribunal's duties, and which would not be allowed in an ordinary court. It is important for journalists to remember, when reporting tribunal cases, that qualified privilege does not extend to any published matter which is not 'of public concern' and the publication of which is not 'for the public benefit'. What flares verbally in some tribunal proceedings as irrelevant, personal abuse may well be such matter.

The Defamation Act 1996 provides absolute privilege for a fair, accurate, and contemporaneous report of proceedings in public of a court, a definition which includes 'any tribunal or body exercising the judicial power of the State'. However, only a few types of tribunal exercise 'judicial power' – see next page. → see ch. 19, pp. 338–340

If a journalist discovers what has been aired in the private proceedings of any tribunal, published reports of such matter will not be protected by either type of statutory privilege, i.e. qualified or absolute.

Under paragraph 14 of Schedule 1 to the 1996 Act, qualified privilege protects fair and accurate reports of the findings (but not of the proceedings) of the disciplinary committees of private associations, e.g. in the field of sport, business, and learning, if, as organisations, they match the criteria in that paragraph. Again, a requirement of this defence against libel actions is that, at the request of anyone defamed by the published report, a reasonable letter or statement of explanation or contradiction must be published. see ch. 19, p. 347

▌ Contempt issues: tribunals which are 'courts'

→
see also
ch. 16
→ glossary

The Contempt of Court Act 1981 states that a 'court', for the purposes of the Act, includes 'any tribunal or body exercising the judicial power of the State'. Few tribunals have such power. But there is no comprehensive case law defining which do. In *A-G v BBC* [1981] AC 303, the House of Lords agreed that a local valuation court, despite its name, was not exercising such judicial power, and so its proceedings could not be protected by contempt law. Another tribunal which is not a court is the professional conduct committee of the General Medical Council. The Court of Appeal decided the GMC does not have the requisite judicial power (*General Medical Council v BBC* [1998] 3 All ER 426).

However, in *Pickering v Liverpool Daily Post* [1991] 1 All ER 622, the House of Lords ruled that a mental health review tribunal – see above, p. 256 – is a court, confirming the view of Lord Donaldson, then Master of the Rolls, who said the power of that tribunal to restore a person to liberty was a classic exercise of judicial power. Mental health review tribunals are now in the First-Tier Tribunal (Mental Health). The Upper Tribunal, the Special Immigration Appeals Commission, and the Employment Appeals Tribunal were each created by statute to be a 'superior court of record'. The High Court has ruled that an employment tribunal is a form of court (*Peach Grey and Co v Sommers* [1995] 2 All ER 513). All these tribunals have procedural rules or other statutory provision permitting them to sit in private, and in some circumstances to forbid matter being disclosed or published from their private hearings.

→
see p.
254, p.
255, and
p. 267

Contempt danger in publishing matter from tribunal hearings held in private

→ glossary

Section 12 of the Administration of Justice Act 1960 makes it an offence of contempt of court to publish, without a court's permission, a report of proceedings it has heard in private, i.e. **in chambers** or **in camera**, or a report of the content of any document prepared for use in those proceedings, if the case being dealt with by the court falls into certain categories listed in the Act. These include mental health; national security; the upbringing of children; secret processes; and any other case where the court, having

power to do so, expressly prohibits publication of information about the
case.

Therefore, when any tribunal which wields 'the judicial power of the
State' – and which therefore is a form of court – considers in a private hearing a case in those categories, a published report of matter from that hearing could be regarded as contempt. The *Pickering* judgment, see above,
means that a mental health tribunal is among those classed as courts. See
also below, p. 267 on employment tribunals.

see also
ch. 9, pp.
130–132

Other contempt dangers if a tribunal is a court

Section 1 of the Contempt of Court Act 1981 prohibits publication of matter which creates a substantial risk of serious prejudice to 'active' court
proceedings, including those of tribunals exercising the judicial power
of the State. Under the Act such a tribunal case is active from the time
arrangements are made for the first hearing, or if no such arrangements
have occurred, from the time that hearing begins, and an appeal hearing
in such a tribunal case is active when commenced by 'originating process',
e.g. application for leave for appeal or for review. The case remains active
until disposed of or discontinued or withdrawn (for all details, see Schedule
1 to the Act, paragraphs 12–16). In *Pickering*, Lord Bridge of Harwich in the
House of Lords, referring to the possibility of media coverage prejudicing a
mental health review tribunal hearing, said he would not expect the tribunal
members or medical witnesses to be consciously influenced by the media,
but that editors and publishers 'will be well advised to exercise great care
not to overstep the mark in this regard'. In respect of all tribunals classed
as courts, judges in them can usually be safely assumed to be resistant to
influence from media reports. However, there is a possibility that matter
published before or during such a tribunal case could be deemed to create
'a substantial risk of serious prejudice' in respect of lay witnesses or of a
tribunal member who is not a judge or lawyer or doctor. Contact with a witness prior to such a hearing could be punished as contempt in **common law**
if it was ruled to amount to interference with him/her, as it was in respect
of an employment tribunal case in *Peach Grey & Co v Sommers* (see above
p. 260, though this contempt did not involve the media). The 1981 Act's general ban on unauthorised use of audio-recording devices in courts has been
held to apply to an employment tribunal (*Neckles v Yorkshire Rider Ltd*
[2002] All ER (D) 111 (Jan)).

see ch.
16, on
contempt
law

→ glossary

see also
ch. 9,
p. 145 on
ban

▌ Employment tribunals

Employment tribunals (formerly called industrial tribunals) adjudicate on complaints against employers, e.g. of unfair dismissal, including 'constructive dismissal' in which a person claims that he/she was forced to quit because improper conduct by another/others in the workplace was not stopped. These tribunals also adjudicate on complaints of discrimination by gender or race or age at work; disputes over contracts of employment, redundancy payments, or health and safety at work; and on complaints against trade unions, e.g. about membership eligibility. Each employment tribunal has three members: a lawyer who is chair, and who is now officially known as an 'employment judge'; and two lay members – someone with experience as an employer and someone whose background is as an employee, e.g. a trade unionist. Employment tribunals sit at 21 permanent centres in England and Wales, and receive more than 100,000 claims each year.

Procedure and information

Employment tribunal staff are instructed to provide to journalists details of the parties in a case, and the nature of the claim, once it is listed for a hearing. The hearings at employment tribunals tend to be informal. Some chairpersons plunge straight into matters of detail. Many fail to ask the parties such basic information as their name, age, and address, and sometimes do not read out relevant documents. These details have to be obtained from tribunal officials, who are instructed to supply them, or the parties themselves. It is normal practice for witnesses to confirm their names and addresses before giving evidence.

In judgments, employment tribunals first decide on *liability* – whether the complaint against the employer is justified. The judgment may be announced quickly, after an adjournment on the day of a hearing, or be 'reserved' to be announced or sent out later. If the employer is held liable, subsequently – often after an adjournment of some weeks – the tribunal decides the '*remedy*', e.g. requiring the employer to pay compensation to someone sacked unfairly.

The Government said in 2008 that a scheme to make employment tribunal judgments available online will be rolled out after pilot tests are complete. Until then, reporters will need to ensure that tribunal officials supply them.

Appeals on points of law from employment tribunal decisions can be made to the Employment Appeals Tribunal (EAT) based in London, see also, pp. 255 and 267. EAT hearings are conducted by a judge of the High Court or a circuit judge, sometimes sitting alone or with two lay members, one each from employer and one from employee backgrounds. Temporary and permanent reporting restrictions can be imposed in employment tribunal and EAT cases, see below. EAT judgments can be read online at its website.

→ see Useful Websites, below

Admission to employment tribunal cases

Under the Employment Tribunals Act 1996, an employment tribunal can decide to sit in private:

- in the interests of national security
- or when a witness's evidence is likely to contain:
  - information which the witness cannot disclose without breaking statutory law or without breaking an obligation of confidence;
  - or information which would cause substantial injury to the witness's or the employer's interests other than interests in collective negotiations over pay and conditions.

A Minister of the Crown can direct an employment tribunal to hear a case in private in the interests of national security, e.g. if the tribunal has not already decided to do so. The EAT too can sit in private in national security cases. See also below, national security restrictions, p. 267.

The High Court has ruled that an employment tribunal is not empowered to sit in private merely because there is to be evidence of a sensitive or salacious nature when sexual misconduct is alleged (*R v Southampton Industrial Tribunal ex p INS News Group Ltd and Express Newspapers plc* [1995] IRLR 247).

Sexual misconduct cases: restricted reporting orders

Under the Employment Tribunals Act 1996, employment tribunals have discretionary power to make temporary anonymity orders, known as 'restricted reporting orders', in cases involving allegations of sexual misconduct. Sexual misconduct is defined as a sexual offence or sexual harassment or other adverse conduct (of whatever nature) related to sex, or to the sexual orientation of the person at whom the conduct is directed.

- The tribunal can forbid the media from including in its reports any matter likely to lead members of the public to identify:
  - the person making the allegation of sexual misconduct; and/or

- anyone 'affected' by it, e.g. the person(s) accused of such misconduct or any witness due to give evidence in such proceedings.

The tribunal can decide in each such case who should have such anonymity, if anyone. It may, for example, decide not to grant anonymity for the accuser but order it in respect of the person accused, to safeguard his/her reputation until judgment on whether the accusation is proved. The anonymity can be imposed by the tribunal even though no request is made for it. Such an order cannot specifically bestow such anonymity on an employer which is a company or institution, so its corporate name can be published if this does not identify a person named in the order (*Leicester University v A* [1999] IRLR 352). But in a case where the employing organisation is small, e.g. a small firm, it may be that to preserve anonymity for the person the firm itself cannot be identified in media reports while the order remains in force, e.g. because reference to the person's gender or age or job description would in itself be enough to identify him/her to people who know he/she works there.

 See also the explanation of the dangers of jigsaw identification, ch. 7. p. 105.

In 1997 the Court of Appeal said it was important that tribunals should recognise that their power to make these orders in cases of sexual misconduct was not to be exercised automatically, and that the public interest in the media's ability to communicate information should be considered (*Kearney v Smith New Court Securities* [1997] EWCA Civ 1211).

Under the Employment Tribunals (Constitution and Rules of Procedure) Regulations 2004 (SI 2004/1861) a tribunal chair can make the restricted reporting order as an interim measure prior to any hearing, and at the first hearing the tribunal can decide whether the order should continue in force as a 'full' order. The regulations state that either type of order must specify who may not be identified, and should be displayed on the noticeboard which lists the hearing and on the door of the hearing room.

Media rights of challenge to a restricted reporting order or its scope

Under the 2004 regulations, any person – i.e. including a journalist – can apply to make representations about an interim restricted reporting order – see above. But once the full order is made, journalists or media organisations can only argue against it, or its scope, by becoming a 'party' in the case, which may leave them liable to pay the legal costs of other parties in respect of argument about the order, if the tribunal requires this (*Dallas McMillan and A v B and Ms F Davidson*, UKEATS/0006/07MT). It is important, then, for a journalist or media organisation to challenge the order while it remains an interim one, if there is objection to it.

In some cases a tribunal has taken account of previous publicity in refusing to make a restricted reporting order. In 2000 a Glasgow employment tribunal refused to make such an order in a case of a businessman accused of sexual harassment. Both parties wanted the order to be made. But the *Daily Record* successfully argued that both parties had previously willingly given information to the press (*Scottish Daily Record and Sunday Mail Ltd v Margaret McAvoy and others*, EAT/1271/01).

The EAT can make a restricted reporting order in cases of alleged sexual misconduct, but only as regards appeals against an employment tribunal's decision about such an order or in other interlocutory appeals.

Lifting or cessation of a restricted reporting order

Once the employment tribunal has made a restricted reporting order:

- it can revoke it at any stage, i.e. lift it while the case is ongoing, to permit media reports to immediately identify the person it formerly covered;
- but, anyway, as soon as the tribunal's judgment in the case is 'promulgated', i.e. announced verbally to the parties at a hearing, or sent out as a document subsequently, the order is automatically no longer in force, and so anyone covered by it can then be identified in media reports, **unless** they are the alleged victim of a sexual offence – see below, p. 266.

The 2004 regulations say that in sexual misconduct cases in which an employment tribunal decides there is '*liability*' (i.e. the judgment is that the complaint against the employer is justified) a restricted reporting order, if one is in force and is not revoked then, remains in force until the subsequent judgment on the '*remedy*' (e.g. on the amount of compensation which the employer must pay) is promulgated. That promulgation may be some weeks or months after the liability judgment, see above, p. 262.

Where a restricted reporting order is imposed, but a settlement is reached without the case proceeding to judgment, the restriction will remain in place indefinitely unless the employment tribunal is persuaded, upon application by the media or a party, to lift it. For example, in 2008 six media organisations persuaded a tribunal and the Employment Appeals Tribunal (EAT) that a restricted reporting order should be lifted to allow reports to identify two sisters who had alleged sexual misconduct in a claim against a firm of City brokers. The case had ended in a settlement, and the sisters wanted the media to be able to identify them. At the EAT, Mr Justice Underhill said the tribunal had been justified in lifting the restriction because there had been a change in circumstances – the media's application and the change in the sisters' position (UKEATPA/1415/08/JOJ and UKEATPA/1417/08/JOJ).

Liability for breach of anonymity

→ glossary

If matter is published which breaches a restricted reporting order, this is a **summary offence** punishable by a fine of up to £5,000. Any proprietor, editor, or publisher held responsible will be liable. It will be a defence for the person or company prosecuted if it can be proved that he/she/it was not aware, and neither suspected nor had reason to suspect, that the published matter breached the order.

Automatic anonymity for alleged victims of sexual offences

→ glossary

see ch. 8 on sexual offences

- An **automatic** reporting restriction, under the Sexual Offences (Amendment) Act 1992, means that anyone alleged in employment tribunal proceedings to be a victim of a sexual offence must not be identified in media reports of the case in his/her lifetime, unless the person gives valid, written consent to be identified.

So, if the allegation of sexual misconduct is or includes an allegation of a sexual crime, e.g. rape, sexual assault, or voyeurism, under the 1992 Act the alleged victim cannot be identified by the media, irrespective of whether a restricted reporting order has been imposed under the Employment Tribunals Act 1996 or whether such an order has been lifted or has expired.

In cases involving allegations of a sexual offence, the tribunal must omit from the register of its judgments, and delete from the relevant judgment and any other document concerning the case which is available to the public, any matter likely to identify any person making or affected by the allegation.

Disability cases: restricted reporting orders

Employment tribunals can make restricted reporting orders when considering claims that an employer unlawfully discriminated on disability grounds, if evidence 'of a personal nature' is likely to be heard. Such an order will be for temporary anonymity, in media reports, of the same duration as bestowed by such orders in cases of sexual misconduct – see above. There is the same liability for breach of the anonymity. Anonymity applies to anyone specified in the order. Evidence of a personal nature is defined as evidence of a medical or other intimate nature likely to cause significant embarrassment if published. The Employment Appeals Tribunal can make these orders too, in the same appeal circumstances as it can in sexual misconduct cases.

National security restrictions

A Minister of the Crown can order an employment tribunal to conceal the identity of a witness in a case concerning national security issues, and order it to keep secret all or part of the reasons for its decision in such a case, or the tribunal on its own initiative can take either of these courses of action. When the tribunal has taken such steps, it is an offence under the Employment Appeals Tribunal Act to publish anything likely to lead to the identification of the witness or to publish any part of a decision the tribunal intended to keep secret. The maximum fine for this offence is £5,000. In terms of who would be prosecuted, the liability covers any person held responsible for the publication. There is a defence available which is similar to that for breach of a restricted reporting order, see p. 266.

Contempt and defamation law affecting coverage of employment tribunals

As this chapter has explained, both employment tribunals and the EAT are classed as courts. Unauthorised publication of matter aired in their private hearings could therefore be deemed to be contempt of court under the Administration of Justice Act 1960 if the particular case falls into any of the relevant categories, which include national security. As these tribunals are classed as courts, the Contempt of Court Act 1981 applies to their proceedings. See pp. 260–261.

Because these tribunals are courts, it can be construed that contemporaneous, fair, and accurate media reports of their proceedings in public are protected by absolute privilege from libel actions. Non-contemporaneous reports will be protected by qualified privilege under paragraph 11 of Part 2 of Schedule 1 to the Defamation Act 1996.

 For more detail on absolute and qualified privilege, see ch. 19, pp. 337–348. See also 258–259.

▶ Public inquiries

Public inquiries can be broadly categorised either as local inquiries, set up routinely in certain circumstances, or those which are set up ad hoc to consider a matter of national concern.

Local public inquiries

Some Acts of Parliament provide that an inquiry hearing must be held before a Minister makes certain decisions affecting the rights of individuals or of public authorities. An inquiry might be held, for example, before land is compulsorily acquired for redevelopment, and also before planning schemes are approved. Such an inquiry is conducted by an inspector on behalf of the Minister. In some cases, the inspector decides the matter at issue. In others he/she must report to the Minister, who subsequently announces a decision and the reasons for it. Some statutes under which inquiries may be held stipulate that they must be held in public. In others, this is discretionary. Local authorities and health trusts also have general statutory powers under which they can fund an ad hoc inquiry into a matter of local (or national) concern, though it will be at their discretion whether it is held in public.

Public inquiries into matters of national concern

Public inquiries initiated ad hoc by government Ministers have in recent years included:

- The Hutton inquiry set up in 2003 into the death of Dr David Kelly – held on a non-statutory basis by a chair appointed by the Secretary of State for Constitutional Affairs see www.the-hutton-inquiry.org.uk/.

- The inquiry set up in 2001 into the death of Victoria Climbié, aged 9, held under powers in three statutes because it examined the functioning of social services, health services, and police. Its chair was appointed by two Secretaries of State, see www.victoria-climbie-inquiry.org.uk/index.htm.

- The inquiry into Bloody Sunday set up in 1998 under the Tribunals of Inquiry (Evidence) Act 1921, with a chair appointed by the Lord Chancellor. See www.bloody-sunday-inquiry.org.uk/.

If an inquiry is held on a non-statutory basis, it has no legal powers to compel witnesses to give evidence, but is seen as a flexible option when full co-operation is anticipated.

In the Inquiries Act 2005, Parliament created what was described as a comprehensive framework of law to replace some of the various pieces of pre-existing legislation under which Ministers could set up statutory inquiries. Under the Act a Minister or an inquiry's chair can decide – on various grounds, e.g. national security or to protect the 'efficiency' of the inquiry – that it should hear evidence in private. The various powers granted to Ministers in the Act, including those to impose or continue reporting restrictions, see below, have led to criticism that it fails to sufficiently embody the idea that a public inquiry should in its proceedings be independent of the Government.

Coverage of public inquiries: defamation law

Media reports of the public sessions of public inquiries enjoy some overlap as regards the statutory provisions which confer privilege against libel actions.

Reports of the public inquiries held under the Inquiries Act 2005 have, according to section 37 of the Act, the same privilege 'as would be the case if those proceedings were proceedings before a court', which means that absolute privilege applies to contemporaneous reports and qualified privilege, under Part 1 of Schedule 1 to the Defamation Act 1996, to non-contemporaneous reports, if the respective requirements of these defences are met.

see ch. 19, pp. 337–348

As regards media reports of public inquiries held under any other statute, these enjoy qualified privilege under paragraph 11 of Part 2 of Schedule 1 to the Defamation Act 1996. This means that if requested by a person defamed by such a report, its publisher must publish a reasonable statement or letter by way of explanation or contradiction. Paragraph 11 applies to reports of the public proceedings or a person appointed to hold an inquiry by any statutory provision, by Her Majesty or by a Minister of the Crown or by a Northern Ireland Department, or by a local authority 'in pursuance of any statutory provision'. But, again, for the privilege to apply, all requirements of the defence must be met. See above, p. 259, where the requirements are set out in respect of reports of tribunals, but these apply to reports of such public inquiries too.

⸬ Point for consideration

Privilege will not apply to media reports of any matter aired in a private session of an inquiry. As is the case with administrative tribunals, proceedings of public inquiries are not as formal as those in an ordinary court of law. This means that some extra care must be exercised in what is reported if qualified privilege under the 1996 Act is relied on – see above, page 259.

Part 1 of the Schedule bestows qualified privilege, without the requirement to publish explanation or contradiction, on a report of the proceedings in public of 'a person appointed to hold a public inquiry by a government or legislature anywhere in the world'. But the Act does not make clear how, in the UK, such an appointment differs from an appointment by a Minister of the Crown (the specification in the Schedule Part 2, paragraph 11).

The *findings* of a public inquiry are usually published by a government department, by Parliament or by the relevant local authority. Under the Defamation Act 1996:

- a fair and accurate media report of such findings, when they have been officially published by a government or legislature anywhere in the world (e.g. the UK Parliament) is protected by qualified privilege which, in that it arises from Part 1 of Schedule 1 to the Act (paragraph 7), has no requirement for anyone's explanation or contradiction to be published.

- a fair and accurate media report of findings officially published by a UK local authority is protected by qualified privilege under Part 2 of the Schedule (paragraph 9), and is therefore subject to a reasonable letter or statement by way or explanation of contradiction being published, if this is requested.

Public inquiries: contempt and other legal issues for journalists

Reporting restrictions

For a public inquiry held under its provisions, the Inquiries Act 2005 gives both the Minister who has commissioned the inquiry and its chair power to restrict the disclosure and publication of an item of evidence or documents, or of the identity of a witness. The restriction can be specified as temporary, but otherwise continues indefinitely, unless varied or revoked. In the Act, the grounds on which such a restriction can be imposed are worded to be wide, e.g. to ensure 'the efficiency' of the inquiry. Another ground is to protect national security. Under the Act, an inquiry chair has power to 'certify' to the High Court that someone has failed to comply with a restriction on disclosure or publication. The High Court would have power to punish non-compliance as contempt of court. The punishment for contempt is up to two years in jail and/or a fine unlimited by statute.

But the Act's 'explanatory notes' state: 'Disclosure restrictions would not prevent a person not involved in the inquiry from disclosing or publishing information that had come into his possession through means unconnected with the inquiry.'

Failure to produce evidence/name a source

The 2005 Act makes it a summary offence to fail to obey an inquiry's order for evidence to be provided, with a maximum jail term of 51 weeks. This power to order production of evidence is similar to that in other statutes relating to local inquiries. But under the 2005 Act, an inquiry chair also has power to 'certify' to the High Court that someone has failed to obey such an order. Thus, though the 2005 Act repealed the Tribunals of Inquiry (Evidence) Act 1921 – the statute under which two journalists were jailed in the 1960s for failing to disclose to the Vassall inquiry their sources of information – there is a prospect of a journalist who refuses to co-operate with an inquiry held under the 2005 Act being punished by the High Court for contempt – see above.

see ch. 32, p. 509

Broadcasting inquiry proceedings/rights to information

The Act gives a chair of an inquiry discretion about what parts of an inquiry, if any, can be filmed for broadcast, and says he/she must take steps to allow the public and reporters to obtain or view a record of evidence and documents, subject to any restriction imposed. Once a public inquiry is over, journalists can make requests under the Freedom of Information Act 2000 for information in evidence or documents not disclosed in public sessions of an inquiry, in that such material will be passed to a public authority, e.g. the government department whose Minister commissioned the inquiry. But requests may be refused under that Act's exemptions.

see ch. 28

⸬ Recap of major points

- Most types of tribunals adjudicate in disputes where the courts do not have the necessary specialist expertise.

- Employment tribunals can make temporary anonymity orders in cases involving sexual misconduct. They can sit in private in certain circumstances, e.g. to protect national security.

- Media reports of the public proceedings of tribunals are protected by qualified privilege and, as regards those classed as courts, by absolute privilege when reports are contemporaneous.

- For any tribunal classed as a court, contempt law applies.

- Public inquiries, broadly speaking, fall into two types: those held routinely at a local level to help decide contested issues; and those set up ad hoc to examine an event which has caused national concern.

- Media reports of the public proceedings of public inquiries are, as regards libel actions, protected by either qualified privilege or absolute privilege, depending on the type of the inquiry and on whether a report is contemporaneous.

- The Inquiries Act 2005 empowers either a Minister or the chairperson of the relevant public inquiry to impose reporting restrictions.

- Under the Act, breach of a reporting restriction or failure to obey an order to produce evidence to the inquiry could be punished by the High Court as contempt of court.

🌐 Useful Websites

www.ajtc.gov.uk/
Administrative Justice and Tribunals Council

www.tribunalsservice.gov.uk/Tribunals/Rules/tribunalprocedurecommittee.htm#link4/
Procedural rules for the First-Tier Tribunal and the Upper Tribunal

www.employmenttribunals.gov.uk/
Employment Tribunals

www.direct.gov.uk/en/Employment/index.htm
Government guidance on employment rights

www.employmentappeals.gov.uk/
Employment Appeals Tribunal

Contempt of court

Chapter summary

Contempt of court is the law which protects the integrity of the administration of justice. It most affects journalists when they publish material which might have an effect on a trial. This chapter explains how prejudicial material might make a juror more likely to find a defendant guilty – or innocent. It might influence the evidence given by a witness. Courts have imposed substantial fines on media organisations guilty of committing contempt by what they published. When deciding what risk of prejudice is created by a media report, judges consider how influential the published material might be; how passage of time may have lessened its impact and how a jury can be properly directed to ignore such material and consider only the evidence given in a trial. This chapter also explains that courts can order the media to postpone reporting of a court hearing, to avoid a risk of prejudice to a later stage of the same case or to another trial. Journalists can also commit contempt if they contaminate a witness's evidence during an interview.

▶ What does contempt of court law protect?

The law of contempt of court protects the judicial process. Anyone who, for example, is disruptive or threatening in a courtroom can be punished immediately for contempt, by being sent by the magistrates or judge to the court's cells, and in some cases subsequently to jail – because contempt is a criminal offence.

 for example, see p. 145

The greatest risk of the media committing contempt is by the publication of material which might prejudice a fair trial, in particular by influencing jurors to think badly of a defendant. This chapter explains, below, what type of material can be prejudicial.

The media could be adjudged to have committed contempt of court in other ways, for example by:

- seeking to discover or publishing matter from the confidential discussions which take place among jurors about a verdict – this too would breach the 1981 Act – see ch. 9 pp. 146–148;

→glossary
- publishing material which is a breach of the **common law** of contempt, e.g. by 'vilifying' a person for having acted as a witness at a trial – see below, p. 298;

- contaminating a witness's evidence by interviewing them in detail, or by offering financial payment to them for their story, prior to trial – see below, p. 298;

- publishing material in breach of a court order made in common law or under the Contempt of Court Act 1981, for example, by naming a blackmail victim in reports of a trial – see ch. 9, pp. 128–130.

⠿ Point for consideration

If material is published in breach of an order made under statute other than the 1981 Act – for example, under the Children and Young Persons Act 1933, see ch. 7 – the offence will usually be punished under the specific provisions of that other statute, rather than as contempt.

◗ Contempt of Court Act 1981

A primary purpose when Parliament passed the 1981 Act was to replace some aspects of the common law of contempt, to provide greater certainty about what constitutes a contempt offence. Section 1 of the Act made con-

→glossary tempt by publication a **strict liability** offence.

- The Act's strict liability rule states that a contempt offence occurs if material is published which creates a substantial risk of serious prejudice or impediment to particular legal proceedings which are 'active'.

For the definitions of 'active' and detail on what type of material if published could create such risks, see below. Strict liability means that the prosecution, when seeking to prove that such contempt has occurred, does <u>not</u> have to prove that an editor or media organisation responsible for the publication had intent to create such a risk. It is the actual or potential prejudicial effect of what was published which is judged. This strict liability ensures that the training of journalists places great weight on the need to avoid committing such contempt. Though prosecutions for contempt are usually of an editor and/or the relevant publishing company, a lower-ranking journalist could be prosecuted too if he/she was felt to be particularly responsible.

→
see also
ch. 3, pp.
35–36
on strict
liability

- The Act defines publication as any writing, speech, broadcast, or other communication addressed to any section of the public.

Breach of the strict liability rule is punishable as contempt, with a maximum of two years' jail and/or an unlimited fine.

Who can prosecute for contempt of court?

Proceedings for contempt under the strict liability rule can be initiated only by a Crown court or higher court, by the Attorney General, or by some other person with the Attorney General's consent.

→
see also
ch. 1 pp.
15–16 on
Attorney
General

Magistrates do not have power to punish contempt of court by publication. Any such contempt in respect of proceedings in a magistrates court (although no such contempt appears to have been recorded) would have to be dealt with by the High Court.

A judge trying a Crown court case has **inherent jurisdiction** to deal with contempt by publication arising during such proceedings. But in 1997 the Court of Appeal ruled that only in exceptional circumstances should trial judges deal with such an alleged contempt themselves (*R v Tyne Tees Television* (1997) *The Times*, 20 October, CA). Crown court judges therefore usually refer such a matter to the Attorney General, who will then decide if the matter should be raised in the High Court for a judgment there on whether contempt by publication has been committed.

→glossary

▶ When are criminal proceedings active?

Under the 1981 Act's strict liability rule, a writer, editor, publisher, proprietor, director, or distributor of a publication can only be held to be in contempt if a substantial risk of serious prejudice or impediment is created in respect of proceedings which are 'active' at the time of that publication.

The Act says a criminal case is active from the time:

- a person is arrested, or
- an arrest warrant is issued, or
- a summons is issued, or
- a person has been charged orally.

A criminal case, if not already active because one of the above four events has occurred, becomes active with the service on the accused of a document specifying the charge(s). See ch. 2 for explanation of these early stages of a criminal case. All of them mean that there is a definite prospect of a particular person facing trial. As that chapter explains, one potential problem for the media is that the police may not make clear, after a crime has been committed, if a person has actually been arrested or is merely 'helping the police with their inquiries'. In some cases, where the police have other suspects in mind, they may not wish to disclose that they have arrested one person, because they fear such news would cause the other suspects to hide from arrest.

See below, p. 284, for detail of when a criminal case ceases to be active. See p. 295, for detail of when a civil case is active. See ch. 15, p. 261, for detail of when cases before certain types of tribunal are active.

▶ What type of material can cause a substantial risk of serious prejudice?

The 1981 Act does not define what material if published will create such a risk to an active case. This, to a large extent, depends on the circumstances of each case. However, from the occasions when editors and media organisations have been convicted of contempt, it is clear that material which *could* be held to be in contempt of court – if published about a person arrested, charged, or summonsed or who is the subject of an arrest warrant – includes:

- reference to any previous convictions(s) he/she has;
- information suggesting he/she is dishonest or is of bad character in other ways;

- any evidence which seems to link him/her directly to the crime of which he/she is suspected or accused;
- any other suggestion that he/she is guilty of it.

If the person is tried, the magistrates or jury will probably not be told of any previous convictions he/she has, and evidence about his/her character and of the crime itself will be admissible only if it meets the standard of evidence acceptable in a trial.

→ see also p. 70 on 'bad character'

It could also be deemed to be contempt to an active case if published material includes:

- a photograph or physical description of such a person when visual identification of him/her as the alleged perpetrator is or is likely to be an evidential issue because:
  - a police identity parade is to be held; and/or
  - a witness is expected to testify at the trial on such visual identification.

If such a photo or description is published a witness may be influenced or confused when giving visual identification evidence, and the court may not be sure if the witness's evidence is based on what he/she saw during the alleged crime or on recollection of a photograph or description which was published subsequently.

Commonly, after a crime is committed the police, in order to get information from the public about who the alleged perpetrator is, ask the media to publish a sketch of or a computer generated image of his/her face, as described by a witness, or a physical description – e.g. 'He was stocky, had short brown hair and a beard'.

The strict liability rule means that the image and description must usually <u>not</u> be published again after the case becomes active.

The Queen's Bench Divisional Court (part of the High Court) ruled in 2004 that a newspaper article revealing the identities of two well-known Premier League footballers being questioned by police over allegations of gang rape at a London hotel created a substantial risk of serious prejudice, because visual identification of the alleged attackers was at issue at the time – i.e. there was a possibility that the alleged victim and/or other witnesses would be asked to pick out from an identity parade or to describe in other evidence the men who allegedly committed the crime. The *Daily Star* was fined £60,000, with costs, for contempt. Lord Justice Rose said the article had created a real, substantial, more than remote risk that the course of justice would be seriously impeded or prejudiced. The aggravating feature of the case was that the media had been repeatedly told not to name or carry photographs of the players under investigation. The Crown Prosecution Service eventually said there was insufficient evidence to prosecute the footballers.

In 1994, a record fine for contempt of court of £80,000 was imposed by the Queen's Bench Divisional Court on the *Sun* after it published a photograph of a man accused of murder. This picture was published six weeks before a police identity parade, in which he was picked out by witnesses. Kelvin MacKenzie, editor at the time of publication, was fined £20,000.

It may also be deemed to be contempt if a witness's detailed account of a relevant event is published after a case becomes active, because there is a risk that:

- the witness may, because such a detailed account has been published, feel obliged to stick to it and therefore may feel less able honestly to retract or vary some detail after further reflection, or that

- the witness's evidence may not figure in the trial at all, because it is ruled inadmissible or has been retracted – but if it has already been published other witnesses, lay magistrates, or people selected as jurors in the case may have read or heard it and been influenced by it.

Though examples of prejudicial material in this chapter relate mainly to the contempt risk in stating or implying that a suspect or a defendant is guilty, it should be remembered too that it is possible to breach the strict liability rule by publishing material suggesting or asserting such a person is innocent.

⬚ Point for consideration

The High Court has power to grant an **injunction**, forbidding publication of matter which, it has been told, is soon to be published and which could in the court's view create a substantial risk of serious prejudice to a particular criminal case. The Attorney General, for example, can ask the court to do this. Such an injunction could also be issued to restrain other media activity regarded as being capable of creating serious prejudice, e.g. attempts by reporters to interview witnesses when a trial is pending – see also p. 298. It has been ruled that a Crown court too has some power to grant such injunctions (*Ex p HTV Cymru (Wales) Ltd, Crown Court at Cardiff* (Aikens J) [2002] EMLR 184).

What can be published after a criminal case becomes active?

The law of contempt does not mean that, after a case becomes active, nothing should be published about the alleged crime. In almost all cases, it will not be contempt to publish the name of the arrested person, because his/her name will feature in any eventual trial. Under the 1981 Act it will not be illegal to publish the names of the alleged victim(s) – though other types of reporting restriction may mean they must have anonymity in media reports. Non-prejudicial, basic information about the alleged crime can continue to be published. For example, it can be reported that there was an alleged robbery, where it allegedly took place, and that later 'a man' was arrested, but not 'the robber was later arrested', because the latter statement asserts that the arrested person is guilty of the alleged crime. See also ch. 2, pp. 28–29 on the risk of libel if a crime report names someone who has been arrested but not charged.

 see chs 7, 8, and 9

 glossary

Common ground

It will not be regarded under the 1981 Act as prejudicial to publish material which is going to be common ground between the defence and prosecution at any eventual trial. Non-prejudicial background material about the alleged perpetrator and any alleged victim falls into this category. Also, in a murder case, there is rarely going to be dispute about where the body was found. In contested cases, the nature and extent of a dead or surviving victim's injuries will probably be common ground because much of the forensic or medical evidence will be beyond dispute – the trial issue will be how these injuries were caused or who caused them.

 When a person appears on a charge in court, **automatic** reporting restrictions may well apply to media reports of the pre-trial hearings – see chs 4, 5, and 6.

 glossary

▶ How the courts interpret the strict liability rule

In respect of cases with potential of jury trial, Lord Justice Schiemann in *A-G v MGN Ltd* [1997] 1 All ER 456, set out the principles for a court to decide whether matter published had created a substantial risk of serious prejudice. He said it should consider what risk occurred at the time it was published. The mere fact that by reason of earlier publications there was already some risk of prejudice did not in itself prevent a finding that the latest publication had created a further risk. He said that the court should consider:

- the likelihood of the publication coming to the attention of a potential juror;

- the likely impact on an ordinary reader;
- and, crucially, the residual impact on a notional juror at the time of the trial.

Juries are told to put pre-trial publicity out of their minds

Judges tell juries, at the beginning of Crown court trials, to decide their verdicts only on what is presented to them in the trial's evidence, and to put any pre-trial publicity about the case, or media coverage of the trial, out of their minds.

The Court of Appeal held in 2003 that defendants who have been the subject of adverse publicity can nevertheless receive a fair trial as long as the judge explains to the jurors how they should approach their task. The Court of Appeal upheld the rejection by the trial judge of a defence submission

 →glossary

that to proceed would be an **abuse of process** in the case of two men charged with a racist attack on a black police officer. These men had previously been subject to adverse publicity because they were suspects in the inquiry into the murder of a black youth, Stephen Lawrence. The trial judge had said the trial process was designed to ensure a fair trial notwithstanding such publicity (*R v Acourt and Norris* [2003] EWCA Crim 929).

As long ago as 1969, Mr Justice (later Lord Justice) Lawton said:

> 66 I have enough confidence in my fellow-countrymen to think that they have got newspapers sized up...and they are capable in normal circumstances of looking at a matter fairly and without prejudice even though they have to disregard what they have read in a newspaper....It is a matter of human experience and certainly a matter of experience for those who practise in the criminal courts first that the public's recollection is short, and secondly, that the drama, if I may use that term, of a trial almost always has the effect of excluding from recollection that which went before (*R v Kray* (1969) 53 Cr App R 412). 99

→
see also
ch. 13, pp.
225–227
for
similar
rulings

More recently, senior judges have firmly endorsed this view that a jury when instructed by the judge is capable of looking at the evidence fairly, even though they may have to disregard what they have read in or heard from media. The Lord Chief Justice, Lord Phillips, said in 2006 that in general the courts had not been prepared to accede to submissions that pre-trial publicity had made a fair trial impossible. Rather, they had held that directions from the judge coupled with the trial process would result in the jury disregarding such publicity (*R v Abu Hamza* [2006] EWCA Crim 2918).

The 'fade factor' and limited publication

The 'fade factor' is a term used to recognise that detail in material published in the early stages of an active, criminal case, e.g. after an arrest or around the time someone is charged, may well have been completely or largely forgotten by members of the public by the time a jury is selected from the public. Another factor a court will take into account when deciding if the strict liability rule has been breached is the geographical area in which the matter was published, and the likely extent to which it was read – or in the case of a broadcast report, seen or heard – in that area.

→ see ch. 6 pp. 76 and 84 on jury selection

The Attorney General said in 2004 that the passage of time might dent or remove the recollection of prejudicial reporting to the point where it no longer put in jeopardy the fairness of a trial. This was especially so when combined with appropriate directions to the jury and the focusing effect of listening over a prolonged period to the evidence.

A leading textbook, *Arlidge, Eady and Smith on Contempt* (2005) observes:

> A long gap between publication and the anticipated trial date may significantly reduce any risk of contamination. Also the fact that publication takes place in the local media, outside the anticipated area of trial, would be a major consideration in reducing the risk of prejudice. On the other hand, some facts are so striking, even when published some time in advance of the hearing, as to render it impossible to be confident that the conscientiousness of jurors, or the directions of a trial judge, would prevent a substantial risk that the course of justice in the trial would be seriously impeded or prejudiced…This is especially so in the case of the revelation of a criminal record.

→ see pp. 276–277 on previous convictions

In 1994 prosecutions for contempt against Independent Television News, the *Daily Mail, Daily Express, Today,* and the *Northern Echo* (Darlington) failed, because the Queen's Bench Divisional Court decided that in respect of the relevant proceedings there was no more than a remote risk of serious prejudice actually occurring. The QBD court held that no contempt had been established because of the length of time between publication and trial, the limited circulation of copies of the papers which contained the offending material, and the ephemeral nature of a single ITN broadcast. The material complained of had been used within two days of the arrest of two Irishmen on charges of murdering a special constable and the attempted murder of another police officer. Lord Justice Leggatt said it was of overriding importance that the lapse of time between the publications and the trial was likely to be nine months, and in the event was.

The lapse of time was a factor in assessing the substantial risk of serious prejudice in a contempt case in 1997. The *Daily Mail* and the Manchester *Evening News*, which had carried stories describing how a home help was caught on video film stealing from an 82-year-old widow, were found not guilty of contempt of court in the Queen's Bench Divisional Court. Mr Justice Owen said his initial view was that the stories were a plain contempt of court carrying as they did the clearest statements that the home help was guilty, at a time when proceedings against her were active. The key issue was whether the stories created a substantial risk that the criminal proceedings against the home help would be seriously prejudiced. The stories were several months old by the time of the trial, however, and he had concluded that the allegation of contempt was not made good. Another judge in that case, Lord Justice Simon Brown, warned the media against taking the view that where a person was apparently caught red-handed there was no possibility of a not guilty plea being entered at trial. There was always a real chance that an accused, however strong the evidence against him, would plead not guilty (*A-G v Unger* [1998] 1 Cr App R 308).

Publication of material shortly before or during a trial

It follows that, as regards a media organisation avoiding a conviction for contempt, the protection of the 'fade factor' is diminished or is non-existent if the material concerned has been published shortly before the relevant trial begins, or after it has begun. For example, in 2008 ITV Central was fined £25,000 for contempt after it broadcast an item about an ongoing trial which included details of a defendant's previous convictions.

The *Sunday Mirror* was fined £75,000 in 2002 for the publication of an article which led to the collapse of the first trial of two Leeds United footballers on assault charges. The article was published while the jury was still considering its verdict and had been sent home for the weekend. It contained an interview with the victim's father who said his son was the victim of a racial attack – a statement that was at variance with a direction which had been given by the trial judge that there was no evidence of a racial motive. → glossary In the contempt proceedings, **counsel** for the Attorney General estimated the cost of the aborted trial at £1,113,000 and the cost of the subsequent retrial £1,125,000.

> →   see also below, p. 284: 'Media could face huge costs…'

In 1981, the *Guardian* was fined £5,000 for contempt because during a trial it published an article in which there was reference to the fact that two of the accused had previously escaped from custody. The jury had not been told of their escape. The trial had to be abandoned and held afresh the following year.

Archive material on news websites

Obviously, the protection of 'the fade factor' does not apply to material which, since it was originally published, remains accessible to the public in a media organisation's online archive. Although UK juries are instructed by judges not to conduct their own research into defendants being tried, it remains a possibility that jurors (and witnesses) will search the internet for such matter. Jurors may find, for example, reference in a news archive to a defendant's previous convictions or detailed accounts of the crime they are trying which were originally published before the case became active or – in the most newsworthy cases – they may find matter about the crime published abroad by foreign media which can ignore UK contempt law.

UK media organisations point out that it would be impossible for them to keep checking whether anything in their online archives from bygone years refers to people who have since become involved in any of the thousands of cases which at any one time are active. However,

- if a media organisation's attention is drawn to archived material which, in the view of the defence or prosecution creates a substantial risk of serious prejudice to a particular active case, the safest course to avoid a contempt problem is to prevent public access to that material until the case ceases to be active.

Lord Falconer, the former Lord Chancellor, suggested in 2008 that the Attorney General should be able to identify twenty or so high-profile cases where there was a distinct contempt risk and write to the media about them, warning the media to remove such prejudicial material from their websites.

The risk posed by material on the internet has been recognised in other jurisdictions. In the Australian state of Victoria a juror commits a criminal offence if he/she uses the internet to research a case being tried.

In 2008 in a trial in the UK of three men for child abduction and sexual assault, one juror used the social networking site *Facebook* to help her decide a verdict. 'I don't know which way to go, so I'm holding a poll,' she wrote. The court was alerted and she was dismissed from the jury.

▶ Media could face huge costs if 'serious misconduct' affects a case

Under the Courts Act 2003 the then Lord Chancellor, Lord Falconer, made regulations in 2004 allowing a magistrates court, a Crown court, or the Court of Appeal to order a third party (which could be a media organisation) to pay costs which are incurred in a court case as a consequence of 'serious misconduct' by that party (Costs in Criminal Cases (General) (Amendment) Regulations 2004 (SI 2004/2408)). It is worrying for the media that the definition of 'serious misconduct' falls short of the statutory test for strict liability for contempt of court – substantial risk of serious prejudice. 'Serious misconduct' could be held to have occurred through publication of material, or through an action of a reporter, even though no contempt is proved to have occurred. The Department of Constitutional Affairs (now the Ministry of Justice) said the new measure was largely inspired by the abandonment, following a *Sunday Mirror* article, of the trial in the Leeds footballers case, which wasted costs of about £1 million. If serious misconduct is held to have occurred in this type of circumstance in future, the media organisation involved would become liable for such huge costs.

→ see above, p. 282

Regulation 3F(4) says that the court must allow the third party against whom such a costs order is sought to make representations, and may hear evidence. An appeal against such an order made by magistrates may be made to the Crown court, an appeal against a Crown court order may be heard in the Court of Appeal. There is no appeal against such an order made in the Court of Appeal.

▶ When do criminal proceedings cease to be active?

Under the Contempt of Court Act 1981 criminal proceedings are no longer active when any of the following events occurs:

→ glossary

- the arrested person is released without being charged (except when released on **police bail** (see ch. 2, p. 24);
- no arrest is made within 12 months of the issue of an arrest warrant (see ch. 2, p. 27);

- the case is discontinued;
- the defendant is acquitted or sentenced; or
- he/she is found unfit to be tried, or unfit to plead, or the court orders the charge to lie on file.

A defendant can be ruled to be unfit to be tried or unfit to plead if he/she suffers acute physical ill-health or mental illness. If a court orders that a charge should 'lie on file' it means that a defendant has been neither con-victed nor acquitted of it, but that the court agrees that the charge is not worth proceeding with. For example, if after a lengthy trial a defendant is convicted of four charges but the jury cannot agree on the fifth charge, the judge may order the fifth charge to 'lie on file' if the expense of a retrial just for that charge seems excessive, and/or it would not, in the event of it being proved, lead to a longer term in prison than the defendant already faces for the four other convictions.

Period between verdict and sentence at Crown court

It will be seen from what is stated above that a Crown court case remains active, even though all verdicts have been reached, until the defendant is sentenced. So it is technically possible that a media organisation could breach the strict liability rule in this period, even though jury involvement has ceased. But a Crown court judge is regarded as too experienced to be influenced by media coverage of a case, so it is considered very unlikely that any substantial risk of serious prejudice will arise whatever is published after all verdicts but before an adjourned sentencing. Media organisations therefore feel safe to publish background features about such a case, includ-ing material which did not feature in the trial, as soon as the last verdict in it is decided.

see also ch. 6, p. 85 on senten-cing

◗ Proceedings become active again when an appeal is lodged

The 1981 Act states that:

- when an appeal is lodged, the case becomes active again, so strict liability for contempt resumes;

- the case ceases to be active when the hearing of any appeal is completed – unless in that appeal a new trial is ordered or the case is remitted to a lower court.

Often a lawyer announces at the end of a criminal or civil case that his/her client will appeal but it usually takes some weeks for any appeal to be prepared and lodged.

Thus there is a 'free-for-all' time (the words of Sir Michael Havers when Attorney General) when the case is not active between, in a criminal case, the sentence and the lodging of any appeal.

see ch. 6, p. 88 on appeals

- As regards an appeal lodged against a conviction in a Crown court, the media still have considerable freedom as regards contempt law in what can be published about such a case, even though it has thus become active again, because the appeal will be heard by the very experienced judges of the Court of Appeal.
- It can safely be assumed that nothing the media can publish will create a substantial risk of serious prejudice to the way these judges approach the case. However, if in the appeal hearing they order that there should be a retrial – i.e. another jury trial – the media must thereafter be very wary of publishing anything which creates such risk to the retrial, because witnesses and potential jurors will be seen as susceptible to publicity about the case before and during the retrial.

Where to check if an appeal has been lodged

Appeals to the Court of Appeal from Crown court trials may be lodged at the Crown court office. Appeals on a point of law to the Queen's Bench Divisional Court from a Crown court appeal hearing must be lodged at the Royal Courts of Justice in London. Appeals from magistrates court summary trials may be lodged at a local Crown court office.

The High Court in Belfast in 2002 refused to impose an injunction preventing Ulster Television broadcasting a programme containing new material which had not been put before the jury in a trial in which two men had been convicted of murder. The men's lawyers said they intended to appeal and, if they were granted a retrial, the material could prejudice a new jury. But Mr Justice Kerr said the possibility of a retrial was a matter of speculation (see also ch. 13, p. 227 for Lord Macfadyen's ruling in similar circumstances).

▌ Police appeals for media assistance

Sometimes when the police have obtained a warrant for a person's arrest, they seek through the media the help of the public in tracing him/her. The warrant has made the case active under the 1981 Act. Police may supply a photograph and/or description of the person for publication, even though visual identification may be an evidential issue in the case, and, if the person is armed or likely to be violent in others ways, the police may state this to warn the public from approaching him/her.

see ch. 2, p. 27 on arrest warrants

- Technically, a media organisation publishing such a photograph, description, or such a warning about the person's character could be accused of thereby creating a substantial risk of serious prejudice to such an active case.

- But the then Attorney General said in the House of Commons during the debate on the Contempt of Court Bill in 1981:

see pp. 276–277

❝ The press has nothing whatever to fear from publishing in reasoned terms anything which may assist in the apprehension of a wanted man and I hope that it will continue to perform this public service. ❞

- There is no known case of a media organisation being held in contempt for publishing such a police appeal.
- But there is no defence in the 1981 Act for assisting the police in this way.

The Attorney General's comments would not apply to such information supplied by the police which is published or repeated <u>after</u> the person was arrested, i.e. when the police no longer need assistance in the case.

▌ Section 3 defence of not knowing proceedings were active

Section 3 of the Act provides a defence for an alleged breach of the strict liability rule. The defence applies if:

- the person responsible for the publication, having taken all reasonable care, did not know and had no reason to suspect when the matter was published that relevant proceedings were active.

But the burden of proof in establishing that all reasonable care was taken is upon the person accused of contempt. Therefore, to be sure that the section 3 defence can be used, a journalist reporting a crime story must check regularly, especially prior to a deadline, with the police to discover whether there has been an arrest or charge, because either event would make the case active. For the same reason, for some news stories it may be necessary for a journalist to check with the magistrates court whether an arrest warrant or summonses has been been issued.If the police or court spokesperson says the case is not active, the journalist should keep a note of what was said and of the time of the check, to prove if necessary that reasonable care was taken to establish if the case was active.

→

see p. 276 on when a case is active

If it turns out from such a check that the case has become active, matter which could create a substantial risk of serious prejudice should be removed from what is due to be published. Such matter is described earlier in this chapter.

▶ Section 4 defence for court reporting

In some circumstances, there is a possibility that a media report of a court hearing could create a substantial risk of prejudice to a later stage of the same case or to another case due to be tried. For examples of such circumstances, see below.

Before the Contempt of Court Act 1981 came into effect even a fair and accurate report of proceedings in open court could be held to create such risk of prejudice, and so be contempt. But as part of Parliament's aim to make contempt law more precise, and fairer, section 4 of the 1981 Act provided a specific defence for the media in this situation.

Section 4 of the Act states that a person cannot be found guilty of breaching the strict liability rule in respect of:

- a report of a court hearing which is held in public;
- if it is a fair and accurate report of that hearing;
- published contemporaneously;
- and in good faith.

For the definition of 'contemparoneous' as regard, publication, see ch. 19, p. 339. 'Good faith' is not defined in the Act, but the overall effect of section 4 is that courts are expected to make a specific order restricting the media if they do not want all, or part of, any hearing to be reported contemporaneously.

It should be noted that the section 4 defence does <u>not</u> protect, as regards the strict liability rule, a report of a court hearing held in private – see also ch. 12.

 → glossary

Inaccurate reporting of a current jury trial

The section 4 defence does <u>not</u> protect a report of a court case held to be unfair or inaccurate. The BBC was fined £5,000 in the Queen's Bench Divisional Court in 1992 for an inaccurate report of a continuing trial before a jury. It was submitted on behalf of the Attorney General that critical issues in the trial were affected by erroneous comment and presentation of facts which could easily and wrongly influence members of the jury. It was held that the report contained errors which had created a substantial risk of serious prejudice since it was foreseeable that publication would delay and obstruct the course of justice (*A-G v BBC* [1992] COD 264).

▌ Section 4(2) orders

In some circumstances, a media report of a court case, even if the report is fair and accurate, could prejudice a later stage of that case or another one.

- For example, if a defendant, or several defendants, are to be dealt with in more than one trial, media reports of the first trial in the series – for example, concerning alleged smuggling of heroin – could arguably if published contemporaneously, and especially if any defendant is convicted, influence people who read such reports and who are then selected as jurors for the next trial in the series, which could concern different allegations of drug-smuggling against the same defendant(s).

- The jury in the second trial, because of the principle of the presumption of innocence for defendants, may well be told nothing in the second trial about the earlier trial. Yet if a juror in this second trial remembers media reports of the first, he/she may be more likely to find a defendant guilty, in that it will be clear that the defendant has featured in more than one drugs case.

→
see ch. 5
p. 70
on 'bad
character'

To avoid such danger of an unfair trial, section 4(2) of the 1981 Act gives a court power to order postponement of the publication of media reports of a hearing. In the example above, a judge could order that no report of the first trial should be published until the second trial is concluded.

Section 4(2) states that:

- a court may order the postponement of the reporting of a case, or part of a case;
- where this appears to be necessary for avoiding a substantial risk of prejudice to the administration of justice in those proceedings;
- or in any other proceedings, pending or imminent;
- the period of postponement may be as long as the court thinks necessary for this purpose.

It should be noted that for a court to make a section 4(2) order the substantial risk need only be of any prejudice, not necessarily of 'serious' prejudice. Publication of matter which breaches a section 4(2) order is punishable as contempt, with a maximum of two years' jail and/or an unlimited fine.

Normally all charges against a defendant can be reported prior to any trial, even under the automatic reporting restrictions of other statutes as described in chs 4, 5, and 6. However, in cases in which a defendant is due to face more than one trial, a Crown court judge may at a stage prior to trial – for example, at the **arraignment** – make a section 4(2) order to postpone publication, before the end of the first trial, of the charge(s) the defendant is due to face in any subsequent trial. The purpose in such circumstances of a section 4(2) order would be to prevent anyone who could be selected for the jury in the first trial knowing that the same defendant is due thereafter to face another trial – knowledge which could prove prejudicial.

see ch. 6, p. 78

See ch. 13, pp. 223–229, for grounds on which the media may choose to challenge the imposition of a section 4(2) order.

▌ What if a section 4(2) order is not made?

Pleas made in a hearing before the trial

Sometimes, a defendant facing a number of charges will plead guilty to some but deny one or more of the others, and then the jury will be brought in to try him/her on the charge(s) he/she has denied. If a media organisation carries a report before the end of that trial which mentions that the defendant has pleaded guilty to or faces some other charge(s), and if the jury has not been told of other charges and/or any such guilty plea (i.e. a previous conviction), the judge may feel it necessary, to ensure fairness to the defendant, to stop the trial and to order a retrial before a fresh jury elsewhere, at great expense to public funds. If the judge had made a section 4(2) order before the trial began, ordering the media to postpone the reporting of the other charge(s)/guilty plea(s), the media's position would have been clear – they should have obeyed the order. But if the judge did not make such an order, the legal position would be less clear as regards whether contempt could be deemed to have occurred by such reporting during the trial of the other charge(s)/guilty plea(s).

In 1981, before the 1981 Act took effect, four evening newspapers were each fined £500 for contempt of court arising in this way. The judge had not indicated to reporters present when the guilty pleas were made that they should not report them at that stage.

In the view of some legal experts, the defence in the Act's section 4 – detailed above – should now provide the media with protection against prosecution for contempt in such circumstances. Their view is that unless the court makes clear, by making a section 4(2) postponement order, that such matter aired in open court should not be contemporaneously published, that defence should apply. However, the section 4 defence is subject to 'good faith' being present in the motive to publish. If it could be proved that the person responsible for what was published had deliberate intent to create prejudice to the subsequent trial, the section 4 defence would fail. Also, if such intent was proved the offence could be regarded not as breach of the 1981 Act but as a graver contempt, in common law. See also below, under 'The law is not clear'.

Matters aired in court in the absence of the jury

Often a judge will be asked to make a ruling, in the course of a trial, about the admissibility of evidence or about another matter. He/she will make that ruling after hearing from defence and prosecution lawyers, while the jury is kept out of the courtroom. The process of making such a ruling – sometimes referred to as 'a trial within a trial' – is still classed as a public proceeding. But it may be that the judge's ruling to the lawyers is that they should not tell the jury about the matter thus discussed. If the media covering the case were then to publish, before the verdict stage is complete, a report of that discussion, this could lead to the trial being aborted – if the jury thereby gets to know of that matter. Yet the judge may not make a section 4(2) postponement order in respect of matter discussed in court in the jury's absence, because he/she expects the media to realise that it should not be published prematurely.

→

see ch. 31, p. 502 on Ponting

In February 1985 during the trial of Clive Ponting, a civil servant, on a charge under the Official Secrets Act, the judge discussed with counsel in the absence of the jury the instructions he should give to the jury on its return to court. The *Observer* published a report of these discussions, while the trial was still in progress. The judge said afterwards that he had not made an order under section 4(2) to postpone publication because it had never occurred to him that the discussions would be publicised before the end of the trial. He referred the matter to the Attorney General who later announced that he had decided not to prosecute the *Observer* for contempt.

The law is not clear

The application of the law of contempt in both the circumstances outlined above – i.e. publication prior to trial of any guilty plea(s)/other charge(s), or contemporaneous publication of matter heard in the jury's absence during a trial – is unclear if no section 4(2) order has been made.

A leading textbook, *Arlidge, Eady and Smith on Contempt* (2005), says:

> 66 Suppose that through oversight or other reason no such [section 4(2)] order is made. Suppose also that information comes to light in the absence of the jury – guilty pleas, or an inadmissible confession for example – which journalists readily appreciate would be likely to prejudice the jury if its members were to find out about it. It may well be in such circumstances that publication of that information would give rise to a substantial risk of serious prejudice, and thus to a **prima facie** contempt under the strict liability rule. It would seem that in principle, provided the publication took place in good faith, the [section 4 defence] protection would prevail. Even if the journalists were conscious of the risk of serious prejudice at the time of publication, it would be difficult to infer any intention on their part to interfere with the administration of justice sufficient to found a common law contempt, since they would presumably (in accordance with the majority view in *R v Horsham Justices, ex p Farquharson* [1982] QB 762) be entitled to assume that the court having the power to order a section 4(2) postponement, knew its own business and had decided on good and sufficient grounds to make no such order. 99

→ glossary

The Judicial Studies Board guidance on reporting restrictions at Crown courts is starker. It states:

 At common law, it is a contempt of court to publish any material which interferes with the course of justice as a continuing process in criminal proceedings. The reporting of that which transpires at times when the jury are asked to withdraw, at any stage before the jury returns its verdict, is therefore likely to be a contempt of court since the report may well defeat the whole purpose of the jury withdrawing. **""**

→ See Useful Websites, below. For more detail of the common law of contempt, see below, p. 297.

Journalists should <u>not</u>, even if no section 4(2) order is made, contemporaneously publish matter discussed or rulings made when the jury is not in the courtroom during a Crown court trial. Even if such publication cannot be held to be contempt, there is presumably a prospect of a media organisation being accused of 'serious misconduct' under the Courts Act 2003, with therefore a risk of it being held liable for the costs of any aborted trial. Such matter can be published after all verdicts are reached, unless the judge orders otherwise. Arguably, the same cautious approach should be taken in respect of publishing any other charge(s) faced, or guilty plea(s) entered, by a defendant who is shortly to be tried on other matters, unless it is clear that the jury will be told of the quilty plea(s)/other charge(s).

see above, p. 284 on Courts Act

▌ Section 5 defence of discussion of public affairs

Section 5 of the Contempt of Court Act states that:

- if a publication is made as, or as part of, a discussion in good faith of public affairs it will not be treated as contempt of court under the strict liability rule if the risk of impediment or prejudice to particular legal proceedings is merely incidental to the discussion.

This defence was introduced because of complaints that freedom of expression in the United Kingdom had been unnecessarily restricted by a ruling given in a case in 1974. The *Sunday Times* wanted to publish an article raising important issues of public interest about the way the drug thalidomide had been tested and marketed. This article had been prepared at a time when civil actions were pending against the manufacturers, Distillers Company (Biochemicals) Ltd, on behalf of children born with deformed limbs because their mothers took the drug during pregnancy. The House of Lords ruled in an appeal that the proposed article would be contempt in respect of those pending cases. Commenting on the decision, the Government-appointed Phillimore Committee said in 1974:

> 66 At any given moment many thousands of legal proceedings are in progress, a number of which may well raise or reflect such issues (matters of general public interest). If, for example, a general public debate about fire precautions in hotels is in progress, the debate clearly ought not to be brought to a halt simply because a particular hotel is prosecuted for breach of the fire regulations. 99

The European Court of Human Rights in 1979 held that the Lords' ruling violated Article 10 of the European Convention on Human Rights, protecting freedom of expression.

The Government's response to the Phillimore Committee and to the ECtHR ruling was to introduce the section 5 defence. The time of liability for contempt in civil proceedings was also changed.

→
see below, p. 295 on civil cases

The Dr Leonard Arthur case

Two newspapers were prosecuted in 1981 for contempt arising from comments published *during* the trial of Dr Leonard Arthur, a paediatrician accused of murdering a baby with Down's syndrome. It was alleged that the doctor, to comply with the parents' wishes, let the new-born baby starve, in a form of euthanasia. The doctor was acquitted of murder. The *Sunday Express* admitted that contempt was committed in an article by John Junor, the editor. The article had complained of the murder trial taking five weeks and said if the Down's syndrome baby had been allowed to live so long he might have found someone apart from God to love him. The editor was fined £1,000 and Express Newspapers £10,000.

The *Daily Mail*, however, denied contempt. The High Court rejected a submission that the *Mails* article, by Malcolm Muggeridge, was protected by section 5. But on appeal, the House of Lords held that while the article did create a substantial risk of serious prejudice to the trial of Dr Arthur, the article *did* meet the criterion of being written in good faith and, because it was written in support of a 'pro-life' candidate at a by-election, it was a discussion of public affairs. Lord Diplock said the article made no express mention of the Arthur case and that the risk of prejudice would be properly described as merely incidental.

- It can be seen, therefore, that to be sure of protection by section 5, a media organisation should not, when publishing a general feature or discussion about a social issue, make any reference in it to any active case in which the issue figures, and in particular should not suggest that the defendant in such a case is guilty or not guilty.

▶ Contempt of civil proceedings under the 1981 Act

- Under the 1981 Act's strict liability rule, civil proceedings are deemed to be active from the time a date for the trial or a hearing is fixed.
- A civil case ceases to be active when it is disposed of, abandoned, discontinued, or withdrawn.

→ ch. 10 explains civil courts

There is generally less possibility of media coverage creating a substantial risk of serious prejudice to active civil cases than to active criminal cases. This is because juries are rarely used in civil cases. Most civil cases are tried by a judge alone. Judges are regarded as highly unlikely to be affected by media coverage. This gives the media fairly broad scope to publish matter about active civil cases.

→ see ch. 10, pp 158–159 on civil cases

- There remains, however, the possibility that witnesses in any civil case could be affected by what the media publish about it, if that coverage delves so deeply into the circumstances of the case that witnesses' evidence given in advance of or at the trial could be coloured or their memories contaminated by detail they have read in the media.

When a jury is involved, particular care must be taken not to breach the strict liability rule, and matter aired in court in the jury's absence should not be published until the jury's involvement in the case ceases.

Mr Justice Poole, in the High Court at Birmingham in 1999, reminded reporters that civil proceedings remained active until the end of the case. A jury had decided in favour of a man's claim against West Midlands Police for malicious prosecution. Before the jury had decided on the damages to be awarded, the *Birmingham Post* suggested that the **claimant** was in line

→ glossary

for an award of £30,000. The judge said the proceedings were therefore tainted. The claimant then abandoned his case rather than go through a retrial.

Sometimes when a journalist seeks a comment about a civil case, a lawyer involved will insist little can be published because it is **sub judice** – a term which indicates merely that the legal action has begun. But this is not the same as the case being active: a civil case becomes active, as stated above, at what may be a later stage, when a date is fixed for the trial or hearing, and even then, media coverage is not prohibited, provided the strict liability rule is obeyed.

 → glossary

> → See also ch. 10, p. 154, for the contempt danger of reporting that a 'payment into court' has been made in a civil case.

Other contempts under the 1981 Act

→

see ch. 9
for more
details
of these
contempts

Section 11 of the Contempt of Court Act also gives power to the courts, when they allow a name or other matter to be withheld from the public, to prohibit the publication of that name or matter in connection with the proceedings. Breach of a section 11 order could be punished as contempt.

It is contempt of court to use or take into court for use any audio recorder (except by permission of the court), and to broadcast any such recordings.

It is contempt of court to seek to discover or to publish how an individual juror voted in a verdict, or what was discussed by a jury to reach a verdict.

Contempt in reports of court hearings held in private

If the media discover that what has been said in a court hearing heard in private, and publishes an account of it, this will under the Administration of Justice Act 1960 be regarded as contempt if the case falls into certain categories. See ch. 9, pp. 130–132.

▶ Contempt in common law

- In the common law of contempt, it is an offence to publish matter which creates a real risk of prejudice to legal proceedings which are imminent or pending, if it can be proved that there was intent to create such a risk.

- The term 'intent' in this context could mean either deliberate intent to create such a risk, or recklessness in publishing matter which the person responsible for the publication should have foreseen would create such a risk.

The Contempt of Court Act 1981 largely superseded this common law by creating the strict liability rule in respect of a case which is active under the Act. The older, common law of contempt still applies in respect of matter published in the period before proceedings become active under the Act (and arguably too in respect of matter published at later stages in the proceedings). However, prosecutions which allege the media have committed such contempt are extremely rare, because for any journalist or editor to be guilty it has to be proved that he/she had intent to create such risk.

In 1988 the *Sun* was fined £75,000 by the High Court for such contempt in common law. The newspaper had offered to fund a private prosecution of a doctor on a charge of raping an eight-year-old girl. It had then published two articles with details of the allegation, made by the girl's mother, which expressed outrage directed at the doctor. Lord Justice Watkins said intent to prejudice those rape proceedings was proved. This was, the judge said, because the editor must have foreseen that the articles he published, which included announcement of steps he was taking to assist the mother to begin the private prosecution, would incur a real risk of prejudicing any eventual trial of the doctor on that accusation. In fact, no trial took place because the doctor was acquitted by a judge at a pre-trial stage, because of insufficient evidence.

In 1991 the *Sport* newspaper and its editor were cleared of common law contempt after they published the previous convictions of a rapist being sought by police for questioning about a missing schoolgirl. No warrant had been issued, so the case was not active under the 1981 Act. The editor said he had ignored police requests not to publish the convictions. He had done so because the rapist was 'on the run and a danger to other women'. The High Court held the Attorney General had not proved intent beyond reasonable doubt.

Witness interviews

see
p. 278,
above

As stated above, publishing detailed accounts of a witness's evidence while a case is active could be regarded as a breach of the 1981 Act's strict liability rule. But even if the intention is not to publish any interview with a witness until after the relevant trial concludes, it may be ruled to be contempt in common law if a reporter interviews a witness about his/her evidence before that witness has given evidence in the case. It may be ruled that the reporter has committed such contempt if he/she contaminated the witness's memory of the relevant events, for example by telling the witness of what other witnesses have said. The reporter may have committed contempt if he/she said anything else which could influence what that witness thinks he/she remembers or which could otherwise affect his/her testimony. It could also be deemed a contempt by 'molestation' if a journalist pestered a witness so much for a pre-trial interview, or in taking photos of him/her that he/she was deterred from giving evidence. If a media organisation offers, before a witness has given evidence, payment to 'buy up' that witness to tell his/her story after the trial (for example, a crime victim describing the effect of his/her ordeal or experiences of the trial) this too could be deemed to be contempt in common law if the offer is held to have influenced how the witness gave evidence. See also clause 15 of the Press Complaints Commission's code of practice – Appendix 2, p. 571, on payments to witnesses.

see also
ch. 9 p.
145 on
photos

Vilifying a witness

If a media organisation, after a trial concludes, publishes criticism of a witness which is so abusive that it could be ruled by a judge as being likely to deter other people from becoming witnesses in future, such 'vilification' of the witness can be punished as a contempt in common law.

Scandalising the court

There is a contempt offence in common law which punishes the publication of scurrilous or very abusive comment about a judge – an offence known as 'scandalising the court'. This law evolved to protect the dignity and standing of the courts, so that the public could have confidence in them. However, there has been no prosecution for this offence for seventy years. Today, a media organisation which questions a judge's good faith or conduct in court is more likely to be sued by the judge for defamation than prosecuted for such contempt. Judges accept that their decisions may be criticised, and so are fairly tolerant of criticism published by the media, much of which can be defended anyway by the libel defence of **fair comment**.

> → See ch. 9, p. 132. for the contempt dangers in publishing matter from some types of court document.

→ see ch. 19, p. 333 on fair comment

◗ Appeals against a contempt conviction

Under section 13 of the Administration of Justice Act 1960, a right of appeal is provided for a person held to be in contempt. Appeals from the High Court (except from the Divisional Court) and the county court go to the Court of Appeal, and appeals from the Divisional Court and the Court of Appeal go to the House of Lords.

▦ Recap of major points

- For the media, the greatest danger of committing contempt of court lies in the publication of material which, under the Contempt of Court Act 1981, could be ruled to have created a substantial risk of serious prejudice to an 'active' case.

- Certain types of material are more likely than others to be regarded as creating such risk – e.g. publication of the previous convictions of a defendant awaiting trial.

- Journalists should know when under the Act a criminal or a civil case becomes active, and when it ceases to be active – because the 'active period' determines what can be published.

- But because juries are rarely used in civil cases, the media have greater leeway as regards what under the Act can be published about active civil cases than they have as regards about active criminal cases.

- In prosecuting under the Act for contempt the Attorney General does not have to prove intent to cause prejudice – the person accused is held to be strictly liable.

- Section 3 of the 1981 Act provides a defence of not knowing that the relevant proceedings were active.

- Section 4 of the Act provides a defence which protects fair, accurate, and contemporaneous reports of court cases.

- Under section 4(2) of the Act a court can order the media to postpone a report of a court case, or part of it, to avoid a substantial risk of prejudice.

- Section 5 provides a defence for a published discussion in good faith of public affairs where the risk of prejudice is merely incidental to the discussion.

- The older, common law of contempt survives, and a journalist could breach it by interviewing a witness in too much detail about evidence he/she is due to give, or by offering payment to the witness prior to trial for his/her story.

- When during a trial there are legal discussions or rulings which occur when the jury is not in the courtroom, the media should not report such matter until all verdicts are reached.

- The Courts Act 2003 introduced law which means that any party, including a media organisation, held to have committed 'serious misconduct' affecting a court case could be liable for huge costs.

🌐 Useful Websites

www.jsboard.co.uk/publications/rrcc/index.htm
  Judicial Studies Board guidance, 'Reporting Restrictions in the Crown Courts'

Part 2

Defamation and related law

Defamation

Chapter summary

This chapter will explain what defamation is and why it is of such a concern to journalists and publishers. It covers the risks of being sued for libel and of losing an action, and therefore having to pay huge costs and damages. In total, in a major case, these could exceed to £1 million. This chapter explains who can sue for defamation and the definitions of what is defamatory. The following chapter will cover what a **claimant** has to do to bring an action. Chapters 19 and 20 will → glossary detail the defences that are available to the media. For anyone who earns his or her living with words and images, defamation presents one of the greatest legal dangers. As this chapter explains, handling a complaint about something published or drafting an apology for it is not a job for an inexperienced journalist.

▶ What is defamation?

Law exists to protect the moral and professional reputation of the individual from unjustified attack. In civil law a statement making such an attack may be found to be a **tort** – that is, a civil wrong for which monetary damages may → glossary be awarded by a court.

Defamatory statements are those published or spoken which affect the reputation of a person, company, or organisation. Broadly speaking, if a defamatory statement is written or is in any other permanent form, the tort is libel, for which damages can be awarded, unless the statement is protected by a defence in libel law, as explained below and in subsequent chapters.

If the statement is spoken or in any other transient form it is, with two exceptions, the tort of slander, also liable to incur damages unless a defence applies.

Slander is explained in ch. 21

The exceptions are that defamatory statements when broadcast on radio or television, including by cable, or when occurring in the public performance of a play are, despite mostly being spoken statements, classed as libel – by the Broadcasting Act 1990 and Theatres Act 1968 respectively – if no defence applies. Libel and slander have different requirements as regards what a claimant must prove, as subsequent chapters explain.

Juries are used to try a defamation case, unless both sides agree for it to be heard by a judge alone, or the judge rules that a jury should not be used (for example, if he/she considers that the case is so complex that having to explain all the paperwork to a jury will add greatly to its length).

see also ch. 10, p. 158 on civil case juries

In a libel case with a jury:

- the judge rules whether a statement complained of is capable of bearing a defamatory meaning;

- if the answer is yes, a jury must decide whether, in the circumstances in which the statement was made, it was in fact defamatory.

→
see p. 310 on damages

A key issue in the case may be the meaning of words in the context of their use. If a jury decides the statement *was* in fact defamatory, it decides how much the publisher must pay in damages to the defamed party.

▶ Definitions of a defamatory statement

There are certain definitions that judges often use when they are trying to explain defamation to juries.

Judges tell juries that a statement about a person is defamatory if it <u>tends to</u> do any one of the following:

- expose the person to hatred, ridicule, or contempt;

- cause the person to be shunned or avoided;

- lower the person in the estimation of right-thinking members of society generally; or

- disparage the person in his/her business, trade, office, or profession.

Notice the words 'tends to', which are important. The person suing does not have to show that the words actually did expose him/her to hatred, etc. These definitions date back to libel cases in the Victorian era and the early twentieth century. They remain unchanged, but what words fit those definitions will change as public attitudes, and so the views of a juror, change.

Judges tell juries that in deciding whether statements are defamatory they should use as their measuring stick the standard of intelligence and judgement of a completely hypothetical creature referred to as the 'reasonable man'.

The test is whether, under the circumstances in which the statement was published, reasonable men and women to whom the publication was made would be likely to understand it in a defamatory sense.

As stated below, even lawyers sometimes find it difficult to decide whether a statement is defamatory. And even judges sometimes disagree. A judge decided that the allegation contained in the following story, about the film stars Tom Cruise and his wife, Nicole Kidman, was not capable of bearing a defamatory meaning, and he struck it out from the couple's claim. He said the allegation was 'unpleasant, maybe; defamatory, no'. The story appeared in the magazine section of the *Express on Sunday*, on 5 October 1997:

> 'Nicole bans brickies from eyeing her up' said the papers last year. Not much of a story, really: the Cruises had the builders in to do a little work on their LA mansion and Nicole ordered the hapless hodwielders to turn and face the wall as she passed. Quite natural, of course: you and I would do the same thing. They were brickies, after all, so they ought to be facing the wall.

The couple challenged the decision in the Court of Appeal, and the court restored the statement to their claim, saying it was 'very much a matter for the jury to consider'. Their **counsel** had told the court that to impute arrogance was plainly capable of being defamatory.

→ glossary

In the third of the definitions above, notice the phrase 'right-thinking members of society generally'. It is not enough for a claimant in a libel action to show that the words of which he/she complains have lowered him/her in the estimation of a limited class in the community who may not conform with that standard.

- It is almost always defamatory to say of a person that he/she is a liar, or a cheat, or is insolvent or in financial difficulties – whether the statement is a libel will depend on whether the publisher has a defence, e.g. it can be proved true.

 see ch. 10, p. 161 on insolvency

▶ Meaning of words

Many statements are capable of carrying more than one meaning.

Inferences

- An inference is a statement with a secondary meaning which can be understood by someone without special knowledge who 'reads between the lines in the light of his general knowledge and experience of worldly affairs'.

For example, an inference is created if someone says: 'I saw the editor leave the pub, and he was swaying and his speech was slurred'. The inference here is indisputably that the editor was drunk, though the term 'drunk' was not used. But for some statements there may be dispute about whether a defamatory inference was created.

The test of what words mean is again the test of the reasonable person. It is not the meaning intended by the person who wrote the words, nor indeed the meaning given to them by the person to whom they were published.

The eminent judge Lord Reid summed up the question of the meaning to be given to words in this way:

❝ Ordinary men and women have different temperaments and outlooks. Some are unusually suspicious, and some are unusually naive. One must try to envisage people between these two extremes and say what is the most damaging meaning they would put on the words in question. ❞

→
see also p. 321 on juxtaposition

The words must be read in full and in their context. A statement innocuous when standing alone can acquire defamatory meaning when juxtaposed with other material. Juxtaposition is a constant danger for journalists, particularly for sub-editors and those dealing with production. Those editing footage must take care how pictures interact with each other, and with any commentary.

Innuendoes

- An innuendo is a statement which may seem to be innocuous to some people but which will be seen as defamatory by people with special knowledge.

For example, to say 'I saw our editor go into that house on the corner of Sleep Street' would not in itself be defamatory, unless the communication is to someone who has special knowledge that the house is a brothel.

The term innuendo comes from a Latin word meaning 'to nod to'.

The libel claimant who argues that he/she has been defamed by an innuendo must show not only that the special facts or circumstances giving rise to the innuendo exist, but also that these facts are known to the people to whom the statement complained of was published.

In 1986 Lord Gowrie, a former Cabinet Minister, received 'substantial damages' after suing over a newspaper article which created the innuendo that he took drugs. He had recently resigned as Minister for the Arts and the *Star* newspaper, under the headline 'A lordly price to pay', stated:

> There's been much excited chatter as to why dashing poetry-scribbling Minister Lord Gowrie left the Cabinet so suddenly. What expensive habits can he not support on an income of £33,000? I'm sure Gowrie himself would snort at suggestions that he was born with a silver spoon round his neck.

Lord Gowrie's counsel said:

> The reference to Lord Gowrie's expensive habits, the suggestion that he was unable to support those habits on his ministerial salary, the use of the word 'snort' and the reference to a 'silver spoon around his neck' all bore the plain implication, to all the many familiar with the relevant terminology, that Lord Gowrie was in the habit of taking illegal drugs, in particular cocaine, and had resigned from the Cabinet because his ministerial salary was insufficient to finance the habit.

- It will be seen from the examples above that a journalist would be mistaken to believe that use of inference or innuendo is any safer in libel law than making a direct allegation.

▌ Bane and antidote

Just as a defamatory meaning may be conveyed by a particular context, so a defamatory meaning may be removed by the context. A judge said in 1835 that, if in one part of a publication something disreputable to the claimant was stated that was removed by the conclusion, 'the bane and the antidote must be taken together'.

The House of Lords applied this rule in 1995 (*Charleston v News Group Newspapers Ltd* [1995] 2 AC 65), when it dismissed a case in which Ann Charleston and Ian Smith, two actors from the television serial *Neighbours*, sued the *News of the World* over headlines and photographs with captions in which their faces had been superimposed on models in pornographic poses.

The main headline read: 'Strewth! What's Harold up to with our Madge?' The text said:

> What would the Neighbours say…strait-laced Harold Bishop starring in a bondage session with screen wife Madge. The famous faces from the television soap are the unwitting stars of a sordid computer game that is available to their child fans…The game superimposes stars' heads on near-naked bodies of real porn models. The stars knew nothing about it.

The actors' lawyers conceded that a reader who read the whole of the text would realise the photographs were mock-ups, but said many readers were unlikely to go beyond the photographs and the headlines.

Lord Bridge, one of the judges, said it was often a debatable question, which the jury must resolve, whether the antidote was effective to neutralise the bane. The answer would depend not only on the nature of the libel a headline conveyed and the language of the text that was relied on to neutralise it but also on the manner in which the whole of the material was set out and balanced. In this case, no reader could possibly have drawn a defamatory inference if he had read beyond the first paragraph of the text.

Lord Nicholls, another of the law lords, warned that words in the text of an article would not always be efficacious to 'cure' a defamatory headline. 'It all depends on the context, one element in which is the layout of the article. Those who print defamatory headlines are playing with fire.' The ordinary reader might not notice words tucked away low down in an article.

▌ Changing standards

Imputations that were defamatory a hundred years ago may not be defamatory today, and vice versa.

For example, in the reign of Charles II it was held to be actionable to say falsely of a man that he was a papist and went to mass. In the next reign similar statements were held not to be defamatory.

During the 1914–18 war a UK court decided that it was a libel to write falsely of a man that he was a German.

Is it defamatory to call someone homosexual? It certainly used to be, but now no 'right-thinking member of society' should think less of someone because they are gay. Therefore, to state wrongly that someone is gay would not in some circumstances be defamatory at all.

→ see p. 304 on defamatory statements

In the case of *Ashby v Sunday Times* (1995) *The Times*, 20 December, where a paper claimed David Ashby, then MP for North West Leicestershire, shared a double bed with another man, the paper's counsel argued this allegation was no longer defamatory. But allegations of homosexuality can prove costly if the claimant argues that the allegation carried other, defamatory inferences. Ashby argued the statement meant he was a liar and a hypocrite in denying that he had left his wife because of a homosexual affair. (However, in his case the jury found for the newspaper.)

▶ Why a media organisation may be reluctant to fight a defamation action

The law of defamation tries to strike a balance between the individual's right to have his/her reputation protected and freedom of speech. So the law provides certain defences for the person who makes a defamatory statement about another for an acceptable reason, as subsequent chapters explain.

Media organisations, however, are often reluctant to fight defamation actions. There are various reasons for this.

Uncertainty of how a jury will interpret meanings

The first is the uncertainty of a how a jury will decide on the meanings of what was published. For example, the statement that seems to one person quite innocuous may, equally clearly, be defamatory to another. It is often difficult, therefore, even for lawyers skilled in the law of defamation, to be able to forecast the jury's decision.

Difficulty of proving the truth

Even if a journalist and his/her editor are convinced of the truth of a story, they may be unable to prove it in court – because, for example, witnesses may be reluctant to give evidence.

→ see ch 19, p. 327 on proving truth

Huge damages could be awarded if trial lost

Because the outcome of a case may be unpredictable, a media organisation has to consider very carefully indeed the money involved if it loses.

For example, in 2000 the magazine *LM* (formerly *Living Marxism*) went into liquidation and ceased publication after a jury awarded a total of £375,000 damages in awards to two television reporters and the ITN company for an article in the magazine that accused them of sensationalising the image of an emaciated Muslim pictured through barbed wire at a Serb-run detention camp in Bosnia.

Media organisations considering whether to contest a libel action brought against them find it difficult to assess what damages might be awarded should they lose. In personal injury cases a judge decides the damages to be paid to a successful claimant – that is, the person suing.

→
see ch. 9,
p. 146 on
confi-
dentality
of jury
delibera-
tions

However, libel damages are normally determined by a jury. We do not know how such juries reach their decisions, but there is little doubt that in general they find it a difficult and confusing job and some have awarded huge sums.

A change in the law in 1990 meant the Court of Appeal can substitute its own award when a jury award is held to be excessive or inadequate.

In 2002 the court reduced to £30,000 damages of £350,000 awarded by a Liverpool jury to a businessman for a *News of the World* story claiming he was a paedophile. The House of Lords has the same power and, again in 2002, cut to £1 a jury award of £85,000 to Bruce Grobbelaar, the former Liverpool goal-keeper, for a *Sun* story claiming he took bribes for match fixing.

In 2002 a leading libel judge said that the ceiling for the most serious defamatory allegations was currently 'reckoned to be of the order of £200,000'. That was the figure he awarded in that year, when trying a case without a jury, to each of two nursery nurses wrongly accused of sexual abuse.

But later the level of awards began to creep up, and in October 2005 a jury awarded £250,000 to Rupert Lowe, chairman of Southampton Football Club, over an article that stated he had behaved 'shabbily' in suspending the club's manager after child abuse allegations. It was the highest award for more than four years.

Huge costs

The damages award, large as it often is, is frequently exceeded by the legal costs, which are generally met largely by the loser. In 1994 the BBC was ordered to pay an estimated £1.5 million costs in a case where a judge, rather than a jury, had heard the case and awarded £60,000 damages. The libel was contained in a *Panorama* programme, 'The Halcion nightmare', which reported that, long before the sleeping drug Halcion was banned in the United Kingdom, evidence existed that it might have had serious adverse side effects.

In 1998 Granada agreed to pay £50,000 damages over a libel contained in a *World in Action* programme which revealed that garments sold by Marks and Spencer and marked 'Made in England' were in fact made by a factory in Morocco employing child labour. Granada also had to pay £600,000 costs.

It may be better to settle out of court

It is not surprising that, faced with these kinds of figures for costs and damages, even the more ardent campaigning editors sometimes decide either not to carry the story or, having carried it, to apologise and settle out of court by payment of agreed damages.

Indeed, the vast majority of libel cases are settled out of court, without any publicity, and for this reason the ongoing cost of libel actions to media organisations is often underestimated.

▌ No win, no fee legal representation

In the book *Libel and the Media: The Chilling Effect* (1997), the authors argued that the libel law exerted a chilling effect on the media, significantly restricting what the public was able to read and hear. The most obvious manifestation occurred when articles, books, or programmes were specifically changed in the light of legal considerations. But, the book warned, the deeper and subtler effect prevented articles being written in the first place. Particular organisations and individuals were considered taboo because of the libel risk; certain subjects were treated as off-limits.

The chilling effect of libel on investigative journalism has been increased by the introduction of **conditional fee agreements** (CFAs), otherwise known →glossary
as 'no win, no fee' agreements, after their use was extended to defamation cases in 1998 under the Conditional Fee Agreements Order (SI 1998/1860).

Legal aid was never available for launching libel actions; this meant that →glossary
historically the libel courts have been beyond the reach of people of modest

incomes; but now litigants without the means to sue can do so and be represented by lawyers who would receive nothing if they lose the case but who can claim up to a 100 per cent increase on fees if it is won.

The media argues that a claimant without means can hold a media defendant to ransom by threatening to sue under a CFA. If the claimant loses the case, the media defendant is unlikely to recover the large sums it has spent in fighting the case. If the claimant wins, the media defendant will have to pay not only damages but also the lawyers' 'success fees', which might be huge. The pressure to settle such a case before it gets to court is considerable, even though a defence may be available.

In 2005, in a case before the House of Lords, Lord Hoffmann referred to the 'blackmailing effect' of CFA-assisted libel cases such as that brought by a convicted Romanian criminal earlier that year. But he concluded that there was little the courts could do about the problem and in the end legislation might be necessary (*Campbell v MGN Ltd* [2005] UKHL 61).

see Late News p. xxxii, on costs

▌ Freedom of expression

Most journalists believe that defamation law, in attempting to 'strike a balance' between protecting reputation and allowing freedom of speech, has been tilted historically in favour of claimants.

But in recent years there have been a number of developments that seemed likely to tilt the balance, to a greater or lesser degree, in favour of freedom of expression.

They were:

see ch. 1 pp. 9–13 on Convention

(1) The Human Rights Act, which took effect on 2 October 2000, requiring courts to pay regard to Article 10 of the European Convention on Human Rights, concerned with freedom of expression. The European Court of Human Rights has said that Article 10 does not involve a 'choice between two conflicting principles' but 'a freedom of expression that is subject to a number of exceptions which must be narrowly construed'.

see ch. 20

(2) The decision of the House of Lords in *Reynolds v Times Newspapers* [2001] 2 AC 127, which greatly extended the ambit of the defence of privilege.

→ glossary

(3) The Defamation Act 1996, which introduced:

(a) a summary procedure for trying defamation cases, which it was hoped would reduce the cost of smaller-scale libel actions. Under the procedure a judge can fix damages up to a ceiling of £10,000. That was the figure awarded in 2002 to a claimant for what the judge described as a 'serious' libel (*Mawdsley v Guardian Newspapers Ltd* [2002] EWHC 1780 (QB));

(b) a new procedure, the offer to make amends.

→ see ch. 19, p. 351 on this procedure

▌A word of warning

Seeking legal advice

Because the law of defamation is so complex, this book can provide nothing more than a rough guide. It can give an indication that a media organisation can sometimes go further, in safety, than many journalists suppose, and ought sometimes, in prudence, to stop and reflect before taking a dangerous course of action.

The golden rule for the journalist is that if publication seems likely to bring a threat of libel, take professional advice first.

But the media's role in exposing wrongdoing is an extremely important one. As Lord Justice Lawton (then Mr Justice Lawton) said in a case in 1965:

❝ It is one of the professional tasks of newspapers to unmask the fraudulent and the scandalous. It is in the public interest to do it. It is a job which newspapers have done time and time again in their long history. ❞

▌Errors and apologies

Sometimes publication of the words that cause the libel problem are not the result of a conscious decision but the result of an innocent error. This results in a solicitor's letter from 'the other side' which may lead eventually to a High Court libel hearing.

Again, the arrival of such a letter is the moment to take legal advice. Libel law is not a matter for an inexperienced person to play with, for the dangers of aggravating the problem by mishandling are too great. A reporter who receives a call which is a complaint about matter published should follow procedure to refer the complaint to the relevant manager or executive.

see ch. 19, pp. 349–351 on apologies

Publishing an apology or an inadequate correction can itself, in certain circumstances, create a further libel problem.

On the other hand, the correct legal steps, including prompt publication of an apology or correction, can remove the heat from a libel threat, and save thousands of pounds even if a settlement is paid.

The most common cause of libel actions against media organisations is the journalist's failure to apply professional standards of accuracy and fairness. The best protection against getting involved in an expensive action is to make every effort to get the story right.

▌ Who can sue, and who cannot?

Individuals

see above, p. 311 on 'no win, no fee'

Although the availability of 'no win, no fee' arrangements has made the libel courts available to greater numbers of people, there are still groups of people who are more litigious than the average person. Anyone with a public persona, quick access to legal representation, and especially a track record of suing for libel is someone of whom a journalist should be wary.

This is not to say that journalists should steer clear of them, but it does reinforce the need for attention to be paid at all times to accuracy and to the defences that are available to the media. It is often useful to approach stories thus:

- Who am I writing about, will they sue?
- Is what I am writing potentially defamatory?
- Do I have a defence?

Corporations

→ glossary   In addition to individuals, a **corporation** can sue for a publication injurious to its trading reputation. And, in general, a corporation, whether trading or non-trading, can sue in libel to protect its reputation.

Should the corporation actually have to prove that it has suffered financial loss in order to collect damages? In 2006 the House of Lords said no (*Jameel v Wall Street Journal* [2006] UKHL 44). Lord Bingham gave some examples of injurious statements:

    ❝ that an arms company has routinely bribed officials of foreign governments to secure contracts; that an oil company has wilfully and unnecessarily damaged the environment; that an international humanitarian agency has wrongfully succumbed to government pressure; that a retailer has knowingly exploited child labour... ❞

Lord Bingham said the good name of a company, as that of an individual, was a thing of value. A damaging libel might lower its standing in the eyes of the public and even its own staff, make people less ready to deal with it, less willing or less proud to work for it. See also below, p. 316, on disparaging of goods.

Local and central government

In an important decision in 1993 (*Derbyshire County Council v Times Newspapers* [1993] AC 534), the House of Lords held that institutions of local or central government could not sue for defamation in respect of their 'governmental and administrative functions' because this would place an undesirable fetter on freedom of speech. They can still sue for libels affecting their property, and they can still sue for malicious falsehood if they can show **malice**.

    Note that it is still possible for individual members or officers of the council to sue. A judge in the House of Lords said:

→ ch. 21 explains malicious falsehood

    ❝ A publication attacking the activities of the authority will necessarily be an attack on the body of councillors which represents the controlling party, or on the executives who carry on the day-to-day management of its affairs. If the individual reputation of any of these is wrongly impaired by the publication any of these can himself bring proceedings for defamation. ❞

As a general rule, an association, such as a club, cannot sue unless it is an incorporated body, but words disparaging an association will almost invariably reflect upon the reputations of one or more of the officials who, as individuals, can sue.

→ see ch. 18 on 'identification'

Trade unions

Trade unions are not corporate bodies. Can they sue for libel? The leading law books differ in their answers to this question. In a case in 1980 a judge held that they cannot sue (*EEPTU v Times Newspapers* [1980] QB 585), and *Carter-Ruck on Libel and Slander* (1997) maintains this is still a correct statement of the law, but *Gatley on Libel and Slander* (2004) doubts whether this decision 'represents the law'. Again, individual officers can sue.

Members of Parliament

The Defamation Act 1996, in a provision that took effect in September 1996, allows Parliamentarians to waive their parliamentary privilege in defamation actions and thus sue. The change enabled Neil Hamilton MP to continue an action against the *Guardian* over allegations that he had accepted cash for asking parliamentary questions. In October that year he abandoned his case.

▶ Disparaging of goods

Can a publication defame a person or a firm by disparaging goods? It is an increasingly important question as product testing becomes commonplace in newspapers, magazines, and other media.

The answer is yes. But it is not sufficient that the statement should simply affect the person adversely in his/her business; it must impute to him/her discreditable conduct in that business, or else tend to show that he/she is ill-suited or ill-qualified to do it.

For example, it is defamatory to write of a businessman that he has been condemned by his trade association or of a bricklayer that he/she does not know how to lay bricks properly.

Not all words that criticise a person's goods are defamatory. For example, a motoring correspondent could criticise the performance of a certain make of car without reflecting upon the character of either the manufacturer or the dealer. (Again, the statement might give rise to an action for malicious falsehood: see ch. 21.)

The imputations that give most problems in this context are dishonesty, carelessness, and incompetence.

In a case in 1994 in which a jury awarded £1.485 million damages to the manufacturer of a yacht, Walker Wingsail Systems plc, an article in *Yachting World* had contrasted the manufacturer's striking claims for the yacht's performance with the drastically poorer performance of the boat when tested by the journalist.

In a case, also in 1994, in which the BBC had to pay £60,000 damages (with an estimated £1.5 million costs) to the makers of the drug Halcion (see above, 'Why a media organisation may be reluctant to fight a defamation action'), the judge was not asked to adjudicate on the question of the safety of the drug but upon whether there had been intentional concealment of information relating to its safety.

Journalists tend to accept without question the journalistic policy of declining to show copy to the traders or companies subject to investigation into their products or services, but this approach can appear less than fair to judges and juries, and could now be important when the journalist is advancing a *Reynolds* defence.

→ see ch. 20 on Reynolds

Which magazine, publisher of perhaps the greatest number of product tests, always sends the factual results of its tests to the subjects before publication but never the comments. Thus it can be, and is, highly critical of products while minimising the danger that its defence of **fair comment** will be lost as a result of challenges on facts. See ch. 19 on fair comment.

→ glossary

⁙ Recap of major points

- A defamatory statement made in permanent form is generally libel; if in transient form it is generally slander.
- A defamatory statement about someone tends to:
  - expose them to hatred, ridicule, or contempt;
  - cause them to be shunned or avoided;
  - lower them in the estimation of right-thinking members of society generally; or
  - disparage them in their business, trade, office, or profession.
- The test of what the words actually mean is the test of what a reasonable person would take them to mean.
- Words may carry an innuendo, a 'hidden' meaning clear to people with special knowledge or create an inference, obvious to everybody.
- A corporation can sue for a publication injurious to its trading reputation.
- But institutions of local or central government cannot sue in respect of their 'governmental and administrative functions'.
- The financial implications of losing a libel action in terms of damages and costs are so punitive that journalists must always consider who they are writing about; what they are writing about them and whether what they are writing will be defensible if a libel action results.
- The decision to publish an apology, and how any apology is worded, needs to be made by a person experienced in handling complaints.

18

What the claimant must prove

Chapter summary

One of the criticisms of libel law made by publishers is the low burden placed
on a **claimant** in bringing an action. This chapter sets out what a claimant has to
prove in court when suing for libel. The court must be satisfied that the words are
capable of bearing a defamatory meaning; that the claimant has been adequately
identified in the publication and that the material has been published to a third
party. Libel law allows a claimant to sue anyone who 'publishes' the libel, which
includes reporters and distributors of the publication. A defence of innocent dissemination affords protection for some categories of people.

→ glossary

▌ The burden on the claimant

A claimant has to show the court three things when suing for libel:

→

see ch.
17, pp.
304–305,
on
defama-
tory
state-
ments

(1) the publication is defamatory;

(2) it may be reasonably understood to refer to him/her, i.e. 'identification';

(3) it has been published to a third person.

It is useful for the journalist to remember what the defamed person does
not have to prove.

First, the claimant does not have to prove that the statement is false. If a
statement is defamatory, the court assumes it is false. If the statement is in
fact true *and the journalist can prove it is true* then there is a defence.

Secondly, the claimant does not have to prove intention: it is normally no use the journalist saying, 'I didn't mean to damage this person's reputation'.

 Intent is relevant in the 'offer of amends' defence, see ch. 19 p. 351.

Thirdly, the claimant does not have to provide any proof of actual damage. The claimant needs to show only that the statement *tends to* discredit. A person may sue for libel even though the people to whom the statement was published knew it to be untrue. The court will presume damage.

The **Reynolds defence** provides protection in some circumstances for publishing untrue statements in the public interest.

 see ch. 20 explains this defence

▶ Identification

The claimant needs to prove that the published matter identifies him/her as the person defamed.

Some journalists believe they can play safe by not naming the person, but such an omission may prove no defence.

- The test in defamation law of whether the published matter identified the person suing is whether it would reasonably lead people acquainted with him/her to believe that he/she was the person referred to.

A judge said in 1826: 'It is not necessary that all the world should understand the libel; it is sufficient if those who know the claimant can make out that he is the person meant.' That is still the law today.

During the late 1980s and 1990s the Police Federation, representing junior police officers, took many actions against newspapers on behalf of their members. During the 33 months to March 1996 the federation fought 95 libel actions, winning all of them and recovering £1,567,000 in damages.

Many of the officers were not named in what was published. In one case, the *Burton Mail* paid £17,500 compensation plus legal costs to a woman police constable who featured anonymously in a story following a complaint about an arrest. It was argued that the story's details identified her.

Derogatory comments about an institution can reflect upon the person who heads that institution. For example, many newspapers have had to pay damages to head teachers, who were not named in the paper, for reports that criticised schools.

Importance of addresses and occupations

→
see ch.
12, pp.
199–200
on
defend-
ant's
details,
and p. 67

It is dangerous to make a half-hearted effort at identification, particularly in reports of court cases. In *Newstead v London Express Newspapers Ltd* [1940] 1 KB 377, the *Daily Express* had reported that 'Harold Newstead, 30-year-old Camberwell man', had been sent to prison for nine months for bigamy.

The paper was successfully sued by another Harold Newstead, who worked in Camberwell, and who claimed that the account had been understood to refer to him. The claimant claimed that if the words were true of another person, which they were, it was the duty of the paper to give a precise and detailed description of that person, but the paper had 'recklessly struck out' the occupation and address of the person convicted. A defendant's age, address and occupation, if mentioned in court, or provided by the court, should be included with his/her name in any report of the case, unless the court directs otherwise.

Blurring identity increases risk

The problem with not fully identifying the subject of any defamatory story is not only that the person may argue in a libel case that he/she was the person referred to but also that another may say the words referred to him/her. A newspaper quoted from a report by the district auditor to a local council, criticising the council's deputy housing manager. The paper did not name him. But a new deputy manager had taken over. He sued, claiming he was thought to be the offending official.

Defamation of a group

If a defamatory statement refers to someone as being a member of a group, and includes no other identifying detail of that person, all members of the group, if it is sufficiently small, may be able to sue successfully for defamation, even though the publisher intended to refer to only one of them.

For example, to say: 'One of the detectives at Blanktown police station is corrupt', without naming the allegedly corrupt detective, will allow all detectives there to sue because the statement 'identifies' them in libel law to their acquaintances and colleagues. Even if the publisher has evidence that one is corrupt, the rest are going to win damages. However, if the group referred to is large, no one in it will be able reasonably to claim to have been identified merely by a reference to the group. For example, to state: 'I know a policeman in London who is corrupt' refers to a group of several thousand people. **Case law** does not set a clear figure for when a group is too large for those in it to claim that reference to the group alone identified them as individuals. In one case, reference to a group of 35 police dog-handlers based in an area of London was ruled to be sufficient to identify them as individuals.

- A case in 1986 concerned a reference published by a newspaper to an allegation that detectives at Banbury CID had raped a woman. The newspaper did not name those allegedly involved, and was successfully sued for reference to this group, which comprised only of 12 detectives (*Riches and others v News Group Newspapers Ltd* [1985] 2 All ER 845).

It should be remembered too that reference to a group may identify those with particular responsibility for it. To state: 'The supermarket in Blanktown Road is run badly' is to refer to a small group of managers, all of whom may sue.

Juxtaposition

The magazine *Stationery Trade News* accurately reported the counterfeiting of some stationery products and named some of those responsible. A company won huge damages against the magazine because it was named in what the editor considered to be a separate part of the article, dealing with another issue, but the jury found that the allegations could be understood as referring to the claimant company as well. The copy referring to the claimants, a firm of envelope manufacturers, was sandwiched between the allegations of counterfeiting and the pictures illustrating counterfeiting.

▌ Publication

The claimant must also prove that the statement has been published. With the exception of criminal libel there is no defamation if the words complained of, however offensive or untrue, are addressed, in speech or writing, only to the person about whom they are made. To substantiate defamation, they must have been communicated to at least one other person. In the case of the news media, there is no difficulty in proving this: publication is widespread.

→ see ch. 21, explains criminal libel

Internet publication

There is an exception to this rule about publication for claimants suing over items on the internet published by foreign parties. In 2005 the Court of Appeal held that it would be an **abuse of process** (resulting in the claim being rejected by the court) for a claimant to bring a libel action over material on the internet unless 'substantial publication' in England could be shown.

 → glossary

The court pointed out that an article in a US-based internet service was downloaded by only five people in England, three of whom were in the claimant's 'camp' (including his lawyer), and the other two were unknown. The court said it did not consider that the article required the provision of a fair and public hearing in relation to an alleged infringement of rights when the alleged infringement was shown not to be 'real or substantial' (*Dow Jones and Co Inc v Yousef Abdul Latif Jameel* [2005] EWCA Civ 75).

The court will not assume that internet publication is necessarily substantial publication (*Amoudi v Brisard* [2006] 3 All ER 294). A court in Canada ruled that hyperlinks to articles containing defamatory material did not amount in that particular case, to substantial publication of defamatory statements by the publisher of the article containing the hyperlinks (*Crookes v Wikimedia Foundation Inc.*, (2008) BCSC 1424).

Repeating statements of others

Every repetition of a libel is a fresh publication and creates a fresh cause of action. This is known as the repetition rule. It is no defence to say that you, the publisher, are not liable because you are only repeating the words of others.

The person who originated the statement may be liable, but also anybody who repeats the allegation may be sued. One of the most common causes of libel actions is repeating statements made by interviewees without being able to prove the truth of the words.

In 1993 and 1994 papers paid damages to defendants in the Birmingham Six case, who had been sentenced to prison for terrorism but later cleared on appeal. Former West Midlands police officers were accused of fabricating evidence in the case, but prosecution of those officers was abandoned. After the abandonment of that prosecution, the *Sunday Telegraph* reported one of the three officers as referring to the Birmingham Six and saying: 'In our eyes, their guilt is beyond doubt.'

The *Sun* newspaper published an article based upon the *Sunday Telegraph*'s interviews. It later carried an apology and was reported to have paid £1 million in damages.

Online archives and repetition

The repetition rule is particularly important for those responsible for online sites that contain archive material. The rule dates from the 1849 case of the Duke of Brunswick, who sued a newspaper for defamation after sending his butler to buy a back copy. Nowadays the duke would be able to call up the archive version on the internet.

It is normally a defence to a libel action that it was not launched until more than a year after the publication. But the law takes the view that every time an article in an archive is accessed this amounts to a new publication and can give rise to a new action.

→ see ch. 354 on limitation period

In 2001 the Court of Appeal confirmed that 'the rule in the Duke of Brunswick case' was still the law and applied to the internet. *The Times* had published articles alleging an international businessman had been involved in criminal activities, and he sued both for the stories in the paper and for those in the paper's archive, available on the internet. The paper argued that the 'single publication' rule should be applied to internet publication so that publication took place only on the day the material was posted.

But the appeal judges rejected this argument.

In 2006 a businessman, Jim Carr, won a second libel damages payout from the *Sunday Telegraph* over the same story, because the newspaper left the piece accessible through its website, as the result of an oversight. In April that year he had won £12,000 and an apology over an article that was published in November 2005. The newspaper had to pay the claimant a further £5,000 in damages as a result of the website story.

Journalists on local newspapers also need to be alert when handling the bygone days column. A doctor received damages for statements published afresh in 1981 in the 'Looking Back' column of the *Evening Star*, Ipswich. The statements, repeated from an article published 25 years previously, had gone unchallenged then.

▌ Who are the 'publishers'?

A person who has been defamed may sue the reporter, the sub-editor, the editor, the publisher, the printer, the distributor, and the broadcaster. All have participated in the publishing of the defamatory statement and are regarded as 'publishers' at **common law**.

→ glossary

▌ The section 1 defence

Newsagents and booksellers have enjoyed a defence of innocent dissemination, saying they are merely the conduit for the passage of the words complained of and thus not responsible for them. But this defence was not available to others, such as distributors and broadcasters.

The Defamation Act 1996, in section 1, extended the defence, and it now applies to anyone who was not the author, editor, or publisher (as defined by the Act) of the statement complained of, who took reasonable care in relation to its publication, and who did not know and had no reason to believe that whatever part he/she had in the publication caused or contributed to the publication of a defamatory statement.

A court deciding whether a person took reasonable care, or had reason to believe that what he/she did caused or contributed to the publication of a defamatory statement, shall have regard to:

- the extent of his/her responsibility for the content of the statement or the decision to publish it;
- the nature or circumstances of the publication; and
- the previous conduct or character of the author, editor, or publisher.

The list of categories of people who are not authors, editors, or publishers for the purposes of the new defence includes broadcasters of live programmes who have no effective control over the maker of the statement complained of.

In 1999 the BBC was sued by the research firm MORI and its head, Bob Worcester, for defamatory remarks made by the controversial politician Sir James Goldsmith during a live radio interview. The BBC said it had a defence under section 1 – but could it be said it had taken 'reasonable care'? It was argued it should have known Sir James was likely to say something defamatory and it should at least have used a 'delay button'. The case was settled before the jury could reach its verdict.

Defence for internet service providers

The section 1 defence is also available for ISPs (internet service providers) which provide as 'host' a service to enable people and companies to publish their own content on their websites. Such ISP hosts play a merely passive role in the process of transmission of any defamatory matter, and are therefore not publishers under section 1. However an ISP could be successfully sued for libel if, in respect of such a site it hosts, it fails to remove defamatory matter quickly after the matter is complained about. In *Godfrey v Demon Internet Ltd* [2001] QB 201 the ISP was successfully sued for matter on a newsgroup it hosted after it left the matter there for about 10 days after a complaint was made. The claim was for damages for those 10 days.

Readers' comments

Newspapers, magazines, TV channels, and radio stations will not be able to use the section 1 defence in respect of content which staff place on such media organisations' websites – because they are clearly publishers. Some media lawyers believe this defence could in some circumstances be used in respect of comments posted directly on to such sites by readers. But if such material is moderated (i.e. checked) by the media organisation's staff before being allowed to appear there, or if a comment which is clearly defamatory, or attracts complaint, is checked by them subsequently but is allowed to remain, or if the organisation has invited comment on a particular issue in a way likely to produce defamatory comment, the section 1 defence is unlikely to apply. The media organisation is likely in these circumstances to be shown in a libel action as being, under section 1, either the editor or the publisher of the comment, or both, or as not having taken reasonable care. The safest course for a media organisation is to remove quickly from its website a reader's comment if there is a complaint that it is defamatory. It can be put back later if after consideration it is deemed safe.

⠿ Recap of major points

- A libel claimant suing over a published statement must prove three things about it: (1) it is defamatory, (2) it may be reasonably understood to refer to him, (3) it has been published to a third person.

- The test of 'identification' is whether the words would reasonably lead people who know the claimant to believe he/she was the person referred to.

- Publication is assumed in the case of traditional media. But this is not always the case with online publication.

- Every repetition is a fresh publication. The journalist is liable for repeating a defamatory statement made by an interviewee or source.

- As for internet publications, the law says every time an article is accessed, that amounts to a new publication.

- A person who has been defamed may sue the reporter, the editor, the publisher, the broadcaster – indeed anyone who has participated in publishing the defamatory statement.

- There is a defence under section 1 of the Defamation Act 1996 for a defendant who can show, among other things, that he/she had no control over the publication.

19

Defences

Chapter summary

Preceding chapters have shown the ever-present danger to journalists of being sued for libel. But the law provides some defences against such lawsuits. If it were not for these defences many of the stories published and broadcast on a daily basis by the media would be suppressed for fear of a libel action. This chapter will explain how these defences work, and provide practical advice on what journalists must do when preparing a story to ensure it complies with the requirements of these defences. The chapter deals with the main defences of justification, fair comment, absolute and qualified privilege, accord and satisfaction, and offer of amends, as well as some other defences.

▌ The main defences

A journalist needs to know how the following defences work. It is often the case that the steps taken by a journalist in researching a story will determine whether a defence will be available. Knowing the requirements of each defence, a journalist can make sure his/her story complies with them and thus avoid a costly libel action.

The main defences are:

- justification;
- fair comment;
- absolute privilege;

- qualified privilege;

- accord and satisfaction;

- offer of amends.

◗ Justification

It has been suggested that the defence of justification should be renamed *truth*, because its requirement is that the published matter complained of can be proved in court to be substantially true. If this requirement is met, the defence provides complete protection against a libel action (the only limited exception arises under the Rehabilitation of Offenders Act 1974 – see ch. 22).

Justification is a difficult defence to use because in a defamation action it is not the task of the **claimant** to shows the published words were untrue. The burden of proof is on the defendant–the publisher–to prove that they <u>were</u> true.

→ glossary

The defence applies to statements of fact. If the words complained of are an expression of opinion they may be defended as fair comment.

Often in a libel action a media organisation will rely on both defences, each applying as appropriate to different statements in what is published.

→ see below, p. 333 on fair comment

- The standard of proof needed for the justification defence to succeed is that used in civil cases generally – the matter must be proved true 'on the balance of probabilities'.

→ ch. 10 explains civil law generally

This is a lower requirement than 'beyond all reasonable doubt', the standard of proof in criminal cases but, nevertheless, demands that a media organisation relying on the justification defence must have sufficient evidence to persuade a jury in a libel trial, or the judge if there is no jury, that its version of the disputed event(s) is the correct one.

Section 5 of the Defamation Act 1952 states that, in a defamation case where two or more 'charges' (i.e. allegations said to affect the claimant's reputation) have been published against the claimant, 'a defence of justification shall not fail by reason only that the truth of every charge is not proved if the words not proved to be true do not materially injure the [claimant's] reputation having regard to the truth of the remaining charges'.

The wording of this requirement means that for a defendant, e.g. a media organisation, to win a libel trial, it is not necessary for it to prove the truth of every defamatory statement in the matter published – but that the most damaging allegation (which lawyers sometimes refer to as the 'sting') does have to be proved, and that the damage to reputation it causes must dwarf the damage caused by any allegation not proved. So if it is published that a politician is cruel to his children and swears at his neighbours, the former allegation would be the sting – the one which is most damaging.

However, in such a case if a media organisation is unable to prove minor allegations, a jury may be harder to persuade that the major allegation is true.

▶ Examples of the justification defence

The *Sun* newspaper successfully used the justification defence when sued in 1994 by Gillian Taylforth, the television actress, and her boyfriend after the paper published a front-page splash headlined 'TV Kathy's "sex romp" on A1' saying the couple had indulged in oral sex in a parked car.

The *Sun* obtained confirmation from the police press office that the boyfriend had been cautioned for indecency, and when sued the paper 'joined' the police in the defence, with the result that the main defence witness was the officer who claimed he saw the incident. The jury found for the paper 10–2.

Cases in which the media plead justification can be extremely complex. In 1992 Scottish Television (STV) successfully defended a libel action brought by Antony Gecas, the former platoon commander of a Lithuanian police battalion under German occupation who settled in Edinburgh after World War Two. In a 1987 programme called 'Crimes of War' STV accused him of involvement in the murder of thousands of Jews.

When sued, STV was faced with the difficult task of proving its account of events that had happened nearly half a century before. The judge found for STV. The case cost an estimated £1.5 million.

In 1997 the *Guardian* newspaper risked the award of huge libel damages and costs when it defended a case brought against it by the former Conservative Cabinet Minister Jonathan Aitken. The paper had reported that he had allowed an Arab business associate to pay his bill at the Ritz hotel in Paris, in breach of ministerial guidelines. Aitken had resigned from the Cabinet in order, he said, to pursue the *Guardian* with 'the sword of truth' and 'the shield of fair play'.

The *Guardian* embarked on a four-year investigation, which culminated in the production of vital evidence at a late stage in the trial, as Aitken appeared to be winning, and the former Minister dramatically abandoned the case. He faced a costs bill of £2 million. Aitken was later jailed for perjury.

Inferences and innuendoes must be proved

Justification means proving not only the truth of each defamatory statement but also any reasonable interpretation that may be understood of the words and any innuendoes lying behind them.

see also ch. 17, pp. 306 and 307 on meanings of words

In 1987 Jeffrey Archer, the politician and novelist (later Lord Archer), was awarded £500,000 against the *Star* newspaper, which said that he had paid a prostitute for sexual intercourse. He also sued the *News of the World* for a story headlined 'Tory boss Archer pays off vice girl'. It was true that Archer had paid £2,000 to the prostitute to go abroad to avoid scandal but he claimed the article implied he had had a sexual relationship with her. The paper said it had never intended such a suggestion, but it had to pay Archer £50,000 damages in an agreed settlement. (In 2001 Archer was found guilty of perjury and perverting the course of justice in the libel action and jailed for four years. He repaid the damages to the two papers, and their costs.)

see below, p. 331 on Archer

Levels of meaning and reporting police investigations

In considering reports linking a claimant with criminal conduct, the courts recognise three levels of meaning:

- the report may mean the person is guilty of the criminal offence (a level 1 meaning);
- or he or she is reasonably suspected of the offence (level 2);
- or there are grounds for an investigation (level 3).

The three categories were set out by Lord Devlin in a case in which two national newspapers said the City of London Fraud Squad was inquiring into the affairs of a company. The statement was true, but the claimant said the words meant (by implication) that he and the company were guilty of fraud, or at least were suspected of fraud, and heavy damages were initially awarded against the newspapers.

On appeal, the House of Lords ruled that the words were not capable of meaning that fraud had been committed, but they were capable of meaning that the claimants were suspected and that whether they had this meaning or not should be left to a jury (*Lewis v Daily Telegraph*, and *Lewis v Associated Newspapers Ltd* [1964] AC 234).

Proving reasonable suspicion

The reason it is defamatory to say a person is <u>reasonably</u> suspected of an offence is that it implies conduct on the person's part that warranted the suspicion, so if you are to succeed in a plea of justification you must show conduct on the person's part giving rise to the suspicion. It is no use saying other people told you about their suspicions (*Shah v Standard Chartered Bank* [1999] QB 241).

In 2003 the *Sun* newspaper had to pay £100,000 damages to a children's nurse for a story headlined 'Nurse is probed over 18 deaths'. The police had been investigating the circumstances of the deaths of a number of terminally ill children whom she had treated but they concluded (after the *Sun*'s story was published) that there were no grounds to suspect her of an offence.

The newspaper tried to show there were reasonable grounds for suspicion, but the Court of Appeal said the newspaper was relying almost entirely upon the fact that a number of allegations had been made against the nurse to the hospital trust and the police. The only respect in which the newspaper focused upon the nurse's *conduct* concerned an allegation made *after* publication, and the court said that could not be taken into consideration (*Elaine Chase v News Group Newspapers Ltd* [2002] EWCA Civ 1772; [2002] All ER (D) 20 (Dec)).

Avoid implying habitual conduct

To say of someone 'He is a thief' may be true in the simple meaning of the words. But if the basis for the statement is just one conviction for stealing a packet of bacon from a shop, a defence of justification might fail.

For that person would argue that the words contained the meaning that he was a persistent thief, and was a person whom no one should trust, whereas he was essentially an honest man who had had a single lapse.

The principle is an important one. Many libel actions result from the journalist implying habitual conduct from a single incident.

Sticking to your story can be expensive

The defence of justification is not only difficult; it can be dangerous. If it fails the court will take a critical view of a media organisation's persistence in sticking to a story which it decides is not true, and the jury may award greater damages accordingly.

In the *Archer* case the *Star* newspaper claimed its story that Archer had sexual relations with the prostitute was true. The £500,000 damages were awarded after the judge told the jury that the newspaper had carried the case through to the bitter end and if it found in Mr Archer's favour the damages should be sufficiently large to 'send a message to the world that the accusations were false'.

see above, p. 329 on Archer

▌ The investigative journalist

Practical advice on procedure

Make sure of your witnesses

Are your witnesses going to be available to give evidence when the case comes to court, which may be years after the events described in the story? The journalist must be sure to keep track of them, noting their various changes of address.

Are they going to be willing to give evidence?

Will they turn up at the trial? If they do, how convincing will their version of events sound when tested by expert cross-examination? What impression will they make on the jury? In particular, will the jury believe their version of events in preference to the version of the person suing? In the libel action that Jeffrey Archer brought against the *Star* the jury accepted the account of the leading Conservative politician in preference to that of the prostitute.

What is the standing of your witness?

UK juries are said to be likely to accept the word of a police officer. In the case brought by the TV actress Gillian Taylforth against the *Sun* (see above) the newspaper won after having the rare experience of having its story backed by police evidence.

Reference has been made to the numerous libel cases brought on behalf of police officers after publications of allegations of bad conduct, such as brutality and harassment. Local editors may see it as their duty to publish such stories in the public interest but they must be aware of the strong likelihood that the libel jury will accept the denial of a police officer rather than the

see ch. 18, p. 319 on police suing

allegation of the source, who, in the nature of things, will often be a person of low social standing, perhaps with a criminal record.

Signed statements are important

If the journalist is working on a story that may be challenged in court, he/she should persuade the witness to make a signed statement at the time and date it.

Or such testimony could be an audio-recording of any witness willing to testify against the claimant. It could be a note of on interview written by the journalist in his/her notebook and signed by the witness who gave it.

Better, it could be a statutory declaration from any such witness. That is a more formal statement made before a magistrate, solicitor, or court officer and it carries greater weight in court.

→ glossary   Best, it could be an **affidavit**, more formal still and sworn on oath. Both this and a statutory declaration put the person giving the statement at risk of being prosecuted for perjury if he/she is not telling the truth–see ch.3, p.40.

If the journalist has a statement, whether written or tape-recorded, from a witness who dies or goes abroad before the trial the statement itself can be produced in evidence.

→ glossary   The Civil Evidence Act 1995 makes **hearsay** evidence acceptable in court subject to certain conditions. For practical purposes, where the statement comprises, or is contained in, a document, it must be signed to make it admissible.

Admissibility of photocopied documents

Suppose you are running a story about council workmen fiddling expenses and you got the story from a photocopy of a confidential council document.

If you can explain why the original is not available, that makes the copy available for evidence. But you would have to persuade the court that the document is authentic – e.g. by evidence from someone within the council. The claimant would no doubt challenge its authenticity.

Make sure you keep the evidence

Often the paper's case is weakened because the journalist has failed to observe the basic editorial discipline of keeping a notebook in good order. When the journalist is required to give evidence, a court will attach weight to a shorthand note, properly dated.

→

see
ch. 20, on
Reynolds
     Keeping a good note is particularly important when a media organisation is using the *Reynolds* defence to contest a libel action.

▌ Fair comment

The defence of fair comment protects published opinion, not any statement put forward as factual. But if a media organisation is using the fair comment defence it will be prepared to rely too on another defence to be run in tandem – it could be justification, absolute privilege, or qualified privilege (the privilege defences are explained later in this chapter).

The main requirements of the fair comment defence, based on decades of case law, can be summarised as being that: → glossary

- the published comment must be the honestly held opinion of the person making it (though it may have been published by another party);
- the comment should be recognisable (i.e. to the reader/viewer/ listener) as opinion – i.e. it should not be worded to be perceived as factual allegation;
- the comment must be based on provably true facts/privileged matter;
- those facts/that matter must be recognisably alluded to or stated in what is published with the comment, unless so widely known that this is not necessary–see also the ruling in *Lowe*, below;
- the subject commented on must be a matter of public interest.

For the defence to succeed, all these requirements must be met. It will be seen from the above list why the justification and privilege defences underpin the fair comment defence.

Only comment, not facts

A judge gave an example of a publication of opinion protected by the fair comment defence. He said that if you accurately report what some public man has done and then say 'Such conduct is disgraceful', that is merely an expression of your opinion, your comment on the person's conduct.

But, the judge said, if you assert that the man has been guilty of disgraceful conduct and do not state what that conduct was, this is an allegation of fact for which there is no defence other than justification or privilege.

This rule seemed to be relaxed by a judge's decision in 2006 (*Lowe v Associated Newspapers* [2006] EWHC 320). Mr Justice Eady said a defendant was not confined to relying in support of the comment on facts actually stated or alluded to in the article itself.

He might in addition rely on facts not to be discerned from the article, but known to the person commenting, either the journalist or the person whose opinion he was reporting, at the time he made the comment. But the defendant could not rely on facts learned by the person making the comment only after publication.

Importantly, Mr Justice Eady said the article did not need to state so much of the facts that readers could decide whether they agreed with the comment; it was enough if the reader could tell that it was comment, not fact.

Sub-editors need to take special care if they introduce comment into headlines on news stories. In 2003 the *Daily Telegraph* published articles making allegations about the left-wing Labour MP George Galloway after a reporter was said to have found documents referring to him in the ruins of a government building in Baghdad, soon after the invasion of Iraq.

One news story was headlined '*Telegraph* reveals damning new evidence on Labour MP'. When sued, the paper did not claim the allegations were true but claimed the headline was an expression of opinion. But the judge said 'damning' had a plain meaning – 'that is to say, that the evidence goes beyond a **prima facie** case and points to guilt'. The MP won his case (*George Galloway MP v Telegraph Group Ltd* [2004] EWHC 2786 (QB).

→ glossary

→

for a fuller account of this case, see ch. 20, p. 363

The exception to the rule that comment must be based on true facts is when the comment is based on privileged material, such as a report of judicial proceedings. This means that a media organisation can, if a defendant is found guilty, make scathing comment about the defendant based on the evidence reported. In such a case, the defence will still succeed, as regards what was published at the time the conviction stood, even if the facts mentioned in the privileged report later turn out to be untrue, e.g. if the defendant is acquitted on appeal. The fair comment defence will also protect publication of criticism of judges and magistrates, based on their actions in court, provided all the defence's requirements are met.

Opinion must be 'honestly held', not 'fair'

The law does not require the 'truth' of the comment itself to be proved; by its nature it cannot be. Comment may be responsible or irresponsible, informed or misinformed, constructive or destructive; but it cannot be true or false. Defendants pleading fair comment do not need to persuade either the judge or the jury to share their views.

What a defendant must do is satisfy the jury that the comment upon established facts represents a view that a person could honestly hold on those facts.

The law was expressed by Lord Diplock (then Mr Justice Diplock) in his summing up to the jury in a case in which Lord Silkin unsuccessfully sued Beaverbrook Newspapers for certain statements by 'Cross Bencher' in the *Sunday Express* (*Silkin v Beaverbrook Newspapers* [1958] 1 WLR 743 (QB)). He said:

> **❝** People are entitled to hold and express strong views on matters of public interest, provided they are honestly held. They may be views which some or all of you think are exaggerated, obstinate, or prejudiced.
>
> The basis of our public life is that the crank and the enthusiast can say what he honestly believes just as much as a reasonable man or woman.
>
> It would be a sad day for freedom of speech in this country if a jury were to apply the test of whether it agrees with a comment, instead of applying the true test of whether this opinion, however exaggerated, obstinate, or prejudiced, was honestly held. **❞**

Proof of malice may undermine the fair comment defence

The word **malice** has a special meaning in the law and, to make things more complicated, has a different meaning depending upon whether the claimant is considering fair comment or qualified privilege, as a defence.

The leading judge, Lord Nicholls, explained in a case in 2000 that, when comment was being considered as a defence, malice covered a situation where a defendant 'put forward as his view something which, in truth, was not his view. It was a pretence. The law does not protect such statements' (*Tse Wai Chun Paul v Albert Cheng*, Court of Final Appeal, Hong Kong [2001] EMLR 777).

But Lord Nicholls also said the defence is not defeated by the fact that the writer is actuated by spite, animosity, intent to injure, intent to arouse controversy, or other motivation, even if that is the dominant or sole motive. He added, however, that proof of such motivation might be evidence from which a jury could infer lack of an honestly held belief in the view expressed.

 →glossary

→
for malice in relation to privilege see below, p. 341

Imputing improper motives

The suggestion that someone has acted out of improper motives has been a frequent cause of libel actions and such a suggestion, if published, has in the past been hard to defend as fair comment.

But judges in the Court of Appeal took a more helpful view in a case in 2001 in a libel action brought by the entrepreneur Richard Branson against his biographer Tom Bower (*Branson v Bower* [2001] EWCA Civ 791; [2001] EMLR 800). Bower, commenting on the attempt by Branson to run the national lottery, said: 'Sceptics will inevitably whisper that Branson's motive is self-glorification.' When sued, Bower claimed this was fair comment but Branson said it was a factual allegation (that he had a questionable intention in bidding for the national lottery) and that this was untrue.

Lord Justice Latham, giving the judgment of the Court of Appeal, said that comment was 'something which is or can reasonably be inferred to be a deduction, inference, conclusion, criticism, remark, observation'.

He said the judge in the lower court had been fully entitled to come to the conclusion that Bower was expressing a series of opinions about Branson's motives.

Reviews

It is the fair comment defence which protects the expressions of opinion contained in reviews of, among other things, performances, books, holidays, and restaurants.

The defence was dealt a blow when a libel jury in Northern Ireland awarded £25,000 damages to the owner of a restaurant called Goodfellas over an unfavourable review in the *Irish News*. But the award was quashed on appeal in 2008, with the Northern Ireland Chief Justice, Sir Brian Kerr, saying:

❝ Only if the jury has a clear understanding of what is capable of constituting comment, can it address the thorny issue of whether the facts on which comment is based are capable of justifying the comment made (*Convery v The Irish News Ltd* [2007] NICA 40). ❞

He said that the jury had been misdirected, but that the court's task had been made more difficult by the confusion generated by the *Irish News* in portraying statements of comment in the article as facts.

Humour, satire, and irony

In 2008 Sir Elton John sued the *Guardian* for libel over a spoof article written by Marina Hyde under the headline 'A peek at the diary of…Sir Elton John' – a regular feature in the paper's Weekend section satirising the activities of celebrities.

Sir Elton claimed the article meant his commitment to the Elton John Aids Foundation was insincere and that once the costs of his White Tie and Tiara fundraising ball were met only a small proportion of the funds raised would go to good causes.

The *Guardian*'s defence was that the words were clearly comment and could not have the meaning claimed by the claimant.

Mr Justice Tugendhat, striking out Sir Elton's claim, accepted the *Guardian*'s argument that the words were a form of teasing, and, had the *Guardian* actually unearthed a story about a charity ball's costs leaving nothing for good causes, it was a serious story that would have been written without any attempt at humour (*Sir Elton John v Guardian News and Media Ltd* [2008] EWHC 3066 (QB)).

▶ Privilege

There are occasions when the public interest demands that there is complete freedom of speech without any risk of proceedings for defamation, even if the statements are defamatory and even if they turn out to be untrue. These occasions are referred to as *privileged*.

Privilege exists under **common law** and statute.   → glossary

Absolute privilege

Absolute privilege, where it is applicable, is a complete answer and bar to any action for defamation. It does not matter whether the words are true or false. It does not matter that they were spoken or written maliciously.

But though a journalist may be reporting what is said on *an occasion* that is protected by absolute privilege it does not follow that his/her report is similarly protected.

Members of Parliament may say whatever they wish in the House of Commons without fear of being sued for defamation. But the reports of parliamentary debates published by the media enjoy only *qualified privilege*, a defence which depends on these being a proper motive in publication.

The reports of parliamentary proceedings in *Hansard* have absolute privilege; so have reports published by order of Parliament (such as White Papers). But the media's coverage of parliamentary publications enjoys only qualified privilege.

→ see below. p. 340 on qualified privilege

→
see also
ch. 15 on
tribunals

The only time journalists enjoy absolute privilege is when they are reporting court cases or the proceedings of certain types of tribunals. In this context the requirements of absolute privilege are that what is published is:

- a fair and accurate report of judicial proceedings held in public within the United Kingdom, published contemporaneously.

The Defamation Act 1996 extended this protection to reports of the European Court of Justice, or any court attached to that court, the European Court of Human Rights, and any international criminal tribunal (a war crimes tribunal) established by the Security Council of the United Nations or by an international agreement to which the United Kingdom is a party.

→
see ch. 12
on open
justice

Privilege for court reports is vital for the media because what is said in court is often highly defamatory. Without privilege, court reporting would be impossible. The law thus recognises that the media help sustain open justice. Privilege does <u>not</u> apply if the court (or tribunal) hearing is held in **private**.

Reports must be fair

For absolute privilege to apply, a report of a court case must be 'fair and accurate'. This does not mean that the proceedings must be reported verbatim; a report will still be 'fair and accurate' if:

- it presents a summary of both sides;
- it contains no substantial inaccuracies;
- it avoids giving disproportionate weight to one side or the other.

In a case in 2006 (*Bennett v Newsquest*, see *Media Lawyer* newsletter, No 64), Mr Justice Eady pointed out that a newspaper story which reported a criminal case and which was the subject of a libel action contained inaccuracies. However, he continued:

❝ The report must be fair overall and not give a misleading impression. Inaccuracies in themselves will not defeat privilege. Omissions will deprive a report of privilege if they create a false impression of what took place or if they result in the suppression of the case or part of the case of one side, while giving the other. ❞

If, however, the report is held to be unfair or inaccurate in any important respect, the media organisation publishing it loses the protection of privilege.

In 1993 the *Daily Sport* paid substantial damages to a police officer acquitted of indecent assault. The paper reported the opening of the case by the prosecution and the main evidence of the alleged victim, but did not include her cross-examination by the defence, which began on the same day, and in which her allegation was undermined. Later the paper had briefly reported the officer's acquittal, but he still decided to sue. The settlement in this case means that it remains something of a grey area in law as to how much of a day's proceedings in court must be covered for a report to be fair.

Trials may last for days, weeks, or months and statements made by the prosecution may subsequently be shown by the defendant to be wrong. Reports of proceedings may be published each day but the safest journalistic practice is that if the publication has reported allegations that are later rebutted those rebuttals should be carried.

Reports must be accurate

All allegations in court reports must be attributed because a report that presents an allegation as if it were a proved fact is inaccurate. Do not write 'Brown had a gun in his hand' but 'Smith said Brown had a gun in his hand'.

A media organisation is left with no protection at all if it wrongly identifies as the defendant someone who is only a witness or unconnected with the case. If a media report is inaccurate about what charge the defendant faces, this too could prove expensive in libel damages.

→
see also ch. 18, p. 320 on need to fully identify a defendant

Journalists must also avoid wrongly reporting that the defendant has been convicted when he has in fact been acquitted. One paper paid damages when it reported a man's acquittal on drug charges but it did so in terms that conveyed the impression he was in fact guilty.

The courts do allow some leeway to publications compressing material in reports, said Mr Justice Eady, in considering an action against the *Worcester News* by a couple who claimed the reports were inaccurate (*Elizabeth and Peter Crossley v Newsquest (Midlands South Ltd)* [2008] EWHC 3054 (QB)).

Reports must be contemporaneous

To have the protection of absolute privilege, court reports should be published contemporaneously with the proceedings. This means 'as soon as practicable', e.g. in the first issue of the paper following that day's session (and the same definition applies in contempt law as regards section 4 of the Contempt of Court Act 1981 – see ch. 16, p. x).

For a weekly paper, contemporaneous publication may mean publishing the following week.

Sometimes the report of court proceedings has to be postponed because a court order compels this. In that case, says the Defamation Act 1996, the story is treated as if it were published contemporaneously if it is published 'as soon as practicable after publication is permitted'.

→
see chs 9 and 16

Even if the report is not contemporaneous, it will still attract qualified privilege under statute and under common law.

 See 'Qualified privilege by statute', 'Statements having qualified privilege', 'Privilege at common law', and 'Reports of judicial and parliamentary proceedings', below, pp. 341, 345 and 348.

Reports of earlier sections of a hearing published to put later reports in context should still be treated as having absolute privilege (*Elizabeth and Peter Crossley v Newsquest (Midlands South Ltd)* [2008] EWHC 3054 (QB)).

Protection only for reports of proceedings

Suppose a 'court report' in the media contains matter that did not originate from the court? In the *Bennett* case referred to above, the judge said:

> 66 Extraneous comments can be included or other factual material but it must be severable, in the sense that a reasonable reader could readily appreciate that the material did not purport to be a report of what was said in court. 99

But such material is not covered by privilege. In general, privilege extends only to the actual report of proceedings held in open court.

- It does not protect, for example, defamatory matter shouted out in court, e.g. from the public gallery by someone who is <u>not</u> part of the proceedings.
- But if the shouted comment is by someone who has given evidence as a witness in that case, privilege would protect its inclusion in a court report, provided all the defence's requirements were met.
- If the shouted comment is not defamatory, it can in libel law be reported safely whoever made it.

Qualified privilege

Qualified privilege is available as a defence where it is considered important that the facts should be freely known in the public interest. There is privilege at common law for the publication of defamatory statements in certain circumstances. See below, and ch 20.

The Defamation Act 1996 lists categories of circumstances in which the statutory form of qualified privilege applies, such as reports of court cases, of public meetings, of council meetings, and of police statements. This is explained below.

Qualified privilege by statute

In general, qualified privilege gives just as much protection to a publication as absolute privilege, provided that the defence's requirements are met. However, it should be noted that these requirements differ from those of absolute privilege. In the latter the motive of the person publishing is irrelevant. But for qualified privilege to apply, there must be no malicious motive – see below.

The basic requirements of the qualified privilege defence are, in respect of the 'statements' i.e. reports of situations and occasions listed by Schedule 1 to the 1996 Act as being capable of being protected by such privilege:

see Schedule on pp. 345–348

- that the published report is fair and accurate, and published without malice.

There is also a general requirement for qualified privilege that:

- the matter published must be a matter of public concern, the publication of which is for the public benefit.

This can be summed up as 'published in the public interest'.

Malice here has a different meaning from malice in the context of fair comment. It means ill-will or spite towards the claimant or any indirect or improper motive in the defendant's mind. Lord Nicholls explained in the *Cheng* case (see above) that the purpose of the defence of qualified privilege is to allow a person who has a duty to perform, or an interest to protect, to provide information without the risk of being sued. If a person's dominant motive is not to perform this duty or protect this interest, he cannot use the defence.

see above, p. 335 on fair comment

In 2005 the BBC failed when pleading it had statutory qualified privilege for a defamatory statement about a health service manager who was named in a BBC West broadcast (*Henry v BBC* [2005] EWHC 2787 (QB)). The broadcast reported the outcome of an inquiry into allegations that the figures for patient waiting lists at Weston General Hospital NHS Trust were falsified and it included film of a press conference in which Mrs Marion Henry was identified, together with two others, by a whistleblower as being responsible for covering up the fact that patients had been removed from the trust's waiting lists.

The judge, Mr Justice Gray, agreed that qualified privilege was available for those parts of the broadcast that summarised the findings of the inquiry because the trust was 'an authority performing governmental functions' in the UK.

But the judge said he was not persuaded it was of public concern or for the public benefit for the BBC to name Mrs Henry and the other two individuals in its report of the allegations of cover-up made at the press conference, so that part of the broadcast was not privileged.

(In the end, the BBC won the case because it proved the defamatory statements were true.)

The *Henry* case shows that the protection of statutory qualified privilege applies only to reports of the actual proceedings or other matters listed in the Act's Schedule 1.

- For example, there is no qualified privilege for a media report of defamatory statements made by a councillor *after* a meeting when asked to expand on statements made during the meeting.

Statements subject to explanation or contradiction

→

see both parts of Schedule, pp. 345–348

Schedule 1 to the Defamation Act 1996 Act sets out in Part I a list of statements having qualified privilege 'without explanation or contradiction' and in Part II a list of statements thus privileged but 'subject to explanation or contradiction'.

- This means that, if required to do so by anyone who is defamed by a report protected by Part II, an editor who has published that report must publish a 'reasonable letter or statement by way of explanation or contradiction' for the qualified privilege to continue to apply to the report.

Failure to publish such a statement would destroy the defence of qualified privilege for what was published earlier. The Act says such a statement must be published 'in a suitable manner', and that this means 'in the same manner as the publication complained of or in a manner that is adequate and reasonable in the circumstances'.

Another reason that the BBC could not rely on statutory privilege in the *Henry* case (see above) was that the BBC had declined to publish the statement supplied by Mrs Henry's solicitors.

Legal advice should be taken if any statement that the complainer asks to be published gives rise to any difficulty, such as the risk of libelling another person. Publication of the statement of 'explanation or contradiction' is not protected by privilege under the 1996 Act, so the statement must be 'reasonable' in this respect. See also replies to attack, below, p. 348.

Public meeting defined

Schedule 1 to the 1996 Act provides in paragraph 12 a legal definition of a 'public meeting', namely:

- a lawful meeting held for the furtherance or discussion of a matter of public concern, whether admission to the meeting is general or restricted.

This definition is fairly wide, covering public meetings about a particular community or ones held about national issues.

- The House of Lords ruled in 2000 that a press conference is a public meeting, an important decision for journalists and the media generally (*McCartan Turkington Breen v Times Newspapers Ltd* [2001] 2 AC 277.

The Times had been sued over its report of a press conference called by a group of people campaigning for the release of a soldier convicted of murdering a joyrider.

During the press conference defamatory comments were made about the solicitors who had represented the soldier, and these were reported by the paper. A jury awarded £145,000 damages. But on appeal, Lord Bingham, the senior law lord, said that press representatives could be regarded either as members of the public themselves or as 'the eyes and ears of the public, to whom they report'.

- The court also ruled that a written press release, handed out at the meeting but not read aloud, and reported by the paper, was in effect part of the press conference proceedings, and so fair, accurate reports of such documents handed out at a press conference have qualified privilege too, in the context of coverage of the press conference.

'Findings' but not proceedings

Paragraph 14 of the Schedule gives protection to reports of findings or decisions of a wide variety of bodies. The protection does not apply to a report of the *proceedings* of such bodies.

see also ch. 15, p. 259

Privilege for sub-committees

Paragraph 11 of the Schedule includes in its definition of local authorities any authority or body to which the Public Bodies (Admission to Meetings) Act 1960 applies, all of which have the protection of qualified privilege.

Protection for reports of statements by government authorities and the police

Paragraph 9 of the Schedule gives privilege, subject to explanation or contradiction, to 'a fair and accurate copy of or extract from' a notice or other matter issued for the public by authorities with governmental functions, including councils and police authorities. This includes, for example, fair and accurate reports of official police statements about people they wish to interview in connection with a crime, and statements made on behalf of local authorities, e.g. about consumer protection or environmental health matters.

There will be many occasions when a reporter will wish to report the misdeeds of a person but may be inhibited by the fear of a libel action. The answer is often to obtain the information in the form of an official statement by a police or local authority spokesman. The paragraph does not protect reports of matter unofficially 'leaked' from such authorities, or of what was said by those who are not official spokespeople.

Not all authorities are covered

It is tempting to assume that the Schedule list covers all statements by people in authority, but it does not cover, for example, statements by the spokespeople of British Telecom, a gas board, a water board, the rail companies, London Regional Transport, British Airport Authority, or other bodies created by statute that are involved in providing day-to-day services to the public. It seems likely, however, that a fair and accurate account of such a body would be held to be covered by privilege at common law.

see below, p. 348 on common law

Cover for comments by press officers

Suppose a reporter telephones the spokesperson of one of the bodies mentioned in the Act and puts questions to him or her. Is the report of the spokesperson's comments protected? In *Blackshaw v Lord* [1984] QB 1, Lord Justice Stephenson said that it would unduly restrict the privilege contained in paragraph 12 [paragraph 12 of the Schedule to the 1952 Act, now paragraph 9] to confine it to written handouts.

❝ It may be right to include…the kind of answers to telephoned interrogatories which Mr Lord [a *Daily Telegraph* reporter], quite properly in the discharge of his duty to his newspaper, administered to Mr Smith [a government press officer]. To exclude them in every case might unduly restrict the freedom of the press…But information which is put out on the initiative of a government department falls more easily within the paragraph than information pulled out of the mouth of an unwilling officer of the department…not every statement of fact made to a journalist by a press officer of a government department is privileged. ❞

Protection for stories from 'statements of case'

There is privilege under paragraph 5 of the Schedule for a fair and accurate copy of or extract from a document which is required by the law to be open to inspection by the public. Until 2006 qualified privilege gave protection

to the reporting of defamatory statements endorsed on a libel **claim form**, →glossary
but not to any accompanying documentation. Under a change in the Civil
Procedure Rules that year journalists reporting on new cases were allowed
access to the full **statement of case** – which would include the claim form, →glossary
particulars of claim, defence, counterclaims, reply to the defence, and 'further information documents'. Such material would now be protected.

→
see also
chs 10
and 12

More categories protected

As stated above, the 1996 Act greatly widened the categories of situations
where privilege applied, including reports of foreign courts, of foreign leg-
islatures, and of all public inquiries appointed by governments, as regards
proceedings held in public.

Reports about companies

The 1996 Act also greatly extended qualified privilege with respect to the
reporting of company affairs. Earlier, only reports relating to proceedings
at general meetings of public companies carried qualified privilege. The
Act extends privilege to documents circulated among shareholders of a UK
public company with the authority of the board or the auditors or by any
shareholder 'in pursuance of a right conferred by any statutory provision'.

Schedule 1 to the Defamation Act 1996

The text of Parts I and II of Schedule 1 to the 1996 Act follows.

❝❞ **Statements having qualified privilege**

Part I: Statements privileged without explanation or contradiction

1 A fair and accurate report of proceedings in public of a legislature any-
    where in the world.
2 A fair and accurate report of proceedings in public before a court anywhere
    in the world.
3 A fair and accurate report of proceedings in public of a person appointed to
    hold a public inquiry by a government or legislature anywhere in the world.
4 A fair and accurate report of proceedings in public anywhere in the world of
    an international organisation or an international conference.
5 A fair and accurate copy of or extract from any register or other document
    required by law to be open to public inspection.
6 A notice or advertisement published by or on the authority of a court, or of
    a judge or officer of a court, anywhere in the world.

7 A fair and accurate copy of or extract from matter published by or on the authority of a government or legislature anywhere in the world.

8 A fair and accurate copy of or extract from matter published anywhere in the world by an international organisation or an international conference.

Part II: Statements privileged subject to explanation or contradiction

9 (1) A fair and accurate copy of or extract from a notice or other matter issued for the information of the public by or on behalf of

   (a) a legislature in any member state or the European Parliament;

   (b) the government of any member state, or any authority performing governmental functions in any member state or part of a member state, or the European Commission;

   (c) an international organisation or international conference.

  (2) In this paragraph 'governmental functions' includes police functions.

10 A fair and accurate copy of or extract from a document made available by a court in any member state or the European Court of Justice (or any court attached to that court), or by a judge or officer of any such court.

11 (1) A fair and accurate report of proceedings at any public meeting or sitting in the United Kingdom of –

   (a) a local authority or local authority committee;

   (b) a justice or justices of the peace acting otherwise than as a court exercising judicial authority;

   (c) a commission, tribunal, committee or person appointed for the purposes of any inquiry by any statutory provision, by Her Majesty or by a Minister of the Crown or a Northern Ireland Department;

   (d) a person appointed by a local authority to hold a local inquiry in pursuance of any statutory provision;

   (e) any other tribunal, board, committee or body constituted by or under, and exercising functions under, any statutory provision.

  (2) This sub-paragraph defines 'local authority' in England and Wales, Scotland, and Northern Ireland.

  (3) A fair and accurate report of any corresponding proceedings in any of the Channel Islands or the Isle of Man or in another member state.

12 (1) A fair and accurate report of proceedings at any public meeting held in a member state.

  (2) In this paragraph a 'public meeting' means a meeting bona fide and lawfully held for a lawful purpose and for the furtherance or discussion of a matter of public concern, whether admission to the meeting is general or restricted.

13 (1) A fair and accurate report of proceedings at a general meeting of a UK public company.

(2) A fair and accurate copy of or extract from any document circulated to members of a UK public company –

(a) by or with the authority of the board of directors of the company,

(b) by the auditors of the company, or

(c) by any member of the company in pursuance of a right conferred by any statutory provision.

(3) A fair and accurate copy of or extract from any document circulated to members of a UK public company which relates to the appointment, resignation, retirement or dismissal of directors of the company.

(4) This sub-paragraph defines 'UK public company'.

(5) A fair and accurate report of proceedings at any corresponding meeting of, or copy of or extract from any corresponding document circulated to members of, a public company formed under the law of any of the Channel Islands or the Isle of Man or of another member state.

14 A fair and accurate report of any finding or decision of any of the following descriptions of association, formed in the United Kingdom or another member state, or of any committee or governing body of such an association –

(a) an association formed for the purpose of promoting or encouraging the exercise of or interest in any art, science, religion or learning, and empowered by its constitution to exercise control over or adjudicate on matters of interest or concern to the association, or the actions or conduct of any persons subject to such control or adjudication;

(b) an association formed for the purpose of promoting or safeguarding the interests of any trade, business, industry or profession, or of the persons carrying on or engaged in any trade, business, industry or profession, and empowered by its constitution to exercise control over or adjudicate upon matters connected with the trade, business, industry or profession, or the actions or conduct of those persons;

(c) an association formed for the purpose of promoting or safeguarding the interests of a game, sport or pastime to the playing or exercise of which members of the public are invited or admitted, and empowered by its constitution to exercise control over or adjudicate upon persons connected with or taking part in the game, sport or pastime;

(d) an association formed for the purpose of promoting charitable objects or other objects beneficial to the community and empowered by its constitution to exercise control over or to adjudicate on matters of interest or concern to the association, or the actions or conduct of any person subject to such control or adjudication.

15 (1) A fair and accurate report of, or copy of or extract from, any adjudication, report, statement or notice issued by a body, officer or other person designated for the purposes of this paragraph –

(a) for England and Wales or Northern Ireland, by order of the Lord Chancellor, and

(b) for Scotland, by order of the Secretary of State.

→glossary

(2) An order under this paragraph shall be made by **statutory instrument** which shall be subject to annulment in pursuance of a resolution of either House of Parliament. "

Privilege at common law

Privilege at common law applies in certain circumstances where the law protects defamatory statements that are untrue, for the convenience and welfare of society.

One such circumstance is where a person makes a defamatory statement in the performance of a legal, moral, or social duty to a person who has a corresponding duty or interest in receiving it.

For example, suppose someone is seeking a job. The potential employer writes to the former employer to ask for a reference. The former employer can reply frankly. The former employer cannot be sued for libel for what is said, even if the facts are wrong, provided the employer is not motivated by malice.

Courts considering whether the defence applied have traditionally applied the 'duty/interest' test.

Replies to attacks

There is also qualified privilege at common law for a defamatory statement made by a person in reply to an attack upon his character or conduct. There would be no privilege for any response wider than necessary to meet the specific allegations. A media organisation publishing a lawful response would share in the privilege.

Reports of judicial and parliamentary proceedings

→

see above, pp. 337–340 on absolute privilege

Finally, there is qualified privilege at common law for fair and accurate reports of judicial proceedings in this country and reports of the proceedings of Parliament, if held in public. If a journalist refers to court proceedings that are not contemporaneous the report does not attract absolute privilege but the reporter may still be able to plead qualified privilege at common law, as well as by statute for any defamatory statements in the report.

▌ Accord and satisfaction

This is a plea that the matter has been otherwise disposed of, for example by the publication of a correction and apology which has been accepted by the claimant in settlement of his complaint.

'Without prejudice'

A complaint to a media organisation may be made by a telephone call to the editor or to another member of the staff; by a letter from the complainer direct, or from his/her solicitors.

A solicitor writing on behalf of a client demanding a correction and apology will always avoid suggesting that this action by the media organisation will be enough in itself to settle the dispute and will make it clear that the request is made 'without prejudice' to any other action that may become necessary.

What does this mean? The basic principle is that parties attempting to settle their differences before going to law should be encouraged to speak frankly. So anything said or written in the course of negotiations to settle is described as 'without prejudice' (that is, off the record) and cannot subsequently be used against a party in court if negotiations fail. The rule applies whether or not the phrase 'without prejudice' is expressly used, but it is generally good practice to do so.

Practical advice on procedure

Journalists speaking with someone complaining about a story need to distinguish between

- discussions over an offer to publish a follow-up story or a correction, and
- discussions over settling a claim.

In the former case, which often involves the journalist and the subject themselves, the discussion need not necessarily be 'without prejudice'; the journalist may well want to refer to this discussion in court, to show fairness or lack of malice, or to mitigate damages.

In the latter case, often involving solicitors and mention of money, the discussion should be 'without prejudice'. A leading lawyer has advised that as a general rule journalists should notify their insurers about potential claims at once and, if there are solicitors 'on the other side', the publisher should probably involve its own lawyer also.

Care with apologies and corrections

It is no defence for a media organisation to publish a correction and apology not accepted by the claimant. Such a publication may be found by a court to constitute an admission that the matter was wrong and possibly that it was defamatory. For example:

- an apology or correction if badly drafted may repeat the libellous matter complained of, angering the person who complained about it;
- an apology or correction if badly drafted may unwittingly libel someone else, e.g. 'In our article yesterday we said Mr Red hit Mr Green. But we wish to point out that Mr Red says Mr Green struck him first'. Mr Green may sue over the apology.

On the other hand, if the jury finds for the claimant, the fact that the media organisation took prompt and adequate steps to correct the error, and to express regret, will provide a plea in mitigation of damages – that is, it will tend to reduce the size of damages awarded.

And an aggrieved person may be prepared to sign a waiver – that is, a statement saying he/she waives his/her right to legal redress in exchange for the publication of a correction and apology – and such a waiver will provide a complete defence of 'accord and satisfaction'.

Practical advice on procedure

The defence of accord and satisfaction does not depend upon the existence of any formal written agreement, but clearly a media organisation has a stronger case if it can produce a signed paper (known as a waiver) in the following terms:

> 66 I confirm that the publication of an apology in the terms annexed in a position of reasonable prominence in the next available issue of the [name of paper] will be accepted in full and final satisfaction of any claim I may have in respect of the article headed [give headline] published in the issue of your newspaper for [date]. 99

A practical danger for an editor who asks a complainer to sign a waiver is that the reader may not have realised previously that he has a claim for damages and, thus alerted, he may consult a lawyer. The waiver is therefore most useful when the complainer has already threatened to consult a lawyer.

Inexperienced reporters will sometimes try to avoid the consequences of their errors without referring them to their editor. They may try to shrug it off, or they may incorporate a scarcely recognisable 'correction' (without apology) in a follow-up story.

Either course of action is highly dangerous. It may further aggravate the offence and annoy the person concerned, and he/she may well take more formal steps to secure satisfaction. In such circumstances the reporter should immediately tell the editor so that the matter can be dealt with.

Payment into court

Another way to 'satisfy' a claimant is by payment into court, a 'Part 36 offer' in lawyers' language. This means that the party being sued, e.g. a media organisation, makes a formal offer of settlement through the court, and the claimant can have this money at any time to end the litigation. If it is not accepted, the action continues.

→ see also ch. 10, p. 154

Neither the judge nor the jury is told at the trial how much money has been paid in. If the award is less than, or the same as, the amount paid in, the claimant will usually be ordered to pay that part of his own and the defendant's costs which were incurred after the date this formal offer was made.

▌ Offer of amends

There are various ways in which the media can defame a person unintentionally. The classic example was the case of Artemus Jones. Here a journalist introduced a fictitious character into a descriptive account of a factual event in order to provide atmosphere – referring to what he thought of as his fictional character at the Dieppe motor festival 'with a woman who is not his wife'.

→ see ch. 18, p. 320 which concerned a report of a court case

Unfortunately the name he chose was that of a real person, a barrister from North Wales. Stung by the comments of his friends the real Artemus Jones sued and recovered substantial damages.

Another example occurs where an account relating to one 'real' person is understood to refer to another. As happened in the case of Harold Newstead in the section on identification.

Another is the case where a statement is on the surface innocuous but, because of circumstances unknown to the writer, is defamatory. In *Cassidy v Daily Mirror Newspapers Ltd* [1929] 2 KB 331, Cassidy, at the races, was photographed with a woman he described as his fiancée, and this was the way she was described in the caption to the photograph used by the newspaper. But Cassidy was already married, and his wife sued on the ground that people who knew her would assume she had been 'living in sin'.

How to make an offer

A person can still be defamed in these various circumstances, but the Defamation Act 1996 provides for a defence known as 'offer to make amends'.

To use this defence, a defendant must make a written offer to make a suitable correction and apology, to publish the correction in a reasonable manner, and to pay the claimant suitable damages.

The defence can only be used where the defendant did not know and had no reason to believe that the statement complained of referred to the claimant and was false and defamatory of him. The claimant has the onus of showing that the publication was not 'innocent'.

If the offer of amends is not accepted, the defendant will have a defence to the action provided the court holds that the defendant did not know and had no reason to believe that the words complained of were false and defamatory.

Don't delay in making the offer

Editors planning to make an offer of amends must not delay. If the resulting compensation is to be assessed by a judge he will start by deciding what would be 'suitable damages' if the editor had made no offer of amends and will then award a 'discount' of perhaps 50 per cent as a 'reward' for making the offer. The *News of the World* received only a 40 per cent discount after it was slow to respond to a complaint and published an apology six months after the original story, and the *Guardian* received only 35 per cent when it failed to provide the 'speedy, unequivocal and prominent apology' the judge said was needed.

The need for a quick and adequate response was illustrated even more clearly by a case in 2006 in which the claimant, a journalist, won damages over an article that accused him of being involved in bomb attacks in London the previous year (*Muhamed Veliu v Xhevdet Mazrekaj and*

Skender Bucpapaj [2006] EWHC 1710 (QB)). He sued both the publisher of the newspaper that had used the story and its editor. The publisher made an unqualified offer of amends, but the editor 'did nothing'. The judge said the publisher and editor were jointly liable for the damages. He set the starting point for compensation at £180,000, then applied a discount of 30 per cent, with respect to the publishers, setting their maximum liability at £120,000. He said the claimant should receive £175,000 damages, and made the editor liable for the whole amount.

Once an offer is made it is binding

The boxing promoter Frank Warren sued Random House, publishers of a book about the life story of boxer Ricky Hatton. Random House initially made an offer of amends, but when new information came to light they sought to withdraw the offer of amends and use a defence of justification instead. The Court of Appeal refused to allow this, treating it almost as a contract. The lesson is: do your research before making an offer.

Claimants cannot sue and keep an offer on the table

Tesco sued the *Guardian* over a story about its tax arrangements. The paper made an offer of amends. Tesco sought to keep the offer open while continuing litigation; however the court would not allow this.

▌ Other defences

Defences that may be available in certain circumstances are:

(1) *That the claimant has died* The action for libel is a personal action. A dead person cannot be libelled. Similarly, an action begun by a claimant cannot be continued by his heirs and executors if he dies before the case is decided. The action dies with him.

→ except in criminal libel: see ch. 21

(2) *That the claimant agreed to the publication* This is known as the 'leave and licence' defence. But short of obtaining a signed statement to that effect before publication, it might be extremely difficult to prove that consent was given. It is no defence to say that you have shown the offending words to the claimant and he has had the chance to respond to the allegations.

(3) *That proceedings were not started within the limitation period* This constitutes a complete defence, unless there is a new publication of offending material (as in a 'bygone days' column: see ch. 18 p. 323). The period, formerly three years, was reduced to one year by the Defamation Act 1996. Reporters should date their notebooks and store them carefully in case they are required to produce them in court.

(4) *That the matter has already been adjudged* The court will not entertain a second action based on the same complaint against the same defendant, or against any other person jointly liable with him for that publication. But the journalist must remember that every repetition is a new publication.

. (5) The defence under section 1 of the Defamation Act 1996, which protects those who were not the author, editor, or publisher of the matter published, and which may protect 'live' broadcasts and internet service providers. This is outlined in ch. 18, pp. 323–325.

⠿ Recap of major points

- The main defences against an action for libel are: justification, fair comment, absolute and qualified privilege.

- It is a complete defence (with one exception arising under the Rehabilitation of Offenders Act 1974) to prove that the words complained of are substantially true. This is the justification defence.

- The justification defence applies only to facts, not to comment. And the defendant must prove not only the plain meaning of the words, but also any innuendo or as reasonable inference the words carry.

- Investigative journalists must make sure they can prove their facts in court.

- A defendant can plead that an article expressing comment was an honestly held opinion on a matter of public interest. This is the fair comment defence.

- This comment must be based upon facts that either are stated in the story complained of, or are otherwise alluded to, or are widely-known. These facts must be true, or privileged.

- In some circumstances, in the public interest, a defamatory statement is privileged and can be made without risk of proceedings.

- Absolute privilege applies to court reports, but reports must be fair, accurate, and contemporaneous.

- Qualified privilege is available on many occasions under statute (e.g. for a report of a public meeting). The defence is qualified because it is lost if the motive in publishing is malicious.

- Other defences include 'accord and satisfaction' and 'offer of amends'.

🌐 Useful Websites

Test whether your story has a defence – see Online Resource Centre.

www.opsi.gov.uk/Acts/acts1996/ukpga_19960031_en_1/
  Defamation Act 1996

20

The *Reynolds* defence

Chapter summary

One of the clichés of journalism is the reporter insisting that information should be given up and a story should be run because 'it's in the public interest', but journalists' faith in the public interest has not always been shared by libel courts. This changed with the *Reynolds* case in 1998, which gave its name to the defence. The court in that case recognised that sometimes journalists have a duty to tell their readers about certain stories and that if they are perform-

→ glossary ing that duty they should have a privilege defence against an action for libel. However, publications trying to mount this defence have found the courts will examine closely the way in which they researched and wrote the story, as well as asking if the story itself was truly in the public interest. This chapter will explain the development of the *Reynolds* defence and detail the steps journalists and publications need to take to make their stories and newsgathering operations '*Reynolds* friendly'.

▌ The birth of the defence

The *Reynolds* defence, put simply, protects the publication of defamatory material, provided that it was a matter of public interest and that it was the product of 'responsible journalism'.

The defence is so named because in 1998 the *Sunday Times* was sued by Albert Reynolds, the former Taoiseach (head of the Government) of the

Republic of Ireland, over a story which he claimed meant he had deliberately and dishonestly misled the Dail (the country's Parliament) by suppressing information concerning the appointment of the country's attorney general to the presidency of its High Court.

The *Reynolds* case and its appeals

→

see ch. 19, p. 348

The *Sunday Times* in its defence said that, in keeping with Article 10 of the European Convention on Human Rights, the public interest in political issues and the conduct of elected politicians should be protected by qualified privilege at **common law**.

→ glossary

The *Sunday Times* lost the case in the first instance, but in 1998, in *Reynolds v Times Newspapers* [1998] 3 All ER 961, the Lord Chief Justice, Lord Bingham, said in the Court of Appeal:

❝ As it is the task of the news media to inform the public and engage in public discussion of matters of public interest, so is that to be recognised as its duty. ❞

In 1999, when the same case reached the House of Lords, on appeal (*Reynolds v Times Newspapers* [2000] 2 AC 127), though Times Newspapers lost, the court confirmed the principle that the media have such a duty and the *Reynolds* defence was born.

Giving judgment in the House of Lords, Lord Nicholls set out a list of circumstances to be examined by the court when looking at this defence.

Lord Nicholls' list

(1) The seriousness of the allegation. The more serious the charge, the more the public is misinformed and the individual harmed, if the allegation is not true.

(2) The nature of the information, and the extent to which the subject matter is a matter of public concern.

(3) The source of the information. Some informants have no direct knowledge of the events. Some have their own axes to grind, or are being paid for their stories.

(4) The steps taken to verify the information.

(5) The status of the information. The allegation may have already been the subject of an investigation which commands respect.

(6) The urgency of the matter. News is often a perishable commodity.

→ glossary

(7) Whether comment was sought from the **claimant**. He may have information others do not possess or have not disclosed. An approach to the claimant will not always be necessary.

(8) Whether the article contained the gist of the claimant's side of the story.

(9) The tone of the article. A newspaper can raise queries or call for an investigation. It need not adopt allegations as statements of fact.

(10) The circumstances of the publication, including the timing.

Following *Reynolds*, judges hearing a case in which a media defendant pleaded this defence customarily went through the 10 points systematically. Journalists too have seen the 10 points as a list of hurdles their story must jump if they are to get the defence. But judges in the House of Lords criticised this approach, saying it was too narrow.

▌ What you need to do to get the defence

Publication in the public interest

Lord Bingham, the senior judge in the *Jameel* case in the House of Lords (*Jameel v Wall Street Journal Europe* [2006] UKHL 44), said the matter published had to be of public interest and the story had to be the product of 'responsible journalism'.

He said: 'The publisher is protected if he has taken such steps as a responsible journalist would take to try and ensure that what is published is accurate and fit for publication'. He recalled that in *Reynolds* Lord Nicholls, who gave the judgment of the court, 'listed certain matters which might be taken into account in deciding whether the test of responsible journalism was satisfied'. He said the rationale of the test was that 'there is no duty to publish, and the public has no interest to read, material which the publisher has not taken reasonable steps to verify'.

In the *Jameel* case, the story was that the US authorities had asked Saudi Arabia to check whether certain individuals and firms had financial links with terrorists. The story named a Saudi Arabian millionaire businessman, Mohammed Jameel, and his companies among those to be investigated. Mr Jameel denied that any such request had been made.

Seeking comment from the claimant

One of the key points in many cases in which the *Reynolds* defence was attempted, was whether the newspaper had properly sought comment from the claimant (Lord Nicholls' seventh point).

⬚ Point for consideration

It is good journalistic practice that a damaging story should be put to the subject before publication. The main argument for this is the obvious one that, as the subject of the story knows more about it than the journalist he will be able to point out any errors in it, including perhaps that there is no truth in the story at all. In the words of Lord Nicholls' seventh point: 'He [the subject] may have information others do not possess or have not disclosed.' The courts reasonably regard observance of the practice as one indication of responsible journalism.

However as point 7 states: 'An approach to the claimant will not always be necessary' and this was the view the court took in the *Jameel* case. There were very special circumstances in that case, so journalists should always attempt to put defamatory allegations to the subject, if they are proposing to report them in the public interest.

In the *Jameel* case the House of Lords overturned High Court and Appeal Court libel judgments in favour of Mr Jameel and his companies. They had sued the *Wall Street Journal Europe*, described by Lord Bingham as 'a respected, influential and unsensational newspaper carrying serious news about international business, finance and politics'.

The paper had reported that, at the request of US law enforcement agencies, the Saudi Arabian central bank was monitoring the bank accounts of prominent Saudis in a bid to prevent them from being used, 'wittingly or unwittingly', for the funnelling of funds to terrorist organisations.

The paper listed those it said were being monitored, including Mr Jameel and his companies.

A spokesman for the Jameel companies had told the *Wall Street Journal*'s reporter that the only person who could speak on the record was Mr Jameel, who was not available. The spokesman asked whether publication could be postponed for 24 hours. The reporter said no, the article would be published with a statement that the Jameel group was not available for comment.

A jury found that the article referred to was defamatory of Mr Jameel and his companies and awarded £30,000 to Mr Jameel and £10,000 to his companies.

It was on this ground that the Court of Appeal upheld the judge's denial of *Reynolds* privilege. The court, turning down the paper's appeal, said:

❝ The judge found that there was no compelling reason why Mr Jameel could not have been afforded 24 hours to comment on the article. We can see no basis for challenging this conclusion. ❞

In the Lords, however, Lord Bingham said that denying *Reynolds* privilege just because the newspaper had failed to delay publication of the claimants' names without waiting long enough for them to comment was a very narrow ground on which to deny the privilege.

The 'responsible journalism' test

The following cases show the courts examining the work of journalists engaged on particular stories to decide whether those stories were 'the product of responsible journalism', to quote Lord Bingham.

Leeds Weekly News case The existence of the reporter's notebook was crucial in the successful defence. Being able to produce a good note is particularly important when attempting to show the 'steps taken to verify the information' (point 4) when using the *Reynolds* defence (see 'The GKR Karate case' below).

The Reynolds case Although the House of Lords in the *Reynolds* case established the existence of the *Reynolds* defence, it also decided, by a majority, that the *Sunday Times* could not take advantage of it. It was held that the paper had conspicuously failed to 'give the gist of the subject's response' (point 8). When the reporter was asked at the trial why his account contained no reference to Mr Reynolds' explanation, he said: 'There was not a word of Mr Reynolds' defence because I had decided that his defence . . . there was no defence.' Mr Reynolds had addressed the Dail (the Irish Parliament) on the matter, but the paper had not reported his statement.

When the court was attempting to establish the steps the reporter had taken to verify his story (point 4), and asked him why he had taken no notes during his inquiries, he replied, 'I was not in note-taking mode'.

The Loutchansky case The *Times* published articles about an international businessman, Grigori Loutchansky. The stories alleged that he controlled a major Russian criminal organisation involved in money-laundering and the smuggling of nuclear weapons. The paper agreed the stories were defamatory, but argued it had a defence of qualified privilege.

The trial judge rejected the defence and the case went to the Court of Appeal, which agreed that the articles dealt with matters of public concern (point 2). However, to implicate him in misconduct of the utmost gravity was manifestly likely to be highly damaging to his reputation. For that reason a proportionate degree of responsibility was required of the journalist and the editor (point 1). But they failed to show this, in particular because the allegations made were vague, the sources were unreliable, sufficient steps had not been taken to verify the information, and no comment had been obtained from Loutchansky before publication.

The judge said 'such steps as were taken' by the reporter in his unsuccessful attempts to contact either Mr Loutchansky or his company, Nordex, or its lawyers were far less diligent than was required by the standards of responsible journalism (point 7).

On the question whether the article met the *Reynolds* test of containing the gist of the claimant's side of the story (point 8), the judge said the article carried the bare statement that Mr Loutchansky had 'repeatedly denied any wrongdoing or links to criminal activity'. This was insufficient, given the seriousness of the unproven allegations to be published.

The reporter was asked in court to produce the note he had made of the vital conversation he claimed to have had with his most important source. He said he thought he must have made the note on a scrap of paper which he had subsequently thrown away (point 4). The Appeal Court rejected the newspaper's appeal (*Loutchansky v Times Newspapers Ltd* [2001] EWCA Civ 1805).

The GKR Karate case In 2000 a judge found for the *Leeds Weekly News*, a free newspaper, which was being sued for an article warning readers against the activities of doorstep salesmen selling karate club membership. It appeared on the front page under the headline, 'Give 'em the chop' and a sub-head, 'Doorstep salesmen flog dodgy karate lessons'.

The judge said the fundamental question was one of public interest. The court had to assess whether it was in the public interest for a newspaper to publish information as it did.

The firm's **counsel** had argued that, given the serious allegations contained in the article, which included allegations of dishonesty, the reporter had fallen far short of the standards of responsible journalism. She had made no adequate investigation before publication (point 4). Working on a hard-hitting story which accused the firm, GKR Karate (UK) Limited, of criminal offences, she had telephoned the firm and left a message with its paging service, but the firm did not reply and in the end the story carried no statement or comment from it (points 7 and 8).

The reporter phoned the trading standards officer in Leeds to ask whether there had been any complaints against the firm locally and was told no. She

→ glossary

did not report this in her story, but she did report the officer saying there had been complaints about GKR clubs 'in other UK cities'.

But the judge said he found the reporter to be an honest, sensible, and responsible person on whose evidence he could rely and who was naturally concerned by the dangers, particularly to children, resulting from this organisation (*GKR Karate Ltd v Yorkshire Post Newspapers Ltd* [2001] 1 WLR 2571).

▶ Neutral reportage

The Al-Fagih case In the *Al-Fagih* case, in 2001, the Court of Appeal ruled that a newspaper was entitled to rely upon the *Reynolds* defence where it had reported, in an entirely objective manner, an allegation about someone made in the course of a political dispute by one of his opponents. The defence was not lost merely because the newspaper had not verified the allegation (*Al-Fagih v HH Saudi Research & Marketing (UK) Ltd* [2001] EWCA Civ 1634).

The newspaper argued that where two politicians had made serious allegations against each other, it was a matter of public importance that the dispute be reported, provided that this was done fairly and accurately and an opportunity was given to the parties to explain or contradict.

At the trial, the judge rejected the defence of qualified privilege. In doing so, she relied heavily on the fact that the journalist had made no attempt to verify the truth of the allegations (point 4). A majority of the Court of Appeal allowed the newspaper's appeal. On the facts of this case, the failure to verify the story did not outweigh the public interest in publication.

The BNP case (Roberts v Searchlight) A case in 2006 indicated that the defence of 'neutral reportage' could be used even when, by contrast with the *Al-Fagih* case, the journal and its staff were clearly *not* neutral. The test is not the stance of the journalists, but the way in which the matter is being reported.

Two British National Party members lost their bid to sue the anti-fascist magazine *Searchlight*, its editor, and a journalist for libel when a judge upheld a qualified privilege defence based on the doctrine of reportage.

In a column entitled 'News from the sewers' the magazine reported a dispute between factions within the party. The defamatory allegations, repeated in *Searchlight*, had been made in the BNP's own bulletin, which reported, among other things, that three members stole money from a party organiser, and that the two claimants had threatened to 'kneecap, torture and kill' BNP members and their families.

The defendants claimed they had a defence of qualified privilege because they were merely reporting the allegations, without adopting or endorsing them (*Christopher Roberts and Barry Roberts v Gerry Gable, Steve Silver and Searchlight Magazine Ltd* [2006] EWHC 1025 (QB)).

The Galloway case In sharp contrast to the *Al-Fagih* case and the *BNP* case, in 2004 the *Daily Telegraph* failed in its claim that its coverage of documents said to have been discovered by a reporter in the ruins of the Foreign Ministry in Baghdad was 'neutral reportage'. A judge held that the paper's allegations that the left-wing MP George Galloway had received funds diverted from Iraq's oil-for-food programme conveyed a defamatory meaning that was not protected by qualified privilege (*George Galloway MP v Telegraph Group Ltd* [2004] EWHC 2786 (QB)).

Mr Galloway was awarded £150,000 damages and the paper had to pay costs estimated at £1.2 million.

The articles and leader comments complained of were published in April 2003, just a month after the invasion of Iraq. Mr Galloway said the articles conveyed the impression that he had taken large sums of money from Saddam Hussein's regime, and had requested more, and that his campaign for medical assistance to Iraq and the lifting of sanctions had been used by him as a front for his own financial advantage.

The newspaper did not say the allegations were true, but disputed the defamatory meaning of the articles and claimed qualified privilege and (as discussed earlier) **fair comment**. The paper argued that the public had →glossary a right to know the contents of the documents, even if they were defamatory of Mr Galloway and irrespective of whether the allegations were true or not. The paper argued that the effect of the words complained of was that the Baghdad documents consisted of strong **prima facie** evidence that →glossary Mr Galloway had arranged for his political campaign against the Iraq war and/or other political activities to be financed by the Iraqi government.

But the judge said *Reynolds* privilege protected the neutral reporting of attributed allegations rather than their adoption by a newspaper and the articles did not 'fairly and disinterestedly' report the context of the Baghdad documents. They went beyond assuming them to be true and drew their own inferences as to the personal receipt of funds diverted from Iraq's oil-for-food programme, something not alleged in the documents themselves.

The Royalty Monthly case The magazine failed in its appeal to overturn Mr Justice Eady's decision to strike out a *Reynolds* defence to an action by Prince Radu of Hohenzollern-Veringen, the husband of Princess Margarita of Romania, who sued *Royalty Monthly* magazine editor Marco Houston and its publisher over an article which he claimed suggests he was an 'imposter'.

The Court of Appeal agreed with the trial judge that such allegations should have been put to the claimant and basic fairness meant that any explanation already given by the claimant ought to be carried *(Prince Radu of Hohenzollern v Houston and Another* [2008] EWCA Civ 921).

Defence extended to cover books

The Court of Appeal dismissed a claim for damages by a former police officer over a book by Graeme McLagan called *Bent Coppers – The Inside Story Of Scotland Yard's Battle Against Police Corruption.* The appeal court judges held Mr McLagan had tried to verify the story and that because of his honesty, expertise on the subject, careful research, and his painstaking evaluation of material, the book was protected. It was the first time *Reynolds* privilege was used to protect a book.

::::: Recap of major points

- The *Reynolds* defence protects publication of material if it can be shown to be a matter of public interest and responsibly reported.

- Lord Nicholls set down a list of pointers to publications indicating what the courts would look at to decide if the defence could be claimed.

- The courts often place emphasis on seeking comment from the person or organisation that is the subject of the story in order to claim this defence.

- Courts will also examine whether the defendant can claim to have been engaged in 'responsible journalism' and 'neutral reportage'.

21

Criminal libel, slander, and malicious falsehoods

Chapter summary

Preceding chapters have looked at libel as a *tort* – a civil wrong for which damages are recoverable. Libel is also a criminal offence, occuring in two forms:

- defamatory libel; and
- seditious and obscene libel

As this chapter explains, each of these forms of criminal libel are relics of a bygone era, and it is unlikely that public prosecutors will use such law these days. But there is still some possibility of private prosecutions.

This chapter also examines the tort of slander, defamation in its spoken form, which can in some circumstances pose a legal risk for journalists.

Another tort, malicious falsehood occurs when statements are published that are not defamatory, but which are false and can be shown to have caused financial loss.

Criminal defamatory libel

Defamatory statements can be dealt with in the civil courts. But law still exists for libel to figure in the criminal courts. In theory the defamer convicted of criminal libel could be sent to prison.

The civil law gives a remedy for defamation, allowing a **claimant** to be compensated for an attack on his or her reputation. →glossary

The rationale behind the criminal law of libel is different. The publication of a libel was considered a crime in some cases because it is an act which might lead to a breach of the peace, e.g. if the target of the libel is inflamed by what was published.

However, it is extremely unlikely that the Crown Prosecution Service would now use the law of criminal libel, which is several centuries old. There are other, more modern and specific offences to control inflammatory behaviour and to prevent disorder. Judges would be reluctant to punish libel as a crime when the civil law enables damages to be awarded against the defamer. During the passage of the Coroners and Justice Bill 2009 there were, as this book went to press, attempts in Parliament to persuade the Government to include clauses in the Bill to abolish both criminal libel and seditious libel – the latter law is explained below. Campaigners see the continued existence of such laws in the UK, even though they are in disuse, as setting a bad example to oppressive regimes abroad which have similar legal powers, used there to curb free speech and to punish dissenters.

Private prosecutions

→
see ch. 2,
p. 27 on
private
prosecu-
tions

But although public prosecutors are very unlikely to prosecute libel as a crime, the law is still available to private prosecutors.

In 1977, a convicted sex offender, Roger Gleaves, began a series of prosecutions for criminal libel against journalists. He had just left prison after serving a sentence for wounding and for committing sexual offences at hostels he ran for homeless young people in London. At his trial, the judge had called him a 'cruel and wicked man with an evil influence on others' (*Gleaves v Deakin* (1980) AC 477).

He prosecuted the two authors of a paperback book, *Johnny Go Home*, based on a TV programme by them which was screened in 1975, and three reporters of the *Sunday People*.

→ glossary

A magistrate committed all five to trial, **remanding** the three newspaper reporters in custody to Brixton prison, because she said she felt they were likely to commit other offences, but they were released the following day by a judge, who granted them bail.

Later the Director of Public Prosecutions took over the case against them and offered no evidence.

The television journalists were not so lucky. Their trial in 1980 lasted two and a half weeks. They had to prove Gleaves's sexual crimes again. They succeeded, and the jury acquitted them.

Publication

To sustain a prosecution for criminal libel the words must be written, or be in some permanent form, but there need be no publication to a third party: it is enough that they are addressed to the person injured by them. This is quite logical because it is the person defamed who is most likely to be angered to the point of attacking the person who insults him, and that would be a breach of the peace.

Libelling the dead

As ch. 19 explains, there can be no civil libel of the dead. But in criminal libel the position is different: words spoken of a dead person may be the subject of a prosecution, but only if it can be proved that they were used with the intention of provoking his/her living relatives to commit a breach of the peace, or that they had a tendency to do so.

Truth as a defence

In civil defamation law, we saw that proving the truth of the offending words constitutes a complete answer to a libel action, see ch. 19.

This defence is available also in criminal proceedings for libel, but in addition the defendant has to satisfy the court that the words were published for the public benefit.

Failure to do so would result in a conviction.

Class libel

A further difference between criminal and civil libel is that it is a crime to libel a class of people, provided the object is to excite the hatred of the public against the class libelled. But a journalist guilty of such conduct is more likely to be prosecuted under the race relations or religious hatred legislation.

see ch. 34

Penalties

For publishing a defamatory libel a person may be sent to prison for up to a year, and/or fined. If it can be proved that he/she knew the libel to be untrue, the period of imprisonment may be doubled.

▌ Sedition, obscenity, and the abolition of blasphemy

The publication of a 'seditious libel' or an 'obscene libel' matter is in law a criminal offence, whether published in writing or by word of mouth.

Though both such offences are termed 'libel', it is no defence to prove that the words complained of are true, or that they form part of a fair and accurate report of what was said on a **privileged** occasion. Only with obscene libel is it any defence to prove that publication of the words was for the public benefit.

→ glossary

These offences too are relics. Statements that in Victorian times might have been held to be obscene or seditious are freely made today. Sex, once almost taboo, is a subject for open discussion in speech and in the printed word today, with many forms of pornography tolerated.

Sedition

Under this law any words that are likely to disturb the internal peace and government of the country constitute seditious libel.

The tests to determine whether words constitute a seditious libel are:

- Do they bring the sovereign or her family into hatred or contempt?
- Do they bring the Government and constitution of the United Kingdom into hatred or contempt?
- Do they bring either House of Parliament, or the administration of justice, into hatred or contempt?
- Do they excite British subjects to attempt, *otherwise than by lawful means* (our italics), the alteration of any matter in Church or State by law established?
- Do they raise discontent or disaffection in British subjects?
- Do they promote feelings of ill-will and hostility between different classes?

From these tests, it seems that this law is very strict, but in fact this law ceased to interfere with an honest expression of opinion so long as it is couched in moderate terms. Thus criticisms of the monarchy and the parliamentary system, constructively advanced, would not be regarded as seditious.

Muslim campaigners tried to prosecute the author Salman Rushdie for sedition on the grounds that his words had created discontent among British subjects, had created hostility between classes, and had damaged relations between Britain and Islamic states.

But a magistrate rejected the attempt, saying that the essential part of the offence of seditious libel is that the seditions action was directed against the State.'

Obscenity

The test of obscene libel is whether the words or matter would tend to deprave and corrupt those likely to read them.

The law used to be that no evidence could be brought to show the literary merits of any work which was the subject of proceedings.

In 1928, for example, *The Well of Loneliness*, a literary work dealing with lesbianism, was condemned as obscene. Evidence as to its literary merit was ruled inadmissible.

The Obscene Publications Act 1959 to a large extent replaced the **com-** →glossary **mon law** offence of obscene libel, and introduced a defence that the publication was 'for the public good...in the interests of science, literature, art, or learning, or of other objects of public concern'.

The publishers of D H Lawrence's *Lady Chatterley's Lover* were acquitted of obscenity as a result of this defence.

Before 1964, the law of obscenity had caught only those who published obscene works. By the Obscene Publications Act of that year, it is an offence to have an obscene article for publication for gain.

Blasphemy

Blasphemy consisted of the use of language having a tendency to vilify the Christian religion or the Bible. As with criminal libel, the law sought to prevent words likely to cause a breach of the peace.

However, there was a general view that these offences of blasphemy and blasphemous libel, which existed in common law, had fallen into disuse and – in that they only sought to protect the sensibilities of followers of the Anglican faith – were in danger of bringing the law into disrepute. In 2008, a measure in the Criminal Justice and Immigration Act abolished them.

❚ Slander

The most obvious difference between libel and slander is that, as ch. 17 explains seen, libel is in some permanent form (e.g. written words, a drawing, or a photograph), while slander is spoken or in some other transient form.

The exceptions are:

- a defamatory statement broadcast on radio or television, or in a cable programme, which by the Broadcasting Act 1990 is treated as libel;

- a defamatory statement in a public performance of a play, by virtue of the Theatres Act 1968.

In slander, as with libel, there must be publication to a third person for a statement to become actionable.

There is one further difference between libel and slander. Whereas actual damage will be presumed in a libel action, it must be proved affirmatively by the claimant in a slander action, except in four cases.

The four cases are:

- any imputation that an individual has committed a crime punishable by death or imprisonment;

- any imputation that an individual is suffering from certain contagious or objectionable diseases, such as venereal disease or leprosy: the test is whether the nature of the disease would cause the person to be shunned or avoided;

- any imputation of unchastity in a woman;

- any statement calculated to disparage an individual in his office, profession, calling, trade, or business.

In these four instances, actual loss does not have to be proved.

Journalists are less likely to become involved personally in a slander action than in a libel action, but they must be aware of the danger of slander.

Let us suppose that X has said that Y, a member of a borough council, has used his position to secure building contracts. This is clearly actionable because it disparages him in his office of councillor. The reporter detailed to check the story will have to interview a number of people to arrive at the truth, and in these interviews he must be wary of being sued for slander as a result of the questions asked during those interviews in which the original slander might be repeated to a third party.

▌ Malicious falsehoods

Publication of a false statement, though it may cast no aspersions on the character of a person, or upon his/her fitness to hold a certain office or to follow a particular calling, may still be damaging to him/her.

For example, to say a solicitor had retired from practice would no doubt cause loss, if false because his/her clients would begin to find other solicitors to do their work. But it is clearly not defamatory, to be considered retired.

If published matter is not defamatory, a wronged person cannot bring an action for either libel or slander.

They may, however, be able to bring an action for malicious falsehood.

The claimant must prove the statement is untrue, in contrast with libel, where the court will assume that a defamatory statement is false.

The claimant in an action for malicious falsehood must also prove that the statement was published maliciously.

As with the defence of qualified privilege in libel, **malice** means a state- → glossary
ment made by a person who knows that it is false or who is reckless as to its truth, or who is actuated by some improper motive (*Spring v Guardian Assurance plc* [1993] 2 All ER 273, CA). Negligence is not malice.

It used to be the case that, to establish malicious falsehood, the claimant had to prove actual damage.

By the Defamation Act 1952, the rule no longer applies to words in permanent form, such as printed words, provided they are calculated to cause financial damage.

Nor does it apply to words, whether spoken or written, that are likely to cause financial damage to the claimant in his office, profession, calling, trade, or business.

In 1990, when the television actor Gorden Kaye was in hospital seriously ill, his representative sued the *Sunday Sport* and its editor for malicious falsehood.

A journalist and a photographer had gained access to the hospital and taken photographs of Kaye, and in a proposed article the *Sunday Sport* planned to say Kaye had agreed to be interviewed and photographed.

The Court of Appeal said the words were false because Kaye was in no see also ch. 24, p. 415 on Kaye case
state to be interviewed or give any informed consent. Any publication would 'inevitably' be malicious because the reporter and photographer knew this (*Kaye v Robertson* [1991] FSR 62 CA).

As to damage, Kaye had a potentially valuable right to sell the story of his accident to other newspapers for 'large sums of money' and the value of that right would be seriously lessened if the *Sunday Sport* were allowed to publish.

Legal aid

Another difference between libel and malicious falsehood used to be that, although claimants could not get **legal aid** for a libel action, they might be able to do so for malicious falsehood. But legal aid for malicious falsehood cases was ended by the Access to Justice Act 1999.

Limitation period

In the past another important difference between libel and malicious falsehood was the 'limitation period'. A claimant had three years from the date of publication in which to sue for libel, but six years for malicious falsehood. The Defamation Act 1996 reduced the limitation period to one year for both actions.

Corrections

An editor may realise that the facts of a story are wrong, but they were not defamatory and it was an honest mistake. In such a case, the editor should act quickly to put the mistake right by means of an adequate correction to avoid any suggestion of malice in a subsequent legal action.

Slander of goods and title

Two types of malicious falsehood are known as slander of goods (false and malicious statements disparaging the claimant's goods), and slander of title (false and malicious denial of the claimant's title to property).

The word slander is misleading in both cases. The damaging statement can be in permanent form or in spoken words.

⁞⁞⁞ Recap of major points

- Libel can be a criminal offence, as well as a civil wrong.
- A prosecution for criminal libel can be brought if the publication is likely to cause a breach of the peace, or it seriously affects the reputation of the person involved.

- Unlike civil libel, an offence of criminal libel can occur if the words are addressed to the person injured by them – that is, there is no need for publication to a third party.

- There is a defence that the words were true *and* published for the public benefit.

- Sedition involves words that are likely to disturb the internal peace and government of the country. The words need to be directed against the State.

- Obscenity involves words that would tend to deprave and corrupt those who are likely to read them.

- However, criminal libel, seditions libel, and obscene libel are offences which are legal relics, unlikely to be prosecuted.

- Slander, a civil wrong (like libel), concerns defamatory words that (unlike libel) are spoken or in some other transient form.

- In slander (unlike libel), actual damage may need to be proved.

- Malicious falsehoods are false statements that, though not defamatory, may still be damaging. The claimant must prove that the statement is untrue (unlike libel, where this is assumed) and malicious.

22

The Rehabilitation of Offenders Act 1974

Chapter summary

This chapter sets out how the Rehabilitation of Offenders Act works in allowing some people to live down previous criminal convictions after a specified period of time. It explains how the Act limits the defences a journalist can use against a libel claim if there is published reference to a 'spent' conviction and a **claimant** can prove **malice**. The amount of time that has to elapse before a conviction becomes spent varies according to the length of the sentence.

 glossary
 glossary

▌ Rehabilitation periods

 glossary The Rehabilitation of Offenders Act 1974 created the concept of **spent convictions**. Such convictions become 'spent' after a length of time known as the rehabilitation period. This period varies according to the severity of sentence.

The philosophy which led to the Act was that people convicted of offences which were not the most serious should be able to 'live down' their criminal past by being given a fresh start in life. There is no legal obligation, for example, to declare a 'spent' conviction when applying for most jobs, whatever the application form says, though for certain jobs there is, e.g. working with children.

As part of this aim to aid rehabilitation, the Act also seeks to prevent the media publishing for no good reason a reference to someone's spent conviction for no good reason.

However, if someone has been sentenced to a jail term of longer than two-and-a-half years, whether the sentence was immediate or suspended, or to a term of more than two-and-a-half years of youth custody or detention in a young offender institution, or of corrective training, that conviction can never become spent, because it denotes a serious crime. Nor can a term of preventive detention, or an extended sentence for public protection, after a violent or sexual offence become spent.

see ch. 5, p. 71 on suspended sentences

The rehabilitation periods determining when less serious convictions become spent vary between 10 years (for a prison sentence greater than six months) and six months (for an absolute **discharge**). But a further conviction during the rehabilitation period can extend it.

 glossary

As indicated above, suspended sentences are treated as if they were put into effect.

see p. 72 on absolute discharge

Journalists requiring further information about rehabilitation periods for particular sentences should consult *Stone's Justices' Manual*.

 See also the Online Resource Centre, ch. 27 for a more detailed breakdown of sentences and rehabilitation periods.

▌ The effect of the Act on the media

The Act limits the defences in libel law available if a media organisation has published reference to a person's spent conviction and is being sued for libel as a result.

(1) If the media organisation pleads **justification** – that is, that the report of the claimant's previous conviction was true – the defence fails if the claimant can prove that the conviction was spent and that the motive behind the published reference to it was malicious.

see ch. 19 for full explanation of all these defences

(2) If the media organisation reports a reference made in a court case to a spent conviction, and that conviction was held in that case to be inadmissible in evidence, it cannot use the defences of absolute or qualified **privilege**.

As regards defence (1) above, the 1974 Act breached for the first time the established principle that truth is a complete defence to an action for defamation. This is because the aim of the Act is to deter the media from publishing a reference to a spent conviction if there is no good reason for airing it.

The Act's effect is best explained by an example. If a media organisation publishes an accurate reference to a criminal conviction in someone's past life, it can, if sued because of this, and if the conviction is not spent, use the libel defences of:

- *Justification* – because it is true that the conviction exists. Defamation law now accepts that the existence of the conviction is proof that the person was guilty of that crime. So a media organisation, once it has proved that the conviction exists, e.g. from a court record, is not required to re-prove, e.g. with witnesses, that the person suing committed that criminal offence.

→
see ch.
19 on
privilege

- *Qualified privilege* – which protects non-contemporaneous reports of court cases if the defence's requirements are met. Mention of a conviction is, in effect, a report of the court case in which the conviction occurred when the defendant pleaded guilty or when magistrates or a jury announced the guilty verdict. This defence will also protect quotation of words from the case, e.g. of the judge calling the convicted defendant 'a scoundrel'.

→
see ch.
19 on fair
comment

- *Fair comment* – as regards opinion expressed about the person based on the fact of the conviction, if the requirements of the defence are met. So, if someone standing in a council election has a criminal conviction, an editorial comment column could safely publish an honestly held opinion, held by the column's author that the conviction renders the person unfit for such public office. Similar comments from others could be published safely too, if this was their honestly held opinion. Even if no such comment is made explicitly, by publishing the conviction in this context a media organisation creates an *inference* that the person could be regarded, because of the conviction, as unfit for such public office. But the fair comment defence will protect the media organisation as regards that inference, if the defence's requirements are met.

→
see ch.
17, on
p. 306 on
inferences

Even if the conviction referred to is 'spent', the above defences will apply, unless the publication of it was malicious, e.g. there was no public interest in referring to it.

But if, for example, a journalist or editor decided to publish reference to the spent conviction maliciously as an act of spite then, if this motive is proved in a libel trial, the 1974 Act means that the defence of justification cannot be used, even though it is true that the conviction exists. Also, proof of malice destroys the defence of qualified privilege. This means that the person suing would, in these circumstances, win the libel case, and receive damages for the effect on his/her reputation of publication of his/her spent conviction. The fair comment defence would be undermined too, e.g. because the published comment has to be based on a matter of public interest. But if reference to the conviction is proved to be malicious, then it becomes harder to justify the comment as being for the public good. Also, a comment has to be based on a privileged statement or a fact defensible by justification.

- However, in most news journalism, e.g. revelation of a council candidate's conviction, or of the criminal record of a dodgy businessperson fleecing customers, the media can publish reference to spent convictions, and comment on them, with no fear of libel consequences, because the public interest is served by the revelation made, and there is no malice.

Spent convictions revealed in court proceedings

If a person is giving evidence in any *civil* proceedings he or she should not be asked any questions about spent convictions.

The Act does not apply to later *criminal* proceedings. If a rehabilitated person appears again before a criminal court after his or her conviction has become spent he or she can still be asked about it.

Absolute or qualified privilege applies to the media's reports of a spent conviction as mentioned in a court case, <u>unless</u> the conviction was ruled by the court to be inadmissible.

Judges have been directed that spent convictions should never be referred to in criminal courts if this could be avoided and that no one should refer in open court to a spent conviction without the authority of the judge.

→ see ch. 19 on privilege requirements

◗ Criminal penalties

The Act does not impose any criminal penalty on the journalist who mentions a spent conviction. But it is an offence for a public servant to reveal details of spent convictions other than in the course of official duties.

Obtaining information of spent convictions from official records by fraud, dishonesty, or bribery is also a criminal offence.

⬚ Recap of major points

- Convictions become spent at the end of the rehabilitation period.
- But a conviction which led to a jail term of more than two-and-a-half years is never spent.
- The rehabilitation period varies between 10 years (for a term of imprisonment exceeding six months) and six months (for an absolute discharge).
- The Act restricts the libel defences available to journalists to refer to 'spent' convictions.
- Previous convictions as revealed in court proceedings can be reported without fear of damaging a libel defence, as long as they have not been ruled inadmissible.

☻ Useful Website

www.nacro.org.uk/data/resources/nacro-2007021302.pdf
Nacro, Rehabilitation of Offenders Act 1974 (2007)

Part 3

Confidentiality, privacy, and copyright

23

Breach of confidence

Chapter summary

Breach of confidence is based upon the principle that a person who has obtained information in confidence should not take unfair advantage of it. This chapter will explain the kind of information and relationships which are considered confidential.

Governments use breach of confidence to protect information they regard as secret. Individuals use it for the same purpose and also as a way to protect privacy, and this use of breach of confidence received a strong boost when the Human Rights Act was implemented in 2000.

This can affect journalists because the main means used to prevent breach of confidence is an interim **injunction** stopping the media from publishing confiden- tial information. This area of law, often linked with privacy, has been developing rapidly in recent years.

▌ Elements of a breach of confidence

Mr Justice Megarry, giving a judgment in 1968, said there are three elements in a breach of confidence:

- the information must have 'the necessary quality of confidence';
- the information must have been imparted in circumstances imposing an obligation of confidence; and

• there must be an unauthorised use of that information to the detriment of the party communicating it (*Coco v AN Clark (Engineers) Ltd* [1969] RPC 41 at 47).

The quality of confidence

The law of breach of confidence safeguards ideas and information imparted or obtained in confidential circumstances. In general, information is not confidential if it is of trivial significance – e.g. a company's canteen menu – or is already in the public domain.

But information already in the public domain cannot always be published with impunity. In 1981, the Court of Appeal confirmed an injunction restraining Thames Television Ltd from showing a programme, *The Primodos Affair*, about a pregnancy-testing drug (*Schering Chemicals v Falkman Ltd* [1981] 2 All ER 321 CA). The decision was based on the fact that the TV producer conceived the idea for the programme while doing private consultancy work for the company concerned, Schering Chemicals Ltd, even though Thames said the programme would contain no material not freely available from other sources.

see below, p. 383

The information, though in the public domain, had been gleaned originally by diligent work, and the conduct leading to the injunction was, in the court's view, reprehensible.

see below, p. 390

However, where information originally confidential has since then already been imparted to a wider audience, as in the *Watford Observer* case, or as in the *Spycatcher* case where the court felt the 'cat was out of the bag', the quality of confidence may be lost.

see ch. 24, p. 409

A series of decisions by judges indicates that the scope for a public domain defence is more limited in privacy claims.

Obligation of confidence

An obligation of confidence can arise in a variety of ways

Contractual relationship The most frequent is a contractual obligation. People working for others may have signed a contract to say that they will not reveal their employer's secrets, but even if they have not there is an implied term in every contract of employment that the employee will not act in a way detrimental to the employer's interests.

Membership of security services

see below, p. 383

Members have no contract of employment with the Crown, but in the *Spycatcher* cases the courts accepted the view that they had a duty of confidence that resulted from the nature of their employment and the requirements of national security and which lasted for life, subject to the defences of public domain and public interest.

Disclosure

Under the process of disclosure (previously known as '**discovery**') in legal →glossary proceedings, parties have to disclose relevant documents to the other side. This information is protected until the information has been read to or by the court or referred to at a public hearing.

Domestic relationship

In 1967 the Duchess of Argyll prevented the *People* newspaper, and her former husband, from publishing marital secrets (*Argyll v Argyll* [1967] Ch 302). By the 1980s the courts were willing to extend the protection to prevent the publication of kiss-and-tell stories originating from less formal relationships. In 1988 a woman was given leave to sue the *Mail on Sunday* for damages for a story about her love affair with another woman.

But information about transient affairs (e.g. with a prostitute) is unlikely to be protected.

 See details of the Theakston and Flitcroft cases in ch. 24, p. 405

Third parties, such as a journalist

The information may have been obtained indirectly from the confider. A third party, such as a journalist, who comes into possession of confidential information and realises it is confidential may come under a legal duty to respect the confidence.

For example, in the *Primodos* case, mentioned above, the chemical company supplied the TV producer with the information about the drug for the purpose of public relations work he was doing for the company. Thames TV, the third party, was prevented by injunction from using the information for a television film.

Unethical behaviour

It was once considered doubtful whether an obligation of confidence could arise when information is acquired through unethical behaviour, because of the reprehensible means used. It now seems to be established that there is an obligation of confidence on those who obtain confidential information by unethical means such as trespass, **theft**, listening devices, or long-range →glossary cameras.

Detriment

The detriment suffered by the confider does not have to be a financial loss.

see
p. 390 on
Spy-
catcher

In the *Spycatcher* case in the Lords (*A-G v Times Newspapers* [1992] 1 AC 191), Lord Keith of Kinkel said it would be a sufficient detriment to an individual that information he gave in confidence was to be disclosed to people he would prefer not to know of it.

But a government was in a different position from an individual. It had to show that publication would be harmful to the public interest.

In the *Spycatcher* case, he said, the book's contents had been disseminated worldwide, and general publication in this country would not bring about any significant damage to the public interest beyond what had already been done.

The party communicating

By 'the party communicating it' is meant the person communicating the information originally, that is, the person to whom the confidence is owed.

▶ Development of the law

For many years judges have granted injunctions preventing breaches of confidence.

In developing this branch of the law over the years the judges were using the discretionary powers available to them when dealing with equitable matters.

see ch.
1, p. 7 on
equity

A landmark in the development of the law of confidentiality was the declaration of the Lord Chief Justice in 1975 that the kind of secrets to be protected could include 'public secrets', which sounds like a contradiction in terms but means simply information emanating from state or public business.

In the 1980s, the law of confidentiality was used for the first time by local authorities against local newspapers.

see ch. 31
on official
secrets

In the late 1980s, the law of confidentiality was used by the British Government in attempts to silence former members of the security services.

In spite of the greater effectiveness of the Official Secrets Act 1989, UK governments have continued to use breach of confidence in an attempt to buttress their powers to impose secrecy on former members of the security services. In the late 1990s and early 2000s the Government used both injunctions and prosecutions under the Act against two former intelligence officers, David Shayler (*R v Shayler* (2002) UKHL 11) and Richard Tomlinson (see below), who made disclosures to the media.

Breach of confidence and privacy

Until 2000, English law recognised no right to privacy. But on many occasions people who believed their privacy was about to be infringed attempted to use the law of breach of confidence to prevent intrusions.

→ see ch. 24, p. 400 on privacy

Their main difficulty lay in 'the essentially different nature of the two kinds of right', as the Law Commission's report on breach of confidence said in 1981 (Cmnd 8388). An obligation of confidence, by definition, arises, first, from the circumstances in which the information is given.

By contrast, said the Commission, a right of privacy in respect of information would arise from the nature of the information itself; it would be based on the principle that certain kinds of information are categorised as private and for that reason alone ought not to be disclosed. In many cases where privacy is infringed this is not the result of a breach of confidence.

Judges were beginning to abandon their strict view on the circumstances in which an obligation of confidence could occur. In the *Spycatcher* case in the House of Lords in 1988 Lord Goff of Chieveley said:

> “a duty of confidence arises when confidential information comes to the knowledge of a person (the confidant) in circumstances where he has notice, or is held to have agreed, that the information is confidential, with the effect that it would be just in all the circumstances that he should be precluded from disclosing the information to others (*A-G v Times Newspapers* (1992) 1 AC 191).”

Lord Goff said he had expressed the duty in wide terms to include the situation where an obviously confidential document was wafted by an electric fan out of a window into a crowded street, or when an obviously confidential document such as a diary was dropped in a public place and then picked up by a passer-by.

Then, when the European Convention on Human Rights was in effect incorporated into English law in 2000, guaranteeing a right to privacy, the judges started to abandon altogether the legal contrivance of implying a relationship where none existed.

→ see ch. 1 pp. 9–13

→
see also
ch. 24 on
Douglas
case

In the *Douglas* case in 2000 Lord Justice Sedley said in the Court of Appeal:

  ❝ The law no longer needs to construct an artificial relationship of confidentiality between intruder and victim: it can recognise privacy itself as a legal principle drawn from the fundamental value of personal autonomy (*Douglas v Hello! Ltd* [2001] 2 All ER 289). ❞

In that case the court was considering whether to lift an injunction that prevented *Hello!* magazine from publishing pictures of the wedding of two film stars who had sold exclusive rights to their wedding photographs to *OK!* magazine. At that time, there was no evidence who had taken the pictures. In fact they were taken by an intruder.

In the following year the House of Lords, in the case involving the model Naomi Campbell, held unanimously that English law provided a cause of action for 'the unjustified publication of private information' (*Campbell v MGN Ltd* [2005] UKHL 61).

→
see ch. 24

In 2001 a judge developed the law of confidence to impose an injunction banning all the media from identifying the two killers of the child James Bulger, who were expected to be given new identities on their release from custody. The

→ glossary

ban was to last throughout the lives of the two. Their **counsel** had argued for the injunction because, among other things, their lives would be at risk if they were identified, and because their rights under the European Convention to life, to privacy, and to protection from torture outweighed the freedom of expression of those who might wish to identify them. The judge, Dame Elizabeth Butler-Sloss, said there was no other means of imposing a ban. See p. 137.

▌ The journalist's dilemma

The law of confidentiality regularly presents journalists with an awkward dilemma, a difficulty reduced but not removed by a measure in the Human Rights Act 1998 (see next section: 'How the media are affected', 'Injunctions'). Suppose a reporter learns about some newsworthy misconduct from a source who has received his information confidentially. The journalist is impelled, both by his instinct for fair play and by his/her respect for the law of libel, to approach the person against whom the misconduct is alleged to get their side of the story.

The BBC Editorial Guidelines tells broadcasters:

> **66** When we make allegations of wrongdoing, iniquity or incompetence or lay out a strong and damaging critique of an individual or institution the presumption is that those criticised should be given a 'right of reply', that is, given a fair opportunity to respond to the allegations before transmission. **99**

→
see ch. 1,
p. 16
on BBC
Guidelines

If the journalist does make such an approach, however, there is a risk that the culprit will immediately obtain an injunction preventing the use of the information and thus killing the story.

In 1977 the *Daily Mail* obtained a copy of a letter from the National Enterprise Board to British Leyland (BL), the nationalised car manufacturer, that appeared to show that BL was paying bribes and conspiring to defraud foreign governments to win overseas orders. It published the story under the headline 'World-wide bribery web by Leyland'.

No doubt the journalists assumed that if they checked the story with BL the firm would immediately get an injunction preventing them from publishing. In fact the letter turned out to be a forgery and the paper had to pay substantial libel damages.

By contrast, in several of the cases mentioned below – e.g. the *Bill Goodwin* case – the journalist attempted to check the story with the source and was then prevented by injunction from using it until it was no longer news.

⠿ Point for consideration

You should certainly check the story if it is defamatory, but in doing so you would be wise to phrase your questions in such a way that you do not reveal that you have confidential material in your possession, thus laying yourself open to an injunction. It is better to use the information at your disposal to try to get the facts from a different, non-confidential, route. You can then return to the original source of the information to check.

▌ How the media are affected

Injunctions

A person who passes information to a journalist may have received it confidentially. If the person to whom the confidence belongs (the confider) discovers, before the paper is published or the programme is broadcast, that the information is to be disclosed, he/she can try to get a temporary injunction prohibiting publication of the confidential material.

→
see also
ch. 1,
pp. 4–5
on 'prior
restraint'

The Human Rights Act 1998 contains a section (section 12) which is intended to provide some protection against injunctions in matters involving freedom of expression.

The confider's lawyer applies to a High Court judge. He/she has to persuade the judge, under section 12, that the confider is 'likely' to establish at the trial that publication should not be allowed.

The limitations of the defence under section 12 were shown in the case where the *Liverpool Echo* wanted to publish a story about financial irregularities at the firm Cream Holdings, an event organiser, based on confidential information it had obtained from the firm's former financial controller.

The paper had published one story, then asked the directors of Cream to answer some questions about their activities. Cream immediately applied for, and was granted by a judge, an injunction to prevent further details being published (*Cream Holdings v Banerjee and Liverpool Post* [2004] UKHL 44).

The paper appealed to the Court of Appeal which, by a 2-1 majority, rejected the paper's case because it considered the firm was likely to win at trial in the sense that it had established a 'real prospect of success'. The paper then took the case to the House of Lords, and the Lords found in its favour.

→ glossary

Before the 1998 Act was implemented, the application might be **without notice**, which meant that only one party was represented, and the newspaper might learn about the proceedings only when it was told that an injunction had been granted. That can still happen.

Section 12 says that if the journalist is not present when the application is made, the court must not grant an injunction unless it is satisfied the person seeking the injunction has taken all practicable steps to notify the journalist or that there are compelling reasons why the journalist should not be notified.

But these matters are generally conducted at speed, and it may not be possible to tell the journalist. In the *Douglas* case, referred to above, *OK!* and the two stars won a temporary injunction from a judge, granted at night over the telephone, banning distribution of the 750,000 print run. The court was told *OK!* had tried to contact the editor of *Hello!* but 'a security guard who answered the phone at their premises had been unable to help'.

In the past injunctions have sometimes been granted at a stage when a newspaper has been printed and ready to go on sale, or a programme has been ready for broadcasting, and such an injunction has caused great inconvenience and expense, but defiance of the order would have been a serious contempt of court.

On many occasions, temporary injunctions which appeared to be harsh and wide-ranging in their terms have been lifted when the newspaper's case was heard. This did not mean that the judges made a mistake, legally speaking, the first time. The purpose of a temporary injunction is to 'hold the ring' (in the words of Lord Donaldson, a former Master of the Rolls), until the matter can be fully argued later.

In the *Douglas* case judges in the Court of Appeal lifted the temporary injunction in 2000. They argued that if *Hello!* published the story, then lost its case at the trial, it would have to pay an 'enormous' bill by way of damages or an account of profits which would be adequate recompense for *OK!*

In fact, *Hello!* did publish the pictures, and when the case came for trial in 2003 a judge awarded *OK!* the huge sum of £1,003,156 damages – as well as £14,600 for the film stars. But in the end *Hello!* did not have to pay enormous damages. In 2005 the Court of Appeal, with a different set of judges, decided that *OK!* (as distinct from the stars) was not entitled to damages. The court said the two stars had a 'virtually unanswerable case' for contending that publication of the unauthorised photographs infringed their privacy, and damages were not an adequate remedy for them, so the earlier court had made a mistake in lifting the injunction. This judgment would seem to indicate that courts may grant interim injunctions more readily in such cases in the future.

→ For their comments on this point, see ch. 24, p. 401

Effect on local papers

In 1982, the *Watford Observer* planned to publish a story based on a document that showed that the publisher Robert Maxwell's printing operation, Sun Printers, was losing money, and he wanted to reduce the workforce.

The day before press day, a reporter telephoned the company asking for comments. At midday on press day, Maxwell telephoned the paper's editor and asked for an assurance that the material would not be published, on the grounds that it was confidential and that negotiations with the trade unions were at a delicate stage.

When the editor declined, Sun Printers' lawyers applied to the High Court for an injunction and telephoned the paper at 4.30 p.m. to say an injunction had been granted. By this time all editorial and typesetting work on the paper would normally have been completed.

Fortunately, the paper, alerted by the call from Maxwell, had prepared alternative material for use in its pages. The injunction was later lifted.

In 1984, Medina Borough Council, on the Isle of Wight, got an injunction preventing the *Southern Evening Echo*, of Southampton, from publishing details of a consultant's report on plans for development in Newport, the island's capital.

As the papers were unloaded from the hydrofoil taking them from the mainland, an officer of the Newport county court stood on the quayside with the injunction. The papers could not be distributed, and another edition had to be sent to the island.

The Spycatcher affair

This affair arose out of attempts by the British Government to prevent publication of information acquired by Peter Wright, a former senior officer of MI5, Britain's internal security service. The Government acted against Wright and a number of newspapers in many courts in several countries. Only a brief summary is given below. Those wishing to study the cases in detail should refer to *The Spycatcher Cases*, by Michael Fysh QC.

see also
ch. 31, p.
503 on
Spy-catcher

In 1985 the British Attorney General began proceedings against Wright in New South Wales, Australia. Wright was then living in Tasmania.

Wright's book recounted his experiences in MI5; among other allegations, it said that MI5 officers had plotted to destabilise the Government led by the Labour Prime Minister Harold Wilson in the mid-1970s, and that officers of the security services had plotted to assassinate President Nasser of Egypt.

see
below,
p. 393 on
profits

The Attorney General sought an injunction or an account of profits, arguing that former members of the security services had an absolute and life-long duty not to reveal any details of their employment.

In June 1986 the *Observer* and *Guardian* newspapers both carried stories reporting the forthcoming hearing in Australia. The stories contained brief accounts of some of the allegations. An English court granted the Attorney General interim injunctions against both newspapers preventing them from disclosing any information obtained by Wright in his capacity as a member of the British security service.

The following year, as mentioned earlier in this chapter, other newspapers published information from *Spycatcher*, believing they were not prevented by the injunctions, but the courts held them guilty of contempt of court.

In 1988, after many legal actions involving the Government and a number of newspapers, both in the United Kingdom and abroad, and after *Spycatcher* had been published in the United States, the House of Lords held, among other things, that the original articles in the *Observer* and *Guardian* in 1986 had not been published in breach of confidence; that the Government was not entitled to a permanent injunction preventing the two papers from further comment on the book and use of extracts from it; and that the Government was not entitled to a general injunction restraining the media from future publication of information derived from Wright or other members or former members of the security service.

By the time the two papers were free to publish the material legally, the story was history rather than news.

Later the European Court of Human Rights (ECtHR) held that the UK Government had been right to obtain the initial injunctions against the *Observer* and the *Guardian* in 1986, but that the injunctions should not have been maintained once the book had been published.

Security service cases

While the *Spycatcher* cases were dragging on the Government became committed to taking legal action whenever members and former members of the security services breached what the Government saw as their lifelong duty of confidence, and many actions followed. (The *Shayler* and *Tomlinson* cases continued the trend into the new millennium.)

→
see ch. 31 on *Shayler* case

A characteristic of the injunctions imposed by courts was their very wide scope. The Government was granted an injunction preventing BBC Radio 4 from broadcasting a series of programmes 'My country: right or wrong'. The injunction was at first in terms that prevented the BBC from broadcasting all information of whatever kind about the security services from former members, or even naming former members of the security services.

But the courts have been willing to make variations if newspapers apply with good supporting evidence that the material is publicly available or there is public interest in publication.

The Bill Goodwin case

In 1989 an engineering company, Tetra Ltd, obtained injunctions against the magazine *The Engineer* and trainee reporter Bill Goodwin. The company, which was in financial difficulties, had prepared a business plan for the purpose of negotiating a substantial bank loan.

A copy of the draft plan 'disappeared' from the company's offices and the next day an unidentified source telephoned Mr Goodwin and gave him information about the company, including the amount of the projected loan and the company's forecast results.

Goodwin phoned the company and its bankers to check the information. The company obtained a without notice injunction restraining the magazine from publishing information derived from the draft plan and later obtained an order requiring Goodwin and *The Engineer* to hand over notes that would disclose the source of the information. Mr Goodwin refused to comply with the order and was fined £5,000. In 1996 the European Court of Human Rights held that the court order and the fine violated his right to freedom of expression under Article 10 of the European Convention on Human Rights (*Goodwin v United Kingdom* (1996) 22 EHRR 123).

Injunction against one is against all

In 1987 the Court of Appeal held that when an injunction is in force preventing a newspaper from publishing confidential information, other newspapers in England and Wales that know of the injunction can be guilty of contempt of court if they publish that information, even if they are not named in the injunction.

The court said papers committed a serious offence against justice itself by taking action which destroyed the confidentiality that the court was seeking to protect and so rendered the due process of law ineffectual. In 1989 two papers were fined £50,000 each for publishing extracts from *Spycatcher* because at the time of publication they knew that interim injunctions were in force against the *Observer* and the *Guardian* preventing them from publishing this material.

The fines were later discharged, but the convictions were upheld and the ruling on the law was confirmed by the House of Lords in 1991.

This legal device for silencing the press is all the more effective because the injunction is sometimes phrased in such a way that journalists are forbidden even to mention the existence of the proceedings.

An injunction obtained in an English court does not prevent publication in another country. In particular, it does not prevent publication in Scotland – though Scottish judges may be asked to impose their own injunction, known as an **interdict**.

→ glossary

Cost of injunctions

As a condition for the granting of an interim injunction the person seeking the injunction has to give a cross-undertaking in damages – that is, an undertaking that he will pay any damages to the defendant if, at the trial, it is held that the interim injunction should not have been granted.

The defendant may also get costs. In a case in 1994, Camelot, organisers of the National Lottery, was granted an injunction preventing the media from identifying the winners of the first major jackpot. When newspapers succeeded in having the injunction lifted, Camelot had to pay them £5,000 costs.

Even so, the cost to a newspaper that decides to challenge an injunction may be considerable. The *Liverpool Echo* risked costs perhaps as high as £600,000 when it took its challenge over the Cream Holdings story to the House of Lords; fortunately it won, but still faced a large bill.

The *News of the World* claimed in 1987 that it had spent £200,000 in an unsuccessful attempt to defeat an injunction granted to a health authority preventing the paper using information from personal medical records supplied by one or more of the authority's employees. The records showed that two practising doctors employed by the authority had the HIV virus.

Fines

Disobeying an injunction can result in an action for contempt of court. The *News of the World* was fined £10,000 for publishing a story headlined 'Scandal of Docs with AIDS' after the granting of the injunction mentioned above.

Order to reveal source

A court can order a journalist to reveal the name of his informant, as happened in the *Bill Goodwin* case.

Delivery up

A court can order that confidential matter be 'delivered up' or destroyed.

Account of profits

A person misusing confidential information to make money may be asked to account for the profits to the person who confided the information, i.e. the person whose confidence was betrayed. A court may rule, after seeing this account, that the person who misused the information should pay some or all of these ill-gotten profits to the party betrayed.

Damages

If confidential matter is published, the person whose confidences have been breached may be able to claim damages. In the *Douglas* case the two film stars were awarded £14,600 for distress and incidental costs.

Supermodel Naomi Campbell was awarded £2,500 damages for distress and injury to her feelings in 2002 against Mirror Group Newspapers when she sued for breach of confidence and infringement of the Data Protection Act 1998. The *Daily Mirror* had published a story about her receiving therapy from Narcotics Anonymous for drug addiction. She was awarded an additional £1,000 for 'aggravated damages' as a result of an additional article published by the paper. The finding was overthrown by the Court of Appeal, but in 2004 the House of Lords restored the trial judge's award (*Campbell v Mirror Group Newspapers* [2004] UKHL 22).

see details of the case in ch. 24, p. 401

◗ Disclosure in the public interest

The Human Rights Act 1998, in section 12, says that when a court is considering imposing an injunction in a matter affecting freedom of expression, and where **journalistic material** is involved, it must have particular regard to the extent to which it is, or would be, in the public interest to be published.

→ glossary

see also
ch. 1 p.
5 on 'the
public
interest'

Even before the Act was implemented, journalists could plead that the disclosure of confidential information would be in the public interest. The *Watford Observer* did in the case referred to above (see under 'Local papers'). The judge, Lord Denning, said that when considering applications for an injunction on grounds of confidentiality, courts had to hold the balance between two competing interests. On the one hand there was the public interest in preserving confidence. On the other was the public interest in making known to people matters of public concern.

In this case, he said, the balance came down in favour of publishing the matters in the report. They were of great interest to all the many people in the Watford area who were concerned with printing. They were fit to be discussed, not only with the immediate workers in Sun Printers' works, but also with those outside connected with the printing industry or interested in it. Other judges have also taken the view that they had to balance the two interests.

In the case *Lion Laboratories v Evans* [1985] QB 526, the Court of Appeal held that the publication of confidential information revealing that a type of breathalyser machine used by police did not work was in the public interest. So was the broadcast of undercover filming by an employee in breach of confidence which showed misconduct at a funeral home (*Service Corp International plc v Channel Four* [1999] EMLR 83).

Section 12(3) of the Human Rights Act says there shall be no prior restraint in a media case 'unless the court is satisfied that the applicant [that is, the person asking for the injunction] is likely to establish that the publication should not be allowed' when the case comes to trial. That means that the person seeking the injunction has the burden of persuading the court, and that the court must assess the likely outcome of a full trial by weighing up the competing factors.

In the *Douglas* case in 2000, after the Act came into force, Lord Justice Sedley said that the right to free expression referred to in Article 10(1) of the European Convention could not have priority over the limitations to the right contained in Article 10(2), which included 'preventing the disclosure of information received in confidence'. He said: 'Everything will ultimately depend on the proper balance between privacy and publicity in the situation facing the court.'

→
see the
wording
of the
Article in
ch. 30

In 2001, the Human Rights Act helped the media to publish material in the face of opposition, in this case from the Government. The *Sunday Times* wanted to publish information that originated from a former intelligence officer, Richard Tomlinson. The paper argued that the material had been published elsewhere and was therefore not confidential, but the Attorney General insisted the paper should prove the information was in the public domain. The Court of Appeal agreed with the newspaper, holding that its application was in harmony with Article 10 of the European Convention and section 12 of the Human Rights Act (*A-G v Times Newspapers Ltd* [2001] EWCA Civ 97; [2001] 1 WLR 885).

In the case in 2002 in which Naomi Campbell sued Mirror Group Newspapers for a story about her receiving therapy from Narcotics Anonymous for her drug addiction, the paper argued that this was published in the public interest because the model had previously gone out of her way to tell the media that, in contrast to other models, she did not take drugs, and this was untrue. Disclosure was necessary, therefore, to correct a false public image.

The House of Lords, in 2004, agreed that in the circumstances it was in the public interest to report the fact of Ms Campbell's drug addiction and that she was receiving treatment for that addiction, but there was no justification for reporting the fact that she was receiving treatment at Narcotics Anonymous, or giving details of the treatment and her reaction to it, or surreptitiously obtaining photographs of her emerging from a treatment session.

Correcting a false public image can indicate that the story is in the public interest. In a case in 2005 (*McKennitt v Ash* [2006] EMLR 10) Mr Justice Eady said:

> ❝ I have little doubt that…where a **claimant** has deliberately sought to mislead the public on a significant issue, that would be regarded as a sufficient reason for putting the record straight, even if it involves a breach of confidence or an infringement of privacy. ❞

→glossary

However, in the case in which he made this comment he rejected the public interest argument. The judge was trying a case in which a well-known Canadian folk singer was suing a former friend who had written and published a book, *Travels with Loreena McKennitt: My Life as a Friend*, which revealed a substantial amount of information about the singer's private life.

The judge said that several references were intrusive and insensitive and should not have been published. He said: 'a very high degree of misconduct must be demonstrated' if behaviour was to trigger the public interest defence. He granted an injunction to restrict further publication and awarded damages of £5,000 for hurt feelings and distress.

Ms Ash appealed unsuccessfully to the Court of Appeal in November 2006. The court said the judge's statement, that 'a very high degree of misconduct must be demonstrated' to trigger the defence, might well go too far, if treated as an 'entirely general statement, divorced from its context'. But that high test had been appropriate on the facts of the case, where the public interest was not said to derive from alleged misconduct by Ms McKennitt, but from the allegation that her conduct 'had previously been lied about or treated with hypocrisy'.

In *Beckham v News Group* an application for an injunction about the state of the Beckhams' marriage failed in part on public interest grounds. It was said that the Beckhams had portrayed a false image about their private life, and that therefore justified a correction (*David Beckham and Victoria Beckham v News Group Newspapers Ltd* [2005] EWHC 2252 (QB)).

In 2006, in the Court of Appeal, the *Mail on Sunday* challenged a decision by a single judge that it had not been in the public interest to publish extracts from the Prince of Wales's 'Hong Kong journal', which he had entitled, 'The Handover of Hong Kong or The Great Chinese Takeaway'. The Prince had attended the ceremony, and referred to the Chinese hierarchy as 'appalling old waxworks'.

At the trial, the newspaper's counsel told the single judge that journals written by the Prince represented his political views while on official business. 'These journals are not "What I did on my holidays". They are records of public events in which the claimant was engaged as a public servant.'

But the judge rejected this argument. He said the contribution that publication made to any public debate or to any process of informing the electorate was 'at best minimal'. It was impossible to say that disclosures from the contents of the journal were necessary in a democratic society.

The Court of Appeal upheld the judge's decision. The Prince's journals were confidential and private; they had been passed to the newspaper by an employee who had broken a contractual obligation of confidentiality; and the arguments that publication was in the public interest were rejected. The Court of Appeal held that, where information had been disclosed in breach of an obligation of confidence, to justify publication the newspaper would have to show not only that the information in question was a matter of public interest but also that, in all the circumstances, it was in the public interest that the duty of confidence should be breached (*HRH the Prince of Wales v Associated Newspapers Ltd* [2006] EWHC 522).

Section 12 of the Human Rights Act also says that a court considering a matter affecting freedom of information must have particular regard to 'any relevant privacy code'. In the *Douglas* case the relevant privacy code, which was considered by the court, was that of the Press Complaints Commission. In this code, privacy is among the topics where the code makes clear that there may be exceptions to the rules set out if the information can be demonstrated to be in the public interest.

→ see ch. 1, p. 17 and Appendix 2, p. 568

This phrase is said to include:

(1) detecting or exposing crime or a serious misdemeanour;

(2) protecting public health and safety; and

(3) preventing the public from being misled by some statement or action of an individual or organisation.

The editor must be able clearly to demonstrate how the public interest is served by publishing private/confidential information.

Examples of what constitutes 'the public interest' are also found in the Ofcom Broadcasting Code.

→ see ch.1, p. 16

People in the public eye

The public interest defence succeeded in 1993 when the *Daily Mirror* published material from *The Downing Street Years*, memoirs of Lady Thatcher, the former Prime Minister. The *Sunday Times*, which had bought exclusive rights to the book, was planning to run lengthy extracts but the *Daily Mirror* obtained a leaked copy and published first, leading on the story three days running. The *Sunday Times* tried to obtain an injunction.

The Conservative Party conference was in progress when the *Mirror* published its first splash 'What she said about him' (referring to John Major, her successor): 'Intellectually he drifted with the tide.' On the following day the paper's headline was 'What she says about them' (leading members of the Party): 'Thatcher sticks the knife in Major's men.'

The judge rejected the application for an injunction. He said that because the Conservative Party was making a public show of unity in Blackpool, the publication of the *Mirror's* claims could be in the public interest. The Court of Appeal agreed.

In 2000, a judge refused an injunction sought by Lord Levy against Times Newspapers. The story was about his tax affairs, and was clearly obtained in breach of confidence. The judge said that Lord Levy was a prominent supporter of the Labour Party, which had a manifesto commitment to closing tax loopholes, and his own tax affairs would shed light on the integrity of that position, which was in the public interest.

In the case brought by Naomi Campbell against the *Daily Mirror* Lord Phillips, Master of the Rolls, said the Court of Appeal did not believe that because an individual had achieved fame, that meant that his/her private life could be laid bare by the media:

> We do not see why it should necessarily be in the public interest that an individual who has been adopted as a role model, without seeking this distinction, should be demonstrated to have feet of clay.

But he said the Human Rights Act, which gave a right to respect for family and private life, must be balanced against freedom of expression in the media. He continued:

> Where a public figure chooses to make untrue pronouncements about his, or her, private life, the press will normally be entitled to put the record straight.

▶ Disclosure to whom?

Even if the information obtained ought to be disclosed in the public interest, it does not necessarily follow that it should be disclosed in the media. The answer to this question depends upon the circumstances.

In the *Operation Snowball* case, which involved allegations of miscarriages of justice and police corruption, the judge lifted an injunction imposed on the *Daily Express*. He said it had been suggested that disclosure should be made not to the public at large, but to certain holders of high office, such as the Commissioner of Police. However, the allegation concerned the administration of justice. Such corruption was properly a matter of public interest as opposed to a matter which should be taken up and dealt with by the authorities.

The *Daily Mirror* was not so fortunate when it wanted to publish information, obtained from tapes made illegally, that revealed alleged breaches of Jockey Club regulations and possibly the commission of criminal offences.

The paper's lawyers argued that the paper would use the tapes to expose iniquity. But the judges rejected the argument, saying the best thing would be for the paper to tell the police or the Jockey Club. Publication would serve the newspaper's interests rather than any public interest.

▦ Recap of major points

- The law says that a person who has obtained information in confidence must not take unfair advantage of it.
- Traditionally, the three elements of a breach of confidence are:

  (1) the information must have 'the necessary quality of confidence';

  (2) the information must have been imparted in circumstances imposing an obligation of confidence; and

  (3) there must be an unauthorised use of that information to the detriment of the party communicating it.
- The person who believes his confidence is to be breached can get an injunction preventing this.
- An injunction preventing one publication from publishing confidential information prevents all the media from publishing it.
- In the absence of a cause of action for privacy, courts use breach of confidence actions to prevent 'the unjustified publication of private information'.
- Section 12 of the Human Rights Act is intended to provide some protection against injunctions in matters involving freedom of expression.
- The person applying for an injunction has to show that he is 'likely' to establish at the trial that publication should not be allowed.
- The Act also says that when a court is considering imposing an injunction in a matter affecting freedom of expression, and where journalistic material is involved, it must have particular regard to the public interest in publication.
- Disobeying an injunction can result in an action for contempt of court.
- A court can order a journalist to reveal the name of the informant who provided confidential information.
- If confidential matter is published, the person whose confidences have been breached may be able to claim damages.

24

Privacy

Chapter summary

Since the last edition of McNae this area of law, coupled with breach of confidence, has seen an increasing number of cases of prominent people, and others, using it to prevent, or seek damages for, breaches of their privacy. In 2008 this fast-developing branch of law attracted widespread publicity with the case of Max Mosley, who successfully sued the *News of the World* and won damages of £60,000. This chapter will explain the development of the legal concept of privacy and the various laws that are used to enforce it.

▶ Development of the law

→

see
p. 402,
below

Until 2 October 2000 the law of England did not specifically recognise the right to privacy, but on that date the Human Rights Act 1998 came into force, in effect incorporating into English law the European Convention on Human Rights, which guarantees under Article 8 the right to privacy.

But though this new right to privacy now existed, it was unclear how the courts would protect it. The remedy most favoured was breach of confidence, an area of the law where many uncertainties existed and still exist.

Journalists were concerned at the potential effect of the right to privacy on their freedom to publish true information of public interest. Section 12 of the Human Rights Act requires courts, when considering granting an **injunction**, to have 'particular regard' to the importance of freedom of expression, guaranteed by Article 10 of the Convention.

→ glossary

But in the *Douglas* case Lord Justice Sedley rejected the view that the section gave greater weight to freedom of expression than to privacy rights. He said: 'Everything will ultimately depend on the proper balance between privacy and publicity in the situation facing the court.'

The *Douglas* case shows the way in which uncertainty about privacy has persisted. In December 2000 the Court of Appeal lifted the injunction that prevented *Hello!* from publishing its snatched pictures of the wedding of two film stars but the court did not have to decide whether such publication was unlawful; and in April 2003 the judge who had that task declined to hold that there was an existing law of privacy under which the stars and *OK!* could recover damages from *Hello!*. He said there were conflicting views in the authorities as to whether such a law existed.

He did decide that they had won the case, but not on the grounds of privacy. He held that the wedding was protected under the law of commercial confidence as a valuable trade asset. The publication of unauthorised photographs by a rival magazine was a breach of that confidence (*Douglas v Hello!* [2003] EWHC 786 (Ch)). But in 2005 the Court of Appeal disagreed on the question of commercial confidence. The court held that the stars' confidence had indeed been breached by *Hello!* and *they* (the stars), could sue the magazine, but *OK!* could not (*Douglas v Hello!* [2005] EWCA Civ 595).

→ see below, p. 410

Meanwhile, in 2004, in a case involving the supermodel Naomi Campbell, the House of Lords authoritatively established 'unjustified disclosure of private information' as a new cause of action. The distinguished judge Sir Charles Gray referred to 'the new (or at least relabelled) **tort**' and said the judgment had, in effect, created a law of privacy for the first time.

→ glossary

The Lords agreed that Ms Campbell was entitled to damages after the *Daily Mirror* reported that she had a drug addiction, for which she was receiving treatment by Narcotics Anonymous. The paper gave details of the treatment and her reaction to it, and surreptitiously obtained photographs, which they published, of her emerging from a treatment session (*Campbell v Mirror Group Newspapers* [2004] UKHL 22).

Another important development was the *Princess Caroline* case, in which the European Court of Human Rights held in 2004 that respect for the private life of Princess Caroline of Monaco was breached by photographs of scenes from her daily life, shopping or on holiday with her family, in public places (*von Hannover v Germany* [2004] ECHR).

English courts had not previously prevented publication of such photographs, and the significance of the decision for the United Kingdom was that the Human Rights Act 1998 says that a court determining a question in connection with a right guaranteed under the European Convention must 'take account' of decisions of the European Court.

In 2008, Max Mosley, the president of the Fédération Internationale de l'Automobile (FIA), which runs Formula 1 grand prix racing, sued the *News of the World* over stories, photos, and video footage of Mr Mosley taking part in sado-masochistic activities.

→

for further detail see below: 'The Max Mosley case', p. 406

Though the case did not establish new principles of privacy – much of what was decided had been said in previous cases – the level of damages awarded was the highest yet and put privacy on a par with other costly legal actions, such as libel.

As well as the remedies described later in this chapter, a person who considers his/her privacy to have been infringed can appeal to the European Court of Human Rights. In 2003 the court ordered the United Kingdom to pay £7,900 (11,800 euros) compensation, plus costs and expenses, to Geoff Peck, after a local authority gave footage of his suicide attempt, recorded on closed-circuit television, to the BBC for its television programme *Crime Beat (Peck v United Kingdom* [2003] ECHR).

▶ Article 8 of the Convention

The right to privacy is guaranteed by Article 8 of the Convention on Human Rights, which says:

❝ 1. Everyone has the right to respect for his private and family life, his home and his correspondence.
2. There shall be no interference by a public authority with the exercise of this right except such as is in accordance with the law and is necessary in a democratic society
   – in the interests of national security, public safety or the economic well-being of the country,
   – for the prevention of disorder or crime,
   – for the protection of health or morals, or
   – for the protection of the rights and freedoms of others. **❞**

The wording of Article 8 suggests it gives protection for privacy only against a 'public authority', but in fact it gives protection also against the media because under the Act a court in the United Kingdom is a public authority and must take account of the judgments of the European Court of Human

Rights (which adjudicates upon Convention matters) whenever it is hearing a case that involves one of the rights guaranteed by the Convention.

'Any relevant privacy code'

The Human Rights Act says in section 12 that where a court is considering imposing an injunction in a matter involving freedom of expression and journalistic, literary, or artistic material, it must have particular regard, among other things, to the extent to which the media defendant has complied with 'any relevant privacy code'.

In the *Douglas* case the judges considered clause 3 of the Press Complaints Commission code relating to privacy, and noted that the pictures taken at the wedding did not have the couple's consent. The current form of the clause states:

→ see also ch. 1, p. 16 and Appendix 2

❝ **Privacy**

i) Everyone is entitled to respect for his or her private and family life, home, health and correspondence, including digital communications. Editors will be expected to justify intrusions into any individual's private life without consent.

ii) It is unacceptable to photograph individuals in a private place without their consent.

Note – Private places are public or private property where there is a reasonable expectation of privacy. ❞

In the code, privacy is one of the topics where there may be exceptions to the rules set out in the code on grounds of public interest, a phrase which includes, in the current wording (the list is not exhaustive):

(1) detecting or exposing crime or serious impropriety;

(2) protecting public health and safety; and

(3) preventing the public from being misled by an action or statement of an individual or organisation.

Lord Justice Brooke (in the *Douglas* case in 2000) said it was not necessary to go beyond section 12 of the 1998 Act and clause 3 of the code to find the ground rules by which the court should weigh the competing considerations of freedom of expression on the one hand and privacy on the other (*Douglas v Hello! Ltd* [2001] 2 All ER 289.

→ see also below and ch. 23, p.389

 See also below, p. 419, on protection of privacy in the Ofcom Broadcasting Code.

▌Laws providing protection

Breach of confidence

Before the development of the 'new cause of action', the only remedies that British citizens had against intrusions into their private lives were those referred to in the introduction to this chapter. If none gave an appropriate remedy, a **claimant** had no legal protection.

→ glossary

As explained in ch. 23, the law of breach of confidence is based on the principle that a person who has acquired information in confidence should not take unfair advantage of it. Originally the obligation was understood to arise only where the parties had a recognised relationship (such as doctor and patient or employer and employee) but more recently the judges had modified the law so that they were ready to infer such a relationship where no obvious relationship existed.

In the *Douglas* case in 2000 Lord Justice Sedley said:

❝ What a concept of privacy does...is accord recognition to the fact that the law has to protect not only those people whose trust has been abused but those who simply find themselves subjected to an unwanted intrusion into their personal lives. The law no longer needs to construct an artificial relationship of confidentiality between intruder and victim: it can recognise privacy itself as a legal principle drawn from the fundamental value of personal autonomy. ❞

The judges' comments in this case gave a considerable boost to the new right of privacy, which received another boost three weeks later when a judge, Dame Elizabeth Butler-Sloss, imposed an unprecedented injunction forbidding the media from revealing the new identities and whereabouts of the two killers of the two-year-old child James Bulger on the ground that such a disclosure would infringe their rights to privacy (Article 8 of the European Convention), Article 2 (right to life), and Article 3 (prohibition of torture).

→ See ch. 9, p. 137, for reference to this case and three others in which the media have been injuncted to forbid publication of the whereabouts of defendants from notorious cases once they have served their sentences.

→

see
ch. 23,
p. 382

The question whether the information has the 'necessary quality of confidence' is an issue that the judges frequently have to consider in privacy cases, particularly in 'kiss and tell' stories – that is, stories in which one of the parties gives the media details of the relationship between them.

In a new approach to the law of confidence, the question is whether Article 8 (the right to privacy) was 'engaged', which depends on whether the information was 'private'. And the touchstone is whether the person claiming had a 'reasonable expectation of privacy'.

In the years immediately following incorporation of the Human Rights Act, courts took the view that not all sexual conduct was entitled to be viewed as confidential or, indeed, deserving of legal protection at all. In 2002 the Court of Appeal lifted an injunction banning publication of details of the extra-marital affairs of a professional footballer, Blackburn Rovers' captain Garry Flitcroft (*A v B (A Company)* [2002] EWCA Civ 337).

The judge who granted the injunction had explained that the law afforded the protection of confidentiality to facts concerning sexual relations within marriage, and he ruled that in the context of modern sexual relations the position should be no different with relationships outside marriage. He granted an injunction preventing the *Sunday People* from identifying Flitcroft and publishing interviews with his former lovers – one a lap dancer he met in a club and the other a nursery teacher who claimed he used his wealth, fame, and position to seduce her.

But the Court of Appeal, lifting the injunction, said there was a significant difference between the confidentiality that attached to what was intended to be a permanent relationship and that which attached to the category of relationships that Flitcroft was involved with in this case.

Earlier that year a judge refused to grant an injunction to 'Top of the Pops' presenter Jamie Theakston banning the *Sunday People* from publishing an article about his activities in a brothel. The judge said a 'fleeting' sexual relationship in a brothel was not confidential (*Jamie Theakston v MGN Ltd* [2002] EWHC 137 (QB)).

But after the *Princess Caroline* case in the Strasbourg court in 2004, English courts began to take a view that was more favourable to claimants on what sort of information should be protected, as the following two cases illustrate.

A High Court judge in 2006 decided that an adulterous relationship could be protected by the law of confidence. An adulterer won a temporary injunction banning the betrayed husband from naming him in the media. Mr Justice Eady imposed the order after the adulterer, a well-known figure in the sports world, faced being named and shamed by the husband, who wanted revenge by selling the story and publishing details on the internet.

The judge decided that even a well-known figure had a right to privacy under Article 8 and, despite his infidelity, had a right to protect his wife and children. Mr Justice Eady conceded that it is was a 'striking proposition' that a spouse whose partner had committed adultery owed a duty of confidence to the third party adulterer to keep quiet about it.

But he added: 'There is a powerful argument that the conduct of an intimate or sexual relationship is a matter in respect of which there is a "reasonable expectation of privacy".'

Also in 2006 the Court of Appeal upheld a ruling by Mr Justice Eady that had been described by commentators as a blow against 'kiss and tell' celebrity exposés after the breakdown of a friendship or relationship (*McKennitt v Ash* [2006] EMLR 10).

The judge had stopped publication of a book on the Canadian folk singer and songwriter Loreena McKennitt by her former friend and confidante Neima Ash.

The protected information covered substantial sections of the book, including details of Ms McKennitt's personal and sexual relationships; her personal feelings, in particular relating to her dead fiancé and the circumstances of his death; matters relating to her health and diet and her emotional vulnerability; and information about a dispute over money Ms McKennitt advanced to Ms Ash and her husband to buy a property, an arrangement that ended in an out-of-court settlement.

The appeal judges held that the interference with private life had to be of 'some seriousness' before Article 8 would be 'engaged' – so that, for example, anodyne or trivial information would not be protected. But they upheld Mr Justice Eady's ruling that even relatively trivial details about an individual's *home* would be protected. The judge had said:

“ To describe a person's home, the décor, the layout, the state of cleanliness, or how the occupiers behave inside it…is almost as objectionable as spying into the home with a long distance lens and publishing the resulting photographs. ”

The Max Mosley case

The *News of the World* printed the story of the involvement of Max Mosley (president of the Fédération Internationale de l'Automobile) in a sado-masochistic orgy with five women, claiming that it had a Nazi theme. It also put secretly filmed footage on its website. The *News of the World*'s informant was one of the women who had taken part in the sado-masochistic activities.

Mr Mosley, the son of the 1930s Fascist leader, Sir Oswald Mosley, said the activities were consensual, harmless, and there were no Nazi overtones.

Mr Justice Eady held that the woman informant owed a duty of confidence, as in previous cases where the relationship was transitory.

He said that if the activities had mocked the ways Jews were treated in concentration camps or parodied Holocaust horror, then there would have been a public interest in revealing Mr Mosley's actvities, at the very least to the FIA. However, he said, there was no such behaviour and the judge could find no public interest to justify the intrusion, the filming, or the publication. He said:

> It is not for journalists to undermine human rights, or for judges to refuse to enforce them, merely on grounds of taste or moral disapproval. Everyone is naturally entitled to espouse moral or religious beliefs to the effect that certain types of sexual behaviour are wrong or demeaning to those participating. That does not mean that they are entitled to hound those who practise them or to detract from their right to live life as they choose.

He added:

> Of course, I accept that such behaviour is viewed by some people with distaste and moral disapproval, but in the light of modern rights-based jurisprudence that does not provide any justification for the intrusion on the personal privacy of the Claimant.
>
> It is perhaps worth adding that there is nothing 'landmark' about this decision. It is simply the application to rather unusual facts of recently developed but established principles. Nor can it seriously be suggested that the case is likely to inhibit serious investigative journalism into crime or wrongdoing, where the public interest is more genuinely engaged.

The judge did, however, refuse to award exemplary damages (*Mosley v News Group Newspapers Ltd* [2008] EWHC 1777).

Mr Mosley announced later in 2008 that he would challenge the UK's privacy laws in the European Court of Human Rights. He said he wanted newspapers to notify someone before publishing private information about them.

He said he had not had an opportunity to seek an injunction to prevent the breach of his privacy as he had not known the allegations were going to be made.

Information concerning health

It is clear that information concerning health will normally be treated as of the utmost confidentiality. In 2002 the *Mail on Sunday* was barred by the Court of Appeal from revealing the identity of a local health authority where a health care worker, referred to as H, had quit his job after being diagnosed as HIV positive. Earlier the paper had won permission in the High Court to name the authority, but not the health care worker.

Lord Phillips, Master of the Rolls, said there was a public interest in preserving the confidentiality of health care workers who might otherwise be discouraged from reporting they were HIV positive. He said the *Mail on Sunday* believed H's patients were entitled to know they had been treated by someone who was HIV positive. But he said that if the authority was identified, it would inevitably lead to the disclosure of H's identity, because only his patients would be offered HIV tests and counselling. The paper was allowed to state that the health care worker was a dentist.

In the case in 2002 in which the supermodel Naomi Campbell sued Mirror Group Newspapers for a story about her therapy for drug addiction, there was no dispute that this information had the 'quality of confidence'. When her case reached the Lords in 2004, the court declared that in any claim based on the publication of private information, the initial question is whether the information is sufficiently private in nature to engage the Article 8 right.

This is determined by asking whether the person suing has 'a reasonable expectation of privacy'. For example, a person could have a reasonable expectation of privacy in relation to the information conveyed by a photograph taken in a public place if the photograph captured a private activity. Thus the picture published by the *Daily Mirror* of Ms Campbell emerging from a therapy session was 'confidential' even though it was taken in a public street.

But although information concerning health will, in general, be treated as of the utmost confidentiality, Michael Stone, convicted of murdering Lin Russell and her six-year-old daughter Megan, failed in 2006 in his attempt to ban the press and public from seeing the full report on his care and treatment.

An independent inquiry report into the treatment Stone received from mental health, probation, and social workers before the attack was due to be published in 2005, but was put on hold pending the legal challenge.

In his ruling the judge said:

> 66 Publication of the report in full can, in my view, only assist the legitimate and ongoing public debate with regard to treatment of the mentally ill and of those with disturbed personalities in the community (*Michael Stone v South East SH* [2006] EWHC 1668). 99

The rapid development of the law of privacy, on the question of quality of confidence, was illustrated in the *Douglas* case in 2005 when the Court of Appeal rejected an appeal by *Hello!* magazine against damages the magazine had been ordered to pay to the film stars at a hearing in 2003 (*Douglas v Hello!* [2005] EWCA Civ 595; [2006] QB 125).

The judgment of the court, delivered by Lord Phillips, Master of the Rolls, showed how far the law of privacy had advanced in the five years since the case first came before the court in 2000, when some were arguing that photographs of an event at a New York hotel attended by 250 guests could not be truly confidential, and that in any case *Hello!* owed no duty of confidence to the stars.

Applying the test propounded by the House of Lords in *Campbell v MGN* ('a reasonable expectation of privacy'), the court held that photographs of the wedding plainly portrayed aspects of the Douglases' private life and fell within the protection of the law of confidentiality, as extended to cover private or personal information.

Lord Phillips said the Douglases appeared to have a 'virtually unanswerable' case for contending that publication of the unauthorised photographs would infringe their privacy. He said the earlier Court of Appeal which in 2000 had lifted an injunction granted to *OK!* had been wrong to do so.

As mentioned above, the single judge who tried the *Douglas* case in 2003 declined to hold that there was an existing law of privacy under which the stars and the magazine *OK!* could recover damages from *Hello!*. He said there were conflicting views in the authorities as to whether such a law existed. But the judges of the Court of Appeal in 2005 did not share his doubts as to the strength of the Douglases' case. (The House of Lords heard an appeal against this decision, and judgment was awaited as *McNae* went to press.)

Can information be confidential if it is in the public domain?

In 2005 a judge granted an injunction restraining a newspaper from publishing the addresses of buildings acquired for housing vulnerable adolescents, although the addresses would be known to neighbours and others who lived nearby and might also be available from the Land Registry (*Green Corns Ltd v Claverley Group Ltd* [2005] EMLR 31). Mr Justice Tugendhat said:

> There will be cases where personal information about a person (usually a celebrity) has been so widely published that a restraint upon repetition will serve no purpose, and an injunction will be refused on that account. It may be less likely that that will be so when the subject is not a celebrity. But in any event, it is not possible in a case about personal information simply to apply [the] test of whether the information is generally accessible, and to conclude that, if it is, then that is the end of the matter…
>
> I conclude that the information as to the addresses which is sought to be restrained is not in the public domain to the extent, or in the sense, that

republication could have no significant effect, or that the information is not eligible for protection at all. 🟥🟥

What is the position with 'widely published' photographs? The Court of Appeal in the *Douglas* case (paragraph 105) said:

> 🟥🟥 Once intimate personal information about a celebrity's private life has been widely published it may serve no useful purpose to prohibit further publication. The same will not necessarily be true of photographs. Insofar as a photograph does more than convey information and intrudes on privacy by enabling the viewer to focus on intimate personal detail, there will be a fresh intrusion of privacy when each additional viewer sees the photograph and even when one who has seen a previous publication of the photograph is confronted by a fresh publication of it. 🟥🟥

Obligation of confidence

In spite of Lord Justice Sedley's comment in the *Douglas* case, that the law no longer needs to construct an artificial relationship of confidentiality between intruder and victim, more recent Court of Appeal decisions suggest that courts hearing cases involving privacy will continue to consider whether an 'obligation of confidence' existed.

Where the relationship is a contractual one the courts will hold the confidant to a very high standard of confidence. Naomi Campbell, whose case against the *Daily Mirror* has been referred to, also won a summary judgment against her former personal assistant, who had given information to the *News of the World* for their story 'Fiery model attacks aide over secret love scenes with heart throb Joseph Fiennes'. (The judgment was overturned on appeal, partly on public interest grounds.)

Ex-employees of celebrities, such as drivers and nannies, are not free to speak freely about the private life of their former boss when the employment ends. The celebrity family the Beckhams obtained an injunction against their former driver and their former nanny to uphold duties of confidence.

Similarly, it is easy to find or infer a relationship of confidence with one's medical advisers, or fellow participants in therapy (as in Naomi Campbell's case against the *Mirror*).

Information obtained covertly

Suppose the information is obtained, for example, by bugging or long-lens photography?

In 2006, in the *McKennitt* case, the Court of Appeal referred to cases where 'confidence' arose from information having been acquired by 'unlawful or surreptitious means'. The court regarded the taking of long-distance photographs as being 'an exercise generally considered to raise privacy issues'.

In the *Douglas* case the wedding pictures were taken by an uninvited freelance photographer. In the *Campbell* case, photographs of the model leaving a Narcotics Anonymous therapy session were also taken surreptitiously. In a 2006 case involving the Prince of Wales's 'Hong Kong Journal', the information was leaked by a 'disaffected secretary' (*HRH the Prince of Wales v Associated Newspapers Ltd* [2006] EWHC 522).

In 2007 former Prime Minister, Tony Blair, and his wife, Cherie won damages from Associated Newspapers over 'long-lens' pictures taken of them while they were on holiday in Barbados at Sir Cliff Richards's villa. The pictures had been taken in secluded and private places and the Blairs said while they accepted a certain level of scrutiny, here the photographers had overstepped the mark. The damages were donated to charity.

In 2008 the pop star Madonna launched a High Court action against the *Mail on Sunday* for more than £5 million in damages over private photographs of her wedding to film director Guy Ritchie. The photographs were copied surreptitiously by an interior designer during work at Madonna's US home, the court was told. The paper admitted breach of copyright and privacy and damages were due to be assessed in 2009.

Public interest

As stated in ch. 23, p. 394, even before the 1998 Act was implemented journalists could plead that the disclosure of confidential information would be in the public interest. Judges may be prepared to accept that the celebrity of the claimant can generate a public interest in private conduct that would otherwise be protected.

The 'role model' status for young people of a disc jockey or a footballer was a real factor against the continuation of injunctions in the *Theakston* and *Flitcroft* cases. In the *Theakston* case the judge drew a distinction between the public interest in the fact of the relationship, which could be published, and in salacious details, which would still be restrained.

In the case involving Naomi Campbell, publication of some of the information was held to be in the public interest, and some not. There were five distinct 'elements' of private information:

- the fact of Ms Campbell's drug addiction;
- the fact that she was receiving treatment for that addiction;
- the fact that she was receiving treatment at Narcotics Anonymous (NA);

- details of the NA treatment and her reaction to it; and,
- surreptitiously obtained photographs of her emerging from an NA treatment session.

Because the model had publicly denied using drugs previously, the first and second facts could be published in the public interest. But the rest could not, because of the intrusiveness of the disclosure and the likelihood that disclosure would interfere with or disrupt her treatment. Three of the judges – the majority – held that Article 10 considerations could not justify publication of the information.

Two of the judges considered that the third, fourth, and fifth categories added little of significance to the disclosure of the first and second and that journalists should be given greater latitude – but as these two were in the minority their views did not prevail. The difference of opinion between the judges illustrates the difficult decisions that have to be taken by journalists when running such stories.

Personality rights

It may be that breach of confidence can be used also to protect commercial interests based upon personality rights. In the 2003 hearing in the *Douglas* case (referred to above) *Hello!* magazine was ordered to pay *OK!* magazine more than £1 million in damages after *Hello!* published the 'snatched' pictures of the wedding of the film stars.

The single judge had decided that *Hello!* had breached the right of confidence of the stars, and that therefore it was liable to pay damages in compensation to *OK!*, which had paid £500,000 for exclusive use of the pictures. But in 2005 the Court of Appeal disagreed and reversed that decision (*Douglas v Hello!* [2005] EWCA Civ 595).

The appeal judges held that the stars' confidence had been breached by *Hello!* and *they* (the stars), could sue the magazine, but *OK!* could not. The court said confidential or private information, which was capable of commercial exploitation but which was protected only by the law of confidence, could not be treated as property that could be owned and transferred. *OK!* appealed against the decision and the ruling of the House of Lords was awaited as this book went to press.

The Data Protection Act

see ch.
25, p. 425

The Naomi Campbell case alerted the media to the implications for the law of privacy of the Data Protection Act (DPA) 1998. She sued the *Daily Mirror* for both breach of confidence and infringement of the DPA.

A journalist collecting personal information intending to put it into a database or extracting information from a database can lay him/herself open to a claim for compensation if the person concerned suffers damage as a result of the unauthorised disclosure of that information.

The advantages, for a claimant, of suing under the DPA rather than for breach of confidence are:

- There is no general public domain defence under the Act.
- If publication has taken place there is no blanket public interest protection for the media.
- The requirements of the first data protection principle are stringent and in most privacy cases are unlikely to be satisfied.
- There is an entitlement to compensation for distress even if no identifiable damage has been caused.

The Act also provides criminal penalties for those unlawfully obtaining personal information under section 55 of the Act. Powers of imprisonment were enacted in 2008 but not implemented at the time this edition of *McNae* went to press.

see ch.
25, p. 438

The Regulation of Investigatory Powers Act 2000

The Regulation of Investigatory Powers Act (RIPA) prohibits intentional and unlawful interception of communications by post or phone or other telecommunication systems. It supersedes the Interception of Communications Act 1985 but, unlike the 1985 Act, it applies to private systems as well as public systems.

The gaps in the previous law were illustrated when a journalist tapped the phone of the actress Antonia de Sancha to record telephone conversations between her and David Mellor, a government Minister. The journalist used a telephone extension leading from de Sancha's flat to the garden. The 1985 Act did not apply because no tap was put on the line between the private property and the operator and in any case the tap was 'authorised' because de Sancha's landlord had given the journalist permission.

RIPA says that the sender or recipient of an intercepted message can sue, even if the person having the right to control the use of a private system gives permission, if such interception is 'without lawful authority'.

The Act provides a means for punishing illegal hacking into mobile phones. Penalties are a maximum of two years in jail, a fine, or both.

In 2006 Clive Goodman, royal editor of the *News of the World*, pleaded guilty with another man on a charge of conspiring to intercept mobile phone voicemail messages under the Criminal Law Act 1977, which covers conspiracy. Each was also charged with eight offences of intercepting communications, by accessing telephone voicemail messages, contrary to RIPA.

The case came to light when Prince William began to fear aides' mobile phone voicemail messages were being intercepted after a story about his knee injury appeared in the paper in November 2005, although few people were aware of it.

How then can one 'intercept' a voicemail message? The Act, in section 2(7), expressly includes the offline storage of messages for later retrieval as still being 'in the course of transmission', and this in effect brings voicemail within the scope of 'interception'.

→
for other information on RIPA, see ch. 32, p. 523

Journalists frequently record their own telephone calls. Under the 2000 Act, interception occurs in the course of transmission, so recording telephone conversations by a device at either end of the communication is not interception and is lawful.

- The Press Complaints Commission has made it clear that a journalist who, when talking in a phone call, records the interview or conversation without telling the other person that he/she is being recorded is <u>not</u> regarded as using a 'clandestine recording device' under clause 10 of the PCC code of practice, even though the journalist has not warned that the call is being recorded (see the PCC adjudication) in *Messrs Lewis Silkin on behalf of Mrs Isobel Stone*, Report 49, 2000).

However, clause 10 does not, unless the code's 'public interest' criterion applies and there is no other way to obtain the information, permit either (a) Conduct classed as subterfuge/misrepresentation – e.g. the journalist failing to declare he/she is a journalist – or (b) a secret recording device being left unattended to eavesdrop or film.

→
ch. 1 p. 17 explains PCC code

The Wireless Telegraphy Act 2006

See Online Resource Centre, ch. 2.

The Act prohibits the use without authority of wireless apparatus with intent to obtain information about the contents, sender, or addressee of any message, and prohibits the disclosure of any such information.

Trespass

Trespass is a direct injury to land, to goods, or to the person. At first sight it would appear to impose significant restrictions on journalists' conduct, but the impression is largely illusory.

Trespass to land

This is a wrongful interference with the possession of 'land', which includes a building such as a house. Wrongful interference includes going there without consent.

It is a tort – a civil wrong – and the occupier of the land can sue for damages or get an injunction to stop it. No one else can.

In a case where a reporter and journalist from the *Sunday Sport* intruded into a hospital room where the TV actor Gorden Kaye was lying semi-conscious, and 'interviewed' and photographed him, Kaye could not sue for trespass because, as a hospital patient, he was not legally the occupier of the land; the hospital authority was (*Kaye v Robertson* [1991] FSR 62 CA).

As a result of this need for the occupier of the land to show unauthorised entry, a journalist cannot be sued for trespass for using binoculars to watch another person on his own land, or photographing that person on his own land, provided the journalist did not enter the land – although he might be sued if he were on a highway that technically formed a part of that person's property.

Note that a journalist's entry is unauthorised if he has obtained permission to enter by fraud – for example, by pretending to be a doctor. And even if his entry is legal, he may be trespassing if he takes advantage of his admission to do things, such as carrying out a search of the property, not covered by his permission to enter. the PCC code bans subter-fuge, unless it can be justified, see p. 17

Even if damages are awarded, they are not likely to be substantial. After all, how much actual damage to land is done, for example, by fixing a microphone to a bed?

But if the trespass has taken some particularly outrageous form the court may award heavy damages, known as exemplary or punitive damages. It may be that a journalist who forced his way into a house to get a story would be liable to pay substantial damages, even though he had done little or no damage to the house.

In addition to seeking damages, the occupier of the land can use reasonable force to eject the trespasser. The police may lawfully assist, though they have no duty to do so and when doing so are not protected by the special powers and privileges of constables.

So there is a civil action for trespass but there is no general criminal offence. for the offence of 'aggra-vated trespass', see ch. 35, p. 548

Trespass to goods

If a journalist visiting a contact picks up and reads a letter on the contact's desk, while the latter has been called out of the room, the journalist commits a trespass to the goods and is liable. Only the person in possession of the letter can bring an action for trespass – even if someone else is injured by the information disclosed. (The injured person may have a claim for breach of confidence.)

The journalist cannot be sued for trespass for reading the letter while it is lying on the desk. If, however, he takes the letter away and intends permanently to deprive the owner of it, he risks the more serious tort of conversion or even the criminal offence of **theft**.

→ glossary

Trespass to the person

This involves actual physical interference with a person, or threats of it. Such action, however, would probably lead to a criminal prosecution for **assault** rather than a civil action.

→ glossary

Harassment

Under the Protection from Harassment Act 1997 harassers can be arrested and imprisoned. The Act declares that a person must not pursue 'a course of conduct' that amounts to harassment of another and which he knows or ought to know amounts to harassment. The Act does not define harassment, but says it includes 'alarming the person or causing the person distress'.

The Act introduced two new criminal offences and a civil measure. A high-level offence, not expected to affect the work of journalists, is intended to catch the most serious cases of harassment, where, on more than one occasion, the conduct is so threatening that victims fear for their safety. This carries a maximum penalty of five years in prison, or an unlimited fine, or both.

A lower-level offence catches harassment which may not cause the victim to fear that violence will be used. The action has to have occurred at least twice. This carries a maximum penalty of six months in prison, or a £5,000 fine, or both.

For these offences to have been committed, there does not have to be an intention on the part of the harasser to cause the victim to fear violence or feel harassed. The prosecution has to prove only that the conduct occurred in circumstances where a reasonable person would have realised that this would be the effect.

Both offences are immediately arrestable, without a warrant, and the police are able to search the harasser's property.

The courts also have the power to make a restraining order immediately after convicting a person of either of the two offences. A breach of this order is a criminal offence with a maximum penalty of five years in prison, or an unlimited fine, or both.

There is also a civil remedy. Victims are able to take action if they are subjected to the conduct described in the low-level offence, and in 2001 the Court of Appeal upheld the ruling of a county court judge that subjects of media reports that cause 'alarm or distress' can sue for damages under the Act. The case concerned a civilian clerk for the City of London police, Esther Thomas, who wanted to sue the *Sun* for articles that reported a complaint by her against the behaviour of four police officers and the following week a selection of readers' letters attacking her. These were followed by another article seeking readers' contributions to a fine imposed on one of the officers.

The publication of one article would not amount to a 'course of conduct', but Ms Thomas's lawyers argued that the publication of two or more did.

The Court of Appeal gave her the go-ahead to sue the paper (*Thomas v News Group Newspapers Ltd and another* [2001] EWCA Civ 1233). Lord Phillips, Master of the Rolls, said it could be argued that publication of the *Sun* articles would lead some readers to send hostile mail to the clerk, causing her distress. Someone who believes himself to be harassed can also attempt to stop the conduct by obtaining an injunction. For example, a journalist might be banned from telephoning the 'victim'. A breach of the injunction would be a criminal offence, carrying the power of arrest, with a maximum penalty of five years in prison, or an unlimited fine, or both.

 See also ch. 35, p. 547, for cases in which photographers have been accused of harassment.

The then Home Secretary said the law would not prevent people going about their lawful activity, and the legitimate work of the police, the security service, journalists, and others would be protected. He was referring to provisions which say that the course of conduct will not amount to an offence if 'in the particular circumstances' it is reasonable or if it is pursued 'for the purpose of preventing or detecting crime'.

But journalists fear that the legislation may be exploited by those who want to gag the press or stop an investigation by a particular journalist. The media can effectively be restrained by police powers of arrest and by applications for injunctions by those who believe they might be subject to media harassment, even if no prosecution is brought, and even if the journalist can successfully defend his conduct as reasonable in particular circumstances.

There have been complaints that journalists in pursuit of a story have harassed people reluctant to be interviewed by massing on the pavement outside their homes. An Act of 1875 makes it a criminal offence, among other things, to besiege people's homes or workplaces with a view to forcing them to do something against their will. But there is no record of this Act being used against journalists.

→

see also
ch. 35
p. 549
on street
trouble
with
police

The police normally move the press aside to allow people to pass, using powers under the Highways Act 1980 to prevent 'wilful' obstruction of the free passage along a highway. These powers include arrest.

Photographers are sometimes arrested and charged under the Public Order Act 1986, which makes it an offence to use 'threatening, abusive, or insulting words or behaviour' or disorderly behaviour 'within the hearing or sight of a person likely to be caused harassment, alarm or distress'.

A bundle of new measures under the Serious Organised Crime and Police Act 2005 included two concerned with harassment. Section 126 makes it an offence to be outside or in the vicinity of someone's home with the intention of persuading the resident or someone else not to do something he is entitled to do, or to do something that he is not under any obligation to do.

Section 127 gives police the power to order someone to leave the vicinity of a person's home, and not to return within a period of up to three months. Penalties, on summary conviction, are imprisonment for up to 51 weeks and/or a fine of up to £2,500.

Copyright

→

see ch.
29

If the journalist is using copyright letters, other documents, or photographs snatched from a family album there is the possibility of an action for infringement of copyright. The Prince of Wales sued the *Mail on Sunday* for infringement of both confidence and copyright when it published extracts from his 'Hong Kong Journal'.

Court reporting restrictions

→

see in
particular
chs 5, 6,
8, and 9

This book has explained the restrictions under which journalists work when reporting court proceedings, and the protection given to juveniles and the victims of sexual assaults, among others.

Contravention of these restrictions normally leads to prosecution before a criminal court.

However, the person who believes he or she has been injured by such a contravention may be able to sue. In 1994 a rape victim won £10,000 damages from a local freesheet that gave sufficient details about her to enable her to be identified. In so doing, the paper was liable for the tort of breach of statutory duty.

What the Ofcom code says on privacy

Guidance on privacy for the print media is contained in the Press Complaints Commission code of practice which is given in full in Appendix 2, pp. 568–572.

The Office of Communications (Ofcom) has responsibility for regulating the UK communications industries, apart from the print media sector and that sector's associated websites. Its guidance on privacy is summarised below.

→
see ch. 1,
p. 16

Section 8 of the Ofcom Broadcasting Code states that the principle aimed for is to ensure that broadcasters avoid any 'unwarranted' infringement of privacy, either in programmes or in connection with obtaining material included in programmes.

Ofcom fined Kiss FM £75,000 for a hoax phone call, in a case which illustrates a number of the issues that concern the regulator – the public interest, the need to obtain consent, surreptitious phone calls, and the need for care when handling people in distress. The programme's presenter, Streetboy, telephoned a man who had been made redundant by his company. The man had called his human resources office to discuss redeployment opportunities, but the officer's phone had inadvertently been redirected to Streetboy's.

Streetboy, posing as the human resources officer, then rang the individual, telling him he should 'go and flip burgers or something'. He told the distressed man: 'You thought you had a chance! Could you not bother calling me again, 'cos you're wasting my time, to be quite frank.'

Ofcom said in its view the broadcast was devoid of any justification of public interest and could have had a serious effect on the individual concerned, whose deep distress was evident.

Ofcom launched an investigation in 2008 after the presenters Jonathan Ross and Russell Brand, left a series of lewd phone messages on the answering machine of veteran actor Andrew Sachs. These referred to the sex life of a relative of his.

Ofcom guidance and unwarranted infringement

The Ofcom code provides a set of principles by way of practical guidance. In dealing with complaints about privacy, Ofcom asks two questions – first, has there been an infringement of privacy, secondly, if so, was it 'warranted'?

What is an 'unwarranted' infringement? The code says that where broad-casters wish to justify an infringement of privacy, they should be able to demonstrate why in the particular circumstances of the case it is warranted. If the reason is that it is in the public interest, then the broadcaster should be able to demonstrate that the public interest outweighs the right to privacy.

Examples of public interest would include revealing or detecting crime, protecting public health or safety, exposing misleading claims made by indi-viduals or organisations, or disclosing incompetence that affects the public.

Private lives, public places

Another term defined in the code is 'legitimate expectation of privacy'. The meaning varies according to the place and nature of the information, activ-ity, or condition in question, the extent to which it is in the public domain (if at all) and whether the individual concerned is already in the public eye. There may be circumstances where people can reasonably expect privacy even in a public place.

Broadcasters should ensure that words, images, or actions filmed or recorded in, or broadcast from, a public place, are not so private that prior consent is required before broadcast from the individual or organisation concerned, unless broadcasting without their consent is warranted.

Need for consent

On consent, the code says that any infringement of privacy in the making of a programme should be with such consent from the person and/or organ-isation concerned – unless the infringement is otherwise warranted. If the broadcast of a programme would infringe the privacy of a person or organ-isation, consent should be obtained before the relevant material is broad-cast, unless the infringement is warranted. (Callers to phone-in shows are deemed to have given consent to the broadcast of their contribution.)

If the privacy of an individual or organisation is being infringed, and they ask that the filming, recording, or live broadcast be stopped, the broadcaster should do so, unless it is warranted to continue.

When filming or recording in institutions, organisations, or other agen-cies, permission should be obtained from the relevant authority or manage-ment, unless it is warranted to film or record without permission. Individual consent of employees or others whose appearance is incidental or where they are essentially anonymous members of the general public will not nor-mally be required.

However, in potentially sensitive places such as ambulances, hospitals, schools, prisons, or police stations, separate consent should normally be obtained before filming or recording and for broadcast from those in sensitive situations (unless not obtaining consent is warranted).

Gathering information

When broadcasters are gathering information, sound, or images, and when they are reusing material, 'the means of obtaining material must be proportionate in all the circumstances, and in particular to the subject matter of the programme'.

One such 'means of obtaining material' is doorstepping, which the code explains is the filming or recording of an interview or attempted interview with someone, or announcing that a call is being filmed or recorded for broadcast purposes, without any prior warning.

Such doorstepping for factual programmes should not take place unless a request for an interview has been refused or it has not been possible to request an interview, or there is good reason to believe that an investigation will be frustrated if the subject is approached openly, or it is warranted to doorstep.

Broadcasters should ensure that the reuse of material – that is, use of material originally filmed or recorded for one purpose and then used in a programme for another purpose or used in a later or different programme – does not create an unwarranted infringement of privacy.

On telephone calls, the code says that broadcasters can record those between themselves and the other party if they have, from the outset of the call, identified themselves, and explained the purpose of the call and that the call is being recorded for possible broadcast (if that is the case) unless it is warranted not to do one or more of these.

Surreptitious filming or recording

Surreptitious filming or recording should be used only where it is warranted, and normally it will be warranted if:

- there is **prima facie** evidence of a story in the public interest; and →glossary
- there are reasonable grounds to suspect that further material evidence could be obtained; and
- it is necessary for the credibility and authenticity of the programme.

Ofcom said that secret filming by a reporter who obtained a job in a prison was justified, to show practices at the prison which, it was claimed, put vulnerable prisoners at risk and which failed to deal with hard drug use.

Suffering or distress

Broadcasters should not take or broadcast footage or audio recordings of people caught up in emergencies, victims of accidents, or those suffering a personal tragedy, even in a public place, where that results in an infringement of privacy, unless it is warranted or the people concerned have given consent.

People in a state of distress should not be put under pressure to take part in a programme or provide interviews, unless it is warranted.

Broadcasters should take care not to reveal the identity of a person who has died or of victims of accidents or violent crimes, unless and until it is clear that the next of kin have been informed of the event or unless it is warranted.

⸬ Recap of major points

- The right to privacy is guaranteed by Article 8 of the Convention on Human Rights.

- The remedy most favoured to protect privacy has been the action for breach of confidence.

- Judges are prepared to infer a relationship requiring confidentiality where no obvious relationship exists.

- Judges use the test of asking whether the claimant had 'a reasonable expectation of privacy'.

- The right to privacy is not necessarily lost because the activity happened in public.

- The model Naomi Campbell received damages when a paper published pictures of her in a public street, emerging from a Narcotics Anonymous therapy session.

- Max Mosley won damages over a story about a sado-masochistic orgy, which the court held was not in the public interest to publish.

- There is a defence that publication was in the public interest.

- Other remedies for breach of privacy include: data protection, the Regulation of Investigatory Powers Act 2000, the Wireless Telegraphy Act 2006, trespass, harassment, copyright, and laws regulating press reports of court proceedings.

The Data Protection Act 1998

Chapter summary

Journalists process data to produce stories and in doing so they are sometimes subject to the provisions of the Data Protection Act 1998. They might also try to obtain information from people or organisations who will cite the Act as a reason for refusing to divulge information. This chapter will explain the way in which the Act can affect journalistic work and what journalists must do to comply with the Act while still protecting their sources.

The 1984 and 1998 Acts

Even before the passage of the Human Rights Act 1998 the law in effect recognised rights of privacy for the vast amount of information held about people on computer and in some manual records.

These rights were provided for information on computer by the Data Protection Act 1984. The Data Protection Act 1998 strengthened those rights and extended them to information about people contained in 'structured manual files'. (In this chapter 'the Act' or 'the DPA' means the 1998 Act.)

The Act requires that the processing of personal data must be in accordance with the Act and the definition of data (see below) is so wide that it comprehensively describes the normal operations of any newspaper or form of media produced with the aid of integrated computerised systems.

A leading lawyer explained: 'Whenever a journalist obtains information which is to be put into a database the principles apply...Whenever a newspaper extracts information from its database and publishes it, that is disclosure' (Michael Tugendhat QC, later Mr Justice Tugendhat, in *The Yearbook of Copyright and Media Law 2000* (2000)).

It is worth noting that the vast majority of breaches of these Acts are not committed by journalists or news organisations, but by public bodies and companies that hold ever-increasing amounts of information about individuals which they either misuse, or, more often, fail to store securely.

Since the 1998 Act there have been numerous examples of the loss of laptops, computer hard drives, and memory sticks containing personal data. The failure by those who hold personal data to do so properly is a source of news on an almost daily basis.

▌ Data protection principles

The Act aims to ensure that people handling personal data comply with eight data protection principles. In brief, data must be:

- fairly and lawfully processed;
- processed for limited purposes;
- adequate, relevant, and not excessive;
- accurate;
- not kept longer than necessary;
- processed in accordance with the data subject's rights;
- secure;
- not transferred to countries without adequate protection.

The Act affects journalists in two ways. First, they may find it difficult to obtain information from authorities that are prevented from releasing such information, or believe themselves to be so prevented, or use the Act as an excuse for refusing to give information they do not wish to give.

Media concerns

In 2004 David Blunkett, then Home Secretary, promised the Newspaper Society, representing the local and regional newspapers, that he would listen to the media's concerns over data protection, after editors in a survey stressed the frequency with which public services tried to block inquiries and obstruct reporting by claiming – rightly or wrongly – that they could not give the information sought because of data protection restrictions.

Elizabeth France, Data Protection Commissioner (later Information Commissioner), said in her annual report in 2000 that 16 years after the original Act there still remained **data controllers** who misrepresented the → glossary nature of data protection law. They 'grasp the Act and wave it as though it were some hybrid garlic which might ward off information hungry vampires'.

Four years later, Ms France's successor as Information Commissioner, Richard Thomas, told the Society of Editors that the data protection law was being used improperly in 'many, many cases' where people found it difficult to respond to a legitimate request. He referred to a case where the organisers of a Women's Institute jam-making competition had not allowed the results to be published 'because of data protection'.

Journalists as 'data processors'

The second way the Act affects journalists is that, as people processing data themselves, they may have problems complying with the privacy rights of those about whom they hold information. In 2002 the supermodel Naomi Campbell was awarded £3,500 damages for breach of confidence and infringement of data protection rights over the *Daily Mirror's* publication of details about her therapy at Narcotics Anonymous (NA). (The finding was first overturned by the Court of Appeal, then, in 2004, upheld by the House of Lords (*Campbell v Mirror Group Newspapers Ltd* [2004] UKHL 22).)

A journalist who obtains personal data unlawfully commits an offence under section 55 of the 1998 Act. The offence forbids not only obtaining and disclosing, but also 'procuring the disclosure of', such data. It is punishable by a fine of up to £5,000 in a magistrates court or an unlimited amount on conviction in the Crown court. see below, p. 437

In 2006 the Information Commissioner urged Parliament to make the offence punishable by up to two years' imprisonment. In a report entitled 'What price privacy?' he said investigations by his office and the police had uncovered evidence of a widespread and organised undercover market in confidential personal information.

Among the 'buyers' were many journalists looking for a story, his report said. In one major case investigated by the commissioner's office the evidence included records of information supplied to 305 named journalists working for a range of newspapers.

▌ Provisions of the 1998 Act

The Act came into effect on 1 March 2000, but data already held in a manual filing system did not need to comply with many aspects of the new law until 2007.

The Act makes considerable use of its own jargon.

For journalists, the definition of 'data' in section 1(1) of the Act is particularly important.

Data means information that (among other things):

- is being processed by means of equipment operating automatically in response to instructions given for that purpose; and
- is recorded with the intention that it should be processed by means of such equipment.

In the Naomi Campbell case, the 'data' were held to include photographs of the model leaving an NA meeting.

Personal data means information which relates to a living individual who can be identified from those data and which either are processed electronically or, if manual, are held in 'a relevant filing system'. In 2003, the Court of Appeal held that incidental references to a person involved in a matter or an event 'that has no personal connotations' is not 'personal information' under the Act (*Durant v Financial Services Authority* [2003] EWCA Civ 1746). Following that decision, the Information Commissioner issued revised guidelines on what 'personal data' means (available at www.ico.gov.uk/ under 'Data Protection').

Processing means:

❝ • obtaining, recording or holding the information or data or carrying out any operation or set of operations on the information or data, including:
  – organisation, adaptation or alteration of the information or data,
  – retrieval, consultation or use of the information or data,
  – disclosure of the information or data by transmission, dissemination or otherwise making available, or
  – alignment, combination, blocking, erasure or destruction of the information or data. ❞

A *relevant filing system* has a lengthy and complicated definition. The Minister introducing the Bill into Parliament said it would apply to highly structured systems such as card indexes, but would exclude collections of paper which only incidentally contained information about individuals. The Court of Appeal in the *Durant* case took the same view.

A *data controller* determines the purposes for which and the manner in which any personal data are processed. Data controllers include magistrates courts, the police, and local authorities, and also all newspapers that keep personal data about people on computer or in structured filing systems.

A *data subject* is a person about whom the information is held – in media terms, the person about whom the reporter is writing his/her story or any third parties who may be referred to or identified in the report.

Under the Act, data are processed for *special purposes* when they are processed for journalistic, literary, or artistic purposes.

▶ The data protection principles

The principles, summarised above, are contained in Schedule 1 to the Act and are, in full:

(1) Personal data shall be processed fairly and lawfully and, in particular, shall not be processed unless certain conditions are met (see 'Fairly and lawfully', below).

(2) Personal data shall be obtained only for one or more specified and lawful purposes, and shall not be further processed in any manner incompatible with that purpose or those purposes.

(3) Personal data shall be adequate, relevant, and not excessive in relation to the purpose or purposes for which they are processed.

(4) Personal data shall be accurate and, where necessary, kept up to date.

(5) Personal data processed for any purpose or purposes shall not be kept for longer than is necessary for that purpose or those purposes.

(6) Personal data shall be processed in accordance with the rights of data subjects under this Act.

(7) Appropriate technical and organisational measures shall be taken against unauthorised or unlawful processing of personal data and against accidental loss or destruction of, or damage to, personal data.

(8) Personal data shall not be transferred to a country or territory outside the European Economic Area unless that country or territory ensures an adequate level of protection for the rights and freedoms of data subjects in relation to the processing of personal data.

'Fairly and lawfully'

As stated, personal data shall be processed fairly and lawfully. In particular, they must not be processed at all unless at least one of a number of conditions set out in Schedule 2 to the Act is met. For the purposes of a journalist attempting to obtain information to write a story the most relevant Schedule 2 conditions would seem to include (either because they apply to the journalist him/herself, or to the data controller from whom he or she hopes to obtain the information):

- Paragraph 1. The data subject has given his consent to the processing.

- Paragraph 3. The processing is necessary for compliance with any legal obligation to which the data controller is subject.

- Paragraph 5. The processing is necessary –
  (a) for the administration of justice,
  (b) for the exercise of any functions conferred on any person by or under any enactment,
  (c) for the exercise of any functions of the crown, a Minister of the crown, or a government department, or
  (d) for the exercise of any other functions of a public nature exercised in the public interest by any person.

- Paragraph 6. The processing is necessary for the purposes of legitimate interests pursued by the data controller or by the third party or parties to whom the data are disclosed, except where the processing is unwarranted in any particular case by reason of prejudice to the rights and freedoms or legitimate interest of the data subject.

Sensitive personal data

The Act provides even stronger protection to 'sensitive personal data', which means information about:

- the racial or ethnic origin of the data subject;
- political opinions;

- religious beliefs or other beliefs of a similar nature;
- membership of a trade union;
- physical or mental health or condition;
- sexual life;
- commission or alleged commission of any offence; or
- any proceedings for any offence committed or alleged to have been committed, the disposal of such proceedings, or the sentence of any court in such proceedings.

The judge in the Naomi Campbell case held that the information about the nature of and details of the therapy that Miss Campbell was seeking was 'sensitive personal data' under the fifth of the above items – physical or mental health.

Sensitive personal data can be processed only if *two* conditions are met, one of them from the Schedule 2 list above and the other from a list contained in Schedule 3: for example, the person gave 'explicit' consent; or he/she deliberately made the information public; or the use to which the information was to be put was necessary for the administration of justice.

As a result of media representations, the Government introduced a **statutory instrument** that extended the Schedule 3 list of conditions and included an additional 'special purposes' condition. The media had been concerned that the new law created new problems over access to information. The statutory instrument widened the grounds for any third party's lawful release of information to the media for publication by adding another 'gateway' for the lawful processing of sensitive personal data. Editors may wish to refer to this measure to resolve disputes with such organisations. It is the Data Protection (Processing of Sensitive Personal Data) Order 2000 (SI 2000/417), which may be read on www.hmso.gov.uk/si/si2000/20000417.htm   →glossary

The statutory instrument sets out 10 circumstances in which sensitive personal data may be processed. Several require that the processing is 'in the substantial public interest'.

For journalists the most important is contained in paragraph 3 which covers disclosures for journalistic, artistic, or literary purposes of personal data relating to:

(1) the commission by any person of any unlawful act (whether alleged or established);

(2) dishonesty, malpractice, or other seriously improper conduct by, or the unfitness or incompetence of, any person (whether alleged or established); or

(3) mismanagement in the administration of, or failures in services provided by, any body or association (whether alleged or established).

Other paragraphs include the following:

- Paragraph 1 covers certain processing for the prevention or detection of any unlawful act, where seeking the consent of the data subject to the processing would prejudice those purposes.

- Paragraph 2 is for cases where the processing is required to discharge functions which protect members of the public from certain conduct which may not constitute an unlawful act, such as incompetence or mismanagement.

- Paragraph 10 covers processing by the police in the exercise of their **common law** powers.

→ glossary

Why did this statutory instrument not provide a defence to the *Daily Mirror* against Naomi Campbell? Remember that the Schedule 2 and Schedule 3 conditions are not exemptions. Even if those conditions are met, processing must also be 'fair and lawful'. As the House of Lords reached the decision that the *Daily Mirror* coverage of Naomi Campbell's therapy for drug abuse breached her confidence, it could not be said to be 'lawful'.

▶ Data protection and the Human Rights Act 1998

Editors in conflict with public bodies proving reluctant to impart information should remind them that the Human Rights Act 1998 (HRA) requires public authorities to act in a way that is consistent with the European Convention on Human Rights (ECHR), which includes a guarantee of freedom of expression, including the right to receive and impart information.

→

see ch.2, p. 29 on ACPO guidelines

'Media Guidelines' circulated by the Association of Chief Police Officers (ACPO) in 2000 remind chief constables that the HRA requires that each police officer and member of the civilian support staff, 'as a "public authority", must act in a way which is at all times consistent with the ECHR'.

The guidelines say that many of the Convention's provisions directly affect the release of information by police to the media. These provisions include Article 3, which provides protection against inhuman and degrading treatment; Article 6, which establishes the right to a fair trial; Article 8, which concerns the right to respect for private and family life; and Article 10, concerning the right to freedom of expression.

The police guidelines say the principles of proportionality, legality, and necessity must all be considered in making decisions where questions of human rights are involved.

▶ Notification

The Information Commissioner keeps a public register of data controllers. The process by which their details are added to the register is called notification.

The fact of notification does not mean that a data user is free to release *any* information it wishes or the journalist wishes to receive. The data controller still needs to ensure that the **disclosure** complies with the data protection principles. → glossary

Data controllers are under a positive obligation to tell data subjects all the purposes to which they are going to put their data.

The requirement to register affects media managements principally, but freelances working from home and keeping their material on computer or in 'structured manual files' should register also because they are not holding that data simply for domestic purposes.

▶ The courts

Some journalists have had difficulty obtaining information from the courts. Magistrates courts use guidelines prepared by the Justices' Clerks' Society which state that a clerk could be found to have unfairly processed information in breach of the DPA if 'restricted' information were to be published. The guidelines were prepared with the assistance of the Data Protection Registrar (now Information Commissioner), who provided the following summary.

❝❝ The guidelines take into account the stage in the judicial process reached by a particular case – that is, whether it is pending, current, or completed.

For current cases, disclosure of information that has been heard in open court may be appropriate. However, with regard to disclosure of information regarding completed cases, disclosure is at the discretion of the clerk because the court register is not a public document and is governed by the Magistrates' Courts Rules....

see ch. 12, p. 199

It is therefore for the clerk to determine disclosure policy. The guidance suggests that disclosure within a specific period might be appropriate but after that the clerk may wish to exercise more discretion.

For that reason, on receipt of a request for disclosure, the clerk will need to consider:

- at what stage the proceedings are;
- whether the information requested has been given in open court; and
- whether there are any unfair implications for the individual. **"**

'Media Guidance' issued to court staff by Her Majesty's Courts Service – which provides adminstration and support for courts, including Crown courts and majestrates courts – makes clear that a defendant's address may be supplied to reporters even if it has not been read out in court, and that the Data Protection Act should not be used as 'a blanket excuse for withholding information' (*Media Lawyer*, Issue 72, 2007).

▌ The police

Journalists, even when engaged in routine reporting tasks, frequently have difficulty obtaining information from the police, who say they are prevented by the provisions of the Data Protection Act. This view is frequently based upon a misunderstanding of the Act.

Two main problem areas are the identification of people involved in road accidents and the victims of crime.

ACPO guidelines

see also
p. 430

The ACPO guidelines say the wishes of the victim, witnesses, or next of kin, where necessary, must be sought at the earliest possible stage before deciding how to publicise a crime, road accident, or any other incident, in accordance with the Data Protection Act.

The guidelines say that when victims or other people who have provided their personal details to police say that their details should not be released to the media, this request should be honoured unless police feel on a case-by-case basis that there is an exceptional reason why such details must be given.

Except in certain circumstances (see below), victims, witnesses, or next of kin are entitled not to have their personal details released without their permission. They are not, however, entitled to ask that police release no information of the incident whatsoever.

The Data Protection Act does not apply to dead people. Victims may therefore be named once positive identification has taken place and immediate relatives have been told.

In certain circumstances, the guidelines say, the Data Protection Act allows for information to be released without the permission of the individual or individuals concerned. The guidelines say that circumstances in which details might be released without the consent of the people concerned would include a major incident involving multiple victims: in such an event it would be a legitimate 'policing purpose' to release casualties' identities before formal authority is obtained, to minimise public alarm and distress, and would thus satisfy the DPA.

The guidelines say there will be frequent occasions when members of the media come to the police seeking further details about information they have received from other sources. Even if authority has not been given, a judgement will have to be made on the course of action to take. Where a person's identity is already in the public domain such a request will often provide an opportunity for the police to give the journalist accurate information or to counter rumour and speculation.

One criticism among many made by journalists is that the police, when asking victims if they object to identification, do so in a manner inviting the answer no. The guidelines say it is important when dealing with all victims, witnesses, or next of kin that police should ask a balanced question to establish consent. In many cases such people are likely to agree.

It is recommended that they should be asked the question, 'We often find it helpful in our inquiries to pass on someone's details to the media. Do you object if we do that in your case?'

ACPO stresses that the notes are for guidance only. It is a matter for chief constables whether and how they should be implemented.

A 'policing purpose'

Data obtained and processed under the Act must be for a specified and lawful purpose. Under the 1984 Act this purpose was registered, in the case of the police, as being for a 'policing purpose'. The Data Protection Registrar (now Commissioner) defined this as:

❝ the prevention and detection of crime, apprehension and prosecution of offenders, protection of life and property, maintenance of law and order, and rendering assistance to the public in accordance with force policies and procedures. 🔊

The ACPO guidelines say that to this should be added 'reducing the fear of crime'.

Children and data protection

see
ch. 26,
'Children
and priv-
acy',
p. 441

The issue of children and data protection is covered in a separate chapter.

▶ Rights of data 'subjects'

People have the right to find out whether an organisation, including a media organisation, holds information about them and if so what it is. They must be told also the purposes for which such information is held and to whom it is or may be disclosed; and also the source of the information.

The 1984 Act had the effect of preserving the confidentiality of journalists' sources by stipulating that a data user did not have to comply with an access request if he could not do so without disclosing information relating to another individual who could be identified by that information – unless that individual consented.

The 1998 Act says the access request must be complied with, even in the absence of the consent of the other individual, if it is reasonable in all the circumstances to comply without that consent. But the lawyer Heather Rowe, a data protection expert, summing up the complex measure for *McNae*, said: 'To my mind the provisions all say, taken together, that you do not have to name a source unless there is something like a court order that makes you do so.'

Under the 1984 Act the data subject could have the data item corrected if it was wrong and claim compensation if he or she had suffered damage. Under the 1998 Act, where rights have been contravened for special purposes (which include journalism), the subject does not have to prove any damage before claiming damages for distress.

Under the 1984 Act the right of compensation arose only from loss from inaccuracy of or unauthorised disclosure of personal data. The right of compensation now is for damage caused by any breach of the Act.

Damages for infringement of rights under the 1998 Act were awarded to the film stars Michael Douglas and Catherine Zeta-Jones, after *Hello!*

magazine published snatched pictures of their wedding. But they were awarded only £50 each.

A data subject has the right in some circumstances to require a data controller to cease processing data referring to him.

Protection from gagging orders

An individual is entitled to require a data controller to cease processing any personal data referring to him or her on the ground that this would cause or be likely to cause substantial damage or substantial distress either to the individual or to another, and that the damage or distress would be unwarranted.

Thus, if there was no protection for the media, a villain being investigated by the press might make a subject access request to obtain a copy of information being held about him, and then use that information as evidence to support an application for an **injunction** ('gagging order') or other civil   → glossary
action.

But the Act does provide such a protection. Under section 32 an injunction to prevent the processing of data must be 'stayed' if the processing relates only to journalistic, literary, or artistic purposes, the material concerned has not previously been published, and the other conditions referred to below are fulfilled.

The stay is until either the claim is withdrawn or the Commissioner determines whether or not the exemption applies.

Exemption for journalistic work

In the Naomi Campbell case, the paper argued that it had a defence under section 32 for its story about the treatment being received by the model, but the trial judge rejected this argument, saying the defence applied only to the processing of data before publication (that is, to prevent gagging orders), not after.

Fortunately for the media, the Court of Appeal rejected that ruling and held that the defence applied both before and after publication; 'fortunately' because the appeal judges said that section 32 provided the *only* defence available to the paper in this case.

Section 32 of the Act says that personal data which are processed only for 'special purposes' (journalistic, literary, or artistic purposes) are exempt from any provisions of the 1998 Act relating to:

(1) the data protection principles (except for requirements to keep data secure – the seventh data protection principle);

(2) subject access;

(3) the right to prevent processing likely to cause damage or distress;

(4) prevention of automated decision-taking; and

(5) rights to rectification, blocking, erasure, and destruction.

The exemption applies only if the processing is undertaken with a view to the publication of special purposes material that has not been published; the Act says 'material which, at the time 24 hours immediately before the relevant time, had not previously been published by the data controller'.

In addition, the exemption applies only if the newspaper or broadcaster reasonably believes that:

(1) having regard in particular to the special importance of the public interest in freedom of expression, publication would be in the public interest; and

(2) in all the circumstances, compliance with the rules in the 1998 Act is incompatible with the journalistic purposes.

In considering whether the belief of the newspaper that publication would be in the public interest is reasonable, regard may be had to its compliance with 'any relevant code of practice'.

The *Daily Mirror* was able to persuade the Court of Appeal (but not the House of Lords) that its story and pictures on Naomi Campbell were fair and lawful and complied with all these requirements. Under section 32(1)(a) of the Act, the processing of the data was undertaken with a view to the publica-

→ glossary   tion of **journalistic material**. Under section 32(1)(b), the data controller reasonably believed that publication would be in the public interest (to correct untruths told by Ms Campbell). Under section 32(1)(c) the data controller reasonably believed that, in all the circumstances, compliance with the provision was incompatible with the 'special purposes' (journalistic purposes) because the paper had approached Miss Campbell's agent, who had refused permission. The paper's case was helped also by the fact that it had complied with the PCC code, in accordance with section 32(3) of the Act.

The House of Lords, however, found for the model after a majority of the judges held that some elements of the *Daily Mirror*'s coverage of her visit to a Narcotics Anonymous session breached her confidence and was therefore unlawful.

▶ Enforcement

If the Commissioner is satisfied that a data controller has contravened a data protection principle, he can serve an enforcement notice requiring compliance. Failure to comply with such a notice is an offence.

The Act includes wide powers of entry and inspection which may be exercised by the information commissioner. These powers can be exercised only under a warrant granted by a **circuit judge** (in Northern Ireland by a →glossary county court judge). A judge must not issue a warrant relating to personal data processed for the 'special purposes' (including journalism) unless the Commissioner has determined whether such data fall within the special purposes exemption.

Although the 1984 Act made it an offence for a data user (now data controller) to disclose data to someone he/she knew was not entitled to receive it, no specific criminal offence was committed by people *obtaining* such information.

Thus in 1992 the *Sun* newspaper was able to reveal, without infringing the Act, that the Chancellor of the Exchequer at that time, Norman Lamont, had exceeded his credit card limit 21 times, information held on computer which could have been obtained only by improper disclosure.

But, as stated earlier, the offence of unlawfully obtaining personal information is now covered by section 55(1) of the 1998 Act. This states that:

  ❝ A person must not knowingly or recklessly, without the consent of the data controller –
  (a) obtain or disclose personal data or the information contained in personal data, or
  (b) procure the disclosure to another person of the information contained in personal data. ❞

Defences are available to those, among others, who act in the reasonable belief they would have obtained permission from the data controller for their actions, and to anyone who shows that obtaining, disclosing, or procuring the information was 'in the public interest'.

Section 55 offences may be prosecuted at the instigation of the Information Commissioner or the Director of Public Prosecutions, and tried in a magistrates court or the Crown court. They are punishable by a fine of up to £5,000 in a magistrates court or an unlimited fine for conviction in the Crown court.

Prison sentences

After two reports by the Information Commissioner entitled, *What Price Privacy?* and *What Price Privacy Now?*, published in 2006, the Government proposed to introduce jail terms of up to two years for anyone who unlawfully obtains or uses information covered by the DPA. The measure was included in section 77 of the Criminal Justice and Immigration Act 2008, but the idea of putting this new law into effect was shelved after lobbying by the media and concern being expressed in Parliament about the measure's potential to deter investigative journalism in the public interest.

There have only been a small number of prosecutions for a breach of section 55 of the DPA. The European Court of Human Rights in *Cumpana v Romania* (2005) 41 EHHR 14 in 2004 said that intrusion on freedom of expression could only be justified in cases of pressing social need, which the prosecution figures for DPA breaches do not appear to bear out.

Before a Secretary of State introduces the imprisonment powers in the Criminal Justice and Immigration Act 2008, he or she must consult first, with media organisations in particular. At the time *McNae* went to press, no such consultation had happened.

The 2008 Act included, after lobbying by the media, a new defence to a charge of unlawfully obtaining personal data. This defence will be inserted into section 55 of the DPA at some future date of the Government's choice. The defence will be available to a person if he/she acted 'with a view to the publication by any person of any journalistic, literary or artistic material', with 'the reasonable belief that in the particular circumstances the obtaining, disclosing or procuring was justified as being in the public interest'.

▓ Recap of major points

- The Data Protection Act 1998 protects information held about people on computers and in 'structured manual files'.
- The definition of personal data is so wide that it covers the normal operations of any media produced with the aid of integrated computerised systems.
- The Act says data must be:
    - fairly and lawfully processed;
    - processed for limited purposes;
    - adequate, relevant, and not excessive;

-    accurate;
-    not kept longer than necessary;
-    processed in accordance with the data subject's rights;
-    secure;
-    not transferred to countries without adequate protection.

- Data are not processed fairly and lawfully unless at least one of a number of specific conditions (e.g. that the subject has given his consent) is met.

- The Act provides even stronger protection to 'sensitive personal data', such as information about the subject's racial or ethnic origin.

- It is acceptable for schools to release examination results to the media, the Information Commissioner says, provided the school has told parents that it is its policy to release such lists. Thus, any parent who does not wish his or her child to be included in the list can object.

- Section 32 of the Act provides that an injunction to prevent the media from publishing personal data must be 'stayed' if the publishing relates only to journalistic purposes and other conditions have been fulfilled.

- The media can have to pay damages for infringing data rights.

- It is a criminal offence to procure the disclosure of personal data.

- The Act includes wide powers of entry and inspection that may be exercised by the Commissioner for the detection both of data protection offences and of breaches of data protection principles.

- Powers of imprisonment have been enacted under the Criminal Justice and Immigration Act 2008, but are subject to a consultation before they can be enforced.

🌐 Useful Websites

www.ico.gov.uk/
    Information Commissioner's website
www.hmso.gov.uk/si/si2000/20000417.htm
    Data Protection (Processing of Sensitive Personal Data) Order 2000

26

Children and privacy

Chapter summary

There are a number of issues particular to media reporting of children that can give rise to legal difficulties. Organisations reluctant to divulge information have often cited data protection law as a reason for refusing the media seemingly innocuous information. This chapter will explain the laws and codes which apply and when such refusals to provide information ought to be challenged by the media.

▌ Do children have any special protection?

Unlike the criminal law, which affords protection of anonymity to children in many circumstances during and after proceedings, in areas such as privacy, children have no special protection. The laws of breach of confidence, privacy, and data protection have not been framed, by statute or **case law**, with special provision for children in mind.

→glossary

However, the parents and guardians of children are sometimes more willing to pursue actions to protect a child's privacy than they would be if the **claimant** was an adult.

→glossary

Schools, in particular, have demonstrated a willingness to cite the law as a reason for refusing to divulge details about children. Their actions may be motivated by a desire to protect the children, but the effect can be to prevent coverage of childhood achievements, which have been the standard fare of regional newspapers for decades and which until now have often provided treasured cuttings for the child subjects and their families.

▶ Laws used to protect children's privacy

The following cases illustrate the way in which a variety of laws are used to prevent disclosure of information about children.

The Data Protection Act 1998

Schools have cited this Act as a reason for refusing to allow photographs of school sports teams; traditional first-year primary school 'starters'; drama productions; and nativity plays.

Part of the reason for this was fear that photographs and video footage might lead to children being targeted by paedophiles. Some local education authorities told newspapers that they would no longer provide the names of children photographed for news items, rendering some stories about individual achievements virtually impossible to report.

It would seem the schools and education authorities had misinterpreted government guidance on the issue relating to placing of images and video on school websites, which they had then applied to photography by press and parents.

In 2003 the Department of Education (now the Department for Children, Schools and Families) sent out advice, which is available on www.teachernet.gov. uk/wholeschool/familyandcommunity/childprotection/usefulinformation/pressphotos/.

It said schools and local education authorities were free to develop their own policies with the press to publish photographs of pupils taking part in school activities and events. It said: 'We recognise that local newspapers play an important part in reporting the achievements and challenges facing local schools and their pupils, and therefore a co-operative arrangement should be beneficial.'

The guidance also quoted Richard Thomas, the Information Commissioner, who said:

- 'Where schools merely allow access to a local newspaper photographer, they are not caught by the DPA unless they provide the personal details of the pupils in the photographs.'

- 'If the names of those in the photograph were collected directly from the participants (subject to the wishes of parents and guardians of pupils) the school would not be releasing personal data subject to the Act at all.'
- 'Alternatively, if the school had canvassed the wishes of parents and guardians and they had agreed to the release then there would be no questions of the DPA preventing disclosure.'

The Information Commissioner's Office issued further guidance in 2007 reiterating that photography and video footage of events such as school nativity plays were not a breach of the DPA. It said the DPA did apply to the taking of photos of children for something such as a security pass.

Exam results and the Data Protection Act

The Information Commissioner's Office issued guidance in 2007 saying it was wrong to use the DPA as a reason to refuse to release exam results to the media.

David Smith, Deputy Commissioner at the Information Commissioner's Office (ICO), said: 'Publishing examination results is a common and accepted practice and many students enjoy seeing their name in print; it is a myth that the Data Protection Act stops this from happening.'

He said schools had to release such results fairly and should tell pupils and parents what the policy was and consider seriously any objections.

Does the law give greater protection to children?

A case which may clarify the extent to which privacy law gives greater protection to children was due to be tried in 2009.

The action was brought by J K Rowling, author of the Harry Potter series of children's books in respect of her son, David. He was photographed when aged 19 months as his parents took him for a walk in his buggy near the family home in Edinburgh.

Ms Rowling, taking the action under her real name, Joanne Murray, and her husband Neil sued claiming the photographs, taken by Big Pictures UK Ltd agency, were an infringement of their son's right to privacy and a breach of the Data Protection Act.

The court's view on this will be interesting, as an adult on a public street would not normally have an expectation of privacy.

In an appeal hearing on the case the Master of the Rolls, Sir Anthony Clarke, sitting with Lord Justice Laws and Lord Justice Thomas, said: 'If a child of parents who are not in the public eye could reasonably expect not to have photographs of him published in the media, so too should the child of a famous parent' (*Murray v Big Pictures UK Ltd* [2008] EWCA 446).

Voyeurism

In 2009, the Holdthefrontpage website reported that a police officer had told a reporter from the *St Albans Review* to destroy pictures he had taken of people sledging in a public park, because they might amount to an act of voyeurism. The reporter was taking pictures after a fall of snow, but was threatened by a man who thought he had been taking images of his children.

When the police arrived they threatened to confiscate the reporter's cameraphone as evidence of an act of voyeurism unless the reporter destroyed the images.

The Ofcom code, people under 16, and vulnerable people

The Ofcom Broadcasting Code says that broadcasters should pay particular attention to the privacy of people under 16. They do not lose their rights to privacy because, for example, of the fame or notoriety of their parents or because of events in their schools.

→ see ch. 1, p. 16

In 2006 Ofcom held that the inclusion in a news broadcast of images of children aged five and two as they accompanied their parents to court to attend a sentencing hearing for another family member was an unwarranted infringement of their privacy. The children were the nieces of Maxine Carr, former girlfriend of the murderer Ian Huntley. Ofcom took into account the vulnerability of the children and the high-profile nature of the case, which involved Ms Carr's mother.

Where a programme features an individual under 16 or a vulnerable person in a way that infringes privacy, consent must be obtained from:

- a parent, guardian, or other person of 18 or over in loco parentis; and
- wherever possible, the individual concerned;

unless the subject matter is trivial or uncontroversial and the participation minor, or it is warranted to proceed without consent.

People under 16 and vulnerable people should not be questioned about private matters without the consent of a parent, guardian, or other person of 18 or over in loco parentis (in the case of people under 16), or a person with primary responsibility for their care (in the case of a vulnerable person), unless it is warranted to proceed without consent.

The code says 'vulnerable people' include those with learning difficulties, those with mental health problems, the bereaved, people with brain damage or forms of dementia, and people who have been traumatised or who are sick or terminally ill.

▌ The Press Complaints Commission code

see ch. 1,
p. 17 on
code

→
see
also ch.
35, pp.
545–546

Clause 6 of the Press Complaints Commission code states that:

- young people should be free to complete their time at school without unnecessary intrusion;

- a child under 16 must not be interviewed or photographed on issues involving their own or another child's welfare unless a custodial parent or similarly responsible adult consents;

- pupils must not be approached or photographed at school without the permission of the school authorities;

- minors must not be paid for material involving children's welfare, nor parents or guardians for material about their children or wards, unless it is clearly in the child's interest;

- editors must not use the fame, notoriety, or position of a parent or guardian as sole justification for publishing details of a child's private life.

⸬ Recap of major points

- The Data Protection Act 1998 has been given as a reason for refusal to provide information concerning children.

- The sorts of events where the media have been denied information include nativity plays, school sports events, and school drama productions.

- The Information Commissioner's Office has issued repeated guidance saying that such bans are not justified by the DPA.

- The Department for Education (now the Department for Children, Schools and Families) has also issued similar advice.

- A case brought by the author J K Rowling in 2009 may resolve some issues concerning privacy, the DPA, and children of celebrities.

- The Ofcom code says particular attention should be paid to the privacy of children under 16.

🌐 Useful Websites

www.teachernet.gov.uk/wholeschool/familyandcommunity/childprotection/
usefulinformation/pressphotos/
DCSF advice on photography

http://www.ico.gov.uk/
Information Commissioner's Office

27

Copyright

Chapter summary

Copyright protects intellectual property. This chapter sets out how the law functions to protect such works; what is protected; and how much of a copyrighted work a journalist may use without fear of an action for breach of copyright. It also explains how long copyright lasts; the penalties for breach of copyright; and measures available to prevent such breaches. The internet has made a great deal of imagery available to journalists, but as this chapter explains, much of it is subject to the protection of copyright.

▶ What is protected by copyright?

Copyright is a branch of intellectual property law and it protects the products of people's skill, creativity, labour, or time.

Under the Copyright, Designs and Patents Act 1988 (the Copyright Act), copyright protects any literary, dramatic, artistic, or musical work, sound recording, film, broadcast, or typographical arrangement. Artistic works include photographs and graphics (see below). Copyright does not have to be registered.

Reproduction of a substantial part of a copyright work may constitute infringement. Whether the part of a copyright work which is copied is a substantial part may depend as much on the quality (the importance) of what is reproduced as on the quantity (*Sweeney v Macmillan Publishers Ltd* [2001] All ER (D) 332 (Nov)).

However, for a work to be protected by copyright it must satisfy the test of originality. Some work or effort must have gone into it. Brief slogans and catch-phrases have been ruled to be too trivial to be protected by copyright.

Copyright in news stories

There is no copyright in facts, news, ideas, or information. Copyright exists in the form in which information is expressed and the selection and arrangement of the material – all of which involves skill and labour.

Sir Nicolas Browne-Wilkinson, Vice-Chancellor (later Lord Browne-Wilkinson), said in the Chancery Division in February 1990 that it was very improbable that the courts would hold there was copyright in a news story, *as opposed to the actual words used*. This idea that there can be no copyright of a fact was reiterated in the judgment when Dan Brown, author of *The Da Vinci Code* was sued, unsuccessfully, for breach of copyright by Michael Baigent and Richard Leigh, two of the three authors of *The Holy Blood And The Holy Grail*, a judgment upheld on appeal (*Michael Baigent and Richard Leigh v Random House Ltd* [2007] EWCA Civ 247).

While there is no copyright in a news story, persistent lifting of facts from another paper, even if there is rewriting each time, may still be an infringement because of the skill, labour, and judgement that went into research on the stories. The defence of **fair dealing** for reporting current events will, however, sometimes allow some quoting from another paper. → see below, p. 451

Literary work is protected by copyright as soon as it is recorded in writing or otherwise and such work includes newspapers and the writing that goes into them.

Material from contributors

Copyright in material supplied to newspapers by outside contributors, whether paid or not, will normally be owned by the contributor. For example, a person sending a reader's letter for publication will by implication have licensed the newspaper to use his or her copyright work freely on one occasion, while still retaining the copyright. On the other hand an editor who uses a freelance writer's article sent in without first negotiating the fee may be in difficulty.

Results and listings

An official of a sporting or trade association may find it part of his duty to make material available to the paper free of charge but the copyright is still the association's and it can withdraw the facility, or start to make a charge, or prevent another journal from copying it.

This applies to much material available to newspapers – TV and radio programmes, sporting fixtures, lists of events, and tide tables. The company whose employee compiled the material owns the copyright.

TV images

Publication without permission of a photograph of the whole or a substantial part of a television image is an infringement under section 17 of the Copyright Act.

Under the Broadcasting Act 1990, those who provide a broadcast service (and own the copyright in the programme listings) must make information about the programmes available to any newspaper or magazine publisher wishing to use it, through a licensing scheme. In case of dispute as to the charge to be made by the broadcasting organisation for the use of the information, the matter is decided by the Copyright Tribunal.

▌ Copyright in maps and drawings

To publish without permission the whole or part of an artistic work such as a map or drawing, where the copyright is owned by another, will constitute infringement, as for example where an artist on a newspaper or magazine adapts a map as a basis for his own sketch to illustrate a story or feature. In 2001, Centrica, the company which owns the Automobile Association, agreed to pay £20 million in an out-of-court settlement to Ordnance Survey for the use of OS maps as its source material to create its own maps. Ordnance Survey had introduced subtle errors into its maps to catch out plagiarists.

▌ Copyright in speeches

Under the 1988 Act, there is copyright in spoken words, even if they are not delivered from a script, as soon as they are recorded, with or without the speaker's permission.

The speaker, as the author of a literary work, owns the copyright in his/her words, unless he/she is speaking in the course of his/her employment.

Under section 58 of the Act, it is not infringement to use the record of the words for reporting current events, subject to four conditions:

(1) The record is a direct record and not taken from a previous record or broadcast.

(2) The speaker did not prohibit the making of the record and it did not infringe any existing copyright.

(3) The use being made of the record, or material taken from it, was not of a kind prohibited by the speaker or copyright owner before the record was made.

(4) The use being made of the record is with the authority of the person who is lawfully in possession of it.

It is possible that limited use of a speaker's words might be covered by fair dealing.

→ see below, p. 451

It seems that surreptitious recording of a speaker's words is not a breach of copyright in itself. Once the words have been recorded, however, there is copyright in them and it will be owned by the speaker. In many cases, there will be a separate copyright in the record because of the skill involved in making it. In certain circumstances there might be an action available for breach of confidence.

→ see ch. 23, p. 383

Copyright in the speaker's words is not infringed in reporting parliamentary or judicial proceedings.

Embargoed speeches

Apart from any copyright in the spoken word, there is a copyright in the manuscript from which a speaker reads.

In this way, Buckingham Palace made legal history in 1993 when it used copyright law to take legal action for breach of an embargo. The *Sun*, together with other newspapers, had been sent copies of the Queen's 1992 Christmas Day message, embargoed until after it had been broadcast. The *Sun* published the message on 23 December under the headline 'Our difficult days, by the Queen'.

In 2006 the Prince of Wales used copyright as part of his case against the *Mail on Sunday* for its publication of his journals written while on a visit to China in which he described the country's leadership as 'appalling old waxworks'.

See ch. 23, p. 396 and ch. 24, where the case brought by the Prince of Wales is discussed in greater detail.

◗ Who owns the copyright?

The first owner of a copyright work created after 31 July 1989 (when the 1988 Act came into force) is the author but in the case of work done in the course of employment the employer is the owner, subject to any agreement to the contrary.

There is no automatic right on the part of a newspaper or magazine or periodical to the copyright of work done by non-members of the staff, even if the work has been ordered.

The copyright can be assigned to the newspaper, or magazine, or periodical but an assignment is not effective unless in writing signed by the copyright owner. The owner can license the publisher to use the work but if it is an exclusive licence this also must be in writing.

Ownership of copyright in photographs

Where a photograph is commissioned from a freelance or commercial photographer today, the copyright is owned by the photographer (or his employer) unless there is an agreement to the contrary. If the photograph was taken before the 1988 Act came into force, however, the copyright will be owned by the person or company who commissioned it, even though the photographer or his employer will own the negatives or film.

Breaches can be expensive. In 2005 English Basketball paid £45,000 in an out-of-court settlement to freelance photographer Chris Tofalos after it used his photographs without authorisation.

In 2007, News Group, publisher of the *News of the World* and the *Sun*, won £30,000 damages with £40,000 costs against the owners of the 'Robbs Celebs' website, which used photographs lifted from News Group publications.

Moral rights in photographs

 →glossary

A person who commissions a photograph for private and domestic purposes is protected by one of the 1988 Act's **moral rights** – the right not to have copies of the photograph issued to the public even if he does not own the copyright.

This has implications for the reporter who borrows a photograph, for example of a wedding, when the bride or bridegroom comes into the news months or years afterwards. The relative who lends the photograph to the reporter is unlikely to own the copyright and may not have commissioned the taking of it in the first place.

If the paper were to publish the photograph (provided it was taken after 31 July 1989) two rights may be said to have been infringed – that of the photographer (who owned the copyright unless there was an agreement to the contrary) and that of the bride/bridegroom who commissioned it and has the right not to have it made available to the public.

The photographer may be glad to accept a fee for publication of his copyright picture but the response of the bridegroom may raise problems under the 1988 Act.

Photographs on social networking sites

The internet has made imagery available that in the past could only have been obtained with the permission of copyright holders. However, downloading and publishing images from social networking sites, even though they are apparently in the public domain, may infringe the copyright of the website, or the person who took the picture uploaded on to the site.

▌ Crown copyright

Work produced by civil servants in the course of their employment is protected by Crown copyright, which has been used in the courts to prevent the publication of material and to threaten former public servants with action for revealing matters concerning their employment.

In 2004 the wife of Charles Bronson, a man sometimes referred to as Britain's most dangerous prisoner, failed in a High Court bid to obtain a ruling that she could use pictures of their wedding in an autobiography. The pictures had been taken by a prison officer using prison equipment, giving rise to Crown copyright in the pictures.

▌ Defence of fair dealing

Fair dealing with a copyright work (apart from a photograph) for the purpose of reporting current events is not an infringement provided it is accompanied by sufficient acknowledgement of the work and its author and provided the work has been made available to the public.

No defence for use of photgraphs

Section 30 of the Copyright Designs and Patents Act 1988 excludes photographs from the defence of fair dealing. This has led to disputes when one paper has lifted exclusive pictures from another. In 2005 the *Daily Mail* and the *Sun* were in dispute after the *Mail* used a cropped picture of the *Sun*'s front page carrying a picture of Prince Harry wearing a Nazi uniform with a swastika armband. The lifting of pictures is common but in the case of *Francois-Marie Banier v News Group Newspapers Ltd* ((1997) *The Times*, 21 June) Mr Justice Lightman said that while the practice might be widespread, it was unlawful.

In 1991, Mr Justice Scott dismissed a copyright action brought by the BBC against British Satellite Broadcasting over the use on the satellite company's sports programme of highlights from BBC coverage of the World Cup finals. The BBC had bought exclusive rights. He held that the use of short clips varying from 14 to 37 seconds, with a BBC credit line, up to four times in 24 hours was protected by the defence of fair dealing for reporting current events.

Criticism and reviews

Fair dealing with a copyright work (including a photograph) for the purposes of criticism or review of that work or of another will also not be treated as infringement, subject again to sufficient acknowledgement and to the work having been made available to the public. This allows for reporting which quotes from books, plays, films, and broadcasts, when writing a criticism, story, or feature.

Works must be available to the public

The importance of a work having been made available to the public is emphasised by changes to copyright law brought about as a result of the implementation of the European Information Society Directive 2001/29/EC by way of the Copyright and Related Rights Regulations 2003 (SI 2003/2498). This directive said that only works that had been lawfully made available to the public could be used for criticism or review by way of fair dealing.

The potential implications of this change for journalists are clear from the use by former royal butler, Paul Burrell, of extracts from letters in a book published in 2003 giving intimate details of the royal family. His book was published shortly before the implementation of the above directive and so he and his publisher were able to rely on fair dealing for protection. This defence will no longer apply to confidential material, such as private letters, and has been seen as a shift in favour of the copyright holder.

How much to use?

If more of the work is quoted than is necessary to make the point in reporting current events or in criticism or review, this may not be fair dealing. It is difficult to put a figure to the proportion of a copyright work that can be used. Authors and publishers tend to think in terms of low percentages.

Parliament and the courts

There is no copyright infringement in reporting Parliament, the courts, or public inquiries, but this does not permit copying of a published report. There is normally no copyright infringement in copying material which must be open to public inspection by Act of Parliament.

Dishonestly obtained material not protected

The use by the *Sun* of stills from a security video showing the length of a visit by Princess Diana and Dodi Al Fayed to the Villa Windsor, a house in Paris, was held by the Court of Appeal in 2000 to be an infringement of copyright which could not be defended either as a publication in the public interest or as fair dealing for reporting current events.

The Court of Appeal allowed an appeal against Mr Justice Jacob's rejection of a claim for damages by Hyde Park Residence Ltd, which provided security services to Dodi's father, Mohamed Al Fayed and family. The *Sun* had maintained that the use of the video was necessary to expose Mohamed Al Fayed as having lied about the marriage plans of the princess and his son and their intention to live at the Villa Windsor. Mr Justice Jacob had said use of the stills to support a matter involving the mother of a future sovereign was of public interest and was fair dealing for reporting current events.

Lord Justice Aldous giving judgment in the Court of Appeal said fair dealing could not provide a defence for the *Sun*.

❝ I do not think a fair-minded and honest person would pay for the dishonestly-taken stills and publish them knowing that they had not been published or circulated when their only relevance was the fact that the Princess and Mr Dodi Al Fayed stayed only 28 minutes at the Villa Windsor – a fact that was known and did not establish that the Princess and Mr Dodi Fayed were not to be married. ❞

The information could have been made available by the *Sun* without infringement of copyright (*Hyde Park Residence Ltd v David Yelland* [2000] EMLR 363).

▌ Public interest defence

→

see ch.1, p. 5 on 'the public interest'

The 1988 Act states that nothing in the Act affects 'any rule of law preventing or restricting the enforcement of copyright on the grounds of public interest or otherwise'. But the extent of a public defence in copyright, and even its existence, remains unclear.

In the *Hyde Park Residence* case, the Court of Appeal also rejected the *Sun*'s submission that the action could be defended on the grounds that publication took place in the public interest. It held that the Copyright Act 1988 did not give a court general power to enable an infringer to use another's copyright in the public interest. Lord Justice Aldous said the basis of a public interest defence in a copyright action was not the same as the basis of such a defence in a breach of confidence action. A court would be entitled to refuse to enforce copyright if the work was:

(1) immoral, scandalous, or contrary to family life;

(2) injurious to public life, public health or safety, or the administration of justice; or

(3) incited or encouraged others to act in a way injurious to those matters.

Lord Justice Aldous said *Lion Laboratories Ltd v Evans* [1985] QB 526 was such a case.

(In that case, the *Daily Express* was successful in asking the Court of Appeal to lift **injunctions** granted to restrain breach of confidence and infringement of copyright. The Court of Appeal held that publication of material which cast doubt on the accuracy of the Lion Intoximeter, a device

→ glossary

providing evidence for **drink-driving** convictions, was such a matter of grave concern as to justify publication in a national newspaper.

→ glossary

→
see also
ch. 23,
p. 394

In 1994 the Department of Trade turned down a suggestion that the Act should be amended to allow a clear statutory defence to copyright infringement for newspapers which publish private photographs issued to them by the police. The department took the view that a public interest defence would be upheld by the courts.

Copyright in newspapers and magazines

There is copyright in the typographical arrangement of newspaper pages. However, the House of Lords held in 2001 that a facsimile copy of the cutting of an article from a page which gave no indication of how the rest of the page was laid out was not a substantial part of the published edition and thus was not an infringement of the copyright of the typographical arrangement (*Newspaper Licensing Agency v Marks & Spencer plc* [2001] UKHL 38; [2001] 3 All ER 977).

In 2005 IPC won a case against the *Sun* when it used a picture of the front cover of IPC's *What's On TV?* magazine alongside pictures of its own TV listings magazine. Mr Justice Hart said the defence of fair dealing was not available when one publication was breaching copyright to advance its own competing purposes (*IPC Media Ltd v News Group Newspapers Ltd* [2005] EWHC 317 (Ch)).

Length of copyright

The Government extended the length of copyright in 1995 from 50 years to 70 years from the end of the year of the author's death, to conform with a European Union directive. Copyright in a broadcast is retained at 50 years.

Under the Copyright and Related Rights Regulations 1996 (SI 1996/2967), a person publishing for the first time a previously unpublished photograph which has gone out of copyright establishes a publication right for 25 years from the end of the year of that first publication.

In 2008 the Government said it was considering extending copyright on sound recordings from 50 to 70 years.

See Online Resource Centre, ch. 27 for updates on this review.

▌ European Convention on Human Rights

→

see ch. 1,
pp. 9–13
on Con-
vention

The right of freedom of expression under Article 10 of the European Convention on Human Rights was held by Sir Andrew Morritt, Vice-Chancellor, in the Chancery Division in 2001, to provide no defence for infringement of copyright over and above those defences already provided by the Copyright Act 1988. The *Sunday Telegraph* had published an article by its political editor which incorporated substantial sections of a confidential note kept by Paddy Ashdown, then leader of the Liberal Democrats, of a meeting with the Prime Minister. The decision was upheld in the Court of Appeal (*Ashdown v Telegraph Group Ltd* (2001) *The Times*, 1 August).

▌ Moral rights

The 1988 Act, to meet the needs of the Berne Convention on copyright, gave moral rights to authors of copyright work.

These gave the author the right to be identified, not to have his work subject to derogatory treatment, and not to have a work falsely attributed to him.

The rights to be identified and not to have the work subject to derogatory treatment do not apply to any copyright work created for publication in a newspaper, magazine, or periodical or to any work made available for such publication with the consent of the author.

▌ Remedies for breach of copyright

Civil action

The owner of the copyright can obtain an injunction in the High Court or county court to restrain a person from infringing his copyright as well as seeking damages and an order for the possession of infringing copies of the work and of material used in the infringement.

Where the court decides there has been a deliberate or reckless infringement of copyright, this can be reflected in the level of damages awarded. In 2002 the *Sun* was ordered to pay £10,450 for its use of a confidential photograph from the medical notes of a convicted killer who had been allowed on day release from Rampton Hospital. The Nottinghamshire Healthcare NHS Trust was awarded £450, plus £10,000 to reflect the flagrancy of the breach (*Nottinghamshire Healthcare NHS Trust v News Group Newspapers* [2002] EWHC 409).

Criminal penalties

Under the 1988 Act a person guilty of infringement can be prosecuted, although such prosecutions usually relate to crimes of video piracy, not journalistic activity.

In 2008 the Government began consultations on increasing criminal penalties for copyright infringement, increasing the maximum fine magistrates could impose to £50,000.

See Online Resource Centre, ch. 27 for updates on this consultation.

Innocent infringement

If the infringer did not know and had no reason to believe the work was subject to copyright, for example if he genuinely believed the copyright had run out, the copyright owner is entitled to an account of profits but not to damages.

Acquiescence

If the owner of a copyright work has encouraged or allowed another to make use of that work without complaint, this may destroy a claim for infringement of copyright.

Recap of major points

- Copyright protects intellectual property such as literary, musical, dramatic, or artistic works, sound recordings, film, broadcast, or typographical arrangements.

- There is no copyright in news in itself, only in the means by which it is expressed to a reader, viewer, or listener.
- A defence of fair dealing is available for the use of short extracts of copyrighted work, properly attributed to their creator.
- Photographs are excluded from the fair dealing defence.
- A copyright owner whose rights have been breached can seek an injunction and/or damages.

🌐 Useful Websites

www.ipo.gov.uk/
Intellectual Property Office

http://ipkitten.blogspot.com/
IPKat Blog

Part 4

Information and expression: rights, sources, and boundaries

Freedom of Information Act 2000

Chapter summary

For democracy to work, citizens must have information to help them plan for the future and to choose which politicians to vote for. The Freedom of Information (FOI) Act 2000, which came into effect in 2005, created the UK's first general right of access to information held by government departments and other public authorities in the United Kingdom. Journalists eagerly began to use the Act's provisions, and this has produced many exclusive stories, some about the highest reaches of Government. But the Act can be frustrating to use, because of bureaucratic delays and its wide-ranging exemptions. A user of the Act must be ready to argue if necessary for the 'public interest' justification for information to be disclosed. This chapter deals with FOI law as it applies in England, Wales, and Northern Ireland, and also refers to information access rights in the Environmental Information Regulations.

▶ Introduction to the Act

A Labour Government came to power in 1997 with a 23-year-old manifesto commitment to give people a legal 'right to know'. The Freedom of Information Act finally became law in January 2005, giving citizens the power to require 'public authorities' to disclose information, e.g. from documents or computer-held data, which would not otherwise be published. These authorities must supply the information without making any financial charge for

→
see also
p. 465
on cost
limits

finding and collating it, if meeting the request costs them no more than £600 (in the case of national government departments) or £450 (in the case of local councils and other types of authorities). The Act has been used extensively by journalists and researchers, sometimes with great success. For example, requests made under the Act have required the Government to disclose:

- the Attorney General's advice on the legality of the UK taking part in the invasion of Iraq;
- an early draft of the controversial dossier published by the Government in 2003 to justify the invasion.

A request by the FOI campaigner and journalist Heather Brooke to the House of Commons made it reveal details of what some Members of Parliament were claiming in expenses to finance and run their second homes.

Disclosures prompted by regional and local journalists using the Act have included:

- the number of under-16s requiring treatment for drug problems and alcohol-related illness at a local hospital;
- the number of police offices arrested for alleged crimes;
- how many crimes reported to police – including alleged sexual assaults – are given no publicity by the police;
- how many children have been excluded from local schools.

Disclosures prompted by BBC journalists using the Act include revelations that:

- only two councils had met Government targets on the welfare of children in council care;
- councils in the South of England had made the same planning procedure mistake 68 times in relation to mobile phone masts;
- elderly residents of a nursing home allegedly suffered verbal and physical abuse.

→
see
Useful
Websites,
below

The Holdthefrontpage website has numerous examples of journalists using the Act.

Although many staff at public authorities have proved helpful when responding to FOI requests, the efficacy of the Act is frequently sapped by delays, e.g. backlogs of several months in some authorities answering requests, and slow consideration of the 'public interest test', see below. And government departments and other public authorities have been officious and self-serving when seeking to use the Act's exemptions, to thwart requests for information – as evidenced by numerous requesters winning appeals made to the Information Commissioner and Information Tribunal, whose roles are explained below. Journalists using the Act need to be systematic and doggedly persistent in pursuing requests. But overall, the FOI Act is continuing to be a worthwhile additional tool for investigative journalism. Heather Brooke, author of the book *Your Right To Know*, summed up the Act well when she said: 'While not quite the sword of truth some had hoped, the new laws are an effective chisel against government secrecy and corruption.' Her website is also a fund of information about the Act.

see Useful Websites, below

▌ What is a 'public authority' under the Act?

In total, around 100,000 major and minor bodies in the public sector are covered by the Act, including:

- national government departments and ministries, e.g. the Home Office, the Foreign Office, the Prime Minister's Office;
- the House of Commons, the House of Lords, the national assemblies of Northern Ireland and Wales;
- the armed forces;
- local government authorities, e.g. metropolitan, county, district, city, and parish councils, transport executives, waste disposal agencies, police forces, fire services;
- national park authorities;
- universities, colleges, and schools – if in the state sector;
- the National Health Service, e.g. primary care trusts, hospital trusts, health authorities, doctors' and dentists' practices;
- various advisory councils, and regulatory bodies with statutory powers, e.g. Ofcom, the General Medical Council.

The Act does not provide a definition of 'public authority', but lists, in its Schedule 1, the bodies and organisations it covers. More have been added by statutory instruments.

see Useful Websites, below

Institutions and agencies not covered by the Act

The UK's security and intelligence agencies – MI5, MI6, and GCHQ – are exempt from the Act, and so are not required to respond to FOI requests.

Courts and tribunals are also not covered by the Act, though some information gathered or created in their functions will be available if an FOI request is made to the relevant government department which holds it, e.g. the Ministry of Justice.

The following are not deemed to be public authorities under the Act: housing associations; charities; private prisons; harbour authorities; Members of Parliament and members of the House of Lords as individuals; schools which have 'academy' status; the Association of Chief Police Officers.

By early 2009 the Government, after a consultation period which ended in February 2008, had yet to announce its decision on whether the Act's scope should be extended to cover more bodies.

Check the Online Resource Centre for FOI law updates.

▶ How the Act works

If a 'public authority' receives a request for information, it must normally make a response within 20 working days, either supplying the information or explaining why it cannot be supplied. It may be that:

- the public authority does not hold the information, in which case the Act's effect is that in most circumstances this must be made clear;

- or the request would exceed the cost limits for the provision of free information – see below;

- or that the information is covered by exemptions under the Act, and therefore need not be supplied.

In the case of some exempt categories, e.g. information held in confidence or which concerns national security, the authority does not have to state what it holds if denial or confirmation of the information's existence would undermine the purpose of the exemption. Most of the exempt categories are outlined below, pp. 467–471.

If a journalist is not sure what information an authority holds, before he/she makes an FOI request he/she should check its website, if it has one and if there is any likelihood of the information being published there by the authority routinely. Each authority is required by the Act to have some form of 'publication scheme' showing what it publishes. If the information is not listed there, then the journalist, if he/she is unsure how to precisely describe in an FOI request the information he/she wants, should ring the authority concerned to ask the relevant person (i.e. an official who co-ordinates FOI matters) about the types of information it holds. The Act requires authorities to offer 'advice and assistance', including on how particular requests should be framed for them to stay within the cost limits for free information. But, as journalists will testify, there are occasions when this advice and assistance is not offered – see below, p. 466.

Under the Act, the motive of the requester in wanting the information should not play any part in the authority's decision on whether it can be provided (unless the request is 'vexatious', e.g. from an obsessive person who asks for the same information repeatedly).

In cases where the authority has to apply the 'public interest test' – see below – to consider if information is exempt, the Act permits it to take longer than 20 working days to make its final response. A public authority is required to consider, even if some information specified in a request is deemed exempt from disclosure, if that request can be met in part by release of non-exempt information.

▶ What is information under the Act?

Information is defined in section 84 of the Act as 'information recorded in any form'. The Act does not require a public authority to gather information it does not already have.. The right under the Act is for *information* to be communicated to the requester, not necessarily in the form of particular documents, though requests often refer to particular documents, and are often met by their being supplied.

▶ The costs limit

A national government department must, if the Act requires it to disclose the requested information, disclose it without making a charge if providing it costs the department £600 or less. Any other public authority covered by the Act (including a local council, a police force, etc.) must provide such information without charge if it costs the authority £450 or less to provide. Cost is estimated by assessing the cost of staff time which will be reasonably needed by the authority to determine whether it holds the information, to locate it, retrieve it, and if necessary to extract the information from a document containing it. Staff time is deemed to cost £25 an hour. If the cost limit is, after a bona fide estimating process, deemed to be exceeded, the authority is not obliged to supply any information specified in the request but can *choose* to supply it without charge, or at a price which reflects the cost of providing it (if the requester is willing to pay that price). If it is possible for the public authority to comply with part, but not all, of a request within the cost limits, then it has a duty under section 16 of the Act to offer advice – see below – to the requester to see if he/she wishes to redefine or limit the scope of the request accordingly. If the information is to be provided in paper form, the requester can be charged a reasonable price for the photocopying. But information can often be sent by email.

Bearing the costs limit in mind, journalists should make requests for information as specific as possible. Asking for data that spans more than a decade, for example, could take much longer to collate than data covering a few years. However, journalists may want records spanning several years to check trends.

To some extent, a requester can get round the cost limit by breaking down a 'large' request into several smaller ones, sent serially. But the public authority has power to 'aggregate' the cost of two or more requests made within 60 days by the same person for the same or a similar type of information – that is, the authority may treat them as being part of a single request, and refuse them, if in total they breach the cost limit for a single request. Nevertheless, an authority should not use its aggregation powers to frustrate a sequence of requests each of which, on the basis of information sent previously, seeks to dig further into a topic by asking for further, different information.

▶ Advice and assistance

Public authorities are required by section 16 of the Act to give someone proposing to make a request, or someone who has already made one, 'advice and assistance, so far as it would be reasonable to expect the authority to do so'.

- The public authority should tell you, **before** you make the request what information of the type you want may be available.
- The public authority should give you guidance to avoid your request breaching the cost limit for such information to be provided without charge.

What happens in reality is that staff within authorities are not always help-ful, and are sometimes brusquely unhelpful, particularly within national government departments, some of which seem hard pressed to cope with the hundreds or thousands of requests received each year.

However, the Information Tribunal has made clear that it expects the Information Commissioner, when adjudicating an appeal made to him against a refusal to supply information, to consider the extent to which the public authority met its obligations to the requester under section 16. Therefore a requester should if necessary remind the authority, in writing, of these obligations. The Act says that any authority which, in relation to this duty to provide advice and assistance, conforms to the Code of Practice issued by the Ministry of Justice (formerly the Department of Constitutional Affairs) is to be taken as complying with that duty.

see Useful Websites, below for this code

Paragraph 8 of the Code states that 'authorities should, so far as is reason-ably practicable, provide assistance to the applicant to enable him or her to describe more clearly the information' requested. The Information Tribunal has said of this duty to provide advice: 'An applicant does not have to ask for it...nothing [in the Act] restricts the duty to advise and assist only to those cases when some form of request has [already] been made....the duty must include at least one to advise and assist an applicant with regard to the for-mulation of an appropriate request' (Appeal number EA/2006/0046).

The Act's Section 1(3) permits a public authority, when it 'reasonably requires' further detail to identify and locate the information requested, to seek to clarify this with the requester, and, if such further detail is not pro-vided, not to comply with the request. The Act does not allow public bodies to distinguish between media requests and requests from 'ordinary' mem-bers of the public. The Information Commissioner has made clear that if a public authority replies to a request that the information is already in the public domain it should, to comply with section 16, specifically point the requester to where the information can be found, e.g. on its website, if the requester seems to need this help.

▌ Exemptions

The Act allows authorities to refuse to supply information on various grounds, known as exemptions. The Information Commissioner's Office website has helpful guidance on these, e.g. it enables searches, categorised usefully by which exemption was claimed, of his decisions on their use.

 see Useful Websites, below

Absolute exemptions

Some exemptions are 'absolute', i.e. under the Act the public authority does not have to give any reason for not disclosing the information, beyond stating that the exemption applies because of the nature of the information. These absolute exemptions include the following categories of information (with the relevant section of the Act indicated):

Section 21 – information reasonably accessible by other means.

Section 23 – information supplied to the public authority by or relating to bodies dealing with security matters, e.g. MI5, MI6, GCHQ.

Section 32 – court records A court itself is not 'a public authority' under the Act – see above. This exemption covers certain documents held by any public authority which *is* covered by the Act, held because it is a litigant or as an interested party in a court case. An example is copies of material which has been filed with a court for the purposes of proceedings there.

→

for detail
of such
law, see
ch. 25

Section 40 – personal information The FOI Act does not override data protection law. A public authority may decide that an FOI request encompasses exempt 'personal data'. In such a case, the authority should nevertheless consider if, by 'redacting', (i.e. editing out) references which could lead to any individual being identified, some non-exempt information could be disclosed. In some cases, the Information Commissioner has considered whether a public authority made any attempt to obtain consent from individuals for disclosure of personal data.

The Commissioner has also made clear that when considering whether personal data should be released, an authority should make a distinction between 'professional personal information', e.g. job descriptions of its staff and details of their professional responsibilities, and 'private personal information', e.g. sickness records.

Section 41 – information provided to the authority in confidence by another party This exemption does not cover information which the public authority has generated itself, so it does not cover any contract the authority has entered into.

⠿ Point for consideration

The Information Tribunal has said that the section 40 or 41 exemptions are not as absolute as they first appear, because the authority will need to apply a public interest test under data protection law and/or the law of confidence when deciding if information can be disclosed.

Section 44 – information the disclosure of which is forbidden by other law For example, the Information Tribunal upheld a ruling that the Independent

Police Complaints Commission could not, because of a provision in the Police Act 1996, disclose under the FOI Act copies of files relating to complaints against the police.

▶ Qualified exemptions

The rest of the Act's exemptions are 'qualified'. This means that if the public authority decides not to supply the information in these categories it must give reasons, showing how it has applied 'the public interest test', as laid down by the Act, to justify its refusal to provide the information. Under the Act, the information may be withheld only if the public interest in withholding it is greater than the public interest in releasing it.

The Act does not define the concept of 'the public interest'. In *The Freedom of Information Act: An Introduction,* the Information Commissioner lists the following public interest factors as among those which should encourage public authorities to disclose information:

- Furthering the understanding and participation in the public debate of issues of the day.

- Promoting accountability and transparency by public authorities for decisions taken by them.

- Promoting accountability and transparency in the spending of public money.

- Allowing individuals and companies to understand decisions made by public authorities affecting their lives.

- Bringing to light information affecting public health and safety.

The Information Commissioner's Office website has further guidance on this.

The Campaign for Freedom of Information has stressed the importance of applicants pursuing their requests, e.g. all the way to the Information Tribunal if necessary, and not accepting an initial rebuff from a public authority. The requester should not assume that the Information Commissioner will automatically recognise the public interest case for the disclosure of the particular information requested, so the requester should spell this out in appeal correspondence.

 see Useful Websites, below

The qualified exemptions include these categories of information:

Section 24 – information which if disclosed is likely to prejudice national security This exemption concerns information other than that already absolutely exempt under section 23, see p. 468.

Section 27 – information which if disclosed is likely to prejudice international relations.

Section 31 – information held by an authority for law enforcement functions.

This is exempt if its disclosure would, or would be likely to, prejudice the prevention or detection of crime, or the apprehension and prosecution of offenders, or the administration of justice. Test cases have established, for example, that information does not have to be disclosed on when a speed camera at a particular site has been active, because this would compromise the camera's effect, in that the information if published could tempt irresponsible drivers to speculate when the camera would be inactive, and therefore to drive at illegal speeds. However more general information, such as how many drivers were caught speeding by a particular camera on a particular day, could be published without such adverse effect.

Section 35 – information which relates to formulation or development of Government policy The Information Tribunal, see below, has been fairly robust in disapproving of some attempts to use this exemption. The tribunal has noted that there is a public interest in involuntary disclosure of information under the Act in that such disclosure acts as a check on information disclosed voluntarily. The older the information, the less sensitive it is as an indication of an authority's policy options.

Section 36 – information the disclosure of which is likely to prejudice effective conduct of public affairs This exemption is controversial in that it is so vague. But it was intended by Parliament to cover material which did not fall into other exempt categories but which, if it was disclosed, would damage the public authority's ability to carry out its duties. Heather Brooke, see above, advises: 'This is the weakest exemption, frequently overturned on appeal. A public authority's reliance on it shows it is desperate and grasping at straws.'

Section 43 – commercial interests This exemption covers trade secrets and information which, if disclosed, 'would, or would be likely to, prejudice the commercial interest of any person (including the public authority holding it)'.

In the case of *John Connor Press Associates* [a freelance news agency] *v Information Commissioner* (EA/2005/0005), the Information Tribunal ruled that the National Maritime Museum should have disclosed financial information concerning its purchase of a particular set of artworks. The Museum had argued that when it received the agency's FOI request, it was in negotiation with another artist about another project, and that its ability to ensure value for public money in that negotiation would have been prejudiced had financial detail about the previous deal been released. But the Tribunal decided that no real and significant risk of such prejudice existed, partly because the deal under negotiation – which included payment for 'performance art' – differed in scope from the museum's previous deal for artworks.

In *Derry City Council v Information Commissioner* [EA/2006/0014], the case concerned a request by an employee of the *Belfast Telegraph* for details of the agreement between the council and Ryanair as regards operation of the Derry City Airport, including how much Ryanair paid for the operation of the airport facility. After an appeal to the Information Commissioner, the council provided information via a document but with information in some financial headings redacted. The Commissioner upheld a complaint about the redaction.

▶ Delays in the public interest test

A significant weakness in the Act is that it does not set public authorities a time limit within which they must complete the 'public interest test' when deciding whether to comply with an FOI request. So consideration of the test can extend for months the normal 20-day deadline for responses to requests.

However, the authority must tell the requester, within the 20 working days, that a qualified exemption potentially applies.

▶ If the information is not supplied

If the authority takes no decision within the 20-day deadline on whether the information will be supplied, or if the authority refuses to supply it because of the cost limit or an exemption, a requester can ask the authority to conduct an 'internal review' into such failure or refusal. The review should be carried out by an official other than one involved in any such refusal. Another weakness of the Act is that there is no statutory timescale within which the internal review must be completed. The Information Commissioner's Office has said that 20 working days (from the time a request for a review is received) is a reasonable time for an authority to complete a review, and that in no case should the time taken exceed 40 working days. If dissatisfied with the result of the authority's review, the requester can appeal to the Information Commissioner.

▶ The Information Commissioner and the Information Tribunal

→

see ch. 25 on data protection

The FOI Act is enforced by the Information Commissioner. This post has a wider remit than the post it replaces, the Data Protection Commissioner. The new title reflects the fact that the Commissioner now supervises both the Data Protection Act 1998 and the Freedom of Information Act. In early 2009 it was announced by the Ministry of Justice, which is responsible for FOI matters, that Christopher Graham, then Director General of the Advertising Standards Authority, had been selected as the preferred candidate to take over as Information Commissioner from the first holder of the post, Richard Thomas, who was due to retire.

The Commissioner can order an authority to release information if he disagrees with a refusal to disclose it. He can query an authority's claim not to hold the requested information. He can query an authority's estimate that the cost limit for the provision of free information would be exceeded.

The Commissioner can, if a requester claims that an authority has not responded within the 20-day limit, serve an enforcement notice on the public authority, requiring it to comply with the Act. As an ultimate sanction, the Commissioner can seek to persuade the High Court to punish as contempt of court the authority's failure to comply with the notice. He can also issue a 'good practice recommendation' under section 48 of the Act, specifying the steps which the authority ought to take to improve compliance with the Act. But FOI campaigners have voiced frustration, in view of the widespread delays in public authorities responding to FOI requests, that the Commissioner has not used his enforcement powers very frequently.

→

see Useful Websites, below

Both requesters and public authorities, if dissatisfied with a decision made by the Information Commissioner, can appeal to the Information Tribunal. The normal deadline is that such appeals should be made within 28 days of receipt of the Commissioner's decision. The Tribunal publishes its decisions online. It is due to be assimilated in 2010 into the over-arching First-Tier Tribunal in the administrative justice system – see ch. 15.

▶ Ministers' power of veto

Notices issued by the Commissioner requiring government departments to disclose requested information can be vetoed by Cabinet Ministers. The Justice Secretary, Jack Straw, made the first use of this power early in 2009. The Commissioner had issued an enforcement notice (upheld by the Information Tribunal) requiring that the Cabinet minutes of the decision to go to war with Iraq be released. However, Jack Straw blocked the notice.

▶ The FOI Act's coverage of media organisations

The BBC, Channel 4, and S4C – because they are public service broadcasters – were made subject to the FOI Act, but in a limited way. The Act states that disclosure provisions only apply, in respect of these broadcast organisations, to information they hold 'for purposes other than those of journalism, art or literature'. By thus protecting **journalistic material** held by these → glossary
broadcast institutions, the Act does not require them to accede to:

a) requests attempting to reveal their journalists' confidential sources;

b) requests by rival news organisations, or by the subjects of journalistic investigations (i.e. 'data subjects'), attempting to secure, prior to or after broadcast, disclosure of material gathered in a journalistic investigation, including any footage/audio not broadcast.

However, the distinction between material held for journalism purposes and management or governance purposes may not, in a particular case, be straightforward. The Commissioner considered the definition of 'journalism' when upholding the right of the BBC to refuse to disclose an internal report which reviewed, and made recommendations about, its coverage of the Middle East, including best practice on matters such as impartiality. The Commissioner agreed with the BBC that the report was held for the purposes of journalism. The Information Tribunal later ruled that the Commissioner's interpretation was wrong. However, in the High Court, after the case went to **judicial review**, Mr Justice Davis ruled that the → glossary
Tribunal had no jurisdiction in the case, and that the Commissioner's decision in it should stand. By early 2009 this case was still unresolved. A

House of Lords ruling meant that the High Court was due to consider it
again.

→
see ch.
1, pp.
16–17 on
PCC and
OFCOM

Ofcom is subject to the FOI Act but the Press Complaints Commission, not
being a public authority, is not.

 ## Environmental information

The Environmental Information Regulations (EIR), the latest version of
which came into force in 2005 (SI 2004/3391), require public authorities to
provide information about environmental matters. These regulations implement a European Union directive and give, in the environmental field, to
the public – and therefore to journalists – more powerful rights of access to
information than those in the FOI Act, as explained below. A public authority receiving a request for information which falls into the scope of the EIR
should automatically deal with it under the EIR rather than under the FOI
Act (but ideally the request should refer to the EIR). For guidance on using
the EIR, see Useful Websites below.

→
see ch. 1,
p. 9 on EU
directives

Information about the environment covers air, water, land, natural sites,
and living organisms – which include GM crops. It covers discharges as well
as noise and radiation. The EIR cover more bodies than the FOI Act and
have fewer exemptions. For example, information about emissions cannot
be withheld for reasons of commercial confidentiality.

All bodies subject to the FOI Act are also subject to the EIR and the same
20-day deadline applies to requests made for information.

The EIR require that public authorities must, as with the FOI Act, assist
those making a request.

EIR requests for information can be turned down on grounds of national
security. However, all refusals are subject to a public interest test and
requests can be turned down only if the public interest in non-disclosure
far outweighs the public interest in disclosure. A 'reasonable' fee can be
charged for EIR requests.

The EIR are enforced by the Information Commissioner, as with the
FOI Act.

The EIR can be used, for example, to ask for reports of hygiene inspec-
tions at factories and restaurants because the EIR cover information on 'the
state of human health and safety, including the contamination of the food
chain'.

▌ Legal issues in using FOI disclosures in stories

Journalists should remember that if they publish matter disclosed to them under the FOI Act or the EIR, and someone claims to have been defamed by it, the published report does not enjoy any special protection in libel law, in that the FOI Act and EIR do not confer statutory qualified **privilege** on such →glossary reports. Depending on content, such reports may well be protected by other libel defences, namely justification (if the published matter is provably true – and information from official records may well be true) or the *Reynolds* defence.

→ see chs 19 and 20 on libel defences

Guidance on the Information Commissioner's Office website states:

> ❝ Disclosure of information under the Act or the [EIR] Regulations will not remove the copyright in it. Any information released may be subject to copyright restrictions that you will have to abide by. If you have any doubts about copyright, consult with the public authority about the status of information. In some cases copyright may be waived or information can be licensed for re-use. ❞

Copyright protects photographs, maps, and diagrams, for example, but – it should be remembered – does not protect facts as such, only the way in which they are recorded. Thus, a journalist drawing on information from matter supplied under FOI and putting it into a news story does not have to fear that those factual revelations will raise copyright issues. Also, in this situation, the **fair dealing** defence applies to citing some text verbatim. Furthermore, a public authority which attempted to use the copyright argument to block publication of its own information released under FOI would be roundly condemned for ignoring the 'public interest' element of the legislation.

→ see ch. 27 on copyright

 →glossary

⠿ Recap of major points

- The Freedom of Information Act gives citizens, including journalists, a general right of access to information held by public authorities, including Government departments, local authorities, the police, and hospitals.

- If a 'public authority' receives a request for information under the Act, it must normally make a response within 20 working days, either supplying the information or explaining why it cannot be supplied.

- The information, if held by the public authority, and if not exempt under the Act, will be provided free of charge (except for any copying fee) if it costs a government department £600 or less to provide, or any other public authority £450 or less to provide.

- However, there are wide-ranging exemptions, and plenty of potential for delays in getting a response from a public authority.

- Public authorities are obliged under the Act to offer advice to requesters to enable them to word their requests in such a way that they are more likely to be successful.

- The Information Commissioner can hear appeals against an authority's decision to refuse to supply information. The Information Tribunal can hear appeals against the Commissioner's decisions.

- The Environmental Information Regulations provide powerful rights of access to information in fields the EIR cover.

🌐 Useful Websites

www.informationcommissioner.gov.uk/
The Information Commissioner

www.informationtribunal.gov.uk/
Information Tribunal

www.cfoi.org.uk/
The Campaign for Freedom of Information

www.yrtk.org/
Heather Brooke's site

www.guardian.co.uk/politics/freedomofinformation/
Guardian newspaper guidance on FOI

www.holdthefrontpage.co.uk/day/foi/foiindex.shtml
Holdthefrontpage stories on journalists using the FOI Act

www.justice.gov.uk/whatwedo/freedomofinformation.htm
Ministry of Justice guidance on use of the FOI Act

www.justice.gov.uk/guidance/foi-code-of-practice.htm
Code of Practice for public authorities as regards FOI requests

www.opsi.gov.uk/Acts/acts2000/ukpga_20000036_en_1/
The Freedom of Information Act

www.ico.gov.uk/what_we_cover/environmental_information_regulation/guidance.aspx/
ICO guidance on Environmental Information Regulations

Other information rights and access to meetings

Chapter summary

As well as the Freedom of Information (FOI) Act 2000 there is various legislation giving the public, and journalists, access to information. This is especially true of local government, which is legally obliged to allow access to information, accounts, and meetings.

This chapter will explain the overlapping laws that allow such access. These laws can be used in conjunction with Freedom of Information requests to obtain material from public bodies. The FOI Act is explained in chapter 28.

▌ Local government

Changes brought about by the Local Government Act (LGA) 2000 had major implications for the access of journalists to decision-making meetings. Previously, decisions were made at meetings that the public (including the media) had the right to attend.

The right applied, under the Local Government (Access to Information) Act 1985 and the Public Bodies (Admission to Meetings) Act 1960, to full council meetings and the meetings of committees and sub-committees except where the information was confidential or exempt. The public still have the right to attend such meetings, except when confidential or exempt matters are under discussion.

The LGA 2000, however, introduced 'cabinet-style' government. Executive decisions are now taken at meetings that may be held **in private** except → glossary where 'key decisions' are to be made. Local authorities have had to reorganise using one of three models, leader and cabinet, directly elected mayor and cabinet, or directly elected mayor and council manager.

Executive decisions are taken at meetings (described below as 'cabinet meetings') that are permitted to be held in private except where 'key decisions' are to be made.

The Government's definition of key decisions appears to give ample opportunity to local authorities to make important decisions in secret if they wish. Even if key decisions are being made, press and public may be excluded if exempt or confidential information or the advice of a political adviser would be disclosed.

▌ The Local Government Act 2000

The Act in brief

Cabinets must meet in public when they are discussing or voting on key decisions, unless the item is confidential or exempt or would disclose the advice of a political adviser.

Agendas and reports for any public meeting must be made available at least five days beforehand.

A written record of all key decisions and other executive decisions must be made available 'as soon as is practicable' after the meeting. This also applies to decisions taken by individual members.

These documents must include a record of the decision, any alternatives considered and rejected, and a record of any conflict of interest.

Every council must publish a 'forward plan', containing details of the key decisions it is likely to make over a four-month period. The plan, which must be updated monthly, must include documents related to those decisions and information on who will take the decision and on those the council will consult.

Meetings of backbench 'scrutiny committees' are open to the press and public, with advance agendas and papers available beforehand.

→ glossary   The regulations covering access to information under the LGA 2000 are contained in a **statutory instrument**, the Local Authorities (Executive Arrangements) (Access to Information) (England) Regulations 2000 (SI 2000/3272). This statutory instrument was amended in 2002 by the Local

Authorities (Executive Arrangements) (Access to Information) (England) Amendment Regulations 2002 (SI 2002/716).

These complex rules are summarised below, but journalists needing to challenge councils may need to refer to the text, which is available at www. opsi.gov.uk/stat.htm. The regulations apply to unitary authorities, London borough councils, county councils, and district councils in England that are operating executive arrangements under the Act.

When cabinets must meet in public

A cabinet meeting must be held in public when a key decision is to be made. A key decision means one that is likely:

- to result in the local authority incurring expenditure or making savings that are significant having regard to the local authority's budget for the relevant service or function; or
- to be significant in terms of its effects on communities living or working in an area comprising two or more wards or electoral divisions.

Who decides when expenditure or savings are 'significant', requiring the meeting to be in public? The guidance notes say, 'It will be for the potential decision-maker to decide'. To help, the full council must agree limits above which items are significant, and the agreed limits must be published.

Papers that must be made available

Records of decisions

'As soon as reasonably practicable' after a cabinet meeting, either in private or public, at which an executive decision has been made, a written statement must be produced. The statement must include:

(1) a record of the decision;

(2) a record of the reasons for the decision;

(3) details of any alternative options considered and rejected;

(4) a record of any conflict of interest and, in that case, a note of any dispensation granted by the authority's standards committee.

An executive decision made by an individual or a key decision made by an officer must be recorded similarly.

The record must be made available for inspection by the public, again 'as soon as is reasonably practicable', at the council offices. With it must be any report considered at the meeting or, as the case may be, by the individual member or officer making the decision.

Where a newspaper asks for a copy of any of the documents available for public inspection, those documents must be supplied on payment of postage, copying, 'or other necessary charge for transmission'.

Reports to be considered

Where an executive member or officer receives a report that he intends to take into consideration when he makes a key decision, he must not make that decision until the report has been available for public inspection for at least five clear days.

Agendas and reports

A copy of the agenda and every report for a public meeting must be available for inspection by the public when they are made available to the members of the cabinet. As a matter of procedure, the regulations say that an item of business shall be considered at a public meeting *only*:

(1) where a copy of the agenda or part of the agenda, including the item, has been available for inspection by the public for at least five clear days before the meeting; or

(2) where the meeting is convened at short notice, a copy of the agenda including the item has been available for inspection by the public from the time that the meeting was convened.

When a meeting is convened at short notice a copy of the agenda and associated reports must be available for inspection at the time the meeting is convened.

When an item that would be available for inspection by the public is added to the agenda, a copy of the revised agenda, and of any report relating to the item for consideration at the meeting, must be available for inspection by the public when the item is added.

On request from a newspaper, a local authority must supply it with:

(1) a copy of the agenda for a public meeting and a copy of each of the reports for consideration at the meeting;

(2) such further statements or particulars, if any, as are necessary to indicate the nature of the items contained in the agenda; and

(3) if 'the proper officer' thinks fit in the case of any item, a copy of any other document supplied to members of the executive in connection with the item.

Forward plans

Each authority must publish every month a 'forward plan' giving details of key decisions to be taken in the following four months. These plans must be available for inspection 'at all reasonable hours' and free of charge. It must also give the dates in each month in the following 12 months on which each forward plan will be published.

A forward plan must include the following information:

- the matter to be decided, the identity of the decision-maker or makers;
- the identity of the principal groups or organisations to be consulted on the decision;
- the means of consultation;
- the way people may make representations; and
- a list of the documents to be considered.

Powers to exclude the press

Even when key decisions are being discussed, a cabinet can exclude the press and public in three situations:

(1) when it is likely that if members of the public were present, confidential information would be disclosed;

(2) when the cabinet has passed a resolution excluding the public because otherwise it is likely exempt information would be disclosed;

(3) when the cabinet has passed a resolution excluding the public because otherwise it is likely the advice of a political adviser or assistant would be disclosed.

'Confidential information' has a special meaning in this context. It means **information** provided to the local authority by a government depart- → glossary
ment upon terms (however expressed) which forbid the disclosure of the information to the public or information the disclosure of which to the public is prohibited by or under any enactment or by the order of a court.

A resolution to exclude on the grounds of exempt information must identify the proceedings, or part of the proceedings, to which the exclusion applies and state the category of exempt information involved.

Exempt information may be summarised as:

(1) information relating to a particular employee, job applicant, or office holder of the council, or an employee, applicant, or official of the magistrates courts or the probationary committee;

(2) information relating to a particular council tenant or a particular applicant for council services or grants;

(3) information relating to the care, adoption, or fostering of a particular child;

(4) information relating to a particular person's financial or business affairs;

(5) information relating to the supply of goods or services to or the acquisition of property by the council, if to disclose the information would place a particular person in a more favourable bargaining position or otherwise prejudice negotiations;

(6) labour relations matters between the council and its employees, if and so long as to disclose the information would prejudice negotiations or discussions;

→ glossary   (7) instruction to and advice from counsel;

(8) information relating to the investigation and prosecution of offenders, if to disclose the information would enable the wrongdoer to evade notice being served on him.

The public can be excluded only for the part of the meeting during which the matter is being discussed.

Obstruction is an offence

A person who has custody of a document that is required to be available for inspection by members of the public commits an offence if he/she intentionally obstructs any person exercising a right conferred under the regulations to inspect the document or make a copy of it, or if he/she refuses to supply a copy of it.

▶ The Local Government (Access to Information) Act 1985

The Local Government (Access to Information) Act (LG(AI)A) 1985 says that all meetings of principal authorities, their committees, and sub-committees must be open to the public unless dealing with confidential or exempt information.

The position regarding working parties and advisory or study groups, which may in effect act as sub-committees without the name, is unclear.

Principal authorities, their committees, and sub-committees must exclude the public when confidential information is likely to be disclosed (for an explanation of confidential information see above, 'Power to exclude the press').

A local authority may, by passing a resolution, exclude the public when it is likely that exempt information will be disclosed (for an explanation of exempt information, see above, 'Power to exclude the press'). The resolution must state to what part of the meeting the exclusion applies and must describe the category in the schedule to which the exempt information applies.

While the meeting is open to the public, 'duly accredited representatives' of newspapers or news agencies reporting the meeting must, under section 5(6)(c) of the LG(AI)A 1985, be afforded reasonable facilities for taking their report and for telephoning it, at their own expense, unless the premises are not on the telephone.

A newspaper or news agency must on request (and on payment of postage or other transmission charge) be supplied with (a) agendas, (b) further particulars necessary to indicate the nature of the items on the agenda, and (c) if the 'proper officer' thinks fit, copies of any other documents supplied to council members. The 'proper officer' may exclude from what he/she sends out any report, or part of a report, relating to items not likely to be discussed in public.

Late items, reports, and supplementary information can be admitted at the meeting only if the chairman regards the matter as urgent and specifies the reason for the urgency. Oral reports will be admissible only if reference to them is on the agenda or is covered by the urgency procedure.

Copies of agendas and of any report for a meeting of a council must be open to public inspection at least five clear working days before the meeting (except for items not likely to be discussed in public). Where a meeting is called at shorter notice they must be open to inspection from the time the meeting is convened.

Copies of minutes and reports and summaries of business discussed in private must be open to public inspection for six years (except for confidential or exempt information).

A list of background papers must be included in each officer's report considered at a meeting, and a copy of each background paper must be open to public inspection for four years. Background papers are those unpublished papers on which a report for a meeting is based and which, in the officer's opinion, have been relied upon to a material extent in preparing the report.

Any person who intentionally obstructs the right of any person to inspect agendas, minutes, and reports is liable to a fine on summary conviction.

The LG(AI)A 1985 applies also to combined police or fire authorities, to meetings of joint consultative committees of health and local authorities, and to some joint boards.

The LG(AI)A 1985 does not apply to parish and community councils. The Public Bodies (Admission to Meetings) Act 1960 still applies to these councils.

❚ The Public Bodies (Admission to Meetings) Act 1960

The Public Bodies (Admission to Meetings) Act (PB(AM)A) 1960 says that these bodies must admit the public to their meetings and to meetings of their committees consisting of all the members of the body.

The PB(AM)A 1960 says, however, that such a body or committee can exclude the public for the whole or part of a meeting, 'whenever publicity would be prejudicial to the public interest because of the confidential nature of the business to be transacted or for other special reasons stated in the resolution and arising from the nature of that business or of the proceedings'.

It says that public notice of the time and place of the meeting must be given by posting it at the offices at least three days before the meeting, or if the meeting is convened at shorter notice, then at the time it is convened.

On request and on payment of postage, if demanded, the body must supply to any newspaper, news or broadcasting agency, a copy of the agenda as supplied to members of the body, but excluding if thought fit any item to be discussed when the meeting is not likely to be open to the public.

The PB(AM)A 1960 says that, so far as is practicable, reporters shall be afforded reasonable facilities for taking their report and, unless the meeting is held in premises not belonging to the body or not having a telephone, for telephoning a report at the reporter's expense.

Rights to admission and to reporting facilities, agendas, and telephones under the terms of the PB(AM)A 1960 also apply to:

(1) parish meetings of rural parishes where there are fewer than 200 electors;

(2) a number of bodies set up under the Water Act 1989. These are: regional and local flood defence committees, regional rivers advisory committees, salmon and freshwater fisheries advisory committees, and customer service committees.

Council meetings held in private

If after a local authority meeting held in private under any of the three Acts referred to above an official statement was issued to the press, a copy of or extract from such a statement would be **privileged** under Schedule 1 to the →glossary Defamation Act 1996.

Information about such meetings, held when the press is excluded, and obtained from an unofficial source, would not be so privileged under the Act should it be defamatory.

Minutes of the proceedings of a parish or community council must, under the Local Government Act 1972, as amended by the LG(AI)A 1985, be open to inspection. Publication of a fair and accurate copy or extract from such minutes is protected by qualified privilege.

Access to council accounts

Many journalists miss the chances to dig out local authority stories provided by the provisions of the Audit Commission Act (ACA) 1998 and the Accounts and Audit Regulations 2003 (SI 2003/533). 'Local authorities' includes police and fire and civil defence authorities.

Under section 15 of the ACA 1998, 'any persons interested' may inspect a local authority's accounts and 'all books, deeds, contracts, bills, vouchers and receipts related thereto', and make copies. The previous version of the regulations said that each authority must make these accounts and documents available for public inspection for 15 full working days before a date appointed by the auditor, but this period was extended to 20 working days in the 2003 update to the regulations. An advertisement about this right must be published in at least one newspaper 14 days before the date on which the accounts and documents become available, but the best way for a journalist seeking to consult these documents is to ask the authority about them directly.

Lawyers differ as to whether the phrase 'any persons interested' includes reporters as such, but if the reporter is also a local elector there is no problem.

The *Express and Star*, Wolverhampton, has used the ACA 1998 to great effect in many stories. It revealed, for example, the details of a Birmingham City car pool equipped with expensive chauffeur-driven cars which were readily available to those in the know. The pool cost about £350,000 a year.

Jonathan Leake, a journalist formerly with the *Express and Star*, points out that the sheer volume of the 'treasure trove' made available by the ACA 1998 is a problem. He recommends alternative approaches.

First, a journalist should go in knowing what he/she is looking for. If the journalist suspects some dubious deals have been struck, he/she should ask for all the original documents relating to them, and go through the ledger to check. He/she should get the original invoices and tenders, and not be palmed off with ledger entries or computer print-outs.

Another approach is for the journalist to go to a particular department equipped for a general trawl. He/she should demand access to the files containing original invoices and receipts and go through them one by one.

A council officer refusing a proper demand for a copy or obstructing a person entitled to inspect one of these documents is in fact committing a criminal offence. The London Borough of Haringey was prosecuted and fined in 1996 for refusing to disclose documents relating to the audit which had been requested by a resident.

An exception to the general rule is that there is no right to examine documents relating to personal expenses incurred by officers of the council. By contrast, the Local Government (Allowances) Regulations 1986 (SI 1986/724) enable electors at any time of the year to demand to see a breakdown of allowances and expenses paid to councillors.

Before 1995 a local authority had to make available to the public information showing the amounts paid to councillors in the previous financial year. Since 1995, local authorities have been required to send this information to the local media.

Under the Local Government Finance (Publicity for Auditors' Reports) Act 1991 a council must make available immediately any report on a matter of particular concern produced by the auditors.

Health authorities and NHS Trusts

Admission to meetings of local health authorities and NHS Trusts, and rights to their agendas, are subject to the Public Bodies (Admission to Meetings) Act (PB(AM)A) 1960.

Department of Health guidance to these bodies in 1998 (Health Service Circular 1998/207) said that the Government was 'committed to ending what it sees as excessive secrecy in decision making in public bodies' and that although authorities and trusts could exclude press and public in the public interest under the terms of the PB(AM)A 1960, they were expected to conduct their business in public in as open a manner as possible.

Under the PB(AM)A 1960, the same rights of admission are given to any committee of a health authority consisting of all members of the authority.

Community health councils (CHCs) in England ceased to operate in September 2003, abolished by the NHS Reform and Health Care Professions Act 2002, although they continued to exist in Wales. The English CHCs were replaced by patient forums (PPI forums – that is, patients and public involvement forums). There are 572 of them, one for each primary care trust and NHS Trust and NHS Foundation Trust in England.

According to the Commission for Patient and Public Involvement in Health, established in January 2003, the forums would:

- be the main vehicle for the public to influence strategic priorities and day-to-day management of health services in their local area;

- be an independent critical friend on wider health matters in their community such as environmental health; and

- review services from the patient perspective and monitor responses from local health services to complaints from patients.

Each forum would comprise 15 to 20 locally recruited volunteers.

The Government has the power to make regulations on access to information from these forums which apply the LG(AI)A 1985 with modifications.

The Health and Social Care Act 2001 provided new powers to overview and scrutiny committees of those local authorities with social services responsibilities (county councils, London borough councils, unitary authorities), and these are subject to similar access to information provisions as other committees covered by LG(AI)A 1985.

An extended set of exemptions applies however, which can be found in Schedule 1 to the Health and Social Care Act 2001. These go further than the exemptions in the LG(AI)A 1985 by exempting also information on: (1) a person providing or applying to provide NHS services, (2) an employee of such person, or (3) information relating to a person's health. Minutes, agendas, and reports are open to public inspection for only three years and background papers for only two years.

Health authorities are required to publish details each year about maximum waiting times for beds in each speciality, the number of complaints received and how long it has taken to deal with them, and how successful the authority has been in relation to national and local standards under the Government's patients' charter.

▌ Police authorities

The Police and Magistrates' Courts Act 1994 gave added power to central Government over policing and the workings of magistrates courts.

The authorities have to draw up local policing plans that acknowledge the objectives set by the Home Secretary. The plan must state the authority's priorities for the year, the financial resources available, and its objectives.

The authority must also issue an annual report as soon as possible after the end of the financial year and arrange its publication. The report must include an assessment of the extent to which the local policing plan has been carried out.

Magistrates courts committees

The public must be admitted to a meeting of the magistrates courts committee at least once a year. The minutes of every meeting must be open to public inspection at the committee's office, except that confidential information can be excluded: in that case, the committee must state its reason. For a fee, copies must be made available.

Schools

Regulations made under the Education Acts 1996 and 1997 require both state and independent schools to provide information on examination results, truancy rates, rates of pupils staying on after 16, and employment or training undertaken by school leavers.

The regulations do not require schools to provide the names of examination candidates, with their results, but some schools do so and papers publish them.

→
see
ch. 26,
p. 442

The governing bodies of every county, controlled, and maintained school must, under the Education (No 2) Act 1986, keep written statements of their conclusions on policy matters. Regulations require the head teacher to make the statement available at all reasonable times.

The governing bodies of grant-maintained schools are required to make an annual report available for inspection at all reasonable times.

Quangos

Many of the day-to-day services to the public that used to be administered by bodies on which representatives of the public served have been hived off to semi-independent agencies on the ground that they would become more efficient when exposed to the disciplines of the market. The managing bodies are staffed by appointees rather than representatives.

The term **quango** (quasi-autonomous non-governmental organisation) is conveniently used to describe non-elected public bodies that operate outside the civil service and that are funded by the taxpayer.

→ glossary

They include grant-maintained schools, further education colleges, urban development corporations, learning and skills councils, and a wide variety of other bodies.

The Government prefers to use the term non-departmental public bodies (NDPBs), which includes only public bodies in the formal sense. It does not cover bodies that in legal terms are private enterprises, even if they are spending public money. The Government divides these bodies into executive NDPBs and advisory NDPBs. Another term used by the Government is 'appointed executive bodies'.

As a result of this difference in definition, estimates of the number of quangos in existence vary from 2,000 to 5,000 and estimates of the amount of money spent annually also vary widely.

Before the rapid increase in quangos in the 1980s and 1990s, it was generally accepted that the bodies that then had corresponding duties were accountable to the public and should provide information about their activities to the public. Many of them – for example, the old water authorities but not the new water companies – were required to admit the press to their meetings. They were generally required to provide documentation. In most cases, fair and accurate reports of their meetings and statements were covered by qualified privilege.

The argument on accountability no longer applies in the same way. Demands for information can be countered by the argument that the body cannot operate in market conditions when the details of its operations are known to its competitors.

The Minister in charge of the water companies justified the clampdown on public access by saying these companies were no longer operating like public corporations but more like private bodies under the Companies Act, with executive and business responsibilities.

In general, there is no right of access to the meetings of quangos but there is now a right to information to most of them under the FOI Act.

▦ Recap of major points

- People have rights to other information from local authorities, such as annual budget figures and agendas, as well as rights to attend meetings.
- In certain circumstances authorities have the right to withhold documents or to deny public access to meetings.

- Laws giving rights to examine accounts can be a very good source of stories, provided the journalist knows where to look.

- There are rights to attend the meetings of health authorities and these bodies are required to publish each year their performance in key areas of health provision.

🌐 Useful Websites

www.communities.gov.uk/
For guidance on the Local Government Act 2000 and exemptions from rights to access meetings

30

Reporting elections

Chapter summary

During elections there are special laws in operation to protect the democratic process. Under the Representation of the People Act 1983 there are penalties in criminal law for those convicted of making or publishing false statements about election candidates. This is in addition to the general, civil law on libel, which also needs to be observed by journalists reporting the heated debate about politics and candidates which occurs in election campaigns. Other law restricts when 'exit polls' can be published. This chapter also refers to the particular duty of broadcast journalists to maintain impartiality during election coverage. It also refers to arrangements for journalists to attend the counting of votes.

▌ False statements about election candidates

Under section 106 of the Representation of the People Act 1983, it is a criminal offence:

- to make or publish a false statement of fact about the personal character or conduct of an election candidate, if the purpose of publishing the false statement is to affect how many votes he/she will get.

To constitute such an offence, the falsity must be expressed as if it were a fact, as distinct from a statement which is clearly merely comment or an opinion about the candidate. It is a defence for anyone accused of publishing such a false statement to show that he/she had reasonable grounds for believing when the statement was published that it was true, and did at that time believe it was true (even if it turns out to be untrue).

It is also an offence under the Act:

- to publish a false claim that an election candidate has withdrawn from the election, if the publisher knows this claim is false and published it for the purpose of promoting or procuring the election of another candidate.

Breach of section 106 is punishable by a fine of up to £5,000. If the publisher is a company, its directors can be convicted. This law aims to deter 'dirty tricks' by those campaigning in an election, or by their supporters, and is not aimed specifically at the media. In 2006 a Labour candidate in a council election in London was convicted of making a false statement that her Liberal Democrat rival was a paedophile. In 1992 the publisher of a leaflet which falsely claimed that the Labour politician Jack Straw 'hated Muslims' was convicted under the Act. This ban in criminal law on such false statements applies only from the time formal notice is given that an election is to take place until the time the election ends. For local government elections, this period is around five weeks. For national Parliamentary elections, the period begins with the date of the dissolution of Parliament or any earlier time at which Her Majesty's intention to dissolve Parliament is announced.

If the false statement is defamatory, the publisher may – of course – also face a libel action. But the criminal sanction in the 1983 Act enables quicker remedial action, in that a candidate who can prove a **prima facie** → glossary case that he/she has been traduced by such a false statement can obtain a court **injunction** preventing its repetition, whereas the legal rule against → glossary 'prior restraint', explained in ch. 1, means it is harder to get an injunction in a libel action, which could take months to be resolved at trial or settled. The 1983 Act also prohibits such false statements even if they are not defamatory. A journalist who in 1997 published false allegations on the internet that an election candidate was a homosexual was fined £250 under the Act. In itself, a statement which inaccurately states that someone is homosexual is not defamatory. But in the context of an election, it could cost a candidate votes if, for example, voters whose religious beliefs are anti-gay decide because of the false statement not to support that candidate.

→ see ch. 17, p. 309 on defamation

▌ Defamation dangers during elections

In the heat of an election, candidates and their supporters may make defamatory allegations about rivals. Terms such 'racist', 'fascist', and 'liar' may be used, for example. A media organisation which publishes them may be successfully sued for libel if it has no defence. There is no specific statutory privilege for the media to publish election material produced by candidates, or what they say. But qualified **privilege** protects fair and accurate reports of public meetings and of press conferences, if all requirements of that defence are met. When reporting speeches by extremist candidates, journalists should remember that such speakers, and reports of their speeches, are subject to the laws against stirring up hatred, including on racial and religious grounds.

→
see ch.
19, pp.
340–346
→
see ch. 34

▌ Election advertisements

In election law, only an election candidate or his/her agent may incur any expenses relating to their campaign, including for the publication of an advertisement. It is an offence for anyone else unless he/she is authorised in writing by the election agent to pay for such an advertisement. This precludes well-wishers from seeking to insert advertisements in a newspaper on behalf of a candidate without his/her express authority.

▌ Broadcasters' duty to be impartial

The Ofcom Broadcasting Code and the BBC Editorial Guidelines, which incorporate the Ofcom Code, have detailed guidance about achieving impartiality in election coverage. Several independent radio stations have been fined by Ofcom after presenters or others broadcast partial declarations of support for political candidates or parties.

→
see also
ch. 1, pp.
16–17

▌ Exit polls

The term 'exit poll' is used to describe any kind of survey in which voters are asked, after they have voted, which candidate and/or political party they voted for. When conducted scientifically, such questioning of people as they leave polling stations can often produce data which accurately predict an election result, hours ahead of its being officially declared. However, a number of democratic nations, including the UK, have imposed legal restrictions on when such data/predictions can be published. The rationale, disputed by some, is that publication of such data, or predictions based on them, at a time when some members of the electorate have yet to vote could skew the election result. The concern is that if people yet to vote are told which candidate/party is apparently due to win the election, with that information being apparently soundly based on votes already cast, these people could alter their original voting intention. Some, for example, may switch their choice to another candidate who appears – from the exit poll data – to have a better chance of winning. Some may decide not to vote at all, believing – for example – that the exit poll data show either that their favoured candidate cannot win, or that he/she will win so easily that no further votes are needed. These possible effects are seen as potential contamination of the democratic process, in that: a) this later group of voters has made choices on data not available to those who voted earlier and b) those data, and any prediction apparently based on them, may be inaccurate or – in the worst cases – may have been falsified to influence voting.

Section 66A of the Representation of the People Act 1983, as inserted by the 2000 Act of the same title, makes it a criminal offence:

- to publish, before a poll is closed, any statement about the way in which voters have voted in that election, where this statement is, or might reasonably be taken to be, based on information given by voters after they have voted.

Under the Act, it is also an offence:

- to publish, before a poll is closed, any forecast – including any estimate – of that election result, if the forecast is based on exit poll information from voters, or which might reasonably be taken to be based on it.

So, for example, it would be illegal to broadcast, or put on a website, before polling stations closed, the statement: 'Fifty-five per cent of the people we have questioned say they have voted today for Labour'. This law applies to Parliamentary and council elections, to those for the Welsh Assembly, and to by-elections. It applies in respect of exit polls conducted to focus on an individual constituency or ward, or on voting nationally. If matter is published in breach of section 66A, the publisher is liable to a fine of up to £5,000 or a jail term of up to six months. Publication of exit polls during polling for European Parliamentary elections is also prohibited (SI 2004/293).

It is perfectly legal to publish, at any time, opinion poll data on voting intentions which have been gathered before voting begins, because such data are not based on how people say they have actually voted. Also, it is legal to report the results of exit polls, and any forecast based on them, as soon as polling has finally closed, as TV programmes frequently do. However, it is not always accurate now to talk of 'an election day'. For example, experiments to encourage more people to vote may mean that in some places voting takes place over several days. It will be an offence to publish an exit poll, or forecast apparently based on it, during any of the polling days, until the polls close on the final day. During elections for the European Parliament in June 2004, *The Times* published an opinion poll which had asked people how they had voted in areas using all-postal ballots. The Electoral Commission, the independent elections watchdog, said this amounted to an exit poll. It referred the matter to the Crown Prosecution Service. The Commission later reported that the CPS, after discussions with *The Times*, had concluded that it would not be appropriate to take any further action.

The regulatory codes for broadcast journalists have, for some time, placed similar controls on the publication of exit polls, and indeed go further, in that the Ofcom Broadcasting Code, which is incorporated into the BBC Editorial Guidelines, states: 'No opinion poll [i.e. not just an exit poll] may be published on the day of the election until the polls close, or in the case of a European election, all the polls have closed across the European Union.'

▌ Election counts

Journalists, including photographers and TV crews, need to be present at election counts, so declarations of the result can be broadcast and quickly published on websites and in newspapers. Admission to counts is at the discretion of the Returning Officer – the official legally responsible for security and procedures at each count. There is no national policy on what rights journalists have to attend counts. But the Electoral Commission's guidance to Returning Officers is to negotiate with media representatives in advance to make what arrangements are possible. According to the Newspaper Society and to the Society of Editors, there is established precedent that if TV crews are allowed into a count, newspaper photographers will also be allowed in.

▦ Recap of major points

- Once an election has been called it is a criminal offence to publish a false statement about the personal character or conduct of a candidate for the purpose of affecting the number of votes he/she gets.
- It is an offence to publish before the end of polling any data obtained in exit polls on how people have voted, or any prediction of the election result based on such data.

🌐 Useful Websites

www.electoralcommission.org.uk/
  Electoral Commission

31

Official secrets

Chapter summary

The UK's official secrets legislation has not been used in recent years to prosecute journalists, despite some State secrets having been published. But it has been used to jail civil servants and others who have supplied sensitive information to journalists. And the potential remains for journalists to be imprisoned

→ glossary under this law. UK governments have used it to gain **injunctions** to prevent such leaked material being published. This chapter gives an outline of this controversial legislation. If a journalist is thought to have breached it, his/her home could be searched by police, and research records seized. There could well be sustained attempts to discover the identity of the journalist's confidential source – the person who has leaked 'inside' information. This law does not contain a 'public interest' defence for anyone prosecuted for leaking or publishing official secrets.

▌ Introduction

The Official Secrets Acts of 1911 and 1989 are concerned with national security and with enforcing the duty of confidentiality owed to the UK State by Crown servants or by employees of companies contracted in military or other sensitive work. Crown servants include all civil servants and members of the armed services, and the police and civilians working for the police. The Act imposes a similar duty on members of the UK's security and intelligence services.

Part of this legislation was designed to punish spies working for foreign powers – those who deliberately betray or incite the betrayal of the UK's defence, intelligence, and diplomatic secrets – or secrets which make vital facilities in the UK vulnerable to sabotage. For example, in 2008 Daniel James, a British army corporal who worked as an interpreter in Afghanistan for a NATO general, was jailed for 10 years for spying for Iran.

However, official secrets law is also used to punish the unauthorised leaking of sensitive information from within UK state agencies to other parties, e.g. to a journalist or to another member of the public, when – it is alleged – such leaking actually or potentially damages the interests of the State or otherwise endangers its citizens. If such information is published, it can, of course, be seen by hostile powers, terrorists, or other criminals, or can embarrass the UK's allies, e.g. if diplomatic correspondence is revealed.

But the use of official secrets law to punish leaks is controversial, because Attorney Generals have approved prosecutions of Crown servants and other people who, on grounds of conscience, leaked or helped to leak information to the media to throw light on controversial government policies. In such cases the rationale for the prosecution is questioned by media and other commentators – is it to protect the State's vital secrets or primarily to stifle debate about a matter of public interest which is embarrassing for the government of the day? Under this law a journalist is open to prosecution if he/she is seen as an accomplice to the leak. Also, the person who receives the sensitive information commits a separate offence if he/she discloses it further when knowing the Act protects it. This leaves a reporter and his/her editor open to prosecution if such information is further circulated or published. The law can also be used to punish a Crown servant who by careless error leaves sensitive information where members of the public may find it.

→ see ch. 1, pp. 15–16 on Attorney General's role

 Because the law is complex, a longer version of this chapter can be read on the Online Resource Centre.

▶ The law's consequences for journalists

Journalists were jailed in 1916 and 1932 for offences under the 1911 Act. But as this book went to press no journalist had been successfully prosecuted under official secrets law, let alone jailed, for many years. Prosecutions under the 1911 and 1989 Acts can be brought only by or with the consent of the Attorney General, except in cases relating to crime or special investigation powers, when the consent of the Director of Public Prosecutions is required.

The underlying reasons for officialdom's reluctance to prosecute journalists are discussed below. However, journalists need to be aware of these Acts and be ready to protect the indentities of their sources of information. Though a journalist may not be sent to prison for his/her story, his/her source may be. A journalist's home may be raided by police seeking to discover who the source is, and the journalist may be arrested and threatened with prosecution, an experience he/she is likely to find intimidating. The journalist may be prevented from publishing the story as a result of an injunction, see p. 503. The Acts are therefore considered to have a chilling effect on journalists investigating and publishing matters that may be in the public interest.

➜   see ch. 32, in particular, pp. 520–523 on police powers to search premises and demand material

▶ Examples of journalists investigated

Here are some examples of the way the legislation has been used against journalists.

In 1998 Tony Geraghty, the former *Sunday Times* defence correspondent, was charged with an offence under the 1989 Official Secrets Act after the publication of his book *The Irish War.* This disclosed the extensive use of computerised surveillance by intelligence agencies in Northern Ireland. Ministry of Defence police raided Geraghty's home and arrested him. It was not until a year later that the charge against him was dropped.

In 2000 Julie-Ann Davies, a broadcast researcher, was arrested and questioned for possible breach of the Act on the basis that she had been in communication with David Shayler, a former MI5 officer who had provided the *Mail on Sunday* with security-related information. She was not prosecuted.

In 2003 armed police raided the home of Liam Clarke, the Northern Ireland editor of the *Sunday Times*, and arrested him and his wife Kathryn Johnston after they published an updated version of their book *From Guns to Government.* The book contained transcripts of tape-recordings, taken from a joint police/MI5 surveillance operation, which detailed bugged telephone conversations that were acutely embarrassing to the UK Government. The two were detained at their home for five hours. Later that year the police admitted the raid had been unlawful because, although a search warrant had been issued under the Police and Criminal Evidence Act 1984, it had been authorised by a magistrate, not by a judge as the law required. In 2006 the two journalists were reported to have received a 'five-figure' sum from the police in settlement of a claim for false imprisonment.

see ch.
32, p. 518
on the
1984 Act

In 2005 the Attorney General, Lord Goldsmith, issued a warning to newspapers after the *Daily Mirror* published a story headlined 'PM halted Bush plan to bomb Arab TV channel off the air'. The story began: 'George Bush's plot to bomb an Arab TV station in friendly Qatar was crushed by Tony Blair, who feared it would spark horrific revenge.'

The paper said the story was based on a leaked memo, which – it said – detailed minutes of a conversation between the Prime Minister and the president in which they discussed the Arabic TV broadcaster Al-Jazeera. It had angered the American and British Governments by broadcasting footage of dead soldiers and others who had died in the Iraq war. The Attorney General warned that newspapers would be contravening official secrets law if they published the contents of the memo. Commentators suggested that Lord Goldsmith had 'read the riot act' to the media because of political embarrassment caused by this sensitive leak of face-to-face exchanges between the Prime Minister and the US president.

▶ The fate of sources

Sources are generally dealt with more severely than journalists are.

Tony Geraghty's source, Nigel Wylde, a former army colonel, was arrested and charged at the same time as Geraghty. The charge against Wylde was eventually dropped, but not until 15 months after his arrest.

Shayler, the former M15 officer, was sentenced to six months' imprisonment in 2002. The stories he had provided to the *Mail on Sunday* in 1997 included the disclosure that the Government kept secret files on certain Labour politicians. The newspaper published the story, but was not prosecuted.

In the Al-Jazeera case, a former civil servant, David Keogh, and Leo O'Connor, who had worked as an MP's researcher were jailed in 2007 for six months and three months respectively for the leak of the memo received by the *Mirror*.

Also in 2007 Thomas Lund-Lack, who worked for the Metropolitan Police's counter-terrorism command, was jailed for eight months after he pleaded guilty to 'wilful misconduct in a judicial or public office', a charge which arose from him leaking documents to the *Sunday Times* about the threat Al-Qaeda poses to the UK. A charge under the Official Secrets Act 1989, which he denied, was dropped.

In 2008 charges, under section 3 of the 1989 Act, against a Foreign Office civil servant, Derek Pasquill, were dropped shortly before he was due to be tried at the Old Bailey, accused of leaking documents to the *Observer* and to the *New Statesman* magazine. Some of the documents concerned the controversial 'rendition' of terrorists suspects, and some the Government's policy of engaging in dialogue with hard-line Islamic radicals. The Government's counsel told the judge that there was no longer a realistic prospect of conviction. It was later reported that internal Foreign Office papers revealed that senior officials had privately admitted that instead of harming the UK's interests, the leaking of some of the documents had helped to provoke a constructive debate about the dialogue policy.

→glossary

In 1985 a jury acquitted Clive Ponting, a senior civil servant who was charged under official secrets law after he leaked to an MP secret information about the controversial sinking of the Argentine battleship the *Belgrano* in the Falklands war.

▌ The media may be excluded from secrets trials

Under section 8 of the Official Secrets Act 1920, the public and the media may be excluded from secrets trials when publication of evidence would be 'prejudicial to the national safety'. There is no generally recognised definition of national safety (or national security). The Act states that a court must sit in open session when sentencing a convicted defendant.

▌ Reluctance to prosecute journalists

The cases referred to above raise the question why the source was so often prosecuted, when the journalist was not. As explained below, section 5 of the 1989 Act, the section under which it is assumed that a journalist in such a case would normally be prosecuted, provides defences that are not available to the source. For example, the journalist will have a defence that the disclosure of the information was not 'damaging' to State interests, e.g. to the work of the intelligence services as defined in the Act.

John Wadham, who when he was director of the civil rights organisation Liberty was Shayler's lawyer, said of the lack of recent prosecutions of journalists:

> ▐▐ It is partly because governments don't like to be seen to be trying to put journalists in prison and partly because juries are less sympathetic to civil servants – who are employed to keep their mouths shut, who are aware of the rules but break them, and who breach the trust with employers and

colleagues – compared with journalists, who are paid to find things out and publish them. 🟥🟥

▮ The use of injunctions

From the 1980s onwards UK governments have made use of injunctions forbidding the publication of leaked official material. This has enabled them to silence the media without a criminal prosecution, i.e. without the risk of a jury deciding that the publication was lawful. Injunctions are granted by judges sitting alone, and it is an offence of contempt of court to disobey an injunction. Several sets of injunctions were issued to stop the media publishing extracts from the book *Spycatcher*, the memoirs of the intelligence officer Peter Wright, which was published abroad. In the legal saga over *Spycatcher* the Court of Appeal set the precedent in 1987 that an injunction against one newspaper, restraining it from publishing confidential information, applied to all the media.

→
see also
ch. 23,
pp. 390
and 392
on *Spycatcher*

▮ The 1911 Act

Section 1 of the 1911 Act is concerned with spying, but journalists need to know about it. Under this section it is an arrestable offence, carrying a penalty of up to 14 years' imprisonment, to do any of the following 'for any purpose prejudicial to the safety or interests of the state':

  (a) approach, inspect, pass over, be in the neighbourhood of, or enter any prohibited place (see below);

  (b) make any sketch, plan, model, or note that might be or is intended to be useful to an enemy;

  (c) obtain, collect, record, or communicate to any person any information that might be or is intended to be useful to an enemy.

Offences under (c) are most relevant for journalists. Section 3 of the 1911 Act gives a lengthy definition of a 'prohibited place'. It includes, for example, 'any work or defence, arsenal, naval or air force establishment or station, factory, dockyard, mine, minefield, camp, ship, or aircraft' and 'any telegraph, telephone, wireless or signal station, or office' when any such property is used by the State. **Statutory instruments** have added British Nuclear Fuels plc and Atomic Energy Authority sites to the list of prohibited places. The Energy Act 2008 added any site where there is equipment or software for the enrichment of uranium, or information about this process. These additions apparently reflect fears that terrorist groups want to build a nuclear bomb or a 'dirty', radio-active one.

⟶ glossary

As can be seen, the definition of a prohibited place is wide. The media has to bear in mind that taking photos or gathering information in the course of routine news coverage outside or near a prohibited place – some of which, for example, are targets for peace protests – could be held to be in breach of the Act and so could publication of such photos or information.

▶ The 1989 Act: the journalist's position

The Act defines offences of disclosure by reference to various classes of information. These include information about security and intelligence; defence; international relations; official investigations into crime, e.g. by the police or other agencies; official phone-tapping, and the official interception of letters or other communications; prison and custody facilities; and matters entrusted in confidence to other States or international organisations.

Section 5 of the Act, for example, says that a person – for the purposes of this example, a journalist – commits an offence if he/she discloses without lawful authority information protected by the Act, knowing or having reasonable cause to believe that it is thus protected against disclosure, if he/she received the information from a Crown servant or government contractor (a) without lawful authority, or (b) in confidence, or received it from someone else who received it in confidence from such a person. But it must also be proved that the journalist knew, or had reasonable cause to believe, that the disclosure of this information would be damaging to State interests as defined in the Act.

 See the Online Resource Centre, ch. 31 for more detail.

Damage test but no public interest defence

Though the 1989 Act can catch journalists and other members of the public, it is directed particularly at members of the security services, other Crown servants, and government contractors who make disclosures without lawful authority. The degree of damage (by disclosure) necessary for conviction under the Act varies according to the class of information and the category of person accused. The damage alleged to have occured could be, for example, to the capacity of the UK's armed forces to carry out certain duties, or to the UK's relations with another state.

There is no public interest defence in official secrets cases. Also, there is no specific defence of prior publication. The information can still be classed as secret even if it has been published previously.

The lawyer David Hooper, author of the book *Official Secrets; the use and abuse of the Act*, has said that he believes the damage test may let in public interest 'by the back door'.

Suppose the journalist being prosecuted had exposed a scandal concerning State activities. A jury, when deciding whether the journalist knew the disclosure would be damaging to the State's interests, may – whatever is stated in the strict letter of official secrets law – choose to take into account when arriving at a verdict, the public interest in the material being published.

Penalties

Penalties for an offence of disclosure under the 1989 Act are a maximum of two years' imprisonment or a fine or both. If the case is tried summarily (by magistrates) the maximum is six months or a fine or both.

▶ Defence Advisory Notices

Guidance on national security is made available to the media by the Defence Press and Broadcasting Advisory Committee by means of Defence Advisory Notices (DA-Notices) (formerly known as D-Notices). There are five standing DA-Notices, see below. They describe the types of subject matter which the Government and media members of the committee consider may damage national security if published. The committee advises, therefore, that as regards such matter caution and guidance is necessary before an editor decides on publication.

The standing DA-Notices are distributed to national and provincial newspapers, radio and television organisations, major internet service providers, and some publishers of periodicals and books on defence and related subjects. The committee is composed of four senior officials of the Cabinet Office, Ministry of Defence, the Home Office, and the Foreign Office, and 15 nominees from newspapers, periodicals, news agencies, and broadcasting organisations. The chairman is the Permanent Under-Secretary of State for Defence. The permanent secretary of the committee (known as the DA-Notice secretary) is normally a retired senior officer from the armed forces. His telephone number is 020 7218 2206. The current secretary is Andrew Vallance. His address is Floor 1 Spine H 21, Ministry of Defence, Main Building, Whitehall, London SW1A 2HB. See below for the address of the committee's website.

Editors, defence correspondents, other journalists, and authors consult him to check whether information being considered for publication comes within a sensitive area. When the secretary learns of media interest in any of the DA-Notice areas, he contacts the editor, publisher, or programme maker to offer advice.

The five DA-Notices in force since 1993 cover the following subjects:

(1) military operations, plans, and capabilities;

(2) nuclear and non-nuclear weapons and operational equipment;

(3) cyphers and secure communications;

(4) identification of specific installations and home addresses;

(5) UK security and intelligence services, and special forces.

They can be read in their entirety at the committee's website, www. dnotice.org.uk.

Procedure exists to issue additional DA-Notices to similarly protect specific pieces of information, but as this book went to press this procedure had not been used for many years. As a result of consulting the DA-Notice secretary, editors sometimes decide to limit what is published and sometimes feel able to publish information that they might otherwise leave out. But the committee has no statutory powers of enforcement. The final decision on whether to publish always rests with the editor or publisher. Editors do not have to seek advice, nor do they have to take any advice that may be offered. In effect, the system is a code of self-censorship by the media in matters of national security. An editor who publishes information of the type covered by a DA-Notice knows that the Government regards such information as sensitive. He/she realises, therefore, that there is a risk of prosecution if what is published is regarded as a breach of official secrets law.

⠿ Recap of major points

- The law of official secrets is complex, and frequently controversial.

- Some of it is for use against foreign spies, terrorists, or other criminals. This law protects national security, other interests of the State, and the safety of citizens.

- But journalists consider that this law is on occasion used to punish those who leak information which is politically embarrassing for the government of the day, and that the law is also used to deter the media from discovering and revealing such information.

- The law has wide definitions of what is secret. There is no public interest defence for anyone prosecuted for breaching it.

- The DA-Notice system is a means by which editors, journalists, and authors can check if material they are considering publishing could be regarded as a breach of national security.

- There is a longer version of this chapter on the Online Resource Centre.

🌐 Useful Websites

www.parliament.uk/commons/lib/research/briefings/snpc-02023.pdf
House of Commons Library, Note on Official Secrecy

www.sis.gov.uk/output/sis-home-welcome.html
Secret Intelligence Service website (MI6)

www.cpbf.org.uk/
Campaign for Press and Broadcasting Freedom

32

The journalist's sources

Chapter summary

It is a matter of professional principle that reporters do not reveal sources of confidential information.

The journalist's job is to discover and publish news but there are many vested interests trying to prevent that. For this reason, to get a story a journalist must often rely on information from people whose safety or careers would be at risk if it became known that they had provided it. Furthermore, if it became common practice to divulge such sources, the job of a journalist would become much more difficult as fewer people would be willing to speak to them.

Various bodies have powers to ask reporters where they got a story. This chapter will explain what those powers are and how journalists can protect their confidential sources from exposure.

▌ Protecting your source: the ethical imperative

→
see also
ch. 1,
p. 17 on
PCC code

Clause 14 of the Press Complaints Commission Code of Practice states simply: 'Journalists have a moral obligation to protect confidential sources of information.' The National Union of Journalists code of conduct has a similar clause.

Journalists' ethical codes in nations all round the world state the same principle. Journalists agree on it more than on any other practice in their professional life. Without such sources being sure that a journalist will not betray their identity, many stories which need to be published in the public interest would never reach journalists, and so would never see the light of day. Clause 14 of the PCC code is not subject to that code's public interest exceptions, so the code does not set out any circumstance which justifies breach of the clause. The NUJ code, too, has no exception to the principle.

→ see Useful Websites below for NUJ Code

▌ Who might ask you to divulge your source?

Judges

In **common law** judges have the power to order disclosure of the identity of wrongdoers (*Norwich Pharmacal Co v Customs and Excise Comrs* [1974] AC 133).

→ glossary

In 1989, Bill Goodwin, a trainee reporter on *The Engineer* magazine, was ordered by a judge to reveal the source of information about an engineering company in financial difficulties and seeking a large loan. He refused to do so and was fined £5,000 for contempt of court (*X Ltd v Morgan-Grampian (Publishers) Ltd* [1991] 1 AC 1).

In 2001 a group of news organisations was ordered to hand over documents wanted by Belgian brewers Interbrew, in an attempt to find the person responsible for circulation of false information that resulted in a fall in share prices (*Interbrew SA v Financial Times Ltd, Independent Newspapers, Guardian Newspapers Ltd, Times Newspapers Ltd and Reuters Group plc* [2002] EWCA Civ 274; [2002] 2 Lloyd's Rep 229).

The organisations refused to do so, and there was a threat by the firm to seek a sequestration order seizing the assets of the *Guardian*. Later the brewer dropped its actions.

→ see 'Statutes giving disclosure powers', below, p. 516

Requests by officials

Sometimes the person asking the journalist for a source will be a tribunal chairman or an official.

In 1963 two journalists appearing before a tribunal of inquiry were jailed for refusing to identify sources of information in stories in the *Vassall* case (*Attorney General v Clough* [1963] 1 QB 773). Vassall had been convicted of spying. The tribunal had been set up under the Tribunals of Inquiry (Evidence) Act 1921, which gave tribunals wide powers to send for and examine witnesses.

Three journalists who refused to name the sources of stories about the Bloody Sunday killings in Northern Ireland were threatened with contempt of court actions by Lord Saville, chairman of the inquiry set up under the same Act to report on the incident. The journalists were Tony Harnden, of the *Daily Telegraph*, the former Channel 4 news producer Lena Ferguson, and Alex Thomson, the station's chief news reporter. Mr Harnden refused to name a soldier whose recollection formed the basis of a story published in 1999. The journalist had given him an undertaking not to say or do anything that might identify him. In 2000 Mr Harnden was 'placed in contempt' of the inquiry and told the matter had been referred to the High Court in Belfast. In 2004 the court was told contempt proceedings were being dropped.

Requests by a police officer

Sometimes the person asking the journalist for his source will be a police officer. Like other citizens, the journalist has no legal duty to provide information to the police for their inquiries, except in the special circumstances mentioned below. This would seem an elementary item of civic knowledge, but in 1990 a *Westmorland Gazette* reporter who declined to tell a police inspector his source for a story about the leak of a council document was threatened with prosecution for obstructing the police in their duties.

 → glossary   If the police need to obtain **journalistic material** to assist their investigations they normally have to apply to a judge first. They also generally need the consent of a judge before searching a journalist's premises for such material. These provisions are contained in the Police and Criminal Evidence Act 1984.

→

see section on the Act, below, p. 518

The opportunities for police officers lawfully to gain access to confidential information held by citizens, including journalists, were increased by the Police Act 1997, the Regulation of Investigatory Powers (RIP) Act 2000, the Terrorism Act 2000 and the Anti-terrorism, Crime and Security Act 2001, and the Serious Organised Crime and Police Act 2005.

 →

see below, p. 517–525

◗ Search powers

Increasingly authorities that have been given the power to demand information are also given the power to search the premises of the person they believe to have the information. This contravenes the traditional principle that 'an Englishman's home is his castle'.

A famous case in 1765 concerned a clerk called Entick whose house had been entered by 'the king's messengers' and his papers seized on the authority of a warrant from the Secretary of State (*Entick v Carrington* (1765) 19 State Tr 1029). The court said firmly the action was unlawful.

That case was referred to and endorsed in the Queen's Bench Divisional Court in 2000 when the court refused an application by the police to order the *Guardian* and the *Observer* to hand over all files, documents, and records in their possession relating to a letter in the *Guardian* from the former M15 officer David Shayler and an article by the reporter Martin Bright in the *Observer*.

Both publications repeated allegations that M16 officers had been involved in a failed attempt to assassinate the Libyan leader, Colonel Gaddafi. The police in particular wanted an email letter sent by Shayler so that they could discover his email address (*R v Central Criminal Court, ex p Martin Bright* [2001] 2 All ER 244; the case is referred to below as the *Martin Bright* case).

Lord Justice Judge said that the Englishman's home principle was linked with freedom of speech. He continued:

> Premises are not to be entered by the forces of authority or the state to deter or diminish, inhibit or stifle the exercise of an individual's right to free speech or the press of its freedom to investigate and inform, and orders should not be made which might have that effect unless a **circuit judge** is personally satisfied that the statutory preconditions to the making of an order are established, and, as the final safeguard of basic freedoms, that in the particular circumstances it is indeed appropriate for an order to be made.

→ glossary

Under the Security Service Act 1996 the security service, which now has police functions, also is enabled to enter on and interfere with property if it is investigating serious crime in the United Kingdom. Again, no authorisation by a judge is necessary, but a warrant from the Home Secretary is required.

Under the Terrorism Act 2000, a court can issue a warrant enabling police investigating a terrorist offence to search premises.

→ see ch. 33, p. 532

In urgent cases a police officer of the rank of superintendent or above can issue the equivalent of a search warrant for excluded or special procedure material, normally available only from a circuit judge. The Secretary of State has to be notified as soon as is reasonably practicable.

▶ Sources and the Human Rights Act 1998

→glossary In the *Martin Bright* case, Lord Justice Judge said that counsel had drawn the attention of the court to a number of decisions of the European Court of Human Rights (ECtHR), but he did not find it necessary to refer to any of these decisions to discover the principles that applied in this case because the principles contained in Article 6 (right to a fair trial) and Article 10 (right to freedom of expression) 'are bred in the bone of the common law'.

→
referred
to above,
p. 509
and,
more
fully, in
ch. 23,
p. 391
In the *Bill Goodwin* case, Goodwin was fined for refusing to comply with a judge's order to reveal his sources in a story that most journalists would have regarded as unexceptional. He appealed against the order unsuccessfully first to the Court of Appeal and then to the House of Lords and all three courts held that disclosure was 'necessary in the interests of justice'.

Then, backed by the National Union of Journalists, he took the case to the ECtHR, where it went first before the European Commission, which at that time had the job of considering matters before they reached the European Court itself. In 1994 the Commission found for Goodwin, saying:

> ❝ Protection of the sources from which journalists derive information is an essential means of enabling the press to perform its important function of 'public watchdog' in a democratic society. ❞

In 1996 the European Court reached the same conclusion in the case (*Goodwin v United Kingdom* (1996) EHRR 123). It said protection of journalistic sources was one of the basic conditions for press freedom, as was reflected in the laws and the professional codes of conduct in a number of contracting states and was affirmed in several international instruments on journalistic freedoms. An order of source disclosure could not be compatible with Article 10 of the Convention unless it was justified by an overriding requirement in the public interest.

In a case involving the *Daily Mirror* report on the Moors murderer Ian Brady, in 2000 Ashworth Security Hospital (where he was held), not knowing at first that the story had come from Robin Ackroyd, applied for and was granted an order against the paper, requiring it to reveal the source. The paper appealed unsuccessfully against the order.

Lord Phillips, Master of the Rolls, said in the Court of Appeal that the decisions of the ECtHR had demonstrated that the freedom of the press had in the past carried greater weight in Strasbourg than it had in the courts of this country. But the court went on to find against the media, after considering the ECtHR test.

Lord Phillips said an English court, when considering whether a production order was 'necessary', should apply the same test as the ECtHR did when considering Article 10 of the Convention. But the hospital could argue that identification of the source was in the interests of the protection of health, the protection of the rights of others, and preventing the disclosure of information received in confidence.

In 2002 the House of Lords agreed and rejected the *Mirror*'s appeal. The judges recognised that the disclosure of sources had a 'chilling effect' on the freedom of the press, but found that it was 'necessary and proportionate and justified' in this case (*Ashworth Security Hospital v MGN Ltd* [2002] UKHL 29; [2002] 4 All ER 193).

So the paper was ordered to reveal its source, but reporter Robin Ackroyd admitted it was he. As mentioned above, *he* refused to identify *his* source, after which he was ordered to do so on the basis that he had no defence after the *Ashworth* case. He appealed.

In May 2003 the Court of Appeal found for the reporter, saying the case against him was different from the earlier case against the paper, and he had an arguable defence that he ought to be allowed to put at trial (*Mersey Care NHS Trust v Robin Ackroyd* [2003] EWCA Civ 663). The court had now learned, as the earlier court had not, that the source for the story (the person who had given the information to Ackroyd) had not been paid for it. If that person had a public interest defence to a claim by the hospital for breach of confidence or contract, a claim based could not succeed against Ackroyd.

Even if Ackroyd failed to establish that his source had a public interest defence, it did not automatically follow that the public interest in non-disclosure of medical records should override the public interest in maintaining the confidentiality of his source.

At the trial that followed, in February 2006, a High Court judge in London rejected arguments by Ashworth Hospital in Merseyside that in this case the need to protect the confidentiality of medical records overrode the public interest in a journalist's right to protect his sources (*Mersey Care NHS Trust v Robin Ackroyd* [2006] EWHC 107 (QB)).

Requiring Ackroyd to disclose his sources 'would not be proportionate to the pursuit of the hospital's legitimate aim to seek redress against the source, given the vital public interest in the protection of a journalist's source', Mr Justice Tugendhat said.

The NHS Trust appealed but the Court of Appeal found for Ackroyd, dismissing the Trust's appeal (*Mersey Care NHS Trust v Robin Ackroyd* [2007] EWCA Civ 101). In a decision handed down in February 2007 the court said that Mr Justice Tugendhat had taken into account the key considerations on each side of the argument, and they did not think there was any basis on which they could properly interfere with the balance he had struck.

In 2007 the House of Lords rejected the Trust's petition to appeal against the Court of Appeal decision.

In 2008 Sally Murrer, a reporter on the Milton Keynes *Citizen*, and Mark Kearney, a former detective accused of leaking information to her, walked free from court after it was ruled that evidence against them was inadmissible. The evidence had been gathered by police bugging of Mr Kearney's car.

Mr Kearney faced charges of misconduct in a public office and Ms Murrer was charged with aiding and abetting misconduct in a public office.

Judge Richard Southwell, in Kingston Crown Court, ruled that the evidence gathered using the listening device was a violation of the defendant's rights under Article 10 of the European Convention on Human Rights and that this was not justifiable. The information in question was not sensitive, let alone 'highly sensitive' and so the police action could not be justified.

Ms Murrer, who was supported by the National Union of Journalists, had to wait 18 months before the case against her collapsed. Her home and office were searched by police and all of her notebooks were seized.

Gavin Millar, QC, representing Ms Murrer, said the police had not considered her status as a journalist when they decided to bug her conversations with Mr Kearney. He said:

> One of the protections of the Strasbourg law is a practical one...It is the right to be brought before a court and have a court decide whether you are required to disclose your source. What they did here was a no-no in Strasbourg terms – and a pretty big no-no (*R v Kearney and Murrer* (2008)).

▶ Contempt of court

Courts claim to recognise that there is a public interest in journalists being able to protect their sources, but have ordered disclosure when they considered it necessary.

In 1980, a court ordered Granada Television to reveal the identity of a 'mole' who had passed on confidential documents belonging to the British Steel Corporation. The documents revealed mismanagement at the corporation, which was then making huge losses. Fortunately for Granada, the mole himself came forward and revealed his identity (*British Steel Corporation v Granada Television Ltd* [1981] 1 All ER 435).

The following year, the Contempt of Court Act 1981 gave statutory form to the courts' recognition of the public interest in allowing journalists to protect their sources.

Section 10 says:

> ❝ No court may require a person to disclose, nor is any person guilty of contempt of court for refusing to disclose, the source of information contained in a publication for which he is responsible, unless it is established to the satisfaction of the court that disclosure is necessary in the interests of justice or national security, or for the prevention of disorder or crime. ❞

Three cases have illustrated that the protection given to the journalist by the section, as interpreted by the courts, has not always proved to be as great as many had hoped (and probably not as great as Parliament had intended).

The first case showed the scope of the phrase 'national security'. In 1983 the *Guardian* newspaper was ordered to return to the Government a leaked photo-stat copy of a Ministry of Defence document revealing the strategy for handling the arrival in Britain of Cruise missiles.

The *Guardian* did not know the identity of its informant, but realised the identity might be revealed by examination of the document, and claimed that as a result of section 10 it did not have to hand it over.

But the House of Lords said the interests of national security required that the identity of the informant must be revealed; publication of the particular document posed no threat to national security, but there was a risk that the person who leaked that document might leak another.

The *Guardian* handed over the document and the informant, a Foreign Office clerk, Sarah Tisdall, was convicted under the Official Secrets Act and jailed for six months (*Secretary of State for Defence v Guardian Newspapers Ltd* [1985] AC 339).

▦ Point for consideration

Journalists should note that had the *Guardian* destroyed the document after it was used to prepare the article but before its handing over was ordered, the paper would have escaped the painful necessity of having to reveal the identity of its source. Sarah Tisdall's identity might not have been revealed and thus she might have avoided a jail sentence.

The case involving Jeremy Warner showed what the courts understood by the word 'necessary' and the phrase 'prevention of crime'.

→

see
below,
p. 517

Inspectors investigating insider dealing asked for a court order compelling Warner to reveal his sources. Action was taken under the Financial Services Act 1986. The Act provides that if a person has no reasonable excuse he/she shall be punished as if he/she had committed contempt of court, and the court therefore considered whether he would have had a defence under section 10 of the Contempt of Court Act 1981.

The House of Lords rejected the idea that disclosure was 'necessary' only if it was the only means of preventing further insider dealing, and that it was the 'key to the puzzle'. Lord Griffiths said 'necessary' had a meaning which lay somewhere between 'indispensable' on the one hand and 'useful' or 'expedient' on the other.

In the case involving Bill Goodwin and *The Engineer*, the House of Lords in 1990 considered the phrase 'interests of justice'. Lord Bridge said the phrase could simply refer to the wish of an employer to discipline a disloyal employee 'notwithstanding that no legal proceedings might be necessary to achieve this end'.

This issue was initially central to the *Ashworth Hospital* case and to the *Interbrew* case in 2002. Some commentators drew the conclusion that judges' interpretation of the words of the section made its protection for journalists' sources illusory.

Earlier, commentators had detected a more benevolent attitude among the judiciary to the media after the pronouncement of the European Commission in the *Goodwin* case in 1994. This attitude was displayed again in the resolution of the *Ashworth hospital* case, see p. 513.

In 1996 two chief constables failed to have a journalist, Daniella Garavelli, jailed over her refusal to reveal the sources of a story to a police disciplinary tribunal. The reporter refused to say who supplied her with information for a front-page exclusive in the *Journal*, Newcastle, over allegations that Northumbria police crime figures had been massaged.

A High Court judge said Garavelli 'put before the public, fully and fairly, a question which had been raised of considerable public importance'. The police had failed to show that the 'interests of justice' outweighed her right not to disclose her source (*Chief constable of Leicestershire Constabulary, Chief constable of Northumbria Police v Daniella Garavelli* [1996] EWHC Admin 51).

▌ Statutes giving disclosure powers

As stated above, increasingly statutes give authorities the power to demand information on *specific* issues and provide penalties under these Acts.

The Criminal Justice Act 1987

This empowers the director of the Serious Fraud Office (SFO) to summon any person believed to have information relevant to an investigation and the person must answer questions or give information. If the person fails to do so he/she faces a maximum prison sentence of six months or a fine.

The director is also empowered to demand from any person documents relating to the investigation. The obligation to hand over information contains no public interest defence similar to that contained in the Police and Criminal Evidence Act 1984.

see below, p. 518

The Serious Organised Crime and Police Act 2005

This extends to the Serious Organised Crime Agency, the police, and HM Revenue and Customs powers to compel the production of documents and to demand information on specific issues. These powers already affect financial journalists when the Serious Fraud Office demands information and when the Department for Business, Enterprise and Regulatory Reform (which has incorporated the former Department of Trade and Industry) is investigating criminal misconduct in the City.

However, there will continue to be protection for journalistic documents and records held in confidence, because the Act provides that no one can be compelled to disclose **excluded material**.

The Financial Services Act 1986

see below, p. 515

This Act was used to prosecute Jeremy Warner (see above), and was enacted after newspaper disclosures of criminal misconduct in the City. It made it an offence for a person without reasonable excuse to refuse to comply with a request to attend before inspectors of the (then) Department of Trade and Industry (now part of the BERR), or to assist them or to answer any question put by them about any matter relevant to their inquiries.

The Financial Services and Markets Act 2000

This places the Financial Services Authority on a statutory basis, and gives its inspectors similar powers. Failure to comply with requests for information and documents could lead to contempt proceedings.

The Criminal Justice Act 1993

This created offences of failing to disclose suspicion or knowledge concerning money laundering and insider dealing. There is a defence of 'reasonable excuse'. The Home Office Minister assured the Guild of Editors (later the Society of Editors) that the legislation on insider dealing would not criminalise the conduct of a financial journalist preparing editorial analysis and news items.

The Police and Criminal Evidence Act 1984 (PACE)

PACE requires the police to make a formal application before a judge to obtain journalistic material they want to help with their investigations. In several of the cases brought under the Act the application has concerned photographs or film taken in public places where disturbances were taking place.

Most editors take the view that they should hand over such material only after careful consideration and generally only after a court order. Their argument is that if it becomes routine for the police to obtain unpublished photographs or untransmitted film journalists will be seen as an arm of the police.

A judge may reject the application if, among other things, he does not consider it in the public interest to grant it. In court, media lawyers have argued that it is not in the public interest that the media should be prevented from doing their job. But in nearly every case that has come to court judges have considered that argument was outweighed by the police's need for evidence to convict.

For example, a judge rejected the media's argument in November 1994 when the police were successful in obtaining film and photographs by the major press and broadcasting organisations after a demonstration against the Bill that became the Criminal Justice and Public Order Act 1994 even though counsel pointed out that at the demonstration 'class war' leaflets were distributed that showed the media were being branded 'agents of the police'.

The provision was intended to provide a new protection for journalistic material, but in practice it has led to accelerating demands for the handing over of such material.

In 2005 a group of media organisations failed in an attempt to overturn a judge's order that they should hand over photographs and film of a pro-hunt rally to the Independent Police Complaints Commission. The order said they had to surrender to the IPCC all film, photographs, and negatives of a protest in Parliament Square.

The order was aimed at helping the IPCC investigate complaints about the behaviour of officers policing the protest.

Special procedure material

Special protection is given to 'journalistic material' in the sections of the Act that lay down the procedure whereby the police may gain access to documents or search premises for evidence of serious offences.

Journalistic material is defined as 'material acquired or created for the purposes of journalism'.

The police have to apply to a High Court judge, a **recorder**, or a circuit → glossary judge if they want to obtain journalistic material under the 'special procedure'. If they succeed the judge will make a 'production order'.

The application will normally be 'on notice' (formerly 'inter partes'), which means that the holder of the evidence is present to argue against disclosure if he wishes.

Before the judge makes an order he has to be satisfied that there are reasonable grounds for believing that a serious offence has been committed; that the evidence would be admissible at a trial for that offence and of substantial value to that investigation; that other methods of obtaining it have been tried without success, or not tried because it appears they are bound to fail; and that its disclosure would be in the public interest, having regard to:

(1) the benefit likely to accrue to the investigation if the material is obtained; and

(2) the circumstances under which the person in possession of the material holds it.

The Act therefore appeared to give useful protection to journalists. However, judges have interpreted the Act in such a way that (as with section 10 of the Contempt of Court Act) the protection is not as valuable as had been hoped.

In 1986, after a police operation in Bristol led to disturbances, the *Bristol Evening Post*, the *Western Daily Press*, and a freelance picture agency were asked by the police to hand over unpublished pictures and refused to do so.

The police applied to the court and the judge ordered that the pictures be produced.

The judge did not require the police to specify the offence which had been committed, nor the value and relevance of the material, nor the *particular material* which was sought; they asked for all the pictures taken between two specific times, and 264 pictures and negatives had to be handed over.

In 1990, 25 newspapers and television companies were ordered to hand over unpublished photographs and untransmitted film of a Trafalgar Square riot against the poll tax. Two weeks later the police applied successfully for similar orders against four other news organisations. The case illustrated again the way in which the courts would apply the test that material must be admissible at trial and of substantial value to the investigation.

At the second hearing the news organisations' counsel said the applications were premature because the police had not yet examined all the material handed over by the other 25 organisations. But the judge said that until the police had seen the material they could not say if it was relevant or not.

A more liberal view of PACE was taken in the *Martin Bright* case in 2000, see p. 511, when the police were using the Act in an attempt to obtain an email sent by David Shayler to the reporter Martin Bright. Lord Justice Judge said that a judge is not restricted in his interpretation of public interest by the 'somewhat limited conditions' referred to above. Other matters such as the importance of open discussion in the media of questions of importance could be considered when a judge decides whether to exercise his discretion over making an order.

Excluded material

Excluded material is exempt altogether from compulsory disclosure. It includes journalistic material which a person holds in confidence and which consists of documents or records.

The protection is not limited to professional journalists, but extends to any material acquired or created for the purposes of journalism.

Evidence which was already liable to search and seizure under the previous law is not protected. For example, if a journalist acquired a stolen document, even on a confidential basis, it would not be excluded material because such documents are already liable to seizure under a warrant issued under the Theft Act 1968.

Search warrants

Instead of asking for an order for a newspaper to produce material, the police can apply to a circuit judge for a search warrant under PACE to obtain either non-confidential or confidential material. The newspaper does not have to be told of the application, and does not have the right to be heard by the judge.

Before the judge grants a warrant, he/she must be satisfied that the criteria for ordering the production of the material are satisfied, and that one of the following four circumstances applies:

- it is not practicable to communicate with anyone entitled to grant entry to the premises;
- it is not practicable to communicate with anyone entitled to grant access to the material;
- the material contains information which is subject to an obligation of secrecy or a restriction on disclosure imposed by statute (for example, material subject to the Official Secrets Act) and is likely to be disclosed in breach of that obligation if a warrant is not issued; *or*
- that to serve notice of an order to produce may seriously prejudice the investigation.

→ see ch. 31, on official secrets law, and p. 522

In the *Zircon* case in 1987, police used a warrant under these provisions to raid the offices of the *New Statesman* and the journalist Duncan Campbell. Although material was 'excluded', it was not protected because a warrant could previously have been issued under the Official Secrets Act.

Once inside a newspaper office, lawfully executing their search warrant, the police have powers under PACE to remove additional journalistic material without getting a new production order or warrant.

As noted earlier, the Serious Organised Crime and Police Act 2005 allows police, subject to the PACE procedure for search warrants for journalistic material (above), to obtain a warrant to search all property occupied or controlled by the person named in the warrant and not merely specific premises.

But the Act adds additional criteria before a judge issues an all-premises warrant. He/she must be satisfied that:

(1) there are reasonable grounds for believing that it is necessary to search premises occupied or controlled by the person in question which are not specified in the application, as well as those which are, in order to find the material in question; and

(2) it is not reasonably practicable to specify all the premises which he/she occupies or controls which might need to be searched.

The Police Act 1997

The Police Act 1997 gives the police the power to authorise themselves to break into premises and place bugs provided they believe this action will help them to investigate serious crime. Under section 89 of the Act, entry to or interference with property or with 'wireless telegraphy' is lawful when a chief constable or, in urgent cases, an assistant chief constable, 'thinks it necessary...on the ground that it is likely to be of substantial value in the prevention or detection of serious crime'.

Under the Act, the Government appoints a small number of commissioners, existing or former High Court judges, and the police have to obtain the prior approval of a commissioner for the bugging of homes, offices, and hotel bedrooms, and in respect of doctors, lawyers, and 'confidential journalistic material'. Prior approval is not necessary in urgent cases, but the chief officer has to apply for approval as soon as reasonably practicable and specify why he/she could not do so before.

A commissioner approves the operation if satisfied that there are reasonable grounds for believing that the action is likely to be of substantial value in the prevention or detection of serious crime and that what the action seeks to achieve cannot reasonably be achieved by other means.

A commissioner can order that an operation be abandoned if it is regarded as 'blatantly unreasonable'. Authorisation lasts for three months.

Serious crime is defined very broadly. It covers offences which involve 'the use of violence, results in substantial financial gain, or is conduct by a large number of persons in pursuit of a common purpose'.

The Act contains no exemption to protect journalists pursuing their inquiries.

Official secrets

The Official Secrets Act 1920, as amended by the Official Secrets Act 1939, operates where a chief officer of police is satisfied that there is reasonable ground for suspecting that an offence under section 1 of the Act, which is concerned with espionage, has been committed and for believing that any person is able to furnish information about the offence.

The officer may apply to the Home Secretary for permission to authorise a senior police officer to require the person to divulge that information. Anyone who fails to comply with any such requirement or knowingly gives false information is guilty of an offence.

Where a chief officer of police has reasonable grounds to believe that the case is one of great emergency and that in the interests of the State immediate action is necessary, he/she may demand the information without the consent of the Home Secretary.

Section 9 of the Official Secrets Act 1911 gives the police wide powers to carry out searches. A magistrate may grant a warrant authorising the police to enter at any time any premises named in the warrant, if necessary by force, and to search the premises and every person found there; and to seize any material which is evidence of an offence under the Act. If a police superintendent considers the case one of great emergency, he/she can give a written order which has the same effect as a warrant.

→

see also ch. 31 for more detail on official secrets law

The Regulation of Investigatory Powers Act 2000

Journalists were concerned about several aspects of this Act. In particular, they feared that the ability of the police to gain access to their emails would prevent them from assuring contacts that their confidentiality would be protected. If the Act had been in force when the police were attempting to access the email sent from David Shayler to the *Guardian* (see above), there would have been no need for the authorities to ask a judge for an order; they could simply have obtained a warrant from the Home Secretary.

Interception

The Home Secretary can issue a warrant authorising interception (that is, disclosure of the contents of communications) after an application from specified officials of the police, security services, and HM Revenue and Customs. He/she must not do so unless he/she believes:

(1) that the warrant is necessary:
 (a) in the interests of national security;
 (b) for the purpose of preventing or detecting serious crime;
 (c) for the purpose of safeguarding the economic well-being of the United Kingdom; or
 (d) for the purpose…of giving effect to the provisions of any international mutual assistance agreement.
(2) that the conduct authorised by the warrant is proportionate to what is sought to be achieved by the conduct.

He/she must consider whether the necessary information could reasonably be obtained by other means.

Disclosure of 'communications data'

The phrase 'communications data' does not include the content of the communications, but does include much information that may be of interest to the police and other investigatory bodies, such as telephone numbers dialled, the date and time of calls, the identity of people to whom emails are sent, and much more. 'Dynamic' metering (obtaining such information while the call is in progress), can help identify the location of a person making calls on a mobile telephone.

The Act allows not only the police but HM Revenue and Customs, any of the intelligence services, and any other 'public authority' specified by the Secretary of State to demand such information on the basis of internal authorisation. The designated person can grant authorisations for others within the authority to engage in such conduct.

The grounds for obtaining communications data are wider than for interception. Such data can be obtained in the interests of public safety; to protect public health; to assess or collect any tax, duty, levy, or other imposition, contribution, or charge payable to a government department; in an emergency, to prevent death or injury, or damage to any person's physical or mental health, or to mitigate any such injury or damage; or for any purpose specified by order of the Secretary of State.

In 2002 the Government announced plans to give access to communications data to many additional public bodies including the Environment Agency, the Information Commission, the Gaming Board, the Food Standards Agency, NHS trusts, the Financial Services Authority, the Royal Mail, and more than 430 local authorities.

The plan caused an outcry. It was denounced as a 'snoopers' charter' by the media and was withdrawn; however the following year it was reintroduced, covering the same bodies, but with additional safeguards against misuse.

Since that time the use of these powers by local authorities to investigate matters considered minor such as fly-tipping, and contravention of school admissions policies, has given rise to much adverse publicity.

If the media are required to disclose communications data, the person giving the authorisation ought to have regard to the need to respect freedom of expression, but there is no express statutory provision within the Act to do so. The procedure will take place in secret, and investigating authorities do not always value freedom of expression.

Surveillance

Surveillance can be 'directed' or 'intrusive'. 'Intrusive surveillance', for the purposes of the Act, is covert and involves use of a surveillance device, or the presence of a person, in residential premises or a private vehicle. Confusingly, any other surveillance is described as 'directed', however intrusive it in fact is.

Schedule 1 to the Act gives a lengthy list of public authorities whose designated representative can give authorisation for directed (but not intrusive) surveillance. The list includes any police force, the intelligence services, the armed forces, the customs and tax authorities, government departments, the National Assembly for Wales, any local authority, and a number of other bodies including the Post Office.

Authorisation for intrusive surveillance, which must be given by a designated person (for example, a chief constable), must be approved by a surveillance commissioner, a person who holds or who has held high judicial office.

In both cases, the grounds are broadly similar to those for interception. The Home Secretary may also give authorisation in intelligence and defence matters.

Investigation of electronic data protected by encryption

A person (including a journalist) may be required to disclose the encryption code of emails, and if he or she tips anybody off that his/her emails are compromised he/she could face a prison sentence. Written permission must be given in England and Wales by a circuit judge, in Scotland by a sheriff, or in Northern Ireland by a county court judge.

The Pensions Act 2004

In 2008 Jenna Towler, news editor of *Professional Pensions* magazine was threatened with prosecution and jail by the Pensions Regulator for refusing to reveal her source of a story concerning the regulator's removal of pension schemes from a trustee company.

The regulator said the information was 'restricted' under the 2004 Act. Section 82 of the Act makes disclosing or receiving such information an offence punishable by up to two years in prison.

Lawyers for the magazine's publisher, Incisive Media, wrote back to the regulator refusing to divulge the source and furthermore the magazine ignored a warning not to follow up the story.

▸ Anti-terrorism legislation

Counter-terrorism legislation includes a number of offences which could relate to journalist's sources, and gives police powers to seize a journalist's research material.

→ see ch. 33, on such law

Subpoenas and witness summonses

Occasionally reporters may be asked to supply evidence of what they themselves have seen, rather than to say where their information came from.

For example, in 1992 a *Wales on Sunday* photographer was asked to give evidence against eight defendants allegedly involved in riots. Cuttings from the paper had been produced in court, and the photographer's byline appeared on the pictures.

In this situation, most journalists will wish to retain their reputation for neutrality and will agree to give evidence only after receiving a **subpoena** (in civil cases) or witness summons (in criminal cases).

→glossary

Whistleblowers

The Public Interest Disclosure Act 1998 (the whistleblowers' charter) provides a defence to disciplinary charges for breach of confidence.

Recap of major points

- It is a matter of professional principle that a reporter does not reveal his/her source of confidential information.
- Judges have the power to order disclosure of the identity of wrongdoers whenever the person against whom disclosure is sought has got 'mixed up' in wrongful conduct that infringes a claimant's legal rights.
- Some tribunals and officials have been given by statute the power to demand information on specific issues. The journalist who refuses to comply faces penalties under these Acts.
- If the police need to obtain 'journalistic material' to assist their investigations they normally have to apply to a judge first but various statutes give them special powers.
- 'Excluded material' is normally exempt altogether from compulsory disclosure. It includes journalistic material that a person holds in confidence and that consists of documents or records.

- Some authorities given the power to demand information are also given the power to search the premises of the person they believe to have the information.

- The European Court of Human Rights has said that an order to disclose the source of information cannot be compatible with Article 10 of the Convention (freedom of expression) unless it is justified by an overriding requirement in the public interest.

- Section 10 of the Contempt of Court Act 1981 says that a disclosure order must not be made 'unless it is established to the satisfaction of the court that disclosure is necessary in the interests of justice or national security, or for the prevention of disorder or crime'.

- The Official Secrets Acts allow the Home Secretary to give the police permission to require a person to disclose information relating to espionage.

- The Acts also give the police wide powers to carry out searches.

- The Home Secretary can also authorise the police and other officials to intercept electronic communications data under the Regulation of Investigatory Powers Act 2000.

🌐 Useful Websites

www.nuj.org.uk/innerPagenuj.html?docid=25
National Union of Journalists Code of conduct

33

Terrorism and the effect of counter-terrorism law

Chapter summary

The heightened threat of terrorism has in recent years led to further wide-ranging prohibitions in the UK's legislation. Some counter-terrorism laws ban the gathering of certain information. Others restrict what can be published, inhibiting freedom of expression. Recent law has also imposed a legal obligation on UK citizens to tell the police about any information gained about potential or actual terrorist activity anywhere in the world. Clearly, the threat posed by terrorism justifies keen laws against it. But, as this chapter explains, the wide scope of counter-terrorism law has potential to deter investigative, journalistic research into the causes and control of terrorism. A journalist was made liable for huge, court costs after failing to prevent police access to his research material. See also ch. 35 for concerns that anti-terrorism law is being cited by police officers seeking to justify interference with the routine work of media photographers.

◗ Definition of terrorism, and its 'glorification'

The definition of terrorism is, of course, a value-loaded one. As has often been said, a terrorist group – e.g. a separatist movement – may be seen to its constituency of supporters as freedom fighters. The UK's legal definition of terrorism, as expressed in section 1 of the Terrorism Act 2000, as amended by the Terrorism Act 2006 and the Counter-Terrorism Act 2008, is as follows:

    ❝ the use or threat of action where the threat is designed to influence the
Government, or an international government organisation, or to intimidate
the public or a section of the public, and the use or threat is made for the
purpose of advancing a political, religious, racial or ideological cause. **❞**

Under the 2000 Act, to meet this definition of terrorism the 'action' must
involve serious violence against a person or serious damage to property, or
endanger a person's life (other than the perpetrator's); or create a serious
risk to the health and safety of the public or a section of the public; or be
designed seriously to interfere with or seriously to disrupt an electronic
system.

It is also illegal in itself – punishable by a maximum jail term of 10 years
– to be a member or to profess to be a member of a 'proscribed group', i.e.
one deemed to be engaged in terrorism or promoting it. The 2000 Act is
the latest legislation to proscribe groups. In early 2009 its Schedule 2, in
a list which can be updated by **statutory instruments**, was proscribing 49
groups from around the world, including Al-Qaeda and the Basque group
ETA. The list includes paramilitary groups with roots in Northern Ireland,
e.g. the IRA and UDA, which have been proscribed for decades. But the
legal definition of terrorism is not confined to the activities of proscribed
groups – it could apply, for example, to 'animal liberation' groups which
threaten violence.

The Terrorism Act 2006 bans dissemination of terrorist publications
and specifically prohibits encouragement of terrorism, including indirect
encouragement through 'glorification' of it. For example, under the Act, a
person commits an offence if he/she publishes, or causes to be published, a
statement which

- glorifies the commission or preparation (whether in the past, in the
  future, or generally) of acts of terrorism, and which

- is a statement from which members of the public could reasonably be
  expected to infer that what is being glorified is being glorified 'as conduct that should be emulated by them in existing circumstances'.

For this 'glorification' offence to occur, the statement must be likely to be
understood by some or all of the members of the public (anywhere in the
world) as an encouragement or other inducement to them to commit, prepare for, or instigate acts of terrorism. Also, the person accused of such
glorification must have intended some people to be thus affected, or been
'reckless' as to the statement's effect though it is irrelevant whether anybody was in fact thus led to actually perpetrate terrorism. Encouragement

→ For
recent
terrorism
cases,
see
Useful
Websites,
below

→ glossary

of terrorism, including through glorification, can be punished by a prison sentence of up to seven years or by a fine or both. This law was created primarily as a response to extremist, Islamic 'preachers of hate'. But, according to the authors of *Media Freedom under the Human Rights Act*, the Act's wording means the glorification offence could catch any praise of any group using political violence anywhere in the world. See Book list, pp. 579–580.

Under the Act – if it has not been proved that the person accused intended the statement to encourage, etc., acts of terrorism – he/she has a defence if he/she can show that the statement published neither expressed his/her views, nor had his/her endorsement, and that it was clear in all the circumstances of the publication that this was the case. This defence, then, would protect journalists, and their publishers, when their journalism includes interviews with or statements from other people glorifying terrorism, if the journalism reports such words in a neutral (or condemnatory) fashion and neither the journalists nor their publishers associate themselves with the glorification. The same defence protects the publisher of a website forum if a member of the public posts such glorification on it. But the law in the Act means that the defence would not apply if the police gave a website publisher notice that a statement encouraging terrorism was being published on the site, but the publisher had then failed to remove it, without reasonable excuse, after more than two working days.

◗ Failure to disclose information

Under section 38B of the Terrorism Act 2000, as amended by the Anti-Terrorism, Crime and Security Act 2001, a person commits a crime if he/she fails to disclose to police, as soon as reasonably practical, information that he/she knows or believes might be of material assistance in preventing the commission by another person of an act of terrorism anywhere in the world, or in securing the apprehension, prosecution, or conviction of another person in the United Kingdom for a terrorist offence. The maximum penalty for such failure to disclose is up to five years in prison or a fine, or both. There is a defence if a person accused of such failure can prove he/she had a 'reasonable excuse'. A reporter may be at risk of prosecution for the offence if he/she discovers information about terrorism by, for example, interviewing a terrorist leader or by witnessing a paramilitary display, but fails to disclose it quickly to police. In section 19 of the 2000 Act similar disclosure obligations are imposed (primarily designed for people in the financial sector) if information is gained which leads to a belief or suspicion that a financial transaction is linked to the funding of terrorism. The Act's section 39 makes it a crime to disclose information which 'tips off' someone that he/she is being investigated by police for terrorist activity, or is due to be.

Collecting and eliciting information

Under section 58 of the 2000 Act, a person commits an offence if he/she 'collects or makes a record of information of a kind likely to be useful to a person committing or preparing an act of terrorism' or 'possesses a document or record containing information of that kind'. There is a defence if the person accused of such collecting/record-keeping can prove that he/she has a reasonable excuse. But there is no specific exemption for journalists as regards their research, or for any other profession. A journalist conducting research, for example, into terrorist manuals available on the internet could, conceivably be prosecuted under this section. In 2008 Sally Hunt, general secretary of the University and College Union, condemned the arrest of a post-graduate student at Nottingham University, whose research was into terrorism, and of a staff administrator there. The student said he had emailed to the administrator, for it to be printed, a declassified open-source document called the Al-Qaeda Training Manual, available on a US government website. Both men were held for six days, then released without charge.

The Counter-Terrorism Act 2008, by inserting a section 58A into the 2000 Act, makes it an offence to 'elicit or attempt to elicit' information about an individual who is or has been a member of Her Majesty's forces, of the UK intelligence services, or a police officer, if the information 'is of a kind likely to be useful to a person committing or preparing an act of terrorism'. The Act also makes it an offence to publish or communicate such elicited information. Both offences have a maximum penalty of a 10-year jail term or a fine or both. Anyone prosecuted for either offence will have a defence if he/she can prove there is a 'reasonable excuse' for his/her actions. The Newspaper Society protested to the Government when these offences were proposed. Santha Rasaiah, head of the Society's political and regulatory affairs department, said that such an 'eliciting' offence was wide enough to potentially catch journalists in a huge number of everyday situations.

🔴 Police powers to seize journalists' material

Schedule 5 to the Terrorism Act 2000 provides the police with a battery of powers to assist in investigations into terrorism. These, as are other powers in current legislation, are re-enactments or successors of parts of the Prevention of Terrorism (Temporary Provisions) Act 1989. It was under the 1989 Act that in 1992 Channel 4 and the independent production company Box Productions were fined £75,000 for contempt of court after refusing to comply with a court order requiring them to disclose to police the identity of a source used in a television programme *The Committee*, part of the 'Dispatches' series, which investigated killings in Northern Ireland *(Director of Public Prosecutions v Channel Four Television Company Limited and another* [1993] 2 All ER 517).

As explained in ch. 32, see pp. 518–521, under the Police and Criminal Evidence Act 1984 (PACE) police in a crime investigation must make an application to a High Court judge, a **recorder** or a **circuit judge** to obtain material held by a journalist, in that **journalistic material** is among the matter classed in that Act as requiring police to use this 'special procedure'. The safeguard is that such an experienced judge – and not a magistrate – should decide whether to make a 'production order' for such material, i.e. an order for it to be disclosed to police. Also, under PACE, if the documents and records involved are held by the journalist in confidence, e.g. from a source whose identity the journalist has promised to keep secret, the material is classed as 'excluded'. This means it cannot usually be made the subject of a production order under PACE. The Terrorism Act 2000 similarly requires that a circuit judge (or in Northern Ireland a Crown court judge), not a magistrate, must decide whether to issue a production order for journalistic material. But the 2000 Act permits such an order to compel disclosure of 'excluded' material as well as 'special procedure' material to assist police in a terrorism investigation. The order will be granted if the judge is satisfied there are reasonable grounds for believing the material will be of substantial value to that investigation and for believing it is in the public interest that the material should be produced or that access to it should be granted to the police. This threshold of justification for compelling disclosure is lower in several respects than in PACE for special procedure material, and – unlike in PACE – there is no requirement under the 2000 Act for a journalist to be usually given notice of police intention to apply for a production order. The 2000 Act therefore gives journalists less protection than PACE against police on

→ glossary
→ glossary

'fishing expeditions' for journalistic material. Nevertheless, a journalist opposing disclosure of his/her material under the 2000 Act can argue that it would not be of substantial value to the police. In 1999 a judge made an order under the 1989 Act, referred to above, that Ed Moloney, northern editor of the Dublin-based *Sunday Tribune*, should hand over to police notes of an interview with a Loyalist later charged with murder. But the order was quashed by the Lord Chief Justice of Northern Ireland, Sir Robert Carswell, who said: 'Police have to show something more than a possibility that the material will be of some use. They must establish that there are reasonable grounds for believing that the material is likely to be of substantial value to the investigation' (*Re Moloney's Application* [2000] NIJB).

Under the 2000 Act, someone made subject to a production order, including a journalist, would normally be given seven days in which to disclose the material to the police. But the order could be for speedier disclosure. If it is disobeyed, a judge can issue a warrant for the material's seizure by police. A police superintendent can issue such a warrant if he/she has reasonable grounds for believing the case is one of great emergency and that immediate seizure is necessary. It is contempt of court, punishable by up to two years in jail, to disobey the order. The police can also apply to a judge for an order requiring any person to provide an explanation of any material seized, produced, or made available. This was the power used under the earlier legislation in the Channel 4 and Box Productions case, see above.

In the 2000 Act, there are different measures for Northern Ireland. Under Schedule 5, the Secretary of State for Northern Ireland can make a written order requiring any person in the province to produce or give access to special procedure material and **excluded material**, and to provide an explana- → glossary
tion of any material thus produced. The Secretary of State may also, by a written order, give to any constable in the province an authority equivalent to a search warrant relating to specified premises.

▶ Huge costs awarded against a journalist

In 2008 the freelance journalist Shiv Malik was required, by a production order granted under the Terrorism Act 2000 by a judge to Greater Manchester police, to hand over all drafts of and source material for a book he had researched and which was due to be published. It had the title *Leaving Al-Qaeda: Inside the Mind of a British Jihadist*. It was about Hassan Butt, who – when co-operating with Malik for the book – had claimed to have been in some way involved, before renouncing terrorism, with an attack in Pakistan which killed 11 people and with recruiting people to a 'proscribed' group, see above, p. 529. The production order required all Malik's notes, audio and video recordings associated with the book. The police had applied for the order after another man, charged with offences under the Act, had claimed in a defence statement that Butt was 'the instigator of certain actions'. The High Court was asked by Malik to consider in **judicial review** if the order was lawful. He argued that it required him to disclose confidential sources, in breach of his rights under Article 10 of the European Convention and that this would affect how sources trusted him, and possibly put him in danger. The High Court judges noted that Malik was a respected journalist. But they ruled that the granting of the production order was valid. However, they limited its scope to include only material disclosed to Malik by Butt, i.e. not material from other sources, and ruled that Malik did not have to surrender his contact lists (*Malik v Manchester Crown Court and the Chief Constable of Greater Manchester Police* [2008] EWHC 1362).They ordered Malik, who complied with the amended order, to pay the police costs for the High Court case, as well as his own. The *Guardian* reported that in total these costs were more than £100,000, but that they were to be funded jointly by the National Union of Journalists and Times Newspapers Ltd, in support of Malik. Butt, interviewed by police when the High Court action was pending, disowned his earlier accounts of involvement in terrorism, and claimed he lied to the media to make money, the court heard.

 → glossary

→ see ch. 32 for case law on protecting sources

 See the Online Resource Centre, ch. 33 for more about this case.

→ See also ch. 35, p. 551 for concerns that anti-terrorism law is being cited by police officers seeking to justify interference with the routine news-gathering work of media photographers.

▌ Anonymity for suspects subject to control orders

The Prevention of Terrorism Act 2005 authorises the system of 'control orders' to restrict the liberty of people suspected of involvement in terrorism but who have not been prosecuted. The evidence said to exist against them, for example, may come from interceptions of phone calls or emails (such 'intercepts' by police or the security services are currently inadmissible as evidence in UK trials) or from intelligence sources which the security services want to keep secret. The Home Secretary can impose temporary orders requiring such suspects, for example, not to travel abroad, associate with certain people, or use the internet or phones. The orders have to be confirmed by a court within seven days, and can then last up to 12 months without renewal. People subject to such orders can apply to the court for anonymity in media reports of the orders. The Act and the Civil Procedure Rules gives judges power to impose such anonymity.

➔ see ch. 12, p. 195 on these rules

▦ Recap of major points

- Terrorism is given a wide definition in UK law.

- It is an offence to publish or cause to be published a statement which 'glorifies' the commission or preparation of acts of terrorism.

- It is an offence to fail to disclose to police information gained about suspected terrorist offences.

- It is an offence to collect or make a record of information 'of a kind likely to be useful to a person committing or preparing an act of terrorism'.

- It is an offence to 'elicit' or publish information about someone who is or has been a member of Her Majesty's forces, of the UK intelligence services, or a police officer, if the information 'is of a kind likely to be useful to a person committing or preparing an act of terrorism'.

- There are some limited defences to the offences listed above. But there is concern among journalists that these defences might not sufficiently protect them in their work.

- Police powers to compel a journalist to surrender research material are stronger under counter-terrorism law than under law covering other police inquiries.

✆ Useful Websites

www.homeoffice.gov.uk/security/terrorism-and-the-law/
   Home Office website, 'Terrorism and the law'
www.cps.gov.uk/publications/prosecution/ctd.html
   Crown Prosecution Service Counter-Terrorism Division site - lists recent terrorism cases
www.cps.gov.uk/publications/prosecution/violent_extremism.html
   CPS site on 'violent extremism' – lists recent terrorism cases

34

The incitement of hate

Chapter summary

Freedom of expression has boundaries. One boundary is that making or publishing some kinds of threatening statement is a crime. As this chapter explains, it is an offence to stir up hatred against people because of their race. In recent years, the statute governing such offences has been amended to specifically outlaw too the stirring up of hatred against people because of their religious beliefs or their sexual orientation.

▌ Stirring up race hatred

Under the Public Order Act 1986, it is an offence for a person:

- to use – e.g. in the street or in a public speech – threatening, abusive or insulting words or behaviour with intent to stir up racial hatred, or
- to display, publish, or distribute written material that is threatening, abusive, or insulting with intent to stir up racial hatred.

Even if there is no such intent, either of the above types of conduct is an offence if, having regard to all the circumstances, such hatred is likely to be stirred up thereby.

Racial hatred is defined as being 'hatred against a group of persons defined by reference to colour, race, nationality (including citizenship), or ethnic or national origins'.

The fact that such an offence can be committed even without intent means that a media organisation reporting with direct or indirect quotes an inflammatory speech or election manifesto (such as that of an extremist politician) or other expression of anti-immigrant propaganda could be prosecuted. However, the phrase 'having regard to all the circumstances' was inserted into the 1986 Act as a response to lobbying by the Guild of Editors (now known as the Society of Editors) because this phrase's inclusion in earlier legislation had been seen as a protection for bona fide news reports of, for example, a racist rally. The phrase requires a court to consider the publication in its context. The Attorney General has to consent to any prosecution. In 1987 the then Attorney General said that when making a decision on whether to allow any such prosecution of a newspaper he would probably take into account the nature of the publication, its circulation, and the market at which it was aimed, as well as any special sensitivity prevailing at the time of publication which might influence the effect on those who read the material.

He warned that a newspaper which published an inflammatory racist letter from a reader would not necessarily escape prosecution merely by publishing, in the same edition, an editorial or letters expressing an anti-racist view.

However, this law is more likely to be used against extremists than against mainstream media. For example, five men who published from an address in Lincolnshire an extreme right-wing magazine and website, which included instructions on how to make bombs to wage a 'racial holy war', were jailed under this law in 2005. Their magazine offered 'team points' to readers who torched synagogues (*Press Gazette*, 11 November 2005). There is some frustration among anti-racism campaign groups that such prosecutions are not more frequent.

For other cases, see Useful Websites, below

▶ Stirring up religious hatred

The Racial and Religious Hatred Act 2006 created a new offence to outlaw specifically the intentional stirring up of hatred against people on religious grounds. It did so by amending the Public Order Act 1986. The crime occurs if a person uses threatening words or behaviour, or displays, publishes, or distributes any written material which is threatening, if he/she intends thereby to stir up religious hatred.

It is also an offence for a person to include threatening visual images or sounds in a broadcast programme if he/she intends thereby to stir up such hatred. The programme provider, producer, or director, or anyone using the words, could be convicted, if such person had such intent.

Under this law, religious hatred is said to be hatred against a group of persons defined by their religious belief or lack of religious belief.

The Act does not seek to define what amounts to a religion or a religious belief. It will be for the courts to determine this in the context of particular cases. However, the definition would certainly include those religions widely recognised in the United Kingdom, such as Christianity, Islam, Hinduism, Judaism, Buddhism, Sikhism, Rastafarianism, Baha'ism, Zoroastrianism, and Jainism. Equally, branches or sects within a religion can be considered as religions or religious beliefs in their own right. By use of the term 'lack of religious belief' this law also seeks to prohibit such stirring up of hatred against a group of persons defined by reference to atheism or humanism.

This 'stirring up' offence applies only to the use of words that are threatening. It does not apply to words that are merely 'abusive or insulting', and therefore it differs in this respect from the offence of stirring up of race hatred. Indeed, one of the amendments made by the 2006 Act to the 1986 Act was to insert what has been referred to as the 'free speech section' to safeguard robust criticism of groups for their religious (or non-religious) beliefs. This section states that the offence of stirring up religious hatred is not intended to restrict 'discussion, criticism or expressions of antipathy, dislike, ridicule, insult or abuse of particular religions or the beliefs or practices of their adherents, or of any other belief system or the beliefs or practices of its adherents, or proselytising or urging adherents of a different religion or belief system to cease practising their religion or belief system'. And, to constitute the offence, the relevant words must be *intended* to stir up religious hatred – it is not sufficient that the words have this effect as a result of recklessness. When Parliament debated this law, the then Home Secretary Charles Clarke said: 'It is there not to stop people criticising religions or the symbols of faith but to prosecute those who seek to set one community against another.' He said police believed hatred stirred up by extremist groups contributed to the Bradford and Burnley riots in 2001. See also Common elements, below, p. 539.

⁙ Point for consideration

 The Criminal Justice and Immigration Act 2008 abolished the **common law** offences of blasphemy and blasphemous libel. See ch. 21, p. 369.

▶ Stirring up hatred on grounds of sexual orientation

The Criminal Justice and Immigration Act 2008 amended the 1986 Act to create an offence of intentional stirring up of hatred on the grounds of sexual orientation. This hatred is defined as 'hatred against a group of persons defined by reference to sexual orientation (whether towards persons of the same sex, the opposite sex or both)'. Although this definition means that heterosexuals are protected by this law's scope, its *raison d'être* is to protect homosexual and bisexual people. In Parliament the then Lord Chancellor Jack Straw said: 'It is a measure of how far we have come as a society in the last 10 years that we are all now appalled by hatred and invective directed against gay people, and it is now time for the law to recognise the feeling of the public.'

The relevant section of the 2008 Act was not in force by the time this book went to press in 2009. But when this section is in effect, this crime occurs if a person uses threatening words or behaviour, or displays, publishes, or distributes any written material which is threatening, if he/she intends thereby to stir up such hatred. There is also a broadcasting offence of such stirring up. The Act's definition of who is liable for such a broadcasting offence is identical to that used for the crime of inciting religious hatred through this medium, see above.

The Act states that discussion or criticism of sexual conduct or practices 'or the urging of people to refrain from or modify such conduct or practices' is not in itself deemed to be illegal (but see also Late News, p. xxix).

▶ Common elements

For each of the stirring up offences outlined above, a magistrate can grant police a warrant to seize inflammatory material. None of the offences applies to the publication of what is said in Parliamentary proceedings or in the Welsh National Assembly, or to contemporaneous reports of court cases or of other judicial proceedings. The Attorney General has to approve all such prosecutions. Penalties for any of these offences are up to six months' imprisonment or a fine or both on summary conviction, and up to seven years' imprisonment or a fine or both on conviction on **indictment**.

→ glossary

See also ch, 33, which explains that the UK's legal definition of terrorist offences includes terrorism with racial or religious motives – i.e. another form of 'hate-crime'.

⠿ Recap of major points

- It is an offence for any person to display, publish, or distribute written material that is threatening, abusive or insulting if he/she intends thereby to stir up racial hatred or if, having regard to all the circumstances, racial hatred is likely to be stirred up thereby.

- It is an offence if a person displays, publishes, or distributes any written material which is threatening if he/she intends thereby to stir up religious hatred.

- When the relevant section of the statute is in effect, there will be a similar offence of stirring up hatred on grounds of sexual orientation.

🌐 Useful Websites

www.cps.gov.uk/Publications/prosecution/rrpbcrpol.html
　　Crown Prosecution Service guidance on prosecuting racist and religious crime
www.cps.gov.uk/publications/prosecution/violent_extremism.html
　　CPS site on 'violent extremism' – lists recent race hate cases

Part 5

Photography, filming, and videoing

Photography, filming, and videoing

Chapter summary

Some elements of the law are more relevant to photographers, journalists using video cameras, and TV crews than to print reporters. This chapter highlights these, and parts of the Press Complaints Commission Code of Practice which apply in particular to photo-journalism. Though most of the public seem happy to view pictures taken by paparazzi, the stalking of celebrities by such photographers has led to lawsuits alleging breach of privacy and harassment, and these project a disreputable image of journalism. But it remains true that a free media needs photographers to have a general liberty to decide when a picture needs to be taken. As this chapter explains, concern has been growing among journalists that police – and sometimes members of the public – increasingly raise invalid objections to media photographers going about their lawful business. This chapter also notes that some photographs or footage supplied by the public may create ethical or legal problems if published. In this chapter, the term 'photography' usually includes filming and videoing.

▌ Privacy considerations

Once there was no specific right of privacy in the United Kingdom. But the law in this field has developed considerably. As chs 23 and 24 show, some of the landmark cases in the UK's evolving privacy law have concerned photographs. One case was resolved by the Court of Appeal in 2005 when Michael Douglas and Catherine Zeta-Jones successfully sued *Hello!* magazine for

 see also p. 547 on harassment

publishing pictures taken surreptitiously of their wedding. Another precedent case was Naomi Campbell's privacy action against the *Daily Mirror*, part of which concerned a picture taken of her as she emerged onto a public street from a Narcotics Anonymous meeting. She won the case in the House of Lords in 2004. The European Court of Human Rights in 2004 ruled that Princess Caroline of Monaco's right to privacy had been infringed by photographers persistently taking pictures of her in public places in her daily life, e.g. shopping – or on holiday with her family. However in 2006 the pop star Elton John failed in the High Court to stop the *Daily Mail* publishing a photograph of him taken in the street. Mr Justice Eady said the photo conveyed nothing private and there had not been persistent harassment of him by photographers (*Media Lawyer*, 28 June 2006).

→ see also ch. 26, p. 442 on J.K. Rowling case

The Code of Practice

→ see also ch. 1, p. 17 and ch. 24, p. 403 on code

The Press Complaints Commission Code of Practice has various clauses which protect aspects of personal privacy. The code is not law, but breach of it could lead to an adjudication against an editor, and its provisions will be considered when relevant in court disputes over privacy. For the photographer, the most pertinent parts of the code are its clauses 3, 4, and 6 (where references to photography should be read, by media organisations covered by the code's provisions, to also include filming and videoing for website publication).

Clause 3: Privacy, states:

> i) Everyone is entitled to respect for his or her private and family life, home, health and correspondence, including digital communications. Editors will be expected to justify intrusions into any individual's private life without consent.
>
> ii) It is unacceptable to photograph individuals in a private place without their consent.
>
> *Note – Private places are public or private property where there is a reasonable expectation of privacy.*

The PCC upheld a complaint by Paul McCartney against *Hello!* magazine for its publication in 1998 of a photo of him and two of his children lighting a candle in a Paris cathedral for his wife Linda, who had died a month earlier. The PCC said it deplored publication of the photograph of the family inside the cathedral which was 'a clear example of a place where there is a reasonable expectation of privacy' (*McCartney v Hello!*: Report 43, 1998). See also the code's clause 5 – intrusion into grief. The code is reproduced in full in Appendix 2, pp. 568–572.

In 2007 the PCC ruled that pictures published in the Scottish *Sun*, taken with a long lens, of Gail Sheridan, wife of Scottish politician Tommy Sheridan, in her back garden did not breach her privacy because she was visible from a public road – and therefore had no reasonable expectation of privacy – and because the photo was 'innocuous' for the reason that she was not doing anything private (*Complaint by Mrs Gail Sheridan against the Scottish Sun*, adjudication issued 3 May 2007). In 2008 the PCC adjudicated against a newspaper for publishing footage of a woman being treated as a road accident victim in which her facial features were shown. The PCC said it was 'particularly concerned about publication of the online image, which had been uploaded before the condition of the victim had been established, shortly after the accident when family members may not have been informed or would have been in a state of shock.' It added: 'There is a clear need for newspapers to exercise caution when publishing images that relate to a person's health and medical treatment, even if they are taken in public places.' The PCC said that the public interest in reporting this accident was not sufficient to override the code's clause 3 (*Complaint by Mr Paul Kirkland against the Wiltshire Gazette & Herald*, adjudication issued 24 April 2008). See below, p. 533, for what the PCC said in this adjudication about major incidents.

Clause 4: Harassment states:

" i) Journalists must not engage in intimidation, harassment or persistent pursuit.

ii) They must not persist in questioning, telephoning, pursuing or photographing individuals once asked to desist; nor remain on their property when asked to leave and must not follow them.

→ see also p. 547 on harassment law

iii) Editors must ensure these principles are observed by those working for them and take care not to use non-compliant material from other sources. "

The PCC upheld a complaint against *OK!* magazine that in 2000 it had printed pictures of Prince William obtained by paparazzi in persistent pursuit of him when he travelled in his 'gap year' in Chile (*Prince William v OK! Magazine*: Report 52, 2000).

Clause 6: Children states:

" i) Young people should be free to complete their time at school without unnecessary intrusion.

ii) A child under 16 must not be interviewed or photographed on issues involving their own or another child's welfare unless a custodial parent or similarly responsible adult consents.

iii) Pupils must not be approached or photographed at school without the permission of the school authorities.

iv) Minors must not be paid for material involving children's welfare, nor parents or guardians for material about their children or wards, unless it is clearly in the child's interest.

v) Editors must not use the fame, notoriety or position of a parent or guardian as sole justification for publishing details of a child's private life. **,,**

The three clauses set out above are subject to the code's public interest exceptions.

It can be seen that the code by no means seeks to inhibit generally the media taking news pictures of children. But it states clearly that when the subject of the story concerns a child's welfare, an appropriate adult must sanction the child being photographed or interviewed, and that pupils must not be photographed at school without the school's consent. The PCC adjudicated against a Scottish newspaper which carried on its website mobile phone footage supplied by a child of disruptive behaviour in class by other pupils at her school. The PCC accepted it was in the public interest to show the behaviour, which the girl said had contributed to her poor exam results, but criticised the paper for not taking steps to disguise in the footage the identities of the children (*Complaint by Mrs Laura Gaddis against the Hamilton Advertiser*, adjudication issued 30 July 2007).

Parental consent for a child to be photographed on a matter concerning the child's welfare can in some instances be implied because of the context in which a photo is taken. In 2006 the PCC ruled that a picture published by *Zoo* magazine of a father and his 10-year-old daughter among a football crowd at Old Trafford stadium did not breach clause 6. It depicted him giving a Nazi salute while his daughter in his arms made a rude gesture. The PCC said that the father must have known that at such an occasion there was a possibility of them being on television or photographed, and so consent was implied. The PCC's adjudication also made clear that 'innocuous' pictures of children in crowds will not normally breach the code (*Complaint by Mr Paschal Quigley against Zoo magazine*, adjudication issued 23 June 2006).

see also
ch. 26

Paranoia about paedophiles frequently prompts irrational objections to photographs being taken of children in everyday activities. For example, in 2006 parents taking photographs at an under-15 football match were told by the referee to stop doing so unless they had the written permission of all parents whose children were playing. The Football Association said the referee was correctly following child protection guidelines.

See ch. 26, p. 441 for information on the invalidity of 'data protection' objections put forward by schools when refusing permission for photographs to be taken. See also ch. 24, pp. 419–422, for detail on privacy protection in the Ofcom Broadcasting Code.

Harassment

It was not the intention of Parliament to target the press with the Protection Against Harassment Act 1997. This law is designed to tackle all stalkers. However, the possibility of using this Act against the media was considered in 2007 when representatives of the Prince of Wales considered what to do about press treatment of Kate Middleton, the girlfriend of Prince William, as she was increasingly targeted by paparazzi photographers.

In 2008 the actress Sienna Miller accepted damages of £53,000 in settlement of civil law claims for harassment and breach of privacy claims against Big Pictures UK Ltd. The case had been due to be tried in the High Court, but the two sides agreed terms which included undertakings by the agency not to pursue Miller by car, motorcycle, or moped, or to place her under surveillance. It also included not taking pictures of her leaving buildings where she had an expectation of privacy. Ms Miller agreed that she did not have such an expectation when leaving a bar, restaurant, or nightclub, on a public footpath, or when attending a red carpet event (*Media Lawyer*, 21 November 2008).

→ See also Late News, p. xxxi, about Lily Allen's action against paparazzi, and see ch. 24, pp. 416–418 for detail on law concerning harassment. See also Kenneth Callaghan case, ch. 9, p. 138

◗ Trespass

The law of trespass forbids unlawful physical entry to land or buildings. The remedy is an action in the civil courts which can result in an **injunction** to prevent further trespass, or damages. → glossary

There is no trespass where a picture is taken from property where the photographer has permission or a right to be, e.g. the public highway, of something or someone on adjoining private land.

Trespass can also include 'trespass to the person', which might amount to compelling a person to be filmed by stopping him from getting into his home or place of work. Trespass to goods means, for instance, picking up a document without permission and photographing it.

 see also ch. 24, pp. 414–416, for detail of trespass law

With the exception of specific laws covering certain sites, e.g. Ministry of Defence (MoD) land and railway property, trespass is not normally a criminal offence and a police officer threatening an arrest for civil trespass is wrong in law. Bye-laws prohibit photography in MoD establishments.

 see also ch. 31, pp. 503–504, for official secrecy law on 'prohibited places'

▌ Aggravated trespass

Section 68 of the Criminal Justice and Public Order Act 1994 created the criminal offence of aggravated trespass. This law was prompted by the actions of some Travellers and those staging noisy 'raves', but it has also been used against protesters, e.g. those occupying a construction site to disrupt the building of a new motorway. It is possible therefore that a photographer or video-journalist or film crew covering such an event will be accused of the offence. The Act's section 68 states that a person commits the offence of aggravated trespass if he/she trespasses on land and, in relation to any lawful activity which other persons are engaged in on that or adjoining land, does anything intended to have the effect:

- of intimidating any of them so as to deter them from engaging in that activity, or
- of obstructing that activity, or
- of disrupting that activity.

The Crown Prosecutions Service guidelines for prosecutors state that 'mere presence as a trespasser' will not be sufficient to charge someone for this offence – the intentional 'additional conduct', as specified above, must have taken place. But, for example, the element of obstruction may be held to have occurred by a person intentionally 'taking up a position' on the land to obstruct. Aggravated trespass carries a penalty of up to three months' imprisonment.

Under the Act's section 69 a senior police officer present at the scene of an aggravated trespass has power to order any person believed to be involved in it to leave the land, and if they fail to leave, or return within a period of three months, that is an offence. The journalist who fails to leave may have a defence under the Act that he/she had 'a reasonable excuse' to stay – but it is, of course, not guaranteed that a court will recognise this defence in any particular case.

▌ Street trouble with the police

Whereas a reporter covering a tumultuous event with a notebook can often make a tactical choice on when to blend into the background, a photographer, video-journalist, or film crew operator cannot – they have to get in close for their pictures. When covering events such as protests, demonstrations, or riots, photographers sometimes find themselves caught in the middle and subject to violence from rioters and to possible arrest, and on occasion, violence, by police.

Police officers covering major incidents can be tense. It has been known for press photographers to be arrested at the scene of an accident, simply because one or other of the emergency services dealing with it did not like them being there. On other occasions police or police community support officers have acted officiously, or in ignorance of the fact that there is no criminal law against citizens taking photos in the street. For example, the Bureau of Freelance Photographers highlighted an incident in Ipswich when an amateur photographer was stopped taking pictures of the Christmas lights by two special constables who escorted him away, insisting he needed 'a licence'.

Concern about apparent deterioration in police treatment of media photographers led in 2008 to a delegation from the National Union of Journalists meeting the Home Office Minister Vernon Croaker. Also in 2008, the Labour MP Austin Mitchell secured widespread support amongst MPs for an 'early day motion' which expressed concern in the House of Commons that police and other officials were infringing on citizens' rights to take photos in public places (see also Late News, p. xxxi).

Public order offences If a police officer warns that a media photographer may be arrested, the arrest is most likely to be under the powers granted by the Public Order Act 1986. This allows arrest if anyone uses behaviour likely to cause 'harassment, alarm or distress'. Though the photographer is not intending to cause such things, in some situations the mere fact that he or she is taking pictures, perhaps of someone or some group who do not want their picture taken, can give rise to this.

In 1995 a BBC cameraman filming scenes of a coach crash was arrested. Police said he had been arrested for his own safety, because he had refused to leave what was a volatile situation. Magistrates bound him over to keep the peace but this bind-over was overturned on appeal. However, at appeal the judge said the cameraman had acted with excessive enthusiasm and that he should remember others had feelings and rights too.

A photographer who took a picture of an army officer defusing an IRA bomb was arrested when the officer complained. He felt the pictures might put him or his family at risk of terrorist reprisals.

Obstructing the highway Under section 137 of the Highways Act 1980 a person commits an offence if he/she 'without lawful authority or excuse, in any way wilfully obstructs the free passage along a highway'. This power allows police to arrest photographers in a public place who do not move on when asked to do so. In 1995 an agency photographer in East Anglia covering an animal rights protest was arrested as he took pictures of police advancing on demonstrators who had sat down to block the road. Despite his protests and those of other media, he was held in a police van, and later, when he refused to accept a caution, he was charged with obstruction of the highway. Although acquitted by magistrates he was not awarded costs.

Obstructing the police Under section 89 of the Police Act 1996 a person commits an offence if he/she 'resists or wilfully obstructs a constable in the execution of his duty, or a person assisting a constable in the execution of his duty'. The obstruction does not have to be a physical act. It can be held to occur, for example, if the person makes it more difficult for the constable to carry out his/her duty. A photographer who persists in taking photographs and engages in argument with a police officer therefore runs the risk of arrest. A freelance photographer was arrested in 2007 as he tried to take pictures of a man threatening to jump from the Tyne Bridge in Newcastle. He was later charged with obstructing the police. But a **district judge** at the city's magistrates courts acquitted the photographer, saying he had acted 'professionally' (*Media Lawyer*, 15 October 2007).

> → For an outline of the police's general powers of arrest, see ch. 2, p. 22.

Police guidelines to officers on helping the media

After talks between journalists' organisations and police chiefs in London, a set of guidelines was produced for police officers about how to deal with the presence of reporters and photographers at the scenes of incidents. These guidelines were adopted in 2007 by the Association of Chief Police Officers (ACPO). These can be read in full on the website of the NUJ London Freelance branch – see Useful Websites below. The guidelines for police includes these passages:

> 📖 Members of the media have a duty to report from the scene of many of the incidents we have to deal with. We should actively help them carry out their responsibilities provided they do not interfere with ours.
>
> …Where it is necessary to put cordons in place, it is much better to provide the media with a good vantage point from which they can operate rather than to exclude them, otherwise they may try to get around the cordons and interfere with police operations. Providing an area for members of the media does not exclude them from operating from other areas to which the general public have access.
>
> …Members of the media have a duty to take photographs and film incidents and we have no legal power or moral responsibility to prevent or restrict what they record. It is a matter for their editors to control what is published or broadcast, not the police. Once images are recorded, we have no power to delete or confiscate them without a court order, even if we think they contain damaging or useful evidence. 🗐

Terrorism Act 2000: section 44 searches

Both professional and amateur photographs have complained of police use of 'stop and search' powers under section 44 of the Terrorism Act 2000. This power, once an area has been designated by a police force as being at potential risk of terrorist attack, authorises a police officer to stop and search a person even if the officer does not have reasonable suspicion that the person is a potential terrorist. The areas which can be designated under the Act can be very large, e.g. all of the London metropolitan police district. The officer who conducts the search is legally empowered to search 'for articles of a kind which could be used in connection with terrorism', and can retain an article if he/she reasonably suspects it is intended to be used for terrorism. But during a search, the officer cannot require the person to remove any clothing in public except for headgear, footwear, an outer coat, jacket, or gloves. It is an offence to wilfully obstruct the officer in the search.

One of the incidents which have prompted criticism about police use of the 2000 Act occurred in Portsmouth in 2008. A man took a photo on his mobile phone of a police car parked at a bus stop, because he considered the parking illegal. Two police officers then questioned him, saying they were using powers under the Act. A police spokesman told the *Daily Mirror* that the officers had been dealing with a nearby domestic incident, and had acted reasonably because they were suspicious about why the man photographed their car. Later in 2008 the NUJ complained that a freelance photographer was detained for 45 minutes after police stopped her under section 44 when she was taking pictures of a wedding close to London City Airport. However, the argument that section 44, by enabling 'random stopping and searching' by police, is in breach of the European Convention on Human Rights has been rejected by the House of Lords (R (on the application of Gillan and another) v Metropolitan Police Commissioner and another [2006] 4 All ER 1041).

In 2008 the National Policing Improvement Agency, on behalf of the ACPO, issued advice to police about section 44 powers, making it clear that these do not prohibit photography in designated areas but that if an officer suspects photos are being taken as part of 'hostile terrorist reconnaissance' he/she can search under section 43 of the Act (which *does* require the officer to reasonably suspect the person to be a terrorist). The advice added: 'Film and memory cards may be seized as part of the search, but officers do not have any legal power to delete images or destroy film.'

The advice adds that all stop and searches under the 2000 Act must comply with the Police and Criminal Evidence Act 1984 (PACE). One of the concerns of journalists about use of the 2000 Act's section 44 search powers is → glossary that under PACE **journalistic material** is protected from seizure by 'special procedures'. But not all lower-ranking officers realise this.

Some media photographers are also concerned that the new 'eliciting' offence in the Counter-Terrorism Act 2008 may be used against them if they take photos of police officers or servicemen. See ch. 33, p. 531.

For detail of police using powers under PACE to obtain from media photographers material they believe would be of substantial value in an investigation into offences by other people, see ch. 32, pp. 518–521.

False imprisonment

If a photographer is subject to unlawful physical restraint, whether this is
→
see ch. 2, p. 23 and ch. 10, p. 158
being locked up in the cells, or physically restrained in some other way by a police officer – or anyone else for that matter – it is possible to sue for false imprisonment. Movement must be completely restricted; barring a photographer from going in one particular direction, e.g. towards the scene of a crash, is not false imprisonment.

In 1995 a freelance photographer, David Hoffman, won £25,000 damages → glossary from the Metropolitan Police for **assault**, malicious prosecution, and unlawful imprisonment as a result of an arrest during a demonstration he was → glossary covering in 1989. False imprisonment is one of the few **torts** for which there is a right to apply for a jury to decide the issue.

▶ Wrong person or wrong picture: libel dangers

Use of file photographs to illustrate news stories or features is fraught with libellous possibilities. A photo of a social function, with people holding drinks, is perfectly acceptable. If it is later used as a stock shot to illustrate the perils of drinking, those pictured may sue, particularly if any of them are teetotal.

A paper in South Wales had to publish an apology after a library picture of football supporters was used to illustrate an article about hooliganism.

In 2007 the High Court heard that the *Daily Mail* had offered substantial damages to a former martial arts world champion whose photograph had been used by mistake in coverage of a **robbery** trial. The man had nothing → glossary to do with the trial, but shared a first name with one of the defendants who was also a martial arts champion. In 2005 the *Sunday Mirror* paid £100,000 in compensation to a man whose photo had been wrongly published as being that of convicted rapist Iorworth Hoare. In 2004 the *Sun* took out advertisements in local papers in East Anglia to make clear it had wrongly identified a local man in a published photo as being a convicted paedophile. It paid compensation.

▶ Other legal and ethical issues for photographers and picture editors

'User-generated content' (UGC) Pictures and footage supplied by readers and viewers are now a regular feature of media coverage, particularly of major events, for example of the tsunami that devastated countries around the Indian Ocean in 2004 and, closer to home, the immediate aftermath of the terrorist attacks in London on 7 July 2005. The PCC has stated: 'Rare and large-scale events such as terrorist attacks and natural disasters involve a degree of public interest so great that it may be proportionate and appropriate to show images of their aftermath without the consent of those involved.' (*Complaint by Mr Paul Kirkland against the Wiltshire Gazette & Herald*, adjudication issued 24 April 2008.)

But journalists handling pictures supplied by readers/viewers should realise that there is a risk in some instances of 'user-generated content' being a breach of the privacy of those depicted. See also p. 546, above on the PCC adjudication on mobile phone footage of unruly children at a school.

In 2007 the PCC condemned *FHM* magazine for publishing a topless picture of a girl aged 14. Her parents complained. The magazine said it thought she was older and had consented to the picture being published. The PCC said the magazine had not taken adequate care to check the picture's provenance (*Complaint by a married couple against FHM magazine*, adjudication issued 15 August 2007).

In some instances, 'UGC' pictures have been published which turned out to be faked or supplied in breach of someone else's copyright (see also Late News, p. xxxii, for PCC guidance on use of pictures from 'social networking sites').

Copyright See ch. 27, for law on copyright in photographs and film.

→
see ch. 9,
p. 143

The courts The Criminal Justice Act 1925 bans photography and filming in courts and their precincts.

→
see chs 9
and 16

Contempt of court There are various circumstances in which the taking of photographs or filming, and/or the publication of such images, could be punishable as contempt or breach of a statutory reporting restriction.

▦ Recap of major points

- Privacy law is evolving in the UK, and if a person has been subject to stalking by photographers, he or she could win damages for being persistently followed and photographed by them in public places.

- Paparazzi could find the law against harassment being used against them.

- The Press Complaints Commission Code of Practice states that people should not be photographed in places where they have 'a reasonable expectation of privacy', unless the circumstances justify this in the public interest.

- The code says children must not be photographed at school without the school's consent, or on any matter concerning their welfare without parental consent, unless the public interest exception applies.

- Photographers, to avoid arrest, need to know the law on aggravated trespass, and the general powers police have to arrest those 'obstructing' them or the highway.

- Police chiefs have issued guidelines to their officers about the need to help the media, and about controversial 'stop and search' powers in section 44 of the Terrorism Act 2000.

- Publishing the wrong photograph or a defamatory caption could lead to a big pay-out for libel.

- Editors need to take care when deciding whether to use 'user-generated content' – pictures and footage supplied by the public – because their provenance may not be clear, and their publication may breach someone's privacy or copyright.

🌐 Useful Websites

www.epuk.org/
   Editorial Photographers website

www.londonfreelance.org/photo/guidelines.html
   National Union of Journalists, London freelance branch website – guidelines for police on media photographers

Part 6

Northern Ireland

Northern Ireland

Chapter summary

In many respects media law in Northern Ireland is the same as in England and Wales. **Preliminary hearings** before magistrates, prior to committal to Crown court, follow Northern Ireland's unique system. Restrictions on reports of criminal proceedings involving juveniles are on the lines of those on the mainland. In non-criminal proceedings a court can ban the identification of anyone under 18. Victims of sexual offences must remain anonymous. It is a statutory offence to disclose the identity of a juror who is serving or has served on a trial in Northern Ireland, or of a person who is on the jury list there.

→ glossary

▌The law is broadly the same as in England and Wales

The law in Northern Ireland, including the courts structure, is broadly the same as that in England and Wales – though Scotland has its own legal system with its basic differences protected by the Act of Union.

→ see ch.1, p. 81

Many of the laws applicable in England and Wales apply to Northern Ireland by means of Orders made by the Secretary of State rather than in Acts of Parliament.

In the few important cases involving the media that have come before the High Court in Northern Ireland, cases in England have been freely cited. The House of Lords (due to be known from October 2009 as the **Supreme Court**) is the final court of appeal for both criminal and civil cases in Northern Ireland.

 → glossary

Defamation

The Defamation Act (Northern Ireland) 1955 is identical to the Defamation Act 1952, which covers the rest of the United Kingdom. Sections 5 and 6 of the Defamation Act (Northern Ireland) 1955 (failure to prove every allegation of fact in the defences of justification and **fair comment**) are still in force. Much of the Defamation Act 1996 is however the main factor in most instances.

→

see also chs 17–21 for defamation law

Contempt of court

The Contempt of Court Act 1981 is effective in Northern Ireland and the many contempt decisions by the High Court in London are equally applicable there.

Special courts (the 'Diplock courts') were introduced in Northern Ireland for the trial by judge alone of terrorists charged with scheduled offences, and it has been contended that the risk of contempt through creating a substantial risk of serious prejudice to these proceedings is much less in the absence of a jury. The danger remains, however, of witnesses being affected in that their evidence might be coloured by accounts given by others.

→

see also ch. 16

▌ Reporting restrictions

Guidelines on reporting restrictions issued in 2008 by the Judicial Studies Board for Northern Ireland, under the chairmanship of Lord Justice Higgins, say courts are encouraged to exercise their discretion to hear media representations when considering discretionary reporting restrictions

▌ Preliminary hearings

Committal proceedings must be in open court except where it appears to the court that the ends of justice would not be served by reports of the whole or part of the hearing. The Magistrates' Courts (Northern Ireland) Order 1981 (SI 1981/1675) prohibits publication of a report of any opening statement made by the prosecution. There is no automatic ban on reporting evidence but a court may prohibit publication of any evidence if it is satisfied that publication would prejudice the trial of the accused. Additional restrictions may be imposed by the court where objection is taken as to the admissibility of the evidence. The court may if satisfied that the objection is made in good faith order that such evidence and any discussion on it shall not be published

▌ Crown courts

Restrictions under the Criminal Justice Act 2003 on reporting prosecution appeals against the termination of a trial by a judge, or against an acquittal, were extended to Ulster under the Criminal Justice (Northern Ireland) Order 2004 (SI 2004/1500).

see also
ch. 6,
p. 83

The Court of Appeal in Belfast held in 1995 that if plea bargaining submissions are heard in open court it could inhibit rather than secure the achievement of justice.

▌ Juveniles in court

A child under 10 cannot be charged with a criminal offence in Northern Ireland. Youth courts (set up in place of juvenile courts in 1999) deal with offences committed by those below the age of 18. The Criminal Justice (Children) (Northern Ireland) Order 1998 (SI 1998/1504), as amended, makes it an offence in reporting the proceedings to publish the name, address, or school, or any particulars likely to lead to the identification of anyone under 18 involved in youth court proceedings, or in an appeal from a youth court, as defendant or witness. It is also an offence to publish a picture of or including anyone under 18 involved. A youth court may lift or relax the restrictions on a convicted young offender in the public interest but must first afford parties to the proceedings an opportunity to make representations.

See ch. 7 for detail of similar law in youth courts in England and Wales.

Under article 22 of the 1998 Order, an adult court may make an order that nothing should be published to identify those under 18 involved in the proceedings as a defendant, witness, or party (see also ch. 7 deals with the comparable section 39 orders used in England and Wales).

The 1998 Order empowers a court in any criminal proceedings to exclude everyone not concerned in the case, where it considers the evidence of a child is likely to involve matter of an indecent or immoral nature. There is no specific provision for the press to remain, unlike the position in England and Wales under section 37 of the Children and Young Persons Act 1933, see p. 193.

▌ Domestic proceedings

see also
ch. 11

Representatives of newspapers and news agencies may attend domestic proceedings but reports must be confined to four points as is the case for family and domestic proceedings in England and Wales. The court may under, the Children (Northern Ireland) Order 1995 (SI 1995/755), direct that any report of non-criminal proceedings must not lead to the identification of any person under 18 as being involved where any power is being exercised under that order, except to the extent which the court may allow.

The court has power to sit **in private** when exercising any power under the 1995 Order.

▌ Sexual offences

The Sexual Offences Act 2003 and the Youth Justice and Criminal Evidence Act 1999 amended the Sexual Offences (Amendment) Act 1992 and the Criminal Justice (Northern Ireland) Order 1994 (SI 2004/2795) as regards media reports of sexual offences in Northern Ireland. This law, which provides anonymity in media reports for victims/alleged victims of sexual offences, is essentially the same as in England and Wales.

 See ch. 8 for more detail, and for when such anonymity does not apply.

However, there is an exception as regards rights of admission to court, in that sometimes in Northern Ireland when a person is charged with incest the prosecution is brought under the Punishment of Incest Act 1908. Section 5 of the Act says that all proceedings under the Act are to be held in private (i.e. excluding press and public). This does not in itself appear, either at common law or under section 12 of the Administration of Justice Act 1960, to prevent publication of any report of the proceedings which may be obtained, unless a court, having power to do so, has specifically prohibited the publication. However, the victim/alleged victim of the incest still has anonymity. The 'in private' rule of section 5 of the 1908 Act does not apply when a prosecution for a sexual offence is brought under any other Act.

→ glossary

→
see ch. 9, p. 130–132 on 1960 Act

Identifying defendants in sexual offence cases

There is nothing in the 1994 Order giving a court discretionary powers, in addition to the automatic restrictions, to impose further restrictions such as prohibiting identification of the defendant. The scope of the Order's article 19 prohibits publication of particulars that would lead to the identification of the complainant and there is no provision in the article for a court to determine *which* particulars they might be. See also ch. 13, p. 222.

A number of Crown courts and magistrates courts have attempted to make orders banning the naming of a defendant, citing the 1994 Order, on the grounds that publication of his name either would lead to the identification of the complainant or would be detrimental to the well-being of the defendant. Such purported orders would seem to be ultra vires.

> → See also ch. 13, p. 217, for details of the judgment in *R v Newtownabbey Magistrates' Court, ex p Belfast Telegraph Newspapers Ltd* (1997).

In 1999 at Newtownabbey Magistrates' Court in the case of a police officer accused of indecently assaulting a child, the prosecution and defence made a joint application for the press to be excluded. Mr Phillip Mateer, a deputy resident magistrate, refused the application, referring to *R v Newtownabbey Magistrates' Court*, cited above.

Identifying jurors

It is an offence to identify a person as being or having been a juror in Northern Ireland, or as being listed as juror or selected for inclusion on the jury list. The offence is contained in the Juries (Northern Ireland) Order 1996 (SI

1996/1141), as amended, which however provides a defence that there was reasonable belief that disclosure of the juror's identity was lawful.

▶ Photography at court

→
see ch. 9,
p. 143

The Criminal Justice (Northern Ireland) Act 1945, operating in a similar way to the mainland Criminal Justice Act 1925 prohibits photography, filming or sketching in a court or its precincts. Guidelines from the Judicial Studies Board say the court can issue guidance, by way of a map, on the extent of the precincts.

▦ Recap of major points

- The law in Northern Ireland, including the courts structure, is broadly the same as in England and Wales, with minor variations.

- Reporting restrictions in Northern Ireland broadly follow those in England and Wales but many of them are contained in Orders made by the Secretary of State rather than in Acts of Parliament.

- When a child is giving evidence involving indecent or immoral matters the court may exclude everyone not concerned in the proceedings and there is no special provision for the press to remain.

- It is an offence to identify a juror, a former juror, or a person selected for jury service.

🌐 Useful Websites

www.jsbni.com/
Judicial Studies Board for Northern Ireland

Appendix 1
Extracts from the European Convention for the Protection of Human Rights and Fundamental Freedoms (known as the European Convention on Human Rights)

Article 2: Right to life

1) Everyone's right to life shall be protected by law. No one shall be deprived of his life intentionally save in the execution of a sentence of a court following his conviction of a crime for which this penalty is provided by law. [see also * below]

2) Deprivation of life shall not be regarded as inflicted in contravention of this Article when it results from the use of force which is no more than absolutely necessary:
   (a) in defence of any person from unlawful violence;
   (b) in order to effect a lawful arrest or to prevent the escape of a person lawfully detained;
   (c) in action lawfully taken for the purpose of quelling a riot or insurrection.

Article 3: Prohibition of torture

No one shall be subjected to torture or to inhuman or degrading treatment or punishment.

Article 6: Right to a fair trial [the article is quoted in part]

1) In the determination of his civil rights and obligations or of any criminal charge against him, everyone is entitled to a fair and public hearing within a reasonable time by an independent and impartial tribunal established by law. Judgment shall be pronounced publicly but the

press and public may be excluded from all or part of the trial in the interest of morals, public order or national security in a democratic society, where the interests of juveniles or the protection of the private life of the parties so require, or to the extent strictly necessary in the opinion of the court in special circumstances where publicity would prejudice the interests of justice.

2) Everyone charged with a criminal offence shall be presumed innocent until proved guilty according to law.

Article 8: Right to respect for private and family life

1) Everyone has the right to respect for his private and family life, his home and his correspondence.

2) There shall be no interference by a public authority with the exercise of this right except such as is in accordance with the law and is necessary in a democratic society in the interests of national security, public safety or the economic well-being of the country, for the prevention of disorder or crime, for the protection of health or morals, or for the protection of the rights and freedoms of others.

Article 10: Freedom of expression

1) Everyone has the right to freedom of expression. This right shall include freedom to hold opinions and to receive and impart information and ideas without interference by public authority and regardless of frontiers.

   This Article shall not prevent States from requiring the licensing of broadcasting, television or cinema enterprises.

2) The exercise of these freedoms, since it carries with it duties and responsibilities, may be subject to such formalities, conditions, restrictions or penalties as are prescribed by law and are necessary in a democratic society, in the interests of national security, territorial integrity or public safety, for the prevention of disorder or crime, for the protection of health or morals, for the protection of the reputation or rights of others, for preventing the disclosure of information received in confidence, or for maintaining the authority and impartiality of the judiciary.

* Article 1 of the Thirteenth Protocol of the Convention, which was adopted into UK law in 2004, stated: 'The death penalty shall be abolished'. It had already been abolished in the UK.

 The full text of the Convention can be read at www.statutelaw.gov.uk/ by using the search facility to access the Human Rights Act 1998, and then accessing the Act's Schedule 1.

Appendix 2
The Press Complaints Commission Editors'
Code of Practice

The Press Complaints Commission is charged with enforcing the following Code of Practice which was framed by the newspaper and periodical industry. This is the code, as ratified by the PCC on 01 August 2007. Clauses marked* are covered by exceptions relating to the public interest.

THE CODE

All members of the press have a duty to maintain the highest professional standards. The Code, which includes this preamble and the public interest exceptions below, sets the benchmark for those ethical standards, protecting both the rights of the individual and the public's right to know. It is the cornerstone of the system of self-regulation to which the industry has made a binding commitment.

It is essential that an agreed code be honoured not only to the letter but in the full spirit. It should not be interpreted so narrowly as to compromise its commitment to respect the rights of the individual, nor so broadly that it constitutes an unnecessary interference with freedom of expression or prevents publication in the public interest.

It is the responsibility of editors and publishers to apply the Code to editorial material in both printed and online versions of publications. They should take care to ensure it is observed rigorously by all editorial staff and external contributors, including non-journalists, in printed and online versions of publications. Editors should co-operate swiftly with the PCC in the resolution of complaints. Any publication judged to have breached the Code must print the adjudication in full and with due prominence, including headline reference to the PCC.

1 **Accuracy**
   i)   The Press must take care not to publish inaccurate, misleading or distorted information, including pictures.

ii) A significant inaccuracy, misleading statement or distortion once recognised must be corrected, promptly and with due prominence, and – where appropriate – an apology published.

iii) The Press, whilst free to be partisan, must distinguish clearly between comment, conjecture and fact.

iv) A publication must report fairly and accurately the outcome of an action for defamation to which it has been a party, unless an agreed settlement states otherwise, or an agreed statement is published.

2 **Opportunity to reply**

A fair opportunity for reply to inaccuracies must be given when reasonably called for.

3 *****Privacy**

i) Everyone is entitled to respect for his or her private and family life, home, health and correspondence, including digital communications. Editors will be expected to justify intrusions into any individual's private life without consent.

ii) It is unacceptable to photograph individuals in a private place without their consent.

Note – Private places are public or private property where there is a reasonable expectation of privacy.

4 *****Harassment**

i) Journalists must not engage in intimidation, harassment or persistent pursuit.

ii) They must not persist in questioning, telephoning, pursuing or photographing individuals once asked to desist; nor remain on their property when asked to leave and must not follow them.

iii) Editors must ensure these principles are observed by those working for them and take care not to use non-compliant material from other sources.

5 **Intrusion into grief or shock**

i) In cases involving personal grief or shock, enquiries and approaches must be made with sympathy and discretion and publication handled sensitively. This should not restrict the right to report legal proceedings, such as inquests.

*ii) When reporting suicide, care should be taken to avoid excessive detail about the method used.

6 *****Children**

i) Young people should be free to complete their time at school without unnecessary intrusion.

ii) A child under 16 must not be interviewed or photographed on issues involving their own or another child's welfare unless a custodial parent or similarly responsible adult consents.

iii) Pupils must not be approached or photographed at school without the permission of the school authorities.

iv) Minors must not be paid for material involving children's welfare, nor parents or guardians for material about their children or wards, unless it is clearly in the child's interest.

v) Editors must not use the fame, notoriety or position of a parent or guardian as sole justification for publishing details of a child's private life.

7 *Children in sex cases

1. The press must not, even if legally free to do so, identify children under 16 who are victims or witnesses in cases involving sex offences.

2. In any press report of a case involving a sexual offence against a child –
   i) The child must not be identified.
   ii) The adult may be identified.
   iii) The word "incest" must not be used where a child victim might be identified.
   iv) Care must be taken that nothing in the report implies the relationship between the accused and the child.

8 *Hospitals

i) Journalists must identify themselves and obtain permission from a responsible executive before entering non-public areas of hospitals or similar institutions to pursue enquiries.

ii) The restrictions on intruding into privacy are particularly relevant to enquiries about individuals in hospitals or similar institutions.

9 *Reporting of Crime

(i) Relatives or friends of persons convicted or accused of crime should not generally be identified without their consent, unless they are genuinely relevant to the story.

(ii) Particular regard should be paid to the potentially vulnerable position of children who witness, or are victims of, crime. This should not restrict the right to report legal proceedings.

10 *Clandestine devices and subterfuge

i) The press must not seek to obtain or publish material acquired by using hidden cameras or clandestine listening devices; or by intercepting private or mobile telephone calls, messages or emails; or by the unauthorised removal of documents or photographs; or by accessing digitally-held private information without consent.

ii) Engaging in misrepresentation or subterfuge, including by agents or intermediaries, can generally be justified only in the public interest and then only when the material cannot be obtained by other means.

11 Victims of sexual assault

The press must not identify victims of sexual assault or publish material likely to contribute to such identification unless there is adequate justification and they are legally free to do so.

12 Discrimination

i) The press must avoid prejudicial or pejorative reference to an individual's race, colour, religion, gender, sexual orientation or to any physical or mental illness or disability.

ii) Details of an individual's race, colour, religion, sexual orientation, physical or mental illness or disability must be avoided unless genuinely relevant to the story.

13 Financial journalism

i) Even where the law does not prohibit it, journalists must not use for their own profit financial information they receive in advance of its general publication, nor should they pass such information to others.

ii) They must not write about shares or securities in whose performance they know that they or their close families have a significant financial interest without disclosing the interest to the editor or financial editor.

iii) They must not buy or sell, either directly or through nominees or agents, shares or securities about which they have written recently or about which they intend to write in the near future.

14 Confidential sources

Journalists have a moral obligation to protect confidential sources of information.

15 Witness payments in criminal trials

i) No payment or offer of payment to a witness – or any person who may reasonably be expected to be called as a witness – should be made in any case once proceedings are active as defined by the Contempt of Court Act 1981.

   This prohibition lasts until the suspect has been freed unconditionally by police without charge or bail or the proceedings are otherwise discontinued; or has entered a guilty plea to the court; or, in the event of a not guilty plea, the court has announced its verdict.

*ii) Where proceedings are not yet active but are likely and foreseeable, editors must not make or offer payment to any person who may reasonably be expected to be called as a witness, unless the information concerned ought demonstrably to be published in the public interest and there is an over-riding need to make or promise payment for this to be done; and all reasonable steps have been taken to ensure no financial dealings influence the evidence those witnesses give. In no circumstances should such payment be conditional on the outcome of a trial.

*iii) Any payment or offer of payment made to a person later cited to give evidence in proceedings must be disclosed to the prosecution and defence. The witness must be advised of this requirement.

16 *Payment to criminals

i)   Payment or offers of payment for stories, pictures or information, which seek to exploit a particular crime or to glorify or glamorise crime in general, must not be made directly or via agents to convicted or confessed criminals or to their associates – who may include family, friends and colleagues.

ii) Editors invoking the public interest to justify payment or offers would need to demonstrate that there was good reason to believe the public interest would be served. If, despite payment, no public interest emerged, then the material should not be published.

The public interest

There may be exceptions to the clauses marked * where they can be demonstrated to be in the public interest.

1.   The public interest includes, but is not confined to:

   i)   Detecting or exposing crime or serious impropriety.
   ii) Protecting public health and safety.
   iii) Preventing the public from being misled by an action or statement of an individual or organisation.

2.   There is a public interest in freedom of expression itself.

3.   Whenever the public interest is invoked, the PCC will require editors to demonstrate fully how the public interest was served.

4.   The PCC will consider the extent to which material is already in the public domain, or will become so.

5.   In cases involving children under 16, editors must demonstrate an exceptional public interest to over-ride the normally paramount interest of the child.

Glossary

Abuse of process Malicious or improper use of legal proceedings.

Affidavit A statement given on oath to be used in court proceedings.

Age of criminality The age above which a child may be accused of a criminal offence and be brought before a court.

Alibi The defence case of a defendant who asserts that he/she was not at the scene of a crime when it occurred and that he/she is therefore innocent of it.

Arraignment The procedure at Crown courts in which charges are put to defendants for them to plead guilty or not guilty.

Assault In legal language, assault is a hostile act that causes another person to fear an attack. Battery is the actual application of force.

Automatic, automatically Terms used of a reporting restriction, banning certain matter from being published, if no court order is needed to put it into effect in respect of a particular court case or individual. Statute specifies the circumstances when it operates. Some such restrictions automatically expire when the case concludes.

Bail The system by which a person awaiting trial, or appeal, may be freed by a court pending the next hearing. *See also* Police bail, below.

Bailiff A representative of the court who enforces its orders.

Bill of indictment An order made by a High Court judge, compelling a person to stand trial at Crown court. A rare procedure, used to cut out the usual committal by the magistrates, or to overcome a decision by the magistrates that there is no case to answer.

Case law The system by which reports of previous cases and the judges' interpretation of the common law can be used as a precedent where the legally material facts are similar.

Circuit judge Judge who has been appointed to sit at Crown court or county court within a circuit – one of the regions of England and Wales into which court administration is divided. Unlike High Court judges, circuit judges do not go on circuit, that is travel to various large centres dispensing justice.

Claim form *Previously known as* Writ or Default summons. A document that begins many forms of civil action.

Claimant *Previously known as* Plaintiff. The person who takes an action to enforce a claim in the civil court. New civil justice rules in 1999 said the word Claimant should be used instead.

Committal hearing Hearing in a magistrates court when the magistrates decide if there is sufficient evidence to commit a defendant facing an either-way charge to Crown court for trial.

Committal for trial When a magistrates court in a Committal hearing, *see above*, decides that there is sufficient evidence for a defendant's case to proceed to Crown court for trial. The defendant may subsequently plead guilty at Crown court, meaning there will be no trial. The term is also used of procedure by which a juvenile accused of a grave offence is committed by a youth court to a Crown court.

Committal for sentence, committed for sentence When a defendant who has at magistrates court admitted an offence or been convicted in a trial there is then sent to Crown court for sentence because the magistrates court decides its powers of punishment are insufficient. (There are no reporting restrictions on committals for sentence.)

Common law Law based on the custom of the realm and the decisions of the judges through the centuries rather than on an Act of Parliament.

Community punishment An order that an offender must carry out unpaid work in the community under the supervision of a probation officer.

Concurrent sentences Two or more sentences of imprisonment imposed for different offences; the longest one is the sentence actually served.

Conditional fee agreements (CFAs) No win, no fee agreements – their use was extended to defamation cases in 1998 under the Conditional Fee Agreements Order 1998 (SI 1998/1860).

Corporation Only individuals and corporations can sue for libel. A corporate body is one that has rights and duties distinct from those of the people who form it. An incorporated company is a corporation formed for the purpose of carrying on a business.

Counsel Barrister (singular or plural), not solicitor.

Data controller A person who alone, jointly, or in common with others determines the purposes for which and the manner in which any personal data are processed or who is responsible for ensuring compliance with the provisions of the Data Protection Act 1998.

Derogations Limitations to the rights conferred by the Human Rights Act 1998.

Derogatory assertions Assertions made in mitigation about a person's character that allege conduct that is immoral, improper, or criminal. May be the subject of a reporting restriction.

Discharge When magistrates decide at a Committal hearing, *see above*, that the evidence for a charge against a defendant is insufficient for the case to proceed to Crown court. This ends that prosecution for that charge. Not to be confused with an absolute discharge, which is a decision by a court after conviction that the defendant should not be punished for the offence.

Disclosure and inspection *Previously known as* Discovery. The process whereby each side in a court action serves a list of relevant documents on the other. The other party then has the right to inspect those documents.

Discovery *See* Disclosure.

District judge An official of the county court who also adjudicates in smaller cases, presides at public examinations in bankruptcy, and deals with cases under the informal arbitration procedure.

District judge (magistrates courts) The title given under the Access to Justice Act 1999 to full-time, legally qualified magistrates, *formerly known as* Stipendiary magistrates.

Drink driving The term to use in headings and Introductions, not Drunk driving.

Either-way offence One triable either summarily at magistrates court or before a jury at Crown court. In an either-way case a defendant who has indicated a plea of not guilty has the right to opt for jury trial at Crown court. But if he/she chooses to be tried by the magistrates court, it may overrule him by deciding the Crown court should deal with his case – *see* Mode of trial hearing, *below*.

Ex parte *See* Without notice.

Excluded material Such material is exempt from compulsory disclosure under the Police and Criminal Evidence Act 1984 (PACE). It includes Journalistic material (*see below*) that a person holds in confidence and that consists of documents or records.

Fair comment A defence to a libel action; the defendant does not have to show the words were fair. But he must show they were honest and published without malice.

Fair dealing A defence to breach of copyright for use of extracts of a copyrighted work, properly attributed to its author.

Habeas corpus, writ of A writ issued by the Queen's Bench Divisional Court to secure the release of a person whom it declares to have been detained unlawfully by the police or other authorities.

Hearsay Evidence of what a witness was told, rather than what they actually saw or heard for themselves.

In camera Proceedings in a courtroom that are heard in the absence of the public and the press (e.g. in Official Secrets Act cases).

In chambers Used to describe the hearing of an application which takes place in the judge's room. If there is no legal reason for such a hearing to be held In private (*see below*), journalists who want to report it should be admitted to it if this is 'practicable' (*see* ch. 12).

In private A term used of a court hearing In camera (*see above*), or one In chambers (*see above*) which the press and public are not entitled to attend.

Indictable offence A charge which may be tried by a jury at Crown court, which therefore is an Either-way offence (*see above*) or Indictable-only offence (*see below*).

Indictable-only offence One that can be tried only by a jury at Crown court.

Indictment A written statement of the charges that are put to the defendant when at the Arraignment (*see above*) at Crown court.

Information A written statement alleging an offence, that is laid before a magistrate who is then asked to issue a summons or warrant for arrest.

Inherent jurisdiction The powers of a court which derive from common law rather than statute. The inherent jurisdiction of lower courts, e.g. magistrates courts, is more limited in scope than that of the higher courts, e.g. the High Court.

Injunction A court order requiring someone, or an organisation, to do something specified by the court, or forbidding a specific activity or act.

Interdict In Scottish law, an Injunction (*see above*).

Journalistic material Material acquired and created for the purposes of journalism. Special protection is given to journalistic material in the sections of the Police and Criminal Evidence Act 1984 that lay down the procedure whereby the police may search premises for evidence of serious arrestable offences.

Judicial review A review by the Queen's Bench Divisional Court, part of the High Court, of decisions taken by a lower court, tribunal, public body, or public official.

Justification The defence in libel actions that the words complained of were true. The word is misleading, because there is no requirement that the words were published justly or with good reason.

Legal aid Public money provided to pay for legal advice and legal representation in court for a party in a civil case or a defendant in a criminal case, if their income is low enough to qualify for such aid.

Lords of Appeal They are usually known as the law lords. They sit in the House of Lords, not the Court of Appeal. Due to sit in the Supreme Court from 2009.

Malice In law not only spite or ill-will but also dishonest or improper motive. Proof of malice can be used by a Claimant (*see* above) in a libel action to deprive the defendant of the defences of fair comment or qualified privilege.

Mode of trial hearing The hearing at a magistrates court which determines whether an Either-way case (*see above*) is dealt with by that court or proceeds to a Committal hearing (*see above*) from which it may be committed to Crown court.

Moral rights The rights of an author of a work, in addition to copyright, to be correctly identified as the author and the right to object to derogatory treatment of that work.

Narrative verdict The system of allowing a coroner or inquest jury to make a short statement of the circumstances of a person's death, rather than the traditional one-word verdicts.

Newton hearing A hearing in which, after a defendant is convicted, the court hears evidence to help it decide on sentence because the prosecution version of the circumstances of the offence differs substantially from the defence version. Newton was the defendant's name in the relevant, precedent case.

Pleadings *See* Statements of case.

Police bail The system administered by police whereby a person under ongoing investigation can be released from arrest on conditions, including that they return to a police station on a later date, at which time they may be questioned again, charged, or be told there will be no charge. They can be arrested if they breach the conditions. After being charged, they can be bailed by police to attend court, or may be taken there in custody.

Preliminary hearing A hearing which occurs at magistrates or Crown court before any trial.

Prima facie At first sight.

Privilege A defence, absolute or qualified, against an action for libel which attaches to reports produced from certain events, documents, or statements.

Quango The term stands for quasi-autonomous non-governmental organisation and is conveniently and loosely used to describe non-elected public bodies that operate outside the civil service and that are funded by the taxpayer.

Queen's Counsel The title given to a senior barrister recommended as counsel to the Queen by the Lord Chancellor.

Recorder An assistant judge at Crown court who is usually appointed to sit part-time (e.g. for spells of a fortnight). Solicitors and barristers are both eligible for appointment as a recorder.

Remand An individual awaiting trial can be remanded on bail, or in custody.

Reynolds **defence** A form of privilege available to journalism that fulfils tests laid down by the courts in the case of *Reynolds v Sunday Times* and subsequent cases.

Robbery Theft (*see below*) by force, or threat of force. The word is often used, wrongly, to describe simple theft.

Sending for trial The fast-track procedure by which an Indictable-only offence (*see above*) is sent from the magistrates court, without any consideration of the strength of evidence against the defendant, to a Crown court.

Spent conviction A conviction that is no longer recognised after the specified time (varying according to sentence) laid down by the Rehabilitation of Offenders Act 1974. After this time, a newspaper referring to the conviction may not have available some of the normal defences in the law of libel.

Statements of case Documents including the Claim form (*see above*), particulars of claim, defence, counterclaims, reply to the defence, and 'further information documents' in a civil action – reports of which are now protected by Privilege (*see above*).

Statutory instrument Secondary legislation which can be enacted without Parliamentary debate by a Minister to make detailed law (e.g. rules and regulations) or amendment to the law, under powers given earlier by a statute (an Act of Parliament, the primary legislation). Statutory instruments are also used to phase in gradually, for administrative convenience, legal changes brought about by Acts.

Stipendiary magistrates *See* District judge (magistrates courts).

Strict liability A strict liability offence does not require the prosecution to show intent on the part of the accused. Statutory contempt of court is a strict liability offence.

Sub judice Literally 'under law'. Often applied to the risk which may arise in reporting forthcoming legal proceedings. Frequently used by authority as a reason for not disclosing information. This is not the test for strict liability under the Contempt of Court Act 1981 (see ch. 16 p. 296).

Subpoena A court order compelling a person to attend court to give evidence.

Summary offence A comparatively minor offence which can usually can only be dealt with by magistrates

Summary proceedings Cases dealt with by magistrates. At the end of a summary trial of an Either-way offence (*see above*), however, magistrates can, if they consider their powers of sentence insufficient, Commit for sentence (*see above*).

Summary trial A trial at a magistrates court.

Supreme Court The name originally given to the Court of Appeal, the High Court, and the Crown court as a combined system. However, from October 2009 the House of Lords appellate committee (the court commonly referred to merely as 'the House of Lords') is due to become known as the Supreme Court.

Surety A person, usually a friend or relative of the defendant, to whom a court entrusts the responsibility to ensure that the defendant, having been given Bail (*see above*), returns to court on the due date. The surety may pledge a sum of money as guarantee that the defendant will answer bail, and risks losing it if the defendant fails to do this.

Theft Dishonest appropriation of property with the intention to permanently deprive another of it.

Tort A civil wrong for which monetary damages may be awarded if the person affected sues in civil law, e.g. defamation, medical negligence.

Without notice *Previously known as* Ex parte, of the one part. An injunction without notice is one granted after hearing only one side of the case.

Book list

Chapter 1, Introduction
Free Speech, E M Barendt (Oxford University Press, 2nd edition, 2007)

Chapter 12, Open justice and access to court information
Contempt of Court, C J Miller (Oxford University Press, 3rd edition, 2000)
Media Law, Geoffrey Robertson and Andrew Nicol (Penguin, 5th edition, 2008)

Chapter 16, Contempt of court
Arlidge, Eady and Smith on Contempt, Sir David Eady and Professor
  A T H Smith (Sweet & Maxwell, 3rd edition, 2007)
Contempt of Court, C J Miller (Oxford University Press, 3rd edition, 2000)

Chapter 17, Defamation
Carter-Ruck on Libel and Slander, Peter F Carter-Ruck (Butterworths, 1997)
Defamation and Freedom of Speech, Dario Milo (Oxford University Press,
  2008)
Defamation: Law, Procedure and Practice, David Price and Korieh Duodu
  (Sweet & Maxwell, 3rd edition, 2004)
Gatley on Libel and Slander, Patrick Milmo QC and Prof W V H Rogers
  (Sweet & Maxwell, 11th edition, 2008)
Libel and the Media, edited by E M Barendt et al (Clarendon Press, 1997)

Chapter 22, The Rehabilitation of Offenders Act 1974
Stone's Justices Manual (Butterworths, 2008)

Chapter 23, Breach of confidence
Confidentiality, Charles Phipps and Roger Toulson (Sweet & Maxwell, 2006)
The Law of Confidentiality: A Restatement, Paul Stanley (Hart Publishing,
  2008)
The Spycatcher Cases, Michael Fysh QC (European Law Centre, 1989)

Chapter 24, Privacy
The Law of Privacy and the Media: Main Work and 2nd Cumulative Supplement,
  edited by Michael Tugendhat QC and Iain Christie (Oxford University Press,
  2006)
Privacy and the Media: the Developing Law, Matrix Media and Information
  Group (Matrix Chambers, 2002)

Privacy and the Press, Joshua Rozenberg (Oxford University Press, 2004)

Chapter 25, The Data Protection Act 1998

Data Protection: A Guide to UK and EU Law, Peter Carey (Oxford University Press, 3rd edition, 2009)

The Yearbook of Copyright and Media Law 2000, Vol 5, edited by E M Barendt and A Firth (Oxford University Press, 2000)

Chapter 27, Copyright

Intellectual Property: Patents, Copyrights, Trademarks and Allied Rights, William Cornish and David Llewelyn (Sweet & Maxwell, 6th edition, 2007)

Chapter 28, Freedom of Information Act 2000

Your Right to Know, Heather Brooke (Pluto Press, 2nd edition, 2007)

Chapter 31, Official secrets

Media Law, Geoffrey Robertson and Andrew Nicol (Penguin, 5th edition, 2008)

National Security and the D-Notice System, Pauline Sadler (Dartmouth Publishing Co Ltd, 2001)

Official Secrets: The Use and Abuse of the Act, David Hooper (Coronet Books, 1988)

Secrecy and the Media: The official History of the D-notice System, Nicholas John Wilkinson (Routledge, 2009)

Chapter 33, Terrorism and the effect of counter-terrorism law

Media Freedom under the Human Rights Act, Helen Fenwick and Gavin Phillipson (Oxford University Press, 2006)

Table of Cases

Table of Statutes

Table of Statutory Instruments

Table of European Conventions and Directives

Page references in **bold** indicate that the text is reproduced in full

Index

Q

Sunday Times
contempt of court
thalidomide drug 293–294
libel actions
Ashby 309
Reynolds 356–358
official secrets
Liam Clarke 500
Surety 45
suspended sentence 71

T

taken into consideration *see* **Offences taken into consideration**
tape recording of proceedings
contempt of court 145–146
telephone calls, recording of 413–414
telephone tapping
official secrets
Liam Clarke case 500
Terrorism
control orders 534
definition of 528–529
Malik case 533–534
offence: collecting information 531
offence: eliciting information 531
offence: encouragement of 529–530
offence: failure to disclose 530–531
offence: glorification of 529–530
police search powers 532
production orders 532–534
proscribed groups 529
section 44 police stop and
search 551–552
see also Table of Statutes on
Terrorism Acts 2000 and 2006;
Counter-Terrorism Act 2008
Theft Act 1968
rewards for stolen goods, ORC ch. 2
theft 38
see also Table of Statutes
Times, The
journalist's sources
Interbrew 509
libel actions
Derbyshire County Council 315
Loutchansky 360–361
support for Shiv Malik 533–534
Torts 150
trafficking *see* **prostitution**
treasure

inquests 250–251
trespass
aggravated trespass 548
goods, to 415–416
land, to 415
person, to 416
tribunals
admission to 257
contempt of court 260–261
employment tribunals
access to information 262
admission 263
challenging orders 264
disability cases 266–267
sexual misconduct cases 263–266
First-tier tribunal 130, 254–258
procedural rules 257–258
Upper tribunal 254–258
Tribunals, Courts and Enforcement Act 254
see also Table of Statutes
typographical arrangements
copyright, and generally 446

U

unpublished material
journalist's sources 520
Upper tribunal *see* **tribunals**
user-generated content
ethical and legal dangers of 553–554

V

valuation tribunals 256
Vassall inquiry 271
videoing *see* **photographers**
Violent Crime Reduction Act
drinking banning orders 111
see also Table of Statutes
voluntary bill of indictment 60
voyeurism 119
vulnerable parties
anonymity 133
vulnerable witnesses 193

W

ward of court 177–179
wasted costs, order to pay 284
wasting police time
criminal offence of 40, 124